■ ■ ■ ■ ■ ■ ■ ■ ■ ■ ■

TO THE STUDENT

This text was created to provide you with a high-quality educational resource. As a publisher specializing in college texts for business and economics, our goal is to provide you with learning materials that will serve you well in your college studies and throughout your career.

The educational process involves learning, retention, and the application of concepts and principles. You can accelerate your learning efforts utilizing the Workbook accompanying this text:

- **Workbook for use with *Basic Business Communication*, Seventh Edition**

This learning aid is designed to improve your performance in the course by highlighting key points in the text and providing you with assistance in mastering basic concepts.

Get your copy at your local bookstore, or ask the manager to place an order for you today.

We at Irwin sincerely hope this text package will assist you in reaching your goals, both now and in the future.

LESIKAR'S
BASIC BUSINESS
COMMUNICATION

LESIKAR'S
BASIC BUSINESS
COMMUNICATION

Seventh Edition

▶ **Raymond V. Lesikar**
Emeritus, Louisiana State University

▶ **John D. Pettit, Jr.**
Austin Peay State University

▶ **Marie E. Flatley**
San Diego State University

IRWIN

Chicago   Bogotá   Boston   Buenos Aires   Caracas
London   Madrid   Mexico City   Sydney   Toronto

© Richard D. Irwin, a Times Mirror Higher Education Group, Inc. company, 1979, 1982, 1985, 1988, 1991, 1993, and 1996

Irwin Book Team

Executive editor:	Craig Beytien
Sponsoring editor:	Karen Mellon
Senior marketing manager:	Jim Lewis
Project editor:	Karen J. Nelson
Production supervisor:	Dina L. Treadaway
Interior designer:	Maureen McCutcheon, Maureen McCutcheon Design
Cover designer:	Maureen McCutcheon, Maureen McCutcheon Design
Art studio:	ElectraGraphics, Inc.
Assistant manager, graphics:	Charlene R. Breeden
Graphics supervisor:	Heather D. Burbridge
Compositor:	Better Graphics, Inc.
Typeface:	10/12 Times Roman
Printer:	Von Hoffmann Press, Inc.

Library of Congress Cataloging-in-Publication Data

Lesikar, Raymond Vincent.
    Lesikar's basic business communication / Raymond V. Lesikar, John D. Pettit,
Jr., Marie E. Flatley. — 7th ed.
        p.   cm.
    Includes bibliographical references and index.
    ISBN 0-256-14078-2
        1. Commercial correspondence.   2. English language—Business
English.   3. Business communication.   I. Pettit, John D.
II. Flatley, Marie Elizabeth.   III. Title.
HF5721.L37   1996
651.7'4—dc20 95–12695

Printed in the United States of America
2 3 4 5 6 7 8 9 0 VH 2 1 0 9 8 7 6

To my dear departed wife and parents whose love, sacrifice, and encouragement made this book possible.   R.V.L.

To my father, J. Douglas "Doug" Pettit whose memory gives special meaning to my work and my life.   J.D.P., Jr.

To my father and niece Mary who continuously model effective you-viewpoint in their e-mail messages.   M.E.F.

About the Authors

JOHN D. PETTIT, JR.

John D. Pettit, Jr., is the Chair of Excellence in Free Enterprise in the College of Business at Austin Peay State University. He earned his Ph.D. from Louisiana State University and his B.B.A and M.B.A from the University of North Texas.

For 33 years Dr. Pettit has taught business communication and other courses at several universities: Wichita State University, University of North Texas, Texas Tech University, Louisiana State University, and Mississippi State University. He has contributed three books and numerous articles to the communication literature.

Dr. Pettit is a Fellow, former president, and former Executive Director of the Association for Business Communication. He is also a member of the Academy of Management and a member and former president of the Southwestern Federation of Administrative Disciplines.

MARIE E. FLATLEY

Marie E. Flatley is a Professor of Information and Decision Systems at San Diego State University, where she teaches various courses in business communication. She received her B.B.A., M.A., and Ph.D. from the University of Iowa. In addition, she has done post-graduate study in AACSB sponsored programs at the University of Minnesota and Indiana University.

Marie is active in numerous professional organizations, including the Association for Business Communication, California Business Education Association, Delta Pi Epsilon, and the National Business Education Association. She has served as Associate Editor for the *Journal for Business Communication* and Editor for the *NABTE Review.* She was recently named Distinguished Member of the Association of Business Communication.

Her current research interests involve using technology to assist with the communication process. And she is currently writing a monograph for Delta Pi Epsilon on electronic communication.

RAYMOND V. LESIKAR

Dr. Raymond V. Lesikar has served on the faculties of the University of North Texas, Louisiana State University at Baton Rouge, The University of Texas at Austin, and Texas Christian University. He served also as a visiting professor at the University of International Business and Economics, Beijing, China. His contributions to the literature include six books and numerous articles.

Dr. Lesikar has been active in consulting, serving over 80 companies and organizations. He is a Fellow, Distinguished Member and former president of the Association for Business Communication, serving ABC in many capacities, including a term as president. He also holds membership in the Southwest Federation of Administrative Disciplines and is a former president of the Southwest Social Science Association.

Preface

This seventh edition continues our efforts to produce the most authoritative, thorough, and technologically current book in the field. We are modestly confident that we have succeeded. We are also confident that more than ever before, we have achieved the two primary goals of the preceding editions: to present business communication in a way that is (1) more learnable for the student and (2) more teachable for the instructor.

AUTHORITATIVE

Our efforts to present the subject matter authoritatively involved a thorough review of the field. The information presented and procedures recommended are not just our ideas and preferences, though we support them. They represent the mainstream of business communication thought developed by researchers, teachers, and practitioners over the years. We are confident they fully meet AACSB and ACBSP accreditation standards for communication.

We are equally confident that our approach to business communication heavily involves the five educational competencies outlined by the Secretary's Commission on Achieving Necessary Skills, U. S. Department of Labor. Certainly the emphasis on the effects of words on human relations helps the student in working with others. Coverage of research and reporting addresses the skill of acquiring and using information. Mastery of complex systems is an obvious goal of our review of procedures involved in analyzing, solving, and presenting report problems. Likewise, the skill of managing resources is a logical product of report preparation. Finally, the computer emphasis throughout the book supports the fifth skill area—technology.

THOROUGH

We worked diligently to cover the subject thoroughly. The content of the earlier editions was based on the results of two extensive surveys of business communication teachers. In this edition we supplemented the results of those surveys with suggestions from the highly competent professionals who reviewed the book. The result is a book whose content has been developed and approved by experts in the field. As well as we can determine, this edition covers every topic that today's business communication leaders say it should have.

TECHNOLOGICALLY CURRENT

Because the computer has affected business communication in so many ways, we worked this subject into the book wherever applicable. Where technology is integral to the way businesses communicate today, we integrated it into the text discussion. In those cases where technology helps students perform special tasks, we presented it in boxes. We believe these efforts will enable students to exploit the power of the computer in saving time and improving work quality.

TEACHABLE AND LEARNABLE

As in the earlier editions, we worked hard to make the book serve both student and teacher in every practical way. For the student, we worked to make the learning experience easy and interesting. For the teacher, we did all in our power to lighten the teaching load.

Successful Plan of the Past. To implement these goals, we continued the following plan that proved to be highly successful in preceding editions:

Readable writing. The writing is in plain, everyday English—the kind the book instructs the students to use.

Chapter objectives. Placed at the beginning of all chapters, clearly worded objectives emphasize learning goals, and are tied in to the chapters' summaries.

Introductory situations. A realistic description of a business scenario introduces the student to each topic, providing context for the discussion and examples.

Preliminary outlines of letters. To simplify and clarify the instructions for writing the basic letter types, outlines of letter plans precede the discussions.

Margin notes. Summaries of content appear in the margins to help students emphasize main points and to review text highlights.

Critical thinking problems. In-depth, realistic business cases are included for all letter and report types—more than any competing text.

Critical thinking questions. End-of-chapter questions emphasize text concepts and provide material for classroom discussion.

Grading checklists. Lists of likely errors keyed to marking symbols are available for letters, reports, and points of correctness. They help the teacher in the grading process and provide the students with explanations for their errors.

Specialized report topics. Lists of research topics by major business disciplines are available for teachers who prefer to assign reports in the student's area of specialization.

Abundant illustrations. Carefully selected examples with handwritten comments show how to apply the text instructions.

Interest-gaining vignettes. Boxes containing exciting, humorous, technology-based, or classic material add interest and make points throughout the book.

Cartoons. Carefully selected cartoons emphasize key points and add interest.

Photographs. Carefully selected full-color photographs throughout the text emphasize key points and add interest to content. Teaching captions provide an enhancement of the textual material.

Chapter summaries by chapter objectives. Ending summaries in fast-reading outline form and by chapter objectives enable students to recall text highlights.

Computer applications. Computer applications have been worked in throughout the book wherever appropriate—into topics such as readability analysis, graphics, research methods, and formatting.

Computer use suggestions. For students who want to know more about how useful computers can be in business communication, pertinent suggestions appear in boxes.

Realistic form illustrations. The letter and report examples have been enhanced to reflect the current state of actual letters and reports (textured paper, letterhead, model computer formatting, fax and e-mail numbers).

New letter and report cases. As in past editions, the realistic and thorough case problems are new.

Teaching-Learning Helps. Teaching-learning helps were available with all earlier editions, but we believe the greatly expanded package for this edition is the most useful and effective ever assembled for a business communication textbook. The support material for this edition consists of these elements:

Workbook. This optional supplement is designed to reinforce the text instructions in the students' minds by providing multiple choice, completion, and application exercises.

Instructor's resource box. Arranged in file folders by chapter, the following support material is assembled for easy use with each lecture:
Sample syllabi and grading systems
Summary teaching notes
Teaching suggestions
Illustrated discussion guides for the transparencies
Answers to end-of-chapter critical thought questions
Answers to end-of-chapter critical thinking exercises
Answers to workbook questions
Case problems from the previous edition text.
Audio-visual list (annotated and with order information

Instructor's manual. All the material found in the Instructor's Resource Box is available in this bound manual.

Transparency package. Fifty-three four-color acetates and 130 transparency masters provide additional examples to critique and summaries of key points for use in lectures and discussion.

Electronic Acetates. For the first time, hundreds of four-color acetates are captured in a Power Point electronic package. The Power Point disks, organized by chapter, contain text information and material created specifically for the electronic format.

The IRWIN Business Communication Video Series. This series consists of self-contained, informative segments covering such topics as writing correctly and the power of listening. Presented in a clear and engaging style, every segment holds students' interest while presenting the techniques for sharpening their communication skills. Contact your IRWIN representative for more information.

Test bank. This comprehensive collection of objective questions covers all chapters.

Computerized Testing Software. This advanced test generator enables the teacher to build and restructure tests to meet specific preferences.

Tele-Test. Customized exam preparation is furnished by the publisher.

ORGANIZATION OF THE BOOK

A major goal in this edition was to cover the essential subject matter more concisely. Thus we made four significant organization changes. First, in response to suggestions of adopters and reviewers, we now cover the basic direct-order letters in a single chapter (Chapter 5). Second, we do the same for the basic indirect-order letters (Chapter 6). Our procedure in these two chapters is first to present in detail a plan for one letter situation. Then we cover the other similar situations briefly, with primary emphasis on differences. This approach to the subject reduces repetition and of course produces conciseness. Even though we reduced overall length of the subject matter involved, we took special care to retain all significant material.

Similarly, our third major change involves combining miscellaneous types of messages. In a single chapter (Chapter 8) we cover memos, collection letters, claim letters, and orders. In the coverage of these topics, we draw on material presented in preceding chapters, again emphasizing differences and reducing duplication. The result is a more concise coverage of these topics with no loss of significant material.

Our fourth major organization change is the movement of the material on producing business documents from the text proper to the appendix (Appendix E). Perhaps more significant than the physical movement of this part is the thorough updating to make this material conform to current standards of electronic word processing.

In spite of these changes, the following basic organization plan that has characterized this book through six successful editions remains unchanged:

PART I   begins with an introductory summary of the role of communication in the organization, including a description of the process of human communication in the organization.

PART II   is a review of the basic techniques of writing. Here the emphasis is on clear writing and the effect of words.

PART III   covers the basic patterns of business letters, beginning with the most common direct and indirect ones.

PART IV   applies the contents of the preceding two parts to other forms of business letters (persuasion, sales, collection, claims, job-search and memorandums).

PART V   concentrates on report writing. Although the emphasis is on the shorter report forms, the long, analytical reports also receive complete coverage.

PART VI   reviews the other forms of business communication. Included here are communications activities such as participating in meetings, interviewing, telephoning, dictating, and listening.

PART VII   comprises a four-chapter group of special communication topics—technology-assisted communication, cross-cultural communication, correctness, and business research methods. Because teachers use them in different ways and in different

sequences, these topics are placed in this final part so that they can be used in the sequence and way that best fit each teacher's needs.

ADDITIONS TO CONTENT

As in the past, this edition was thoroughly updated throughout. We expanded coverage wherever we and our reviewers thought it would improve content. Our most significant additions or expansions are the following:

Ethics.   In support of both AACSB and ACBSP accreditation standards, the role of ethics in business communication is addressed wherever it applies throughout the book.

Updated technology chapter.   Thoroughly revised, this chapter focuses attention on the technology used in each step of the writing process—discussing both software and hardware as they assist the writer.

Cross-cultural communication.   Coverage of this timely subject was revised and expanded to support AACSB and ACBSP standards.

Collaborative writing.   Because of its widespread use in business, the subject is covered in the report writing section.

Document production.   Thoroughly updated coverage of letter and report format to include processing electronically (Appendix E).

Documentation.   This appendix part was revised and expanded to cover electronic sources of information.

Job search, resumes, and application letters.   As in every past edition, this material was expanded and revised to reflect today's standards and practices including examples and discussion of electronic résumés.

ACKNOWLEDGMENTS

Any comprehensive work such as this must owe credit to a multitude of people. Certainly, we should acknowledge the contributions of the pioneers in the business communication field, especially those whose teachings have become a part of our thinking. We should acknowledge also those colleagues in the field who served as reviewers for this edition. They are primarily responsible for the improvements that have been made. Although all identification was removed from the reviews given us, we were told that these people served as reviewers:

Frank Andera, *Central Michigan University*

Connie Jo Clark, *Lane Community College*

Edna Jellesed, *Lane Community College*

Pamela Johnson, *California State University, Chico*

Mary Miller, *Ashland University*

Rita Thomas Noel, *Western Carolina University*

Diana Reep, *University of Akron*

Elizabeth Regimbal, *Cardinal Stritch College*

Phyllis Taufen, *Gonzaga University*

Without exception, their work was good and helpful.

Because this seventh edition has evolved from all the previous editions, we also acknowledge those who contributed to those editions. They include:

Barbara Alpern, *Walsh College.*

Stuart Brown, *New Mexico State University*

Joan Feague, *Baker College*

Robert Insley, *University of North Texas*

Charles Marsh, *University of Kansas*

Deborah Roebuck, *Kennesaw State College*

Diane Reep, *University of Akron*

Carolyn Rainey, *Southeast Missouri State University*

Marilyn Price, *Kirkwood Community College*

Doris Phillips, *University of Mississippi*

George Walters, *Emporia State University*

Joan Beam, *Ferris State University*

Ben Crane, *Temple University*

Jerry Sullivan, *University of Washington*

Shelby Kipplen, *Michael Owens Technical College*

Jim Rucker, *Fort Hays State University*

Edwina Jordan, *Illinois Central College*

Cheryl Shearer, *Oxnard College*

Sandy Thomas, *Kansas City Kansas Community College*

Dolores Osborn, *Central Washington University*

Ruth Walsh, *University of South Florida*

Michael Wunsch, *Northern Arizona University*

C. Douglas Spitler, *University of Nebraska–Lincoln*

Barbara Shaw, *University of Mississippi*

James Bell, *Southwest Texas State University*

Jon N. Loff, *Allegany Community College*

Lila B. Stair, *Florida State University*

Frank E. Nelson, *Eastern Washington State College*

Judy F. McCain, *Indiana University*

James J. Weston, *California State University–Sacramento*

Kathy Wessel, *South Suburban College*

Julia Newcomer, *Texas Woman's University*

Ethel A. Martin, *Glendale Community College*

David Ramsey, *Southeastern Louisiana University*

Peter Bracher, *Wright State University*

John J. Brugaletta, *California State University–Fullerton*

Carol L. Huber, *Skagit Valley College*

Gay Sibley, *University of Hawaii at Manoa*

Douglas H. Shepard, *State University of New York*

Dwight Bullard, *Middle Tennessee State University*

Andrea Corbett, *University of Lowell*

Phyllis Howren, *University of North Carolina*

Dan Armstrong, *Oregon State University*

Tim Sabin, *Portland Community College*

Evelyn Morris, *Mesa Community College*

Suzanne Lambert, *Broward Community College*

In addition, over the life of this book many of our professional colleagues have made a variety of inputs. Most of these were made orally at professional meetings. Our memories will not permit us to acknowledge these colleagues individually. Nevertheless, we are grateful to all of them.

Finally, on our respective home fronts, we acknowledge the support of our loved ones. Marie acknowledges husband Len Deftos. John acknowledges wife Suzanne, son David B., daughter Melanie, and Melanie's husband Jamie Wilson. Ray acknowledges all his family members, both present and departed, who have provided love and inspiration over the years. Without the support of all these dear people this book would not exist.

Raymond V. Lesikar
John D. Pettit, Jr.
Marie E. Flatley

Contents in Brief

Contents

PART ONE
▶ Introduction

PART TWO
▶ Fundamentals of Business Writing

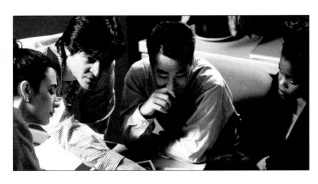

PART FIVE
▶ Fundamentals of Report Writing

PART SIX
▶ Other Forms of Business Communication

PART SEVEN
▶ Special Topics in Business Communication

LESIKAR'S
BASIC BUSINESS
COMMUNICATION

INTRODUCTION

1 **COMMUNICATION IN THE WORKPLACE**

C　　H　　A　　P　　T　　E　　R

Communication in the Workplace

1

CHAPTER OBJECTIVES

Upon completing this chapter, you will understand the role of communication in business. To achieve this goal, you should be able to

1 Explain the importance of communication to you and to business.

2 Describe the three main forms of communication in the business organization.

3 Describe the formal and informal communication networks in the business organization.

4 Explain the process of communication among people.

5 Explain three basic truths about communication.

6 Describe the plan of this book.

THE ROLE OF COMMUNICATION IN BUSINESS

Your work in business will involve communication—a lot of it—because communication is a major and essential part of the work of business.

• Communication is important to business.

The Importance of Communication Skills to You

Because communication is so important in business, businesses want and need people with good communication skills. All too often they do not get them, however, because most employees, even the college trained, do not communicate well. Among the recent studies that support this observation, perhaps the most notable[1] reports that one of the four major criticisms of today's college-trained people is their "poor communication and interpersonal skills." This study further reports that the shortcomings are in "both oral and, especially, written communication."

• Business needs good communicators, but most people do not communicate well.

The communication shortcomings of employees and the importance of communication in business explain why you should work to improve your communication skills. Whatever position you have in business, your performance will be judged largely by your ability to communicate. If you perform (and communicate) well, you are likely to be rewarded with advancement. And the higher you advance, the more you will need your communication ability. One study reports that top-level administrators spend about 85 percent of their work time communicating.[2] The evidence is clear: Improving your communication skills improves your chances for success in business.

• By improving your communication ability, you improve your chances for success.

Why Business Needs to Communicate

To understand how important communication is to business, note how much communication business requires. Take, for example, a pharmaceutical manufacturer. Throughout the company workers send and receive information. They process information with computers, write messages, fill out forms, give and receive orders, and talk over the telephone. More specifically, salespeople receive instructions and information from the home office and send back orders and weekly summaries of their activities. Executives use letters and telephone calls to initiate business with customers and other companies and respond to incoming letters and calls. Production supervisors receive work orders, issue instructions, and submit production summaries. Research specialists receive problems to investigate and later communicate their findings to management. Similar activities occur in every niche of the company. Everywhere workers receive and send information as they conduct their work.

• Communication is vital to every part of business.

Oral communication is a major part of this information flow. So, too, are various types of forms and records, as well as the storage and retrieval facilities provided by computers. Yet another major part consists of various forms of written communication—letters, memorandums, and reports.

• Communication takes many forms: oral, written, and computer.

All of this communicating goes on in business because communication is essential to the organized effort involved in business. Communication enables human beings to work together. In a business, it is the vehicle through which management performs its basic functions. Managers direct through communication, coordinate through communication, and staff, plan, and control through communication.

• All organized effort, including the work of business, requires communication.

---

[1] Lyman W. Porter and Lawrence E. McKibbin, *Management Education and Development: Drift or Thrust into the 21st Century* (New York: McGraw-Hill Book Company, 1988), p. 99.

[2] Martha H. Rader and Alan P. Wunsch, "A Survey of Communication Practices of Business School Graduates by Job Category and Undergraduate Major," *Journal of Business Communication* 7, no. 4 (Summer 1980), pp. 37–38.

Main Forms of Communication in Business

The importance of communication in business becomes even more apparent when we consider the communication activities of an organization from an overall point of view. These activities fall into three broad categories: internal operational, external operational, and personal.

Internal-Operational Communication.

All the communication that occurs in conducting work within a business is classified as internal operational. This is the communication among the business's workers that is done to implement the business's operating plan. By *operating plan* we mean the procedure that the business has developed to do whatever it was formed to do—for example, to manufacture products, provide a service, or sell goods.

Internal-operational communication takes many forms. It includes the orders and instructions that supervisors give workers, as well as oral exchanges among workers about work matters. It includes reports and records that workers prepare concerning sales, production, inventories, finance, maintenance, and so on. It includes the memorandums and reports that workers write in carrying out their assignments.

Much of this internal-operational communication is performed on computer networks. Workers send electronic mail through networks to others throughout the business, whether located down the hall, across the street, or around the world. As you will learn in Chapter 16, the computer also assists the business writer and speaker in many other aspects of communication.

External-Operational Communication.

The work-related communicating that a business does with people and groups outside the business is external-operational communication. This is the business's communication with its publics—suppliers, service companies, customers, and the general public.

External-operational communication includes all of the business's efforts at direct selling—salespeople's "spiels," descriptive brochures, telephone callbacks, follow-up service calls, and the like. It also includes the advertising the business does, for what is advertising but communication with potential customers? Radio and television messages, newspaper and magazine advertising, and point-of-purchase display material obviously play a role in the business's plan to achieve its work objective. Also in this category is all that a business does to improve its public relations, including its planned publicity, the civic-mindedness of its management, the courtesy of its employees, and the condition of its physical plant. And of very special importance to

- There are three categories of communication in business:

- (1) Internal operational—the communicating done in conducting work within a business,

- such as giving orders, assembling reports, writing memorandums, and communicating by computers.

- (2) External operational—work-related communication with people outside the business,

- such as personal selling, telephoning, advertising, and letter writing.

"Gentlemen, it's only a suggestion but just remember who made it." (*From The Wall Street Journal, with permission of Cartoon Features Syndicate*)

our study of communication, this category includes all the letters that workers write in carrying out their assignments.

Technology assists workers with external-operational communication in both constructing and transmitting documents. For example, salespeople can keep database information on customers; check their company's computers for new product information and inventory information; and construct sales, order confirmation, and other letters for their customers. These letters can be transmitted by fax, electronic mail, or printed copy.

- Technology (computers, fax) assists in constructing and sending these communications.

The importance of external-operational communication to a business hardly requires supporting comment. Every business is dependent on outside people and groups for its success. And because the success of a business depends on its ability to satisfy customers' needs, it must communicate effectively with them. In today's complex business society, businesses depend on each other in the production and distribu-

- Both internal and external communications are vital to business success.

In the large business, much of the work done involves internal-operational communication.

tion of goods and services. This interdependence requires communication. Like internal communication, external communication is vital to business success.

Personal Communication.   Not all the communication that occurs in business is operational. In fact, much of it is without purpose as far as the business is concerned. Such communication is called personal.

Personal communication is the exchange of information and feelings in which we human beings engage whenever we come together. We are social animals. We have a need to communicate, and we will communicate even when we have little or nothing to say.

We spend much of our time with friends in communication. Even total strangers are likely to communicate when they are placed together, as on an airplane flight, in a waiting room, or at a ball game. Such personal communication also occurs at the workplace, and it is a part of the communication activity of any business. Although not a part of the business's plan of operation, personal communication can have a significant effect on the success of that plan. This effect is a result of the influence that personal communication can have on the attitudes of the workers.

The workers' attitudes toward the business, each other, and their assignments directly affect their willingness to work. And the nature of conversation in a work situation affects attitudes. In a work situation where heated words and flaming tempers are often present, the workers are not likely to make their usual productive efforts. However, a rollicking, jovial work situation is likely to have an equally bad effect on productivity. Somewhere between these extremes lies the ideal productive attitude.

Also affecting the workers' attitudes is the extent of personal communication permitted. Absolute denial of personal communication could lead to emotional upset, for most of us hold dear our right to communicate. On the other hand, excessive personal communication could interfere with the work done. Again, the middle ground is probably the best.

Communication Network of the Organization

Looking over all of a business's communication (internal, external, and personal), we see an extremely complex network of information flow. We see an organization feeding on a continuous supply of information. More specifically, we see dozens, hundreds, or even thousands of individuals engaging in untold numbers of communication events throughout each workday.

Most of the information flow of operational communication is downward and follows the formal lines of organization (from the top administrators down to the workers). This is so because most of the information, instructions, orders, and such needed to achieve the business's objectives originate at the top and must be communicated to the workers. However, most companies recognize the need for more upward communication. They have found that administrators need to be better informed of the status of things at the bottom. They have also found that information from the lower levels can be important in achieving company work goals.

The Formal Network.   In simplified form, information flow in a modern business is much like the network of arteries and veins in the body. Just as the body has arteries, the business has major, well-established channels of information flow. These are the formal channels—the main lines of operational communication. Through these channels flows the bulk of the communication that the business needs to operate. Specifically, the flow includes the movements of information by reports, memorandums, records, and such within the organization; of orders, instructions, and messages down the authority structure; of working information through the organization's computer network; and of externally directed letters, sales presentations, advertising, and publicity. These main channels should not just happen; they should be carefully thought out and changed as the needs of the business change.

Marginal notes (left column):

- (3) Personal communication—non-business-related exchanges of information and feelings among people.

- Personal communication affects worker attitudes.

- And attitudes affect worker performance.

- The extent of personal communication permitted affects worker attitudes.

- Information flow in a business forms a complex network.

- The flow is mainly downward, but upward communication is also important.

- The main (formal) lines of flow are like the network of arteries in the body.

FIGURE 1–1 Formal and Informal Communication Networks in a Division of a Small Manufacturing Company

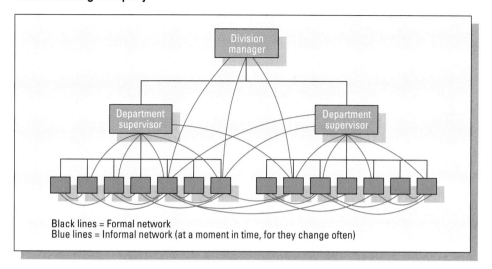

Black lines = Formal network
Blue lines = Informal network (at a moment in time, for they change often)

The Informal Network. Parallel to the formal network lies the informal network, a secondary network consisting primarily of personal communication (see Figure 1–1). Just as the formal network is like the arteries, the informal one is like the veins. It comprises the thousands upon thousands of personal communications that occur in a business. Such communications follow no set pattern; they form an ever-changing and infinitely complex structure linking all the members of the organization.

The complexity of this informal network, especially in larger organizations, cannot be overemphasized. Typically, it is really not a single network but a complex relationship of smaller networks consisting of groups of people. The relationship is made even more complex by the fact that these people may belong to more than one group and that group memberships and the links between and among groups are continually changing. Truly, the informal network in a large organization is so complex as to defy description.

- The secondary (informal) network is like the veins.

- This secondary network is highly complex and continually changing.

The informal communication network of a business consists of all the communication of its employees whenever they get together.

Known as the *grapevine* in management literature, this communication network is far more effective than a first impression might indicate. Certainly, it carries much gossip and rumor, for this is the nature of human conversation. And it is as fickle and inaccurate as the human beings who are a part of it. Even so, the grapevine usually carries far more information than the formal communication system; and on many matters it is more effective in determining the course of an organization. Wise managers recognize the presence of the grapevine. They give the talk leaders the information that will do the most good for the organization. That is, they keep in touch with the grapevine and turn it into a constructive tool.

Variation in Communication Activity by Business

• The extent of a business's
communication depends on the
nature of the business, its
operating plan, and the people
involved.

Just how much communicating a business does depends on several factors. The nature of the business is one. For example, insurance companies have a great need to communicate with their customers, especially through letters and mailing pieces, whereas housecleaning service companies have little such need. The business's operating plan affects the amount of internal communication. Relatively simple businesses, such as repair services, require far less communication than complex businesses, such as automobile manufacturers. Also, the people who make up a business affect its volume of communication. Every human being is different. Each has different communication needs and abilities. Thus, varying combinations of people will produce varying needs for communication.

THE PROCESS OF HUMAN COMMUNICATION

• The following review describes
how communication among
people works.

Although we may view the communication of a business as a network of information flow, we must keep in mind that a business organization consists of people and that the communication in the organization occurs among people. Thus, it is important to our basic understanding of business communication to know how communication among people occurs. The following review of the human communication process will give you that knowledge.

In many small businesses, little need for operational communication exists. Much of the communicating done is with customers.

The Beginning: A Message Sent

To describe the communication process, we will use a situation involving two people—Marci and Kevin (see Figure 1–2). Although the steps described may suggest that Kevin and Marci are communicating in separate actions, the actions occur simultaneously. As one is sending, the other is receiving. Our description begins with Marci communicating a message to Kevin. Her message could be in any of a number of forms—gestures, facial expressions, drawings, or, more likely, written or spoken words. Whatever the form, Marci sends the message to Kevin.

• The process begins when Marci sends a message to Kevin.

Entry in the Sensory World

Marci's message then enters Kevin's sensory world. By *sensory world* we mean all that surrounds a person that the senses (sight, hearing, smell, taste, touch) can detect. As we will see, Kevin's sensory world contains more than Marci's message.

• The message enters Kevin's sensory world,

Detection by the Senses

From his sensory world Kevin picks up stimuli (messages) through his senses. We must note, however, that Kevin's senses cannot detect *all* that exists in the world around him. Just how much they can detect depends on a number of factors. One is the ability of his senses. As you know, not all eyes see equally well and not all ears hear equally well. And so it is with the other senses. Another factor is Kevin's mental alertness. There are times when he is keenly alert to all that his senses can detect, and there are times when he is dull—in a stupor, a daydream, or the like. Furthermore, Kevin's cultural background has sensitized him more to some stimuli than others. Yet another limiting factor is Kevin's will. In varying degrees, the mind is able to tune in or tune out events in the sensory world. In a noisy room full of people, for example, the conversation of a single person can be selected and the other voices ignored.

• where his senses may detect it.

FIGURE 1–2   The Communication Process: Marci and Kevin Communicate

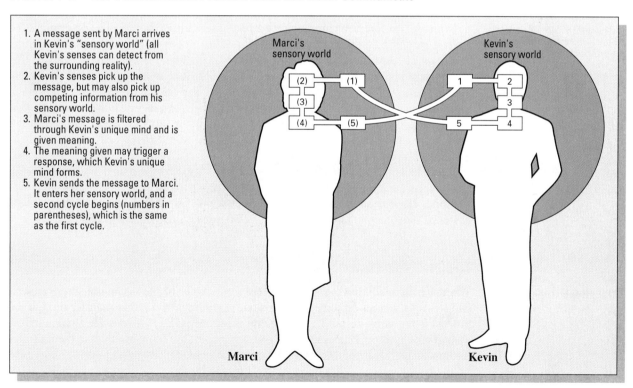

1. A message sent by Marci arrives in Kevin's "sensory world" (all Kevin's senses can detect from the surrounding reality).
2. Kevin's senses pick up the message, but may also pick up competing information from his sensory world.
3. Marci's message is filtered through Kevin's unique mind and is given meaning.
4. The meaning given may trigger a response, which Kevin's unique mind forms.
5. Kevin sends the message to Marci. It enters her sensory world, and a second cycle begins (numbers in parentheses), which is the same as the first cycle.

When Kevin's senses pick up Marci's message, they relay it to his brain—that is, as much or as little of the message as they detect. But Marci's message may not be all that Kevin's senses pick up. In addition to Marci's message, his sensory world may contain outside noises, movements of objects, facial expressions, and the like. In fact, his senses are continually picking up messages from the world around him. Marci's message is just the primary one at the moment. The others are there, and they might interfere with Marci's message.

- What Kevin's senses detect, they send to his brain,

The Filtering Process

When Marci's message gets to Kevin's brain, it goes through a sort of filtering process. Through that process Kevin's brain gives meaning to Marci's message. In other words, the message is filtered through the contents of Kevin's mind. Those contents include all his experience, knowledge, biases, emotions, cultural background—in fact, all Kevin is and has been. Obviously, no two people have precisely identical filters, for no two people have minds with precisely the same contents.

- where it goes through a filtering process.

Because people's filters differ, the meanings they give to comparable messages may differ. Thus, the meaning Kevin gives Marci's message may not be precisely the same as the one that someone else would give it. And it may not be the meaning Marci intended. For example, assume that Marci used the word *liberal* in her message. Now assume that Marci and Kevin have had sharply differing experiences with the word. To Marci the word is negative, for her experience has made her dislike things liberal. To Kevin the word is positive. Thus, the message Kevin receives from the word would not be precisely the message Marci sent. And so it could be with other words in Marci's message.

- Because minds differ, message meanings differ.

Formation and Sending of the Response

After his mind has given meaning to Marci's message, Kevin may react to the message. If the meaning he received is sufficiently strong, he may react by communicating some form of response. This response may be through words, gestures, physical actions, or some other means.

- Kevin's mind reacts to the meaning, and he may respond.

When Kevin elects to communicate a response, through his mind he determines the general meaning that the response will take. This process involves the most complex workings of the mind, and we know little about it. There is evidence, however, that ability, here and throughout this stage, is related to one's intelligence and the extent that one permits the mind to react. Kevin's ability to evaluate filtered information and formulate meaning is also related to his ability with language. Ability with language equips one with a variety of symbols (words and other ways of expressing meaning). And the greater the number of symbols one possesses, the better one can be at selecting and using them.

- Through his mind and its contents, Kevin determines the meaning of the response.

Kevin ends this stage of the communication process by forming a message. That is, he converts meanings into symbols (mainly words), and then he sends these symbols to Marci. He may send them in a number of ways—as spoken words, written words, gestures, movements, facial expressions, diagrams on paper, and so on.

- Kevin forms a message and sends it.

The Cycle Repeated

When Kevin sends his message to Marci, one cycle of the communication process ends. Now a second cycle begins. This one involves Marci rather than Kevin, but the process is the same. Kevin's message enters Marci's sensory world. Her senses pick it up and send it through her nervous system to her brain. There her unique mental filter influences the meaning she gives Kevin's message. This filtered meaning may also bring about a response. If it does, Marci, through her mind, selects the symbols for her

- Then the cycle is repeated.

response. Then she sends them to Kevin, and another cycle of communication begins. The process may continue, cycle after cycle, as long as Marci and Kevin want to communicate.

The Communication Process and Written Communication

Although our description of the communication process illustrates face-to-face, oral communication, it also fits written communication. But there are some differences. Perhaps the most significant difference is that written communication is more likely to involve creative effort. It is more likely to be thought out, and it may even begin in the mind rather than as a reaction to a message received.

- Written communication differs from oral communication in tha (1) is more likely to involve creative effort,

A second difference is the time between cycles. In face-to-face communication, cycles occur fast, often in rapid succession. In written communication, some delay occurs. How long the delay will be varies. Fax messages may be read a few minutes after they are transmitted, letters in a few days, reports perhaps in days, weeks, or months. Because they provide a record, written communications may communicate over extremely long time periods.

- (2) has longer cycles, and

A third difference is that written communication usually involves a limited number of cycles and oral communication usually involves many. In fact, some written communication is one-cycle communication. That is, a message is sent and received, but none is returned.

- (3) usually has fewer cycles.

Some Basic Truths about Communication

Analysis of the communication process brings out three underlying truths that will help us understand its complexity.

- The communication process reveals some basic truths.

Meanings Sent Are Not Always Received. The first underlying truth is that the meanings transmitted are not necessarily the meanings received. No two minds have identical filters. No two minds have identical storehouses of words, gestures, facial expressions, or any of the other symbol forms. And no two minds attach exactly the

- Because our mental filters differ, meanings sent may differ from meanings received.

C O M M U N I C A T I O N   I N   B R I E F

A Sure Way of Getting a Response

In oral communication the cycles can go on indefinitely. In sharp contrast, written communication may end after a single cycle. How one imaginative mother used a written communication to assure a second cycle makes a classic story.

The mother was having difficulty in getting her college-student son to answer her letters. She wrote regularly but rarely received a reply. In desperation, she resorted to psychology. She wrote the usual letter filled with news from home. Then she ended with a reference to an enclosed check and instructions to "use it as you like." She mailed the letter, but she did not include the check.

In short order the son responded. His letter was filled with the kind of information mothers like to hear. At the end was a thank-you for the check, "which must have been forgotten, so please send it."

The son got the check, the mother got a letter, and, of course, a second communication cycle occurred.

same meanings to all the symbols they have in common. Because of these differences in minds, errors in communication are bound to occur.

• Meanings are in the mind—not in symbols.

Meaning Is in the Mind.   A second underlying truth is that meaning is in the mind—not in the words or other symbols used. How accurately one conveys meaning in symbols depends on how skillful one is in choosing symbols and on how skillful the person receiving the symbols is in interpreting the meaning intended. Thus, you should look beyond the symbols used. You should consider the communication abilities of those with whom you want to communicate. When they receive your messages, they do not look at the symbols alone. They also look for the meanings they think you intended.

• Because symbols are imperfect and people differ in their ability to communicate, communication is far from perfect.

The Symbols of Communication Are Imperfect.   The third underlying truth is that the symbols used in communication are imperfect. One reason for this is that the symbols we use, especially words, are at best crude substitutes for the real thing. For example, the word *man* can refer to billions of human beings of whom no two are precisely alike. The word *dog* stands for any one of countless animals that vary sharply in size, shape, color, and every other visible aspect. The word *house* can refer equally well to structures ranging from shanties to palatial mansions. The verb *run* conveys only the most general part of an action; it ignores countless variations in speed, grace, and style. These illustrations are not exceptions; they are the rule. Words simply cannot account for the infinite variations of reality.

Communication is also imperfect because communicators vary in their ability to convey thoughts. Some find it very difficult to select symbols that express their simplest thoughts. Variations in ability to communicate obviously lead to variations in the precision with which thoughts are expressed.

• Communication across cultures is especially difficult.

Communication across cultures is especially imperfect, for often there are no equivalent words in the cultures. For example, usually there is no precise translation for our jargon in other cultures. Words such as *condo, computer virus,* and *yuppie* are not likely to have equivalents in every other culture. Similarly, other cultures have specialized words unique and necessary to them that we do not have. For instance, the Eskimos have many words for *snow,* each describing a unique type. Obviously, such distinctions are vital to their existence. We can get along very well with the one word. As you will see in Chapter 17, this subject is so vital to today's business communication that an entire chapter is devoted to it.

• Even so, we communicate reasonably well.

Although the foregoing comments bring to light the difficulties, complexities, and limitations of communication, on the whole we human beings do a fairly good job of communicating. Still, miscommunication often occurs. And people who attach precise meanings to every word, who believe that meanings intended are meanings received, and who are not able to select symbols well are likely to experience more than their share.

Resulting Stress on Adaptation

• The communication process shows the need for adaptation—an underlying principle in our study of communication.

Understanding the communication process can help you become a better communicator. The process shows that communication is a unique event—that every mind is different from every other mind. No two of us know the same words; and no two of us know equal amounts about all subjects. Obviously, such differences make communication difficult. Unless the words (or other symbols) used in a message have the same meanings in the minds of both the sender and the recipient, communication suffers. Communication scholars have tried to solve this problem by stressing the adaptation of messages to the minds of their recipients. By *adaptation* we mean fitting the message to the recipients—using words and other symbols that they understand. As you will see, adaptation is the foundation for our review of communication principles in the pages ahead.

THE GOAL, PLAN, AND PHILOSOPHY OF THIS BOOK

The preceding discussion shows that communication is important to business, that it is performed in various and complex ways, and that it is imprecise. These observations suggest that communicating in business is not to be taken lightly. If you want to excel at it, you must develop your communication skills. Helping you to do this is the goal of this book.

• The goal of this book is to help you improve your communication skills.

The Plan: Situations, Solutions, Summaries

To achieve this goal, the book introduces each major topic through a business communication situation that realistically places you in the business world. Each situation describes a possible communication problem. Then the following material instructs you on how to solve the problem. For your study convenience, summaries of the text material appear in the margins. A general summary by chapter objectives appears at the ends of the chapters.

• The book introduces topics by situations—then it shows solutions. Summaries help your study.

The Philosophy: Communicate to Communicate

In presenting this subject matter, the book takes a practical, realistic approach. That is, it views business communication as having one primary goal—to communicate.

• Successful communication is the purpose of communicating.

Although this statement may appear elementary, it has significant meaning. All too often other goals creep in. For example, communicators sometimes seek to impress—perhaps by using big words and involved sentences. Or they seek to entertain with a clever choice of words. Good business communicators rarely have these goals. They primarily seek to communicate. They use words and sentences that communicate clearly and quickly. If the message has any difficulty, the reason is that the subject matter is difficult. In no way should the words and the sentence structures add to the difficulty.

• Some writers have other goals (to impress, to entertain). Business communicators should seek only to communicate.

SUMMARY ▶ by Chapter Objectives

1. Business needs and rewards people who can communicate, for communication is vital to business operations.
   • But good communicators are scarce.
   • So, if you can improve your communication skills, you increase your value to business and business will reward you.

① Explain the importance of communication to you and to business.

2. The communicating in business falls into three categories:
   • The communicating a business does to implement its operating plan (its procedure for doing what it was formed to do) is called *internal-operational* communication.
   • The communicating a business does with outsiders (suppliers, other businesses, customers, and such) is *external-operational* communication.
   • Informal exchanges of information not related to operations are called *personal* communication.

② Describe the three main forms of communication in the business organization.

3. The flow of communication in a business organization forms a complex and ever-changing network. Information continually flows from person to person—upward, downward, and laterally.
   • The communicating that follows the formal structure of the business forms the *formal* network. Primarily, operational information flows through this network.
   • The flow of informal (personal) communication forms the *informal* network.

③ Describe the formal and informal communication networks in the business organization.

4. The human communication process is as follows:
   • A message arrives in one's sensory world (all that one can detect with the senses).

④ Explain the process of communication among people.

- The senses pick up the message and relay it to the brain.
- The brain filters the message through all its contents (knowledge, emotions, biases, and such) and gives it a unique meaning.
- This meaning may trigger a response, which the mind then forms.
- The person then sends (by voice, marks on paper, gestures, or such) this message into the sensory world of another person.
- Within this person the process described above is repeated (another cycle begins).
- The process continues, cycle after cycle, as long as the people involved care to communicate.

5 Explain three basic thruths about communication.

5. The communication process reveals these truths:
   - Meanings sent are not always received (our mental filters differ).
   - Meaning is in the mind—not in the symbols (mainly words) used.
   - The symbols we use are imperfect, primarily because the reality they describe is so complex.

6 Describe the plan of this book.

6. The plan of this book is to introduce you to the primary types of business communication problems through realistic situations.
   - You are placed in a business communication situation.
   - Then you are shown how to handle it.

CRITICAL THOUGHT QUESTIONS

1. Is the ability to communicate more important to the successful performance of a supervisor's job than to that of a company president's job? Defend your answer.

2. Make a list of types of companies requiring extensive communication. Then make a list of types of companies requiring little communication. What explains the difference in these two groups?

3. List the types of external-operational and internal-operational communication that occur in an organization with which you are familiar (school, fraternity, church, or such).

4. Identify the types of technology used primarily in internal- and external-operational communication to transmit messages. Explain what you think might account for the differences.

5. Discuss the question of how much personal communication should be permitted in a business organization. Defend your view.

6. Describe the network of communication in an organization with which you are familiar (preferably a simple one). Discuss and explain.

7. Describe what is in your sensory world at this moment. Contrast the parts that are usually in your awareness with the parts that are usually not in your awareness.

8. Using the model for the communication process as a base, explain how people reading or hearing the same message can disagree on its meaning.

9. Give an example of a simple statement that could be misunderstood. Explain why. Then revise the statement for more precise understanding.

CRITICAL THINKING EXERCISES

1. Megan Cabot is one of 12 workers in Department X. She has strong leadership qualities, and all her co-workers look up to her. She dominates conversations with them and expresses strong viewpoints on most matters. Although she is a good worker, her dominating personality has caused problems for you, the new supervisor of Department X. Today you directed your subordinates to change a certain work procedure. The change is one that has proven superior wherever it has been tried. Soon after giving the directive, you noticed the workers talking in a group, with Megan the obvious leader. In a few minutes she appeared in your office. "We've thought it over," she said. "Your production change won't work." Explain what is happening. How will you handle the situation?

2. After noticing that some workers were starting work late and finishing early, a department head wrote this memorandum to subordinates:
   It is apparent that many of you are not giving the company a full day's work. Thus the following procedures are implemented immediately:
   a. After you clock in, you will proceed to your workstations and will be ready to begin work promptly at the start of the work period.
   b. You will not take a coffee break or consume coffee on the job at the beginning of the work period. You will wait until your designated break times.
   c. You will not participate in social gatherings at any time during the workday except during designated break periods.
   d. You will terminate work activities no earlier than 10 minutes prior to the end of the work period. You will use the 10 minutes to put up equipment, clean equipment, and police the work area.
   e. You will not queue up at the time clock prior to the end of the work period.
   The memorandum was not well received by the workers. In fact, it led to considerable anger, misunder-

standing, and confusion. Using the model of communication as a base, analyze the memorandum and explain the probable causes of the difficulties.

3. After being introduced to a candidate for the presidency of their company, two workers had the following discussion. One worker is Scott, a young college-age man who is holding a full-time job while going to school part-time. The other is Will, an old-timer—a self-made man and master craftsman.
   Scott: I like the candidate. He appears young, energetic, and bright.
   Will: He's young all right. Too young! Too bright! That fancy Harvard degree won't help him here. Why, I'll bet he hasn't spent one day in a working-man's shoes.
   Scott: Now that's not fair. He was trained to be an administrator, and he has had experience as an administrator—high-level experience. You don't need experience as a soldier to be a general.
   Will: Don't tell me what this company needs. I've spent 40 years here. I know. I was here when old J.P. (the company founder) was president. He started as a machinist and worked to the top. Best president any company could have. We loved the man. He knew the business and he knew the work we do.
   Scott: But that doesn't happen today. Administrators have to be trained for administration. They have to know administration, finance, marketing—the whole business field. You don't get that in the shop.
   Will: All you kids think that knowledge only comes from books. You can't substitute book sense for experience and common sense. I've been here 40 years, son. I know.

   The dialogue continued to accelerate and soon led to angry words. Neither Scott nor Will changed positions. Analyze the dialogue using the model of communication as the base.

FUNDAMENTALS OF BUSINESS WRITING

Adaptation and the Selection of Words

Upon completing this chapter, you will be able to adapt your language to specific readers and to select the most effective words for use in business communication. To reach this goal, you should be able to

1 Explain the role of adaptation in selecting words that communicate.

2 Simplify writing by selecting the short and familiar words.

3 Use technical words appropriately.

4 Discuss the differences in the strength of words and select the words that communicate your message best.

5 Write concretely and stress active voice.

6 Write with clarity and precision by avoiding camouflaged verbs, by selecting the right words, and by using idioms correctly.

7 Use words that do not discriminate.

▶ to Choosing Words that Communicate

As a means of introducing yourself to business communication, place yourself in a hypothetical situation. You are the office manager of a manufacturing company. You have before you a memorandum from Max Schlitz, one of your assistants. Following your instructions, Max investigated your company's use of available space. He has summarized his findings in a memorandum report.

At first glance you are impressed with Max's report and with his ability. But after reading the report, you are not sure just what his investigation uncovered. Here is a typical paragraph:

> In the interest of ensuring maximum utilization of the subterranean components of the building currently not apportioned to operations departments, it is recommended that an evaluation of requisites for storage space be initiated. Subject review should be initiated at the earliest practicable opportunity and should be conducted by administrative personnel not affiliated with operative departments.

Max's problem is altogether too commonplace in business. His words, though properly used, do not communicate quickly and easily. This and the following chapter show you what you can do about writing like this. ■

THE BASIC NEED FOR ADAPTATION

The study of clear writing logically begins with adaptation. By *adaptation* we mean fitting the message to the specific reader. Obviously, readers do not all have the same ability to understand a message. They do not all have the same vocabulary, the same knowledge of the subject, or the same mentality. Thus, to communicate clearly you should first know the person with whom you communicate. You should form your message to fit that person's mind.

• For writing to be clear, it must be adapted to the reader.

Visualizing the Reader

In adapting your message, you begin by visualizing your reader. That is, you form a mental picture of what he or she is like. You imagine what the reader knows about the subject, what his or her educational level is, and how he or she thinks. In general, you consider whatever you believe could have some effect on your reader's understanding of your message. With this in mind, you form the message.

• Adaptation begins with visualizing the reader—imagining what he or she knows, feels, thinks, and such.

Technique of Adapting

In many business situations, adapting to your reader means writing on a level lower than the one you would normally use. For example, you will sometimes need to communicate with people whose educational level is below your own. Or you may need to communicate with people of your educational level who simply do not know much about the subject of your message.

• Often you will need to write at levels lower than your own.

To illustrate, assume that you need to write a memorandum to a group of less-educated workers. You know that their vocabularies are limited. If you are to reach them, you will have to use simple words. If you do not, you will not communicate. On the other hand, if you had to write the same message to a group of highly educated people, you would have a wider choice of words. These people have larger vocabularies than the first group. In either case, however, you would select words that the intended readers understand.

• In writing to less-educated workers, for example, you may need to simplify. You may write differently for highly educated people.

Adaptation Illustrated

The following paragraphs from two company annual reports illustrate the basic principle of adaptation. The writer of the first report apparently viewed the readers as people who were not well informed in finance.

Last year your company's total sales were $117,400,000, which was slightly higher than the $109,800,000 total for the year before. After deducting for all expenses, we had $4,593,000 left over for profits, compared with $2,830,000 for 1995. Because of these increased profits, we were able to increase your annual dividend payments per share from the 50 cents paid over the last 10 years.

The writer of the second report saw the readers as being well informed in finance. Perhaps this writer believed the typical reader would come from the ranks of stockbrokers, financial managers, financial analysts, and bankers. So this writer adapted the annual report to these readers with language like this:

The corporation's investments and advances in three unconsolidated subsidiaries (all in the development stage) and in 50 percent-owned companies was $42,200,000 on December 31, 1992, and the excess of the investments in certain companies over net asset value at dates of acquisition was $1,760,000. The corporation's equity in the net assets as of December 31, 1995, was $41,800,000 and in the results of operations for the years ended December 31, 1995 and 1994, was $1,350,000 and $887,500, respectively. Dividend income was $750,000 and $388,000 for the years 1995 and 1992, respectively.

Which writer was right? Perhaps both. Perhaps neither. The answer depends on what the stockholders of each company were really like. Both examples illustrate the technique of adaptation. They use different words for different audiences, which is what you should try to do.

Adapting to Multiple Readers

- If you write for one person in a group, you may miss the others.

Adapting your message to one reader is easy. But how do you adapt when you are communicating with two or more readers? What if your intended readers vary widely in education, knowledge of the subject, and so on? Writing to the level of the best-educated and best-informed persons would miss those at lower levels. Adapting your message to the lowest level runs the risk of insulting the intelligence of those at higher levels.

- To communicate with all of them, write for the lowest member of the group.

The answer is obvious. You have to adapt to the lowest level you need to reach. Not doing so would result in not communicating with that level. Of course, by writing for readers at the lowest level, you run the risk of offending those at higher levels. You can minimize this risk by taking care not to talk down. For example, you can carefully

---

C O M M U N I C A T I O N   I N   B R I E F

A Classic Case of Adaptation

There is a story told around Washington about a not-too-bright inventor who wrote the Bureau of Standards that he had made a great discovery: Hydrochloric acid is good for cleaning clogged drains.

He got this response: "The efficacy of hydrochloric acid is indisputable, but the corrosive residue is incompatible with metallic permanence."

Believing that these big words indicated agreement, this not-so-bright inventor wrote back telling how pleased he was that the bureau liked his discovery.

The bureaucrat tried again: "We cannot assume responsibility for the production of toxic residue with hydrochloric acid and suggest alternative procedure."

The inventor was even more gratified. He again expressed his appreciation to the bureau for agreeing with him.

This time the bureaucrat got the message. He replied in words any inventor would be certain to understand: "Don't use hydrochloric acid. It'll eat hell out of pipes."

In talking to a child, we naturally adapt the language to the child. Similarly, in business communication we need to adapt the language to the reader.

work in "as you know" and similar expressions to imply that you know the reader knows what you are writing about.

Governing Role of Adaptation

The preceding discussion shows that adaptation is basic to communication. In fact, it is so basic that you will need to apply it to all the writing and speaking instructions in the pages ahead. For example, much of what will be said about writing techniques will stress simplicity—using simple words, short sentences, and short paragraphs. You will need to think of simplicity in terms of adaptation. Specifically, you will need to keep in mind that what is simple for one person may not be simple for another. Only if you keep in mind the logical use of adaptation will you fully understand the intended meaning of the writing instructions.

* Adaptation underlies all that will be said about writing. Apply it to the other writing instructions.

SUGGESTIONS FOR SELECTING WORDS

A major part of adaptation is selecting the right words. These are the words that communicate best—that have correct and clear meanings *in the reader's mind.*

Selecting the right words depends on your ability to use language, your knowledge of the reader, and your good judgment. Few hard-and-fast rules apply. Still, you should keep in mind the suggestions presented in the following paragraphs. As you review them, remember that you must use them with good judgment. You must consider them in light of the need to adapt the message to your reader or readers.

As you will see, most of the suggestions support simplicity in writing. This approach is justified by three good reasons. The first is that many of us tend to write at too difficult a level. Instead of being ourselves, we change character when we write. Rather than being friendly, normal people, we become cold and stiff. We work to use big words and complex structures. Winston Churchill referred to this tendency when he made his classic remark: "Little men use big words; big men use little words." We would do well to follow the example of this big man.

* Selecting the right words is a part of adaptation. Following are some suggestions to help you select such words.

* These suggestions stress simplicity for three reasons: (1) many people tend to write at a difficult level;

In the Lord's Prayer, you will find 66 words—48 are of one syllable, a percentage of 72.

In "All the world's a stage" (Shakespeare's *As You Like It*), there are 212 words—150 are of one syllable, a percentage of 70.

In Abraham Lincoln's Gettysburg Address, there are 268 words—196 are of one syllable, a percentage of 73.

• (2) the writer usually knows the subject better than the reader; and

The second reason for simplicity is that the writer usually knows the subject of the message better than the reader. Thus, the two are not equally equipped to communicate on the matter. If the writer does not work at reducing the message to the reader's level, communication will be difficult.

• (3) the results of research support simplicity.

The third reason for simplicity is that convincing research supports it. According to the research of such experts as Gunning, Dale, Chall, and Flesch, writing slightly below the reader's level of understanding communicates best.

Use Familiar Words

• Familiar words communicate. Use them. Use your judgment in determining what words are familiar.

The foremost suggestion for word selection is to use familiar words. These are the everyday words—the words with sharp and clear meanings in the mind. Because words that are familiar to some people may be unfamiliar to others, you will need to select familiar words with care. You have no choice but to rely on your judgment.

Specifically, using familiar words means using the language that most of us use in everyday conversation. We should avoid the stiff, more difficult words that do not communicate so precisely or quickly. For example, instead of using the more unfamiliar word *endeavor,* use *try.* Instead of using *terminate,* use *end.* Prefer *use* to *utilize, do* to *perform, begin* to *initiate, find out* to *ascertain, stop* to *discontinue,* and *show* to *demonstrate.*

• Difficult words are not all bad. Use them when they fit your needs and are understood.

The suggestion to use familiar words does not rule out some use of more difficult words. You should use them whenever their meanings fit your purpose best and your readers understand them clearly. The mistake that many of us make is to overwork the more difficult words. We use them so much that they interfere with our communication. A good suggestion is to use the simplest words that carry the meaning without offending the readers' intelligence. Perhaps the best suggestion is to write the words you would use in face-to-face communication with your readers.

The following contrasting examples illustrate the communication advantages of familiar words over less familiar ones.[1] As you read the examples, consider the effect on communication of an entire letter or report written in the styles illustrated.

UNFAMILIAR WORDS	FAMILIAR WORDS
This machine has a tendency to develop excessive and unpleasant audio symptoms when operating at elevated temperatures.	This machine tends to get noisy when it runs hot.
Ms. Smith's idiosyncrasies supply adequate justification for terminating her employment status.	Ms. Smith's peculiar ways justify firing her.
This antiquated mechanism is ineffectual for an accelerated assembly-line operation.	This old robot will not work on a fast assembly line.

[1] For some of these examples, we are indebted to students and friends who gave them to us over the years.

UNFAMILIAR WORDS	FAMILIAR WORDS
The most operative assembly-line configuration is an unidirectional flow.	The most efficient assembly-line design is a one-way flow.
The conclusion ascertained from a perusal of pertinent data is that a lucrative market exists for the product.	The data studied show that the product is in good demand.
Company operations for the preceding accounting period terminated with a substantial deficit.	The company lost much money last year.

An example supporting the use of familiar words came from Cape Kennedy while scientists were conducting research in preparation for long spaceflights. In one experiment, a monkey was placed in a simulated spaceship with enough food to last many days. With an unlimited supply of food available, the monkey simply ate too much and died. A scientist used these words to record the incident: "One monkey succumbed unexpectedly apparently as a result of an untoward response to a change in feeding regimen." Most readers of the report missed the message. Why didn't the scientist report in everyday language, "One monkey died because it ate too much"?

Another real-life example involved President Franklin D. Roosevelt. Across his desk came a memorandum advising federal workers to do the following in the event of an air raid:

Such preparations shall be made as will completely obscure all federal buildings and non-federal buildings occupied by the federal government during an air raid for any period of time from visibility by reason of internal or external illumination. Such obscuration may be obtained either by blackout construction or by termination of the illumination.

Irked by the heavy wording, FDR sent this memorandum to the author:

Tell them that in buildings where they have to keep the work going to put something over the windows; and, in buildings where they can let the work stop for a while, turn out the lights.

In this and the preceding examples, the familiar words are clearly better. Readers understand them.

Choose Short Words

According to studies of readability, short words generally communicate better than long words. Of course, part of the explanation is that short words tend to be familiar words. But there is another explanation: A heavy use of long words—even long words that are understood—leaves an impression of difficulty that hinders communication.

• Generally, short words communicate better.

The suggestion that short words be chosen does not mean that all short words are easy and all long words are hard. Many exceptions exist. Few people know such one-syllable words as *gybe, verd,* and *id.* Even children know such long words as *hippopotamus, automobile,* and *bicycle.* On the whole, however, word length and word difficulty are related. Thus, you should concentrate on short words and use long words with caution. Use a long word only when you believe that your readers know it.

• Some exceptions exist.

This point is illustrated by many of the examples presented to support the use of familiar words. But the following illustrations give it additional support. In some of them, the long word versions are likely to be understood by more highly educated readers. Even so, the heavy proportion of hard words clouds the message. Without question, the short-word versions communicate better. Note that the long words and their short replacements are in italics.

LONG WORDS	SHORT WORDS
The decision was *predicated* on the *assumption* that an *abundance* of *monetary* funds was *forthcoming.*	The decision was *based* on the *belief* that there *would be more money.*

LONG WORDS	SHORT WORDS
They *acceded* to the *proposition* to *terminate* business.	They *agreed to quit* business.
During the *preceding* year the company *operated* at a *financial deficit*.	*Last year* the company *lost money*.
Prior to *accelerating productive operation*, the supervisor inspected the machinery.	Before *speeding up* production, the supervisor inspected the machinery.
Definitive action was *effected subsequent* to the reporting date.	*Final* action was *taken after* the reporting date.
The *unanimity* of current forecasts is not *incontrovertible evidence* of an *impending* business *acceleration*.	*Agreement* of the forecasts is not *proof* that business *will get better*.
This *antiquated merchandising* strategy is *ineffectual* in *contemporary* business *operations*.	This *old sales* strategy *will not work* in *today's* business.

Mark Twain understood the value of using short words when he made this often quoted statement: "I never use a word like *metropolis* when I can get the same price for *city*." One bureaucrat who did not understand the principle created a position to improve communication and gave it the title of Coordinator for the Obliteration of Proliferation of Obfuscation!

Use Technical Words and Acronyms with Caution

- All fields have technical words.

Every field of business—accounting, computer science, engineering—has its technical language. This language can be so complex that in some cases specialized dictionaries are compiled. Such dictionaries exist for computers, law, finance, and other business specialties. There are even dictionaries for subareas such as databases, desktop publishing, and real estate.

- These words are useful when you communicate with people in your field. But they do not communicate with outsiders. Use them with caution.

As you work in your chosen field, you will learn its technical words and acronyms. In time you will use these terms freely in communicating with people in your field. This is as it should be, for such terms are useful. Frequently, one such word will communicate a concept that would otherwise take dozens of words to describe.

A problem comes about, however, when you use technical terms with people outside your field. Because these words are everyday words to you, you tend to forget that not everyone knows them. The result is miscommunication. You can avoid such miscommunication by using technical words with extreme caution. Use them only when your readers know them.

- Some examples are *covered employment, cerebral vascular accident, annuity, bobtail*. These words are well known to people in special fields, but not to most outsiders.

Examples of misuse of technical writing are easy to find. To a worker in the Social Security Administration, the words *covered employment* commonly mean employment covered by social security. To some outsiders, however, they would mean working under a roof. When a physician uses the words *cerebral vascular accident* with other physicians, they understand. Most people would get little meaning from these words, but they would understand a *little stroke*. *Annuity* has a clear meaning to someone in insurance. *A contract that guarantees an income for a specified period* would have more meaning to uninformed outsiders. Computer specialists know *C + +* and *LISP* to be popular programming languages; but these words are meaningless to most others. To a trucker *bobtail* means a tractor cab without trailer. Nontruckers might get other meanings from that word—or perhaps no meaning at all.

- Use initials cautiously. Spell out and define as needed.

Initials (including acronyms) should be used with caution, too. While some initials, such as IBM, are widely recognized, others, such as CIM (computer integrated manufacturing), are not. Not only might the readers not know the initials, they might confuse them with others. For example, if you saw IRA, you might think of the Irish Republican Army, and someone else might think of individual retirement account. And your instructor might think of a committee named Instructionally Related

Technical Language?

When an ordinary person wants to give someone an orange, he or she would merely say, "I give you this orange." But when a lawyer does it, the words are something like this: "Know all persons by these present that I hereby give, grant, bargain, sell, release, convey, transfer, and quitclaim all my right, title, interest, benefit, and use whatever in, of, and concerning this chattel, otherwise known as an orange, or *Citrus orantium,* together with all the appurtenances thereto of skin, pulp, pip, rind, seeds, and juice, to have and to hold the said orange together with its skin, pulp, pip, rind, seeds, and juice for his own use and behoof, to himself and his heirs, in fee simple forever, free from all liens, encumbrances, easements, limitations, restraints, or conditions whatsoever, any and all prior deeds, transfers, or other documents whatsoever, now or anywhere made, to the contrary notwithstanding, with full power to bite, cut, suck, or otherwise eat the said orange or to give away the same, with or without its skin, pulp, pip, rind, seeds, or juice."

Activities. If you have any question as to whether your reader is familiar with the initials, the best practice is to spell out the words the first time you use them and follow them with the initials. Also, if you are writing a long document with several pages between where you defined initials originally and where you use them again, it is courteous to your reader to spell out again.

Probably the most troublesome technical language is that of the legal profession. Legal terms have too often worked their way into business communication. The result has been to add unnecessary words as well as words not understood by many business readers. Such words also produce a dull and formal effect.

- Legal language has worked its way into business writing.

Among the legal words that may add little real meaning are *thereto, therein, whereas, herewith,* and *herein.* For example, "the land adjacent thereto" can be written "the adjacent land" without loss in meaning. In addition, legal wordings such as *cease and desist* and *bequeath and devise* contain needless repetition.

- Words like *thereto, herewith,* and *ipso facto* are examples.

Some legal words can be replaced with plain words. *Despite* can replace *notwithstanding. Ipso facto, sub judice,* and other such Latin phrases can be replaced by plain language with the same meaning.

- Replace legal language with plain words.

Your technical language may not be any of the ones illustrated. But you will have one. You will need to be careful not to use it when you write to people who do not understand it.

Select Words with the Right Strength and Vigor

In a way, words are like people; they have personalities. Some words are strong and vigorous. Some are weak and dull. And some fall between these extremes. Good writers know these differences, and they consider them carefully. They use the words that do the best job of carrying the intended meaning. As a rule, they make the stronger words stand out.

- Words have personalities. Select the stronger ones.

Selecting words with just the right personalities requires that you learn language well—that you learn to distinguish shades of difference in the meanings of words. For example, you should recognize that *tycoon* is stronger than *eminently successful businessperson,* that *bear market* is stronger than *generally declining market,* that *boom* is stronger than *a period of business prosperity,* and that *mother* is stronger than *female parent.*

- To select words wisely, you should consider shades of difference in meanings.

You will not always want the strongest and most vigorous words. Sometimes, for good reason, you will choose weaker ones. The word *bill* is strong. Because it has a harsh meaning in some minds, you may prefer *statement* in some instances. The same

- Sometimes weaker words serve your purpose best.

goes for *debt* and *obligation, die* and *passed on, spit* and *saliva, labor boss* and *union official,* and *fired* and *dismissed.*

In selecting the stronger words, you should keep in mind that the verb is the strongest part of speech. Second is the noun. Verbs are action words, and action carries interest. Nouns are the doers of action—the heroes of the sentence. Thus, they also attract attention.

Adjectives and adverbs are weak words. They add length and distract from the key words, the nouns and the verbs. As Voltaire wrote, "The adjective is the enemy of the noun." In addition, adjectives and adverbs are judgment words. As we will see, objectivity—which is opposed to judgment—is a requirement of much business communication. But you should know that adjectives and adverbs are among the weaker words, and you should use them sparingly.

Use Concrete Language

Good business communication is marked by words that form sharp and clear meanings in the mind. These are the concrete words. You should prefer them in your writing.

Concrete is the opposite of abstract. Abstract words are vague. In contrast, concrete words stand for things the reader can see, feel, taste, or smell. Concrete words hold interest, for they refer to the reader's experience.

Among the concrete words are those that stand for things that exist in the real world. Included are such nouns as *chair, desk, computer, road, automobile,* and *flowers.* Also included are words that stand for creatures and things: *John Jordan, Mary Stanley, Mickey Mouse, Spot,* the *Metropolitan Life Building,* and *Mulberry Street.*

Abstract nouns, on the other hand, cover broad meanings—concepts, ideas, and the like. Their meanings are general, as in these examples: *administration, negotiation, wealth, inconsistency, loyalty, compatibility, conservation, discrimination, incompetence,* and *communication.* Note how difficult it is to visualize what these words stand for.

Concreteness also involves how we put words together. Exact or specific wordings are concrete; vague and general wordings are abstract. For example, take the case of a researcher who must report the odor of a newly developed cleaning agent. The researcher could use such general words as "It has an offensive, nauseating odor." Now note how much more concrete language communicates: "It has the odor of decaying fish." The second example is concrete because it recalls an exact odor from memory. Notice the difference in communication effect in these contrasting pairs of wordings:

ABSTRACT	CONCRETE
A significant loss	A 53 percent loss
Good attendance record	100 percent attendance record
The leading company	First among 3,212 competitors
The majority	62 percent
In the near future	By Thursday noon
A laborsaving robot	Does the work of seven workers
Light in weight	Featherlight
Substantial amount	$3,517,000

Now let us see the difference concreteness makes in the clarity of longer passages. Here is an example of abstract wording:

It is imperative that the firm practice extreme conservatism in operating expenditures during the coming biennium. The firm's past operating performance has been ineffectual for the reason that a preponderance of administrative assignments has been delegated to personnel who were ill-equipped to perform in these capacities. Recently instituted administrative changes stressing experience in operating economies have rectified this condition.

Written for concreteness, this message might read as follows:

We must cut operating expenses at least $2 million during 1995–96. Our $1,350,000 deficit for 1993–94 was caused by the inexperience of our two chief administrators, Mr. Sartan and Mr. Ross. We have replaced them with Ms. Pharr and Mr. Kunz, who have had 13 and 17 years, respectively, of successful experience in operations management.

Another illustration of concreteness is the story of the foreign nation that competed strenuously with the United States in an international automobile show. In one category, only automobiles from these two countries were entered. One would surely win first place, the other second. The U.S. automobile won. The government-controlled press of the losing country gave this report to its people: "In worldwide competition, our excellent entry was judged to be second. The entry from the United States was rated next to last." The words sound concrete—*second, next to last*. But they omitted one fact needed for meaningful concreteness—that only two automobiles were entered.

Use the Active Voice

You should prefer the active voice to the passive voice. Active voice produces stronger, livelier writing. It emphasizes the action, and it usually saves words.

In active voice, as you will recall, the subject does the action. In passive voice, the subject receives the action. For example, the sentence "The auditor inspected the books" is in active voice. In passive voice, the sentence would read: "The books were inspected by the auditor."

These two sentences show the advantages of active voice. Clearly, the active-voice sentence is stronger. In it the doer of action acts, and the verb is short and clear. In the passive-voice sentence, the extra helping word *were* dulls the action. In addition, placing the doer of the action (*auditor*) in a prepositional phrase presents the information indirectly rather than directly. Note also that the active-voice sentence is shorter.

For further proof of the advantages of active over passive voice, compare the following sentences:

- Prefer the active voice to the passive voice.

- In active voice, the subject does the action. In passive voice, it receives the action.

- Active voice is stronger and shorter.

PASSIVE	ACTIVE
The results were reported in our July 9 letter.	We reported the results in our July 9 letter.
This policy has been supported by our union.	Our union supported this policy.
The new process is believed to be superior by the investigators.	The investigators believe that the new process is superior.
The policy was enforced by the committee.	The committee enforced the policy.
The office will be inspected by Mr. Hall.	Mr. Hall will inspect the office.
A gain of 30.1 percent was reported for hardware sales.	Hardware sales gained 30.1 percent.
It is desired by this office that this problem be brought before the board.	This office desires that the secretary bring this problem before the board.
A complete reorganization of the administration was effected by the president.	The president completely reorganized the administration.

The suggestion that active voice be preferred does not mean passive voice is incorrect or you should never use it. Passive voice is correct, and it has a place. The problem is that many writers tend to overuse it, especially in report writing. Our writing would be more interesting and would communicate better if we used more active voice.

- Passive voice has a place. It is not incorrect.

Your decision on whether to use active or passive voice is not simply a matter of choice. Sometimes passive voice is preferable. For example, when identifying the doer of the action is unimportant to the message, passive voice properly de-emphasizes the doer.

Advertising is often criticized for its effect on price.
Petroleum is refined in Texas.

Passive voice may enable you to avoid accusing your reader of an action:

The damage was caused by exposing the material to sunlight.
The color desired was not specified in your order.

Passive voice may also be preferable when the performer is unknown, as in these examples:

During the past year, the equipment has been sabotaged seven times.
Anonymous complaints have been received.

Yet another situation in which passive voice may be preferable is one in which the writer does not want to name the performer:

The interviews were conducted on weekdays between noon and 6 P.M.
Two complaints have been made about you.

In other instances, passive voice is preferable for reasons of style.

Avoid Overuse of Camouflaged Verbs

An awkward construction that should be avoided is the camouflaged verb. When a verb is camouflaged, the verb describing the action in a sentence is changed into a noun. Then action words have to be added. For example, suppose you want to write a sentence in which *eliminate* is the action to be expressed. If you change *eliminate* into its noun form, *elimination,* you must add action words—perhaps *was effected*—to have a sentence. Your sentence might then be: "Elimination of the surplus was effected by the staff." The sentence is indirect and passive. You could have avoided the camouflaged construction with a sentence using the verb *eliminate:* "The staff eliminated the surplus."

Here are two more examples. If we take the good action word *cancel* and make it into a noun, *cancellation,* we would have to say something like "to effect a cancellation" to communicate the action. If we change *consider* to *consideration,* we would have to say "give consideration to." So it would be with these examples:

ACTION VERB	NOUN FORM	WORDING OF CAMOUFLAGED VERB
acquire	acquisition	make an acquisition
appear	appearance	make an appearance
apply	application	make an application
appraise	appraisal	make an appraisal
assist	assistance	give assistance to
cancel	cancellation	make a cancellation
commit	commitment	make a commitment
discuss	discussion	have a discussion
investigate	investigation	make an investigation
judge	judgment	make a judgment
liquidate	liquidation	effect a liquidation
reconcile	reconciliation	make a reconciliation
record	recording	make a recording

Margin notes:

- Passive is better when the doer of the action is not important.

- Passive helps avoid accusing the reader.

- Passive is better when the performer is not known.

- It is also better when the writer prefers not to name the performer.

- Avoid camouflaged verbs. You camouflage a verb by changing it to a noun form and then adding action words.

- For example, if *cancel* becomes *cancellation,* you must add "to effect a" to have action.

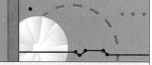

Grammar and Style Checkers: Tools for Selection of Words

Grammar and style checking programs help writers proofread documents by searching for errors in grammar, style, usage, punctuation, and spelling. Like yesterday's versions, the writer still decides whether to follow the suggestions the software recommends.

However, unlike yesterday's programs, today's versions offer the writer an explanation for the recommendation. This helps one decide while understanding the reason behind changes.

The accompanying example identified passive voice and suggested the writer revise based on rules commonly applied to formal memo and letter writing. The writer may decide to replace, edit, or ignore the recommendation. What would you do?

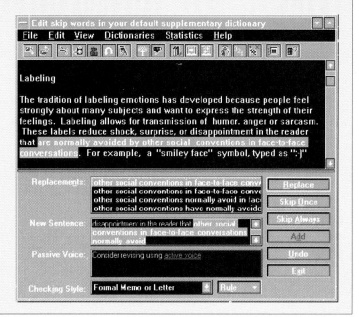

Note the differences in overall effect in these contrasting sentences:

CAMOUFLAGED VERB	CLEAR VERB FORM
Amortization of the account *was effected* by the staff.	The staff *amortized* the account.
Control of the water *was not possible.*	They *could not control* the water.
The new policy *involved the standardization of* the procedures.	The new policy *standardized* the procedures.
Application of the mixture *was accomplished.*	They *applied* the mixture.
We must *bring about a reconciliation of* our differences.	We must *reconcile* our differences.
The *establishment* of a rehabilitation center *has been accomplished* by the company.	The company *has established* a rehabilitation center.

From these illustrations you can see that our suggestion on camouflaged verbs overlaps our two preceding suggestions. First, camouflaged verbs are abstract nouns. We suggested that you prefer concrete words over abstract words. Second, camouflaged verbs frequently require passive voice. We suggested that you prefer active voice.

You can comply with these related suggestions by following two helpful writing hints. The first is to make the subjects of most sentences either persons or things. For example, rather than write "consideration was given to . . . ," you should write "we considered . . ." The second is to write most sentences in normal order (subject, verb, object), with the doer of the action as the subject. Involved, strained, passive structures often result from attempts at other orders.

* Avoid camouflaged verbs by (1) writing concretely and (2) preferring active voice. To comply with these suggestions, (1) make subjects persons or things and (2) write sentences in normal order.

Select Words for Precise Meanings

Obviously, writing requires some knowledge of language. In fact, the greater your knowledge of language, the better you are likely to write. Unfortunately, all too many

* Writing requires a knowledge of language.

Illustrating word precision are excerpts from a spirited debate in Parliament between the nimble-tongued Benjamin Disraeli and his arch adversary, William Gladstone. At the height of a particularly bitter argument, Gladstone asked Disraeli to define two words he had used in his attack on Gladstone's position: *misfortune* and *calamity*. Taking full advantage of the situation, Disraeli responded, "If you were to fall into the River Thames, Mr. Gladstone, that would be a misfortune. If someone were to pull you out, that would be a calamity."

of us treat language routinely. We use the first words that come to mind. We use words without thinking of the meanings they convey. We use words we are not sure of. The result is vague writing.

- You should study language and learn the shades of difference in the meanings of similar words.

If you want to be a good writer, you will need to study words carefully. You will need to learn their precise meanings, especially the shades of difference in the meanings of similar words. For example, *weary, tired, pooped, fagged out,* and *exhausted* all refer to the same thing. Yet in most minds there are differences in the meaning of these words. In a rather formal message, *weary* would certainly be more acceptable than *pooped* or *fagged out.* Similarly, *fired, dismissed, canned, separated,* and *discharged* refer to the same action but have different shades of meaning. So it is with each of these groups of words:

die, decease, pass on, croak, kick the bucket, check out, expire, go to one's reward
money, funds, cash, dough, bread, finances
boy, youth, young man, lad, shaver, stripling
fight, brawl, fracas, battle royal, donnybrook
thin, slender, skinny, slight, wispy, lean, willowy, rangy, spindly, lanky, wiry
ill, sick, poorly, weak, delicate, cachectic, unwell, peaked, indisposed, out of sorts

- You should learn the specific meanings of other words.

Knowledge of language also enables you to use words that carry the meanings you want to communicate. For example, *fewer* and *less* mean the same to some people. But careful users select *fewer* to mean "smaller numbers of items" and *less* to mean "reduced value, degree, or quantity." The verbs *affect* and *effect* are often used as synonyms. But those who know language select *affect* when they mean "to influence" and *effect* when they mean "to bring to pass." Similarly, careful writers use *continual* to mean "repeated but broken succession" and *continuous* to mean "unbroken succession." They write *farther* to express geographic distance and *further* to indicate "more, in addition." They know that *learn* means "to acquire knowledge" and *teach* means "to impart knowledge."

- Use correct idiom. Idiom is the way ideas are expressed in a language.

In your effort to be a precise writer, you should use correct idiom. By *idiom* we mean the way things are said in a language. Much of our idiom has little rhyme or reason, but if we want to be understood, we should follow it. For example, what is the logic in the word *up* in the sentence "Look up her name in the directory"? There really is none. This is just the wording we have developed to cover this meaning. "Independent of" is good idiomatic usage; "independent from" is not. What is the justification? Similarly, you "agree to" a proposal, but you "agree with" a person. You are "careful about" an affair, but you are "careful with" your money. Here are some additional illustrations:

- There is little reason to some idioms, but violations offend the reader.

FAULTY IDIOM	CORRECT IDIOM
authority about	authority on
comply to	comply with

FAULTY IDIOM	CORRECT IDIOM
different than	different from
enamored with	enamored of
equally as bad	equally bad
in accordance to	in accordance with
in search for	in search of
listen at	listen to
possessed with ability	possessed of ability
seldom or ever	seldom if ever
superior than	superior to

SUGGESTIONS FOR NONDISCRIMINATORY WRITING

Although discriminatory words are not directly related to writing clarity, our review of word selection would not be complete without some mention of them. By discriminatory words we mean words that do not treat all people equally and with respect. More specifically, they are words that refer negatively to groups of people, such as by sex, race, nationality, age, or disability. Such words run contrary to acceptable views of fair play and human decency. They have no place in business communication.

Many discriminatory words are a part of the vocabularies we have acquired from our environments. We often use them innocently, not realizing how they affect others. We can eliminate discriminatory words from our vocabularies by examining them carefully and placing ourselves in the shoes of those to whom they refer. The following review of the major forms of discriminatory words should help you achieve this goal.

Avoid Sexist Words

All too prevalent in today's business communication are sexist words—words that discriminate against a person because of his or her sex. Although this form of discrimination can be against men, most instances involve discrimination against women. The reason is that many of our words suggest male superiority. This condition is easily explained: Our language developed in a male-dominated society. For reasons of fair play, you would do well to avoid sexist words. Suggestions for avoiding some of the more troublesome sexist words follow.

Masculine Pronouns for Both Sexes. Perhaps the most troublesome sexist words are the masculine pronouns (*he, his, him*) when they are used to refer to both sexes, as in this example: "The typical State University student eats *his* lunch at the cafeteria." Assuming that State is coeducational, the use of *his* suggests male supremacy. Historically, of course, the word *his* has been classified as generic—that is, it can refer to both sexes. But many modern-day businesspeople do not agree and are offended by the use of the masculine pronoun in this way.

You can avoid the use of masculine pronouns in such cases in three ways. First, you can reword the sentence to eliminate the offending word. Thus, the illustration above could be reworded as follows: "The typical State University student eats lunch at the cafeteria." Here are other examples:

SEXIST	NONSEXIST
If a customer pays promptly, *he* is placed on our preferred list.	A customer who pays promptly is placed on our preferred list.
When an unauthorized employee enters the security area, *he* is subject to dismissal.	An employee who enters the security area is subject to dismissal.

- Avoid words that discriminate against sex, race, nationality, age, or disability.

- We often use discriminatory words without bad intent.

- Avoid using the masculine pronouns (he, him, his) for both sexes.

- You can do this (1) by rewording the sentence;

In business today, men and women, the young and the old, and people of all races work side by side in roles of mutual respect. It would be unfair to use words that discriminate against any of them.

SEXIST	NONSEXIST
A supervisor is not responsible for such losses if *he* is not negligent.	A supervisor who is not negligent is not responsible for such losses.
When a customer needs service, it is *his* right to ask for it.	A customer who needs service has the right to ask for it.

- (2) by making the reference plural,

A second way to avoid sexist use of the masculine pronoun is to make the reference plural. Fortunately, the English language has plural pronouns (*their, them, they*) that refer to both sexes. Making the references plural in the examples given above, we have these nonsexist revisions:

- as illustrated here;

If customers pay promptly, *they* are placed on our preferred list.
When unauthorized employees enter the security area, *they* are subject to dismissal.
Supervisors are not responsible for such losses if *they* are not negligent.
When customers need service, *they* have the right to ask for it.

- or (3) by substituting neutral expressions,

A third way to avoid sexist use of *he, his,* or *him* is to substitute any of a number of neutral expressions. The most common are *he or she, he/she, s/he, you, one,* and *person.* Using neutral expressions in the problem sentences, we have these revisions:

- as in these examples.

If a customer pays promptly, *he or she* is placed on our preferred list.
When an unauthorized employee enters the security area, *he/she* is subject to dismissal.
A supervisor is not responsible for such losses if *s/he* is not negligent.
When service is needed, *one* has the right to ask for it.

- Neutral expressions can be awkward; so use them with caution.

You should use such expressions with caution, however. They tend to be somewhat awkward, particularly if they are used often. For this reason, many skilled writers do not use some of them. If you use them, you should pay attention to their effect on the flow of your words. Certainly, you should avoid sentences like this one: "To make an employee feel he/she is doing well by complimenting her/him insincerely confuses her/him later when he/she sees his/her co-workers promoted ahead of him/her."

- Avoid words suggesting male dominance,

Words Derived from Masculine Words. As we have noted, our culture was male dominated when our language developed. Because of this, many of our words are masculine even though they do not refer exclusively to men. Take *chairman,* for example.

This word can refer to both sexes, yet it does not sound that way. More appropriate and less offensive substitutes are *chair, presiding officer, moderator,* and *chairperson.* Similarly, *salesman* suggests a man, but many women work in sales. *Salesperson, salesclerk,* or *sales representative* would be better. Other sexist words and nonsexist substitutes are as follows:

SEXIST	NONSEXIST
man-made	manufactured, of human origin
manpower	personnel, workers
congressman	representative, member of Congress
businessman	business executive, businessperson
mailman	letter carrier, mail carrier
policeman	police officer
fireman	fire fighter
fisherman	fisher
cameraman	camera operator

• such as these examples.

Many words with *man, his,* and the like in them have nonsexist origins. Among such words are *manufacture, management, history,* and *manipulate.* Also, some clearly sexist words are hard to avoid. *Freshperson,* for example, would not serve as a substitute for *freshman.* And *personhole* is an illogical substitute for *manhole.*

• But not all man-sounding words are sexist.

Words that Lower Women's Status.   Thoughtless writers and speakers use expressions belittling the status of women. You should avoid such expressions. To illustrate, male executives sometimes refer to their female secretaries as *my girl,* as in this sentence: "I'll have my girl take care of this matter." Of course, *secretary* would be a better choice. Then there are the many female forms for words that refer to work roles. In this group are *lady lawyer, authoress, sculptress,* and *poetess.* You should refer to women in these work roles by the same words that you would use for men: *lawyer, author, sculptor, poet.*

• Do not use words that lower the status of women.

Examples of sexist words could go on and on. But not all of them would be as clear as those given above, for the issue is somewhat complex and confusing. In deciding which words to avoid and which to use, you will have to rely on your best judgment. Remember that your goal should be to use words that are fair and that do not offend.

I love being a partner Mr. Jenkins! There's just one problem. *(From The Wall Street Journal, with permission of Cartoon Features Syndicate)*

Avoid Words that Stereotype by Race or Nationality

• Words depicting minorities in a stereotyped way are unfair and untrue.

Words that stereotype all members of a group by race or nationality are especially unfair. Members of any minority vary widely in all characteristics. Thus, it is unfair to suggest that Jews are miserly, that Italians are Mafia members, that Hispanics are lazy, that blacks can do only menial jobs, and so on. Unfair references to minorities are sometimes subtle and not intended, as in this example: "We conducted the first marketing tests in the ghetto areas of the city. Using a sample of 200 black families, we . . ." These words unfairly suggest that only blacks are ghetto dwellers.

• Words that present members of minorities as exceptions to stereotypes are also unfair.

Also unfair are words suggesting that a minority member has struggled to achieve something that is taken for granted in the majority group. Usually well intended, words of this kind can carry subtle discriminatory messages. For example, a reference to a "neatly dressed Hispanic man" may suggest that he is an exception to the rule— that most Hispanics are not neatly dressed, but here is one who is. So can references to "a generous Jew," "an energetic Puerto Rican," "a hardworking black," and "a Chinese manager."

• Eliminate such references to minorities by treating all people equally and by being sensitive to the effects of your words.

Eliminating unfair references to minority groups from your communication requires two basic steps. First, you must consciously treat all people equally, without regard to their minority status. You should refer to minority membership only in those rare cases in which it is a vital part of the message to be communicated. Second, you must be sensitive to the effects of your words. Specifically, you should ask yourself how those words would affect you if you were a member of the minorities to which they are addressed. You should evaluate your word choices from the viewpoints of others.

Avoid Words that Stereotype by Age

• Words that label people as old or young can arouse negative reactions.

Your sensitivity in not discriminating by sex should also be extended to include by age—both against the old and the young. While those over 55 might be retired from their first jobs, many lead lives that are far from the sedentary roles in which they are sometimes depicted. They also are not necessarily feeble, forgetful, or forsaken. While some do not mind being called *senior citizens,* others do. Be sensitive with terms such as *mature, elderly,* and *golden ager,* also. Some even abhor *oldster* as much as the young detest *youngster.* The young are often called *teenagers* or *adolescents* when *young person, young man,* and *young woman* are much fairer. Some slang terms show lack of sensitivity, too—words such as *brat, retard,* and *dummy.* Even harsher are *juvenile delinquent, truant,* and *runaway,* for these labels are often put on the young based on one behavior over a short time period. Presenting both the old and young objectively is only fair.

As we have suggested, use labels only when relevant, and use positive terms when possible. In describing the old, be sensitive to terms such as *spry,* which on the surface might be well intended but can also imply a negative connotation. Present both groups fairly and objectively when you write about them.

Avoid Words that Typecast Those with Disabilities

• Disabled people are sensitive to words that describe their disabilities.

People with disabilities are likely to be sensitive to discriminatory words. While television shows those with disabilities competing in the Special Olympics, often exceeding the performance of an average person, common sense tells us not to stereotype these people. However, sometimes we do anyway. Just as with age, we need to avoid derogatory labels and apologetic or patronizing behavior. For example, instead of describing one as *deaf and dumb,* use *deaf.* Avoid slang terms such as *fits, spells, attacks;* use *seizures, epilepsy,* or other objective terms. Terms such as *crippled* and *retarded* should be avoided since they degrade in most cases. Work to develop a non-biased attitude, and show it through carefully chosen words.

In Conclusion about Words

The preceding review of suggestions for selecting words is not complete. You will find more—much more—in the pages ahead. But you now have in mind the basics of word selection. The remaining are refinements of these basics.

As you move along, you should view these basics as work tools. Unfortunately, the tendency is to view them as rules to memorize and give back to the instructor on an examination. Although a good examination grade is a commendable goal, the long-run value of these tools is their use in your writing. So do yourself a favor. Resolve to keep these basics in mind every time you write. Consciously use them. The results will make you glad you did.

- More about words appears in the following pages.

- The preceding suggestions are realistic ways to improve your writing. Use them.

....

SUMMARY ▶ by Chapter Objectives

1. To communicate clearly, you must adapt to your reader.
   - Adapting means using words the reader understands.
   - It also involves following the suggestions below.
2. Select words that your reader understands.
   - These are the familiar words (words like *old* instead of *antiquated*).
   - They are also the short words (*agreed to quit* rather than *acceded to the proposition to terminate*).
3. Use technical words with caution.
   - For example, use *a little stroke* rather than *a cerebral vascular accident.*
   - However, technical words are appropriate among technical people.
4. Select words with adequate strength and vigor.
   - Develop a feeling for the personalities of words.
   - Understand that words like *bear market* are stronger than *generally declining market.*
5. Prefer the concrete words and active voice.
   - Concrete words are the specific ones. For example, *57 percent majority* is more concrete than *majority.*
   - In active voice, the subject acts; in passive voice, it receives the action. For example, use *we reported the results* rather than *the results were reported by us.*
   - Active voice is stronger, more vigorous, and more interesting. But passive voice is correct and has a place in writing.
6. Write more clearly and precisely by following these suggestions:
   - Avoid overuse of camouflaged verbs—making a noun of the logical verb and then having to add a verb (*appear* rather than *make an appearance*).
   - Select words for their precise meanings (involves studying words to detect shades of difference in meaning—for example, differences in *fight, brawl, fracas, donnybrook, battle royal.*)
   - Also, learn the specific ways that words are used in our culture (called *idiom*).
7. Avoid discriminatory words.
   - Do not use words that discriminate against women. (For example, using *he, him,* or *his,* to refer to both sexes and words such as *fireman, postman, lady lawyer,* and *authoress.*)
   - Do not use words that suggest stereotyped roles of race or nationality (blacks and menial jobs, Italians and the Mafia), for such words are unfair and untrue.
   - Do not use words that discriminate against age or disability.

1 Explain the role of adaptation in selecting words that communicate.

2 Simplify writing by selecting the short and familiar words.

3 Use technical words appropriately.

4 Discuss the differences in the strength of words and select the words that communicate your message best.

5 Write concretely and stress active voice.

6 Write with clarity and precision by avoiding camouflaged verbs, by selecting the right words, and by using idioms correctly.

7 Use words that do not discriminate.

CRITICAL THOUGHT QUESTIONS

1. A fellow student says, "So I'm not a good writer. But I have other places to put my study time. I'm a management major. I'll have secretaries to handle my writing for me." Give this student your best advice, including the reasoning behind it.

2. Evaluate this comment: "Simplifying writing so that stupid readers can understand it is for the birds! Why not challenge readers? Why not give them new words to learn—expand their minds?"

3. Explain how you would apply the basic principle of adaptation to each of the following writing assignments:

   a. An editorial in a company newspaper.

   b. A memorandum to Joan Branch, a supervisor of an assembly department, concerning a change in assembly operations.

   c. A report to the chief engineer on a technical topic in the engineer's field.

   d. A letter to a laborer explaining pension benefits.

   e. A letter to company stockholders explaining a change in company manufacturing policy.

4. "Some short words are hard, and some long words are easy. Thus, the suggestion to prefer short words doesn't make sense." Discuss.

5. "As technical language typically consists of acronyms and long, hard words, it contributes to miscommunication. Thus, it should be avoided in all business communication." Discuss.

6. Using illustrations other than those in the book, discuss differences in word strength. Be sure to comment on strength differences in the parts of speech (nouns, verbs, adjectives, adverbs).

7. Define and illustrate active and passive voice. Explain when each should be used.

8. Discuss this statement: "When I use *he, him,* or *his* as a generic, I am not discriminating against women. For many years these words have been accepted as generic. They refer to both sexes, and that's the meaning I have in mind when I use them."

9. List synonyms (words with similar meanings) for each of the following words. Then explain the differences in shades of meaning as you see them.

   a. fat
   b. skinny
   c. old
   d. tell
   e. happiness
   f. understand
   g. dog
   h. misfortune
   i. inquire
   j. stop

10. Discuss this statement: "The boss scolded Susan in a grandfatherly manner."

CRITICAL THINKING EXERCISES

Instructions, Sentences 1–20: Assume that your readers are at about the 10th-grade level in education. Revise these sentences for easy communication to this audience.

1. We must terminate all deficit financing.

2. The most operative assembly-line configuration is a unidirectional flow.

3. A proportionate tax consumes a determinate apportionment of one's monetary flow.

4. Business has an inordinate influence on governmental operations.

5. It is imperative that consumers be unrestrained in determining their preferences.

6. Mr. Casey terminated John's employment as a consequence of his ineffectual performance.

7. Our expectations are that there will be increments in commodity value.

8. This antiquated mechanism is ineffectual for an accelerated assembly-line operation.

9. The preponderance of the businesspeople we consulted envision signs of improvement from the current siege of economic stagnation.

10. If liquidation becomes mandatory, we shall dispose of these assets first.

11. Recent stock acquisitions have accentuated the company's current financial crisis.

12. Mr. Coward will serve as intermediary in the pending labor-management parley.

13. Ms. Smith's idiosyncrasies supply adequate justification for terminating her employment.

14. Requisites for employment by this company have been enhanced.

15. The unanimity of current forecasts is not incontrovertible evidence of an impending business acceleration.

16. People's propensity to consume is insatiable.

17. The company must desist from its deficit financing immediately.

18. This antiquated merchandising strategy is ineffectual in contemporary business operations.

19. Percentage return on common stockholders' equity averaged 23.1 for the year.

20. The company's retained earnings last year exceeded $2,500,000.

Instructions: Exercise 21 concerns adaptation and technical language. As you must find your own sentences for it, this exercise differs from the others.

21. From one of your textbooks, select a paragraph (at least 150 words long) that would be difficult for a student less advanced in the subject than you. Rewrite the paragraph so that this student can understand it easily.

Instructions, Sentences 22–58: Revise these sentences to

make them conform to the writing suggestions discussed in the book. They are grouped by the suggestion they illustrate.

USING STRONG, VIGOROUS WORDS

22. I have an idea in mind of how we can enhance our savings.
23. Ms. Jordan possesses qualities that are characteristic of an autocratic executive.
24. Many people came into the store during the period of the promotion.
25. We are obligated to protect the well-being of the hired employees.
26. Companies promoting their products in the medium of the newspaper are advised to produce verbal messages in accord with the audience level of the general consuming public.

SELECTING CONCRETE WORDS

27. We have found that young men are best for this work.
28. She makes good grades.
29. John lost a fortune in Las Vegas.
30. If we don't receive the goods soon, we will cancel.
31. Profits last year were exorbitant.
32. Some years ago she made good money.
33. His grade on the aptitude test was not high.
34. Here is a product with very little markup.
35. The cost of the on-line database search was reasonable.
36. We will need some new equipment soon.

LIMITING USE OF PASSIVE VOICE

37. Our action is based on the assumption that the competition will be taken by surprise.
38. It is believed by the typical union member that his or her welfare is not considered to be important by management.
39. We are serviced by the Bratton Company.
40. Our safety is the responsibility of management.
41. You were directed by your supervisor to complete this assignment by noon.
42. It is believed by the writer that this company policy is wrong.
43. The union was represented by Cecil Chambers.
44. These reports are prepared by the salespeople every Friday.
45. Success of this project is the responsibility of the research department.
46. Our decision is based on the belief that the national economy will be improved.

AVOIDING CAMOUFLAGED VERBS

47. It was my duty to make a determination of the damages.

48. Harold made a recommendation that we fire Mr. Schultz.
49. We will make her give an accounting of her activities.
50. We will ask him to bring about a change in his work routine.
51. This new equipment will result in a saving in maintenance.
52. Will you please make an adjustment for this defect?
53. Implementation of the plan was effected by the crew.
54. Acceptance of all orders must be made by the chief.
55. A committee performs the function of determining the award.
56. Adaptation to the new conditions was performed easily by all new personnel.
57. Verification of the amount is made daily by the auditor.
58. The president tried to effect a reconciliation of the two groups.

Instructions, Sentences 59–70: Following is an exercise in word precision. Explain the differences in meaning for the word choices shown. Point out any words that are wrongly used.

59. Performance during the fourth quarter was (average) (mediocre).
60. This merchandise is (old) (antique) (secondhand) (used).
61. The machine ran (continually) (continuously).
62. The mechanic is a (woman) (lady) (female person).
63. His action (implies) (infers) that he accepts the criticism.
64. Her performance on the job was (good) (topnotch) (excellent) (superior).
65. On July 1 the company will (become bankrupt) (close its door) (go under) (fail).
66. The staff members (think) (understand) (know) the results were satisfactory.
67. Before buying any material, we (compare) (contrast) it with competing products.
68. I cannot (resist) (oppose) her appointment.
69. Did you (verify) (confirm) these figures?
70. This is an (effective) (effectual) (efficient) plan.

Instructions, Sentences 71–80: These sentences use faulty and correct idioms. Make any changes you think are necessary.

71. The purchasing officer has gone in search for a substitute product.
72. Our office has become independent from the Dallas office.
73. The retooling period is over with.
74. This letter is equally as bad.
75. She is an authority about mutual funds.
76. When the sale is over with, we will restock.
77. Our truck collided against the wall.

78. We have been in search for a qualified supervisor since August.
79. Murphy was equal to the task.
80. Apparently, the clock fell off the shelf.

AVOIDING DISCRIMINATORY LANGUAGE

Instructions, Sentences 81–90: Change these sentences to avoid discriminatory language.

81. Any worker who ignores this rule will have his salary reduced.
82. The typical postman rarely makes mistakes in delivering his mail.
83. A good executive plans his daily activities.
84. The committee consisted of a businessman, a lawyer, and a lady doctor.
85. A good secretary screens all telephone calls for her boss and arranges his schedule.
86. An efficient salesman organizes his calls and manages his time.
87. Our company was represented by two sales representatives, one Hispanic engineer, and one senior citizen.
88. Three people applied for the job, including two well-groomed black women.
89. Handicap parking spaces are strictly for use by the crippled.
90. He didn't act like a Mexican.

3

Construction of Clear Sentences and Paragraphs

Upon completing this chapter, you will be able to construct clear sentences and paragraphs by emphasizing adaptation, short sentences, and effective paragraph design. To reach this goal, you should be able to

(1) Explain the role of adaptation in writing clear sentences.

(2) Write short, clear sentences by limiting sentence content and economizing words.

(3) Design sentences that give the right emphasis to content.

(4) Employ unity and clarity in writing effective sentences.

(5) Compose paragraphs that are short and unified, use topic sentences effectively, show movement, and communicate clearly.

▶ to Writing Sentences and Paragraphs that Communicate

Continuing in your role as Max Schlitz's boss (preceding chapter), you conclude that not all his writing problems involve word choice. True, his words detract from the readability of his writing. But something else is wrong. His sentences just do not convey sharp, clear meanings. Although grammatically correct, they appear to be needlessly complex and heavy. His long and involved paragraphs also cause you concern.

What you have seen in Max's writing are problems concerning two other determinants of readability—the sentence and the paragraph. As you will learn in the pages ahead, these two writing units play major roles in communicating. This chapter will show you (and Max) how to construct sentences and paragraphs that produce readable writing. ∎

FOUNDATION OF ADAPTATION

As you have seen, choosing the right words is basic to clear communication. Equally basic is the task of arranging those words into clear sentences. Just as with choosing words, constructing clear sentences involves adaptation to the minds of the intended readers.

Fitting sentences to the minds of readers requires the reader analysis we discussed in the preceding chapter. You should simply study your readers to find out what they are like—what they know, how they think, and such. Then construct sentences that will communicate with them.

In general, this procedure involves using the simpler sentence structures to reach people with lower communication abilities and people not knowledgeable about the subject. It involves using the more complex sentence structures only when they are appropriate, usually when communicating with knowledgeable people. As we will see, even with knowledgeable people, simplicity is sometimes needed for the best communication effect.

In adapting sentences, you should aim a little below the level of your reader. Readability research tells us that writing communicates best when it does not tax the mind. Thus, some simplification is best for all readers. Keep this point in mind as you read through the rest of this chapter.

- Sentences should be adapted to readers.

- Use the simpler sentence structures for those less able to understand; use the more complex structures when appropriate.

EMPHASIS ON SHORT SENTENCES

Writing simpler sentences largely means writing shorter sentences. Readability research tells us that the more words and the more relationships there are in a sentence, the greater is the possibility for misunderstanding. Apparently, the mind can hold only so much information at one time. Thus, to give it too much information is to risk miscommunication.

What constitutes a short, readable sentence is related to the reader's ability. Readability studies show that writing intended to communicate with the middle-level adult reader should average about 16 to 18 words per sentence. For more advanced readers, the average may be higher. For less advanced readers, it should be lower.

This emphasis on short sentences does not mean that you should never use long sentences. You may use them occasionally, and you should—if you construct them clearly. Longer sentences are sometimes useful in subordinating information and in increasing interest by adding variety. The information needed to complete a thought sometimes requires a long sentence. What you should be concerned about is the average length of your sentences.

- Short sentences communicate better because of mind limitations.

- Short means about 16–18 words for middle-level readers.

- Sometimes longer sentences are justified.

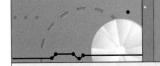

Grammar and style checkers are useful in helping you diagnose problems. They can help you improve clarity by both pointing out long sentences and counting words, sentences, and paragraphs.

Today's programs let you modify acceptable length as well as other rules. In the accompanying example, the software identified long sentences as any with more than 20 words. While it did find three long sentences, the overall words per sentence at 15.59 still fell within an acceptable word range. Therefore, the writer of this document should not feel compelled to shorten the long sentences if they are clear. However, the writer should examine the long sentences the software points out for the opportunity to improve clarity.

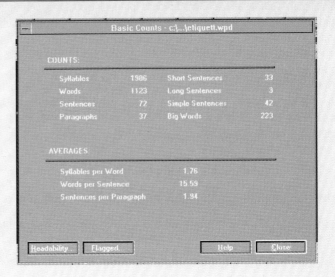

The following sentence from an employee handbook illustrates the effect of long sentences on communication:

When an employee has changed from one job to another job, the new corresponding coverages will be effective as of the date the change occurs, provided, however, if due to a physical disability or infirmity as a result of advanced age, an employee is changed from one job to another job and such change results in the employee's new job rate coming within a lower hourly job-rate bracket in the table, the employee may, at the discretion of the company, continue the amount of group term life insurance and the amount of accidental death and dismemberment insurance that the employee had prior to such change.

The chances are that you did not get a clear message from this sentence when you first read it. The explanation is not in the words used; you probably know them all. Neither is it in the ideas presented; they are relatively simple. The obvious explanation is the length of the sentence. So many words and relationships are in the sentence that they cause confusion. The result is vague communication at best—complete miscommunication at worst.

- Short sentences are achieved in two ways.

You can write short, simple sentences in two basic ways: (1) by limiting sentence content, (2) by using words economically. The following pages contain specific suggestions for doing this.

Limiting Sentence Content

- Limiting content is one way to make short sentences.

Limiting sentence content is largely a matter of mentally selecting thought units and making separate sentences of most of them. Sometimes, of course, you should combine thoughts into one sentence, but only when you have good reason. You have good reason, for example, when thoughts are closely related or when you want to de-emphasize content. The advantage of limiting sentence content is evident from the following contrasting examples:

LONG AND HARD TO UNDERSTAND	SHORT AND CLEAR
This memorandum is being distributed with the first-semester class cards, which are to serve as a final check on the correctness of the registration of students and are to be used later as the midsemester grade cards, which are to be submitted prior to November 16.	This memorandum is being distributed with the first-semester class cards. These cards will serve now as a final check on student registration. Later, they will be used for midsemester grades, which are due before November 16.
Some authorities in human resources object to expanding normal salary ranges to include a trainee rate because they fear that through oversight or prejudice probationers may be kept at the minimum rate longer than is warranted and because they fear that it would encourage the spread from the minimum to maximum rate range.	Some authorities in human resources object to expanding the normal salary range to include a trainee rate for two reasons. First, they fear that through oversight or prejudice probationers may be kept at the minimum rate longer than is warranted. Second, they fear that this would increase the spread between the minimum and the maximum rate range.
Regardless of their seniority or union affiliation, all employees who hope to be promoted are expected to continue their education either by enrolling in the special courses to be offered by the company, which are scheduled to be given after working hours beginning next Wednesday, or by taking approved correspondence courses selected from a list, which may be seen in the training office.	Regardless of their seniority or union affiliation, all employees who hope to be promoted are expected to continue their education in either of two ways. (1) They may enroll in special courses to be given by the company. (2) They may take approved correspondence courses selected from the list in the training office.

Without question, the long sentences in the examples are hard to understand, and the shorter versions are easy to understand. In each case, the difference is primarily in sentence length. Clearly, the shorter sentences communicate better. They give more emphasis to content and to organization of the subject matter.

However, you can overdo the writing of short sentences. A succession of short sentences can give the impression of elementary writing and draw attention from the content of the sentences to their choppiness. You should avoid these effects by varying the length and order of your sentences. But you should keep the length of your sentences within the grasp of your readers.

- Avoid overdoing this suggestion. Too many short sentences give a choppy effect.

Economizing on Words

A second basic technique of shortening sentences is to use words economically. Anything you write can be expressed in many ways, some shorter than others. In general, the shorter wordings save the reader time and are clearer and more interesting.

- Another way to shorten sentences is through word economy.

Economizing on words generally means seeking shorter ways of saying things. Once you try to economize, you will probably find that your present writing is wasteful and that you use uneconomical wordings.

- Seek shorter ways of saying things.

To help you recognize these uneconomical wordings, a brief review of them follows. This review does not cover all the possibilities for wasteful writing, but it does cover many troublesome problems.

- Following are some suggestions.

Cluttering Phrases. An often used uneconomical wording is the cluttering phrase. This is a phrase that can be replaced by shorter wording without loss of meaning. The little savings achieved in this way add up.

- Avoid cluttering phrases. Substitute shorter expressions.

Here is an example of a cluttering phrase:

In the event that payment is not made by January, operations will cease.

That no person in the classified civil service of the United States shall be removed therefrom except for such cause as will promote the efficiency of said service and for reasons given in writing, and the person whose removal is sought shall have notice of the same and of any charges preferred against him, and be furnished with a copy thereof, and also be allowed a reasonable time for personally answering the same in writing; and affidavits in support thereof; but no examination of witnesses nor any trial or hearing shall be required except in the discretion of the officer making the removal; and copies of charges, notice of hearing, answer, reasons for removal, and of the order of removal shall be made a part of the records of the proper department or office, as shall also the reasons for reduction in rank or compensation; and the copies of the same shall be furnished to the person affected upon request, and the Civil Service Commission also shall, upon request, be furnished copies of the same: *Provided, however,* that membership in any society, association, club, or other form of organization of postal employees not affiliated with any outside organization imposing an obligation or duty upon them to engage in any strike, or proposing to assist them in any strike, against the United States, having for its objects, among other things, improvements in the condition of labor of its members, including hours of labor and compensation therefore and leave of absence, by any person or groups of persons in said postal service, or the presenting by any such person or groups of persons of any grievance or grievances to the Congress or any Member thereof shall not constitute or be cause for reduction in rank or compensation or removal of such person or groups of persons from said service.

The phrase *in the event that* is uneconomical. The little word *if* can substitute for it without loss of meaning:

If payment is not made by January, operations will cease.

Similarly, the phrase that begins this sentence adds unnecessary length:

In spite of the fact that they received help, they failed to exceed the quota.

Although makes an economical substitute:

Although they received help, they failed to exceed the quota.

You probably use many cluttering phrases. The following partial list (with suggested substitutions) should help you cut down on them:

CALVIN & HOBBES *by BILL WATTERSON*

CLUTTERING PHRASE	SHORTER SUBSTITUTION
Along the lines of	Like
At the present time	Now
For the purpose of	For
For the reason that	Because, since
In accordance with	By
In the amount of	For
In the meantime	Meanwhile
In the near future	Soon
In the neighborhood of	About
In very few cases	Seldom
In view of the fact that	Since, because
On the basis of	By
On the occasion of	On
With regard to, with reference to	About
With a view to	To

Surplus Words.   To write economically, eliminate words that add nothing to sentence meaning. As with cluttering phrases, we often use meaningless extra words as a matter of habit. Eliminating these surplus words sometimes requires recasting a sentence. But sometimes they can just be left out.

• Eliminate surplus words.

This is an example of surplus wording from a business report:

It will be noted that the records for the past years show a steady increase in special appropriations.

The beginning words add nothing to the meaning of the sentence. Notice how dropping them makes the sentence stronger—and without loss of meaning:

The records for past years show a steady increase in special appropriations.

With the advent of computers, the way business messages are composed has changed, but the mental process involved remains unchanged. One still must select words and build sentences that form precise meanings in the minds of readers.

Here is a second example:

His performance was good enough *to enable* him to qualify for the promotion.

The words *to enable* add nothing and can be dropped:

His performance was good enough to qualify him for the promotion.

The following sentences further illustrate the use of surplus words. In each case, the surplus words can be eliminated without changing the meaning.

CONTAINS SURPLUS WORDS	ELIMINATES SURPLUS WORDS
He ordered desks *that are of the* executive type.	He ordered executive-type desks.
There are four rules *that* should be observed.	Four rules should be observed.
In addition to these defects, numerous other defects mar the operating procedure.	Numerous other defects mar the operating procedure.
The machines that were damaged by the fire were repaired.	The machines damaged by the fire were repaired.
By *the* keeping *of* production records, they found the error.	By keeping production records, they found the error.
In the period between April and June, we detected the problem.	Between April and June we detected the problem.
I am prepared to report *to the effect* that sales increased.	I am prepared to report that sales increased.

• Avoid roundabout ways of saying things.

Roundabout Constructions.   As we have noted, you can write anything in many ways. Some of the ways are direct and to the point. Some cover the same ground in a roundabout way. Usually the direct ways are shorter and communicate better.

This sentence illustrates roundabout construction:

The department budget *can be observed to be decreasing* each *new* year.

Do the words *can be observed to be decreasing* get to the point? Is the idea of *observing* essential? Is *new* needed? A more direct and better sentence is this one:

The department budget decreases each year.

Here is another roundabout sentence:

The union *is involved in the task of reviewing* the seniority provision of the contract.

Now if the union is *involved in the task of reviewing,* it is really *reviewing.* The sentence should be written in these direct words:

The union *is reviewing* the seniority provision of the contract.

The following sentence pairs further illustrate the advantages of short, direct wording over roundabout wording:

ROUNDABOUT	DIRECT AND TO THE POINT
The president *is of the opinion that* the tax was paid.	The president *believes* the tax was paid.
It is essential that the income be used to retire the debt.	The income *must* be used to retire the debt.
Reference is made to your May 10 report *in which you concluded* that the warranty is worthless.	Your May 10 report *concluded* that the warranty is worthless.
The supervisors *should take appropriate action to determine* whether the time cards are being inspected.	The supervisors *should determine* whether the time cards are being inspected.

ROUNDABOUT	DIRECT AND TO THE POINT
The price increase *will afford* the company *an opportunity* to retire the debt.	The price *will enable* the company to retire the debt.
During the time she was employed by this company, Ms. Carr was absent once.	*While* employed by this company, Ms. Carr was absent once.
He criticized everyone he *came in contact with.*	He criticized everyone he *met.*

Unnecessary Repetition of Words or Ideas. Repeating words obviously adds to sentence length. Such repetition sometimes serves a purpose, as when it is used for emphasis or special effect. But all too often it is without purpose, as this sentence illustrates:

We have not received your payment covering invoices covering June and July purchases.

It would be better to write the sentence like this:

We have not received your payment covering invoices for June and July purchases.

Another example is this one:

He stated that he believes that we are responsible.

This sentence eliminates one of the *thats*:

He stated that he believes we are responsible.

Repetitions of ideas through the use of different words that mean the same thing (*free gift, true fact, past history*) also add to sentence length. Known as redundancies, such repetitions are illogical and can rarely be defended. Note the redundancy in this sentence:

The provision of Section 5 provides for a union shop.

The duplication, of course, is in the meaning of *provides*. By definition, a *provision* provides. So the repetition serves no purpose. This sentence is better:

Section 5 provides for a union shop.

You often hear this expression:

In my opinion, I think the plan is sound.

Do not *in my opinion* and *I think* express the same thought? Could you possibly think in an opinion other than your own? This sentence makes better sense:

I think the plan is sound.

Here are other examples of redundancies and ways to eliminate them:

- Repeat words only for effect and emphasis.

- Avoid repetitions of ideas (redundancies).

NEEDLESS REPETITION	REPETITION ELIMINATED
Please endorse your name on the back of this check.	*Please endorse* this check.
We must *assemble together* at 10:30 A.M. *in the morning.*	We must *assemble* at 10:30 A.M.
Our new model is *longer in length* than the old one.	Our new model is *longer* than the old one.
If you are not satisfied, *return it back* to us.	If you are not satisfied, *return* it to us.
Tod Wilson is the *present incumbent.*	Tod Wilson is the *incumbent.*
One should know the *basic fundamentals* of clear writing.	One should know the *fundamentals* of clear writing.
The *consensus of opinion* is that the tax is unfair.	The *consensus* is that the tax is unfair.

NEEDLESS REPETITION	REPETITION ELIMINATED
By acting now, we can finish *sooner than if we wait until a later date.*	By acting now, we can finish *sooner.*
At the present time, we are conducting two clinics.	We are conducting two clinics.
As a matter of interest, I am interested in learning your procedure.	I am *interested* in learning your procedure.
We should plan *in advance for the future.*	We should *plan.*

Determining Emphasis in Sentence Design

- You should give every item its due emphasis.

The sentences you write should give the right emphasis to content. Any written business communication contains a number of items of information, not all of which are equally important. Some are very important, such as a conclusion in a report or the objective in a letter. Others are relatively unimportant. Your task as writer is to form your sentences to communicate the importance of each item.

- Short sentences emphasize contents.

Sentence length affects emphasis. Short, simple sentences carry more emphasis than long, involved ones. They stand out and call attention to their contents. Thus, they give the reader a single message without the interference of related or supporting information.

- Long sentences de-emphasize contents.

Longer sentences give less emphasis to their contents. When a sentence contains two or more ideas, the ideas share emphasis. How they share it depends on how the sentence is constructed. If two ideas are presented equally (in independent clauses, for example), they get about equal emphasis. But if they are not presented equally (for example, in an independent and a dependent clause), one gets more emphasis than the other.

To illustrate the varying emphasis you can give information, consider this example. You have two items of information to write. One is that the company lost money last year. The other is that its sales volume reached a record high. You could present the information in at least three ways. First, you could give both items equal emphasis by placing them in separate short sentences:

The company lost money last year. The loss occurred in spite of record sales.

Second, you could present the two items in the same sentence with emphasis on the lost money.

Although the company enjoyed record sales last year, it lost money.

Third, you could present the two items in one sentence with emphasis on the sales increase:

The company enjoyed record sales last year, although it lost money.

Which way would you choose? The answer depends on how much emphasis each item deserves. You should think the matter through and follow your best judgment. But the point is clear: Your choice makes a difference.

• Determining emphasis is a matter of good judgment.

The following paragraphs illustrate the importance of thinking logically to determine emphasis. In the first, each item of information gets the emphasis of a short sentence and none stands out. However, the items are not equally important and do not deserve equal emphasis. Notice, also, the choppy effect that the succession of short sentences produces.

The main building was inspected on October 1. Mr. George Wills inspected the building. Mr. Wills is a vice president of the company. He found that the building has 6,500 square feet of floor space. He also found that it has 2,400 square feet of storage space. The new store must have a minimum of 6,000 square feet of floor space. It must have 2,000 square feet of storage space. Thus, the main building exceeds the space requirements for the new store. Therefore, Mr. Wills concluded that the main building is adequate for the company's needs.

In the next paragraph, some of the items are subordinated, but not logically. The really important information does not receive the emphasis it deserves. Logically, these two points should stand out: (1) the building is large enough, and (2) storage space exceeds minimum requirements. But they do not stand out in this version:

Mr. George Wills, who inspected the main building on October 1, is a vice president of the company. His inspection, which supports the conclusion that the building is large enough for the proposed store, uncovered these facts. The building has 6,500 square feet of floor space and 2,400 square feet of storage space, which is more than the minimum requirement of 6,000 and 2,000 square feet, respectively, of floor and storage space.

The third paragraph shows good emphasis of the important points. The short beginning sentence emphasizes the conclusion. The supporting facts that the building exceeds the minimum floor and storage space requirements receive main-clause emphasis. The less important facts, such as the reference to George Wills, are treated subordinately. Also, the most important facts are placed at the points of emphasis—the beginning and ending.

The main building is large enough for the new store. This conclusion, reached by Vice President George Wills following his October 1 inspection of the building, is based on these facts: The building's 6,500 square feet of floor space exceed the minimum requirement by 500 square feet. The 2,400 square feet of storage space exceed the minimum requirement by 400 square feet.

The preceding illustrations show how sentence construction can determine emphasis. You can make items stand out, you can treat them equally, or you can de-emphasize them. The choices are yours. But what you do must be the result of good, sound thinking and not simply a matter of chance.

Giving the Sentences Unity

- All parts of a sentence should concern one thought.

Good sentences have unity. For a sentence to have unity, all of its parts must combine to form one clear thought. In other words, all the things put in a sentence should have a good reason for being together.

- There are three causes of unity error.

Violations of unity in sentence construction fall into three categories: (1) unrelated ideas, (2) excessive detail, and (3) illogical constructions.

- First, placing unrelated ideas in a sentence violates unity.

Unrelated Ideas.   Placing unrelated ideas in a sentence is the most obvious violation of unity. Putting two or more ideas in a sentence is not grammatically wrong, but the ideas must have a reason for being together. They must combine to complete the single goal of the sentence.

- You can avoid this error by (1) putting unrelated ideas in separate sentences, (2) subordinating an idea, or (3) adding words that show relationship.

You can give unity to sentences that contain unrelated ideas in three basic ways: (1) You can put the ideas in separate sentences. (2) You can make one of the ideas subordinate to the other. (3) You can add words that show how the ideas are related. The first two of these techniques are illustrated by the revisions of this sentence:

Mr. Jordan is our sales manager, and he has a degree in law.

Perhaps the two ideas are related, but the words do not tell how. A better arrangement is to put each in a separate sentence:

Mr. Jordan is our sales manager. He has a law degree.

Or the two ideas could be kept in one sentence by subordinating one to the other. In this way, the main clause provides the unity of the sentence.

Mr. Jordan, our sales manager, has a law degree.

Modern executives often are extremely busy. They want and need their incoming messages to communicate easily and quickly.

Adding words to show the relationship of ideas is illustrated in the revision of this example:

Our production increased in January, and our equipment is wearing out.

The sentence has two ideas that seem unrelated. One way of improving it is to make a separate sentence of each idea. A closer look reveals, however, that the two ideas really are related. The words just do not show how. Thus, the sentence could be revised to show how:

Even though our equipment is wearing out, our production increased in January.

The following contrasting pairs of sentences further illustrate the technique:

UNRELATED	IMPROVED
Our territory is the southern half of the state, and our salespeople cannot cover it thoroughly.	Our territory is the southern half of the state. Our salespeople cannot cover it thoroughly.
Operation of the press is simple, but no machine will work well unless it is maintained.	Operation of the press is simple, but, like any machine, it will not work well unless it is maintained.
We concentrate on energy-saving products, and 70 percent of our business comes from them.	As a result of our concentration on energy-saving products, 70 percent of our business comes from them.

Excessive Detail. Putting too much detail into one sentence tends to hide the central thought. If the detail is important, you should put it in a separate sentence.

• Excessive detail is another cause of lack of unity. If the detail is important, put it in a separate sentence. This means using short sentences.

This suggestion strengthens another given earlier in the chapter—the suggestion that you use short sentences. Obviously, short sentences cannot have much detail. Long sentences—full of detail—definitely lead to lack of unity, as illustrated in these contrasting examples:

EXCESSIVE DETAIL	IMPROVED
Our New York offices, considered plush in the 1980s, but now badly in need of renovation, as is the case with most offices that have not been maintained, have been abandoned.	Considered plush in the 1980s, our New York offices have not been maintained properly. As they badly need repair, we have abandoned them.
We have attempted to trace the Plytec insulation you ordered from us October 1, and about which you inquired in your October 10 letter, but we have not yet been able to locate it, although we are sending you a rush shipment immediately.	We are sending you a rush shipment of Plytec insulation immediately. Following your October 10 inquiry, we attempted to trace your October 1 order. We were unable to locate it.
In 1995, when I, a small-town girl from a middle-class family, began my studies at Darden University, which is widely recognized for its information systems program, I set my goal for a career with a major consulting firm.	A small-town girl from a middle-class family, I entered Darden University in 1995. I selected Darden because of its widely recognized information systems program. From the beginning, my goal was a career with a major consulting firm.

Illogical Constructions. Illogical constructions destroy sentence unity. These constructions result primarily from illogical thinking. Illogical thinking is too complex for meaningful study here, but a few typical examples should acquaint you with the possibilities. Then, by thinking logically, you should be able to reduce illogical constructions in your writing.

• Illogical constructions can rob a sentence of unity.

The first example contains two main thoughts in two correct clauses. But one clause is in active voice (*we cut*), and the other is in passive voice (*quality was reduced*).

• Active and passive voice in the same sentence can violate unity.

First we cut prices, and then quality was reduced.

We achieve unity by making both clauses active, as in this example:

First we cut prices, and then we reduced quality.

• So can mixed constructions.

The mixed constructions of the following sentence do not make a clear and logical thought. The technical explanation is that the beginning clause belongs with a complex sentence, while the last part is the predicate of a simple sentence.

Because our salespeople are inexperienced caused us to miss our quota.

Revised for good logic, the sentence might read:

The inexperience of our salespeople caused us to miss our quota.

These sentences further illustrate the point:

ILLOGICAL CONSTRUCTION	IMPROVED
Job rotation is when you train people by moving them from job to job.	Job rotation is a training method in which people are moved from job to job.
Knowing that she objected to the price was the reason we permitted her to return the goods.	Because we knew she objected to the price, we permitted her to return the goods.
I never knew an executive who was interested in helping workers who had got into problems that caused them to worry.	I never knew an executive who was interested in helping worried workers with their problems.
My education was completed in 1995, and then I began work as a sales representative for Microsoft.	I completed my education in 1995 and then began work as a sales representative for Microsoft.

Arranging Sentences for Clarity

• Clear writing requires that you follow the established rules of grammar.

As you know, various rules of grammar govern the structure of sentences. You know, for example, that modifying words must follow a definite sequence—that altering the sequence changes meaning. "A venetian blind" means one thing. "A blind Venetian" means quite another. Long-established rules of usage determine the meaning.

• These rules are based on custom and logical relationships.

Many such rules exist. Established by centuries of use, these rules are not merely arbitrary requirements. Rather, they are based on custom and on logical relationships between words. In general, they are based on the need for clear communication.

• For example, dangling modifiers confuse meaning.

Take the rule concerning dangling modifiers. Dangling modifiers confuse meaning by modifying the wrong words. On the surface, this sentence appears correct: "Believing that the price would drop, our purchasing agents were instructed not to buy." But the sentence is correct only if the purchasing agents did the believing—which is not the case. The modifying phrase dangles, and the intended meaning was probably this: "Believing that the price would drop, we instructed our purchasing agents not to buy."

• So do unparallel constructions, pronouns without antecedents, and subject-verb disagreements.

Other rules of grammar also help to make writing clear. Unparallel constructions leave wrong impressions. Pronouns that do not clearly refer to a definite preceding word are vague and confusing. Subject-verb disagreements confuse the reader. The list goes on and on. The rules of grammar are useful in writing clear sentences. You should know them and follow them. You will want to study Chapter 18 for a review of these rules and complete the diagnostic exercise at the chapter end for feedback on your understanding of them.

CARE IN PARAGRAPH DESIGN

• Paragraphing shows and emphasizes organization.

Paragraphing is also important to clear communication. Paragraphs show the reader where topics begin and end, thus helping organize information in the reader's mind. Paragraphs also help make ideas stand out.

How one should design paragraphs is hard to explain, for the procedure is largely mental. Designing paragraphs requires the ability to organize and relate information. It involves the use of logic and imagination. But we can say little that would help you in these activities. The best we can do is give the following points on paragraph structure.

Giving the Paragraphs Unity

Like sentences, paragraphs should have unity. When applied to paragraph structure, unity means that a paragraph builds around a single topic or idea. Thus, everything you include in a paragraph should develop this topic or idea. When you have finished the paragraph, you should be able to say, "Everything in this paragraph belongs together because every part concerns every other part."

• The contents of a paragraph should concern one topic or idea (unity).

Unity is not always easy to determine. As all of a letter or a report may concern a single topic, one could say that the whole letter or report has unity. One could say the same about a major division of a report or a long paper. Obviously, paragraph unity concerns smaller units than these. Generally, it concerns the next largest unit of thought above a sentence.

• But unity can vary in breadth. Paragraph unity concerns a narrow topic.

A violation of unity is illustrated in the following paragraph from an application letter. As the goal of the paragraph is to summarize the applicant's coursework, all the sentences should pertain to coursework. By shifting to personal qualities, the third sentence violates paragraph unity. Taking this sentence out would correct the fault.

At the university I studied all the basic accounting courses as well as specialized courses in petroleum, fiduciary, and systems. I also took specialized coursework in the behavioral areas, with emphasis on human relations. Realizing the value of human relations in business, I also actively participated in organizations, such as Sigma Nu (social fraternity), Delta Sigma Pi (professional fraternity), YMCA, and Men's Glee Club. I selected my elective coursework to round out my general business education. Among my electives were courses in investments, advanced business report writing, financial policy, and management information systems. A glance at my résumé will show you the additional courses that round out my training.

Keeping Paragraphs Short

As a general rule, you should keep your paragraphs short. This suggestion overlaps the suggestion about unity, for if your paragraphs have unity, they will be short.

• Generally, paragraphs should be short.

As noted earlier, paragraphs help the reader follow the writer's organization plan. Writing marked by short paragraphs identifies more of the details of that plan. In addition, such writing is inviting to the eye. People simply prefer to read writing with frequent paragraph breaks.

• Short paragraphs show organization better than long ones.

This last point is easily proved by illustration. Assume you have a choice of reading either of two business reports on the same subject. One report has long paragraphs. Its pages appear solid with type. The second report has short paragraphs and thus provides frequent rest stops. You can see the rest stops at first glance. Now, which would you choose? No doubt, you would prefer the report with short paragraphs. It is more inviting, and it appears less difficult. Perhaps the difference is largely psychological, but it is a very real difference.

• Most readers prefer to read short paragraphs.

How long a paragraph should be depends on its contents—on what must be included to achieve unity. Readability research has suggested an average length of eight lines for longer papers such as reports. Shorter paragraphs are appropriate for letters.

• About eight lines is a good average length.

Keep in mind that these suggestions concern only an average. Some good paragraphs may be quite long—well over the average. Some paragraphs can be very short—as short as one line. One-line paragraphs are an especially appropriate means of emphasizing major points in business letters. A one-line paragraph may be all that is needed for a goodwill closing comment.

• But length can and should vary with need.

• A good practice is to question paragraphs over 12 lines.

A good rule to follow is to question the unity of all long paragraphs—say, those longer than 12 lines. If after looking over such a paragraph you conclude that it has unity, leave it as it is. But you will sometimes find more than one topic. When you do, make each topic into a separate paragraph.

Making Good Use of Topic Sentences

• Topic sentences can help make good paragraphs. But not every paragraph must have a topic sentence.

One good way of organizing paragraphs is to use topic sentences. The topic sentence expresses the main idea of a paragraph, and the remaining sentences build around and support it. In a sense, the topic sentence serves as a headline for the paragraph, and all the other sentences supply the story. Not every paragraph must have a topic sentence. Some paragraphs, for example, introduce ideas, relate succeeding items, or present an assortment of facts that lead to no conclusion. The central thought of such paragraphs is difficult to put into a single sentence. Even so, you should use topic sentences whenever you can. You should use them especially in writing reports that discuss a number of topics and subtopics. Using topic sentences forces you to find the central idea of each paragraph and helps you check paragraph unity.

• Placement of the topic sentence depends on the writer's plan.

How a topic sentence should fit into a paragraph depends primarily on the subject matter and the writer's plan. Some subject matter develops best if details are presented first and then followed by a conclusion or a summary statement (the topic sentence). Other subject matter develops best if it is introduced by the conclusion or the summary statement. Yet other arrangements are possible. You must make the decision, and you should base it on your best judgment. Your judgment should be helped, however, by a knowledge of the paragraph arrangements most commonly used.

• The topic sentence can come first.

Topic Sentence First.   The most common paragraph arrangement begins with the topic sentence and continues with the supporting material. As this arrangement fits most units of business information, you should find it useful. In fact, the arrangement is so appropriate for business information that one company's writing manual suggests that it be used for virtually all paragraphs.

To illustrate the writing of a paragraph in which the topic sentence comes first, take a paragraph reporting on economists' replies to a survey question asking their view of business activity for the coming year. The facts to be presented are these: 13 percent of the economists expected an increase; 28 percent expected little or no change; 59 percent expected a downturn; 87 percent of those who expected a downturn thought it would come in the first quarter. The obvious conclusion—and the subject for the topic sentence—is that the majority expected a decline in the first quarter. Following this reasoning, we would develop a paragraph like this:

A majority of the economists consulted think that business activity will drop during the first quarter of next year. Of the 185 economists interviewed, 13 percent looked for continued increases in business activity, and 28 percent anticipated little or no change from the present high level. The remaining 59 percent looked for a recession. Of this group, nearly all (87 percent) believed that the downturn would occur during the first quarter of the year.

• It can come last.

Topic Sentence at End.   The second most common paragraph arrangement places the topic sentence at the end, usually as a conclusion. Paragraphs of this kind usually present the supporting details first, and from these details they lead readers to the conclusion. Such paragraphs often begin with what may appear to be a topic sentence. But the final sentence covers their real meat, as in this illustration:

The significant role of inventories in the economic picture should not be overlooked. At present, inventories represent 3.8 months' supply. Their dollar value is the highest in history. If considered in relation to increased sales, however, they are not excessive. In fact, they are well within the range generally believed to be safe. Thus, inventories are not likely to cause a downward swing in the economy.

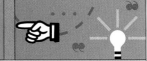
Topic Sentence within the Paragraph.   A third arrangement places the topic sentence somewhere within the paragraph. This arrangement is rarely used, for good reason. It does not emphasize the topic sentence, although the topic sentence usually deserves emphasis. Still, you can sometimes justify using this arrangement for special effect, as in this example:

• Or it can come in the middle.

Numerous materials have been used in manufacturing this part. And many have shown quite satisfactory results. *Material 329, however, is superior to them all.* When built with material 329, the part is almost twice as strong as when built with the next best material. It is also 3 ounces lighter. Most important, it is cheaper than any of the other products.

Leaving out Unnecessary Detail

You should include in your paragraphs only the information needed. The chances are that you have more information than the reader needs. Thus, a part of your communication task is to select what you need and discard what you do not need.

• In writing paragraphs, leave out unnecessary information.

What you need, of course, is a matter of judgment. You can judge best by putting yourself in your reader's place. Ask yourself questions such as these: How will the information be used? What information will be used? What will not be used? Then make your decisions. If you follow this procedure, you will probably leave out much that you originally intended to use.

• But deciding what to include is a matter of judgment.

The following paragraph from a memorandum to maintenance workers presents excessive information.

In reviewing the personnel history form you filled out last week, I found an error that needs to be corrected. The section titled "work history" has blank lines for three items of information. The first is for dates employed. The second is for company name. And the third is for type of work performed. On your form you wrote company name only, and it extended across all three blanks. You did not indicate years employed or your duties. This information is important. It is reviewed by your supervisors every time you are considered for promotion or for a pay increase. Therefore, it must be completed. I request that you come by my office and complete this form at your earliest convenience.

The message says much more than the reader needs to know. The goal is to have the reader come to the office, and everything else is of questionable value. Even if some explanation is desirable, would it not be better to explain at the office? This revised memorandum is better:

Please come by my office at your earliest convenience to correct an error in the personnel form you filled out last week.

Giving the Paragraphs Movement

Good writing has movement. Movement is the writing quality that takes the reader toward the goal in definite and logical steps, without side trips and backward shifts.

• Each paragraph should move an additional step toward the goal.

The progress is steadily forward—step by step. The sentences move step by step to reach the paragraph goal, and the paragraphs move step by step to reach the overall goal.

Perhaps movement is best explained by example:

Three reasons justify moving from the Crowton site. First, the building rock in the Crowton area is questionable. The failure of recent geologic explorations in the area appears to confirm suspicions that the Crowton deposits are nearly exhausted. Second, the distances from the Crowton site to major consumption areas make transportation costs unusually high. Obviously, any savings in transportation costs will add to company profits. Third, the obsolescence of much of the equipment at the Crowton plant makes this an ideal time for relocation. The old equipment at the Crowton plant could be scrapped.

The flow of thought in this paragraph is orderly. The first sentence sets up the paragraph structure, and the parts of that structure follow.

SUMMARY ▶ by Chapter Objectives

1 Explain the role of adaptation in writing clear sentences.

1. Writing that communicates uses words that the reader understands and sentence structures that organize the message clearly in the reader's mind. It is writing that is *adapted* to the reader.

2 Write short, clear sentences by limiting sentence content and economizing on words.

2. In general, you should use short sentences, especially when adapting to readers with low reading ability. Do this in two ways:
   - Limit sentence content by breaking up those that are too long.
   - Use words economically by following these specific suggestions:
     —Avoid cluttering phrases (*if* rather than *in the event that*).
     —Eliminate surplus words—words that contribute nothing (*It will be noted that*).
     —Avoid roundabout ways of saying things (*decreases* rather than *can be observed to be decreasing*).
     —Avoid unnecessary repetition (*In my opinion, I think*).

3 Design sentences that give the right emphasis to content.

3. Give every item you communicate the emphasis it deserves by following these suggestions:
   - Use short sentences to emphasize points.
   - Combine points in longer sentences to de-emphasize them.
   - But how you combine points (by equal treatment, by subordination) determines the emphasis given.

4 Employ unity and clarity in writing effective sentences.

4. Achieve unity and clarity in your sentences.
   - Make certain all the information in a sentence belongs together—that it forms a unit. These suggestions help:
     —Eliminate excessive detail.
     —Combine only related thoughts.
     —Avoid illogical constructions.
   - Ensure clarity by following the conventional rules of writing (standards of punctuation, grammar, and such).

5 Compose paragraphs that are short, unified, use topic sentences effectively, show movement, and communicate clearly.

5. Design your paragraphs for clear communication by following these standards:
   - Give the paragraphs unity.
   - Keep the paragraphs short.
   - Use topic sentences effectively, usually at the beginning but sometimes within and at the end of the paragraph.
   - Leave out unessential details.
   - Give the paragraphs movement.

CRITICAL THOUGHT QUESTIONS

1. How are sentence length and sentence design related to adaptation?
2. Discuss this comment: "Long, involved sentences tend to be difficult to understand. Therefore, the shorter the sentence, the better."
3. What is the effect of sentence length on emphasis?
4. How can unity apply equally well to a sentence, to a paragraph, and to longer units of writing?
5. What are the principal causes of lack of unity in sentences?
6. Discuss this comment: "Words carry the message. They would carry the same meanings with or without paragraphing. Therefore, paragraphing has no effect on communication."
7. Defend the use of short paragraphs in report writing.
8. "Topic sentences merely repeat what the other sentences in the paragraph say. As they serve only to add length, they should be eliminated." Discuss.

CRITICAL THINKING EXERCISES

Instructions, Sentences 1–8: Break up these sentences into shorter, more readable sentences.

1. Records were set by both the New York Stock Exchange Composite Index, which closed at 263.27, up 1.65 points, topping its previous high of 261.62, set Wednesday, and Standard & Poor's Industrial Average, which finished at 573.61, up 2.20, smashing its all-time record of 571.41, also set in the prior session.
2. Dealers attributed the rate decline to several factors, including expectations that the U.S. Treasury will choose to pay off rather than refinance some $4 billion of government obligations that fall due next month, an action that would absorb even further the available supplies of short-term government securities, leaving more funds chasing skimpier stocks of the securities.
3. If you report your income on a fiscal-year basis ending in 1995, you may not take credit for any tax withheld on your calendar-year 1995 earnings, inasmuch as your taxable year began in 1994, although you may include, as a part of your withholding tax credits against your fiscal 1996 tax liability, the amount of tax withheld during 1995.
4. The Consumer Education Committee is assigned the duties of keeping informed of the qualities of all consumer goods and services, especially of their strengths and shortcomings, of gathering all pertinent information on dealers' sales practices, with emphasis on practices involving honest and reasonable fairness, and of publicizing any of the information collected that may be helpful in educating the consumer.
5. The upswing in business activity that began in 1995 is expected to continue and possibly accelerate in 1996, and gross domestic product should rise by $65 billion, representing an 8 percent increase over 1995, which is significantly higher than the modest 0.05 percent increase of 1994.
6. As you will not get this part of medicare automatically, even if you are covered by social security, you must sign up for it and pay $7.75 per month, which the government will match, if you want your physician's bills to be covered.
7. Students with approved excused absences from any of the hour examinations have the option of taking a special makeup examination to be given during dead week or of using their average grade on their examinations in the course as their grade for the work missed.
8. Although we have not definitely determined the causes for the decline in sales volume for the month, we know that during this period construction on the street adjacent to the store severely limited traffic flow and that because of resignations in the advertising department promotion efforts dropped well below normal.

Instructions, Sentences 9–38: Revise the following sentences for more economical wording.

9. In view of the fact that we financed the experiment, we were entitled to some profit.
10. We will deliver the goods in the near future.
11. Mr. Watts outlined his development plans on the occasion of his acceptance of the presidency.
12. I will talk to him with regard to the new policy.
13. The candidates who had the most money won.
14. There are many obligations that we must meet.
15. We purchased coats that are lined with wolf fur.
16. Mary is of the conviction that service has improved.
17. Sales can be detected to have improved over last year.
18. It is essential that we take the actions that are necessary to correct the problem.
19. The chairperson is engaged in the activities of preparing the program.
20. Martin is engaged in the process of revising the application.
21. You should study all new innovations in your field.
22. In all probability, we are likely to suffer a loss this quarter.
23. The requirements for the job require a minimum of three years of experience.

24. In spite of the fact that the bill remains unpaid, they placed another order.

25. We expect to deliver the goods in the event that we receive the money.

26. In accordance with their plans, company officials sold the machinery.

27. This policy exists for the purpose of preventing dishonesty.

28. The salespeople who were most successful received the best rewards.

29. The reader will note that this area ranks in the top 5 percent in per capita income.

30. Our new coats are made of a fabric that is of the water-repellent variety.

31. Our office is charged with the task of counting supplies not used in production.

32. Their salespeople are of the conviction that service is obsolete.

33. Losses caused by the strike exceeded the amount of $14,000.

34. This condition can be assumed to be critical.

35. Our goal is to effect a change concerning the overtime pay rate.

36. Mr. Wilson replaced the old antiquated machinery with new machinery.

37. We must keep this information from transpiring to others.

38. The consensus of opinion of this group is that Wellington was wrong.

Instructions, Paragraphs 39–43: Rewrite the following paragraphs in two ways to show different placement of the topic sentence and variations in emphasis of contents. Point out the differences in meaning in each of your paragraphs.

39. Jennifer has a good knowledge of office procedure. She works hard. She has performed her job well. She is pleasant most of the time, but she has a bad temper, which has led to many personal problems with the work group. Although I cannot recommend her for promotion, I approve a 10 percent raise for her.

40. Last year our sales increased 7 percent in California and 9 percent in Arizona. Nevada had the highest increase, with 14 percent. Although all states in the western region enjoyed increases, Oregon recorded only a 2 percent gain. Sales in Washington increased 3 percent.

41. I majored in marketing at Darden University and received a B.S. degree in 1996. Among the marketing courses I took were marketing strategy, promotion, marketing research, marketing management, and consumer behavior. These and other courses prepared me specifically for a career in retailing. Included, also, was a one-semester internship in retailing with Olympic Department Stores.

42. Our records show that Penn motors cost more than Oslo motors. The Penns have less breakdown time. They cost more to repair. I recommend that we buy Penn motors the next time we replace worn-out motors. The longer working life offsets Penn's cost disadvantage. So does its better record for breakdown.

43. Recently China ordered a large quantity of wheat from the United States. Likewise, Germany ordered a large quantity. Other countries continued to order heavily, resulting in a dramatic improvement in the outlook for wheat farming. Increased demand by Eastern European countries also contributed to the improved outlook.

Writing for Effect

Upon completing this chapter, you will be able to write business communications that emphasize key points and have a positive effect on human relations. To reach this goal, you should be able to

1 Explain the need for effect in writing business letters.

2 Use a conversational style that eliminates the old language of business and "rubber stamps."

3 Use the you-viewpoint to foster goodwill in letters.

4 Employ positive language to achieve goodwill and other desired effects.

5 Explain the techniques of achieving courtesy in letters.

6 Use the four major techniques for emphasis in writing.

7 Write letters that flow smoothly through the use of a logical order helped by the four major transitional devices.

▷ to Affecting Human Relations through Writing

To prepare yourself for this chapter, once again play the role of Max Schlitz's supervisor. As you review Max's work, you note that he writes more than reports. Like many people in office positions, he writes more letters than anything else.

The fact that he writes many letters causes you to think. What if he writes letters the way he writes reports? Letters go outside the company and are read by customers, fellow businesspeople, and others. Because poorly written letters would give bad impressions of the company, you decide to review Max's letters. Typical of what you find is this letter denying a request for an adjustment:

Dear Mr. Morley:

Your Dec. 3d complaint was received and contents noted. After reviewing the facts, I regret to report that I must refuse your claim. If you will read the warranty brochure, you will see that the shelving you bought is designed for light loads—a maximum of 800 pounds. You should have bought the heavy-duty product.

I regret the damage this mistake caused you and trust that you will see our position. Hoping to be of service to you in the future, I remain,

Sincerely yours,

In this letter, you detect more than just the readability problem you saw in Max's reports. You see problems of human relations. The words appear tactless, unfriendly, and lacking in warmth and understanding. Overall, they leave a bad impression in the reader's mind.

Clearly, Max needs to know more about letter writing. What specifically does he need to know? The answer is the subject of this chapter. ■

NEED FOR EFFECT

As noted in the preceding chapters, clarity will be your major concern in much of the writing you will do in business. It will be your major concern in most of the writing you will do to communicate within the organization—reports, memorandums, procedures, proposals, and so on. In such writing, your primary concern will be to communicate information. Whatever you do to communicate information quickly and easily will be appropriate.

- Written communication within a business primarily requires clarity.

When you write letters, however, you will be concerned about communicating more than information. The information in the letters will be important, of course. In fact, it will probably be the most important part. But you will also need to communicate certain effects.

- Letter writing requires clarity and planned effect. The goodwill effect is valuable to business.

One effect that you will need to communicate is the goodwill effect. Building goodwill through letters is good business practice. Wise business leaders know that the success of their businesses is affected by what people think about the businesses. They know that what people think about businesses is influenced by their human contact with the businesses and that letters are a major form of human contact.

The goodwill effect in letters is not desirable for business reasons alone. It is, quite simply, the effect most of us want in our relations with people. The things we do and say to create goodwill are the things we enjoy doing and saying. They are friendly, courteous things that make relations between people enjoyable. Most of us would want to do and say them even if they were not profitable.

- Most people enjoy building goodwill.

As you read the following chapters, you will see that other effects sometimes ensure the success of letters. For example, in writing to persuade a reader to accept an unfavorable decision, you can use the techniques of persuasion. In applying for a job, you can use writing techniques that emphasize your qualifications. And in telling bad

- For their success, letters often require other effects.

news, you can use techniques that play down the unhappy parts. These are but a few of the effects that you may find helpful in letter writing.

Getting such effects in letters is largely a matter of skillful writing and of understanding how people respond to words. It involves keeping certain attitudes in mind and using certain writing techniques to work them into your letters. The following review of these attitudes and techniques should help you get the effects you need.

- Getting the desired effects is a matter of writing skill and of understanding people.

CONVERSATIONAL STYLE

- Writing in conversational language has a favorable effect.

One technique that helps build the goodwill effect in letters is to write in conversational language. By conversational language we mean language that resembles conversation. It is warm and natural. Such language leaves an impression that people like. It is also the language we use most and understand best.

Resisting Tendency to Be Formal

- Writing in conversational language is not easy, for we tend to be stiff and formal.

Writing conversationally is not as easy as you might think, because most of us tend to write formally. When faced with a writing task, we change character. Instead of writing in friendly, conversational language, we write in stiff and stilted words. We seek the big word, the difficult word. The result is a cold and unnatural style—one that doesn't produce the goodwill effect you want your letters to have. The following examples illustrate this problem and how to correct it.

STIFF AND DULL	CONVERSATIONAL
Reference is made to your May 7 letter, in which you describe the approved procedure for initiating a claim.	Please refer to your May 7 letter in which you tell how to file a claim.
Enclosed herewith is the brochure about which you make inquiry.	Enclosed is the brochure you asked about.
In reply to your July 11 letter, please be informed that your adherence to instructions outlined therein will greatly facilitate attainment of our objective.	By following the procedures you listed in your July 11 letter, you will help us reach our goal.
This is in reply to your letter of December 1, expressing concern that you do not have a high school diploma and asking if a Certificate Attainment would suffice as prerequisite for the TAA Training Program.	The Certificate of Attainment you mention in your December 1 letter qualifies you for the TAA Training Program.
I shall be most pleased to avail myself of your kind suggestion when and if prices decline.	I'll gladly follow your suggestion if the price falls.

Avoiding the Old Language of Business

- The early English business writers developed an unnatural style for letters. This "language of business" was influenced by legal language and the language of the nobility.

Adding to our natural difficulty in writing business letters conversationally are some deep-rooted historical influences. Unfortunately, the early English business writers borrowed heavily from the formal language of the law and from the flowery language of the nobility. From these two sources they developed a style of letter writing that became known as the "language of business." It was a cold, stiff, and unnatural style.

We beg to advise and wish to state

That yours has arrived of recent date.

We have it before us, its contents noted.

Herewith enclosed, the prices we quoted.

Regarding the matter, and due to the fact

That up until now your order we've lacked,

We hope you will not delay it unduly

And beg to remain yours very truly,

Anonymous

But it was generally accepted throughout the English-speaking world. The following expressions typify this style:

IN OPENINGS	IN CONTENTS	IN CLOSINGS
Your letter of the 7th inst. received and contents duly noted	Please be advised	Thanking you in advance
	Said matter	Trusing this will meet with your favor
We beg to advise	In due course	
In compliance with yours of even date	Inst., prox., ult.	We beg to remain
	Kind favor	Anticipating your favorable response
Your esteemed favor at hand	Kind order	
	Re:	Assuring you of our coop- eration
This is to inform you	In re	
We have before us	Said matter	Hoping to receive
Responding to yours of even date	Deem it advisable	I am, Dear Sir, yours respectfully
	Wherein you state as per our letter	Trusting to be favored by your further orders, we are, Gentlemen, yours faithfully
Yours of the 10th ultimo to hand	In reply wish to state	
Your favor received	Attached hereto	

This style of writing business letters reached a peak in the late 1800s, and it was still in much use in the early years of this century. A typical business letter of this period would begin something like this: "Yours of the 7th inst. received and contents duly noted. In reply wish to state . . ." It would end something like this: "Hoping to hear from you at your earliest convenience, I remain, Yours Sincerely . . ." The text between these parts would be equally stiff and unnatural. Further illustrating writing in the old language of business is this model letter from a leading letter book of the day:

* This style reached a peak in the late 1800s. "Yours of the 7th inst. received and contents duly noted" typifies this manner of writing.

Gentlemen,

We have to thank you for yours of the 28th inst., enclosing cheque for $95.12 in payment of our invoice of the 17th inst. Formal receipt enclosed herewith. Trusting to be favored with your further orders,

We are, Gentlemen,
Yours faithfully,[1]

- The old language of business has faded away, but some of its expressions remain (*please be advised, enclosed please find*). Do not use them.

Although the old language of business has faded away, some of its expressions remain with us. These include "enclosed please find," "please be advised," "this is to inform," "deem it advisable," and "take the liberty." You should not use them. Perhaps the most common remnants of the old language of business are the dangling closes (endings that trail off into the signature). Typical examples are "trusting to hear from you," "thanking you in advance, I remain," and "hoping to hear from you." These closes may express sincere feeling, but they belong to the past. You should leave them there.

Cutting Out "Rubber Stamps"

- Rubber stamps are expressions used by habit every time a certain type of situation occurs.

Rubber stamps (also called *clichés*) are expressions used by habit every time a certain type of situation occurs. They are used without thought and do not fit the present situation exclusively. As the term indicates, they are used much as you would use a rubber stamp.

- They give the effect of routine treatment. It is better to use words written for the present case.

Because they are used routinely, rubber stamps communicate the effect of routine treatment, which is not likely to impress readers favorably. Such treatment tells readers that the writer has no special concern for them—that the present case is being handled in the same way as others. In contrast, words specially selected for this case are likely to impress. They show the writer's concern for and interest in the readers. Clearly, specially selected wording is the better choice for producing a goodwill effect. Some examples of rubber stamps you have no doubt heard before are listed below. These phrases, while once quite appropriate, have become stale with overuse.

a blessing in disguise
as good as gold
back against the wall
call the shots
last but not least
learning the ropes
leave no stone unturned
to add insult to injury

- Expressions from the old language of business are rubber stamps. Some new ones exist.

Expressions from the old language of business account for many of the rubber stamps now in use. But modern business writers have developed many more. A widely used one is the "thank you for your letter" form of opening sentence. Its intent may be sincere, but its overuse makes it routine. Also overused is the "if I can be of any further assistance, do not hesitate to call on me" type of close. Other examples of modern business-letter rubber stamps are the following:

I am happy to be able to answer your letter.
I have received your letter.
This will acknowledge receipt of . . .
According to our records . . .
This is to inform you that . . .
In accordance with your instructions . . .

---

[1] Pitman's Mercantile Correspondence (London: Sir Isaac Pitman & Sons, n.d.), p. 18.

TECHNOLOGY IN BRIEF

Grammar and Style Checkers: Tools for Identifying Clichés

While helpful, grammar and style checkers can catch only some clichés that creep into our writing. All the examples listed below are from *The Dictionary of Clichés;* one grammar and style checker properly identified two as clichés and missed five.

a whole new ball game
avoid like the plague
go along for the ride
have your cake and eat it too
last but not least <cliché>
leave no stone unturned <cliché>
spill the beans

Although the programs can help, you still need to be able to identify the trite and overused expressions the software misses. Also, you will need to be able to recast the sentences to show your readers you are sincere.

You do not need to know all the rubber stamps to stop using them. You do not even need to be able to recognize them. You only need to write in the language of good conversation, for these worn-out expressions are not a part of most conversational vocabularies. If you use rubber stamps at all, you learned them from reading other people's letters. You did not learn them from oral communication experiences.

• You can avoid rubber stamps by writing in your conversational vocabulary.

Proof through Contrasting Examples

The advantages of conversational writing over writing marked by old business language and rubber stamps are best proved by example. As you read the following contrasting sentences, note the overall effects of the words. The goodwill advantages of conversational writing are obvious.

In face-to-face communication, words, voice, facial expressions, gestures, and such combine to determine the effect of the message. In writing, the printed word alone must do the job.

DULL AND STIFF	FRIENDLY AND CONVERSATIONAL
This is to advise that we deem it a great pleasure to approve subject of your request as per letter of the 12th inst.	Yes, you certainly may use the equipment you asked about in your letter of August 12.
Pursuant to this matter, I wish to state that the aforementioned provisions are unmistakably clear.	These contract provisions are clear on this point.
This will acknowledge receipt of your May 10th order for four dozen Hunt slacks. Please be advised that they will be shipped in accordance with your instructions by Green Arrow Motor Freight on May 16.	Four dozen Hunt slacks should reach your store by the 18th. As you instructed, they were shipped today by Green Arrow Motor Freight.
The undersigned wishes to advise that the aforementioned contract is at hand.	I have the contract.
Please be advised that you should sign the form before the 1st.	You should sign the form before the 1st.
Hoping this meets with your approval . . .	I hope you approve.
Submitted herewith is your notification of our compliance with subject standards.	Attached is notification of our compliance with the standards.
Assuring you of our continued cooperation, we remain . . .	We will continue to cooperate.
Thanking you in advance . . .	I'll sincerely appreciate . . .
Herewith enclosed please find . . .	Enclosed is . . .
I deem it advisable . . .	I suggest . . .
I herewith hand you . . .	Here is . . .
Kindly advise at an early date.	Please let me know soon.

. . . .

YOU-VIEWPOINT

- The you-viewpoint produces goodwill and influences people favorably.

Writing from the you-viewpoint (also called *you-attitude*) is another technique for building goodwill in letters. As you will see in following chapters, it focuses interest on the reader. Thus, it is a technique for persuasion and for influencing people favorably.

- The you-viewpoint emphasizes the reader's interests. It is an attitude of mind involving more than the use of *you* and *yours*.

In a broad sense, you-viewpoint writing emphasizes the reader's interests and concerns. It emphasizes *you* and *your* and de-emphasizes *we* and *our*. But it is more than a matter of just using second person pronouns. *You* and *your* can appear prominently in sentences that emphasize the we-viewpoint, as in this example: "If you do not pay by the 15th, you must pay a penalty." Likewise, *we* and *mine* can appear in sentences that emphasize the you-viewpoint, as in this example: "We will do whatever we can to protect your investment." The point is that the you-viewpoint is an attitude of mind. It is the attitude that places the reader in the center of things. Sometimes it just involves being friendly and treating people in the way they like to be treated. Sometimes it involves skillfully handling people with carefully chosen words to make a desired impression. It involves all these things and more.

The You-Viewpoint Illustrated

Although the you-viewpoint involves much more than word selection, examples of word selection help explain the technique. First, take the case of a person writing a letter to present good news. This person could write from a self-centered point of view, beginning with such words as "I am happy to report . . .". Or he or she could begin with the you-viewpoint words "You will be happy to know . . .". The messages are much the same, but the effects are different.

Next, take the case of a writer who must inform the reader that a request for credit has been approved. A we-viewpoint beginning could take this form: "We are pleased to have your new account." Some readers might view these words favorably. But some would sense a self-centered writer concerned primarily with making money. A you-viewpoint beginning would go something like this: "Your new charge account is now open for your convenience."

The third case is that of an advertising copywriter who must describe the merits of a razor. Advertising copywriters know the value of the you-viewpoint perhaps better than any other group. So no advertising copywriter would write anything like this: "We make Willett razors in three weights—light, medium, and heavy." An advertising copywriter would probably bring the reader into the center of things and write about the product in reader-satisfaction language: "So that you can choose the one razor that is just right for your beard, Willett makes razors for you in three weights—light, medium, and heavy."

The you-viewpoint can even be used in bad-news messages. For example, take the case of an executive who must write a letter saying no to a professor's request for help on a research project. The bad news is made especially bad when it is presented in we-viewpoint words: "We cannot comply with your request to use our office personnel on your project, for it would cost us more than we can afford." A skilled writer using the you-viewpoint would look at the situation from this reader's point of view, find an explanation likely to satisfy this reader, and present the explanation in you-viewpoint language. The you-viewpoint response might take this form: "As a business professor well acquainted with the need for economizing in all phases of office operations, you will understand why we must limit our personnel to work in our office."

- Even a bad-news situation can benefit from you-viewpoint wording.

The following contrasting examples demonstrate the different effects that changes in viewpoint produce. With a bit of imagination, you should be able to supply information on the situations they cover.

WE-VIEWPOINT	YOU-VIEWPOINT
We are happy to have your order for Kopper products, which we are sending today by Mercury Freight.	Your selection of Kopper products should reach you by Saturday, as they were shipped by Mercury Freight today.
We sell the Forever cutlery set for the low price of $4 each and suggest a retail price of $6.50.	You can reap a $2.50 profit on each Forever set you sell at $6.50, for your cost is only $4.
Our policy prohibits us from permitting outside groups to use our equipment except on a cash-rental basis.	As your tax dollar pays our office expense, you will appreciate our policy of cutting operating costs by renting our equipment.
We have been quite tolerant of your past-due account and must now demand payment.	If you are to continue to enjoy the benefits of credit buying, you must clear your account now.
We have received your report of May 1.	Thank you for your report of May 1.
So that we may complete our file records on you, we ask that you submit to us your January report.	So that your file records may be completed, please send us your January report.
We have shipped the two dozen Crown desk sets you ordered.	Your two dozen Crown desk sets should reach your with this letter.
We require that you sign the sales slip before we will charge to your account.	For your protection, you are charged only after you have signed the sales slip.

A Point of Controversy

- Some say that the you-viewpoint is insincere and manipulative. It can be insincere, but it need not be. Using the you-viewpoint is just being courteous. Research supports its use.

The you-viewpoint has been a matter of some controversy. Its critics point out two major shortcomings: (1) it is insincere and (2) it is manipulative. In either event, they argue, the technique is dishonest. It is better, they say, to just "tell it as it is."

These arguments have some merit. Without question, the you-viewpoint can be used to the point of being insincere; and it can be obvious flattery. Those who favor the technique argue that insincerity and flattery need not—in fact, should not—be the result of you-viewpoint effort. The objective is to treat people courteously—the way they like to be treated. People like to be singled out for attention. They are naturally more interested in themselves than in the writer. Overuse of the technique, the defenders argue, does not justify not using it. Their argument is supported by research showing that a majority of personality types, especially the friendlier and more sensitive, react favorably to you-viewpoint treatment.[2] A minority, mainly the less sensitive and harsher personalities, are less susceptible.

- The you-viewpoint can manipulate. But condemn the goal, not the technique.

On the matter of manipulative use of the you-viewpoint, we must again concede a point. It is a technique of persuasion, and persuasion may have bad as well as good goals. Supporters of the you-viewpoint argue that it is bad goals and not the techniques used to reach them that should be condemned. Persuasion techniques used to reach good goals are good.

- A middle-ground approach is best. Use the you-viewpoint when it is the right thing to do.

The correct approach appears to lie somewhere between the extremes. You do not have to use the you-viewpoint exclusively or to eliminate it. You can take a middle ground. You can use the you-viewpoint when it is friendly and sincere and when your goals are good. In such cases, using the you-viewpoint is "telling it as it is"—or at least as it should be. With this position in mind, we apply the technique in the following chapters.

······································

ACCENT ON POSITIVE LANGUAGE

- Of the many ways of saying anything, each has a unique meaning.

Whether your letter achieves its goal will often depend on the words you use. As you know, one can say anything in many ways, and each way conveys a different meaning. Much of the difference lies in the meanings of words.

Effects of Words

- Positive words are usually best for letter goals, especially when persuasion and goodwill are needed.

Positive words are usually best for achieving your letter goals. This is not to say that negative words have no place in business writing. Such words are strong and give emphasis, and you will sometimes want to use them. But your need will usually be for positive words, for such words are more likely to produce the effects you seek. When your goal is to change someone's position, for example, positive words are most likely to do the job. They tend to put the reader in the right frame of mind, and they emphasize the pleasant aspects of the goal. They also create the goodwill atmosphere we seek in most letters.

- Negative words stir up resistance and hurt goodwill.

Negative words tend to produce the opposite effects. They may stir up your reader's resistance to your goals, and they are likely to be highly destructive of goodwill. Thus, to reach your letter-writing goals, you will need to study carefully the negativeness and positiveness of your words. You will need to select the words that are most appropriate in each case.

- So beware of strongly negative words (*mistake, problem*), words that deny (*no, do not*), and ugly words (*itch, guts*).

In doing this you should generally be wary of strongly negative words. These words convey unhappy and unpleasant thoughts, and such thoughts usually detract from your goal. They include such words as *mistake, problem, error, damage, loss,* and *failure.*

---

[2] Sam J. Bruno, "The Effects of Personality Traits on the Perception of Written Mass Communication," doctoral dissertation, Louisiana State University, Baton Rouge, 1971.

There are also words that deny—words such as *no, do not, refuse,* and *stop.* And there are words whose sounds or meanings have unpleasant effects. Examples would differ from person to person, but many would probably agree on these: *itch, guts, scratch, grime, sloppy, sticky, bloody,* and *nauseous.* Or how about *gummy, slimy, bilious,* and *soggy?* Run these negative words through your mind and think about the meanings they produce. You should find it easy to see that they tend to work against most of the goals you may have in your letters.

Examples of Word Choice

To illustrate your positive-to-negative word choices in handling letters, take the case of a company executive who had to deny a local civic group's request to use the company's meeting facilities. To soften the refusal, the executive could let the group use a conference room, which might be somewhat small for its purpose. The executive came up with this totally negative response:

We *regret* to inform you that we *cannot* permit you to use our clubhouse for your meeting, as the Ladies Book Club asked for it first. We can, however, let you use our conference room, but it seats *only* 60.

The negative words are italicized. First, the positively intended message "We *regret* to inform you" is an unmistakable sign of coming bad news. "*Cannot* permit" contains an unnecessarily harsh meaning. And notice how the good-news part of the message is handicapped by the limiting word *only.*

Had the executive searched for more positive ways of covering the same situation, he or she might have written:

Although the Ladies Book Club has reserved the clubhouse for Saturday, we can instead offer you our conference room, which seats 60.

Not a single negative word appears in this version. Both approaches achieve the letter's primary objective of denying a request, but their effects on the reader differ sharply. There is no question as to which approach does the better job of building and holding goodwill.

For a second illustration, take the case of a correspondent who must write a letter granting the claim of a woman for cosmetics damaged in transit. Granting the claim, of course, is the most positive ending that such a situation can have. Even though this customer has had a somewhat unhappy experience, she is receiving what she wants. The negative language of an unskilled writer, however, can so vividly recall the unhappy aspects of the problem that the happy solution is moved to the background. As this negative version of the message illustrates, the effect is to damage the reader's goodwill:

We received your claim in which you contend that we were responsible for *damage* to three cases of Madame Dupree's lotion. We assure you that we sincerely *regret* the *problems* this has caused you. Even though we feel in all sincerity that your receiving clerks may have been *negligent,* we will assume the *blame* and replace the *damaged* merchandise.

Obviously, this version grants the claim grudgingly, and the company would profit from such an approach only if there were extenuating circumstances. The phrase "in which you contend" clearly implies some doubt about the legitimacy of the claim. Even the sincerely intended expression of regret only recalls to the reader's mind the event that caused all the trouble. And the negatives *blame* and *damage* only strengthen the recollection. Certainly, this approach is not conducive to goodwill.

In the following version of the same message, the writer refers only to positive aspects of the situation—what can be done to settle the problem. The job is done without using a negative word and without mentioning the situation being corrected or suspicions concerning the honesty of the claim. The goodwill effect of this approach is likely to maintain business relations with the reader:

Three cases of Madame Dupree's lotion are on their way to you by Mercury Freight and should be on your sales floor by Saturday.

For additional illustrations, compare the differing results obtained from these contrasting positive-negative versions of letter messages (italics mark the negative words):

NEGATIVE	**POSITIVE**
You *failed* to give us the fabric specifications of the chair you ordered.	So that you may have the one chair you want, will you please check your choice of fabric on the enclosed card?
Smoking is *not* permitted anywhere except in the lobby.	Smoking is permitted in the lobby only.
We *cannot* deliver until Friday.	We can deliver the goods on Friday.
Chock-O-Nuts do not have that *gummy, runny* coating that makes some candies *stick* together when they get hot.	The rich chocolate coating of Chock-O-Nuts stays crispy good throughout the summer months.
You were *wrong* in your conclusion, for paragraph 3 of our agreement clearly states . . .	You will agree after reading paragraph 3 of our agreement that . . . .
We *regret* that we *overlooked* your coverage on this equipment and apologize for the *trouble* and *concern* it must have caused you.	You were quite right in believing that you have coverage on the equipment. We appreciate your calling the matter to our attention.
We *regret* to inform you that we must deny your request for credit.	For the time being, we can serve you only on a cash basis.
You should have known that the Peyton fryer *cannot* be submerged in water, for it is clearly explained in the instructions.	The instructions explain why the Peyton fryer should be cleaned only with a cloth.
Your May 7 *complaint* about our Pronto minidrier is *not* supported by the evidence.	Review of the situation described in your May 7 letter explains what happened when you used the Pronto minidrier.

. . . .

COURTESY

- Courtesy is a major contributor to goodwill in business letters.

A major contributor to goodwill in business letters is courtesy. By courtesy we mean treating people with respect and friendly human concern. Used in business letters, courtesy leads to friendly relations between people. The result is a better human climate for solving business problems and doing business.

- Courtesy involves the preceding goodwill techniques.

Developing courtesy in a letter involves a variety of specific techniques. First, it involves the three discussed previously: writing in conversational language, employing the you-viewpoint, and choosing words for positive effect. It also involves other techniques.

Singling Out Your Reader

- It also involves writing directly for the one reader.

One of the other techniques is to single out and write directly to your reader. Letters that appear routine have a cold, impersonal effect. On the other hand, letters that appear to be written for one reader tend to make the reader feel important and appreciated.

- This means writing for the one situation.

To single out your reader in a letter, you should write for the one situation. What you say throughout the letter should make it clear that the reader is getting individual treatment. For example, a letter granting a professor permission to quote company material in the professor's book could end with "We wish you the best of success on

A French General's Justification of Politeness

> Once, at a diplomatic function, the great World War I leader Marshal Foch was maneuvered into a position in which he had to defend French politeness.
>
> "There is nothing in it but wind," Foch's critic sneered.
>
> "There is nothing in a tire but wind," the marshal responded politely, "but it makes riding in a car very smooth and pleasant."

the book." This specially adapted comment is better than one that fits any similar case: "If we can be of further assistance, please let us know." Using the reader's name in the letter text is another good way to show that the reader is being given special treatment. We can gain the reader's favor by occasionally making such references as "you are correct, Mr. Brock" or "as you know, Ms. Smith."

Refraining from Preaching

You can help give your letters a courteous effect by not preaching—that is, by avoiding the tone of a lecture or a sermon. Except in the rare cases in which the reader looks up to the writer, a preaching tone hurts goodwill. We human beings like to be treated as equals. We do not want to be bossed or talked down to. Thus, writing that suggests unequal writer-reader relations is likely to make the reader unhappy.

- The effect of courtesy is helped by not preaching (lecturing).

Preaching in letters is usually not intended. It often occurs when the writer is trying to convince the reader of something, as in this example:

- Usually preaching is not intended. It often results from efforts to persuade.

> You must take advantage of savings like this if you are to be successful. The pennies you save pile up. In time you will have dollars.

It is insulting to tell the reader something quite elementary as if it were not known. Such obvious information should be omitted.

Likewise, flat statements of the obvious fall into the preachy category. Statements like "Rapid inventory turnover means greater profits" are obvious to the experienced retailer and would probably produce negative reactions. So would most statements including such phrases as "you need," "you want," "you should," and "you must," for they tend to talk down to the reader.

- Elementary, flat, and obvious statements often sound preachy.

Another form of preachiness takes this obvious question-and-answer pattern: "Would you like to make a deal that would make you a 38 percent profit? Of course you would!" What intelligent and self-respecting retailer would not be offended by this approach?

Doing More than Is Expected

One sure way to gain goodwill is to do a little bit more than you have to do for your reader. We are all aware of how helpful little extra acts are in other areas of our personal relationships. Too many of us, however, do not use them in our letters. Perhaps in the mistaken belief that we are being concise, we include only the barest essentials in our letters. The result is brusque, hurried treatment, which is inconsistent with our efforts to build goodwill.

- Doing more than necessary builds goodwill.

The writer of a letter refusing a request for use of company equipment, for example, only needs to say no to accomplish the primary goal. This answer, of course, is blunt and totally without courtesy. A goodwill-conscious writer would explain and justify the refusal, perhaps suggesting alternative steps that the reader might take. A wholesaler's brief extra sentence to wish a retailer good luck on a coming promotion is worth the effort. So are an insurance agent's few words of congratulations in a letter to a policyholder who has earned some distinction.

Likewise, a salesperson uses good judgment in an acknowledgment letter that includes helpful suggestions about using the goods ordered. And in letters to customers a writer for a sales organization can justifiably include a few words about new merchandise received, new services provided, price reductions, and so on.

To those who say that these suggestions are inconsistent with the need for conciseness, we must answer that the information we speak of is needed to build goodwill. Conciseness concerns the number of words needed to say what you must say. It never involves leaving out information vital to any of your objectives. On the other hand, nothing we have said should be interpreted to mean that any kind or amount of extra information is justified. You must take care to use only the extra information you need to reach your goal.

Avoiding Anger

Expressing anger in letters—letting off steam—may sometimes help you emotionally. But anger helps achieve the goal of a letter only when that goal is to anger the reader. The effect of angry words is to make the reader angry. With both writer and reader angry, the two are not likely to get together on whatever the letter is about.

To illustrate the effect of anger, take the case of an insurance company correspondent who must write a letter telling a policyholder that the policyholder has made a mistake in interpreting the policy and is not covered on the matter in question. The correspondent, feeling that any fool should be able to read the policy, might respond in these angry words:

If you had read Section IV of your policy, you would know that you are not covered on accidents that occur on water.

One might argue that these words "tell it as it is"—that what they say is true. Even so, they show anger and lack tact. Their obvious effect is to make the reader angry. A more tactful writer would refer courteously to the point of misunderstanding:

As a review of Section IV of your policy indicates, you are covered on accidents that occur on the grounds of your residence only.

Most of the comments made in anger do not provide needed information but merely serve to let the writer blow off steam. Such comments take many forms—sarcasm, insults, exclamations. You can see from the following examples that you should not use them in your letters:

No doubt, you expect us to hold your hand.
I cannot understand your negligence.
This is the third time you have permitted your account to be delinquent.
We will not tolerate this condition.
Your careless attitude has caused us a loss in sales.
We have had it!
We have no intention of permitting this condition to continue.

Being Sincere

Courteous treatment is sincere treatment. If your letters are to be effective, people must believe you. You must convince them that you mean what you say and that your efforts to be courteous and friendly are well intended. That is, your letters must have the quality of sincerity.

The best way of getting sincerity into your letters is to believe in the techniques you use. If you honestly want to be courteous, if you honestly believe that you-viewpoint treatment leads to harmonious relations, and if you honestly think that tactful treatment spares your reader's sensitive feelings, you are likely to apply these techniques sincerely. Your sincerity will show in your writing.

- As the extras add length, they appear not to be concise. But conciseness means word economy—not leaving out essentials.

- Rarely is anger justified in letters. It destroys goodwill.

- Efforts to be courteous must be sincere.

- Sincerity results from believing in the techniques of courtesy.

The language used in a letter communicates more than the message. It tells how friendly, how formal, how careful the writer is—and more.

Overdoing the Goodwill Techniques. There are, however, two major areas that you might alertly check. The first is the overdoing of your goodwill techniques. Perhaps through insincerity or as a result of overzealous effort, the goodwill techniques are frequently overdone. For example, you can easily refer too often to your reader by name in your efforts to write to the one person. Also, as shown in the following example, you-viewpoint effort can go beyond the bounds of reason.

* The goodwill effort can be overdone. Too much you-viewpoint sounds insincere.

So that you may be able to buy Kantrell equipment at an extremely low price and sell it at a tremendous profit, we now offer you the complete line at a 50 percent price reduction.

This example, included in a form letter from the company president to a new charge customer, has a touch of unbelievability:

I was delighted today to see your name listed among Morgan's new charge customers.

Or how about this one, taken from an adjustment letter of a large department store?

We are extremely pleased to be able to help you and want you to know that your satisfaction means more than anything to us.

Avoiding Exaggeration. The second area that you should check is exaggerated statements. It is easy to see through most exaggerated statements; thus, they can give a mark of insincerity to your letter. Exaggerations are overstatements of facts. Although some exaggeration is conventional in sales writing, even here bounds of propriety exist. The following examples clearly overstep these bounds:

* Exaggerated statements are obviously insincere.

Already thousands of new customers are beating paths to the doors of Martin dealers.
Never has there been, nor will there be, a fan as smooth running and whispering quiet as the North Wind.
Everywhere coffee drinkers meet, they are talking about the amazing whiteness Cafree gives their teeth.

Many exaggerated statements involve the use of superlatives. All of us use them, but only rarely do they fit the reality about which we communicate. Words like

* Superlatives (*greatest, finest, strongest*) often suggest exaggeration.

greatest, most amazing, finest, healthiest, and *strongest* are seldom appropriate. Other strong words may have similar effects—for example, *extraordinary, stupendous, delicious, more than happy, sensational, terrific, revolutionary, colossal,* and *perfection.* Such words cause us to question; we rarely believe them.

····························

THE ROLE OF EMPHASIS

- Emphasis also determines effect. Every item communicated should get the proper emphasis.

Getting desired effects in writing often involves giving proper emphasis to the items in the message. Every message contains a number of facts, ideas, and so on that must be presented. Some of these items are more important than others. For example, the main goal of a letter is very important. Supporting explanations and incidental facts are less important. A part of your job as a writer is to determine the importance of each item and to give each item the emphasis it deserves.

- There are four basic emphasis techniques.

To give each item in your message proper emphasis, you must use certain techniques. By far the most useful are these four: position, space, structure, and mechanical devices. The following paragraphs explain each.

Emphasis by Position

- Position determines emphasis. Beginnings and endings carry emphasis.

The beginnings and endings of a writing unit carry more emphasis than the center parts. This rule of emphasis applies whether the unit is the letter, a paragraph of the letter, or a sentence within the paragraph. We do not know why this is so. Some authorities think that the reader's fresh mental energy explains beginning emphasis. Some say that the last parts stand out because they are the most recent in the reader's mind. Whatever the explanation, research has suggested that this emphasis technique works.

- The first and last sentences of a letter, the first and last sentences of a paragraph, and the first and last words of a sentence all carry more emphasis than the middle parts.

In the letter as a whole, the beginning and the closing are the major emphasis positions. Thus, you must be especially mindful of what you put in these places. The beginnings and endings of the internal paragraphs are secondary emphasis positions. Your design of each paragraph should take this into account. To a lesser extent, the first and last words of each sentence carry more emphasis than the middle ones. Thus, even in your sentence design, you can help determine the emphasis that your reader will give the points in your message. In summary, your organizational plan should place the points you want to stand out in these beginning and ending positions. You should bury the points that you do not want to emphasize between these positions.

"Has it ever occurred to you, Leland, that maybe you're too negative?" *(From* The Wall Street Journal, *with permission of Cartoon Features Syndicate.)*

Space and Emphasis

The more you say about something, the more emphasis you give it; and the less you say about something, the less emphasis you give it. If your letter devotes a full paragraph to one point and a scant sentence to another, the first point receives more emphasis. To give the desired effect in your letter, you will need to say just enough about each item of information you present.

- The more space a topic is given, the more emphasis the topic receives.

Sentence Structure and Emphasis

As we noted in Chapter 3, short, simple sentences call attention to their content and long, involved ones do not. In applying this emphasis technique to your writing, carefully consider the possible sentence arrangements of your information. Place the more important information in short, simple sentences so that it will not have to compete with other information for the reader's attention. Combine the less important information, taking care that the relationships are logical. In your combination sentences, place the more important material in independent clauses and the less important information in subordinate structures.

- Sentence structure determines emphasis. Short, simple sentences emphasize content; long, involved ones do not.

Mechanical Means of Emphasis

Perhaps the most obvious emphasis techniques are those that use mechanical devices. By *mechanical devices* we mean any of the things that we can do physically to give the printed word emphasis. The most common of these devices are the underscore, quotation marks, italics, boldface type, and solid capitals. Lines, arrows, and diagrams can also call attention to certain parts. So can color, special type, and drawings. These techniques are infrequently used in letters, with the possible exception of sales letters.

- Mechanical devices (underscore, color, diagrams, and the like) also give emphasis to content.

COHERENCE

Your letters are composed of independent bits of information. But these bits of information do not communicate the whole message. A part of the message is told in the relationships of the facts presented. Thus, to communicate your message successfully, you must do more than communicate facts. You must also make the relationships clear. Making these relationships clear is the task of giving coherence to your letter.

- Letters should be coherent. The relationships of parts should be clear.

The best thing you can do to give your letter coherence is to arrange its information in a logical order—an order appropriate for the strategy of the one case. So important is this matter to letter writing that it is the primary topic of discussion in following chapters. Thus, we will postpone discussion of this vital part of coherence. But logical organization is usually not enough. Various techniques are needed to bridge or tie together the information presented. These techniques are known as *transitional devices*. We will discuss the four major ones: tie-in sentences, repetition of key words, use of pronouns, and use of transitional words.

- Presenting information in logical order helps coherence.

Tie-In Sentences

By structuring your letter so that one idea sets up the next, you can skillfully relate the ideas. That is, you can design the sentences to tie in two successive ideas. Notice in the following example how a job applicant tied together the first two sentences of the letter:

- Sentences can be designed to tie together succeeding thoughts.

As a result of increasing demand for precision instruments in the Billsburg boom area, won't you soon need another experienced and trained salesperson to call on your technical accounts there?
With seven successful years of selling Morris instruments and a degree in civil engineering, I believe I have the qualifications to do this job.

Now substitute the following sentence for the second sentence above and note the abrupt shift it makes.

I am 32 years of age, married, and interested in exploring the possibilities of employment with you.

For another case, compare the contrasting examples of the sentence that follows the first sentence of a letter refusing an adjustment on a trenching machine. As you can see, the strategy of the initial sentence is to set up the introduction of additional information that will clear the company of responsibility.

THE INITIAL SENTENCE

Your objective review of the facts concerning the operation of your Atkins Model L trencher is evidence that you are one who wants to consider all the facts in a case.

GOOD TIE-IN	**ABRUPT SHIFT**
In this same spirit of friendly objectivity, we are confident that you will want to consider some additional information we have assembled.	We have found some additional information you will want to consider.

Repetition of Key Words

- Repetition of key words connects thoughts.

By repeating key words from one sentence to the next, you can make smooth connections of successive ideas. The following successive sentences illustrate this transitional device (key words in italics). The sentences come from a letter refusing a request to present a lecture series for an advertising clinic.

Because your advertising clinic is so well planned, I am confident that it can provide a really *valuable* service to practitioners in the community. To be truly *valuable,* I think you will agree, the program must be given the *time* a thorough preparation requires. As my *time* for the coming weeks is heavily committed, you will need to find someone who is in a better position to do justice to your program.

Use of Pronouns

- Pronouns connect with the words they relate to.

Because pronouns refer to words previously used, they make good transitions between ideas. So use them from time to time in forming idea connections. Especially use the demonstrative pronouns (*this, that, these, those*) and their adjective forms, for these words clearly relate ideas. The following examples (demonstrative pronouns in italics) illustrate this technique:

Ever since the introduction of our Model V 10 years ago, consumers have suggested only one possible improvement—automatic controls. During all *this* time, making *this* improvement has been the objective of Atkins research personnel. Now we proudly report that *these* efforts have been successful.

Transitional Words

- Use transitional words in your writing.

When you talk in everyday conversation, you connect many of your thoughts with transitional words. But when you write, more than likely you do not use them enough. So be alert for places that need to be connected or related. Whenever sharp shifts or breaks in thought flow occur, consider using transitional words.

- Transitional words tell the thought connection between following ideas.

Among the commonly used transitional words are *in addition, besides, in spite of, in contrast, however, likewise, thus, therefore, for example,* and *also.* A more extensive list appears in Chapter 10, where we review transition in report writing. That these words bridge thoughts is easy to see, for each gives a clue to the nature of the connection between what has been said and what will be said next. *In addition,* for example, tells the reader that what is to be discussed next builds on what has been discussed. *However* clearly shows a contrast in ideas. *Likewise* tells that what has been said resembles what will be said.

A Word of Caution

The preceding discussion does not suggest that you should use these transitional devices arbitrarily. Much of your subject matter will flow smoothly without them. When you use them, however, use them naturally so that they blend in with your writing.

• Do not use transitional words arbitrarily. Make them appear natural.

··

SUMMARY ► by Chapter Objectives

1. Although clarity is a major concern in all business writing, in letters you will also be concerned with effect.
   • Specifically, you will need to communicate the effect of goodwill, for it is profitable in business to do so.
   • Sometimes you will need to communicate effects that help you persuade, sell, or the like.
   • To achieve these effects, you will need to heed the following advice.

   1 Explain the need for effect in writing business letters.

2. Write letters in a conversational style (language that sounds like people talking).
   • Such a style requires that you resist the tendency to be formal.
   • It requires that you avoid words from the old language of business (*thanking you in advance, please be advised*).
   • It requires that you avoid the so-called rubber stamps—words used routinely and without thought (*this is to inform, in accordance with*).

   2 Use a conversational style that eliminates the old language of business and "rubber stamps."

3. In your letters, you will need to emphasize the you-viewpoint (*you will be happy to know . . . rather than I am happy to report . . .*).
   • But be careful not to be or appear to be insincere.
   • And do not use the you-viewpoint to manipulate the reader.

   3 Use the you-viewpoint to foster goodwill in letters.

4. You should understand the negative and positive meanings of words.
   • Negative words have unpleasant meanings (*We cannot deliver until Friday*).
   • Positive words have pleasant meanings (*We can deliver Friday*).
   • Select those negative and positive words that achieve the best effect for your goal.

   4 Employ positive language to achieve goodwill and other desired effects.

5. You should strive for courtesy in your letters by doing the following:
   • Practice the goodwill techniques discussed above.
   • Single out your reader (write for the one person).
   • Avoid preaching or talking down.
   • Avoid displays of anger.
   • Be sincere (avoiding exaggeration and overdoing the goodwill techniques).

   5 Explain the techniques of achieving courtesy in letters.

6. Use the four major techniques for emphasis in writing.
   • Determine the items of information the message will contain.
   • Give each item the emphasis it deserves.
   • Show emphasis in these ways:
     —by position (beginnings and endings receive prime emphasis),
     —by space (the greater the space devoted to a topic, the greater is the emphasis.
     —by sentence structure (short sentences emphasize more than longer ones).
     —by mechanical means (color, underscore, boldface, and such).

   6 Use the four major techniques for emphasis in writing.

7. You should write letters that flow smoothly.
   • Present the information in logical order—so that one thought sets up the next.
   • Help show the relationships of thoughts by using these transitional devices:
     —Tie-in sentences,
     —Word repetitions,
     —Pronouns, and
     —Transitional words.

   7 Write letters that flow smoothly through the use of a logical order helped by the four major transitional devices.

CRITICAL THOUGHT QUESTIONS

1. Discuss this comment: "Getting the goodwill effect in letters requires extra effort. It takes extra time, and time costs money."

2. "Our normal conversation is filled with error. Typically, it is crude and awkward. So why make our letters sound conversational?" Discuss.

3. "If a company really wants to impress the readers of its letters, the letters should be formal and should be written in dignified language that displays knowledge." Discuss.

4. After reading a letter filled with expressions from the old language of business, a young administrative trainee made this remark: "I'm keeping this one for reference. It sounds so businesslike!" Evaluate this comment.

5. "If you can find words, sentences, or phrases that cover a general situation, why not use them every time that general situation comes about? Using such rubber stamps would save time, and in business time is money." Discuss.

6. Discuss this comment: "The you-viewpoint is insincere and deceitful."

7. Evaluate this comment: "It's hard to argue against courtesy. But businesspeople don't have time to spend extra effort on it. Anyway, they want their letters to go straight to the point—without wasting words and without sugar coating."

8. "I use the words that communicate the message best. I don't care whether they are negative or positive." Discuss.

9. "I like letter writers who shoot straight. When they are happy, you know it. When they are angry, they let you know." Discuss.

10. A writer wants to include a certain negative point in a letter and to give it little emphasis. Discuss each of the four basic emphasis techniques as they relate to what can be done.

11. Using illustrations other than those in the text, discuss and illustrate the four major transitional devices.

CRITICAL THINKING EXERCISES

Instructions: Rewrite Sentences 1–16 in conversational style.

1. I hereby acknowledge receipt of your July 7 favor.

2. Anticipating your reply by return mail, I remain . . .

3. Attached please find receipt requested in your May 1st inquiry.

4. We take pleasure in advising that subject contract is hereby canceled.

5. You are hereby advised to endorse subject proposal and return same to the undersigned.

6. I shall appreciate the pleasure of your reply.

7. Referring to yours of May 7, I wish to state that this office has no record of a sale.

8. This is to advise that henceforth all invoices will be submitted in duplicate.

9. Agreeable to yours of the 24th inst., we have consulted our actuarial department to ascertain the status of subject policy.

10. Kindly be advised that permission is hereby granted to delay remittance until the 12th.

11. In conclusion would state that, up to this writing, said account has not been profitable.

12. Replying to your letter of the 3rd would state that we deem it a great pleasure to accept your kind offer to serve on the committee.

13. I beg to advise that, with regard to above invoice, this office finds that partial payment of $312 was submitted on delivery date.

14. In replying to your esteemed favor of the 7th, I submit under separate cover the report you requested.

15. In reply to your letter of May 10, please be informed that this office heretofore has generously supported funding activities of your organization.

16. Kindly advise the undersigned as to your availability for participation in the program.

Instructions, Sentences 17–32: Write you-viewpoint sentences to cover each of the situations described.

17. Company policy requires that you must submit the warranty agreement within two weeks of sale.

18. We will be pleased to deliver your order by the 12th.

19. We have worked for 37 years to build the best lawn mowers for our customers.

20. Today we are shipping the goods you ordered February 3.

21. (From an application letter) I have seven years of successful experience selling office machinery.

22. (From a memorandum to employees) We take pleasure in announcing that, effective today, the Company will give a 20 percent discount on all purchases made by employees.

23. Kraff files are made in three widths—one for every standard size of record.

24. We are happy to report approval of your application for membership.

25. Items desired should be checked on the enclosed order form.

26. Our long experience in the book business has enabled us to provide the best customer service possible.

27. So that we can sell at discount prices, we cannot permit returns of merchandise.

28. We invite you to buy from the enclosed catalog.

29. Tony's Red Beans have an exciting spicy taste.

30. We give a 2 percent discount when payment is made within 10 days.

31. I am pleased to inform you that I can grant your request for payment of travel expenses.

32. We can permit you to attend classes on company time only when the course is related to your work assignment.

Instructions, Sentences 33–48: Underscore all negative words in these sentences. Then rewrite the sentences for positive effect. Use your imagination to supply situation information when necessary.

33. Your misunderstanding of our January 7 letter caused you to make this mistake.

34. We hope this delay has not inconvenienced you. If you will be patient, we will get the order to you as soon as our supply is replenished.

35. We regret that we must call your attention to our policy of prohibiting refunds for merchandise bought at discount.

36. Your negligence in this matter caused the damage to the equipment.

37. You cannot visit the plant except on Saturdays.

38. We are disappointed to learn from your July 7 letter that you are having trouble with our Model 7 motor.

39. Tuff-Boy work clothing is not made from cloth that shrinks or fades.

40. Our Stone-skin material won't do the job unless it is reinforced.

41. Even though you were late in paying the bill, we did not disallow the discount.

42. We were sorry to learn of the disappointing service you have had from our sales force, but we feel we have corrected all mistakes with recent personnel changes.

43. We have received your complaint of the 7th in which you claim that our product was defective, and have thoroughly investigated the matter.

44. I regret the necessity of calling your attention to our letter of May 1.

45. We have received your undated letter, which you sent to the wrong office.

46. Old New Orleans pralines are not the gummy kind that stick to your teeth.

47. I regret to have to say that I will be unable to speak at your conference, as I have a prior commitment.

48. Do not walk on the grass.

Instructions, Numbers 49 and 50: The answers to these questions should come from letter examples to be found in following chapters.

49. Find examples of each of the four major emphasis techniques discussed in this chapter.

50. Find examples of each of the four transitional devices discussed in this chapter.

PART THREE

BASIC PATTERNS OF BUSINESS LETTERS

⑤ **Directness in Good News and Neutral Situations**

⑥ **Indirectness in Bad News Letters**

Directness in Good News and Neutral Situations

Upon completing this chapter, you will be able to write direct order letters effectively. To reach this goal, you should be able to

1 Describe the process of writing business letters.

2 Use the direct approach, orderly arrangement, and goodwill in favorably answering inquiries.

3 Phrase personnel evaluations so they systematically present the essential information and are fair to all concerned.

4 Compose adjustment-grant letters that regain any lost confidence.

5 Write order acknowledgment letters that cover problems positively and build goodwill.

6 Write clear, well-structured routine requests for information.

7 Compose orderly and thorough inquiries about prospective employees that show respect for human rights.

THE PROCESS OF WRITING LETTERS

With this chapter you will begin writing business letters. As you write the letters, you should keep in mind what is involved in the process of writing. As you will see, following the process guidelines will enable you to get more from your writing efforts. The following brief review of this process should guide you in your efforts.

• Following is a review of the process of writing letters.

Planning the Letter

Your first step in writing a business letter should involve planning. This is the prewriting stage—the stage in which you think through your writing project and develop a plan for doing it.

• Begin by planning.

First, you determine the objective of the letter—what the letter must do. Must it report information, acknowledge an order, ask for something, request payment of a bill, evaluate an applicant, or what?

• Determine the objective of the letter.

Next you predict the reader's likely reaction to your objective. Will that reaction be positive, or negative, or somewhere in between? Of course, you cannot be certain of how the reader will react. You can only apply your knowledge of the reader to the situation and use your best judgment. Your prediction will determine the plan of the letter you write.

• Predict how the reader will react.

Gathering and Collecting the Facts

The next step in writing a business letter is to get all the information you will need. In a business situation, this means getting past correspondence; consulting with other employees; getting sales records, warranties, product descriptions, and inventory records—in fact, doing whatever is necessary to inform yourself fully of the situation. Without all the information you need, you may make costly mistakes. Moreover, if you do not have all the information you need, you will have to look for it in the midst of your writing. This breaks your train of thought and causes you to lose time.

• Get the information (facts) you need.

In a classroom situation, the write-up of the problem is likely to contain the information you need. So you will need to study the problem carefully, making certain that you understand all the information.

Analyzing and Organizing Information

If you predict the reader will react to your letter positively, or even neutrally, you will usually organize the letter in a direct plan. That is, you will get to your objective right away—at the beginning. In positive situations, you are likely to have no need for opening explanations or introductory remarks, for these would only delay achieving your objective. You simply start with the objective of the letter. This plan, commonly called the *direct order,* is easy to use. Fortunately, it is appropriate for most business letters.

• Select the letter plan. Use direct order for favorable reactions.

If you predict that your letter will produce a negative reaction, you should usually write it in indirect order. *Indirect order* is the opposite of direct order. This plan gets to the objective after preparing the reader to receive it. As you will see, such a letter typically requires a more skillful use of strategy and word choice than does one written in direct order.

• Use indirect order for unfavorable reactions.

Writing the Letter

After you have the plan in mind, you write the letter. You should write it in the clear and effective manner discussed in the preceding chapters—choosing words the reader understands, constructing sentences that present their contents clearly, using words that create just the right effect. In addition, you should follow carefully the text

• Then write the letter, striving for clarity and effect.

instructions for the letter you are writing. The end product of this effort is a first draft. As you will see, the process does not end here.

Rewriting Your Work

• When time permits, review your work.

In actual business practice, your first draft may well be the final draft, for often time does not permit additional work on the document. But now you are in a learning situation. You are preparing for the time when you will not have time. Your efforts now should be directed toward improving your writing skills—toward learning writing techniques that can become reflexive in the years ahead when you will write under time pressures. Even so, when you reach the stage of your career when you must write under time pressures, you would be wise to employ as many of the following suggestions as time will permit.

• Then revise it.

After completing your first draft, you should review it carefully. Look at each word. Is it the right one? Would another one be more precise? Are there better, more concise ways of saying it? Did you say what you mean? Could someone read other meanings into your words? Is your organization the best for the situation? What we are suggesting is that you be your own critic. Challenge what you have done. Look for alternatives. Then, after you have conducted a thorough and critical review, make any changes that you think will improve your work.

• Get input from others,

Input from others can also benefit your refinement of your writing. As you know, it is often difficult to find errors or weaknesses in your own work; yet others seem to find them easily. Thus, if your instructor permits or encourages any input from associates, use them. Receive these criticisms with an open mind, objectively evaluating them and using those that meet your review. Unfortunately, most of us are thin-skinned about such criticisms, and we tend to be defensive when they are made. You should resist this tendency.

• including your instructor.

The most valuable input may be the written comments your instructor makes about the work submitted. Perhaps this input comes too late to benefit you gradewise. But it does not come too late to benefit your learning. You would be wise to take these comments and revise a final time, ending with your best possible product.

Editing and Presenting the Final Document

• Then process, edit, and proof the final draft.

After you have made all the changes you think are needed, you should construct the final draft. Here you become a proofreader, looking for errors of spelling, punctuation, and grammar. You determine that the format is appropriate. In general, you make certain the final letter represents your very best standards—that it will reflect favorably on you and (in later years) your company. Then you present the letter. This final letter is the best you are capable of writing, and you have learned in the process of writing it.

· ·
PLAN OF THE PRESENTATION

• This chapter covers favorable responses and inquiries.

• First, we cover a general type of response—then three similar types.

We begin our study of business letters with the most common of direct-order types: favorable responses and inquiries. As we have noted, these are the easiest to write.

Favorable responses are the positive answers to inquiries the business has received. Our study of this type begins with a general form of this letter—one giving information requested or positive answers to questions asked. We cover this letter type in detail. Then we cover three similar but more specific types—responses to inquiries about personnel, favorable responses to requests for adjustment, and order acknowledgments. Because the plans for these three types are similar to those for the general favorable response, our coverage of them is brief. We emphasize mainly special considerations and differences.

In similar fashion, we cover routine inquiry letters, which are letters likely to encounter little negative feeling. They seek information or answers to questions. First, we review in detail the techniques for handling the general type of inquiry. Then we review in summary fashion a similar but more specific type: the inquiry about personnel.

Other types of routine responses and inquiries exist, of course, and by learning the patterns and techniques reviewed in this chapter, you should be able to adapt to them.

- Then we cover inquiries about personnel.

▶ to General Favorable Response Letters

Introduce yourself to favorable response letters by assuming you are the assistant to the vice president for administration of Pinnacle Manufacturing Company. Pinnacle is a small manufacturer of an assortment of quality products. Because the company is small, your duties involve helping your boss cover a wide assortment of activities. Many of these activities require that you answer the incoming correspondence.

Most of the incoming correspondence you answer favorably. That is, you tell the reader what he or she wants to know. In today's incoming correspondence, for example, you have a typical problem of this type. It is a letter from a prospective customer for Pinnacle's Chem-Treat paint. In response to an advertisement, this prospective customer asks a number of specific questions about Chem-Treat. Foremost, she wants to know whether the paint is really mildewproof. Do you have evidence of results? Do you guarantee results? Is the paint safe? How much does a gallon cost? Will one coat do the job?

You can answer all but one of the questions positively. Of course, you will report this one negative point (that two coats are needed to do most jobs), but you will take care to give it only the emphasis it deserves. The letter will be primarily a good-news message. Because the reader is a good prospect, you will work for the best goodwill effect. ■

GENERAL FAVORABLE RESPONSES

When you write letters that answer inquiries favorably, your primary goal is to tell your readers what they want to know. As their reactions to this goal will be favorable, you should use the direct order. Of course, you could write such letters, as well as the other letters covered in this chapter, in the indirect order and still get the job done. But, as the indirect letter is slow and takes more time, it is inconsistent with the needs of business in such situations. As noted previously, you should use directness except when there is good reason not to use it. The direct plan recommended below generally follows these steps:

- Favorable reader reaction justifies this direct plan for the letter.

- Begin with the answer, or state that you are complying with the request.
- Identify the correspondence being answered either incidentally or in a subject line.
- Continue to give what is wanted in orderly arrangement.
- If negative information is involved, give it proper emphasis.
- Consider including extras.
- End with a friendly, adapted comment.

Beginning with the Answer

Using the direct order means giving readers what they want at the beginning. What they want are the answers to their questions. Thus, you should begin by answering. When a response involves answering a single question, you begin by answering that

- Begin by answering. If there is one question, answer it; if there is more than one, answer the most important.

question. When it involves answering two or more questions, you begin by answering one of them—preferably the most important. In the Chem-Treat case, this opening would get the response off to a fast start:

Yes, Chem-Treat will prevent mildew if used according to instructions.

• Or begin by saying that you are complying with the request.

An alternative possibility is to begin by stating that you are giving the readers what they want—that you are complying with their request. Actually, this approach is really not direct, for it delays giving the information requested. But it is a favorable beginning, and it does not run the risk of sounding abrupt, which is a criticism of direct beginnings. These examples illustrate this type of beginning:

The following information should tell you what you need to know about Chem-Treat.
Here are the answers to your questions about Chem-Treat.

• The traditional information beginnings are slow and obvious.

Either of these beginnings is an improvement over the indirect beginnings that are used all too often in business. Overworked indirect beginnings such as "Your April 3 inquiry has been received" and "I am writing in response to your letter" do little to accomplish the goal of the letter. They also give obvious information. Although acceptable because of its courtesy, even the "Thank you for your April 7 inquiry" delays getting to the objective of answering.

Identifying the Correspondence Being Answered

• You should identify the letter being answered.

Even though the indirect examples in the preceding paragraph have shortcomings, they do something desirable. They identify the letter being answered. This identification information is useful for filing purposes. It also helps the reader recall or find the letter being answered.

• The subject line is one good way of identifying that letter. Include subject identification and the date of the letter being answered.

One good way of identifying the letter being answered is the use of a *subject line*, a mechanical device usually placed after the salutation. Typically, the subject line contains an identifying term such as *Subject:, About:,* or *Re:,* followed by appropriate descriptive words. The words identify the nature of the letter and the situation. For example, for the inquiry about Chem-Treat, these subject lines would be appropriate:

Subject: Your April 3 inquiry about Chem-Treat
Re: Your April 3 inquiry concerning Chem-Treat

• Identification can also be made incidentally early in the response.

Another way of identifying the letter being answered is to refer to it in the text of your letter. You should make such references incidentally, for they usually do not deserve strong emphasis. Illustrating this technique is the phrase "as requested in your April 3 letter."

Logically Arranging the Answers

• If one answer is involved, give it directly and completely

If you are answering just one question, you have little to do after handling that question in the opening. You answer it as completely as the situation requires, and you present whatever explanation or other information you need to do so. Then you are ready to close the letter.

• If more than one answer is involved, arrange the answers so that each stands out.

If, on the other hand, you are answering two or more questions, the body of your letter becomes a series of answers. As in all clear writing, you should work for a logical order, perhaps answering the questions in the order your reader used in asking them. You may even number your answers, especially if your reader numbered the questions. Or you may decide to arrange your answers by paragraphs so that each stands out clearly.

Skillful Handling of Negatives

• Emphasize favorable responses; subordinate unfavorable responses.

When your response concerns some bad news along with the good news, you may need to handle the bad news with care. Bad news stands out. Unless you are careful,

it is likely to receive more emphasis than it deserves. Sometimes you will need to subordinate the bad news and emphasize the good news.

In giving proper emphasis to the good- and bad-news parts, you should use the techniques discussed in Chapter 4, especially position. That is, you should place the good news in positions of high emphasis—at paragraph beginnings and endings and at the beginning and ending of the letter as a whole. You should place the bad news in secondary positions. In addition, you should use space emphasis to your advantage. This means giving less space to bad-news parts and more space to good-news parts. You should also select words and build sentences that communicate the effect you want. Generally, this means using happy and pleasant words and avoiding unpleasant and sad words. Your overall goal should be to present the information in your response so that your readers get just the right effect.

- Place favorable responses at beginnings and ends. Give them more space. Use words skillfully to emphasize them.

Consideration of Extras

For the best in goodwill effect, you should consider including extras with your answers. These are the things you say and do that are not actually required. Examples are a comment or question showing an interest in the reader's problem, some additional information that may prove valuable, and a suggestion for use of the information supplied. In fact, extras can be anything that does more than skim the surface with hurried, routine answers. Such extras frequently make the difference between success and failure in the goodwill effort.

- The little extra things you do for the reader will build goodwill.

Illustrations of how extras can be used to strengthen the goodwill effects of a letter are as broad as the imagination. A business executive answering a college professor's request for information on company operations could supplement the requested information with suggestions of other sources. A technical writer could amplify highly technical answers with simpler explanations. In the Chem-Treat problem, additional information (say, how much a gallon covers) would be helpful. Such extras genuinely serve readers and promote goodwill.

Cordiality in the Close

As in most routine business letter situations, you should end routine responses with friendly, cordial words that make clear your willing attitude. As much as is practical,

- End with friendly words adapted to the one case.

your words should be adapted to the one case. For example, you might close the Chem-Treat letter with these words:

If I can help you further in deciding whether Chem-Treat will meet your needs, please write me again.

Or an executive answering a graduate student's questions concerning a thesis project could use this paragraph:

If I can give you any more of the information you need for your study of executive behavior, please write me. I wish you the best of luck on the project.

Notice that both of the examples above close with an offer of further help. Not only does this increase cordiality in the close, but it also signals the readers that all of their concerns have already been addressed. Using terms such as "further," "additional," and "any more" tells the reader the writer is willing to go a little extra if needed.

Contrasting Illustrations

• Following are bad and good examples of response letters.

Contrasting letters in answer to the Chem-Treat inquiry illustrate the techniques of answering routine inquiries. The first letter violates many of the standards set in this and earlier chapters. The second meets the requirements of a good business letter. These examples include only the texts of the letters. But the examples that follow show complete letters (on letterhead paper and with inside address, salutation, complimentary close, signature, and such) along with handwritten comments pointing out highlights. These two illustration forms are used throughout the letter portion of this book.

An Indirect and Hurried Response.   The not-so-good letter begins indirectly with an obvious statement referring to receipt of the inquiry. Though well intended, the second sentence continues to delay the answers. The second paragraph begins to give the information sought, but it emphasizes the most negative answer by position and by wording. This answer is followed by hurried and routine answers to the other questions asked. Only the barest information is presented. The close belongs to the language of business in great-grandfather's day.

• The poor one is indirect and ineffective.

Dear Ms. Motley:

I have received your April 3 letter, in which you inquire about our Chem-Treat paint. I want you to know that we appreciate your interest and will welcome your business.
In response to your question about how many coats are needed to cover new surfaces, I regret to report that two are usually required. The paint is mildewproof. We do guarantee it. It has been well tested in our laboratories. It is safe to use as directed.
Hoping to hear from you again, I remain

Yours sincerely,

Effectiveness in Direct Response.   The better letter uses a subject line to identify the inquiry. Thus, it frees the text from the need to cover this detail. The letter begins directly, with the most favorable answer. Then it presents the other answers, giving each the emphasis and positive language it deserves. It subordinates the one negative answer, by position, volume of treatment, and structure. More pleasant information follows the negative answer. The close is goodwill talk, with some subtle selling strategy thrown in. "We know that you'll enjoy the long-lasting beauty of this mildewproof paint" points positively to purchase and successful use of the product.

• This direct letter does the better job.

Dear Ms. Motley:

Subject: Your April 3 inquiry about Chem-Treat.

Yes, Chem-Treat paint will prevent mildew or we will give you back your money. We know it works, because we have tested it under all common conditions. In every case, it proved successful.

PART 3   Basic Patterns of Business Letters

This letter responds to a professor's request for production records that will be used in a research project. The writer is giving the information wanted but must restrict its use.

DYNAMIC LTD

March 17, 1996

Professor Clyde C. Garland
No. 1602-22 McGuffy Drive
Fort McMurray, Alberta T9H 4H4

Dear Professor Garland:

Direct reports a favorable response

Enclosed with our compliments is a copy of the production records you asked for in your May 2 letter. We think you will find it useful in your project. As you will understand, much of the information concerns company secrets our competitors should not know; so we request anonymity in any published use of the data.

Shows friendly attitude

Skillfully handles negative point in positive language

Goodwill adapted to one cause

The work you are doing will be valuable to all of us in the industry. We wish you the best of luck in your work and look forward to reading your results.

Sincerely,

Reba O. Whitehead

Reba O. Whitehead
Production Manager

ROW:klo

Enclosure

4510 S. Madison Ave.
Mesilla, NM 88046
505-708-8960
Fax: 505-708-8971
Whitehead@dynamic.com

Answering an inquiry about a company's experience with a word processing center, this letter numbers the answers as the questions were numbered in the inquiry. The opening appropriately sets up the numbered answers with a statement that indicates a favorable response.

PROBST
INDUSTRIES

August 7, 1996

Ms. Ida Casey, Office Manager
Liberty Insurance Company
1309 Nolte Street
Philadelphia, PA 19123

Dear Ms. Casey:

Direct— tells that writer is complying

Following is the information about our word processing center that you requested in your August 3 letter. For your convenience, I have numbered my responses to correspond with the sequence you used. — *Sets up listing*

Orderly listing of answers

1. Our executives have mixed feelings about the effectiveness of the center. At the beginning, majority opinion was negative, but it appears now that most of the antagonism has subsided.

2. The center definitely has saved us money. After normal attrition has eliminated unnecessary workers, we estimate that the monthly saving will be about $5,400. — *Complete yet concise answers*

3. The changeover did create a morale problem among the secretaries, even after we had assured them that we would reduce employment only by attrition.

4. We created our center from our own secretarial staff. We lost no one during the changeover period.

5. We are quite willing to share our center operating procedures with you. I am enclosing a copy of our procedures directive, which describes center operations in detail.

Friendly— Adapted to the one case

If after reviewing this information you have other questions, please write me again. And if you feel that an inspection of our operation would help, you are welcome to visit us. I wish you the best of luck in implementing your center. — *This extra builds good-will*

Sincerely,

David M. Earp

David M. Earp
Office Manager

DME:GT

Enclosure

102 N. Halsted Ave.
Laveen, AZ 85339
602-890-5647
Fax: 602-890-5642

Skillful (?) Handling of a Complaint

A traveling man once spent a sleepless night in a hotel room, tormented by the sight of cockroaches walking over the ceiling, walls, and floor. Upon returning home, he indignantly protested the condition in a letter to the hotel management. Some days later, to his delight, he received a masterfully written response. It complimented him for reporting the condition, and it assured him that the matter would be corrected—that such a thing would never happen again. The man was satisfied, and his confidence in the hotel was restored. His satisfaction vanished, however, when he discovered an interoffice memo that had been accidentally inserted into the envelope. The memo said, "Send this nut the cockroach letter."

When you carefully follow the directions on each can, Chem-Treat paint is guaranteed safe. As the directions state, you should use Chem-Treat only in a well-ventilated room—never in a closed, unvented area.

One gallon of Chem-Treat is usually enough for one-coat coverage of 500 square feet of previously painted surface. For the best results on new surfaces, you will want to apply two coats. For such surfaces, you should figure about 200 square feet per gallon for a good heavy coating that will give you five years or more of beautiful protection.

We sincerely appreciate your interest in Chem-Treat, Ms. Motley. We know that you'll enjoy the long-lasting beauty of this mildewproof paint.

Sincerely,

I N T R O D U C T O R Y   S I T U A T I O N

▷ to Personnel Evaluations

A request for an evaluation of a Pinnacle employee is the next letter you take from the in-basket. The writer, Ms. Mary Brooking, president, Red Arrow Transport, Inc., wants information about George Adams, Pinnacle's assistant shipping clerk. Ms. Brooking is considering Adams for the position of manager of a Red Arrow branch office. In her letter she asks some specific questions about him and about his ability to do the job. As Adams works under the supervision of your office, he listed you as a reference.

You are well acquainted with Adams and his work. Just last week he came by your office to tell you that he was looking at an employment opportunity that offered advancement—something that Pinnacle, unfortunately, could not offer soon. Everything you have observed in his work supports your opinion that he is industrious and capable. He knows the shipping business, and he is an able supervisor. He tends to stick to his own ideas too strongly, and this has caused some friction with his superiors—you included. But you feel that this tendency reflects his independence and self-reliance, qualities that may be desirable in a branch manager with no immediate supervisors on the grounds.

Because you believe that Adams has earned the position he seeks, you want to write a letter that will help him. But because you are an honest person, you will report truthfully. Thus, you will write a letter that will be fair to all concerned—to Adams, to Ms. Brooking, and to you. ■

PERSONNEL EVALUATIONS

When you receive a request to evaluate a former employee, company policy may prohibit you from answering. For legal reasons, many companies do not permit such letters. But if you do write such a letter, you should organize it in the direct order. The

• Personnel evaluations satisfy the reader. Thus, they justify the direct order, as outlined in this general plan.

justification for the direct order is that the message is favorable, since you are doing what the reader requested. It is favorable regardless of whether it contains positive or negative information about the employee because the reader is getting the information requested. As described in the following paragraphs, this procedure will produce a good direct-order letter:

- Begin by (1) answering a question or (2) saying that you are complying with the request.
- Refer to the inquiry letter incidentally or in a subject line.
- Report systematically, giving each item proper emphasis, taking care to be fair, and stressing fact rather than opinion.
- End with adapted, goodwill comment.

General Plan of Personnel Evaluations

As you can see, the plan for this letter type is much like the plan previously discussed. You begin it either with an answer to one of the questions asked, as in this example:

Mr. Chester Bazzar, the subject of your May 11 inquiry, worked under my supervision for four months in 1993.

Or you begin it with a statement indicating that you are complying with the request:

As you requested in your May 8 letter, here is my evaluation of Mr. Carlton I. Bowes.

Somewhere in or near the beginning, you refer to the letter being answered by incidental reference or in a subject line. Then you give the information requested in some orderly and logical fasion. In doing this, you may choose to organize around the questions asked. You may even number the responses, especially if the questions were numbered in the inquiry. Finally, you close with some appropriate, friendly words.

Special Need for Fair Reporting

The one unique concern in writing this letter is the need to report the information fairly—to present an accurate picture. It is important because what you write affects the lives of people. Presenting your information too positively would be unfair to your reader. Presenting it too negatively would be unfair to the applicant.

In conveying an accurate picture, you should carefully distinguish between facts and opinions. For the most part, you should report facts. But sometimes a reader wants your opinions. If you present opinions, you should clearly label them as such. You should support all opinions with facts.

Conveying an accurate picture of the subject also involves giving the facts proper emphasis. Even if every fact you present is true, the report could be unfair. The reason is that negative points stand out. They overshadow positive points. Thus, sometimes you may need to subordinate the negative points. Not to do so would be to give them more emphasis than they deserve.

This suggestion for subordinating negative points does not mean you should hide shortcomings or communicate wrong information. Quite the contrary. If the subject has a bad work record, you should report this. Purely and simply, your task is to communicate an accurate picture.

For legal reasons, sometimes you will need to leave out certain information. In the United States, laws and court decisions have affected the exchange of information about job applicants. Reports about an applicant's age, race, religion, sex, marital status, and pregnancy are generally prohibited. So are reports about an applicant's criminal record, citizenship, organization memberships, and mental and physical handicaps. Exceptions may be made in the rare cases in which such information is clearly related to the job.

Marginal notes:

- Begin directly, either with significant information requested . . .
- or a statement saying you are complying.
- Refer to the inquiry, present the information requested, and end with goodwill.
- It is especially important to present a true picture.
- Prefer facts to opinions.
- Proper emphasis may require subordination.
- But subordination does not mean altering truth.
- Abide by legal requirements regarding information that may be reported.

Examples in Contrast

Illustrating good and bad technique in personnel evaluations are the following contrasting letters about George Adams.

A Slow, Disorganized, and Unfair Report. The weaker letter begins indirectly—and with some obvious information. The first words are wasted. The letter shows little concern for proper emphasis. Note that the main negative point (the personality problem) receives a major position of emphasis (at a paragraph beginning). Even the information about the applicant's future at Pinnacle (which does not reflect on his abilities) gets negative treatment. The organization is jumbled. Information about personal qualities and about job performance, for example, appears in two different paragraphs. The close is an attempt at goodwill, but the words are timeworn rubber stamps.

Dear Ms. Brooking:

I have received your May 10 letter in which you ask for my evaluation of Mr. George Adams. In reply I wish to say that I am pleased to be able to help you in this instance.

Probably Mr. Adams' greatest weakness is his inability to get along with his superiors. He has his own ideas, and he sticks to them tenaciously. Even so, he has a good work record with us. He has been with us since 1983.

Mr. Adams is a first assistant in our shipping department. He is thoroughly familiar with rate scales and general routing procedure. He gets along well with his co-workers and is a very personable young man. In his work he has some supervisory responsibilities, which he has performed well. He is probably seeking other work because there is little likelihood that we will promote him.

Mr. Adams' main assignment with us has placed him in charge of our car and truck loadings. He has done a good job here, resulting in significant savings in shipping damages. We have found him a very honest, straightforward, and dependable person.

Trusting that you will hold this report in confidence, I remain

Sincerely,

- This bad example violates the techniques emphasized.

Good Organization and Fairness in Direct Report. The better letter begins directly, reporting a significant point in the first sentence. Use of the subject line frees the text of the need to identify the inquiry, which makes for a faster-moving beginning. The text presents the information in logical order, with like things being placed together. The words present the information fairly. The major negative point is presented almost positively, which is how it should be viewed in regard to the job concerned. The letter closes with an appropriate goodwill comment.

Dear Ms. Brooking:

Subject: Your May 10 inquiry about George Adams

Mr. Adams has been our assistant shipping clerk since March 1985 and has steadily improved in usefulness to our company. We want to keep him with us as long as he wants to stay. But with things as they are, it will apparently be some time before we can offer him a promotion that would match the branch managership for which you are considering him.

Of course I am glad to give you in confidence a report on his service with us. As first assistant, he has substituted at the head clerk's desk and is thus familiar with problems of rate scales and routing. His main assignment, however, is to supervise the car and truck loadings. By making a careful study of this work, he has reduced our shipping damages noticeably within the last year. This job also places him in direct charge of the labor force, which varies from six to ten workers. He has proved to be a good boss.

We have always found Mr. Adams honest, straightforward, and dependable. He is a man of strong convictions. He has his own ideas and backs them up. He is resourceful and works well without direction.

I recommend Mr. Adams to you highly. If you need additional information about him, please write me again.

Sincerely,

- Directness, good organization, and correct emphasis mark this good letter.

Evaluating a well-qualified office worker with no significant deficiencies, this letter presents its information systematically. The opening comment is general, but by informing the reader of a favorable response, it has the effect of directness.

McMILLAN, INC.
WHOLESALE GROCERY

May 16, 1996

Mr. Brooke I. Crump, Manager
Bennett-Bond Instruments, Inc.
11731 Alvin Boulevard
Arlington, TX 76010

Dear Mr. Crump:

Identifies subject and inquiry letter

Subject: Report on Ms. Patricia Heine, requested by you May 10

Direct— tells that writer is complying

Following are my answers to your questions about Ms. Heine. For your convenience, I have arranged them in the numbered sequence used in your letter.

Numbering systematical-ly arranges the answers for the reader's convenience

1. Ms. Heine worked for us from January 1990 to June 1992.

2. For the first six months, Ms. Heine worked as an administrative trainee. Her assignments rotated through the major departments of the company. Following the training period, she was placed in charge of customer services, where she remained until she left the company. On this assignment she demonstrated good adminis-trative ability and a practical knowledge of dealing with people.

3. In all her assignments I found Ms. Heine a very capable worker. She worked hard, and she demonstrated good administrative potential. In fact, I had selected her to groom for a position of administrative responsibility.

Answers are complete, yet concise

4. I found Ms. Heine a most personable young woman. She got along with all her associates. I believe she is a person of integrity and good morals.

5. Ms. Heine left us for a higher paying job—one she felt offered her faster advancement. We wanted her to stay with us.

Summary of evaluation in a recommendation

I have a high regard for Ms. Heine. I recommend her to you for any work for which her experience has prepared her.

I am pleased to give you this confidential report on Ms. Heine.

Goodwill ending

Sincerely,

Mary L. Lamme

Mary L. Lamme
Office Manager

MLL:tt

1313 N. Palm Ave.
Palm Harbor, FL 34683
305-465-3200
Facsimile: 305-465-3256

INTRODUCTORY SITUATION

▶ to Adjustment-Grant Letters

This time you pull an unhappy customer's letter from your in-basket. It seems that Ms. Bernice Watson, owner of Tri-City Hardware, is upset because the fire extinguishers Pinnacle sent her arrived badly damaged. She had ordered them for a special sale. In fact, she had even featured them in her newspaper advertising. The sale begins a week from next Saturday, and she has no fire extinguishers to sell. She wants a fast adjustment—either the merchandise by sale time or her money back.

You want to keep this unhappy customer's business. So you check out the situation immediately and plan to fax your response as soon as possible. You find that you can get more fire extinguishers to her in time for her sale. You also find that you can explain what happened. Now you will write Ms. Watson, handling her claim in the best way possible. You will tell here that the goods are on the way. You will try to regain any lost confidence in your company or its products with convincing explanation. Your goal is to hold onto this good customer. ■

....

ADJUSTMENT GRANTS

When you can grant an adjustment, the situation is a happy one for your customer. You are correcting an error. You are doing what you were asked to do. As in other positive situations, a letter written in the direct order is appropriate. The direct-order plan recommended below follows these general steps:

- Begin directly—with the good news.
- Incidentally identify the correspondence that you are answering.
- Avoid negatives that recall the problem.
- Regain lost confidence through explanation or corrective action.
- End with a friendly, positive comment.

• Good news in adjustment grants justifies directness, as in this general plan.

In most face-to-face business relations, people communicate with courteous directness. You should write most business letters this way.

Special Needs of Adjustment Grants

- Follow the good-news pattern, but consider two special needs.

This plan has much in common with the two letter types discussed. You begin directly with the good-news answer. You refer to the correspondence you are answering. And you close on a friendly note. But because the situation stems from an unhappy experience, you have two special needs. One is the need to overcome the negative impressions the experience leading to the adjustment has formed in the reader's mind. The other is the need to regain any confidence in your company, its products, or its service the reader may have lost from the experience.

- Negative impressions remain; so overcome them.

Need to Overcome Negative Impressions. To understand the first need, just place yourself in the reader's shoes. As the reader sees it, something bad has happened—goods have been damaged, equipment has failed, or sales have been lost. The experience has not been pleasant. Granting the claim will take care of much of the problem, but some negative thoughts may remain. You need to work to overcome any such thoughts.

- Overcome them through positive writing.

You can attempt to do this using words that produce positive effects. For example, in the opening you can do more than just give the affirmative answer. You can add goodwill, as in this example:

The enclosed check for $89.77 is our way of proving to you that we value your satisfaction highly.

Throughout the letter you should avoid words that recall unnecessarily the bad situation you are correcting. You especially want to avoid the negative words that could be used to describe what went wrong—words such as *mistake, trouble, damage, broken,* and *loss.* Even general words such as *problem, difficulty,* and *misunderstanding* can create unpleasant connotations.

- Even apologies may be negative.

Also negative are the apologies often included in these letters. Even though well intended, the somewhat conventional "we sincerely regret the inconvenience caused you . . ." type of comment is of questionable value. It emphasizes the negative happenings for which the apology is made. If you sincerely believe that you owe an apology, or that one is expected, you can choose to apologize and risk the negative effect.

In most instances, however, your efforts to correct the problem show adequate concern for your reader's interests.

Need to Regain Lost Confidence.
Except in cases in which the cause of the difficulty is routine or incidental, you also will need to regain the reader's lost confidence. Just what you must do and how you must do it depend on the facts of the situation. You will need to survey the situation to see what they are. If something can be done to correct a bad procedure or a product defect, you should do it. Then you should tell your reader what has been done as convincingly and positively as you can. If what went wrong was a rare, unavoidable event, you should explain this. Sometimes you will need to explain how a product should be used or cared for. Sometimes you will need to resell the product.

• Regain lost confidence through convincing explanation.

Contrasting Adjustments

The techniques previously discussed are illustrated by the following adjustment letters. The first, with its indirect order and grudging tone, is ineffective. The directness and positiveness of the second clearly make it the better letter.

• Following are good and bad adjustment grants.

A Slow and Negative Treatment.
The ineffective letter begins with an obvious comment about receiving the claim. It recalls vividly what went wrong and then painfully explains what happened. As a result, the good news is delayed for an additional paragraph. Finally, after two delaying paragraphs, the letter gets to the good news. Though well intended, the close leaves the reader with a reminder of the trouble.

Dear Ms. Watson:

• This bad letter is needlessly slow.

We have received your May 1 claim reporting that our shipment of Fireboy extinguishers arrived in badly damaged condition. We regret the inconvenience caused you and can understand your unhappiness.

Following our standard practice, we investigated the situation thoroughly. Apparently, the fault was in our failure to check the seals carefully. As a result, the fluid escaped in transit, damaging the exteriors of the fire extinguishers. We have taken corrective measures to assure that future shipments will be more carefully checked.

I am pleased to report that we are sending a replacement order. It will be shipped today by Red Line Motor Freight and should reach you by Saturday.

Again, we regret all the trouble caused you.

Sincerely,

The Direct and Positive Technique.
The better letter uses a subject line to identify the transaction. The opening words tell the reader what she most wants to hear in a positive way that adds to the goodwill tone of the message. With reader-viewpoint explanation, the letter then reviews what happened. Without a single negative word, it makes clear what caused the problem and what has been done to prevent its recurrence. After handling the essential matter of disposing of the damaged merchandise, the letter closes with positive resale talk far removed from the problem.

Dear Ms. Watson:

• This better letter is direct and positive.

Subject: Your May 1 report on invoice 1348

Two dozen new and thoroughly tested Fireboy extinguishers should reach your sales floor in time for your Saturday promotion. They were shipped early today by Red Line Motor Freight.

As your satisfaction with our service is important to us, we have thoroughly checked all the Fireboys in stock. In the past, we have assumed that all of them were checked for tight seals at the factory. We learned, thanks to you, that we must now systematically check each one. We have set up a system of checks as part of our normal handling procedure.

This letter grants the action requested in the claim of a customer who received sterling flatware that was monogrammed incorrectly. The writer has no excuse, for human error was to blame. His explanation is positive and convincing.

Ivers and Sons Jewelers

October 5, 1996

Ms. Charlotte W. Brown
1414 Midland Avenue
Lexington, KY 40507

Dear Ms. Brown:

Direct— good news begins letter

Subject: Your October 1 inquiry concerning order No. A4170

Identifies claim and transaction

Your Mecca sterling flatware properly monogrammed with an Old English B should reach you in a day or two. It is our evidence to you that Mecca's century-old record for satisfaction is as genuine as the sterling itself.

Relates action to reader concern

Because we value your satisfaction so much, we carefully looked into the handling of your order. We found it was just one of those situations that even the most careful human beings occasionally get into. Two people read and checked the order, and two people overlooked the "Old English monogram" specification. You will agree, I feel sure, that such things happen even in the best-run businesses. Even so, we are redoubling our efforts to continue to give the fast, dependable service Mecca customers have come to expect over the years.

Frank and convincing explanation

Good persuasion technique

Goodwill specially adapted

We know that your Mecca sterling will enhance many a dinner party through the years ahead. We wish you the best in enjoyment from your set.

Sincerely,

Jonathan Batte

Jonathan Batte
Manager
Customer Relations

eom

71650 Old Mill Rd.
Minneapolis, MN 55440
612-670-4242
Fax: 612-670-4221

When you receive the new Fireboys, will you please return the original group by motor freight? We will pay all transportation charges.

As you may know, the new Fireboys have practically revolutionized the extinguisher field. Their compact size and efficiency have made them the top seller in only three months. We are confident they will play their part in the success of your sale.

Sincerely,

INTRODUCTORY SITUATION

▶ to Order Acknowledgment Letters

The next work you take from your in-basket is an order for paints and painting supplies. It is from Mr. Orville Chapman of the Central City Paint Company, a new customer whom Pinnacle has been trying to attract for months. You usually acknowledge orders with individually typed letters, but this case is different. You feel the need to welcome this new customer and to cultivate him for future sales.

After checking your warehouse and making certain that the goods will be on the way to Chapman today, you are ready to write him a special letter of acknowledgment. ■

ORDER ACKNOWLEDGMENTS

As the description of the preceding situation implies, acknowledgments are sent to let people who order goods know the status of their orders. Most acknowledgments are routine. They simply tell when the goods are being shipped. Many companies use form letters for such situations. Some use printed, standard notes with checkoff or write-in blanks. But individually written acknowledgment letters are sometimes justified, especially with new accounts or large orders.

- Businesses usually acknowledge orders with form notes, but they sometimes use letters.

Skillfully composed acknowledgment letters can do more than acknowledge orders, though this task remains their primary goal. These letters can also build goodwill. Through a warm, personal, human tone, they can reach out and give a hearty handshake. They can make the reader feel good about doing business with a company that cares. They can make the reader want to continue doing business with that company. To maintain this goodwill for repeat customers, you will want to revise your form acknowledgments on a regular basis. If your company offers goods or services that are consumed often, you'll need to revise these letters more frequently than a business offering durable goods or services.

- Acknowledgment letters build goodwill, as shown in this general plan.

The sequence below illustrates how you should approach such letters.

- Acknowledge the order, giving its status.

- Include some goodwill—sales talk, reselling, or such.

- Include a thank-you.

- Report frankly or handle tactfully problems with vague or back orders.

- Close with adapted, friendly comment.

Favorable Response Pattern with Goodwill Emphasis

In writing the acknowledgment letter outlined above, you emphasize goodwill building throughout. Your direct beginning can begin this goal by emphasizing receiving the goods rather than sending them, as in this example:

- Directly acknowledge the order.

The Protect-O paints and supplies you ordered April 4 should reach you by Wednesday. They are leaving our Walden warehouse today by Blue Darter Motor Freight.

In addition, when the situation permits, you can include a warm expression of thanks for the order. When you are acknowledging a first order, a warm welcome can enhance your goodwill message. When such information is of service, you can even include some words about new products or services. And you can end the goodwill message with friendly talk in the close—perhaps a specially adapted forward look to continued business relations.

Need for Tact in Shipment Delays

• When goods must be delayed, handle this news tactfully.

Sometimes the task of acknowledging is complicated by your inability to send the goods requested right away. You could be out of them; or perhaps the reader did not give you all the information you need to send the goods. In either case, a delay is involved. In some cases, delays are routine and expected and do not pose a serious problem. In others, they are likely to lead to major disappointments. When this is the case, you will need to use tact.

• In vague orders, request the needed information positively.

Using tact involves minimizing the negative effect of the message. In the case of a vague order, for example, you should handle the information you need without appearing to accuse the reader of giving insufficient information. To illustrate, you gain nothing by writing, "You failed to specify the color of umbrellas you want." But you gain goodwill by writing, "So that we can send you precisely the umbrellas you want, please check your choice of colors on the enclosed card." This sentence handles the matter positively and makes the action easy to take.

• Emphasize receipt of the items in back orders.

Similarly, you can handle back-order information tactfully by emphasizing the positive part of the message. For example, instead of writing, "We can't ship the Crescent City pralines until the 9th," you can write, "We will rush the Crescent City pralines to you as soon as our stock is replenished by a shipment due May 9." If the back-order period is longer than the customer expects or longer than the 30 days allowed by law, you may choose to give your customer an alternative. You could offer a substitute product or service. Giving the customer a choice among alternatives builds goodwill. A more complete discussion of how to handle such negative news is provided in the following chapter.

Contrasting Acknowledgments

• Following are contrasting examples.

The following two letters show bad and good technique in acknowledging Mr. Chapman's order. As you would expect, the good version follows the plan described in the preceding paragraphs.

Slow Route to a Favorable Message.   The bad example begins indirectly, emphasizing receipt of the order. Although intended to produce goodwill, the second sentence further delays telling what the reader wants most to hear. Moreover, the letter is written from the writer's point of view (note the *we*-emphasis).

• This one is bad.

Dear Mr. Chapman:

Your April 4 order for $1,743.30 worth of Protect-O paints and supplies has been received. We are pleased to have this nice order and hope that it marks the beginning of a long relationship.

As you instructed, we will bill you for this amount. We are shipping the goods today by Blue Darter Motor Freight.

We look forward to your future orders.

Sincerely,

Fast-Moving Presentation of the Good News.   The better letter begins directly, telling Mr. Chapman that he is getting what he wants. The remainder of the letter is customer

This letter concerns an order that cannot be handled exactly as the customer would like. Some items are being sent, but one must be placed on back order and one cannot be shipped because the customer did not give the information needed. The letter skillfully handles the negative points.

F&W SUPPLY

1701 Westminster Avenue
Toronto, Ontario M6P 3B9
416-470-4884
Facsimile 416-470-4817

October 7, 1996

Mr. Fred K. Fletcher, President
Fletcher Machine Works
4772 Worth Road
Detroit, MI 48201

Dear Mr. Fletcher:

Direct— tells about goods being sent

By noon tomorrow, your three new Baskin motors and one Dawson 110 compressor should reach your Meadowbrook shops. As you requested, we marked them for your West Side loading dock and sent them by Warren Motor Express.

Positive emphasis on delivery

Negative information presented with you- viewpoint emphasis

So that we can be certain of sending you the one handcart for your special uses, will you please review the enclosed description of the two models available? As you will see, the Model M is our heavy-duty design, but its extra weight is not justified for all jobs. When you have made your choice, please mark it on the enclosed card and mail the card to us. We'll send your choice to you as soon as we know it.

Helpful explanation— aids reader in making choice

Tactful— emphasis on receipt of goods

Your three dozen 317 T-clamps should reach you by the 13th. As you may know, these very popular clamps have been in short supply for some time now, but we have been promised a limited order by the 11th. We are marking three dozen for rush shipment to you.

We are always pleased to do business with your organization and will continue to serve you with quality industrial equipment.

Friendly forward look

Sincerely,

Shannon E. Kurrus

Shannon E. Kurrus
Sales Manager

SEK:bim
Enclosure

This letter to a longtime customer routinely reports that all the items ordered will be sent. Appropriately, the letter is short and direct.

FARMER'S FRIEND, INC.

• 2703 Cross Timbers Road •
• Jackson, MS 39206 •
• (601) 978-7800 • Fax: (601) 978-5432 •

June 10, 1996

Ms. Virginia T. Wells, Owner
Wells Farm Store
1317 Cameron Road
Magnolia, MS 39652

Dear Ms. Wells:

Direct reports handling of order

The assorted Farmer's Friend chemicals you ordered June 7 should reach you by June 14. They were shipped this morning by Rapid Freight Lines. As you specified, we will add the $785.40 charge to your account.

Emphasis on receipt of goods

Method of payment covered

Friendly close

We sincerely appreciate your order, Ms. Wells. We look forward to the privilege of serving you again.

Sincerely,

Victor V. Potts

Victor V. Potts
Sales Manager

ccs

---

welcome and subtle selling. Notice the good use of reader emphasis and positive language. The letter closes with a note of appreciation and a friendly, forward look.

Dear Mr. Chapman:

• This letter is better.

Your selection of Protect-O paints and supplies should reach you by Wednesday, for the shipment left today by Blue Darter Motor Freight. As you requested, we are sending you an invoice for $1,743.30, including sales tax.

As this is your first order from us, I welcome you to the Protect-O circle of dealers. Our representative, Ms. Cindy Wooley, will call from time to time to offer whatever assistance she can. She is a highly competent technical adviser on paint and painting.

Here in the home plant we will also do what we can to help you profit from Protect-O products. We'll do our best to give you the most efficient service. And we'll continue to develop the best possible paints—like our new Chem-Treat line. As you will see from the enclosed brochure, Chem-Treat is a real breakthrough in mildew protection.

We genuinely appreciate your order, Mr. Chapman. We are determined to serve you well in the years ahead.

Sincerely,

I N T R O D U C T O R Y   S I T U A T I O N

▶ to Routine Inquiries

Introduce yourself to routine inquiry letters by continuing in your role at Pinnacle. As assistant to the vice president for administration, often you must write letters for your boss. Today you must do just that.

The letter you must write will request information that the Pinnacle executive team needs in selecting a site for the company's expansion plant. As a member of this team, your boss has been assigned the task of finding suitable sites as well as certain basic information about each site. Of course, your boss has delegated much of this work to you.

Already you have found a number of possible locations. An advertisement you found in the classified section of today's *Wall Street Journal* may produce another. The advertisement describes a 120-acre tract on the Mississippi River 12 miles upstream from New Orleans. The location and price are right. So now you must get the other information the executives need. Does the land have deep frontage on the river? What about the terrain? Is the land well drained? How accessible is it by public roads? Your task is to write the letter that will get the information Pinnacle needs. If the answers are favorable, the executives probably will want to inspect the tract. ■

●
ROUTINE INQUIRIES

Letters that ask for information are among the most common in business. Businesses need information from each other. They consider requests for information routine, and they cooperate in exchanging information.

• Letters asking for information are routine.

Because businesses usually cooperate in such situations, you can write most requests for information in the direct order. That order saves time for both the writer and the reader. It gets right down to business without delaying explanation or description.

• In such letters, there is usually no need to delay the request.

Directness is not preferred in some situations. As you will see in Chapter 6, directness may be inappropriate when there is doubt that the reader will respond favorably. In such cases, you may need to use the indirect order to explain or persuade.

• An exception occurs if negative reader reaction is likely.

From the preceding discussion, you can see that before writing a request for information you must determine how your reader will receive the letter. If you believe that the reader will not consider the request routine, you should use indirect order. But if

• Thus, the first step in planning the inquiry letter is to determine the reader's probable reaction.

CHAPTER 5   Directness in Good News and Neutral Situations   103

Answering inquiry letters that do not include adequate explanation can be frustrating.

you think the reader will consider the request routine, you should use direct order. Specifically, you should use this direct-order plan:

• Then follow this general plan.

- Begin directly with the objective—either a specific question that sets up the entire letter or a general request for information.
- Include necessary explanation—wherever it fits.
- If a number of questions are involved, give them structure.
- End with goodwill words adapted to the one case.

This plan is discussed and explained in the following pages.

Beginning with the Objective

• When a favorable response is likely, you should begin with the request.

Because you normally have no reason to waste time in routine inquiries, you should begin them with the objective of the letter. As your objective is to ask for information, you can start with a question. A question beginning moves fast—the way most people want their work to go. Also, questions command attention and are, therefore, likely to communicate better than other sentence forms.

• You may use either of two types of question beginnings: (1) a specific question that sets up the information wanted or

The direct beginning of an inquiry letter can be either of two basic types. First, it can be a specific question that sets up the information wanted. If your objective is to ask a number of questions, it would be one that covers these questions. For example, if your objective is to get answers to specific questions about test results of a company's product, you might begin with these words:

Will you please send me test results showing how Duro-Press withstands high temperatures and long exposures to sunlight?

In the body of the letter you would include the precise questions concerning temperatures and exposures to sunlight. For example, you might ask questions such as these:

What is the effect when subjected to constant temperatures between 80 and 90 degrees?
What is the effect when subjected to long periods of below-freezing temperatures?
What are the effects of long exposure to direct sunlight?

The second type of beginning is a general request for information. This sentence meets the requirement:

Will you please answer the following questions about your new Duro-Press fabric.

• (2) a general request for information.

The "will you" here and in a preceding example may appear unnecessary. The basic messasge would not change if the words were eliminated. In the minds of some authorities, however, including them softens the request and is worth the additional length.

Perhaps both of these direct approaches appear illogical to some. Our minds have been conditioned to the indirect approach that old-style writers have used over the years. Such writers typically begin with an explanation and follow the explanation with the questions. Clearly, this approach is slower and less businesslike. Contrasting examples on following pages illustrate the point.

• Either question beginning is better than the explanation-first plan.

Informing and Explaining Adequately

If your reader needs information or explanation to help in answering your questions, you will need to include explanation or information. If you do not explain enough or if you misjudge the reader's knowledge, you make the reader's task difficult. For example, answers to questions about a computer often depend on the specific needs or characteristics of the company that will use it. The best-informed computer expert cannot answer such questions without knowing the facts of the company concerned.

• Somewhere in the letter, explain enough to enable the reader to answer.

Where and how you include the necessary explanatory information depend on the nature of your letter. Usually, a good place for general explanatory material that fits the entire letter is following the direct opening sentence. Here it helps reduce any startling effect that a direct opening question might have. It often fits logically into this place, serving as a qualifying or justifying sentence for the letter. In letters that ask more than one question, you will sometimes need to include explanatory material with the questions. If this is the case, the explanation fits best with the questions to which it pertains. Such letters may alternate questions and explanations.

• Place the explanation anywhere it fits logically.

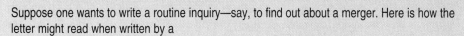

COMMUNICATION IN BRIEF

How One Might Write a Routine Inquiry

Suppose one wants to write a routine inquiry—say, to find out about a merger. Here is how the letter might read when written by a

12-year-old public school student: "What gives on this merger?"

21-year-old college graduate: "Kindly inform me on current general economic and specific pertinent industrial factors relating to the scheduled amalgamated proposals."

40-year-old junior executive: "J.P.—Please contact me and put me in the picture regarding the mooted merger. I have nothing in my portfolio on it. Sincerely, W.J."

55-year-old member of the board, with private secretary: "Without prejudice to our position vis-à-vis future developments either planned or in the stage of actual activating, the undersigned would appreciate any generally informative matter together with any pertinent program-planning data specific to any merger plans that may or may not have been advanced in quarters not necessarily germane to the assigned field of the undersigned."

65-year-old executive, now boss of the company and very busy: "What gives on this merger?"

Structuring the Questions

- If the inquiry involves just one question, begin with it.

If your inquiry involves just one question, you can achieve your primary objective with the first sentence. After any necessary explanation and a few words of friendly closing comment, your letter is done. If you must ask a number of questions, however, you will need to consider their organization.

- If it involves more than one, make each stand out. Do this by (1) placing each question in a separate sentence,

Whatever you do, you will need to make your questions stand out. You can do this in a number of ways. First, you can make each question a separate sentence with a bullet, a symbol (●, ○, ■, and so on) used to call attention to a particular item. Combining two or more questions in a sentence de-emphasizes each and invites the reader's mind to overlook some.

- (2) structuring the questions in separate paragraphs,

Second, you can give each question a separate paragraph, whenever this practice is logical. It is logical when your explanation and other comments about each question justify a paragraph.

- (3) ordering or ranking the questions, and

Third, you can order or rank your questions with numbers. By using words (*first, second, third,* and so on), numerals (1, 2, 3, etc.), or letters (a, b, c, and so on), you make the questions stand out. Also, you provide the reader with a convenient check and reference guide to answering.

- (4) using the question form of sentence.

Fourth, you can structure your questions in question form. True questions stand out. Sentences that merely hint at a need for information do not attract much attention. The "It would be nice if you would tell me . . ." and "I would like to know . . ." types are really not questions. They do not ask—they merely suggest. The questions that stand out are those written in question form, those using direct requests: "Will you please tell me . . . ?" "How much would one be able to save . . . ?" "How many contract problems have you had . . . ?"

- But take caution in asking questions that produce *yes* or *no* answers.

You may want to avoid questions that can be answered with a simple *yes* or *no.* An obvious exception, of course, would be when you really want a simple *yes* or *no* answer. For example, the question "Is the chair available in blue?" may not be what you really want to know. A better wording probably is "In what colors is the chair available?" Often you'll find that you can combine a yes/no question and its explanation to get a better, more concise question. To illustrate, the wording "Does the program run on an IBM? We have a Think Pad 755." could be improved with "What models does the program run on?" or "Does the program run on the Think Pad 755?"

Ending with Goodwill

- End with a friendly comment.

Because it is the natural thing for friendly people to do, you should end routine inquiry letters with some appropriate, friendly comment. This is how you would end a face-to-face communication with the reader, and there is no reason to do otherwise in writing. Ending your letter after the final question is like turning your back on someone after a conversation without saying good-bye. Such an abrupt ending would register negative meanings in your reader's mind and would defeat your goodwill efforts.

- When possible, make the close fit the one case.

The facts of the case determine just what you should say in the close to make a goodwill impression. Your letter will receive a more positive reaction if you use words selected specifically for the one case. Such general closes as "A prompt reply will be appreciated" and "Thank you in advance for your answer" are positive, for they express a friendly "thank you." And there is nothing wrong with a "thank you" sincerely expressed here or elsewhere in business writing. The problem is in the routine, rubber-stamp nature of many expressions including it. A more positive reaction results from an individually tailored expression such as, "If you will get this refrigeration data to me by Friday, I will be very grateful."

Contrasting Inquiry Examples

Illustrating bad and good techniques are the following two routine inquiry letters about land for a possible Pinnacle plant site. The first example follows the old-style indirect pattern. The second is direct.

• The following examples show bad and good inquiries.

The Old-Style Indirect Letter. The less effective letter begins slowly and gives obvious information. Even if one thinks that this information needs to be communicated, it does not deserve the emphasis of the opening sentence. The second sentence does refer to the objective of the letter, but it is not in the interest-gaining form of a question. The information wanted is covered hastily in the middle paragraph. There are no questions—just hints of needs for information. The items of information wanted do not stand out but are listed in rapid succession. They are not in separate sentences. The close is friendly, but old style. "By return mail" originated in the days when sailing ships shuttled mail across the seas.

• First is the bad example. Its indirect beginning makes it slow.

Dear Mr. Piper:

We have seen your advertisement for a 120-acre tract on the Mississippi River in the July 1 *Wall Street Journal*. In reply we are writing you for additional information concerning said property.

We would be pleased to know the depth of frontage on the river, quality of drainage, including high and low elevations, and the availability of public roads to the property.

T E C H N O L O G Y   I N   B R I E F

Bullets: Symbols for Listing Items

Most high-end, full-featured word processing programs have a feature that will let you easily insert a variety of symbols in your documents. Of course, one of the most useful symbols in textual material is the bullet. It is used most often to list items of equal importance, items not needing ranking or ordering. While the traditional bullet—•—is the symbol that most often comes to mind, you may want to use others for variety and attention-getting purposes.

•	●	○	◦
■	□	◇	▷
☞	✏	✔	✗
☆	❄	⇨	➔

Try exploiting the power of your word processor and add some variety to your bullets to increase their impact and add interest to your document.

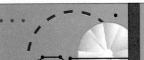

Tables: A Tool for Organizing Data

Setting up tables with a document is now an easy task. Most word processors have a tables feature that allows you to create tables as well as import spreadsheet and database files. In both instances, you can arrange information in columns and rows, inserting detail in the cells. You can even format the column headings in addition to calculating with formulas. You can see these features illustrated in the accompanying example. This table could be the detail you would normally put in the body paragraphs of a document.

Name	Address	Phone	Purchase Anniversary
Perry O. Hansen	2437 27th Street Moline, IL 61265	762-1965	June 1
Carole Hoeh Weissmann	1208 51st Street Moline, IL 61265	764-0017	June 25
Sally M. Peterson	1301 Tudor Ct. Moline, IL 61265	762-5987	March 26

Organizing information with tables makes it easier for both you and your reader. You will be sure to include all information since the headings prompt you for complete detail; your reader will be able to extract needed information both quickly and accurately.

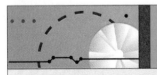

Templates and Macros: Shortcut Tools for Improved Productivity and Quality

Shortcuts can save time and improve quality. Templates are shortcuts for formatting documents; macros are shortcuts for executing a series of commands.

Appendix B reviews using basic templates. Usually you are prompted to enter basic header and closing facts in a form so the template can set up your document in standard format. However, you can set up personalized, special-use templates, too.

Macros can be set up for many of the repetitive tasks in communicating. For example, you could create macros for names—people names, titles, company names, division and department names, etc. Macros can also be created to answer commonly asked questions in both sentence and paragraph form. And they can be used to spell out acronyms or terms familiar to the writer but not necessarily the reader. A macro called SASE could call up "self-addressed, stamped envelope" spelled in full.

Both templates and macros save you time because you enter only a few keystrokes or click a button, and they improve quality by issuing the correct commands each time. Take advantage of shortcuts to eliminate the work of document preparation and improve the quality of your final document.

Some Words of Advice on Letter Writing from the Old Masters

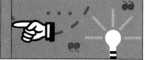

A letter is a deliberate and written conversation.

Gracian

Remember this: write only as you would speak; then your letter will be good.

Goethe

There is one golden rule to bear in mind always: that we should try to put ourselves in the position of our correspondent, to imagine his feelings as he writes his letters, and to gauge his reaction as he receives ours. If we put ourselves in the other man's shoes we shall speedily detect how unconvincing our letters can seem, or how much we may be taking for granted.

Sir Ernest Gowers

Do not answer a letter in the midst of great anger.

Chinese Proverb

Seeing an epistle hath chieflie this definition hereof, in that it is termed the familiar and mutual task of one friend to another: it seemeth the character thereof should according there-unto be simple, plain and of the lowest and neatest stile utterly devoid of any shadow of lie and lofty speeches.

Angel Day, *The English Secretorie,* 1586
(early book on letter writing)

And to describe the true definition of an Epistle or letter, it is nothing but an Oration written, containing the mynd of the Orator, or wryter, thereby to give to him or them absent, the same that should be declared if they were present.

William Fulwood, *The Enemie of Idlenesse,* 1568
(earliest known book on letter writing in English)

If the information you supply us is favorable to our needs, we will be pleased to inspect the property. Hoping to hear from you by return mail, I am,

Sincerely,

The Direct and Effective Letter.   The second example begins directly by asking for information. As the reader will welcome the inquiry, no need exists for delaying explanation. Because the direct opening may have a startling effect, explanatory information that justifies the inquiry follows. Next comes the remaining questions, with explanations worked in wherever they help the readers in answering. The letter closes with a courteous request for quick handling. In addition, the close suggests the good news of possible quick action on the property.

Dear Mr. Piper:

Will you please answer the following questions about the 120-acre tract you advertised in the July 1 *Wall Street Journal?* We are seeking such a site for a new plant, and it appears that your property could meet our needs.
• How deep is the frontage on the river as it shallowest and deepest points?
• What are drainage conditions on the land? A written description of the tract terrain should answer this question. In your description, please include a contour map showing minimum and maximum elevations.
• What is the composition and condition of the existing access road?

If your answers indicate that the site meets our needs, we will want to inspect the property. As we must move fast on the building project, may I have your answers soon?

Sincerely,

• This direct and orderly letter is better.

This letter to a hotel inquires about convention accommodations for a professional association. In selecting a hotel, the organization's officers need answers to specific questions. The letter covers these questions.

NATIONAL
MANAGEMENT
▉▉▉ FORUM ▉▉▉

July 17, 1995

Ms. Connie Briggs, Manager
Lakefront Hotel
10017 Lakefront Boulevard
Chicago, IL 60613

Dear Ms. Briggs:

Direct—a courteous general request that sets up the specific question

Will you please help the National Management Forum decide whether it can meet at the Lakefront? The Forum has selected your city for its 1996 meeting, which will be held August 16, 17, and 18. In addition to the Lakefront, the convention committee is considering the De Lane and the White House. In making our decision, we need the information requested in the following questions.

Explanation of situation provides background information

Can you accommodate a group such as ours on these dates? Probably about 600 delegates will attend, and they will need about 400 rooms.

What are your convention rates? We need assurance of having available a minimum of 450 rooms, and we could guarantee 400. Would you be willing to reserve for us the rooms we would require?

Specific questions— with explanations where needed

What are your charges for conference rooms? We will need eight for each of the three days, and each should have a minimum capacity of 60. On the 18th, for the one-half-hour business meeting, we will need a large assembly room with a capacity of at least 500. Can you meet these requirements?

Questions stand out— in separate paragraphs

Also, will you please send me your menu selections and prices for group dinners? On the 17th we plan our presidential dinner. About 500 can be expected for this event.

As convention plans must be announced in the next issue of our bulletin, may we have your response right away? We look forward to the possibility of being with you in 1996.

Individually tailored goodwill close

Sincerely,

Patti Wolff

Patti Wolff, Chair
Site Selection Committee

tr

17306 Milldale Avenue • St. Louis, MO 63118 • 314-878-4461 • Fax: 314-878-4462

CASE ILLUSTRATION   **Routine Inquiries.** (Getting Information about a Training Program)

This letter is from a company training director to the director of a management-training program. The company training director has received literature on the program but needs additional information. The letter seeks this information.

SORBET INDUSTRIES

September 21, 1996

Ms. Katherine O. Hrozek
Director
Moissant Training Institute
1771 Poindexter Drive
Albany, NY 12224

Dear Ms. Hrozek:

Direct— a general request sets up the specific question

Please send me the additional information we need in determining whether to send some of our executives to your Western Management Institute. We have your illustrated brochure and the schedule you mailed August 17. Specifically, we need the answers to these questions:

Reference to brochure tells what writer knows— helps reader in responding

Numbered questions stand out— helps reader in responding

1. What are your quantity discount rates? We could send about six executives each session.

2. At what background level is your program geared? We have engineers, accountants, scientists, and business administrators. Most have college degrees. Some do not.

Explanations worked into questions where needed

3. Can college credit be given for the course? Some of our executives are working on degrees and want credit.

4. What are the names and addresses of training directors of companies that have sent executives to the program?

We will appreciate having your answers for our October 3 staff meeting, and we look forward to the possibility of sending our executives to you in the years ahead.

Favorable forward look makes good will close

Sincerely,

Ronald I Dupre

Ronald I. Dupre
Director of Training

po

941 Rue Sherbrooke Quest Montreal, Quebec
H3A 2T4 514-890-6767 Fax: 514-890-6739

▶ to Inquiries about People

From time to time, your work at Pinnacle involves investigating applicants for employment. Of course, in your position you do no hiring. The Personnel Department conducts initial interviews, administers aptitude tests, and performs all the other screening tasks. Then it refers the best applicants to the executives in charge of the jobs to be filled. The executives, including your boss, make the final decisions.

This morning Personnel sent your boss a Mr. Rowe W. Hart, its selection for the vacant position of office manager. Mr. Hart appears to be well qualified—good test scores and employment record. After talking with him, your boss feels that he is bright and personable. Because your boss feels that he cannot judge ability from a single interview, he has asked you to follow your usual practice of writing the applicant's references for their evaluations. In Hart's case, the best possibility appears to be Ms. Alice Borders, who was his immediate supervisor for three years.

Your task now is to write Ms. Borders a letter that will get the information needed. The following discussion and illustrations show you how. ■

....

INQUIRIES ABOUT PEOPLE

• Letters asking questions about people should follow this general plan.

Letters asking for information about people are a special form of routine inquiry. Normally, they should follow this general plan:

- Begin directly, with a general question seeking information or a specific question that sets up the entire letter.

- Explain the situation.

- Cover the questions systematically, with explanations as needed.

- End with adapted goodwill words.

• The letter involves two special considerations.

As you can see from this outline, the plan for the inquiry about personnel is virtually the same as that for the routine inquiry. But writing the letter involves two special considerations, which is why we review this letter separately.

• 1. Respect human rights, both legal and moral.

First, as we noted in the review of responses to inquiries about personnel (which are answers to this letter), is the need to respect the rights of the people involved. These rights are both legal and moral. In fact, because of the legal aspects, some companies do not permit their personnel to correspond about personnel. Those companies that do permit such exchanges of information should try to protect the rights of the people involved.

• Ask only for information related to the job.

When you write these letters, for legal as well as ethical reasons, you should ask only questions related to the job. Specifically, you should avoid questions about the applicant's race, religion, sex, age, pregnancy, and marital situation.[1] Even questions about the applicant's citizenship status and arrest and conviction record are better not asked. So are questions about mental and physical handicaps and organization (especially union) memberships.

---

[1] As required by the following acts and court cases relating to them: Wagner Act of 1935, Immigration and Nationality Act of 1952, Civil Rights Act of 1964, Vocational Rehabilitation Act of 1973, Age Discrimination Act of 1975, and Pregnancy Discrimination Act of 1978.

Answering inquiries about people requires the most careful thought, for the lives and rights of human beings are affected.

In protecting these rights, you must seek truth and act in good faith. You should ask only for information you need for business purposes. You should ask only when the subject has authorized the inquiry. You should hold any information received in confidence. And you would do well to include these points in your letter, either in words or by implication.

A second concern in writing this letter is the need to structure the questions around the job involved. Specifically, the information you seek should be determined by your needs. What you need is information that will tell you whether the subject is qualified for the one job involved. Thus, you should analyze the job to determine the information you should have in selecting a person to do it. The questions you would ask about an applicant for a sales job, for example, would be quite different from those you would ask about an applicant for work as an accountant.

* Stress fact, write for business use and when authorized, and treat confidentially.

* 2. Structure the questions around the job.

Examples in Contrast

In applying the preceding instructions to Rowe Hart's application for the position of office manager at Pinnacle, assume that analysis of the applicant and the job tells you that you should ask four questions. First, is Hart capable of handling the responsibilities involved? Second, does he know the work? Third, how hard a worker is he? Fourth, is he morally responsible? Now, how would you arrange these questions and the necessary explanation in a letter?

* Following are good and bad examples of a personnel inquiry.

A Scant and Hurried Example.   The first letter example shows a not-so-good effort. The opening is indirect. The explanation in the opening is important, but does it deserve the emphasis that the beginning position gives it? Although the question part gives the appearance of conciseness, it is actually scant. It includes no explanation. It does not even mention what kind of position Hart is being considered for. The items of information wanted do not stand out. In fact, they are not even worded as questions but are run together in a single, declarative sentence. Though courteous, the closing words are old style.

"First the good news—if I cure you, I'll become world famous." (From The Wall Street Journal, with permission of Cartoon Features Syndicate.)

• This bad one is slow and scant.

Dear Ms. Borders:

Mr. Rowe W. Hart has applied to us for employment and has given your name as a reference. He indicates that he worked under your supervision during the period 1990–95.

We would be most appreciative if you would give us your evaluation of Mr. Hart. We are especially interested in his ability to handle responsibility, knowledge of office procedures, work habits, and morals.

Thanking you in advance for your courtesy, I remain,

Sincerely yours,

An Orderly and Thorough Example. The next example gives evidence of good analysis of the job and the applicant. The letter begins directly with an opening question that serves as a topic sentence. The beginning also includes helpful explanation. But this part is not given unnecessary emphasis, as was done in the preceding example. Then the letter presents the specific questions. Worded separately and in question form, each stands out and is easy to answer. Worked in with each question is explanation that will help the reader understand the work for which Hart is being considered. The close is courteous and tailored for the one case. Note also, throughout the letter, the concern for the rights of the people involved. Clearly, the inquiry is authorized, is for business purposes only, and will be treated confidentially.

• This good example shows careful study of the job and the applicant.

Dear Ms. Borders:

Will you help me evaluate Mr. Rowe W. Hart for the position of office manager? In authorizing this inquiry, Mr. Hart indicated that he worked for you from 1990 to 1995. Your candid answers to the following questions will help me determine whether Mr. Hart is the right person for this job.

What is your evaluation of Mr. Hart's leadership ability, including human-relations skills, to run an office of 11?

How able is Mr. Hart to manage a rapidly expanding office system? Ours is a growing company. The person who manages our office will not only need to know good office procedures but will also need to know how to adapt them to changing conditions.

What is your evaluation of Mr. Hart's stamina and drive? The position he seeks often involves working under heavy pressure.

What is your evaluation of Mr. Hart's moral reliability? Our office manager is responsible for much of our company equipment as well as some company funds.

We will, of course, hold your answers in strict confidence. And we will appreciate whatever help you are able to give Mr. Hart and us.

Sincerely,

This is the case of a freight-line executive who is looking for a manager for one of the company's branches. The top applicant is a shipping clerk for a furniture company. With the applicant's permission, the executive has written this letter to the applicant's employer.

ARROW FREIGHT

7171 INDIGO LAKE RD.
AUSTIN, TX 78710
512-212-8908
Fax: 512-212-8904

February 17, 1996

Mr. Amos T. Dodgson, Manager
Easterbrook Furniture, Inc.
3970 Burnham Avenue
Seattle, WA 98125

Dear Mr. Dodgson:

Direct— Interest- gaining question tells reader what is needed

Will you do George Barton and me the favor of providing an evaluative report on him? He is an assistant shipping clerk with you who wants to manage a branch office for us. He has authorized this inquiry.

Explanation softens possible startling effect of opening

Human rights respected

Bullets make questions stand out— questions cover work to be done

• How well does he know packing and hauling techniques?

• How do you judge his administrative ability to run an office of one secretary and a work force of six?

• What is your appraisal of his ability to meet customers and generally build goodwill with the community?

• What do you know about his honesty and integrity? Our managers are solely responsible for their branch's assets—equipment as well as all receipts.

Explanation as needed

• As a final question, is there anything else you can tell me that might indicate whether Mr. Barton is the right person for our job?

I will be grateful for your answers. Of course, whatever you report will be held in close confidence.

Friendly close and respect for human rights

Sincerely,

Mary E. Caperton

Mary E. Caperton
Manager

det

OTHER DIRECT LETTER SITUATIONS

• Other direct letter situations occur.

In the preceding pages, we have covered the most common direct letter situations. Others occur, of course. You should be able to handle them with the techniques that have been explained and illustrated.

• You should be able to handle them by applying the techniques covered in this chapter.

In handling such situations, remember that whenever possible, you should get to the goal of the letter right away. You should cover any other information needed in good logical order. You should carefully choose words that convey just the right meaning. More specifically, you should consider the value of using the you-viewpoint, and you should weigh carefully the differences in meaning conveyed by the positiveness or negativeness of your words. As in all cordial human contacts, you should end your letter with appropriate and friendly goodwill words.

SUMMARY ▶ by Chapter Objectives

① Describe the process of writing business letters.

1. The process of writing business letters begins with planning.
   • Begin by determining the objective of the letter (what it must do).
   • Next, predict the reader's probable reaction to the objective.
   • Then assemble all the information you will need.
   • Select the letter plan (direct order if positive or neutral reaction; indirect order if negative reaction).
   • Write the letter, applying your knowledge of conciseness, readable writing, and effect of words.
   • Review your work critically, seeking ways of improving it.
   • Get input from others.
   • Evaluate all inputs.
   • Revise, using your best judgment. This end product is an improved letter, and you have had a profitable learning experience.

② Use the direct approach, orderly arrangement, and goodwill in favorably answering inquiries.

2. When responding to inquiry letters favorably, you should begin directly.
   • If the response contains only one answer, begin with it.
   • If it contains more than one answer, begin with a major one or a general statement indicating you are answering.
   • Identify the letter being answered early, perhaps in a subject line.
   • Arrange your answers (if more than one) logically.
   • And make them stand out.
   • If both good- and bad-news answers are involved, give each answer the emphasis it deserves, perhaps by subordinating the negative.
   • For extra goodwill effect, consider doing more than was asked.
   • End with appropriate cordiality.

③ Phrase personnel evaluations so that they systematically present the essential information and are fair to all concerned.

3. Handle personnel evaluations directly.
   • Do so even if they contain negative information, for you are doing what the reader asked.
   • You have two logical choices for beginning the letter.
     —You can begin by answering a question asked, preferably one deserving the emphasis of the opening position.
     —You can begin with a statement indicating you are complying with the request.
   • Refer to the letter you are answering early in the letter (perhaps in the subject line).
   • Present the information in a logical order, making each answer stand out.
     —Numbering the responses is one way of doing this.
     —Arranging answers by paragraphs also helps.
   • Report fairly and truthfully.
     —Stress facts and avoid opinions.

—Give each item the emphasis it deserves.

- End with appropriate friendly comment.

4. As letters granting adjustments are positive responses, write them in the direct order.
   - But they differ from other direct-order letters in that they involve a negative situation.
     —Something has gone wrong.
     —You are correcting that wrong.
     —But you should also overcome the negative image in the reader's mind.
   - You do this by first telling the good news—what you are doing to correct the wrong.
   - In the opening and throughout, emphasize the positive.
   - Avoid the negative—words like *trouble, damage,* and *broken.*
   - Try to regain the reader's lost confidence, maybe with explanation or with assurance of corrective measures taken.
   - End with a goodwill comment, avoiding words that recall what went wrong.

4 Compose adjustment-grant letters that regain any lost confidence.

5. Write order acknowledgments in the form of a favorable response.
   - Handle most by form letters or notes.
   - But in special cases use letters.
   - Begin such letters directly, telling the status of the goods ordered.
   - In the remainder of the letter, build goodwill, perhaps including some selling or reselling.
   - Include an expression of appreciation somewhere in the letter.
   - End with an appropriate, friendly comment.

5 Write order acknowledgment letters that cover problems positively and build goodwill.

6. The routine inquiry is another basic direct order letter.
   - Begin it with a request—either (1) a request for specific information wanted or (2) a general request for information.
   - Somewhere in the letter explain enough to enable the reader to answer.
   - If the inquiry involves more than one question, make each stand out—perhaps as separate sentences or separate paragraphs.
   - Consider numbering the questions.
   - And word them as questions.
   - End with an appropriate friendly comment.

6 Write clear, well-structured routine requests for information.

7. Inquiries about people follow much the same order as described above.
   - But they require special care, as they concern the moral and legal rights of people.
   - So seek truth, and act in good faith.
   - Also, adapt your questions to the one applicant and the one situation rather than follow a routine.

7 Compose orderly and thorough inquiries about prospective employees that show a respect for human rights.

1. Discuss why just reporting truthfully may not be enough in handling negative information in letters answering inquiries.
2. Defend a policy of doing more than asked in answering routine inquiries. Can the policy be carried too far?
3. What can acknowledgment letters do to build goodwill?
4. Discuss situations where each of the following forms of an order acknowledgment would be preferred: form letter, merged letter, and a special letter.
5. Discuss how problems (vague orders, back orders) should be handled in letters acknowledging orders.
6. Discuss the relationship of positive and negative words to fair treatment in employee evaluation letters.
7. Why is it usually advisable to do more than just grant the claim in an adjustment-grant letter?
8. When is the direct order appropriate in inquiry letters? When would you use the indirect order? Give examples.
9. "Explanations in inquiry letters merely add length and should be eliminated." Discuss.
10. What should the letter writer do to respect the rights of people in inquiries about them?
11. "In writing inquiries about people, I do not ask specific questions. Instead, I ask for 'everything you think I should know' about the person." Discuss this viewpoint.

1. Point out the shortcomings in this response letter. The letter is a reply to an inquiry about a short course in business communication taught by a professor for the company's employees. The inquiry included five questions: (1) How did the professor perform? (2) What was the course format (length, meeting structure)? (3) What was the employee evaluation of the instruction? (4) Was the course adapted to the company and its technical employees? (5) Was homework assigned?

Dear Mr. Braden:

Your January 17 inquiry addressed to the Training Director has been referred to me for attention as we have no one with that title. I do have some training responsibilities and was the one who organized the in-house course in clear writing. You asked five questions about our course.

Concerning your question about the instructor, Professor Alonzo Britt, I can report that he did an acceptable job in the classroom. Some of the students, including this writer, felt that the emphasis was too much on grammar and punctuation, however, He did assign homework, but it was not excessive.

We had class two hours a day from 3:00 to 5:00 p.m. every Thursday for eight weeks. Usually the professor lectured the first hour. He is a good lecturer but sometimes talks over the heads of the students. This was the main complaint in the evaluations the students made at the end of the course, but they had many good comments to make also. Some did not like the content, which they said was not adapted to the needs of a technical worker. Overall, the professor got a rating of B– on a scale of A to F.

We think the course was good for our technical people, but it could have been better adapted to our needs and our people. I also think it was too long—about ten hours (five meetings) would have been enough. Also, we think the professor spent too much time lecturing and not enough on application work in class.

Please be informed that the information about Professor Brett must be held in confidence.

Sincerely,

2. Point out the shortcomings in this letter granting a claim for a fax machine received in damaged condition.

Inspection of the package revealed that the damage did not occur in transit.

Dear Ms. Orsag:

Your May 3 letter in which you claim that the Rigo FAX391 was received in damaged condition has been carefully considered. We inspect all our machines carefully before packing them, and we pack them carefully in strong boxes with Styrofoam supports that hold them snugly. Thus we cannot understand how the damage could have occurred.

Even so, we stand behind our product and will replace any that are damaged. However, we must ask that first you send us the defective one so we can inspect it. After your claim of damage has been verified, we will send you a new one.

We regret any inconvenience this situation may have caused you and assure you that problems like this rarely occur in our shipping department.

Sincerely,

3. List your criticisms of this letter inquiring about a convenience store advertised for sale:

Dear Mr. Meeks:

This is in response to your advertisement in the May 17 *Daily Bulletin* in which you describe a convenience store in Clark City that you want to sell. I am very much interested as I would like to relocate in that area. Before I drive down to see the property, I need some preliminary information. Most important is the question of financing. I am wondering whether you would be willing to finance up to $50,000 of the total if I could come up with the rest, and how much interest would you charge and for how long. I would also like to have the figures for your operations for the past two or three years, including gross sales, expenses, and profits. I need to know also the condition of the building, including such information as when built, improvements made, repairs needed, and so on.

Hoping that you can get these answers to me soon so we can do business.

Sincerely yours,

4. List your criticisms of this letter asking for information about an applicant for a job:

Dear Ms. Bentley:

Inez Becker has applied to us for a job as inventory clerk in our parts department. She listed you as a reference and claims that she worked for you as a records clerk in your parts department for the period May 1992 to August 1995. As I am impressed with Ms. Becker, I would like to have your evaluation of her.

I am especially interested in her work ethic and how she gets along with other workers. I am curious about why she left the job with you. Also, please tell me whether you would hire her back if you had an opening. In addition, I would like to know about her honesty, character, and attitude.

Thank you in advance for your prompt response.

Sincerely yours,

....

CRITICAL THINKING PROBLEMS

FAVORABLE RESPONSES

1. As owner of Learn How, a new neighborhood business specializing in selling videos that show one how to do various things, you were delighted to receive the following inquiry from Sally Peterson, president of the local Friends of the Library club.

June 1, 1996

Mr. Jim Andrews
Learn How
Seminole Mall
Seminole, FL 34642

Dear Mr. Andrews:

Several items listed in your advertisement in last Sunday's *St. Petersburg Times* interested several members of our group, Friends of the Library. We would like to learn more about the items and their availability as well as their costs.
• What level of expertise are the videos on deck building, personal computer maintenance, and Visual Basic programming?
• How can we arrange to review these videos before recommending them for purchase?
• How long would it take to get six copies of each of these videos?
• Will you let us know the total costs for 18 of these videos including any discounts for volume purchases or for community groups?
As a group of volunteer local citizens, we try to supplement the holdings of the local library with items of interest to those in our area. Your immediate help in providing the answers to the above questions will be greatly appreciated.

Sincerely,

Sally Peterson, President
Friends of the Library

Not only can you answer all the questions positively, but you also believe it gives you an opportunity for some free promotion, telling those in the organization more about your business. For example, in responding that the videos they were interested in were basic, you can also make a pitch on others your ad didn't mention. You can let them know about advanced videos in these and other areas. And, of course, you'll want to include a copy of the video descriptions along with your money-back guarantee if they are not satisfied. At the moment you have six copies of each on hand and would be happy to hold them; you also are happy to special order any other videos for the Friends. Additionally, for the Friends you'll be happy to extend a 10 percent discount on all purchases—both regular and sale items. Furthermore, you decide to offer to provide a public showing in the library's community room of these or other videos available in your store. Your response is clearly favorable; you believe in supporting the community that supports your business.

2. Acting as Joan Marian, public relations director for the American Dietetic Association, write a letter responding to Mr. Thomas McLaughlin of McLaughlin Body Company in Moline, Illinois. He requested information on ways to get healthy meals at airports. He referred to the report of a study in *USA Today* done by the association's members on 20 major airports in the United States. He's interested in passing this information along to his employees who travel regularly.

You're always happy to help educate the public about eating right. And while hot dogs and beer are still the most popular items at airports, airport food is getting healthier. However, some airports are better than others. Your members found that all airports had fresh fruit such as apples, bananas, strawberries, and melon. Also, widely available were non- and low-fat items such as yogurt, bagels, and pretzels.

At Chicago's O'Hare Airport, one Mr. McLaughlin's employees most likely would connect through, the above items were readily found as well as spinach salads and turkey breast sandwiches. New York's La Guardia Airport has the widest variety of healthy choices, including vegetable dishes and Greek and garden salads. Even dried fruit such as papaya, mangoes, and apricots could be found there. However, Atlanta's Hartsfield Airport won overall on healthiest food. Choices included Chinese dishes to low-fat turkey and ham sandwiches.

Of course, you can also recommend Mr. McLaughlin's employees bring their own food. Many hotels' room services will prepare special order meals to go. And now most airlines allow one to place requests for low-fat or vegetarian meals up to 24 hours before departure time. Include in your response the association's most recent list of recommended reading on healthy eating.

3. What a delight! In today's e-mail you heard from a longtime friend, Cyril Kesten. Cyril's a former classmate of yours. Last you heard from him, he was headed to Canada to teach at the University of Regina in Saskatchewan. Yes, he's still there and enjoying it tremendously. One of his newest activities is starting special interest discussion groups on Usenet. Apparently, he got your e-mail address when he saw you participating in an on-line discussion group. He tells you he's learned from members of the discussion group that you're quite an expert on creating multimedia. And he'd love to have you come to Canada to visit him and share your expertise with his student teachers. And you'd love to go.

   In responding, not only agree to speak to his students, but also confirm all the other details involving both the speaking and the visit. Discuss the content or focus of your presentation and the equipment you'll need. Also, confirm the dates, times, and hotel reservations. Do tell him you're looking forward to seeing his wife, Helene, again as well as meeting his children.

4. You, Paul Adami, vice president of marketing for Greyhound, are proud of your company and especially the success of its recent promotional fares. The recent fare campaign is targeted at the customer who might grab some of the discount rates the airlines are offering. The response to the new promotional fares has been so great that you realize you need to create a form letter to respond to the inquiries for detailed information you're getting by phone, fax, and e-mail.

   Write the form letter for Mr. Adami. Explain to potential customers that to get the low fares, tickets must be purchased at least three days in advance for Monday through Thursday and Saturday departures. Holidays, of course, are blacked out. You might also mention that on major routes such as Los Angeles to San Francisco or Atlanta to Washington, D.C., you've lowered your walk-up fares $20 to $40. Even the fares for long trips such as New York to Los Angeles have been cut more than 50 percent on one-way tickets.

   While this is strictly a favorable response to an inquiry about a special promotional program, do make it easy for the reader to call and purchase a ticket by including Greyhound's national 800 number reservation line.

5. You recently received a request from Dr. Jennie Hunter for information on places to stay and to take young people in your town. She'll be bringing six of her best Western Carolina University students to town to compete with students from [your school] as part of an intercollegiate business competition. Since the budget for the group is tight, she'd like you to recommend the safest, cleanest, and most reasonable places to stay. The competition is the second week of August, so she'd like to know what kind of weather

to expect at that time of year. Additionally, she'd like you to recommend restaurants and places of interest for these students to visit. Are there any special museums or exhibits that would interest these students? None of them have visited your city before. She'd also like to know what kind of nighttime entertainment is available for college students. Will a nearby county or state fair be running? Will any special concerts be in town or on the campus? What kinds of facilities are available for golf, tennis, and swimming?

   As coordinator of the Intercollegiate Business Competition Program, respond to Dr. Hunter, addressing all her questions. You might even include additional information you think would interest her or her students. Do welcome them to your town and congratulate them on making it into the quarterfinals of this national competition.

6. Carol Weissmann, manager of a large travel agency in the Champaign/Urbana area in Illinois, requested information about Princess Cruises' new ship featuring a virtual-reality theater. Apparently, she's had a request from a campus group to book a block of rooms.

   Yes, tell her you indeed do have a new ship being built that will have a virtual-reality theater. The ship, scheduled for delivery in late 1997, will be home ported in Fort Lauderdale, Florida. It'll have year-round service in the Caribbean.

   In addition to the virtual-reality theater and traditional cruise ship facilities, it'll have a nightclub, three show lounges, and three dining rooms. It's expected to carry 2,600 passengers in its 750 cabins; 28 of these are wheelchair accessible.

   You expect that Ms. Weissmann has good potential to book numerous trips since she's located in a college town. In addition to providing the information for her, work to build goodwill.

7. One of your favorite co-workers, Ron Lycan, told you last week that he's looking for new employment now that he's completed his MBA and asked you for permission to list you as a reference. Today's mail brought a request from Rosemary Lenaghan, a partner at Arthur Andersen, to evaluate Ron's work attitude and interpersonal skills. You are confident you can speak positively about Ron on both these factors. In some ways you're certain the reason he's already being considered seriously by such a prestigious firm is that his strength on these qualities comes through clearly on his résumé.

   You've been working with Ron for nearly three years in a maintenance programming environment in a local bank. You've seen him in a variety of settings and in a variety of circumstances. To you he seems just as comfortable working with technical people as with end users in a variety of positions and at a variety of management levels. Additionally, while you might be tempted to say he's laid back because under stress he's always levelheaded, never flustered, you've also watched him take charge when needed.

And he seems to enjoy working in a variety of roles. Perhaps that's why you enjoy working with Ron so much; his attitude is always positive and he completes his work competently.

Another important interpersonal skill Ron possesses is the ability to help people learn and understand how the computer can serve and support them. In training others, he demonstrates the ability to target the level of instruction appropriately, empowering users to believe they can master the tool. He chooses good examples, presents them in a light but serious way, and communicates that he is approachable for further help.

In addition to working effectively with others one on one, getting along well on teams is another particularly important interpersonal communication skill. He often serves as catalyst in moving teams forward on projects but is willing to step in and out of the leadership role when appropriate. Therefore, you might say that he's an effective team player, adjusting to roles as needed.

You really hate losing Ron as a colleague; however, you know that he'll be happier working in a more challenging position. And you're confident that he'll bring a positive work attitude and effective interpersonal skills to a new position. Write a positive letter for him.

8. As safety manager for Spritz Bottling Company, you receive today an inquiry letter from Mrs. Dana Haddon, the executive director for NETS (see Problem 46, Routine Inquiries, for background details). Mrs. Haddon indicates in her letter that you are one of 10 industry leaders she has chosen to sample before she constructs a questionnaire to be distributed to all companies within the NETS umbrella. She will use the information you and others provide to construct her questionnaire instrument. To be sure, you are pleased to give the benefit of your Spritz experience in safe driving planning and control.

Yes, you have total responsibility for the safe driving program at Spritz, a program you designed five years ago. Much of the actual work, however, is completed by your three assistants. You believe that the program is unique in its use at Spritz, although the program uses basic concepts inherent in most training and behavior change strategies.

When drivers first join the company, they must take and pass a two-day course in safe driving. The lecture part (one and one-half days) is primarily awareness training in which you cover safe driving practices, what to do in case of accidents, company policy on safe driving, hazards that create accident conditions, and such. Trainees must pass a written test on this coverage with a score of 90 percent before they can participate in the performance part of the training (one-half day). If trainees score less than 90 percent, they may retake the exam once. If they fail twice, their employment is terminated.

Once trainees pass the cognitive part of the training, they next must pass a performance test with a score of 90 percent. This part involves a 30-minute driving test involving scenarios that the drivers will likely encounter in their work. You assess their performance on how skillfully they handle the driving situations to which they are exposed—their judgment, their response skills, their anticipation, their caution, and the like. Trainees have one chance to repeat the performance aspect of the exam to attain a 90 percent or better score. If they do not, they are terminated from employment.

You conduct the performance part of the exam on two simulators you've designed for the training program. These simulators allow different scenarios to be flashed on a video screen and then record the trainees' reaction to the situation. So that there will be no response bias in the training, a computer alternates the situations slightly so that each performance session consists of new driving situations for trainees taking the performance test. Each test is reviewed thoroughly with the driver.

In addition, you place monitoring equipment on your delivery trucks—computers that measure weight shift, braking, sharp turns, and such. The daily records they produce are reviewed monthly to assure that drivers are not taking unnecessary chances or developing bad driving habits. New drivers are assigned for one year to a senior driver (one with five years of experience with the company without an accident). This senior-junior mentor system has worked well in terms of esprit de corps in the delivery team and in terms of experienced drivers sharing their trade tips with their beginning counterparts. To make the process worthwhile to both parties, you offer a $1,000 bonus to both parties if the beginning drivers maintain an accident-free second year of employment.

For experienced drivers, you offer a 1 percent increase in their commissions for each five continuous years of accident-free driving. It's your conviction that rewards must be linked with correct behavior. The bonus system and the increased commission tie rewards to the expected consequences. In addition, you'd rather pay the results of good driving in wages than the results of bad driving in increased insurance premiums. All of your route sales personnel work on commission.

You also stress the value of time management and effective accident control. Your experience shows that most accidents occur when drivers try to do more than conditions will allow. Thus, you stress that drivers should avoid certain times in particular traffic flows. For example, most traffic flows increase before noon and 5 P.M. During these times, you suggest that route salespeople call on customers outside the traffic zones, do prospective selling, or perform some other productive activity.

As a last item, you believe that most large companies have the resources to attack the problem of company vehicle accidents. It's more likely that the smaller companies are the ones who incur the significant losses because they cannot control traffic problems as the larger companies can. Your experience shows you reduced accident losses by 20 percent over the last three years. It would be interesting to know the losses incurred by companies with different sales volumes.

Because of this belief you think that a NETS Safe Driving Institute might find good use among the smaller companies who do not have accident prevention programs. Perhaps the larger companies could provide the lead in developing the institute. It would be difficult to individualize training because of the diversity of companies that would be involved. But the institute would be a start in the right direction. Having similar characteristics of the buddy system you use at Spritz, the institute could provide a needed effort to help all those in the traffic safety business. You'll mention this idea in your letter.

Using the foregoing ideas, construct a favorable response letter to Mrs. Dana Haddon, executive director of NETS. Make the letter as "clean" as the safe driving records of your route people who benefit from your traffic safety program.

9. As head tennis professional at Las Colinas Country Club, you react with much interest to the letter you received today from Kristine Strifler, general manager at Lakeview Country Club. "They are doing this thing right," you think to yourself as you finish the letter. "They're emphasizing the *what* before the *who*—just like the book says!" (see Problem 47, Routine Inquiries, for background information).

In your 20 years of experience as a tennis professional at three private clubs, you've seen some good and bad colleagues come and go. And you think there's a pattern to those who are successful. Yes, you will gladly share these ideas with Strifler in her selection and assessment work.

As you see it, the work of a successful tennis professional requires two sets of knowledge, skills, and abilities. First, there are those you refer to as *core qualifications*. Second, there are *fringe qualifications* because they are essential only to the extent that the core qualifications exist first.

Core qualifications are those that involve attitudes. Enthusiasm for the job, integrity, ethics, and such fit into this core category specifically. In addition, being able to adapt and adjust to various groups of people and personalities is another area that exists in the core category. Yet verbal behavior is not what is needed here. A balance between verbal expression and non-verbal tangible results is essential to sustain the performance of a teaching tennis professional.

In addition to these core qualifications, there are fringe attributes—those that are important, but only after the core characteristics are established. Here you would place teaching ability, experience, education, pro shop management, technical skill, and such. These characteristics are what would usually be listed on a résumé. But their application to the uniqueness of Lakeview Country Club might need special attention.

How do you assess and measure these core and fringe characteristics? The fringes are easier to do, but their applications could pose some problems. The manager and tennis committee would need to know of any special circumstances that need identification. Core elements would require the most immediate attention. And their measurement would involve many inferences. Perhaps the tennis committee could create certain scenarios in which to assess such qualities as ethics, enthusiasm, motivation, etc. If candidates were placed in the scenarios/situations in the interviews, then various reactions could be observed and compared. Of course, a close check of references would be needed as well.

Using these ideas, compose a meaningful response to Kristine Strifler. Make it a complete, concise, and professional "set" of answers that will assist her and the tennis committee in conducting their search for a tennis professional at Lakeview Country Club.

10. Yes, you'll help Ronald Ivy as he prepares his speech, "Workplace Diversity: 2005," for presentation to groups that request it (see Problem 48, Routine Inquiries, for background details). You are senior researcher at Hanigan Consulting Group in New York, and you directed the study about which Ivy inquires in his letter.

Your media relations department at Hanigan released some preliminary findings of the study to the press. And that's what Ivy saw in *The Wall Street Journal*. You are still compiling the complete report, and it should be ready in about a month. For now, you will give your reactions to the questions Ivy asks. As soon as the final report is ready, you'll send him a copy. The report is based on interviews with this year's college graduates.

Your study found that the top-tier new hires of color began their job searches long before their white classmates did. And they conducted their searches by different rules. Specifically, about 27 percent of the minority hires started looking into potential employers before they were juniors in college compared with 7 percent of whites. Four of five nonwhite graduates participated in corporate internships or co-op programs compared with two of three whites. All of the minority hires said they planned to go to graduate school compared with 74 percent of whites.

In focus groups, black, Hispanic, and Asian students indicated their assessment of a firm's racial environment far outweighed its name or industry position. Minority groups also developed extensive grapevines in which they gathered and shared information about potential employers. They based this information on their internships or employment experiences. Overall, successful minority students who make the grade are determined not to lose because of credentials or lack of information.

Based on your study, minorities do try harder—in almost every phase of the game. They take more difficult courses, they are out front in assessing companies, and they share information freely among themselves. If minority students had unpleasant internship experiences, a firm's reputation among good, desirable, nonwhite candidates could be significantly damaged for a long time. Perhaps the facts tell an old story with modern application: Successful college hires work harder and longer. Such a conclusion could mean much for diversity planning and management in the years to come. It could also be a breath of fresh air to those who worry about values and future prosperity in the nation.

Organize the foregoing information so that it answers Ivy's questions. You are responding favorably, but you will personalize the message so that it relates directly to the speech Ivy must prepare.

11. The inquiry letter you receive today from Diana Robben, president of Office Essentials, confirms your belief that demand in the wholesale/industrial segment of the market does indeed exist for your ecofurniture products. In her letter, she asks if your Going Green business produces a line of products for the office (see Problem 49, Routine Inquiries, for background information).

When you began to produce ecofurniture five years ago, you thought your market would exist with ultimate consumers—people who would purchase primarily for the home. Since that time, individual businesses, churches, government agencies, and other institutional consumers have purchased your products. You now sell the same products to both the consumer and industrial markets—chairs, coffee tables, sofas, and the like. These products are truly ecologically manufactured with recycled wood, paper, and plastic. And they are finished with water-based paints. It would appear that those in the industrial market want to decorate their workplace environment with safe products.

At present, 25 percent of your sales are to the industrial market and 75 percent to the consumer market. Originally, it was your intent to create products and not distribute them. Accordingly, you sell your product directly to large chains that resell them to ultimate consumers and to wholesalers that service retailers. What you do best, you firmly believe, is manufacture—not market. For the business/industrial orders you've received, you've handled sales directly from your facilities without any middle marketers. With 25 percent of your sales in the industrial market, it might be time for you to push sales to appropriate distribution channels to service this important market opportunity. Mrs. Robben's inquiry and several others you've received convince you the time is right for you to expand your distribution policy.

Also, you have already begun to expand the product line available to industrial buyers. New products such as computer desks, bookshelves, executive chairs, and office desks/tables should roll off your production lines in two months. All of them, of course, are ergonomically engineered for comfort as well as ecologically designed for safety and quality.

You anticipate that the products will grow at a constant 4 percent per year of your total sales until it reaches 40 percent.

Next week, your printer will deliver the new catalogs you designed to promote the more complete office line of ecofurniture. The catalogs have a price list and quantity/advertising discounts in them. You've talked with the printing company, and it can deliver an "early first-off-the-press" brochure by the end of this week—in two days. You'll include the brochure with your response letter to Robbens. One point you will need to make clear, however—ecofurniture is not inexpensive. It takes a different process and unique equipment to produce the furniture. Thus, there are costs that you must recoup in addition to a certain profit margin you must attain to stay in business. On the other hand, the products are not lavish and expensive. They are moderately to highly moderately priced; but they do create a green, ecologically positive Earth. And this is a core value in all your business and production efforts. To date, you have sold your products to 126 industrial customers; and they have been quite satisfied with them.

Using this information, prepare a "green light" letter to Ms. Diana Robben. Make it positive and specific so that she will want to add Going Green furniture to her product line for the industrial buyer.

12. Mr. Edward Vandermeulen's inquiry letter you open today is just one of three you have received as a result of the ad you ran in *Corporate Executive* last week (see Problem 50, Routine Inquiries, for details). With these three and several others, you just might be able to solve your capital and executive talent needs sooner than you thought.

Mr. Vandermeulen wants to know some solid evidence about your company—its market position, its potential, its history of revenues, incomes, profits, and other such hard data items. To be sure, you will give these facts to him to establish your credibility as a young growth-oriented company. Although he does not say so explicitly, you infer that he wants to make sure you are not one of those sinking companies clutching at the financial walls to stay alive in the market. Many such companies raise quick money to solve cash flow problems by hiring executives and offering them ownership for up-front money.

As executive assistant to Bernard Coda, owner of Chem Temp, you have seen the company grow and prosper in your five years of employment. It is well positioned to continue the legacy of success that the Coda family started in 1910. Through internal product expansions and external acquisitions, Chem Temp now is a global player. Specifically, the company produces specialty chemical products that are bromine based for flame retardants and water sanitizing. Also, the product line includes plastic and petroleum additives. Recently, contracts were signed for $100 million for water treatment options in several European locations and for bromine extractions in the Dead Sea.

Amid the growth and market positioning, the company needs senior executive personnel to lead the company in the coming years. Still a family-owned, nonpublic operation, Chem Temp is offering base salary positions at $100,000 to $125,000, with 5 percent performance bonuses if revenue, income, and profit levels exceed projections. Moreover, senior executives can set aside 5 percent of their base salaries for special accounts that will be used to purchase stock options once the company goes public. This public status is expected to occur during the next five years. The money set aside would draw minimum interest until it is used for stock purchase. When the company does go public, senior executives may purchase 5 percent of their base salaries each year in stock options and may use case bonuses to purchase options as well.

These equity opportunities would be supplemented by the usual fringes (medical/life insurance, disability coverage, etc.) and some special perks—car allowances and country club memberships, for example. Indeed, you believe the top executive pay package you've assembled should attract a pool of talent that will lead Chem Temp to the next level in its growth potential.

Although equity and compensation are important, you believe the opportunity to be a part of the future of the Chem Temp team, the feeling of creative freedom to decide and direct, and the opportunity to develop new markets are the prime attractions you have to offer to the possible entrepreneurial executives. With these ideas in mind, sit down at your computer and compose the response to Edward Vandermeulen's inquiry. You can use it as a model letter to adapt to the two other inquiries you have received and to others who undoubtedly will inquire about your unique career opportunity.

13. "This could be a good account for a long time," you think as you read the inquiry letter from Kay T. Moore, executive vice president of marketing at Senseney, Inc. (see Problem 51, Routine Inquiries, for background information).

As sales manager for Kurdian Travel, Inc. (a large travel agency near your locale), your writing project for the moment is to respond favorably to Moore's questions about your cruise vacations. You'll want to include "some little extras" as well—but not to the extent that you lose money on the deal you want to strike with Senseney, Inc. Mrs. Moore plans to offer a free cruise for two to her top performers at Senseney as a compensation extra—a visible reward for performance excellence. Indeed, you have many cruises to select from. Your agency represents four cruise lines that sail the Eastern and Western Caribbean, Mediterranean, Canada, Alaska, and the Greek Isles. Twenty-one scenic and fun cities are regular ports-of-call for these cruise lines.

Usually, three ports of call are visited during a week's cruise; the other days are "fun days at sea" with culinary elegance, lounge entertainment, relax-

ation facilities, and other amenities from which travelers can select to suit their vacation appetites.

On the matter of price, you can offer a 25 percent discount on regular cruise prices if 20 or more persons book one-week or more reservations. This discounted price would include moderate-level cabin accommodations; however, if people wanted to upgrade their facilities, they could do so at a 25 percent discount, the same as the discount for the cruise. The 25 percent rate would apply to the salesperson and one "significant other." If additional family members, friends, and such want to join the twosome, they would qualify for a 15 percent discount. And if some employees want to book 10-day or two-week excursions, the 25 percent discount would apply as well.

You'll send descriptive catalogs from each of the four cruise lines to Moore. Also, you'll send four 10-minute videos that visually describe the leisure experience of each cruise line. You hope these selling supplements will give Moore the insight she needs to select your agency to book passage for her superior sellers.

In addition, you'll pay for 50 percent of the round-trip airfare to the closest metropolitan airport to wherever a cruise ship embarks. Limo fares, transport fees, and such to and from the dock location of the ship are part of the total cruise package. You'll track all guests daily to make sure they do not incur problems in their itineraries. The guests will also receive a bottle of champagne, compliments of you, as a bon voyage expression of your professional service.

Cover these ideas in a well-organized response to Kay T. Moore's inquiry. Make your words so inviting that she will be one of the first people to select a cruise. Top executives of Senseney can qualify also for the travel plan you offer to the salesperson.

PERSONNEL EVALUATIONS

14. As Len Deftos, a medical research scientist in a major university, you were forced by cutbacks in funding to terminate employees you never would under normal circumstances. Therefore, you're happy to write a positive letter for Jane Adami, one of your very best employees on a training grant that wasn't renewed last year. You know Jane's been out of work for almost a year, but you think she's used the time wisely learning more about the computer as well as doing some freelance editing work.

Jane's formal education is strong in the sciences. In fact, you know that at one point she even seriously considered going to medical school. For you she's trained medical students, gathered and collected data, reviewed research, analyzed findings, and written reports. Therefore, you think you can highly recommend her for the sales representative position with Merck. She has both the people skills and ability to complete the paperwork demanded of sales representatives. Also, she's a good listener, a quality useful in sales work. Furthermore, she's been using a laptop computer for several years, so she's familiar with a major tool sales representatives use.

Jane's also a creative self-starter. Her work on the training grant involved designing innovative ways to help medical students learn and carry out the design. While she had no regular, prescribed routine, she successfully completed many projects in a timely fashion. As a sales representative she would also have to design her own work plan and carry through on it.

Jane's outgoing, pleasant personality is also a plus. She's a middle child, one known for easily getting along with others. Her friends would probably choose her as one they enjoy being with. Write the letter to Merck's human resources director, stating objectively what she's done for you and interpret how these skills would be assets for working as a sales representative for Merck.

15. Today you received a request for information from Lisa Miller on the quality of the work done for you and work skills of your financial planner, Stephen Acord. While you use him on fee-for-service basis, he did get your permission to use you as a reference for potential clients.

Steve has been a good friend of yours ever since you met 10 years ago when he helped you and your spouse set up educational funds for your children. While your children aren't quite old enough for college, their college funds have done well. And you've used him to help guide you in your other financial decisions. To you, he seems to take a personal interest in your family, your goals, and your life-style choices. He doesn't force his values and definitely not any financial products on you. However, he does encourage you to verbalize reasons for your decisions. And on several occasions, he has posed numerous questions you overlooked in analyzing your needs and their match with certain financial products. You're definitely convinced that without Steve's help your net worth would be substantially less. You even think you may have made some serious errors without his guidance. Not only is he well-versed on a wide variety of financial services and products, but he also knows how to act in a timely fashion. It's clear to you that you've learned a lot from Steve, and you really appreciate the way he's helped you learn to match your needs and desires with appropriate actions.

The quality of Steve's work is superb, and his skills are exceptional. You have the highest regard for him personally, too. Write the letter, making certain you sound sincere.

16. As Janet Baker, manager of a local drugstore that is part of a national chain, you've been asked by the regional manager of the chain to evaluate the performance of one of your employees, Megan Adami. Megan's been working as a clerk for the last three years in your store while she's been attending college. When you hired her, she thought she wanted to become a pharmacist; however, she changed her major to management two years ago. And now she's

applying for one of the few manager trainee spots in your chain.

Her university is highly respected for the quality of its business program. In fact, her major department has won recognition for its special programs in both international business and total quality management. Despite working to provide 100 percent of her college expenses, Megan's been able to maintain a 3.5 grade point average. This places her in the top 10 percent of all graduates in her major. And you know she's been able to apply many of the concepts she has learned in various projects involving store management. In fact, she used you as an expert source in a report her group wrote on casual dress policies.

Additionally, Megan's work record has been impeccable. She has always completed work asked of her extremely well. And her attitude is upbeat and sincere. In the three years at your store, she has never missed a work shift. She plans both her vacations and her schoolwork around the needs of the store. Her flexibility in adjusting her schedule is greatly appreciated by you and her co-workers. She's always willing to work on holidays so co-workers can be with their children and families.

While Megan hasn't been in a formal supervisory position, you've noticed she's taken a lead in helping new employees learn the ropes. In fact, they often seek out her advice on basic management problems such as communicating with customers, preventing shoplifting, and stocking shelves.

You realize the chain takes only a select few into its management trainee program. But you are convinced that she is clearly one that would be a great asset to the chain. Write the letter.

17. Today's Exchange in-box brought a request from Kate M. Meersman of the Houston area company Krug for information on a former student of yours, Terry Lenaghan. Kate tells you Terry is applying for a position requiring a broad sense of business skills, particularly accounting, and highly developed, mature interpersonal communication skills. You remember Terry clearly not only for his red hair but also for his bright insights and his congeniality. You're confident he has the ability to do well in almost any job that interests him, and you'll respond to the request positively.

Terry was a superb student in your business communication class. Not only did he attend regularly, but he also frequently added comments and provided analogies that you believe helped other students see the material clearly. He was a disc jockey for the campus radio station, playing music and handling on-the-air requests. His writings always seemed to reflect a special, creative flair that was unique, yet quite appropriate. He seemed to understand how to write both to get the message across clearly and to keep the reader interested. You remember once checking on his background and learning that he was also an A student in English. And you vividly remember that he had exceptional ACT scores, scoring in the upper 90 percentile on both the math and English components. Therefore, his decision to emphasize accounting didn't surprise you since you realized he was just as good with analytical tasks.

Terry was well liked by both you and his classmates. He exhibited good team skills when working on a group report. He seemed to be able to step into the leadership role when needed and to step back when it was appropriate for others to lead. He also encouraged his team members to write their report together using a group writing tool recently installed on the network. While not required as part of the assignment, students were exposed to group writing tools and encouraged to use them. Terry took the challenge and provided the initiative his team needed. The result was a superb report written in one voice and using everyone's input. All team members reported satisfaction with both their product and the process.

You believe Terry has superior innate abilities to successfully meet challenges and identify opportunities with varied, creative perspectives. In addition, you think he has the interpersonal skills to work effectively, efficiently, and pleasantly with others. Write Kate Meersman a letter to show that Terry not only meets Krug's needs but also far exceeds them. He would be an extremely valuable asset to the company.

18. As CEO of Guardian Insurance Company and president of the Vista Ridge School Board, you will respond positively to the job inquiry you receive from Melanie Wilson at Prologic (see Problem 57, Inquiries, Prospective Employees, for background details).

You had hoped that Melinda McMahan would stay with her career in public education because you saw such great potential in her. But she is a single parent and she probably needs a career fast track. Thus, the lure of the benefits, money, and advancement opportunities of the private sector are too much for the public sector to compete with. Also, Melinda would have had to make several lateral moves in her career in public education before she could ascend to a higher position. Right now, her best bet is to move to the human resources job that Prologic offers. You will support her totally in her efforts even though you know the educational world will sorely miss a dedicated professional.

When McMahan joined VRISD, she did so as curriculum coordinator for elementary education. After working in this capacity for two years, she was promoted to overall curriculum supervisor for the entire district. In effect, she is an assistant superintendent with one high school, three middle school, and eight elementary school principals reporting directly to her. In her role, she is responsible for the total design of the district curriculum and for making certain it is complete, up-to-date, and relevant.

To acquire this knowledge, she is continually traveling to workshops and seminars to acquire new ideas and concepts in her work. Many of these are sponsored by IBM, Xerox, and other such businesses that provide educational technology for instruction. Thus, you believe that much of the transfer of learning to industry and multiple interactions with business about which Melanie Wilson at Prologic inquires has already occurred. You are convinced she could make the transition to the private sector with ease.

Moreover, Melinda has designed specific studies to assess the impact of the curriculum on student learning and development. In fact, she has an admirable publication record in the education literature from studies she has conducted. Her work has not been superficial or solely conceptual. To the contrary, she has followed the typical scientific model using empirical research—theoretical development, derivation of hypotheses, testing of variables, and deriving conclusions. Her work has included both correlation and longitudinal studies. To be sure, she has the mastery of technical skill and the conceptual capability to serve as an objective assessor of learning efforts—in a public school system, in a training room as an organizational development consultant, or what have you.

In answer to Wilson's question about interpersonal skills, you will have to be somewhat indirect. As you have known Melinda for five years, she has always presented herself pleasantly and professionally. At the same time, she has in certain situations appeared shy. Throughout the schools she works with, however, she conducts numerous workshops for teachers. And the reports on her performance are nothing less than glowing. Thus, her personal shyness is most probably a good complement to her professional personality. In the arena of work, her social skills appear to be balanced to support her technical competence.

All told, you can respond favorably to the questions Wilson asks. You'll fill in details so that she will be convinced you know her well enough to assess her capabilities. You hate to lose a dedicated educator of her caliber; but that seems to be a trend these days. Write the evaluation of Melinda McMahan's abilities for the job at Prologic.

19. "Joan D. Bruno was one of three research assistants I've ever seen that is capable of original research," you say to yourself as read the letter you receive from Dr. Hyler Bracey (see Problem 58, Inquiries, Prospective Employees, for background information). "We had good times learning and working together during the three years she was completing her studies at Central State University." You'll gladly respond to the questions that Dr. Bracey asks of you about Ms. Bruno's qualifications.

Yes, Ms. Bruno was your research assistant for three years when she was working on her master's degree. At the time, you had several research grants to investigate dysfunctional effects of stress on organizational performance. Ms. Bruno did much of the field research for the studies. And she worked meticulously to enter the data into files for analysis. You remember one weekend that she labored three days—with little sleep or rest—to make sure that a statistical program would run and analyze the data in the way you specified. Indeed, she is a tireless and dedicated worker, and you will tell Dr. Bracey so in your letter.

During her course work on her master's degree, you had Ms. Bruno as a student in two courses: Psychometric Testing and Industrial Psychology. In both courses, she earned a top A. In addition to her mastery of techniques, she exhibited a unique intellectual curiosity for the subject matter, viewing each course with insight and inquisitiveness as well as genuine respect for the traditions of the discipline itself. You remember especially that she formed a study group in your Industrial Psychology class that met each week for lunch to discuss current concepts and issues. Her enthusiasm for learning was evident by her drive, ambition, and intellectual perspective. You talked with her about continuing for a Ph.D., but money problems and the need to relate concepts with actual practice dictated that she forgo intellectual pursuits for the world of work. However, she had an unquestionable capability for an academic career.

Because of her intellectual instincts and devotion to duty, you asked that she join you as co-author on three manuscripts you had in progress. You felt that this offer was only fair because Ms. Bruno had helped conduct much of the research legwork. Eventually, the manuscripts were published in practitioner magazines. In this publication process, Ms. Bruno did her fair share of the work—writing, editing, and rewriting the manuscripts for publication. She handles language well, especially in her analytical writing efforts.

On the matter of business courses in her curriculum, you must report that she took only psychology courses. The extent of her work experience since graduation and the fieldwork she performed for you, however, should certainly attest to her understanding of organizational dynamics. She also possesses the necessary interpersonal skills to relate well to others in both business and personal situations.

You will convey these sentiments to Dr. Hyler Bracey in a favorable evaluation of Ms. Joan D. Bruno's qualifications for organizational development consultant at Change Strategies, Inc. You had high expectations for her career when you trained her; thus, you believe that she has significant potential for success at Change Strategies, Inc.

20. In the role of Stephanie Vanatta, video productions supervisor at KAKE, write an evaluation letter of Clyda Pendarvis, a member of your production team (see Problem 59, Inquiries, Prospective Employees, for background information). You knew about Clyda's job hunting activities. It appears that she has been successful in her efforts.

Clyda has performed well in her various work assignments over the past five years. When she first joined your unit, you assigned her to routine and ordinary tasks. In general, she did whatever you needed her to do at the moment; but these various assignments gave her good insight and perspective on the

value of the unit to the station's activities. Because of her consistent work on whatever she was assigned to do, you gave her more responsibilities with the unit.

For a time (about 18 months), Clyda worked in video editing for your daily news telecasts. After reporters and camera workers in the field would bring her a tape, she would work with them, along with the newscast anchors, to put it into final form for use in the daily/nightly news. In this process, there was obviously much time pressure and need for exacting, error-free work. As the people who work with her speak glowingly of her performance, you believe Clyda has met the technical and personal demands of her job in excellent fashion.

After her 18-month stint in news support, you appointed her to work as video director of special programming—interviews, features, special reports, and such. In this role, she directed the entire production cycle: set design, taping, and editing. To do her job better, she signed up for two art classes at a local junior college—one in lighting and effects and the other in creative filming. The work of the department improved with her performance; she indeed provided good visibility for your technical staff.

With the depth and breadth of her work experience at KAKE, you believe she is ready to make a significant career move. Since there are no more moves for her in your unit, she must look outside to get a position in keeping with her increasing skills and abilities. The job at Doolin-Shaw would appear to fit her quite appropriately.

Write the personnel evaluation letter recommending Clyda Pendarvis for the job at Doolin-Shaw, Inc. You'll miss the cheerful, optimistic personality of Clyda, but you cannot hold her back. She has too much talent. Make Clyda as good on paper in your letter as she is in the work that she does for you.

21. "Donald Mounce is an excellent process trainer. They couldn't do better for their job than him!" you think to yourself as you read the letter from Brian Jacques asking about Mounce's qualifications for the job (see Problem 60, Inquiries, Prospective Employees, for background information). He's worked for you for five years and has always completed his assignments successfully and competently.

When Mounce joined C & G Consultants, he had a master's degree in educational assessment and eight years of direct and indirect experience in consulting. His references from his previous job were excellent, extolling his good work and the superb potential that he possessed for consulting/development work in general and behavior change strategies in particular. You have seen much of that potential come to fruition in his five years with you.

In the first assignment you gave him, you tried to build his confidence and self-esteem. As he quickly grew in experience and professional stature, you assigned him to more and more difficult and complex clients. In each work role, Mounce has grown and flourished as the consummate professional that he truly is. Presently, you assign him to your larger and more senior accounts because you are confident in his abilities to work with and solve the more complex problems that these clients present. Usually, his assignments with a client last about 12 months. And you know he has interpersonal skills to supplement his professional competency. Clients report that his total commitment to his work, his adaptable presence, and his pleasant disposition accommodate his change agent's role in the organization he serves.

Moreover, his army reserve training provides a good and valuable source of professional updating. On his monthly weekend of reservist training, he hears lectures and sees the latest techniques in professional training in small group behavior. He spends his two-week active duty each year in a Veterans Administration hospital learning and practicing the most recent techniques in mental reconditioning and rehabilitation. Thus, his army reserve training acts as a catalyst for the professional competence he continually uses for the benefit of clients at C & G Consultants.

Also, you know that Mounce is active in many community affairs. He's especially active in Habitat for Humanity, a group devoted to providing housing for the poor. Moreover, he's a member of the Rotary Club and the local community chorus. Such a variety of interests undoubtedly gives him versatility in his interpersonal skills and shows the values of a significant, nurturing human being.

You will write to Jacques and answer favorably the questions he asks about Mounce. You wish you could keep him at C & G Consultants, but right now you don't have a job as broad in scope as the one at Entergy. He has the qualifications and the proven record to succeed in the reengineering of the job structure at Entergy.

ADJUSTMENT GRANTS

22. As Janet Wingler, customer relations director for Pacific Data Products, you've just received a fax from James Andrews, a computer consultant in St. Petersburg, Florida, requesting an adjustment. He placed a phone order for additional memory for his computer from you just over 90 days ago and now wants to return it for a full credit of $159.90.

Mr. Andrews states his main reason for wanting to return the memory is that he has decided to replace the computer with a new, faster one. Therefore, he does not need the additional memory since he'll be disposing of the computer he had originally intended to upgrade. Furthermore, he tells you that it is still in its original shrink-wrap packaging.

While you believe your current policy of accepting all product returns within 90 days is a generous one, especially in an industry with such rapid developments, you decide to grant the adjustment and accept the return. Not only is Mr. Andrews gracious in his request, but he's in a position as a consultant and trainer to recommend your products to many others.

Also, your records show he has bought and paid for promptly several other products from your company in the past.

In granting the adjustment, do remind Mr. Andrews of the 90-day cut-off for future returns. However, be sure to retain his goodwill. You may want to let him know you are both crediting his account for the full amount and handling it without any charges for restocking or shipping.

23. As manager of the local Chart House, one of the area's top-rated restaurants, you respond to special letters like the following one from Lee McLaughlin.

Dear Manager:

The quality of both the service and the food we experienced on February 14 at your Solana Beach restaurant was miserable.

Since this was Valentine's Day, I made reservations nearly a month in advance to insure that I could bring my wife, Buffy, to your Solana Beach restaurant. This location is known for both its fine food, good atmosphere, and beautiful ocean views. I specially requested a 5:00 p.m. seating so that we could enjoy our meal as the sun went down. Your receptionist assured me of both the time and a window table.

When we arrived, the place was so crowded the overflow was spilling out both the front doors and the deck. However, I felt confident we'd be seated since my reservation was a long-standing one. However, I quickly learned that we'd have a 20-minute wait. While disappointed, we waited the 20 minutes. But the 20 minutes stretched to 60. And on top of that, we did not get a window table nor a view of the sunset both since it was late and since the crowd on the deck blocked the view.

In trying to make the best of a bad situation, we ordered fine wine and expensive meals. But we were rushed by the waiter. Our bill came to over $130.

I'm so disappointed now in the Chart House, you'd have to convince me why I would want to return. And I definitely will not recommend it to anyone, especially for special occasions. If things can be changed, let me know.

Sincerely,

Lee McLaughlin

Since Mr. McLaughlin did not totally close the door on your restaurant, you believe you can persuade him to return. Give him a reason [you supply the reason] why you had such an unusual crowd at 5:00 P.M. Additionally, to encourage him to return and to retain his goodwill you can enclose a coupon for complimentary meal and drink. Of course, do include some resale on the quality of the food, the service, and the atmosphere.

24. Angeli Ramirez, a recent college graduate, sent you an e-mail message, complaining about wasting money for your on-line job databank service. Angeli told you she had been listed in the databank for over three months without even as much as one call. Not only did she pay $50 to be listed in the databank, but she relied solely on it while she completed the last 18 units for her degree. Now she feels as though she was falling behind both financially and careerwise as her classmates enter career-related jobs. In her field, information systems, there are numerous opportuni-

ties, particularly in the data communications area, which interests her most. And you know she would be a good employee based on her excellent academic record and her top-notch summer internship at Andersen Consulting. While she'd like her money back, she's most interested in getting started in a career-related job as soon as possible.

As Mel Short, director of E-span, you decide both to refund the $50 registration fee (which should not have been collected) and help her get some good interviews. Angeli is clearly a good candidate and an appropriate user of your service, which is targeted at college-educated, computer-literate, and technically proficient job seekers. Encourage Angeli to continue to access E-span through her Compuserve connection, reminding her there is no additional cost other than her Compuserve connection charge. You may want to suggest that she investigate other areas listed on the E-span menu in Compuserve that give tips and ideas for getting a job.

25. As Barbara DuBois, general manager of Book Stacks Unlimited, Inc., an on-line book store, you're faced with an unusual request by a customer. The customer, Carolyn Winship, is a longtime, well-established customer. She recently ordered six copies of the H. R. Haldeman book, *The Haldeman Diaries: Inside the Nixon White House,* for members of her book club. A copy was sent to each member and the total billed to Ms. Winship. She assumed we would send the CD-ROM version as we do with all her orders, but our warehouse shipped the print copy. She'd like us to immediately ship the CD-ROM versions for overnight delivery, charge the price difference to her account, and absorb the shipping costs. She assures us that the members will return the print copies. But she doesn't want to be billed for both versions, and she doesn't want to be bothered gathering and mailing the books.

In checking into this matter, we discovered that the Haldeman book was the first title we sold in both the print and CD-ROM versions. At the time, our inventory system was not set up to handle identical titles on different media, so the error was an understandable one. As new titles were released in both print and CD-ROM, our inventory management program was updated to handle them. However, we entered titles separately only from that point on, choosing not to enter old titles unless they were re-stocked.

Ms. Winship tells you that her group is definitely interested in some of the quotes attributed to Nixon but found only in the CD-ROM version, the more complete version. You decide to grant Ms. Winship's reasonable yet unusual request. You want to retain her goodwill as well as the goodwill of the book club members; so you'll include pre-addressed, postage-paid return labels and bag for the books. Feel free to promote some of your new titles that are in line with the types of books she's been ordering the last three years.

26. Today you need to respond to a letter from Veronica De La Rosa. While on a recent trip to New Orleans,

she rented one of your special business cars. These cars include cellular phone/faxes and are extremely popular during the week. In fact, on occasion your airport office has even leased the same car within an hour of its return.

As general manager of Avis's downtown location, you are sure this quick turnaround may have contributed to Ms. De La Rosa's claim. Apparently, the car received a parking ticket the day Ms. De La Rosa returned it. One of your company's clerks forwarded the ticket to her for payment. However, the time of the ticket was after she had returned the car.

In fact, as proof it could not have been her responsibility, she included a copy of her airline ticket and her boarding pass. She asked that the parking ticket be removed from her record. You can clearly see she was not driving the car when it was ticketed. Not only will you grant her request, but you also will work to regain her goodwill while doing some resale of Avis's fine line of cars.

27. George Kent was the manager of Super Bowl Supplies, a San Diego-based supplier of football novelties. In early January, he received an order from Down Memory Lane, a Tampa-based chain selling sporting goods. The order was for 100,000 T-shirts featuring the quarterback of the Super Bowl champions.

Being from San Diego and a Chargers fanatic, George was so sure that the Chargers would whip the 49ers that he made arrangements for Bobby Humphry's picture to be printed on all the T-shirts. On the day of the Super Bowl, George began his partying early and impulsively gave the final, irrevocable order for the printing job to be completed on all the T-shirt shipments. He and other San Diego fans had planned a big bash that evening, and George wanted to make sure that the printing job was taken care of so that he could enjoy himself and the festivities.

Missy Weber, the manager of Down Memory Lane, was enraged when she received the 100,000 T-shirts two days later with the wrong quarterback's picture on them. She complained to Super Bowl Supplies in a claim letter (see Problem 28, Claims, for background information) and asked the company to send a fresh consignment with Steve Young's picture on the T-shirts.

Assume you are Lisa Franklin, the new manager of Super Bowl Supplies (George Kent was fired the day after the Super Bowl). Your company has agreed to send the new order. Explain in your letter to Ms. Weber why the wrong order was sent to her and what steps the company is taking to make sure such a mistake will not happen again. Resell her on the company's products and services as you want her as a regular customer.

(Note: This case situation may be adapted to other sporting events such as basketball, baseball, hockey, etc., and other activities as the course instructor may choose.)

28. Assume the role of Nicole Jarvis, sales manager of

Jarvis, Inc., a leading manufacturer of monogrammed work clothes. This morning, you received a letter from an irate Ron Gallela, the supplies manager for QuickBurger, Inc. Reading his letter and reviewing the antecedents to the case, you are terribly embarrassed because it is obvious your company is at fault.

Mr. Gallela had ordered 2,000 shirts monogrammed with the QuickBurger logo of a smiling employee handing out a burger. The color of the shirt as specified by Mr. Gallela was light blue, which was also the color of all QuickBurger outlets. Your assistant, Tina Johnson, had written on the production schedule form the exact logo requirements of the customer but had forgotten to specify the color of the shirt. It was obviously a mistake; but, as Tina pointed out to you, the production schedule form does not have a column for color specification. The production department followed Tina's specification exactly except that when it came to the shirt's color, the production head unfortunately chose the color of QuickBurger's arch rival—McDonald's. Imagine Ron Gallela's chagrin when he saw the results.

In his letter to you, Ron Gallela has pointed out the fact that the mix-up was unproductive and untimely for QuickBurger because employees in several stores did not have the company shirt to wear to work. You know you have to do something quickly to appease Mr. Gallela; otherwise, your company will lose an important customer. Also, the company procedure must be changed so that such an error will not occur again. So, you add a column for color specification to the production scheduling form and also insist from now on that every job must be double-checked for specifications before the order is sent.

As Nicole Jarvis, write a letter to Mr. Gallela that will accompany a new shipment of 2,000 shirts completed according to his exact specifications. Work hard to explain what went wrong in a positive way. Convince Mr. Gallela that your intentions are to serve customers efficiently and correctly. Resell him on the products and services of Jarvis, Inc.

29. You are Pat Morita, the manager of Satisfaction Guaranteed Travels, Inc. You have just received a letter from an obviously irate customer, Shannon Fox (see Problem 30, Claims for background information).

Ms. Fox is the president of Dallas Dowagers Association, a group of elderly ladies who are out to have a good time. It seems that the group took a trip to the Grand Canyon, and the entire travel arrangements were handled by your company. Apparently the new tour guide assigned to Ms. Shannon Fox's group confused this group with one scheduled for Ms. Samantha Fox and a group of British musicians. The Samantha Fox group did not have overnight accommodations included in its tour.

When the tour guide called to the home office to determine whether overnight accommodations were included for the group, the clerk answering the call pulled the Samantha Fox records rather than the Shannon Fox records. So no overnight accommoda-

tions showed for the group. Thus, the elderly ladies of the Shannon Fox group had to spend a rather painful and uncomfortable night in the open air amid the howling of wolves and cold winds. It was not a night they would ever want to repeat, and Ms. Fox's letter to you contained some pretty strong words about the mishandling of the situation.

Now you will write Ms. Shannon Fox an adjustment-grant letter. With it, you will send a check for the $100 owed her personally, the amount your company had charged each member of the tour group for overnight accommodations. You will explain what happened as convincingly as you can in an effort to regain any lost confidence in your company. Also in your letter to Ms. Fox, you will explain that your company is sending out similar letters granting refunds to all members of the tour group. The situation is negative throughout. But you will work hard to prove that Satisfaction Guaranteed Travels does the right thing for all of its clients.

30. As director of sales for the Whisper Manufacturing Company, grant the claim described in Problem 29, Claims. You were not surprised to receive this claim, for it is the third one you have received this month; all are based on the same defect in your product.

You already know the problem and its explanation, as you thoroughly investigated the situation after receiving the first claim. Back in April the production people decided to try a new motor for Whisper fans— an import that sold for 15 percent less than the Dillard-Hix motors that have been used in all Whisper fans for the past 20 years. Preliminary tests on the imported motors indicated they would do the job. But evidence now accumulated after months of operation indicates these motors don't hold up. They become noisy.

Of course, as soon as Whisper executives learned about the weakness of the imported motors, they returned to the old and reliable Dillard-Hix motors. Management doesn't intend to change again. And they want to do all they can to correct any damage to customer relations caused by the mistake. Specifically, they have decided that all defective fans brought to the company's attention will be replaced with good fans—at the company's expense.

So now you'll write the complaining real estate broker and present the good-news answer. And you will explain the situation in a way that will mend the damaged image of Whisper fans. Waldon Electric of the real estate broker's city will do the actual work of exchanging the fans. The broker should hear from Waldon soon. Your letter must convince the broker that you stand behind the products you offer to the consuming public.

31. You are a bank officer in the credit card division of the State Street National Bank, and you are trying to reply to the day's mail. Mark Whiting has filed a claim asking you to remove the charges on his account from PCs-By-Mail, a mail-order computer supply house located in Chicago.

Mr. Whiting has been a customer of the bank for many years and has several very significant accounts there. He states that he ordered a printer for his computer over 90 days ago and requested By-Mail to charge the $473.95 to his credit card. They promptly billed his credit card, but they never shipped the printer, despite repeated promises to do so. Mr. Whiting's letter adds that the Chicago Better Business Bureau has informed him that PCs-By-Mail filed for bankruptcy a week ago and no longer answers its telephone.

A telephone call to an officer in your associated Chicago bank verifies that PCs-By-Mail has indeed filed for bankruptcy. By law, your bank is required to remove the charges from Mr. Whiting's account and refund the payments he has made (he has paid the full amount with interest of $11.47 for the period of time before he made the payment). State Street National Bank will have to file as an unsecured creditor with the bankruptcy judge in Chicago to get its money back.

You have sent a letter to PCs-By-Mail requesting that it return the money your bank had transferred to it, with interest. And you have sent a memorandum to the Legal Department to tell it to file the claim in Bankruptcy Court. You included the court, the docket number, the date of filing, and other relevant information from your file. Now, you must explain to Mr. Whiting what you have done. Write the letter to him that will adjust his account and give him assurance that your handling of the matter is just and credible.

ACKNOWLEDGMENTS (OF VAGUE AND BACK ORDERS)

32. As Kurt Messersmith, marketing manager for Irwin-One, the business trade division of Richard D. Irwin, you received a large order from Professor Julie Jahn of the University of San Diego for one of your management books. Normally, most of your books are sold to the trade market rather than the university; nevertheless you are just as pleased to get the order. In placing the order, Professor Jahn was a bit vague when she requested your series book on teams. She'd like it in paperback since it'll be a supplement to the regular management text.

While you'd like to place the order, you want to be sure to send her the book she wants. Even though she mentioned it was a bit like a workbook with lots of exercises, you have a couple of titles that would fit that description. Furthermore, she remembered its cover was basically light gray or brown. Unfortunately, that doesn't help too much since most of your books for the business series have varying shades of gray and brown as their basic color. However, the size of the book may help or perhaps even the last name of one of the authors.

When you acknowledge Professor Jahn's order, you could ask for the ISBN number to be exactly sure you are providing the right book. However, perhaps she won't have the book in front of her, so you might want to ask the book's size and author's name. Of course, any other identifying information would help. And you could provide her with the list of titles that fit her description to see if any of them sound familiar to her. Do make it as easy as possible for her to respond.

33. As Michael Deftos, vice president of marketing for Thomson Consumer Electronics, you received an order today that was both thrilling and gut-wrenching, thrilling because it was for a new item you recommended producing that seemed risky and gut-wrenching because it was so large you will have trouble shipping it in a timely manner. The product is your 18-inch satellite dish. Buyers will receive more than 150 channels of programming, including HBO, Showtime, Lifetime, and some other 30 cable networks and 40 to 50 movie channels. However, no broadcast stations are participating because they don't want to compete with their local affiliates. Many in your company thought this would limit sales drastically.

You realized, though, that the quality would sell it. Its use of digital compression technology results in sharper pictures. And the on-screen menu lets users easily find the kind of programs that interest them. Furthermore, its list price of only $699 and monthly charges comparable to local cable charges make it very price competitive. Apparently, your customer recognizes the good buy these small satellite dishes represent to television owners and wants to be a major supplier in the Southeast.

The demand for these dishes has far exceeded your forecasts and your present capacity. Since this customer is placing such a large order, you want to keep the order and retain goodwill. You can offer to ship one-third of the order within 30 days and the rest within 90 days. Furthermore, you are presently retooling some of your other production lines for handling this product and expect your backlog to be cleared within 120 days. Therefore, you can assure the customer of timely shipments in the future. Write a letter that will retain the order and gain the customer's goodwill for future orders for both this product and other Thomson products.

34. Eleanor Braaten, an apartment complex owner and wife of a prominent Seminole-area developer, placed an order today for your compact washer-dryers for all the units in her 126-unit Redington Beach property. She told you she was delighted to learn that you were importing the perfect solution for her beachfront units. The EZ1000, made by an Italian appliance maker, is targeted at singles, couples, and the elderly living in condos or apartments, not the suburban family.

Not only is this machine thrifty on water and energy, but it is also space saving. It takes up only about 60 percent of the space of a single standard-size unit while handling both washing and drying tasks. While its capacity is smaller, those living in apartments and condos usually don't have as many people to wash for as those in large homes. Additionally, it eliminates the need to wait until the washer is done and remove clothes from one unit and place in another. With the EZ1000 the user simply puts the load in and returns to clean, dry clothes.

While the list price on the units is $795, Ms. Braaten thinks it actually will save money in the long run. Additionally, she sees providing these unique, easy-to-use appliances as a feature that will set her rental units apart from others on the strip. Most of her units are rented to vacationers who don't want to think about laundry and will see this appliance as fitting nicely with their expectations for leisure. She'd like to have the washer-dryer units installed as soon as possible so she can start promoting her apartments as equipped with them.

As Derrick Wingler, customer relations director for Equator Corporation of Houston, the importer for the EZ1000, you'll have to tell Ms. Braaten the units are back-ordered. In fact, her order for 126 units would account for most of your next shipment. Therefore, you'll have to let her know that while you can immediately ship 26 units, the following 100 may take as long as 60 days. But you are confident that your Italian supplier is reliable and can assure her she will have the units in time to start her new advertising campaign. Write the message to retain Ms. Braaten's goodwill. You may want to do some resale on the fine choice she has made.

35. As Marybeth Bola, a Kodak marketing manager for on-site processing, you need to clear up an order you received today from Matt Lenaghan, buyer for the Springfield area Wal-Mart. He told you he's received requests for self-service photofinishing, and he's interested in your kiosks. He understands these photofinishing kiosks work much like ATMs or card-creation kiosks. He wants the kiosks that will make prints from prints, slides, and photo CDs. He'd like three of these kiosks in place by December to capture the Christmas business.

Write Matt Lenaghan an acknowledgment letter, confirming that you'll ship the new Creation Stations in time for Christmas. However, he didn't tell you where he wanted them shipped or how he'd handle payment. Additionally, he didn't place an order for any supplies, which you are sure he'll need to have on hand during the busy Christmas season.

In your letter, do some resale on the photofinishers. Tell him that not only do they handle the formats he specified, but they also handle negatives and allow users to add text, graphics, and backgrounds. Furthermore, they'll make enlargements as well as standard-size prints. You may want to relate these features to the kinds of papers and supplies he'll want to order to keep his kiosks stocked and making money for Wal-Mart. Work to retain the order and his goodwill.

36. As Hal Monk, sales manager for Archeological Tours, 271 Madison Avenue, New York 10016, you must acknowledge the tour bookings you received by fax today from Brookings Travel Tours, Chicago.

Your company arranges tours of world historical significance in large numbers (20 or more) for smaller agencies. You will book tours for one agency or you will combine travelers from two or more agencies to meet the minimum 20 requirement for a tour. Your concern of the moment is to get things straight for the four groups Brookings Tours wants to schedule for archaeological adventures across the globe. The groups and their preferences are the substance of the fax you received. Each of the tours has a tour guide who travels with the groups, gives introductory lectures before visiting historic sites, and answers questions.

Yes, you can book the Rotary group for the Egypt archaelogical tour November 14–28. Dr. Nabil Abufadl, a respected authority on Egyptian history, will accompany the group on the tour.

The second and third groups that Monk wants to book present some problems. Rather than book the groups and then have to change the arrangements, you decide to ask Monk for more information before you proceed. The First Baptist Church group wants to take the Eastern Turkey tour and the St. Paul Lutheran Church group wants the Anatolian Turkey tour. But there are two dates for each tour—May 5–19 and October 15–29. You'll need to know which tour each group prefers before you can make the arrangements.

The fourth group, the Oak Brook Retired Teachers, wants the Himalayan Kingdoms tour on October 2–16. But that tour is filled. You can schedule the group for November 1–17; but you'll need the OK before you do.

On the matter of credit, Brookings Tours asks for 30 days to pay for the tours after they are confirmed. Your policy is to require one-half payment with each tour you book. You then require the remaining one-half within 45 days. If there is a cancellation within two months of the tour, you will refund the full payment. After that two-month cancellation, you will refund one-half of the payment until two weeks before the tour dates at which time you will no longer refund any payments. Indeed, Brookings should encourage each group to take out traveler's insurance, which will protect against certain risks of not being able to take the tour.

Write the acknowledgment letter to Brookings Travel Tours that will get the information you need to complete the travel bookings for the group. As this is a first contact with Brookings Travel Tours, work especially hard to show the detail and thoroughness of your service.

37. You are Robert Golladay, manager of mail-order sales at Valley Orchards. The advertisements you've been running in *The Wall Street Journal, Forbes,* and *Fortune* have certainly stimulated sales, as evidenced by the many orders you have received in the last month. Although you intended the ads to spark sales

to consumers, you are surprised that you've received as many orders from businesses as you have. At the moment, you must deal with an order from Advantage PCs, who asks you to send gift fruit boxes to 25 of its best customers as special Christmas gifts (Note: Holiday occasions can be changed to fit different seasons depending on the instructor's preference.)

You will acknowledge the order and certainly you can send the first 10 people on Advantage's list the boxes of assorted fruits (grapefruits, oranges, lemon, etc.) that are requested. But you'll have to wait on the next 15 because your harvesters are in the fields picking the fruit. The unexpected upsurge in demand prompted by your advertising depleted most of your inventory. Most likely, the orders can be filled in two weeks and they will arrive before Christmas. But you want to give Advantage a status report of its shipment and the opportunity to cancel if it prefers. Moreover, there was a laborers' strike last month, and you've had difficulty getting consistent workers to gather the fruits.

Also, five of the people on the list are designated a "single fruit only." You guess that this wording means you would send grapefruit or oranges only rather than the assorted box you usually send. Rather than send the wrong order, you'll ask Advantage exactly what the wording means. If it is consistent with your meaning, you will ask them to specify what fruit they'd like.

You advertised the assorted fruit at $49.99 including tax and freight. But because of the magnitude of the order, you can offer a 5 percent discount. You've checked Advantage's credit and it has a "good pay" record. Your normal billing procedure is for all accounts to be paid within 30 days.

Write the order acknowledgment letter to Advantage PC that will keep it sold on your business. This account will be a profitable one, and you want to have it as a repeat customer for many years to come.

38. Assume you are sales manager for the Dow Jones & Company, Inc., publisher of *The Wall Street Journal*. In addition to your daily newspaper, which is world famous for its financial news coverage, you also publish various supplements. Often these supplements are inserts to one of the issues of the *Journal;* in some instances, they are produced for free distribution to students and other interested groups who request them. You believe that these supplements are good investments in your future as they are usually aimed at markets where potential sales of the *Journal* exist. Thus, you distribute them free in liberal quantities as long as the groups seem legitimate. You advertise the availability of the supplements widely in the *Journal,* in direct-mail promotion letters, and through brochures and other promotional literature distribution at booths at conventions and such.

Today, you must handle the order you receive from (your school). The professor of the Introduction to Business course, a beginning course for freshmen, sent you forms for 10 students who wish to take *The*

Wall Street Journal for 15 weeks at the educational discount price of $25. Indeed, you will enter the names of the students in your database and they should begin to receive their subscriptions in approximately one week. You will bill them individually for the amount they owe at the addresses listed on the form.

Professor _____ (an instructor at your university who teaches the Introduction to Business class) also wants some of the supplements you provide for classes. The first one requested, "How to Read and Make Sense of *The Wall Street Journal,*" will be sent by regular mail. The professor requests 60 copies, which seems reasonable. They should arrive in about one week. In addition, the professor wants 60 copies of each of these supplements: "Managing Your Career" and "How to Invest in the Stock Market." The "Managing Your Career" supplement is revised yearly. You can send the 60 copies requested now; but if the professor will wait for one month, you can send the edition presently being revised. The publication is chocked full of suggestions on interviewing, preparing employment letters/résumés, networking, identifying skills needed by the market, etc. You believe the professor would want to wait for the latest coverage in an area that lacks structure and direction. You'll ask him what he wants to do.

On the matter of providing the supplement "How to Invest in the Stock Market," you have two publications that use the same title. One publication emphasizes the individual investor and the other emphasizes the institutional investor. Although these options were provided on the order form, neither one was checked. So, you'll need to determine which one the professor wants before you fill the order. Most probably, you think the professor wants the personal investor option, but you will also check this out before you send the copies. As soon as you get the preference, you'll send the materials by regular mail; they should arrive in one week.

Write the letter that will handle the various details of this account. You want it to sell because of the potential it has for future accounts. At the same time, you want it to be clear and complete so that you can provide the information the professor wants. Tell what you can send and what you can't (and why) in this smooth and thorough order acknowledgment.

39. As sales director of MEDLINE, you must acknowledge the order request of Dr. John Anderson, president of the Sedgwick County Medical Society. He has ordered several of your on-line services for medical doctors in his county (see Problem 63, Orders, for background information).

Your MEDLINE service offers on-line computer information services to doctors to help them make accurate diagnoses, confirm them, or learn about specialized diseases outside their areas of expertise. Usually, they are useful to primary care physicians who need to refer patients to a specialist; in the process, the primary care physicians must determine which specialist to refer to. Also, medical specialists frequently work with one another; jointly they often must determine other specialists in other medical specialties to consult.

For example, a patient recently visited his family practice physician and complained of half of his face being flushed and red and the other half not so. Confronted with unknown symptoms, the family care specialist consulted MEDLINE and referred the patient to a neurologist who, in turn, consulted a nutritionist. The patient had eaten a certain food substance and it had caused an allergic reaction through a bilateral neurological disorder. Thus, technology linked with diagnostic skill resulted in accurate treatment for the patient.

Dr. Anderson wants three of your services: MEDNET–general, PEDNET, and OBGYNET. You can provide the MEDNET–general; in fact, you can have the Sedgwick County Medical Society on-line in three working days. But there are problems with the other two. The PEDNET (an on-line service in pediatrics) consists of two subdirectories—one in general pediatrics and the other in neuropediatrics. The cost of the general pediatric service is $1,000 per month; but for the other service, NEUROPEDNET, the cost is $500 per month, or $1,500 total per month for subscription service. You'll check with Dr. Anderson before you provide the service. He indicates he will pay $1,000 for PEDNET. You wonder, however, if he knows about the subdirectories.

In addition, the OBGYNET is missing two years of information, 1991–93. In the classifying and updating process completed about a month ago, certain files were lost. Your staff will need four weeks to retrieve them. You will add Sedgwick County Medical Society whenever the service is complete. In the meantime, you'll tell Dr. Anderson about the glitch and give him the opportunity to take alternate action if he so desires.

Prepare the acknowledgment order that will get the Sedgwick County Medical Society on-line and will determine the extent of the services wanted. You'll need to clear up the details about the vague and back orders to do so. As this is your first contact from Sedgwick County Medical Society, make sure your words reflect your sales and goodwill intent. Send the message to them through Internet.

ROUTINE INQUIRIES

40. You recently read about a company, Message Check, that prints checks for fund-raising projects. Priscilla Beard, the president and founder, was a fund-raiser for several Seattle-area nonprofit organizations including the symphony, ballet, and the arts center. Her idea to raise money with a product that would be useful to many people brought her into the check printing business. By cutting out the bank, she is able to raise money for nonprofits. In addition, the checks promote the worthiness or activities of the organiza-

tion. She's been successful with checks designed for Greenpeace, Mothers Against Drunk Drivers, and Vietnam Veterans.

You think this idea would be a great success on your campus. Not only might current students use these checks, but alumni would use them, too.

Write a letter to Mrs. Beard inquiring about projected revenue estimates and the initial costs for designing two styles with your school's logo. Be sure to give her demographics about your student body. In addition to size, age, and gender statistics, try to give her an accurate life-style picture of students. Do they live in dorms, apartments, or at home? Do they commute or live on campus? Do they work in addition to going to school? This kind of data will help her project a more accurate estimate of anticipated revenues. Also, you think you need to have two styles designed—one style that's very traditional and one that's more contemporary with space to promote current student concerns such as [name two concerns popular now on your campus].

Ask her to fax you her response by the first of the month so you can propose the idea at a meeting on the 10 complete with supporting detail.

41. As Marina Munson, owner and president of Diversified Talent in Los Angeles, you provide actors and actresses to companies for their print and video advertising. As more and more of your client base enter global markets, they are asking for people they use in videos to speak languages in addition to English. While you feel you can do a good job for your current talent pool, you are reluctant to dilute it with others solely because they speak a second language. And since a high percentage of your current talent is college graduates, you believe training them may be your best bet to meet your current demands for bilingual talent.

Interestingly, the majority of your clients are reaching out to Japanese markets, asking for actors and actresses that speak Japanese. For the last several years, you've been using a CD-ROM system at home with a dictionary that will pronounce words. And you've recently learned that BayWare brought out an interactive program called Power Japanese. Like the dictionary you've used, this program combines text and sound to teach the basics of Japanese. Supposedly, in just two months a user can pick up enough of the language to understand a few hundred words and conduct simple conversations.

While you think the $175 list price is reasonable, you want evidence it works since you'll be asking your people to spend two months in training. In your letter of inquiry, ask at least three questions that will help you decide whether it would be appropriate for your talent. You might want to know if it is self-paced, what kind of feedback a user gets, and whether the vocabulary taught is suitable for the businesses your clients run. You could ask for copies of reviews or letters of recommendations from satisfied users. And you'll want to know about the expertise or qualifications of the creator of the program. Of course, since you'll be buying at least half a dozen of these, do ask about discounts for volume pricing.

42. You recently learned about a travel program just for students called the National Collegiate Travel Club. For $50 you and your parents are entitled to discounts on airlines and car rentals. While the traveling to and from school at the beginning and end of semesters and holidays is easy to plan, other unexpected needs for students to travel often come up. Some of the needs you and your friends have had concerned sick parents or grandparents, homesickness, needed breaks, and special events. Often the sky-high prices prohibit travel or make it a financial hardship. While the Collegiate Travel Club provides discount coupons and special rates, you want to know a bit more about it before signing up. Send your questions to Robert Edwards, regional manager, at CSBK34D@ prodigy.com.

    In addition to asking questions about which airlines are included, find out whether there are any blackout dates. Asking for sample fares is a good idea, too. Find out if the tickets are reserved in advance or if you are on some type of standby status. Also, you'll want to know if your whole family is eligible. Can your parents use it for other trips as well as making trips to campus to see you perform in a [play, recital, sports event, or special program]? You know that many of your friends have had trouble renting cars because they weren't 25. So ask what age you have to be to rent a car in the club. Feel free to ask any other questions you think would be important to you or add value to the club. Some of these might include a newsletter, an on-line reservation service, e-mail responses, fax-on-demand flight information, an electronic bulletin board service, and an 800 number. Write the questions to elicit the exact information that will help you make a decision on whether to sign up.

43. Recently you read a story in *The Wall Street Journal* about companies offering fax-on-demand services, and you think it might work for your company—a small family-owned music store. As prices drop on fax machines and fax modems, their use will explode. So you think your timing for such a service is perfect. The service can operate a couple of ways. Users could call your computer-based message system and respond to a series of prompts by touching keys on their telephone. They could key in code numbers and their fax number; then your system would almost instantaneously fax the material they requested. The material could be product information, price lists, regulations, etc. It would allow you to extend the hours of your business, making you more competitive with larger stores and providing your customers with additional service. Of course, they could send orders by fax as well. It could also work by communicating fax to fax. Some claim this fax-on-demand service will be the marketing tool of the future.

    One provider company mentioned in the article was Brooktrout Technology, Inc., in Needham, Massachusetts. Write to Mike McLaughlin, vice president of sales and marketing, inquiring about the product. Ask at least three questions, providing sufficient detail where needed. You need to know about costs, equipment needed, and levels of service and technical support available.

44. As Butch Trevor, owner and buyer for Trevor Hardware in Moline, Illinois, you saw a story in the local paper on Sunday about a new gadget that saves money by cutting voltage. It is designed primarily for appliances such as refrigerators, freezers, or window air conditioners that run constantly and have both peak and normal operating levels. When unneeded electricity enters the appliance, it turns to heat and is lost. But one still pays for the lost electricity.

    This new gadget senses the electrical needs of the appliance and delivers only that amount, saving on energy consumption and cost of operating the appliance. In most cases the appliance will also be quieter. Additionally, it protects against damaging electrical surges. You think your conservation-minded customers would really appreciate this gadget.

    However, before ordering these plugs you'd like to ask about availability, warranty, and price along with other concerns you have. Write a letter of inquiry to GreenPlugs in Boulder, Colorado.

45. As a buyer for Sam's, a warehouse discount business, you've recently received requests for hair straighteners. And you've noticed that several companies are promoting new relaxers. Supposedly the new products are easy to use and less damaging on hair than earlier products in this category. Furthermore, some of the milder forms can be used for children and teenagers. You're certain a big part of this demand is the trend toward short, straight hair. Not only do singer Toni Braxton and members of the rap group Salt-N-Pepa sport straight hair, but television celebrity Oprah Winfrey does, too.

    Since you've never carried this type of product, you want to know more about it, so you decide to send an inquiry to several companies' general managers. Ask at least three questions you need answered to make a good decision on whether to carry the product. In addition to asking about the safety, you'll want to know about the market size in your area since this product might have the potential to bring in new customers. You've heard that users tend to touch up every six to eight weeks, indicating that perhaps the product is a long-term repeat purchase. Perhaps you'll want to know about volume pricing discounts and sales estimates or market share for that company in your area. Maybe the demographics of the potential buyers would interest you. As an astute businessperson, you're probably interested in the company's plans for advertising the product in your area.

    Create a form letter and use the mail merge feature to send the letter to Alberto-Culver, Softsheen Products, Johnson Products Co., and Revlon Group, Inc.

46. "Tragic, but interesting!" you think as you muse the

current statistics you will soon distribute to your member organizations. As executive director of the Network of Employers for Traffic Safety, you are responsible for attending to the safety interest of the 1,200 members you represent. This you do through statistical summaries, newsletters, and special reports that relate to all phases of traffic safety management—detection, prevention, control, and such.

The tragic-but-interesting thought in your mind at present concerns the statistics on your computer screen. The spreadsheet report compiled by your staff shows that moving vehicle (auto, truck, bus, etc.) crashes were the leading cause of on-the-job deaths last year. More specifically, these crashes cost employers $55 billion last year in lost work time, medical expenses, and legal bills. You predict that the figure will increase this year unless something is done to control the moving vehicle losses. That the loss figure is correct you don't doubt, but what companies are doing to control losses stimulates your administrative thinking.

As you reflect on the problem, you recall some isolated cases that members have shared with you in your many trips to numerous states and countries. For example, you remember that several firms have set up precautionary measures: Roadway Express has its "Million Mile Challenge," an interactive video with 40 road scenarios; Commonwealth Electric drivers attend skid school; Art Van Furniture in Michigan has drivers take "dedicated runs" to keep them familiar with routes and traffic patterns; and Melody Foods, a Detroit dairy company, takes vehicles away from salespeople who have poor safety records and offers cash and prizes to drivers with no accidents.

On the other hand, you know that companies also place equipment on cars and trucks to control driving practices. Leaseway Transportation (Cleveland) puts computers in trucks to monitor speed, hours driven, and hard braking. Supervisors then review a log from the computer. Roadway Express puts speed cars in trucks to keep them below 60 miles per hour. These bits and pieces of prevention exist, but you wonder how widespread such practices are among your members. Your first thought is to conduct a formal survey to determine company traffic control practices. As you ponder the situation further, however, you determine that a more indirect method would be more prudent before you conduct the survey—one that would allow you to experiment with questions (their wording, content, sequence, etc.) before you ask them formally in a questionnaire.

Thus, you decide to write to 10 of the largest firms you represent (excluding the ones already mentioned) to assess the extent of their reactive and/or proactive practices regarding driving control. It's likely that the format and responses you get will provide the substance and structure of a questionnaire you will distribute to all firms later as the project develops. For now, you will collect ideas from a select few—the largest among the membership.

As you plan the letter, you decide that a direct approach is best in this inquiry situation—that is, you will begin immediately with an important question. Then you give a concise explanation of your need for the information. This explanation could also cover other items that relate to the situations as well. Thereafter, you will ask other groups of questions that will make one writing effort do the job.

What topics will you need in your questions? Actual driving losses; costs of them broken down by medical, legal, and other categories of expenses; programs developed to deal with the issue; insurance rates; and reward systems for safe driving are among the broad areas that cross your mind. No doubt there are others that will need to be covered. Also, you will need to provide explanations where appropriate to get specific answers to questions. These explanations will need to be skillfully interwoven with the questions you construct.

Prepare a model letter that you will send to the 10 largest members in your association. Select a real company to use in the inside address of the letter. (You may refer to Chapter 19 for sources from which you may select a real-life company.)

47. Your assignment for today is to switch roles with Kristine Strifler, general manager of the Lakeview Country Club. At its monthly meeting on Wednesday, the board accepted the resignation of Jim Risser, the tennis professional who had served Lakeview faithfully and diligently for the last seven years. It was Jim's feeling that he needed to move to the next level in his career ladder—as the head tennis pro at a larger club. The parting of the ways was friendly and professional.

With Jim's anticipated leaving, the board has charged you, as club manager, to begin the search for a replacement. Although the tennis committee of the board will do the interviewing and selecting, it is your job to begin the advertising process to alert the market about the job opening. It is now May 31, and Jim will see the tennis program through the summer months, leaving officially on August 31. Thus, you have a three-month window in which to fill the position so that your tennis program will have continuity from the summer to the fall programs.

In an effort to broadcast the word in a general way to the employment market, you plan to design a classified ad to run in *Tennis Pro,* a monthly trade magazine for tennis professionals. But you think this strategy needs to be preceded by a letter to selected, established professionals who could help you identify the critical factors of success for a practicing club professional. If you could identify a list of core essentials for the job, you could use the list to word your broadcast advertising, to assess each applicant's credentials, to serve as a guide in interviewing candidates, to become the basis of a job description for the position, and to serve as performance criteria against which to assess actual behavior with expected behavior. Thus, you decide to write a model letter that will be sent individually to respected tennis professionals whose names have been passed along to you through the tennis professional informal network.

In the letter, you will ask what the criteria are for success as a tennis professional at a private club. But you cannot ask the question generically, lest you get a massive list of all types of factors and characteristics. Thus, you will need to ask specific questions about pro tour experience, certifications, teaching experience, pro shop operations, and management skills. Also, leadership skills, personality factors, and such would certainly be a part of the ideal tennis professional. Asking such questions is one thing, but providing explanations about the uniqueness of Lakeview is another. Both questions and explanations of them will be needed so that you will receive the specific type of information you need to determine the predictors of success at Lakeview Country Club.

Prepare this model inquiry letter to be sent to nine tennis pro elites you have identified. Make sure it "serves" your purpose well.

48. Today's role projects you into the work of human resource manager at Electronic Data Systems (EDS). Each year EDS requires its managers to do 40 hours of public service for the local and/or professional communities. Since the company began the public service policy several years ago, you have worked with school districts in their human resource needs, started an adopt-a-school program for the company, and established equitable compensation systems in several municipal governments in the area.

This year, however, you want to take a different direction in the public service you provide. About a month ago, you decided that giving speeches to various groups would offer you the best opportunity to work with the general citizens and to tap into your 20 years of experience in human resources work. Fortunately, EDS prepares a speakers' directory each year and distributes it throughout its service areas. You turned in the topic "Workplace Diversity: 2005" several weeks ago to be published in the directory. Now you must prepare the speech for those who might request it—civic groups, university professional societies, professional associations, and such. Since you turned in the topic for directory printing, you've been surveying the literature and making notes of random ideas you've had. It's your hope to delve into the legal, social, and political forces that have created diversity presently and to make projections for the next 10 years.

Today's "Labor Letter" of *The Wall Street Journal* catches your eye with an item mentioned in it. The Hanigan Consulting Group of New York recently conducted a study of minority college hires and found that nonwhites received an average of three job offers compared to two for whites as well as higher average starting salaries. This type of information is what you could use in your speech. So you decide to write to the Hanigan Group to inquire further about the findings.

The reasons the nonwhites receive more offers and better salaries than the whites are what you truly want to know from Hanigan. Do nonwhites try harder? Do they prepare themselves differently? If so, what differences exist—in curriculum preparations, in part-time jobs, and in other areas?

Perhaps, too, there might be special support groups that offer employment services to nonwhites. If they do, who are they and what do they provide? Something must account for the differences in salary and job offers; so this information will make good content for the projection part of your speech. You'd like a complete copy of the report if they would send one.

Write a direct-inquiry letter to the Hanigan Consulting Group, 565 Lexington Avenue, New York 07651, that will get you the items you want to make your speech a current and substantive one whenever you are called upon to give it.

49. As president of Office Essentials, a large office furniture supplier in Chicago, you are constantly on the alert looking for ways to satisfy the needs of your business, government, and industrial customers by adding to your line of quality furniture products. Of course, you are interested as well in expanding your profit margin—a measure of how well you satisfy market needs.

Today, a brochure you receive from Going Green, a small manufacturer in Vermont that offers ecofurniture, catches your eye. Ecofurniture is a specialized type of furniture made from recycled wood, plastics, or paper. Usually, the finishes on the products are water-based, not chemical or resin-based. Often, resin-based finishes produce harmful gases and cause allergy and asthma reactions in people who are sensitive to such allergens.

You know that many of your institutional buyers are quite concerned about workplace safety, air quality, and preserving the environment. Thus, to provide these elements, many have begun ecological programs such as paper/container recycling, carpooling, and the like. It's your feeling that employees and others might see the results of their ecological efforts if they can see products that are ecologically produced.

Accordingly, you decide to try to find out more about ecofurniture's use in the modern office. The brochure you received emphasized furniture for the home. As an example, the brochure cites papier-mâché-like children's furniture, bookshelves/coffee tables of recycled wood from buildings scheduled for demolition, and mattresses filled with recycled, chemically free plastics from 520 one-and-one-half-liter bottles. But you wonder whether products for the office are available. Thus, you believe a direct-inquiry letter will give you the information you want to consider adding the products to your product mix.

In the letter, you will begin directly by asking about what products the company has for the institutional (business, government, etc.) market. You assume that Going Green does produce such products because the brochure mentioned ecofurniture for the home "and office." It did not mention anything more about the office, however; thus, you infer that the promotional material you received was aimed at the retail segment of the market and not the institutional.

Also, you will want to inquire about prices, quantity discounts, and advertising allowances offered by the seller. Then, too, there is the issue of other vendors' success with carrying the line. You'll want names of businesses to contact, and how much success the ecofurniture has had in the market thus far by number of suppliers, sales, and such. You'd like an estimate of future demand, too. These points and perhaps others you will need to cover in your inquiry letter. As you envision the inquiry, it will alternate questions with explanations so that you can get specific information.

Write the letter to Going Green, Inc., 2011 North Porter Colchester, VT. Your letter will need to be direct and complete so that one writing effort will do the job.

50. When you graduated from college five years ago, you did what other top-ranking graduates were doing. You took a job with a large, global company as a management trainee. After a successful nine-month stint in training at Vaught Industries, you landed an "assistant to" position with the company. And now, two years later, you are busily involved in a junior manager's position with excellent opportunities for career advancement to senior and top management.

Although you have worked diligently, your career, as you see it, will still involve labor that far exceeds the rewards. Thus, your career options include staying with the large corporation, looking for transfers to other large firms, or finding a position with a smaller, nonpublic firm that has growth opportunities and that will offer a possible share of the company's ownership.

You've thought about this lost option frequently. Several of your friends at other companies have chosen it with good success. Thus, the following ad catches your eye as you scan the pages of this month's *Corporate Executive,* a magazine for leaders of $1 billion-plus sales companies.

Tired of working for "the same company"? Try us. We're a growing firm. And we need executive talent. Competitive salary with long-term ownership opportunity in equity—stock options, bonuses for performance, accelerated vesting, and equity stakes available based on performance goals for company and individual. Creative freedom, less bureaucracy, and feeling of being part of a team. For more information write Box 4475, Burr Ridge Station, Chicago, or send letter of interest and résumé.

This opportunity could very well provide a new spark and a new direction for your career path—one that might be more profitable in the long run. The odds of your being able to qualify for stock ownership options with your present company are quite remote because such a fringe benefit is reserved for only the elite of top management. Thus, the idea of reaping more directly the fruits of your labor appeals to you.

But you will need more specific information and details before you decide to apply. You know, for instance, that most young (not necessarily small) businesses need capital; so a huge equity package may be a sign of a deep problem with financial status. Nevertheless, you decide to write to the company and to ask for more facts.

What should you include in the letter? First, you will need to ask about growth patterns of the company and its industry competitive niche. Also, there is the question about how much stock is available. And you'd like to know some details about how individual performance is related to vesting and equity opportunities. Moreover, you have basic questions about salary levels offered. Perhaps other ideas will emerge for you to ask as questions as you think more deeply about the issues involved.

Prepare the direct inquiry that will get you the details you need to properly assess this career option. If your letter is successful, you will use it to send to other companies to get similar facts.

51. Today's assignment projects you into the role of Kay T. Moore, executive vice president of marketing at Senseney, Inc. Your company produces cellular phones and accessories and distributes the products internationally through 450 salespeople.

Presently you are returning on the corporate jet from the annual national sales meeting, held for the past two days in Vail, Colorado. At the beginning of the meeting, you announced that sales were climbing to an all-time high and that enthusiasm was abundant throughout the entire organization.

Because of the growth of sales, most salespeople's commissions were also growing, thus creating momentum and a motivating climate for pay as an extrinsic work reward. Yet, you feel at this point that you must develop a compensation extra—to reward peak performance and to acknowledge the excellence that your star performers have achieved. As in most sales organizations, you have your nonquota people, although they are few; and you have your plateauers—those whose sales level off. You'd like to spark these people's efforts to move forward with their sales performances.

But what type of "extra" to design into the compensation package still has to be decided. In fact, you thought about the matter for several days and even checked out some of your thoughts with some key sales personnel at the annual meeting. You've considered cash bonuses, sabbaticals, and increased vacation; but none of these extras seem to fit the recognition features you'd like to achieve with the award.

As you browse through *Business Travel* on the jet, an ad catches your eye. It's from Travel World, a company offering luxury cruises in different parts of the world—the Caribbean, the Mediterranean, Alaska, Mexico, and such. As you think about it, your mind clicks—a cruise could very well be the way to link recognition with excellence in sales achievement. As the idea forms in your mind, you notice ads from several other travel agencies as well that emphasize cruises.

The next day as you are back in your headquarters office, you are even more convinced that a free cruise offered at the top 5 percent of your Senseney sales force would be an excellent way to recognize superior sales. But you must now collect the necessary details before you can complete the compensation idea.

You decide to write to three of the travel agencies to ask them about their cruise packages. (You will select three real-life agencies for this assignment.) Of course, you need information about costs, accommodations, and ports of call to be able to compare the cruises and to select the best one.

As this extra will be paid for by the company, you believe a one-week cruise would be best. The salesperson may be accompanied by a spouse, child, friend, and such, which the company will pay for. But you'll pay for only one. Thus, you will want to inquire about costs for additional family members, friends, etc.

Because cruises vary extensively by types of accommodations and other features, you will want to be specific in the questions you ask. Most of them will need explanations so that you can get definite answers. In addition to costs, accommodations, and destinations, you will want to inquire about possible corporate discounts, extensions to the package you will provide, and other details that will relate to your sales force.

Sit down now at your computer and rough out a routine inquiry letter that will give you the information you need to design the compensation extra for Senseney, Inc. Your final decision will be announced in a memo to the sales force after you collect and compare the information you receive. You will start with a question beginning and include other specific questions and explanations in the body of the letter.

Write a "smooth sailing" letter that will get the information you need about cruises as a compensation extra.

INQUIRIES ABOUT PEOPLE

52. As Leonard Johns, general manager of the Palm Springs Hilton, you have been busy reviewing several applications you've received for the front office manager position. You're primarily interested in someone who possesses good written, verbal, and interpersonal skills. Additionally, some work experience where the candidate has demonstrated reliability, honesty, and the willingness to learn new systems is valuable.

One applicant that interests you is Mary Adami.

Not only is she a college student near graduation, but she also is interested in working in hotel management when she graduates. She's willing to finish her last year's worth of credits by going part time since she believes a job in her field is worth it. Her college transcript shows she has taken courses in English composition and business communication. Furthermore, her school required a basic speech class, too. She also elected a course in speaking for business and the professions as one of her management electives. And in the interview she said she definitely plans to take the report writing class that will fill a writing proficiency requirement as well as an elective. You're impressed that she doesn't shy away from courses in writing and speaking; many of the applicants do. In fact, she was selected by her instructor to be a communication tutor, evaluating the work of others and further polishing her own skills. While this was the only experience she listed on her résumé, you believe it is in line with the requirements for the job.

Therefore, you decide to contact her business communication professor. While you fully expect the instructor to report that Mary is extremely good in business communication, you want to know more about how she performed as a tutor. Did she show up on time for meetings? Could the instructor depend on her to evaluate the students' work fairly? Even the work of her friends? How did she get along with the other tutors? Did she take any leadership roles? Was she able to relinquish them when it was more appropriate for others to lead? You'd also like the instructor's opinion on Mary's maturity and nature. Could she be lighthearted and good-natured with others while still being fair and serious in her role as a tutor? You'll try to ask open-ended questions that will allow the professor to answer the questions and provide supporting examples.

53. "Extraordinary!" This word clearly described the candidate you interviewed this morning for a systems analyst position. The candidate, Julie Smith, stands head and shoulders over everyone else in the candidate pool. In addition to having top grades, some work experience, and a superb summer internship experience, she's often stepped into leadership roles in her school. She served as president of a team that competed successfully in intercollegiate games, sweeping nearly all categories. Furthermore, she has served as an officer of the Data Processing Management Association's student chapter and is currently its president. While her résumé exudes strengths scholastically, you want to know more about her interpersonal skills and her self-initiative, so you decide to contact both her university and work references.

Ask questions of both references that will elicit responses to help you make the decision as to whether or not to offer her a position. Professors might have observed her interpersonal skills both in how she worked in groups on assigned projects as well as on the business team with a less clear objective. Was she able to work effectively in those situations? Ask them to elaborate through examples they know of firsthand. Also, ask them to cite examples of where she may have demonstrated some initiative. Perhaps there were times when she went beyond what was required or took a new perspective when sticking to a traditional one may have been safer. You're also interested in how she performed in the workplace. Did she get along with colleagues—superiors and subordinates as well as peers? Ask employers to cite examples that were typical of her normal level of interpersonal skills and initiative.

Since you want to extend the offer to her before other companies beat you to it, give the references many ways to reach you at EDS. In addition to your 800 phone number, you'll want to give them your fax number, cellular number, and your e-mail address. Of course, you can assure them that their remarks will be confidential since Julie has signed a waiver that prevents her from seeing their remarks. Ask for their response by a specific date so that you can give Julie an accurate estimate of when she may expect to hear from you.

54. As Clay Shelton, manager of the local MacTemps, you recently interviewed Sally Short for graphic designer assignments. Sally said she came to your firm because of its national reputation for specializing in computer-skilled personnel. In addition, she's learned through her instructors in the Blackhawk College Adult Education Program that you provide great work and high pay as well as offer long-term assignments. She knows that you offer the best benefits in the industry. But she's primarily interested in the flexibility the job provides.

Sally's résumé shows she has both training in PCs and work experience requiring creative expression. In addition to a college degree, Sally has taken courses through the local adult education programs on a variety of software applications. She's worked on both PCs and Macs with programs such as Corel, QuarkXpress, Freehand, Illustrator, and Canvas. While she has no formal professional experience, she has produced brochures for the floral shop where she has been working. In using Pagemaker and Photoshop with these brochures, she demonstrates an exceptional talent for layout and design. And she reports she's helped her husband prepare graphics for presentations and proposals.

Sally's enthusiasm for graphics work is extremely high. While she recognizes her lack of formal work experience, she displays a willingness and an ability to learn quickly. You think she'd be competent in most jobs your company has calls for, but you want to be assured that she works effectively on teams and is a good listener. Your clients want products, not solely artwork. She'll need to work under deadlines and effectively with others from various parts of organizations. While she presented herself extremely well in the interview, you'll check her references to assure you that she is someone you'd

like to have as part of the MacTemps team.

Contact Mrs. Sharon Garbett, an instructor at Blackhawk College, for information about Sally's team skills. Be sure to ask how well she met deadlines for class projects. Leave the door open for Mrs. Garbett to give you further examples that reflect the quality of her work. Also, ask Mrs. Garbett to explain the extent of hands-on experience Sally got with scanners in the Blackhawk program.

55. As Stephen Robbins, director of human resources for a large HMO in your area, you have been interviewing applicants for a human resources supervisor position. One applicant, Maria Perez, seems to fit the job description perfectly. Not only is she Spanish/English bilingual, but she's also been working in the university personnel department while completing courses toward her bachelor's degree in management. Over the years she's been involved in nearly all aspects of human resources including recruiting, testing, training, and affirmative action programs. While none of the memos to university employees have gone out under her signature, she had drafted many of them for audiences with various levels of education. Furthermore, she's minoring in Information Systems, taking advanced courses in statistics, computing, and communications.

In checking on her work references, be sure to ask which word processing and spreadsheet programs she had used on the job. Also, ask whether she's had any experience in interviewing, delivering orientation programs, and writing or updating job descriptions. If she has no direct experience, ask whether they think she has the ability to handle such tasks. Invite unsolicited comments on her ability to supervise others in human resources work.

In checking with her academic references, ask about performance in classes and about her attitude in general. Also, ask her professors to comment on her interpersonal skills, skills highly valued in this supervisory position. Of course, you'll be sure to ask them to comment on both her written and oral communication skills.

56. As Jason Wong, director of professional staffing at Intuit, you're interested in learning more about Lydia Jerome, an applicant for tax quality assurance analyst. Ms. Jerome has a unique background in the financial/accounting field. She has a degree in accounting from the state's most respected program, where she took several courses in tax preparation. Additionally, she's been teaching accounting courses at a local university. And she's worked at nationally known brokerages, passing the brokerage exam with ease on her first attempt. She was exceptionally good working with a full list of clients. Through her work she has gained skills in working several financial computer applications. And she is very interested in working with state-of-the-art software.

You'll write to her work references to learn about her competence and knowledge in individual and business taxes. Also, you want their opinion on her attention to quality. Was she a stickler for details? Was she willing to put in overtime to get jobs done right?

Her academic references and perhaps her colleagues at the university should be able to comment on her ability to write. Ask whether they think she'll be able to write clear, concise user manuals and on-line help. Ask whether they know of any experience she's had that supports their opinions. Also, invite comments on her general willingness to learn new things and her enthusiasm and attitude toward tax.

57. As manager of the human resources department at Prologic, a technical computer service provider, you are responsible for providing human resource services—compensation/benefits, employee relations, training/development, and such—to the 600 employees of the firm.

Your concern of the moment is the training activities you provide. You have always evaluated the instruction and other training you've offered primarily through trainee questionnaires that rated the instruction and relevance of the contents covered. Top management, however, wants to make sure the training dollar they approve is paying off. Thus, they have authorized a new position—that of assessment/appraisal of training.

When the executive team approved the position, you quickly began the search process because you definitely need the right person for your professional human resource group. Your classified ad in the larger newspapers in the region provided 12 résumés that you would consider as definite possibilities for the job. You have reviewed each of the 12 specifically and narrowed the selections to the top 3. Your number one choice is Melinda McMahan, and you decide to write her first reference, James Collier, before you interview her. Comments from Collier would guide you in the conduct of the interview.

As you see the work of the new specialist in assessment/appraisal of training, it involves curriculum development and a long-term appraisal of transfer of learning to the jobs of the organizations. Quite obviously, the work would require a person of high social skills because of the myriad of relationships in the job. More important, perhaps, is the technical proficiency needed for the assessment work. The successful applicant will need a solid foundation of statistics and curriculum design as they relate to the training function in industry.

Melinda has many of the qualities listed and annotated on her résumé. She majored in adult education at Carson University and taught for three years at Mojave Community College. During that time, she earned an educational administration certification from a local university. On the surface, you believe she has good educational knowledge. Her coursework reveals that she has had several statistics courses and,

of course, significant work in curriculum construction and assessment.

After teaching in the community college, she joined an independent school district as curriculum coordinator where she has worked for the past five years. Although she has excellent educational credentials, you wonder about her ability to transfer what she has done in public education to the world of work in the private sector. That and other questions about her you will ask in a personnel inquiry to James Collier, the president of the school board. She lists him as her first reference, and he's president of a large insurance company. He should be able to speak about her capabilities in the organizational world with significant authority.

Write the inquiry to Mr. Collier that will get you the information you need about Melinda. You'll interview her based on what Collier reports.

58. The classified ad you ran in *The Wall Street Journal* and in several metropolitan newspapers throughout a five-state region has generated 15 applications for your organizational development consultant's job. You have pruned the list to three, and the best candidate appears to be Joan D. Bruno. Before you proceed any further in the selection process, you ask Ms. Bruno to supply a list of references as she indicated on her résumé. She does so, and the first person on the list is Dr. Morris E. Massey. You will write to him about Ms. Bruno's qualifications. If you are impressed with the assessments, you will write similar letters to the other references listed to determine whether you should interview the candidate.

As owner/manager of Change Strategies, Inc., you began your consulting service as a one-person operation. After a distinguished 20-year career as a senior manager in corporate life, you decided to branch out on your own—and the results have proved higher than your wildest imagination. Presently, you have 10 consultants assisting you with various programs spread over several industries—electronics, petrochemicals, and financial services. Because your business continues to grow, you began the search for your 11th partner/problem solver—hence, the application and availability of Joan Bruno.

As you see the job of your 11th partner, it will demand more professionalism from the successful applicant than any of the others you've hired. Economic fluctuations, right-sizing, and such will demand the highest skills from your consultant representatives when they enter a client's firm to help it solve the myriad of business problems that exist—given the cultural, political, and economic milieu in which organizations compete to survive. Thus, the education, experience, and personal qualities of the person you select will need to be impeccable.

More specifically, the successful candidate will need to be well educated in the scientific approach to problem solving. Thus, a research orientation is essential to the job—one not only in orientation but in tangible results/applications as well. In addition, the candidate will need to have relevant experience on which to draw and to relate to clients' problems and needs. Even more important is proficiency in more than one language because of the global nature of business and cultural diversity in the work force. And perhaps most of all the successful applicant will need to have superb interpersonal skills to initiate and to maintain relationships with clients. Successful skills would also apply to the cohesion and operation of your OD team itself. Overall, the successful new hire will need all of the knowledge, skills, and abilities of an organizational problem solver—a keen mind, a depth and breadth of experience, and professional manners so that the consultant's message is both understood and accepted.

Ms. Bruno lists Dr. Morris E. Massey of Central State University as her first reference. After completing an undergraduate degree in industrial technology at Collins College, she began graduate work at Central State University and majored in Organizational and Industrial Psychology. During her master's work, she was a research assistant to Dr. Massey. You also notice that she lists three publications in human resource practitioner journals written with him. Her grades on both degrees were excellent. When she graduated, she joined a psychological testing firm where she worked for two years. After that, she worked for two large firms—one in training assessment for five years and the other in instructional development for five years. You can see the career progression in her job pattern, but later you'll want to verify her reasons for leaving her jobs. You can see perseverance, dedication, and adaptability in her background. But you'll need to check these out with Dr. Massey.

Write him about the education, experience, and personal qualities of Ms. Bruno. It's obvious that he is her mentor. You presently have five Ph.D.'s on your staff; so she'll need to be especially talented. Also, you wonder if she took any business courses in her training. She would need them to give perspective in her work since 80 percent of your clients are in the private sector. You will especially need to ask questions about interpersonal skills—writing/speaking ability, flexibility, likability, ethics, and such. Prepare the letter that will get the information you need before you proceed to the next step in the selection process.

59. Assume the role of vice president of sales for Doolin-Shaw, Inc., a medium-sized manufacturer of steel and vinyl siding for houses, buildings, and the like. Last week, your video productions specialist gave you notice that she intends to leave. Thus, you must find a replacement. You have advertised the job and interviewed several applicants. At the moment, you favor Clyda Pendarvis, who currently works in technical support at KAKE, the ABC affiliate in the greater Phoenix area. Ms. Pendarvis gives you her supervisor's name, Stephanie Vanatta, as a reference. She

says Vanatta knows about her job-hunting activities, and she has willingly agreed to serve as a reference.

Before you check out her job skills and performance, you will get a clear picture of the job that Clyda will perform. Then, you will write to Ms. Vanatta and ask questions that you hope will determine whether or not Clyda will be a good fit for the job.

The job of video production specialist, as you view it, entails conceiving, designing, taping, editing, and producing sales promotion videos of company products for sales representatives and Doolin-Shaw customers. Some videos will be custom designed for one account, particularly those that are large ones. Other videos will fit a number of situations and products and can be used repeatedly. The central part of the video specialist's job is to interact with representatives successfully to please customers. Technical competence is essential, but people skills are required as well. Because most all work performed is crisis specific to commission-hungry representatives, time management and fast turnaround are crucial. The job would be split with three-fourths time in sales promotion and one-fourth time in training support. Overall, you need someone who has a good balance of educational training, practical experience, pleasant personality attributes, and a good work ethic.

Ms. Pendarvis received a degree from Patterson College in radio, TV, film with a minor in business. Since graduation, she has worked as a wedding photographer as well as a freelance commercial artist. Both of these jobs led to her present position with the television station, where she has worked for five years in various phases of technical support. In the interview with her, you liked her affability and her goal-oriented behavior, characteristics that are often lacking among those in the creative professions.

With these job and background factors in mind, write to Ms. Stephanie Vanatta to get her opinion of Clyda Pendarvis's qualifications. Be complete and thorough in the questions you ask so that you can make a good employment decision.

60. You are the manager of the training and development department with a staff of 75 at Entergy. Recently you were authorized by the Executive and Compensation Committee to seek a new addition to your staff—a specialist in process consultation. The person selected for the work will need to have short-run skills and focus and long-term perspectives of organizational growth and design.

You and those on the ECC believe the structure of Entergy has changed over the years and will continue to do so. Workplace empowerment, participative techniques, self-directed work teams, and such have created a flatter, less hierarchical organization. And along with the flatter organization is an increased span of control for most managers. In many cases, it might be that subordinates and their peers can solve problems that bosses cannot mainly because subordinates are closer to the actual situation and its daily impact on operations. Thus, many organizations have used peer appraisals of work performance, but applications have successfully occurred in manufacturing and engineering units where there are project teams and units naturally assembled. The ECC believes that all employees at Entergy need to be trained in peer appraisal and feedback for its benefits to performance measures, planning, rewards, and organizational control.

The idea of peer appraisal is not without its problems, however. Isolated studies show that peers give all positive reviews when they know their feedback will be used directly for salary increases. Moreover, when employees are honest with one another, they tend to retaliate against others; thus, they destroy the very cohesiveness that is needed in small work groups. The result of all these problems is mistrust of management intentions and deliberate distortions of the appraisal feedback itself. Accordingly, the ECC instructs you specifically about the importance of the position staffing: "We don't need to make selection and staffing errors in the job. We're talking about a cultural change in Entergy. And we'll need someone who will see this thing through for at least two to three years."

After receiving the go-ahead from the ECC on the position, you called several "hired gun" process consultants to determine key criteria for the job. You decided not to bring in part-time consultants because of the long-term nature of the job. With these relevant criteria, you developed with your own training and development staff leaders a job ad that you broadcast throughout the professional market in newspapers, trade magazines, and releases to several private personnel firms. This effort drew 31 applicants and résumés. You pruned the list to nine initially. And then you rank-ordered the nine candidates. From the list, you have interviewed the top three and all have

been impressive. The most impressive is Donald Mounce.

Mounce has a varied background in education and in experience. He received a counselor education degree from St. Louis University and upon graduation accepted a job as school counselor at Coral Gables ISD High School. He kept the job for three years but left to return to the University of Miami to complete his master's degree, which he began during night school, in educational assessment. With his graduate degree completed, he joined Marco, Inc., as a staff member in its measurement and assessment group. He stayed in the job for five years but left in good graces for a higher paying job with C & G Consultants. Over the past four years, he has worked in performance appraisal and evaluation, being assigned to a number of large company clients and conducting stand-up training. In addition, he's an army reservist assigned to a mental health unit that is responsible for combat rehabilitation. He appears to have good credentials for the job.

The work of the new process consultant will involve continuous assessment and professional diagnosis. Largely, the person selected for the job will design and implement the peer appraisal concept. Thus, the job will need formal training and informal follow-up, conceptual design, small group reinforcement, development of sensitivity, and the ability to adjust and adapt throughout the program's implementation. Moreover, the job will require a person of high interpersonal competence to relate to the different personalities in your workplace.

Mounce lists Dr. Walter Jack Duncan at C & G Consultants, his senior manager, as his first reference. Write to Dr. Duncan about Donald's professional and personal qualities. Ask pertinent questions so that you can evaluate his qualifications for the work of process consultant at Entergy.

Indirectness in Bad-News Letters

Upon completing this chapter, you will be able to write indirect responses to convey bad news. To reach this goal, you should be able to

1 Determine which situations require using the indirect order for the most effective response.

2 Use tact and courtesy in refusals of requests.

3 Write adjustment refusals that minimize the negative and overcome bad impressions.

4 Compose tactful yet clear credit-refusal letters that foster goodwill.

▶ to Refused Request Letters

To introduce yourself to the refused request letter, assume again the role of assistant to the Pinnacle vice president. Today your boss assigned you the task of responding to a request letter from the local chapter of the National Association of Peace Officers. This worthy organization has asked Pinnacle to contribute to a scholarship fund for certain needy children.

The request letter is very persuasive. It points out that the scholarship fund is terribly short. As a result, the association is not able to take care of all the needy children. Many of them are the children of officers who were killed in the line of duty. You have been moved by the letter, and you would like to comply. But you cannot.

You cannot contribute now because Pinnacle policy does not permit it. Even though you do not like the effects of the policy in this case, you think the policy is good. Each year Pinnacle earmarks a fixed amount—all it can stand—for contributions. Then it doles out this amount to the causes that a committee of its executives considers the most worthy. Unfortunately, all the money earmarked for this year has been given away. You will have to say no to the request, at least for now. You can offer to consider the association's cause next year.

Your letter must now report the bad news, though it can hold out hope for the future. Because you like the association and because you want it to like Pinnacle, you will try to handle the situation delicately. The task will require your best strategy and your best writing skills. ■

SITUATIONS REQUIRING INDIRECTNESS

As explained in Chapter 5, when the main message of a letter is bad news, you should usually write in the indirect order. The indirect order is especially effective when you must say no or convey other disappointing news. The main reason for this approach is that negative messages are received more positively when an explanation precedes them. An explanation may even convince the reader that the writer's position is correct. In addition, an explanation cushions the shock of bad news. Not cushioning the shock makes the letter unnecessarily harsh, and harshness destroys goodwill.

• Usually bad-news letters should be in the indirect order.

You may want to use directness in some bad-news situations. If, for example, you think that your negative answer will be accepted routinely, you might choose directness. You also might choose directness if you know your reader well and feel that he or she will appreciate frankness. And you might choose directness anytime you are not concerned about goodwill. But such instances are not the rule. Usually you would be wise to use indirectness in refusals.

• There are exceptions, as when the bad news is routine or when the reader prefers frankness.

The following pages analyze some common letter situations that are usually best handled in the indirect order. As in the preceding chapter, the first situation is a common one—the refusal of a request. We cover it in detail. Then we cover two other common letter types: the refusal of a request for adjustment and the refusal of credit. Since handling these two situations is similar to the handling of the first one, we cover them briefly. The focus here is on special considerations involving each type. We keep repetition to a minimum.

• Following are typical letter situations calling for the indirect order.

REFUSED REQUEST

Refusal of a request is definitely a bad-news message. Your reader has asked you for something, and you must say no. How bad the news is varies from case to case. Even so, it is hard to imagine a refusal that is good news. Because the news is bad, you should usually write the request refusal in the indirect order.

• Refusing a request calls for the indirect order.

Your reason for refusing indirectly has been mentioned, but its importance warrants repeating it. In the refusal letter you have two goals. The main one is to say no. The other is to maintain goodwill. You could achieve the first goal by simply saying no—plainly and directly. Maintaining goodwill, however, requires more. It requires that you convince your reader that the no answer is fair and reasonable. If you began with the no answer, you would put your reader in an unhappy frame of mind. Then the reader would not be in the mood to read your explanation. Your best strategy is to explain or justify first. From your explanation or justification, you can move logically to your refusal.

- In refusals you have two goals: (1) to refuse, and (2) to maintain goodwill. The first goal alone would be easy, but the second goal makes both goals hard.

Developing the Strategy

- Begin the letter by thinking through the situation. Look for the best explanation.

In deciding on what explanation to use, you should think through the facts of the case. First, you should consider why you are refusing. Then, assuming that your reasons are just, you should try to find the best way of convincing your reader. In doing this, you might well place yourself in your reader's shoes. Try to imagine how the explanation will be received. What comes out of this thinking is the strategy you should use in your letter.

- Do not hide behind company policy. Justify it.

Sometimes you must refuse because of company policy. When this is the case, you should be careful how you explain the refusal. Do not just say that you are refusing because it is company policy to do so. Instead, justify the policy. Explain its fairness to all concerned. For example, take a retailer's policy of refusing to return goods bought on sale. This policy clearly protects the retailer. But close inspection shows that it also benefits the customer. Only by cutting the costs of returns can the retailer give the customer the low sale price. Thus, the policy works to the benefit of both the customer and the retailer. Refusals based on that policy should say so.

- When the reader is clearly wrong, appeal to a sense of fair play.

Sometimes you must refuse simply because the facts of the case justify a refusal. When those facts show that you are right and the reader is wrong, your goodwill goal is hard to reach. In such cases, you can use little you-viewpoint reasoning. Probably the best course is to review the facts of the case, taking care not to accuse or insult, and to appeal to the reader's sense of fair play.

There are other refusal problems—too many to cover in this brief review. Your procedure for each of these problems should be the same. You should study the facts of the one case and develop the strategy that best fits those facts. Then you should present that strategy in a letter following this general pattern:

- This is the letter plan you should follow.

- Begin with words that indicate response to the request, are neutral as to the answer, and set up the strategy.

- Present your justification or explanation, using positive language and you-viewpoint.

- Refuse clearly and positively, including a counterproposal or compromise when appropriate.

- End with an adapted goodwill comment.

Setting Up the Strategy in the Opening

- Do not begin explaining abruptly.

Having developed your strategy, you should put it into letter form. In general, your plan should be to explain before refusing. But you must be careful. You cannot just blurt out the explanation. Such directness would be just as awkward as beginning with the refusal.

- The opening should (1) be on subject, (2) be neutral, and (3) set up the explanation.

Instead, you should begin indirectly with words that meet three requirements. First, they should clearly indicate that you are responding to the request. Second, they should be neutral. By *neutral* we mean that they imply neither no nor yes—that they should not give away the answer. Third, they should set up the strategy of your letter.

How these requirements should be met is best explained through illustration. First, take the case described at the beginning of this chapter—refusing an association's request for a donation. The following opening meets this case's requirements well:

Your organization is doing a commendable job of educating its needy children. It deserves the help of those who are in a position to give it.

The beginning, on-subject comment clearly marks the letter as a response to the inquiry. It implies neither a yes nor a no answer. The statement "It deserves the help of those who are in a position to give it" sets up the explanation, which will point out that the company cannot help. Also, it puts the reader in an agreeable or open frame of mind—ready to accept the explanations that follow.

Presenting the Reasoning

The reasoning that justifies your refusal should flow logically from your opening. After all, your opening was designed to set up that reasoning. Of course, you should present the reasoning convincingly.

To do this, you should use the writing techniques that help in persuasion. You should choose your words carefully, taking care to avoid the negative ones. You should use the you-viewpoint. In particular, you should use emphasis techniques. Play up the bright parts of your message, and play down the gloomy parts. In general, you should use all your writing skills in your effort to sell the reader on your reasoning.

- The reasoning that supports the refusal comes next.

- Handle this part skillfully. Use emphasis, you-viewpoint, positive wording.

Positively Handling the Refusal

Your handling of the refusal follows logically from your reasoning. If you have built the groundwork of explanation and fact convincingly, the refusal comes as a logical conclusion and as no surprise. If you have done your job well, your reader may even support the refusal. Even so, because the refusal is the most negative part of your message, you should not give it too much emphasis. You should state it quickly, clearly, and positively. You should keep it away from positions of emphasis, such as paragraph endings.

To state the refusal quickly, you should use as few words as possible. Laboring the refusal for three or four sentences when a single clause would do gives it too much emphasis.

To state the refusal clearly, you should make certain that the reader has no doubt about your answer. In the effort to be positive, writers sometimes become evasive and unclear. Take, for example, a writer who attempts to show that the facts of the case justify the company policy on which a refusal is based. Such words as "these facts clearly support our policy of . . ." would not communicate a clear refusal to some people. Another example is that of a writer who follows justifying explanation with a compromise offer. In this case, such words as "it would be better if . . .". would make for a vague refusal.

To state the refusal positively, you should study carefully the effects of your words. Such harsh words as *I refuse, will not,* and *cannot* stand out. So do such timeworn apologies as "I deeply regret to inform you . . ." and "I am sorry to say . . .". You can usually phrase your refusal in terms of a positive statement of policy. For example, instead of writing "your insurance does not cover damage to buildings not connected to the house," write "your insurance covers damage to the house only." Or instead of writing "We must refuse," a wholesaler could deny a discount by writing "We can grant discounts only when . . .". In some cases, your job may be to educate the reader. Not only will this be your explanation for the refusal, it will also build goodwill.

If you can make a compromise, you can use it to include your refusal. That is, by saying what you can do, you can imply clearly what you cannot do. For example, if you write "The best we can do is . . ." you make it clear that you cannot do what the reader has requested. Yet you do this in the most positive way that the situation will permit.

- The refusal should flow logically from the reasoning. Do not emphasize it.

- State the refusal quickly,

- clearly, and

- positively.

- If you can compromise, let what you can do imply what you cannot do.

Writing letters the old-fashioned way can be wasteful and inefficient. Today's progressive business correspondents enjoy the advantages of electronic word processing.

Closing with Goodwill

- End with a pleasant off-subject comment.

Even a skillfully handled refusal is the most negative part of your message. As the news is disappointing, it is likely to put your reader in an unhappy frame of mind. That frame of mind works against your goodwill goal. To reach your goodwill goal, you must shift your reader's thoughts to pleasanter matters.

- Adapt the close to the one case.

The best closing subject matter depends on the facts of the case, but it should be positive talk that fits the one situation. For example, if your refusal involves a counterproposal, you could say more about the counterproposal. Or you could make some friendly remark about the subject of the request as long as it does not remind the reader of the bad news. In fact, your closing subject matter could be almost any friendly remark that would be appropriate if you were handling the case face to face. The major requirement is that your ending words have a goodwill effect.

- Avoid ending with the old, negative apologies.

Ruled out are the timeworn, negative apologies. "Again, may I say that I regret that we must refuse" is typical of these. Also ruled out are the equally timeworn appeals for understanding, such as "I sincerely hope that you understand why we must make this decision." Such words emphasize the bad news.

Contrasting Refusals

The advantage of the indirect order in refusal letters is evident from the following contrasting examples. Both refuse clearly. But only the letter that uses the indirect order gains reader goodwill.

Harshness in the Direct Refusal. The first example states the bad news right away. This blunt treatment puts the reader in a bad frame of mind. The result is that the reader is less likely to accept the explanation that follows. The explanation is clear, but note the unnecessary use of negative words (*exhausted, regret, cannot consider*). Note also how the closing words leave the reader with a strong reminder of the bad news.

- This bad letter is harsh because of its directness.

Dear Ms. Cangelosi:

We regret to inform you that we cannot grant your request for a donation to the association's scholarship fund.

CASE ILLUSTRATION Refused Request Letters. (Refusing a Request for Letter Examples)

Tact and strategy mark this refusal, in which an office manager turns down a textbook author's request. The author has asked for model letters that can be used as examples in a correspondence guidebook. The office manager reasons that complying with this request would take more time than should be expected.

October 3, 1996

Dr. Ruth A. Howard
College of Business
Dorman University
1901 Finny Street
Calgary, Alberta T2M 2Y9

Dear Dr. Howard:

On-subject beginning— ties in with request ⎯ Your <u>Correspondence Guidebook</u> described in your September 21 letter should be a really practical aid to the business executive.

Sets up explanation

You-viewpoint explanation ⎯ The practical value of the book, as I see it, depends largely on the quality of its illustrations. Your book demands illustrations that meet all the criteria of good correspondence. But getting the quality of illustration you need will require careful checking by someone who knows good writing, and going through the 40,000 letters in our files will take considerable time and skill. For this reason, I am sure you will understand why the best we can do is to make our files open to you or your staff. We would, of course, be happy to provide working space for you, and we assure you our very best cooperation. If you wish to use our files in this way, please let us know.

Refusal logically flows from explanation

Note positive wording of refusal

Goodwill close— off subject and pleasant ⎯ Please let us know, also, if we can help you further. We look forward to seeing the book.

Sincerely,

Raphael E. Pattillo

Raphael E. Pattillo
Office Manager

ced

334 N. Hampton St.
Stanley, NY 14561
716-773-4422
FAX 716-773-4416

This example shows good strategy in turning down a request to speak at a convention.

WILKERSON ASSOCIATES
Consultants to Management

January 20, 1996

Mr. Thelbert H. Gooch
Executive Director
National Association of Administrators
7112 Avondale Road
Phoenix, AZ 85017

Dear Mr. Gooch:

On-subject beginning—compliment gains reader's favor

Your January 13 invitation to address the National Association of Administrators is a most distinct honor to me personally. I am well aware of the high quality of NAA's membership.

Sets up explanation

Offer of alternative shows concern—builds goodwill

Presenting a major paper to this quality group deserves a thorough and competent effort. Obviously, such an effort requires time. Because my time is fully committed to a writing project for the months ahead, I must suggest that you get someone who has the time to do the job right. May I recommend Ms. Paula Perkins of my staff? Paula is an outstanding speaker and an expert on the subject of women's progress in management.

Reasonable, convincing explanation

Goodwill close—adapted to this one case

If I can help you further in your efforts to get speakers, please write me again. I wish you good luck with the program.

Sincerely,

Forrest Y. Wilkerson

Forrest Y. Wilkerson
President

FYW:et

67800 W. Ninovh St. • Neenah, WI 54956 • 608-989-7865 • FAX: 608-989-7661 • Forrest@wa.com

On Controlling Anger in Letters: Some Words of Advice from Abraham Lincoln

An officer in the field had blundered badly, and Secretary of War Stanton was furious. "I feel that I must give this man a piece of my mind," he said to President Lincoln. "By all means, do so," said Lincoln. "Write him now while it's fresh on your mind. Make the words sting. Cut him up." Thus encouraged, Stanton wrote the letter, a masterpiece of angry words. He then pridefully took his letter to Lincoln.

After reading the letter, the president responded. "This is a good one," he said. "Now tear it up. You have freed your mind on the subject, and that is all that's necessary. You never want to send such letters. I never do."

So many requests for contributions are made of us that we have found it necessary to budget a definite amount each year for this purpose. Our budgeted funds for this year have been exhausted, so we simply cannot consider additional requests. However, we will be able to consider your request next year.

We deeply regret our inability to help you now and trust that you understand our position.

Sincerely,

Tact and Courtesy in an Indirect Refusal.   The second example skillfully handles the negative message. Its opening words are on subject and neutral. They set up the explanation that follows. The clear and logical explanation ties in with the opening. Using no negative words, the explanation leads smoothly to the refusal. Note that the refusal is also handled without negative words, and yet is clear. Saying "the best we can do is . . ." also says what cannot be done. The friendly close fits the one case.

Dear Ms. Cangelosi:

Your efforts to build the scholarship fund for the association's needy children are most commendable. We wish you good success in your efforts to further this worthy cause.

We at Pinnacle are always willing to assist worthy causes whenever we can. That is why every January we budget for the year the maximum amount we believe we are able to contribute to worthy causes. Then we distribute that amount among the various deserving groups as far as it will go. As our budgeted contributions for this year have already been made, we are placing your organization on our list for consideration next year.

We wish you the best of luck in your efforts to help educate the deserving children of the association's members.

Sincerely,

• This letter using the indirect approach is better.

▶ to Adjustment Refusal Letters

Sometimes your job at Pinnacle involves handling an unhappy person. Today you have to do that, for the morning mail has brought a strong claim for adjustment on an order for Pinnacle's Do-Craft fabrics. The claim writer, Ms. Arlene Sanderson, explains a Do-Craft fabric that her upholstering company used on some outdoor furniture has faded badly in less than 10 months. She even includes sample cuts of the fabric to prove her point. She contends that the product is defective, and she wants her money back—all $2,517 of it.

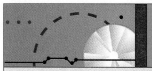
Inspection of the fabric reveals that it has been subjected to strong sunlight for long periods. Do-Craft fabrics are for inside use only. Both the Pinnacle brochures on the product and the catalog description stress this point. In fact, you have difficulty understanding how Ms. Sanderson missed it when she ordered from the catalog. Anyway, as you see it, Pinnacle is not responsible and does not intend to refund the money. At the same time, it wants to keep Ms. Sanderson as a customer and friend. Now you must write the letter that will do just that. The following discussion tells you how. ■

ADJUSTMENT REFUSALS

- Letters refusing claims for adjustment are bad news.

Letters that refuse claims carry bad news. As with other bad-news situations, you should usually handle them indirectly. The indirect approach is especially necessary when there is reason to be concerned about your reader's sensitive feelings. Of course, not all claims are refused. Most are legitimate, and most companies try hard to correct for legitimate damages. But some claims are not well founded. They may be based on wrong information, or they may be dishonest. In such cases a company is likely to say no.

Determining the Basic Strategy

- Your first step is to determine your explanation and the strategy for presenting it.

Your first step in writing a letter refusing a claim for adjustment is to decide how to explain your decision. Probably your best course is to base your explanation on the facts of the case. You should review them, and from your review determine precisely why a refusal is justified. Then, with these facts in mind, you should search for the best possible way of presenting your position. This mental effort requires that you think through the situation thoroughly—especially from your reader's point of view. It should end with the development of a strategy for presenting your case clearly and convincingly.

- Then present your strategy following this plan.

After you have determined what to say, you write the letter. Although variations may be justified, usually you should follow this general order:

- Begin with words that are on subject, are neutral as to the decision, and set up your strategy.

- Present the strategy that explains or justifies, being factual and positive.

- Refuse clearly and positively, perhaps including a counterproposal.
- End with off-subject, friendly words.

Applying the Indirect Plan

The plan above clearly is much like that for the refused request previously discussed. It should be, for a refused adjustment is really a special type of refused request. Both letters have the same need to identify the correspondence being answered near the beginning—either incidentally or in a neutral subject line. Likewise, both have the same need to begin with words that set up the strategy that will justify the refusal. And here lies the primary difference between this letter and other refused requests. The strategies you are likely to use are different.

• Follow the general plan for bad-news letters.

As we have noted, the strategy you select should be based on the legitimate reason for your refusal and the facts of the case. Of the many strategies available to you, one is to begin on a point of common agreement and then explain how the case at hand is an exception. To illustrate, a case involving a claim for adjustment for failure of an air conditioner to perform properly might begin thus:

• Set up your strategy in the opening, as in these examples.

You are correct in believing that a 2-ton Deep Kold window unit should cool the ordinary three-room apartment.

The following explanation will show that the apartment in question is not an ordinary apartment.

Another strategy is to build the case that the claim for adjustment goes beyond what can reasonably be expected. A beginning such as this one sets it up:

Assisting families to enjoy beautifully decorated homes at budget prices is one of the most satisfying goals. We do all we reasonably can to reach it.

The following explanation, of course, will show that the requested adjustment goes beyond what can be reasonably expected. Many such strategy possibilities are available to you.

Following comes the explanation that supports the refusal. Here you should use a minimum of negative language. Especially should you avoid words that question the reader's honesty. And as in other refused request letters, you follow the explanation with the refusal. Your refusal should be clearly worded, yet you want it to be as positive as the situation permits. For example, this one is clear, yet it contains no negative language:

• Avoid negatives in explaining and refusing.

For reasons you will understand, we can pay only when your employees pack the goods.

If a compromise is in order, you might present it in positive language like this:

In view of these facts, the best we can do is repair the equipment at cost.

As in all bad-news letters, you should end this one with some appropriate, positive comment not directly related to the situation involved. You could write about new products or services, industry news, or such. Neither negative apologies nor words that recall the problem are appropriate here.

• Close positively and off subject.

Contrasting Adjustment Refusal Letters

Bad and good treatment of Pinnacle's refusal to give money back for the faded fabric are illustrated by the following two letters. The bad one, which is blunt and insulting, destroys goodwill. The good one, which uses the techniques described in the preceding paragraphs, stands a good chance of keeping goodwill.

• The following examples show the value of the preceding plan.

Bluntness in a Direct Refusal.   The bad letter begins bluntly with a direct statement of the refusal. The language is negative (*regret, must reject claim, refuse, damage,*

Crusty old Mr. Whiffle bought an umbrella from a mail-order company. As the umbrella did not function to his requirements, Mr. Whiffle wrote the company a letter asking for his money back.

The mail-order company answered with a well-written letter of refusal.

Again Mr. Whiffle wrote, and again the company replied with a nicely written refusal.

Mr. Whiffle wrote a third time. The mail-order company refused a third time.

So angry was Mr. Whiffle that he boarded a bus, traveled to the home office of the mail-order company, and paid a visit to the company's adjustment correspondent. After a quick explanation of his purpose, Mr. Whiffle broke the umbrella over the adjustment correspondent's head. The correspondent then gave Mr. Whiffle his money.

"Now why didn't you do this before?" Mr. Whiffle asked. "You had all the evidence."

Replied the correspondent, "But you never explained it so clearly before."

inconvenience). The explanation is equally blunt. In addition, it is insulting ("It is difficult to understand how you failed . . ."). It uses little tact, little you-viewpoint. Even the close is negative, for it recalls the bad news.

• The bad letter shows little concern for the reader's feelings.

Dear Ms. Sanderson

Subject: Your May 3 claim for damages.

I regret to report that we must reject your request for money back on the faded Do-Craft fabric.

We must refuse because Do-Craft fabrics are not made for outside use. It is difficult for me to understand how you failed to notice this limitation. It was clearly stated in the catalog from which you ordered. It was even stamped on the back of every yard of fabric. As we have been more than reasonable in trying to inform you, we cannot possibly be responsible.

We trust that you will understand our position. We regret very much the damage and inconvenience our product has caused you.

Sincerely,

Tact and Indirect Order in a Courteous Refusal.   The good letter begins with friendly talk on a point of agreement that also sets up the explanation. Without accusations, anger, or negative words, it reviews the facts of the case, which free the company of blame. The refusal is clear, even though it is made by implication rather than by direct words. It is skillfully handled. It uses no negatives, and it does not receive undue emphasis. The close shifts to helpful suggestions that fit the one case. Friendliness and resale are evident throughout the letter but especially in the close.

• This better letter is indirect and tactful.

Dear Ms. Sanderson

Subject: Your May 3 letter about Do-Craft fabric.

Certainly, you have a right to expect the best possible service from Do-Craft fabrics. Every Do-Craft product is the result of years of experimentation. And we manufacture each yard under the most careful controls. We are determined that our products will do for you what we say they will do.

Because we do want our fabrics to please, we carefully ran the samples of Do-Craft Fabric 103 you sent us through our laboratory. Exhaustive tests show that each sample has been subjected to long periods in extreme sunlight. As we have known from the beginning that Do-Craft fabrics cannot withstand exposure to sunlight, we have clearly noted this in all our advertising, in the catalog from which you ordered, and in a stamped reminder on the back of every yard of the fabric. Under the circumstances, all we can do concerning

CASE ILLUSTRATION   Adjustment Refusal Letters. (Refusing a Refund for a Woman's Dress)

An out-of-town customer bought an expensive dress from the writer and mailed it back three weeks later, asking for a refund. The customer explained that the dress was not a good fit and that she really did not like it anymore. But perspiration stains on the dress proved that she had worn it. This letter skillfully presents the refusal.

103 BREAKER RD. HOUSTON, TX 77015 713-454-6778 Fax: 713-454-6771

Febuary 19, 1996

Ms. Maud E. Krumpleman
117 Blackjack Road
College Station, TX 77840

Dear Ms. Krumpleman:

On-subject opening—neutral point from claim letter — We understand your concern about the exclusive DiVella dress you returned February 15. As always, we are willing to do as much as we reasonably can to make things right. ⎤ *Sets up explanation*

Review of facts supports writer's position — What we can do in each instance is determined by the facts of the case. With returned clothing, we generally give refunds. Of course, to meet our obligations to our customers for quality merchandise, all returned clothing must be unquestionably new. As you know, our customers expect only the best from us, and we insist that they get it. Thus, because the perspiration stains on your dress would prevent its resale, <u>we must consider the sale final.</u> We are returning the dress to you. With it you will find a special alteration ticket which assures you of getting the best possible fit free of charge. ⎤ *Good restraint—no accusations, no anger*

Note positive language in refusal ⎦ ⎤ *Emphasis on what store can do helps restore goodwill*

Friendly goodwill close — So, whenever it is convenient, please come by and let us alter this beautiful DiVella creation to your requirements. We look forward to serving you.

Sincerely,

Marie O. Mitchell

Marie O. Mitchell
President

dm

Happenings such as this are bitter disappointments to those involved. Letters about the matter should not recall this scene unnecessarily.

your request is suggest that you change to one of our outdoor fabrics. As you can see from our catalog, all of the fabrics in the 200 series are recommended for outdoor use.

You will probably also be interested in the new Duck Back cotton fabrics listed in our 500 series. These plastic-coated cotton fabrics are most economical, and they resist sun and rain remarkably well. If we can help you further in your selection, please call on us.

Sincerely,

INTRODUCTORY SITUATION

▶ to Credit Refusal Letters

Although Chester Carter, your boss at Pinnacle, is in charge of the credit department, you do not normally get involved in credit work. But exceptions occur. Today, for example, the credit manager consulted with Chester about a request for credit from Bell Builders Supply Company, one of Pinnacle's longtime cash customers. The financial information Bell submitted with the request does not justify credit. Bell has more debt than it can afford, and still more debt would only make matters worse.

Because a refusal appears to be best for all concerned, Pinnacle will turn down Bell's request. The decision is fair, but it will not be good news to Bell. In fact, it might even end this firm's cash business with Pinnacle. Handling the situation is obviously a delicate task.

The importance of the case prompts Chester to ask you to write the refusal letter for his signature. A refusal letter from a top executive, Chester thinks, just might be effective. Now you are faced with the task of writing the letter that will refuse as well as keep the reader a cash customer. ■

CREDIT REFUSALS

Letters that refuse credit are more negative than most refusals. The very nature of credit makes them so. Credit is tied to personal things, such as morals, acceptance in society, character, and integrity. So, unless skillfully handled, a credit refusal can be viewed as a personal insult. For the most positive results, such a refusal requires the indirect order and a tactful strategy.

Some will argue that you need not be concerned about the reader's feelings in this situation. As you are turning down the reader's business, why spend time trying to be tactful? Why not just say no quickly and let it go at that? If you will study the situation, the answer becomes obvious.

In the first place, being kind to people is personally pleasing to all of us. At least, it should be. The rewards in business are not all measured in dollars and cents. Other rewards exist, such as the good feelings that come from treating people with courtesy.

In the second place, being kind to people is profitable in the long run. People who are refused credit still have needs. They are likely to satisfy those needs somewhere. They may have to buy for cash. If you are friendly to them, they just might buy from you. In addition, the fact that people are bad credit risks now does not mean that they will never be good credit risks. Many people who are good credit accounts today were bad risks at some time in the past. By not offending bad risks now, you may keep them as friends of your company until they become good risks.

Determining the Strategy

Your first step in writing a credit refusal letter is to work out your explanation. That explanation will depend on the reason for the refusal. If you are refusing because the applicant is a bad moral risk, you have a very difficult assignment. You cannot just say bluntly that you are refusing because of bad character. Even people with low morals would bristle at this approach. In such cases, you might choose a roundabout approach. For example, you might imply the reason. As the applicant knows his or her credit reputation, a mere hint is often enough to indicate that you also know it.

Some credit authorities in the United States prefer a more direct approach for bad moral risks, citing the Equal Credit Opportunity Act of 1975 as support. This act states that applicants refused credit are entitled to written explanation of the reasons for the refusal. One way of implementing this approach is to follow the refusal with an invitation to come in (or telephone) to discuss the reasons. This discussion could be followed by a written explanation, if the applicant wants it. Opponents of this approach argue that the applicants already know the facts—that very few of them would pursue the matter further.

If you are refusing because your applicant's financial condition is weak, your task is easier. Weak finances are not a reflection on character, for they are related not to personal qualities, but to such factors as illness, unemployment, and bad luck. Thus, with applicants whose finances are weak, you can talk about the subject more directly. You also can talk more hopefully about granting credit in the future. In actual practice, cases do not fit neatly into these two groups. But you should be able to adapt the suggestions that follow to the facts of each case.

In any case, as described below, your letter should follow this general plan of organization:

■ Begin with words that set up the strategy (explanation), are neutral as to the decision, and tie in with the application.

■ Present the explanation.

■ Refuse tactfully—to a bad moral risk, by implication; to a person with weak finances or in a weak economic environment, positively and with a look to the future.

■ End with adapted goodwill words.

Margin notes: Because credit is personal, use tact in refusing it. • Some think tact is not necessary. • But treating people tactfully pleases us personally. • It also gains future customers for your business. • Begin by working out the refusal strategy. You can imply the reason with bad moral risks. • But some authorities favor offering an explanation. • Frank discussion is effective with weak financial risks. • Follow this organization plan.

Bad-news letters should show the same friendly concern for others that caring people display in their face-to-face relations.

Adapting the Bad-News Plan

- Following the bad-news pattern, set up strategy with on-subject and neutral words—perhaps a reference to an order accompanying the request.

You will recognize the preceding letter pattern as the same one suggested for the two preceding refusal situations. The opening sets up your strategy, it is neutral as to decision, and it is on subject. Again, the significant difference between this and the preceding refusals is in the strategies that can be used. In this case, for example, the beginning words might refer to the order involved (if one accompanied the request), as in this example.

Your January 22 order for Rock-Ware roofing shows good planning for the rush months ahead. As you will agree, it is good planning that marks the path of business success.

The strategy this opening sets up is to explain that well-managed businesses hold down indebtedness—something the reader needs to do.

- A thank-you for the request is appropriate and popular strategy.

A popular and appropriate strategy is to begin with a simple expression of gratefulness for the credit application and then lead into a courteous explanation and refusal. Although it is usually effective, the timeworn "Thank you for your application" variety is better replaced with different wording, such as this:

We are sincerely grateful for your credit application and will do all that we reasonably can to help you get your business started.

The following explanation will show that the facts of this case make granting credit something beyond what the writer can reasonably do.

- Explanations to bad moral risks can be vague.

The explanation set up by the opening can be an additional point of difference. If you are refusing because of the reader's bad credit morals, you need to say little. Bad moral risks know their records. You need only to imply that you also know. For example, this sentence handles such an explanation well, and it also gives the answer.

Our review of your credit record requires that we serve you only on a cash basis at this time.

- Explanations to weak financial risks with good morals can be more open.

Your explanation to applicants with good morals but weak finances can be more open financial discussions of the facts of the case. Even so, you should select your words carefully to avoid any unintended negative effect. In some cases, you might want to show concern for the reader's credit problem.

"No."

(From The Wall Street Journal, with permission of Cartoon Features Syndicate.)

Whatever explanation you use, your words should lead to a clear but positive refusal. For a good moral risk with bad finances, this one does the job well:

• Refuse clearly and positively.

Thus, for the best interest of both of us, we must postpone extending credit until your current assets-to-liabilities ratio reaches 2 to 1.

As in the other bad-news letters, you should end the credit refusal letter with words of goodwill. Preferably, avoid anything routine, and make the words fit the one case. A suggestion for cash buying or comments about merchandise can be effective. So can a forward look to whatever future relations appear appropriate. This closing meets these requirements:

• Close with positive, friendly words that fit the one case.

As one of Meyers' cash customers, you will continue to receive the same courtesy, quality merchandise, and low prices we give to all our customers. We look forward to serving you soon.

Contrasting Credit Refusal Illustrations

The following two contrasting letters refusing Bell's credit application clearly show the advantages of tactful indirect treatment. The bad letter does little other than refuse. The good one says no clearly, yet it works to build goodwill and cultivate cash sales.

• The following letters contrast credit refusal techniques.

Harshness as a Result of Tactless Treatment.   The weaker letter does begin indirectly, but the opening subject matter does little to soften the bad news. This obvious subject matter hardly deserves the emphasis that the opening gives it. Next comes the refusal—without any preceding explanation. It uses negative words (*regret, do not meet, weak, deny*). Explanation follows, but it is scant. The appeal for a cash sale is weak. The closing words leave a bad picture in the reader's mind.

Dear Mr. Bell:

• This one is tactless.

We have received your May 3 order and accompanying request for credit.
After carefully reviewing the financial information you submitted, we regret to report that you do not meet our requirements for credit. It is our considered judgment that firms with your weak assets-to-liabilities ratio would be better off buying with cash. Thus, we encourage you to do so.
We would, of course, be pleased to serve you on a cash basis. In closing, let me assure you that we sincerely regret that we must deny you credit at this time.

Sincerely,

As the merge information in the address area indicates, this is a department store's form letter refusing credit to bad moral risks. Such stores ordinarily use form letters because they must handle credit on a mass basis. Because form letters must fit a variety of people and cases, they tend to be general.

White-Horton & Co.

102 W. Euclid Dr.   Irasburg, Vermont 05845   802-789-9850   FAX: 802-789-9714   Wunch@wh.com

Date

FIELD(Personal Title) FIELD(First Name) FIELD(Last Name)
FIELD(Company Name)
FIELD(Street Address)
FIELD(City), FIELD(State) FIELD(Zip)

Dear FIELD(Personal Title) FIELD(Last Name):

Favorable beginning contact—routine but appropriate

We sincerely appreciate your interest in an account with White-Horton & Company. Whenever we can, we are always willing to serve you.

Sets up explanation

Positive suggestion of cash buying

In determining what we can do for you regarding your FIELD (Request Date) request for credit, we made the routine checks you authorized. The information we have received permits us to serve you only as a cash customer. But, as you know, cash buying here at White-Horton's discount prices can make a very real saving for your budget.

Explanation is clear and positive—implies that writer knows credit record

Positively worded refusal

We hope to see you in the store again very soon, and we look forward to the opportunity of serving you.

Friendly closing words

Sincerely,

Cynthia R. Wunch

Cynthia R. Wunch
Credit Manager

hts

Courtesy and Tact in a Clear Refusal.   The better letter generally follows the plan outlined in preceding pages. Its on-subject, neutral opening sets up the explanation. The explanation is thorough and tactful. Throughout, the impression of genuine concern for the reader is clear. Perhaps the explanation of the values of cash buying would be out of place in some cases. In this case, however, the past relationship between reader and writer justifies it. The letter ends with pleasant words that look to the future.

Dear Mr. Bell:

> • This good letter refuses tactfully.

Your May 3 order for Pinnacle paints and supplies suggests that your company is continuing to make good progress.

To assure yourself of continued progress, we feel certain that you will want to follow the soundest business procedures possible. As you may know, most financial experts say that maintaining a reasonable indebtedness is a must for sound growth. About a 2-to-1 ratio of current assets to liabilities is a good minimum, they say. In the belief that this minimum ratio is best for all concerned, we extend credit only when it is met. As soon as you reach this ratio, we would like to review your application again.

We appreciate your interest in Pinnacle paints and look forward to serving you.

Sincerely,

OTHER INDIRECT LETTERS

The types of indirect letters covered in preceding pages are the most common ones. There are others. Some of these (sales, collections, and job applications) are rather special types. They are covered in the following chapters. You should be able to handle all the other indirect types that you encounter by adapting the techniques explained and illustrated in this chapter.

> • Adapt the techniques of this chapter.

SUMMARY ▶ by Chapter Objectives

1. When the main message of the letter is bad news, use the indirect order.
   • But exceptions exist, as when you believe that the news will be received routinely.
   • Make an exception also when you think the reader will appreciate directness.
2. The refusal of a request is one bad-news situation that you will probably choose to treat indirectly.

> (1) Determine which situations require using the indirect order for the most effective response.
>
> (2) Use tact and courtesy in refusals of requests.

- In such situations, strive to achieve two main goals:
  —to refuse, and
  —to maintain goodwill.
- Begin by thinking through the problem, looking for a logical explanation (or reasoning).
- Write an opening that sets up this explanation.
- Then present your explanation (reasoning), taking care to use convincing and positive language.
- Refuse clearly yet positively.
- Close with appropriate, friendly talk that does not recall the bad news.

3. Refusals of adjustments follow a similar pattern.
   - First, determine your explanation (reasoning) for refusing.
   - Begin with neutral words that set up your reasoning and do not give away the refusal.
   - Then present your reasoning, building your case convincingly.
   - Refuse clearly and positively.
   - Close with appropriate friendly talk that does not recall the refusal.

4. Letters refusing credit are more negative than most other types of refusal letters, for the refusal is tied to personal things.
   - As with other types of refusals, begin by thinking through a strategy.
   - If you are refusing because of the applicant's bad credit character, use a round-about approach.
   - If you are refusing because of the applicant's weak finances, be more direct.
   - In either case, choose opening words that set up your strategy, are neutral, and tie in with the request being answered.
   - To the bad moral risk, imply the facts rather than state them bluntly.
   - In refusals because of weak finances, look hopefully to credit in the future.
   - End all credit refusals with appropriate positive words, perhaps suggesting cash buying, customer services, or other appropriate topics.

CRITICAL THINKING QUESTIONS

1. Give examples of when directness is appropriate for responses giving negative (bad-news) information.

2. Writing in the indirect order usually requires more words than does writing in the direct order. Since conciseness is a virtue in writing, how can the indirect order be justified?

3. What strategy is best in a letter refusing a request when the reasons for the refusal are strictly in the writer's best interests?

4. Apologies in refusal letters are negative, for they call attention to what you are refusing. Thus, you should avoid using them. Discuss.

5. An adjustment correspondent explained the refusal of an adjustment request by saying that company policy did not permit granting claims in such cases. Was this explanation adequate? Discuss.

6. Is there justification for positive writing in a letter refusing credit? You are not going to sell to the reader, so why try to maintain goodwill?

7. Discuss the difference between refusing credit to a good moral risk with bad finances or in a poor economic environment and refusing credit to a bad moral risk.

CRITICAL THINKING EXERCISES

1. Point out shortcomings in the following letter from a sports celebrity declining an invitation to speak at the kickoff meeting for workers in a fund-raising campaign for a charity.

Dear Ms. Chung:

As much as I would like to, I must decline your request that I give your membership a free lecture next month. I receive many requests to give free lectures. I grant some of them, but I simply cannot do them all. Unfortunately, yours is one that I must decline.

I regret that I cannot serve you this time. If I can be of further service in the future, please call on me.

Sincerely yours,

2. Criticize the following letter refusing the claim for a defective riding lawn mower. The mower was purchased 15 months earlier. The purchaser has had difficulties with it for some time and submitted with the claim a statement from a local repair service verifying the difficulties. The writer's reason for refusing is evident from the letter.

Dear Mr. Skinner:

Your May 12 claim of defective workmanship in your Model 227 Dandy Klipper riding mower has been reviewed. After considering the information received, I regret to report that we cannot refund the purchase price.

You have had the mower for 15 months, which is well beyond our one-year guarantee. Even though your repair person says that you had problems earlier, he is not one of our authorized repair people. If you will read the warranty you refer to in your letter, you will see that we honor the warranty only when our authorized repair people find defects. I think you will understand why we must follow this procedure.

If you will take the machine to the authorized service center in your area (La Rue Lawn and Garden Center), I am confident they can correct the defect at a reasonable charge.

If I can be of additional service, please contact me.

Sincerely,

CRITICAL THINKING PROBLEMS

REFUSED REQUESTS

1. You own a travel agency near campus and cater to the college-age client. While a good portion of your business is travel to and from students' hometowns, another significant portion is vacation travel. While European travel dominates the summer season travel, skiing destinations are popular during both winter and spring breaks. In fact, you offer special packages to destinations in Colorado, Utah, New England, as well as California. Organized groups of students are important customers because these groups can be counted on to book trips year after year.

One of your regular customers has requested you book the same package at the same price you've offered the past three years. However, this year you

must raise your price. You've been able to keep your prices down in the past only by getting competitive bids from all providers—the airlines, charter buses, and hotels. However, the lift ticket prices have been rising steadily the past three years at over 10 percent a year. This year they average over $50 for one-day lift tickets—$10 more than last year's rates. Now you must raise your prices to meet all your increasing costs.

Write a letter that refuses the request but keeps the booking. You can keep everything the same as in the past for an increase of only $25 for the two-day package. You may decide to offer a counterproposal such as a lowering the quality of the hotel, scheduling the trips midweek, increasing the length of the package one day to take advantage of multiday lift ticket rates, or other reasonable alternatives. Remember in delivering the bad news you want to retain the business; regular business is important to your agency.

2. As Rodel Simpauco, manager of CD Club of America, you need to respond to the following angry request from a customer. From the letter, you suspect that the customer clearly doesn't understand how the club works. While you could stand behind the legal contract the customer has signed, you'd like to see him a satisfied, continuing member of the club or at least a satisfied customer. Part of your task in refusing the request is to educate the customer and work to regain his goodwill.

Dear Manager:

Your record club stinks! Not only am I being sent CDs I didn't order and don't want, I'm being billed for ones I've returned. On top of that you are unfairly charging me finance charges and postage. And I've had to pay the return postage, too.

Immediately credit my account for the full amount due and drop me from the club. Also, the quality of the CDs I have kept is poor. I will NOT recommend that any of my friends join your club unless you take care of my account immediately.

Sincerely,

Casey Schroeder

To keep this customer satisfied, you may want to offer a counterproposal. For example, you may offer to exchange the unwanted CDs for ones of the customer's choosing, to change the plan to receive CDs only when ordered rather than automatically, or to eliminate the finance charge and reimburse for postage. Any reasonable counterproposal that retains the customer's goodwill should work.

3. As George Pappas, the manager of a unique Greek restaurant in Tarpon Springs, Louis Pappas' Riverside, you received a letter from Perry Hansen that both pleased and disappointed you. Mr. Hansen told you how much he enjoyed a recent visit to your restaurant. He reported that he enjoyed the unique view of sponge boats and pleasure vessels as well as the excellent food and wide selection of Greek and American foods. He reports he's never had a better Greek salad and his wife's seafood was the freshest she could remember. He enjoyed the entertainment and thought the pricing was reasonable. And he said the service was superb! That's the good part.

In fact, it was so good that he would like to rent the whole restaurant on either a Friday or Saturday night for a family reunion next December. He's even willing to pay full menu prices; he's not asking for any special pricing. While you are delighted he enjoyed your restaurant so much, you must refuse his request. Not only are Friday and Saturday nights your regular business nights for other customers, but December is also the beginning of peak tourist season. You don't want to have to turn regular customers

away for a onetime affair. However, you are willing to make your restaurant available on Monday nights. To encourage him, you may even want to offer some special menu or special volume pricing discount. While you must refuse his request, try to keep Mr. Hansen's business and goodwill.

4. As Mike McLaughlin, manager of the Washington, D.C., branch of the World Bank, you've recently been inundated with requests from employees for a compressed workweek schedule. In a recent scheduling experiment, you decided to offer a compressed workweek schedule where employees work for nine extended days and take the 10th day off. The schedule was designed to address the work-family issue, luring more skilled women, reducing stress, and easing single parent's problems.

An evaluation of the program revealed that morale had improved, particularly among those participating rather than those left to cover for them on days off. Also, absenteeism was down and productivity was unchanged. Therefore, you decided to continue the program's trial. However, the enthusiasm for the schedule attracted 1,500 requests—nearly one-sixth of your employees. So you've decided to draft a form letter refusing current requests for the schedule. You can cite reasons such as the experimental nature of the trial, the need to evaluate the bank's requirements to cover areas, and the need for time to establish fair policies and procedures should the compressed schedule become a permanent scheduling option.

5. As regional sales manager for InFocus, the manufacturer of computer projection equipment, you've received a request from Susan Collins for free use of your equipment. As chair of the Association for Business Communication's program for next year, Susan would like you to donate your equipment for use at its annual meeting in Chicago in November. She reports that more than 400 people attend this meeting, all of whom use and teach the use of presentation equipment in their college classes.

While she makes a good case that those attending are indeed part of your market and influential in training many others, you decide to refuse a pure donation. For one thing, you think many other organizations would expect you to do the same for their groups. And, of course, this practice could get out of hand rapidly, distracting you from your primary business purpose. However, since these participants are clearly potential customers, you'd like them to be exposed to your equipment, and this meeting might just be a good way to do that. Therefore, while you must clearly refuse the donation, you will offer an alternative barter arrangement. You would provide the computer projection equipment and Susan's group would both distribute literature on it and post a sign noting your company's generosity to this group.

6. As director of human resources at Krug in Houston, part of your job involves handling requests related to employee benefits. Most of the time you simply need to explain benefits, but today you need to write a

refusal to fund an activity an employee appears to have viewed as a benefit.

The employee, Mary Adami, requested both time and funding to take a course in Spanish at a local college. While your company clearly supports, even encourages, employees to continually improve their knowledge and skills, the training you support with time and covered educational expenses has to be directly related to their current job or one they will be doing in the near future. Mary's job as a biomedical engineer for Krug doesn't require the use of Spanish. In refusing to support this request, explain the types of educational courses you would support for someone in her position. Some of the courses others in her position have taken that have been approved include advanced science and math courses, computer courses such as Unix, and courses in speaking, writing, and interpersonal communications. Of course, you can always offer to review the request again if she can show how it directly relates to the work she's doing now or will be doing soon. Do work to maintain her interest in continuing to improve her knowledge and skills.

7. As manager of a local Merrill Lynch office, one part of your job is public relations and another part is community involvement. You work hard at these aspects for you recognize that both a positive image of Merrill Lynch and a prospering community contribute to your business. Besides sponsoring local PBS programs, you make yourself and other staff members available to conduct free, informational seminars on all aspects of investing. In addition, you often address special groups on financial topics. In fact, this past year you've been speaking regularly to senior citizen groups on various types of investments, informing them of the nature, risks, and returns. This year your company is holding informational programs for working people, explaining tax-deferred investments and helping untangle the complexities of planning for retirement.

So when you received Professor Linda Hittle's request for you to speak to her Introductory Finance students, you were willing to go. In fact, you had been planning to target these young, future high-income earners next year for your educational programs. However, you noted that his class met from 12:00 to 1:00 P.M.—the exact time of your seminars to the downtown workers. And because the market is still open then, you can't afford to pull another person away for a couple of hours. Therefore, you'll have to refuse his request. But because you want to build both Professor Hittle's's and her student's goodwill toward Merrill Lynch, you may want to offer an alternative. Depending on the class, you may want to offer to send special videos that Merrill Lynch has produced, to supply some clearly written, informational packets on topics that relate to the class, or even to speak to them after the market has closed in the late afternoon or evening or even on Saturday. In any case, you want to retain goodwill but still need to refuse the request clearly.

8. As manager of the sales center at A.S.A.P. Vending Machine Company, you have a rather interesting situation confronting you today. For the last six months, Local 414 of the United Federation of Electricians has rented one of your Dispense-a-Cup hot drink machines at a fee of $45 per month. But now the local wants to purchase one. The price of a new Dispense-a-Cup machine is $1,835 plus tax. But that's only part of the story.

Jim Mellon, the union office manager, has requested that you apply the rental fees for the past six months to the sales price of a new machine. "Other companies do this," he notes in his letter to you. "So I ask that you do this for our group; it's only fair!" Perhaps other firms make such arrangements, but you can't—or rather won't! If you are to stay in business, you'll need to keep your product and rental prices as they are. If other firms have more flexible arrangements, you are willing to bet they charge higher prices. And your price structures are stable and fair. Thus, you believe you have good reasons for saying no to the union and friend Mellon. What would happen if you granted the request? You would have to charge higher prices to make up for the money you would lose. And your customers (including the union) wouldn't like that.

So sit down at your computer and map out a tentative plan for the letter—buffer, reasons, refusal, off-subject close. You need to plan the message around the reasons for the refusal. Think through them specifically for you-viewpoint strategy. Then prepare the letter for the union that will say no and keep the business.

9. You are the public relations director of the private foundation established by Kay Miller, widow of Herbert Miller, the founder of a highly successful fast-food empire. Since 1985, the year after her husband died, Ms. Miller has given more than $35 million to a variety of causes. Among her donations are these: $12 million for a "think tank" to study peace issues at the University of Notre Dame; $5 million for AIDS research; $10 million to local charities, mostly those benefiting children; and others. Miller has also channeled money to environmentalist and nuclear freeze groups, not to mention $1 million to the American Red Cross for African famine relief.

Today is a typical day at the Miller Foundation. On your desk you have a large stock of requests for aid. Among these requests is a letter from the Intercity Homeless Advocacy Coalition asking for $50,000 to renovate two apartment complexes for homeless individuals in a metropolitan city close to you. (Your instructor will select the city.) Well aware of Miller's current sympathies, you know that this request cannot be funded. Particularly severe situations that have possible global ramifications (such as the current famine condition in Africa) are top priorities. In addition, Miller prefers to support research activities that contribute to the long-term alleviation of social problems rather than simply meet temporary needs. In this case, Miller would be more likely to fund academic field research on the plight of the homeless in the intercity than apartment renovations. She believes that there are enough government programs to provide for the temporary needs of the group.

As public relations director of the Miller Foundation, write a letter to the Intercity Homeless Advocacy Coalition presenting the foundation's position. Your letter will refuse the funding requested. But it will do so in a tactful and convincing manner. Address the letter to Robert Golladay, executive director.

10. You, the sales manager for the Washington Hilton Hotel in Washington, D.C., have just received a letter from Mrs. Modine Johnson, executive director of the National Association of Educators, requesting the use of the Kennedy Suite for the Friday luncheon during the NAE's annual convention November 3–7. Mrs. Johnson indicates the association will need the suite from 12:00–2:30 P.M. for the NEA President's Address and for making various awards to the members. NEA has blocked 1,500 room nights at your hotel and will have five catered hospitality functions. It goes without saying that you want NEA's business, and you want to make and keep the organization happy.

The Kennedy Suite is your most popular and lavish room for banquet functions. Because of its design, decor, and ostentation, the suite particularly appeals to professional organizations. NEA members would be genuinely impressed with the suite's elegance, dignity, and distinction. After checking your room reservation schedule for November 5, however, you discover that the suite has been reserved for quite some time by the Association of Entrepreneurs, a smaller group meeting at the hotel during the same dates as NEA. Quite obviously, you have a conflict; so you will have to refuse Mrs. Johnson's request. It just wouldn't be fair to reschedule the room now. Besides, that's not the way you do business.

You do think about an alternative, however. The Lincoln Suite, a not-so-extravagant or lavish banquet room, is available and has a capacity for 400 people. The rate for the use of the room is $1,000, which is $500 less than the fee for the Kennedy Suite. And you would do your professional best to equip the room to meet the NEA's needs. If NEA wants the room, you will need to know right away.

Write the letter that will refuse the request of Mrs. Johnson. After you have refused, you can present the alternative. Do not make this a direct-response letter saying, in effect, "Yes, you can use the Lincoln Suite." You are not granting NEA's request; so you'll use an indirect strategy. Think specifically about the reasons before you write the letter.

11. You are the president of Sun Belt Savings and Loan. Your firm has a tradition of supporting the local symphony, both with funds and with paid time of your executives. Not only has this support helped to build the community, but it also has provided excellent publicity for your organization and has been a morale booster for your employees.

It is that time of year again to renew your commitment to the symphony. You have just received your annual request from James Ataya, chair of the Symphony Fund Raising Committee, asking for your donation and for the time of two of your vice presidents to assist in the fund-raising effort.

Although Sun Belt Savings did not participate in the more risky oil and real estate ventures that caused so many other S&Ls to go under, you lent over $500,000 to a bank that was later forced into bankruptcy by the FDIC. There is little likelihood that this loss will be recovered. In addition, the recent changes in federal law have increased the amount of capital Sun Belt must maintain to continue making loans. The situation requires a great deal of management attention and control.

You conclude, regretfully, that you cannot spare any of your officers nor will Sun Belt be able to make its normal corporate donation of $20,000. Thus, you will write a clear, firm refusal to Mr. Ataya. While making it clear that Sun Belt cannot participate in the symphony fund-raising this year, you also cannot give the impression that Sun Belt might go bankrupt soon. There is little chance that this will occur, but the rumor that it might happen could create conditions that might cause you problems. You would like to offer to participate in future efforts, but the predictions for the savings and loan industry are so uncertain that you do not foresee that you can make that commitment either.

Write the letter to James Ataya. Your refusal to participate this year does not mean you dislike the symphony or that you do not support the community. Your decision is based on austere business conditions. Use these reasons strategically in your refused request letter to Mr. Ataya.

12. Today's mail brings you a challenging situation with which to deal. A letter from Mr. Chris Bancroft, business manager of *The Production Manager,* a professional periodical for college production/operations management students, requests that you send him news pictures that are related to production/operations work. You are the manager of the special services department of the National Photographic News Service. Your organization provides photos to magazines, newspapers, and such for a price—but not free!

Because of the market to which *The Production Manager* caters, Mr. Bancroft has a rather slim budget you suspect. But as much as you would like to help him, you cannot do so for logical, sound economic reasons. You simply cannot afford to provide a free service for him and his publication. Certainly he doesn't give free subscriptions to his customers nor can you give "freebies" to yours. Thus, you must refuse his request. Your news service's fixed rate for pictures to the media is $15. Your news service has rather high costs of production because your staff covers a wide area in geographic regions and in types of pictures.

If Mr. Bancroft could afford the $15 rate per picture, you could do some research for him. If he would provide a list of specific subjects in which he is interested, your staff would reseach the subjects and send him all related photos. You would charge him only for those he could use, based on his acceptance of the photos. All the rejected ones would need to be returned. This alternative is the best you can offer him, given the circumstances of his request.

Prepare the letter for Mr. Chris Bancroft. You believe his request is rather naive. But don't belittle him. You still want to keep his goodwill. He might have a stronger need for your services in the future.

13. In your role of regional director of the Disaster Assistance Program Division of the Federal Emergency Management Agency (FEMA) in region _____,* you must write a refusal letter to Governer _____ of (state).

Several days ago, you received an impassioned letter from the governor asking that the president declare the region a disaster area. According to the governor, homes and business buildings in the region have been damaged by the recent storm that hit the area. Many citizens are in makeshift shelters with little hope of immediately recovering their personal and business property. It is your job to conduct investigations in disaster areas to determine the extent of damages and the merit of such requests from high-ranking state officials.

After conducting a joint damage assessment with (state) officials, you conclude that indeed some homes and businesses sustained damages as the result of the storm. However, there are no unmet emergency needs and no families are isolated. The majority of families are no longer in shelters and most have returned home to clean up. Damage estimates represent only the cost of limited furniture replacement, very minor structural repair, and loss of equipment stored outdoors. To be sure, there is loss. But the facts of the case do not warrant federal assistance and intervention.

The American Red Cross has agreed to provide assistance for unmet needs. Also, the Small Business Administration gives disaster loans to small businesses that sustain damages in natural disasters as long as the SBAs requirements are met. And, of course, there is insurance.

The severity and magnitude of the storm are not assessed to be beyond the response capability of the state as required by federal law. The FEMA office in Washington asks that you write the letter that will deny the governor's request for disaster help. Prepare it skillfully, specifically, and tactfully. Your writing effort will get the review of many government officials and citizens.

ADJUSTMENT REFUSALS

14. You've had a terrible week as public relations director for the San Diego Padres. The estimates of opening day ticket sales were far below the actual number of fans that arrived. So the demand for food exceeded the supply, and the number of workers you had on hand couldn't handle the crowds. Additionally, the computer for TicketMaster, your official ticketing agency, went down the day of the game, causing long delays at the ticket windows. These delays were not only for those buying tickets at the last minute but also for fans who had prepaid and arranged for will-call pickups. As a result, you've had to troubleshoot numerous problems. And today's mail brought the following letter.

Dear Public Relations Director:

Your organization really needs to get its act together! For a losing team with untested players of questionable ability, you need to extend yourself to your faithful core of supporters even more than ever.

My boss gave me tickets and the afternoon off to attend the game and support the team. The tickets were prepaid by credit card and to be picked up at the stadium. Much to my surprise, arriving nearly an hour before the game was not enough to avoid major traffic problems and the hunt and seek parking game. After struggling just to get into the stadium and finding parking on the far North edge of the lot (seemed about a mile or more walk to the ticket window), the line for tickets was unbelievably long. Not only did I miss almost one third of the game, but my favorite player, Tony Gwynn, only played one inning while I was there. Additionally, I did not get one of the autographed baseball hats, which was one of the major reasons for going to the game.

On top of that the food vendors, ushers, and bathroom cleanup crews were slow or nonexistent when needed. Why can't the Padres at least provide an enjoyable atmosphere to watch a losing team?

The only way you'll make me a true supporter again is to refund the cost of my tickets and assure me that my next visit will be an enjoyable one.

Sincerely,

Leah Alipio

Many of the problems this fan experienced were out of your control, so you'll want to refuse the adjustment. However, you do want to build goodwill and support for the Padres, so you can make a reasonable counterproposal. You'll also need to do some resale on the Padres' fine organization. You might mention some of the accomplishments of Tony Gwynn and allude to seeing him accomplish more of these at future games. You could mention other players, too. And talk about the enjoyable atmosphere and excitement baseball games bring. While clearly refusing the adjustment, work to gain the goodwill of this faithful supporter.

15. Today's mail brought a steamy request for a $215 refund from a customer in Moline, Illinois, Kim Nguyen. Apparently, she recently flew round-trip between Moline and San Francisco on your airline. While she does not even bring up any of the conditions of the flight, she is angry that she had to pay $515 for her ticket while her seat partner paid only $298. She states that her partner flew nearly twice as far, originating in Boston. She puts the blame on your ticket agent for not giving her the lower fare. In fact, she repeatedly accuses your airline of gouging her and other small-town residents.

Of course, your agent didn't gouge her or any

other small-town residents. And you'll have to refuse the adjustment in her ticket price. But this patterns response clearly demands tact and education. You could present the case for price competition in the Boston area as the reason behind the seat partner's lower fare. You might also want to suggest ways she could lower her ticket costs through advance purchase, Saturday night layover, and midweek flights. You might even suggest that when she's beginning to book her future flights that she check fares out of both Des Moines and Chicago; she may find it pays to drive or ride a bus or shuttle to a larger city. Do make it clear that the $515 fare was the best fare available on the date she booked her flight. Furthermore, you'll want to do some resale on your good service, friendly flight attendants, etc.

16. Many small companies are being choked by big customers paying their bills late, 30 to 90 days late. The late payments often cause these small-business owners to borrow against expensive lines of credit or to mortgage their own homes just to pay their bills. Sometimes they even have to lay off employees or delay paying them. But Thomas Banks, owner of Truck Brokers, Inc., a transportation brokerage company in Bethany, Ohio, believes in cracking down on slow-paying customers even if it costs some sales. He firmly believes he's in the transportation business, not the money-lending business. With this philosophy in mind, it's clear that you'll have to refuse a request Mr. Banks received today from one of your new customers, Ameritech Corporation, to extend its payment from 30 to 45 days.

    While Ameritech cites the need to control costs and optimize cash flow, your boss believes your company needs to do the same. In fact, in your refusal, you may want to remind Ameritech that one reason you are the lowest-cost provider is that you don't build in fees to cover the cost of borrowed money or have undue collection expenses. Make it clear that you will not extend payment due dates now or in the future. Work to retain Ameritech's goodwill.

17. As Butch Trevor, owner and president of Trevor True Value Stores, you need to refuse a request for adjusting a shipment date from one of your long-term suppliers. The supplier has requested that you take delivery of your full order of snow shovels on December 1 rather than October 1—a full 60 days late. The supplier has offered you a 10 percent discount on the price as compensation for later delivery.

    You realize that most of your customers who buy shovels buy them at the start of the winter season. That often means purchasing them on the day of the first snowfall or just before a major storm is predicted. While it's possible that you won't have snow before December 1, you definitely want to have the shovels on hand for the early rush. And a 10 percent discount would not make up for the lost sales or the lost goodwill of your customers. And while you've never measured the amount precisely, you realize that customers who come in to buy one item will often buy other items if they have been successful in get-

ting the one item they needed immediately. Plus you've read in the newspaper that one of your major competitors had some major restructuring after some recent downsizing. You suspect that your distributor is trying to fill a late order from this competitor. You'd hate to send your customers to them if it snowed before December 1. Therefore, you'll clearly refuse the delivery date adjustment. In attempting to retain your supplier's goodwill, you may want to remind the supplier of your long and mutually profitable business association as well as your expectation for a continued good relationship in the future.

18. As Edward Sanchez, manager of your local Wherehouse Records, you believe your return policy is extremely fair, especially in comparison to your competitors. For example, you take back opened merchandise as well as most merchandise without receipts. One customer recently returned a CD that was said to skip; but when you inspected it, you could see it was merely dirty and full of hand prints. However, unless a customer is returning merchandise with a receipt within 30 days of purchase, you hesitate to refund cash. For most items, your store policy is to accept the merchandise and issue a merchandise credit to the customer.

    Today you received a package from a customer about 30 miles from your store. The package included 10 CDs—all titles you have in current stock. In fact, most of them are among your current best-sellers. The customer, Vikki Harding, asked for a credit on her Visa.

    Since all the CDs appeared in good condition and since your normal practice is to accept returns without receipts, you initially decided to comply with Ms. Harding's request. But when one of your sales associates attempted to return the CDs to stock by scanning the bar codes, your computer system refused to match the codes with your inventory of the same items. As you inspected the CDs more closely, you discovered that two were marked with RC. This marking is commonly used by record clubs for their inventory purposes. Therefore, you recognize these CDs as ones not purchased at a Wherehouse outlet and change your mind, deciding to refuse this adjustment.

    In writing your refusal, you'll explain that you accept only stock purchased at Wherehouse outlets and that the bar codes don't match your chain's inventory records. Since the customer does live in your store's region, you'll want to be sure you keep this customer's goodwill. You might even do a bit of resale on Wherehouse, its lenient policies, its up-to-date inventory, and its wide selection. Perhaps you can regain the record club member as a regular Wherehouse customer.

19. Place yourself for this writing assignment in the role of Ms. Judy Webb, public relations director for Continental Cyclery. Three months ago, Bill Yarbrough purchased one of your custom racing bicycles, a Trex L-2 used by many racing teams throughout the world.

Today, a UPS truck delivered a box with Yarbrough's broken bicycle in it. As you visually inspect it after unpacking the box, you find the bicycle has a broken steering tube. In a letter that accompanies the returned bicycle, Yarbrough states that his bike was defective and asks that you replace the steering tube free. Also, he notes that he was injured when the tube broke as he was riding and wants you to pay medical costs amounting to $510.36 (he says there were no witnesses to the incident).

After inspecting the damaged bicycle more thoroughly, your master frame builder reports that the brazing on the bicycle was not faulty. Rather, he indicates that the break in the steering tube is a stress fracture, most likely resulting from a severe jolt such as a head-on impact. The frame builder is certain of this conclusion because of a bend he discovered in the down-tube, which could only happen through a collision.

It appears that Yarbrough is trying to get his bicycle repaired free when he was the one who abused it. But you can't and won't call him a cheat and a liar. You will refuse his request with tact, grace, and diplomacy. It's highly probable that Yarbrough is a member of a racing club; so you don't want him bad-mouthing you there. That could cost you sales; so ride easy and firm on this biking enthusiast with your words that will tell him no and make him like you and your products.

20. You are the sales manager for Midwestern Discount Software (MDS). As part of your job, you handle all customer complaints that the department managers can't resolve. You have received a letter from Lynn Judd in which he requests that you refund his money for the disk drive he purchased recently.

Mr. Judd states that he purchased a drive to add to his computer. He says he was told by the floor salesperson that the drive would work with any IBM personal computer. He has installed the disk drive in the proper slot of the IBM-type computer he owns made by Packard-Bell, and it is getting the correct power. The computer, however, does not recognize that the drive is attached.

MDS sells microcomputer software and components at discounts of up to 50 percent off normal retail prices. In order to justify those discounts, the company provides no support services to customers. It caters to people who are familiar with microcomputers and do not need explanations or training. The patrons are expected to understand the complexities of the parts and programs they buy. Since the patrons understand these complexities, MDS has a firm policy of never accepting returns. This policy permits MDS to offer such low prices. The frequent newspaper ads run by MDS clearly say that all sales are final. This wording also appears in large print at the top of each sales receipt.

You recognize that the computer made by Packard-Bell is a "clone." While it runs IBM programs, it is not made by IBM. Your phone call to a Packard-Bell distributor reveals that the company has never tested its machine with the brand of disk drive Mr. Judd bought. It is very likely that the disk drive will not work on his computer.

Your salesperson provided the correct information to Mr. Judd. He simply did not understand the difference between an IBM computer and an IBM clone.

Logically, you conclude that the no-return policy applies to Mr. Judd's request. Write a letter to him telling him your decision. But you still want him to remain a customer of MDS. He will buy computer parts and programs somewhere in all likelihood. It might as well be at MDS, right? Write!

21. Assume that you are the director of the Have Fun While You Learn Institute of Vocational Training. In today's mail comes a letter from Ms. Clarisa Vanmeter, who was enrolled last semester in the six-week Basic Accounting course conducted by Professor Luca Pacioli.

Ms. Vanmeter claims in her letter that she is entitled to a refund for most of her tuition payment and for most of her room and board. According to her, the course was worthless. She couldn't balance her checkbook before the course and neither could she after the course. So she dropped out at the end of the second week. She did not use her room, nor did she eat meals after that date. As Ms. Vanmeter sees it, she is entitled to two-thirds of the $600 tuition cost and the four-week room and board at $120 per week.

After reading Ms. Vanmeter's letter, you check with Professor Paciolo and learn some additional facts. Vanmeter did drop out, as she claims; but it was after the first test, on which she scored 32 after a 30-point curve. The class average was 83. The lady displayed little interest in the class; in fact, according to her classmates, she displayed more interest in Wayne Newberry, a fellow student who thought he was Tom Cruise. She was absent at least three days during the first two weeks and rarely did her homework. According to the other students, Vanmeter spent most evenings watching videos on the VCR. About her claim that the class was worthless, Professor Pacioli pointed to the students' evaluations. Not one of the 34 other students rated it lower than 8 on a 10-point scale.

As you see it, the lady has no right to a refund. The Have Fun While You Learn Institute kept its end of the bargain. If refunds were permitted, losses would result. The institute contracted with the hotel for meals and rooms; so it had to pay for them even if they were not used.

Write a letter that will give this illogical young woman your answer. As much as you'd like to tell her off, resist the temptation and maintain the dignity that is appropriate for the institute.

22. *Schindler's List, Dances with Wolves,* and other videotapes on which you own copyrights and that are over two hours in length are creating problems for your customers—primarily video stores and renters of tapes. As claims adjuster for Orion Pictures, you are going to have to deal with this difficult situation in the claims work you do for the corporation.

Specifically, Video Fantasy of Boston, a chain of 25 stores, wants its money back on 20 films that were purchased from you four weeks ago. Writes Ms. Linda Hardy, president of the chain, in a claim letter to you: "We keep running out of the titles because of defective tapes. It's embarrassing and I lose money." You've had similar comments for other dealers, as well. And unless you determine the problem and correct it, you will continue to receive claims; even worse, customers will likely stop buying your films.

To determine the problem so that you can deal with it effectively, you take the returned defective tapes to your product development team for inspection. After several hours of work with the tapes and several phone calls to distributor plants of the company, the team believes it has some answers about the tapes. First, "high-speed" rewinders used by some rental stores can rewind tapes tighter than some consumers' VCRs. Thus, when retailers rewind tapes, they do so at high speeds; and the end of the tape breaks off at the reel, making it unusable for other renters. But this problem is the retailers' responsibility, not yours. As you recognized a difference in the rewinding speeds of various VCRs, you had printed on each label of a rental tape, "Rewind Slowly."

In addition, tapes that separate from reels and often jam in rewinding are those longer than the normal two-hour videos. The complaints about jamming and breaking concern titles that fit into this group. In deciding whether to use one cassette or two, you consulted your marketing research department. Their surveys and product feedback indicated that retail distributors preferred one cassette. The 24-hour return "drop boxes" didn't have room for two cassettes. For cost and return convenience, you decided on the one-cassette product design. But the product should not break or jam if it is rewound properly.

Given both findings, you can't grant Video Fantasy's or any other retailer's claim for adjustment. The retailers must do their part to care for the product so they can provide damage-free cassettes to movie viewers. Your production department indicates that 5 percent of the 665,000 tapes it has released could be faulty. As you quickly assess, that's about 33,000 tapes that retailers could have trouble with. So you will develop a tactful, firm refused adjustment letter for this market segment. It will be a model letter you can easily use repeatedly for other retailers who may contact you. But you don't want it to sound routine.

Prepare the adjustment refusal for Ms. Hardy at Video Fantasy that will serve as a model letter for others. Because retailers have a choice in what they purchase, you want the letter to sound warm even though it must refuse. Make it a "movey"—a message that will move customers to Orion for other sales.

CREDIT REFUSALS

23. As manager of the credit division of a local department store (you choose the store), you work hard to extend credit to those who both want your merchan-

dise and who can pay for it. Most of your credit applications are handled by staff using standard formulas you've developed over the years to identify only the most creditworthy.

Today's mail brought an extremely persuasive letter from Michael Richards, a newcomer to your area. Upon moving to your city, Mr. Richards immediately applied for credit. In his letter he reports that he is a new business teacher at your local high school. While this is his first job, he reminds you that it is a responsible one. He also stresses that since he is just starting out he needs everything to set up an apartment with a home office. He states he wants to do business with your store based on its fine reputation and quality merchandise.

While Mr. Richards could become one of those fine customers you want to cultivate, you still need to refuse his request for credit since he has no established record of paying his own bills and no history of holding employment longer than the summer jobs he worked during college. Since he does need to purchase many items when starting out, you might tell him about the sales you have throughout the year such as furniture over Labor Day, household items in January and July, and office equipment in September, November, and January. You even have a 90 days same as cash plan on furniture, which would be a way to establish a good payment record. Clearly refuse his credit request but encourage him to re-apply after he has worked six months and paid all his bills in a timely fashion.

24. As Karen Sampson, an owner and the manager of small strip mall near your campus, you often lease space to businesses targeting their products and services at students. Generally, this has worked out well since the retail space immediately adjacent to the campus is limited and the student population has remained large enough to support it, even in years of declining enrollments. You try to lease space to a variety of businesses so as not to split their market share so much that their businesses would not be profitable. This strategy seems to have worked quite successfully for the past 10 years. In fact, the turnover rate of your tenants is far below the average for strip malls located in similar areas.

Today, July 1, one of your tenants asked you to extend credit for rent due until September 1. The business is a small T-shirt and sunglasses boutique. In fact, until this year it had been profitable and popular with students. The tenant blames the economy for poor business, stating merchandise did not move last May even when prices were drastically reduced. She expects the fall business to be better, making up for the slow summer months and enabling her to pay the rent in full then.

While you might normally extend credit to one of your tenants during an economic turndown, the circumstances appear different to you from the way your tenant has presented them. First, none of your other tenants has even mentioned problems with lower profit levels. Second, enrollments, while down a few years ago, have remained stable for the last three years. And third, and perhaps subjectively, you think the T-shirt craze is over and that this tenant hasn't presented an inventory that appeals to the market today. Furthermore, you've been approached by an independent bookstore owner for the space. Since you do have a prospective tenant already, you could offer to release the current tenant from the lease without penalty. However, be sure that you clearly refuse to extend credit on the lease. You want the rent when due or the tenant out so that you can replace her with a paying tenant.

25. Running a bicycle repair shop has been a good business for generations in the Laviaguere family. For the current owner, John Laviaguere, it has been both personally and economically profitable. He believes that by charging fair prices, he will be encouraging more people to ride bicycles. Not only is it an economical means of transportation, but it also is both good exercise and good for the environment.

   To keep prices low, John needs to keep overhead low. For generations members of his family have provided repair services for cash. By eliminating accounts receivable, he's been able to manage cash flow adequately. In fact, not since the first day the business opened has anyone borrowed to meet current cash flow needs. John's father instilled in him another important reason for not extending credit. His father explained that once he repaired a bicycle, his service was consumed and shortly thereafter forgotten. And a service cannot be repossessed nor can the time consumed be recovered; the customer must pay in full at delivery of the repaired bicycle.

   Therefore, when the company that was John's largest client asked for a credit line, John knew he had to refuse. However, he also recognized that in doing so he needed to promote his repair services since he did not want this client taking the business elsewhere.

26. As Brian. Lenz, president and owner of Lenz and Associates, you run a business to lend to businesses. Most of the time you do this by buying their accounts receivables, but occasionally you buy their equipment and/or inventory.

   As an experienced lender, you have learned that the best loans are for equipment that immediately starts generating a profit for the business. You have provided the funds (through a variety of your funding sources) for everything from manufacturing equipment to fitness machines in health clubs. Loans for inventory are much more difficult decisions. In fact, when you first started, you provided the funds for boats. Unfortunately, they sat on the lot and the owner couldn't pay you anything since he couldn't sell them. And you had a difficult time recovering the boats.

   Today you received a request for a credit line for some computer kiosks. The owner of these particular kiosks is targeting a niche market—those needing computer graphics. These kiosks would contain a wealth of graphics, which users could copy to their own floppy disks for a fee collected through credit card numbers on-line at the time for the transaction. The kiosks would be placed near business centers as well as at copy centers. While you think this idea is a unique one, you wonder how you would be paid back if no one downloaded the graphics. What if the kiosks just sat? While not quite the same as the boats since the price range is different, the target market is questionable. Yes, copying is much easier than searching the Internet and Bulletin Boards for graphics and downloading or FTPing them, but the market is probably not well defined.

   You decide to refuse this request for credit. However, you like the innovative idea and want to assure the potential customer that you will welcome other proposals for credit. Refuse clearly but work to retain this customer's goodwill.

27. Ever since Jennifer Clare can remember, she has always had an inventive, creative streak. So her new computer software business and the excitement she's enjoyed since it started last year have been very rewarding. In fact, the computer game she and her colleague developed is catching on rapidly. At a recent trade show, they took several orders including one for $10,000. It was their largest order yet. But on the last day of the show in the last hour, a Russian company presented an order for $100,000. Jennifer said it was exciting and scary.

   However, shortly after their initial celebration, the Russian company asked for a line of credit for the full amount. How devastating! Her company did not have the cash to handle that request. Also, never having done business with a Russian company, she was not sure how she could convert rubles to dollars since rubles are not currently on any currency exchange.

   As much as she'd like to keep this order, she needs to refuse the credit request. Perhaps by doing some resale on the product she can salvage some of the sale.

28. When Melinda and Jerry Magarret moved to Midvale, they had been married for two months. Both were beginning teachers in the Midvale school system—he a biology teacher and junior varsity basketball coach at the high school and she a first-grade teacher. During their first year in the community, they lived in a small apartment and built up their savings to be used as a down-payment on their first home.

   With their frugal ways, their savings, and a small inheritance from a grandparent, they were able to pay the 20 percent down payment on a new three-bedroom, 1,500-square-foot house. Their salaries qualified them for the 30-year note on the house, barely! And after one year of living in the house, they appear to be solid financially, concentrating on the possibility of a family and contributing to the community. Indeed, these young people and others like them are vital to the future growth of Midvale.

   Several weeks ago, the couple visited your store, Elegant Furnishings. They were looking for dining room furniture for their new house. And they located it—a three-piece cherry wood set including a table with six chairs, china cabinet/hutch, and server. It sells for $8,999 and the Magarrets truly want it.

When they filled out the credit application form you require, they willingly furnished the financial information needed. And the credit check you ran on them shows they are a "good pay" account. Thus, everything appears on the surface to be a "go" for the couple to purchase the dining room furniture they want. As you study the financial inventory more, however, you become increasingly more convinced that the Magarrets should wait to purchase the furniture. It's quite normal for a young couple to begin modestly and then want to overextend themselves as they begin to accumulate physical possessions. This situation might very well apply to the Magarrets.

For example, they are meeting their current payments and credit obligations, but you cannot determine from their monthly budget how they would handle the $400 per month payment for the next two years unless they gave up eating. Right now, they have little leverage for increased credit. Both work in the summer—Melinda as a workshop leader in teacher training and in summer school and Jerry as a driver education and basketball camp instructor. If they would save this money from their summer income and apply the amount to the purchase price, then you could extend credit on the balance of $4,000. And you can guarantee them the same price of $8,999. Either way you figure it, however, you will have to deny them credit for the full amount now.

With their best interest in mind, write the Magarrets the credit refusal that you must. In time, they will qualify for larger credit amounts. Right now, they are cutting their financial pie too thin. You will be extremely tactful in your letter because you want their business. They are a definite credit account for you in the future. The youth of their experience should not prohibit them from many future sales on credit. And they might purchase smaller items for cash with someone; so it might as well be you.

Write this young account with definite future credit possibilities the credit refusal that will keep them loyal to your Elegant Furnishings business.

29. The credit request letter you receive today from the Allied Business Federation, a group of college professors who meet yearly to share research, is typical of many you receive in your job as credit manager of the Hammond Hotel chain. The ABF through its executive director, Geraldine Chertz, plans to hold its annual meeting in your New Orleans hotel on March 15. In doing her preconvention planning work, she asks for a 60-day pay account. She sends along the compilation report from her accountant as proof that her organization is solvent and can pay its bills. The ABF is a nonprofit organization under section 506C of the IRS code.

Your usual policy is to require a standard 30-day pay account to groups such as these. Based on your estimate, the ABF will have accounts payable of about $15,000 for a banquet, one cocktail reception, and coffee/soft drink breaks during the three-day meeting. The 350 to 400 members who stay at your

hotel will pay for their own rooms, and they will spend good money in hotel restaurants for food. Also, several publishing companies will host receptions and parties for the members. So you will make good money from the group—but not enough to grant the 60-day master account that Chertz desires.

Your reason for the 30-day policy is much the same as the ABF's request for the 60-day account: both of you need the money. You need the cash for operations and cash flow purposes while ABF wants to retain the funds for short-term interest and liquidity. But you are going to say no to the request. A 60-day account is not standard in the industry and not warranted by the money involved. Besides, if you granted the request, then other groups would want the same terms and that would compound your cash flow problems. Simply put, you cannot grant the 60-day account, and you will write the group telling it that 30 days is "max." To be sure, though, you don't want to make ABF members angry because you want ABF to return several years down the road. Also, remember there is more at stake than a 30-day account; there are the publishers and members who will pay for the services you offer as well. So, you'll need to be extremely tactful in handling the situation.

As your course instructor indicates, consider this case in two parts. The situation probably repeats itself frequently enough to be handled by a form letter. But there are two situations to deal with. One involves a credit situation where you must require 50 percent of the estimated costs in cash and the other 50 percent due in 30 days. A second involves restricting all accounts to 30 days. Your instructor will choose the situation you will write about in the letter you construct for ABF as a typical organization that would request a credit account with Hammond Hotels.

30. Courthouse Collectibles is a two-year-old retail business that sells antiques, quilts, maps, posters, wall hangings, paintings, and other unique gifts. So successful has been its business (sales volume, profit, etc.) that the owners are opening a second store 100 miles away, close to an outlet mall on a major interstate highway. The strategy is to appeal to travelers as they seek shopping breaks in their journeys along the highway. This location strategy is complemented by a promotion strategy of advertising the new business through highway signs at selected points approaching the store location.

But the new location has not been fully stocked with inventory yet. Although the merchandising policy for the new location will remain basically the same as the original store, there will be some differences because of the nature of the customers who will visit the new store. This is where you enter the Courthouse Collectibles' picture.

As owner of Mary Laura's Native American Jewelry, you receive today an order from Barbara Ivy of Courthouse Collectibles for 100 of your dream catcher earrings that you sell for $68 each. The earrings are one of your more popular jewelry items. In either pierced or clip styles, they are made from sterling silver and gem turquoise. The design consists of three feathers connected to the bottom of a circle that surrounds a webbed net with a turquoise rock within the webbing. In Indian mythology, the Oneida Indians (located in the northeast part of the United States) placed a dream catcher above a baby's cradleboard. The web of the catcher would filter all dreams and let only the good dreams through the open circle at the center of the net. The dream catcher was kept throughout life to maintain its magical power.

Indeed, you believe your dream catcher earrings would be a logical addition to the product line of Courthouse Collectibles. Because the order is the first you have received from Courthouse Collectibles, you run your standard credit check and receive mixed signals from it. First you note that cash discounts were taken on all credit accounts until the last two months when payments revealed a 35-day pay record on 30-day accounts. Also, more accounts have been added within the last six months; but their terms have rarely been met. Thus, what started as a "good pay" account has turned into one of "slow pay." You suspect the location expansion might be the reason for this recent slow record, but you don't know exactly. Perhaps the demands created by additional creditors have caused cash flow problems. Regardless of the reasons, you will not grant the business credit. Another financial obligation is not what this business needs right now. There's just too much surplus drain. And now you must tell them so in writing.

Prepare the credit refusal letter to Barbara Ivy of Courthouse Collectibles. If the new location generates additional revenues and proves to be successful, you can foresee granting credit later after the business has proven itself. In your letter, you will need to discuss your logic frankly but not tactlessly. So watch the effect of your words. Also, you still want the cash business now. At the quantity requested, you can offer a 2 percent discount but you need the cash before you will fill the order. Maybe Courthouse Collectibles could finance locally and get the cash. It might also be able to factor some of its accounts receivables. Your letter will attempt to be helpful with telling Courthouse Collectibles what to do. Write the credit refusal letter that will keep the goodwill of the potentially good account.

31. After his father died several years ago, Al Yacas took over the Yacas Lawn Sprinkler Company the elder Yacas had started. Al was a vocational woodshop/mechanics teacher in another state with 15 years of experience. When he inherited the lawn sprinkler business, he decided to take early retirement to devote full-time efforts to the ongoing concern. Since that time, he has held his own in terms of lawn sprinkler sales. To diversify the seasonal business for variations in demand, Harry added a nursery, which his wife manages. He also added landscaping service. Along with these new business lines, he also has service calls throughout the year on sales of his existing sprinkler systems. All told, Al has a good, keen business mind; and he has used this sense to maintain and

improve the business he inherited from his father.

But now Al wants to diversify the business even more, this time into the sale of spas and hot tubs. He believes that good market potential exists for the product; and he can use his training in mechanics, woodwork, and the like to build decks and install hot tubs. Also, he thinks he can promote a complete landscaping service for backyards, gardens, and houses to be constructed. Indeed, he is enthusiastic in his entrepreneurial spirit.

As sales manager for Coleman Spas, you read with interest the persuasive credit request letter from Al Yacas, asking for 20 Coleman hot tub shells at $1,195 each to be delivered to his business (f.o.b. destination) as soon as possible. He wants to pay for the hot tubs as he installs them; but he does not want to exceed 90 days on his account. His request is unusual to say the least and not consistent with industry practice. You run the usual credit check and receive the report on Yacas Lawn Sprinkler. You notice that in the last two years cash discounts have rarely been taken and that payments on 30-day accounts average 29.5 days and on 45-day accounts, 44.5. These results indicate that Al apparently needs his money for operations and thus squeezes his payments in at the last moment. Such a strategy in itself is not bad; but combined with other market factors, it means you are going to have to refuse his request for credit.

You know, for example, that five large competitors carry your products in the local area. Because you do not have exclusive dealerships, the competition for the product would be intense. Also, Al indicates he has an "in" with many building contractors and that his contacts would guarantee him a stable market for his services. Based on the financial sources you consult, however, the home improvement loan market will soon cease to exist because of gradually increasing interest rates. And most builders in the industry take an average of 120 days to complete a contracted job. Thus, the people on whom Al would depend are taking longer to complete jobs than the 90 days Al requests for credit, assuming he could contract for spas to generate a sufficient volume of sales for him. Given these findings, it's highly unlikely that Al could meet the credit terms he requests. He would be cutting things too thin.

Write a letter refusing credit to the enterprising and ambitious account. Perhaps if you had some tangible record of success from him, you could talk about credit. Maybe he could arrange for financing locally. If so, you could provide him the hot tubs he wants. You do have a sound, good product. But you'll need cash before he gets it. Also, Al might rearrange his internal operations differently and generate the money for the hot tubs. It appears he's committed to adding to his line, so keep him as a friend of your business. You want his cash business now and hopefully his credit business later when he proves he can handle the additional indebtedness.

APPLICATIONS TO SPECIFIC SITUATIONS

Indirectness in Persuasion and Sales Writing

Upon completing this chapter, you will be able to use persuasion effectively in making requests and composing sales letters. To reach this goal, you should be able to

(1) Use imagination in writing skillful persuasive requests that begin indirectly, use convincing reasoning, and close with goodwill and action.

(2) Describe the choices available in determining the structure of a sales mailing.

(3) Describe the preliminary steps of studying the product or service and selecting the appeals to use in a sales letter.

(4) Discuss the choices of letter mechanics available to the sales writer.

(5) Compose sales letters that gain attention, persuasively present appeals, and effectively drive for action.

NEED FOR INDIRECTNESS IN PERSUASION

Although letters in which you ask for something that your reader may be reluctant to give need not involve bad news, they are also handled in the indirect order. For example, with a letter requesting a favor that will require some personal sacrifice, your chances for success will be greater if you justify the request before making it. This approach, of course, follows the indirect order. Or, for another example, when you write a letter selling a product or service, your readers will usually resist your efforts. To succeed, therefore, you have to begin by convincing them that they need the product or service. This approach also follows the indirect order. Such indirect letters involving persuasion are the subject of this chapter.

* Certain requests and sales letters are best written in the indirect order.

INTRODUCTORY SITUATION

▷ to Persuasive Requests

Introduce yourself to the next business letter situation by returning to your hypothetical position at Pinnacle. As a potential executive, you spend some time working for the community. Pinnacle wants you to do this for the sake of good public relations. You want to do it because it is personally rewarding.

Currently, as chair of the fund-raising committee of the city's Junior Achievement program, you head all efforts to get financial support for the program from local businesspeople. You have a group of workers who will call on businesspeople. But personal calls take time, and there are many people to call on.

At its meeting today, the Junior Achievement board of directors discussed the problem of contacting businesspeople. One director suggested using a letter to sell them on giving money. The board accepted the idea with enthusiasm. With just as much enthusiasm, it gave you the assignment of writing the letter (for the president's signature).

As you view the assignment, it is not a routine letter-writing problem. Although the local businesspeople are probably generous, they are not likely to part with money without good reason. In fact, their first reaction to a request for money is likely to be negative. So you will need to overcome their resistance in order to persuade them. Your task is indeed challenging.   ■

PERSUASIVE REQUESTS

Letters making requests that are likely to be resisted require a slow, deliberate approach. The direct order suggested for routine requests (Chapter 5) just will not do the job. Persuasion is necessary. By persuasion, we mean reasoning with the reader—presenting facts and logic that support your case. In this approach, which is discussed in detail below, you should generally follow this indirect plan.

* Requests that are likely to be resisted require persuasion.

■ Open with words that (1) set up the strategy and (2) gain attention.

* Generally follow this indirect plan.

■ Present the strategy (the persuasion), using persuasive language and you-viewpoint.

■ Make the request clearly and without negatives (1) either as the end of the letter or (2) followed by words that recall the persuasive appeal.

Determining the Persuasion

Planning the persuasive request letter requires imagination. You begin by thinking of a strategy that will convince your reader. To do this, put yourself in your reader's shoes. Look at the request as the reader sees it, and determine the reader's objections. Think about what you can say to overcome those objections. From this thinking, you should develop your plan.

* The persuasion is planned to overcome reader objections.

Persuasive requests and sales letters arrive uninvited. They have goals that are likely to encounter reader resistance. Unless they gain the reader's attention at the beginning, they are likely to end up in a wastebasket.

* Many persuasive appeals may be used—money rewards, personal benefits, and so on.

The specific plan you develop will depend on the facts of the case. You may be able to show that your reader stands to gain in time, money, or the like. Or you may be able to show that your reader will benefit in goodwill or prestige.

In some cases, you may persuade by appealing to the reader's love of beauty, excitement, serenity, or the like. In other cases, you may be able to persuade by appealing to the pleasant feeling that comes from doing a good turn. Many other possibilities exist. You select the one that best fits your case.

Gaining Attention in the Opening

* The opening sets the strategy and gains attention.

In the indirect letters previously discussed, the goal of the opening is to set up the explanation. The same goal exists in persuasion letters, but persuasion letters have an additional goal. It is the goal of gaining attention.

* Attention is needed to get the reader in a mood to receive the persuasion.

The need to gain attention in the opening of persuasion letters is obvious. You are writing to a person who has not invited your letter and probably does not agree with your goal. So you need to get that person in a receptive mood. An interesting beginning is a good step in this direction.

* What you write to gain attention is limited only by your imagination.

Determining what will gain attention also requires imagination. It might be some statement that arouses mental activity, or it might be a statement offering or implying a reader benefit. Because questions arouse mental activity, they are often effective openings. The following examples indicate the possibilities.

From the cover letter of a questionnaire seeking the opinions of medical doctors:

What, in your opinion as a medical doctor, is the future of the private practice of medicine?

From a letter requesting contributions for handicapped children:

While you and I dined heartily last night, 31 orphans at San Pablo Mission had only dried beans to eat.

From a letter seeking the cooperation of business leaders in promoting a fair:

What would your profits be if 300,000 free-spending visitors came to our town during a single week?

Presenting the Persuasion

Following the opening, you should proceed with your goal of persuading. Your task here is a logical and orderly presentation of the reasoning you have selected.

As with any argument intended to convince, you should do more than merely list points. You should help convey the points with convincing words. Since you are trying to penetrate a neutral or resistant mind, you need to make good use of you-viewpoint. You need to pay careful attention to the meanings of your words and the clarity of your expression. Because your reader may become impatient if you delay your objective, you need to make your words travel fast.

- Your persuasion follows.

- Present the points convincingly (selecting words for effect, using you-viewpoint, and the like).

Making the Request Clearly and Positively

After you have done your persuading, you move to the action you seek. You have prepared the reader for what you want. If you have done that well, the reader should be ready to accept your proposal.

Like negative points, your request requires care in word choice. You should avoid words that detract from the request. You should also avoid words that bring to mind pictures and things that might work against you. Words that bring to mind reasons for refusing are especially harmful, as in this example:

I am aware that businesspeople in your position have little free time to give, but will you please consider accepting an assignment to the board of directors of the Children's Fund?

The following positive tie-in with a major point in the persuasion strategy does a much better job:

Because your organizing skills are so desperately needed, will you please serve on the board of directors of the Children's Fund?

Whether your request should end your letter will depend on the needs of the case. In some cases, you will profit by following the request with words of explanation. This procedure is especially effective when a long persuasion effort is needed. In such cases, you simply cannot present all your reasoning before stating your goal. On the other hand, you may end less involved presentations with the request. Even in this case, however, you may want to follow the request with a reminder of the appeal. As illustrated in the second example letter (p. 181), this procedure associates the request with the advantage that saying yes will give the reader.

- Follow the persuasion with the request.

- Word the request for best effect.

- Do not use a negative tone.

- Be positive.

- The request can end the letter or be followed by more persuasion.

- Ending with a reminder of the appeal is also good.

Contrasting Persuasion Letters

The persuasive request is illustrated by contrasting letters that ask businesspeople to donate to Junior Achievement. The first letter is direct and weak in persuasion; the second letter is indirect and persuasive. The second letter, which follows the approach described above, produced better results.

- The following letters illustrate good and bad persuasion efforts.

Obvious Failure in Directness.   The weaker letter begins with the request. Because the request is opposed to the reader's wishes, the direct beginning is likely to get a negative reaction. In addition, the comments about how much to give tend to lecture rather than suggest. Some explanation follows, but it is weak and scant. In general, the letter is poorly written. It has little of the you-viewpoint writing that is effective in persuasion. Perhaps its greatest fault is that the persuasion comes too late. The old-style close is a weak reminder of the action requested.

Dear Mr. Williams:

Will you please donate to the local Junior Achievement program? We have set $50 as a fair minimum for businesses to give. But larger amounts would be appreciated.

The organization badly needs your support. Currently, about 900 young people will not get to participate in Junior Achievement activities unless more money is raised. Junior

- This bad letter has no persuasion strategy.

Achievement is a most worthwhile organization. As a business leader, you should be willing to support it.

If you do not already know about Junior Achievement, let me explain. Junior Achievement is an organization for high school youngsters. They work with local business executives to form small businesses. They operate the businesses. In the process, they learn about our economic system. This is a good thing, and it deserves our help.

Hoping to receive your generous donation by return mail, I am,

Sincerely,

Skillful Persuasion in an Indirect Order.   The next letter shows good imagination. It follows the indirect pattern described above. Its opening has strong interest appeal and sets up the persuasion strategy. Notice the effective use of you-viewpoint throughout. Not until the reader has been sold on the merits of the request does the letter ask the question. It does this clearly and directly. The final words leave the reader thinking about a major benefit that a yes answer will give.

- This better letter uses good persuasion strategy.

Dear Mr. Williams:

Right now—right here in our city—620 teenage youngsters are running 37 corporations. The kids run the whole show, their only adult help being advice from some of your business associates who work with them. Last September they applied for a charter and elected officers. They selected products for manufacture—antifreeze, candles, and chairs, to name a few. They issued stock—and they sold it, too. With the proceeds from stock sales, they set up a production operation. Now they are producing and marketing their products. This May they will liquidate their companies and account to their stockholders for their profits or losses.

You, as a public-spirited citizen, will quickly see the merits of the Junior Achievement program. You know the value of such realistic experience to the kids—how it teaches them the operations of business and how it sells them on the merits of our American system of free enterprise. You can see, also, that it's an exciting and wholesome program, the kind we need more of to combat delinquency. After you have considered these points and others you will find in the enclosed brochure, I know you will see that Junior Achievement is a good thing.

Like all good things, Junior Achievement needs all of us behind it. During the 13 years the program has been in our city, it has had enthusiastic support from local business leaders. But with over 900 students on the waiting list, our plans for next year call for expansion. That's why I ask that you help make the program available to more youngsters by contributing $50 (it's deductible). Please make your check payable to Junior Achievement, and send it right away. You will be doing a good service for the kids in our town.

Sincerely,

In this letter a trade publication editor seeks information from an executive for an article on desirable job application procedures. The request involves time and effort for the executive. Thus, persuasion is necessary.

THE
OFFICE
ADMINISTRATOR

November 20, 1996

Ms. Adelade O. Romano
Director of Personnel
Chalmers-DeLouche, Inc.
17117 Proden Road
St. Paul, MN 55108

Dear Ms. Romano:

Question opening gets attention

Opening topic sets up explanation

What clues have you found in application letters that help you estimate a person's character and desirability to your firm?

Explanation follows logically

Young people entering business are eager for any clue that will put them on the other side of the fence. They want to know what goes on in your mind when you are judging the people behind the letters. In our column, "Letters That Talk," we want to send a message especially to those people. To make the article as practical as possible, we are drawing our information from people in the field who really know.

Explanation is straight-forward—appeals subtly to good feeling from helping others

A mutual friend of ours, Max Mullins, told me of your recent problem of finding the most desirable person behind 250 application letters. What specific points did you look for in these letters? What clues distinguished some people from the others? When the going got hard, what fine points enabled you to make your final choice? The young people of today are eager for you to answer these questions.

Request evolves from presentation of appeal

You can help solve the young person's problem if you will jot down your personal comments on these letters and allow me to study them in confidence as the basis for an article. Will you do that for us and them? It is just possible, you know, that through this article to young businesspeople you may contribute to the success of a future leader in your own company. At least, you will be of service to the mass of young people who are trying to get "that" job that is so important to them right now.

Clear and direct request

Final words recall basic appeal

Sincerely,

Charlotte C. Clayton

Charlotte C. Clayton
Associate Editor

405 Perrin Ave.
Austin, TX 78716
512-437-7080
FAX: 512-437-7081
Clayton@officea.com

▶ to Sales Letters

Introduce yourself to the next letter type by assuming the role of Anthony A. Killshaw, a successful restaurant consultant. Over the past 28 years, you have acquired an expert knowledge of restaurant operations. You have made a science of virtually every area of restaurant activity—menu design, food control, purchasing, kitchen organization, service. You have also perfected a simple system for data gathering and analysis that quickly gets to the heart of most operations' problems. Testimonials from a number of satisfied clients prove that the system works.

Knowing that your system works is one thing. Getting this knowledge to enough prospective clients is another. So you have decided to publicize your work by writing restaurant managers and telling them about what you have to offer.

At the moment, your plan for selling your services by mail is hazy. But your direct-mail package will probably consist of a basic letter, a printed brochure, and a form to be checked by prospective customers. The letter will carry the major message, and the brochure will cover the details. The recipients will be the major restaurant operations that are on the roster of the American Restaurant Association.

Because sales writing requires special skills, you have decided to use the help of a local advertising agency—one with good direct-mail experience. However, you have a pretty good idea of what you want, so you will not leave the work entirely up to the agency's personnel. You will tell them what you want included, and you will have the final word on what is acceptable. ■

VALUE OF SALES WRITING

- Professionals usually write sales letters, so why study the subject?

You will probably never write a sales letter—a real one, that is. Except in some small business operations, sales letters are written by professional writers. They achieve this status by having a talent for writing and by practicing long and hard. Why, then, you might ask, should you study sales letters?

- The answer: Knowing selling techniques helps you in writing other types of letters.

The answer is that even an amateurish effort to write sales letters gives you knowledge of selling techniques that will help you in many of your other activities. For one thing, it will help you in writing other types of letters, for in a sense every letter is a sales letter. In every letter you are selling something—an idea, a line of reasoning, your company, yourself.

- It also helps in your daily life, for much of what you do involves selling.

Even in your daily life you will find good use for selling techniques. From time to time, all of us are called on to sell something. If we are employed in selling goods and services, our sales efforts will, of course, be frequent. In other areas of business, our sales efforts may consist only of selling such intangibles as an idea, our own competence, or the goodwill of the firm. In all such cases, we use selling techniques. Thus, sales writing and selling techniques are more valuable to you than you might think. After you have studied the remainder of this chapter, you should see why.

PRELIMINARY EFFORTS

- Usually brochures, leaflets, and the like accompany sales letters.

As you probably know from experience, most direct-mail efforts consist of more than just a letter. Typically, such efforts include a coordinated group of pieces—brochures, leaflets, booklets, foldouts, and so on. But a letter is usually the main piece. It carries the main message, and the other pieces carry the supporting details.

- But the emphasis in the following pages is on the letter.

The following discussion emphasizes the letter, for it would be beyond the scope of this book to cover more. But much of what is said about the letter applies to other forms of sales literature. After you have studied the following material, you should have a general idea of how to sell by mail.

Knowing the Product or Service and the Reader

Before you can begin writing, you must know about the product or service you are selling. You simply cannot sell most goods and services unless you know them and can tell the prospects what they need to know. Before prospects buy a product, they may want to know how it is made, how it works, what it will do, and what it will not do. Clearly, a first step in sales writing is careful study of your product or service.

In addition, you should know your readers. In particular, you should know about their needs for the product or service. Anything else you know about them can help—their economic status, age, nationality, education, and culture. The more you know about your readers, the better you will be able to adapt your sales message.

In large businesses, a marketing research department or agency typically gathers information about prospective customers. If you do not have such help, you will need to gather this information on your own. If time does not permit you to do the necessary research, you may have to follow your best logic. For example, the nature of a product can tell you something about its likely buyers. Industrial equipment would probably be bought by people with technical backgrounds. Expensive French perfumes and cosmetics would probably be bought by people in high-income brackets. Burial insurance would appeal to older members of the lower economic strata. If you are purchasing a mailing list, you usually receive basic demographics such as age, sex, race, education, income, and marital status of those on the list. Sometimes you know more—interests, spending range, consumption patterns, and such.

Determining the Appeal

With your product or service and your prospects in mind, you are ready to create the sales letter. This involves selecting and presenting basic appeals. By *appeals*, we mean the strategies you use to present a product or service to the reader. You could, for example, present a product's beauty or its taste qualities. You could stress that a product will provide hours of fun or that it will make one more attractive to the opposite sex. Or you could present a product through an appeal to profits, savings, or durability.

For convenience in studying appeals, we can divide them into two broad groups. In one group are emotional efforts to persuade. Such efforts affect how we feel, taste, smell, hear, and see. They also include strategies that arouse us through love, anger, pride, fear, and enjoyment. In the other group are rational appeals. These are appeals to the reason—to the thinking mind. Such appeals include strategies based on saving money, making money, doing a job better, and getting better use from a product.

In any given case, many appeals are available to you. You should consider those that fit your product or service and those that fit your readers best. Such products as perfume, style merchandise, candy, and fine food lend themselves to emotional appeals. On the other hand, such products as automobile tires, tools, and industrial equipment are best sold through rational appeals. Automobile tires, for example, are not bought because they are pretty but because they are durable, because they grip the road, and because they are safe.

How the buyer will use the product may be a major basis for selecting a sales strategy. Cosmetics might well be sold to the final user through emotional appeals. Selling cosmetics to a retailer (who is primarily interested in reselling them) would require rational appeals. A retailer would be interested in their emotional qualities only to the extent that these make customers buy. A retailer's main questions about the product are: Will it sell? What turnover can I expect? How much money will it make for me?

- Begin work on a sales letter by studying the product or service to be sold.

- Also, study your readers.

- Research can help you learn about prospective customers. If research is not possible, use your best logic.

- Next, decide on what appeals and strategies to use.

- Appeals may be emotional (to the feelings) or rational (to the reason).

- Select the appeals that fit the product and the prospects.

- The prospects' uses of the product often determine which appeal is best.

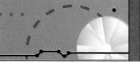

Sales letters and their supplements often include art that increases visual appeal as well as attracts attention to documents. Today's business writers need not be artists to use good art in their documents since word processing software includes a variety of graphics as well as providing some basic drawing tools. And most programs accept a variety of graphics from other sources. Some readily available sources of prepared graphics inclinclude the following:

- Graphics bundled with graphics, spreadsheet, and word processing programs.
- Clip art from both commercial and shareware sources, which can be bought off the shelf or downloaded from the on-line sources including the Internet.
- Scanned graphics from printed sources.

Here is a sampling of a variety of graphics easily combined with text in documents.

··

STRUCTURE OF THE SALES LETTER

- Writing sales letters involves imagination.

After selecting the appeal, you should write the sales letter. At this point, your imagination comes into the picture. Writing sales letters is as creative as writing short stories, plays, and novels. In addition to imagination, it involves applied psychology and skillful word use. There are as many different ways of handling a sales letter as there are ideas. The only sure way of judging each way is by the sales that the letter brings in.

- Sales-letter plans vary in practice, but this plan is used most often.

Because sales letters can vary greatly, it is hard to describe their order. But you should usually follow this conventional pattern:

- Gain favorable attention in the opening.
- Create desire by presenting the appeal, emphasizing supporting facts, and emphasizing reader viewpoint.

- Include all necessary information—using a coordinated sales package (brochures, leaflets, and such).

- Drive for the sale by urging action now and recalling the main appeal.

- Possibly add a postscript.

This pattern is similar to the classic AIDA model (attention, interest, desire, action) developed almost a century ago. The techniques used in developing this pattern are discussed below. As you study them, bear in mind that in actual practice only your imagination will limit the possibilities open to you.

Determining Letter Mechanics

A part of your effort in planning a sales letter is to determine its makeup. The physical arrangements of sales letters may differ in many ways from those of ordinary business letters. With few exceptions, sales letters are mass-produced rather than individually processed. They may use individually processed inside addresses. This effective technique is often replaced by impersonal salutations, such as "Dear Students," "Dear Homeowner," or "Dear Sir." One technique eliminates the salutation and inside address and places the beginning words of the letter in the form of these parts. As shown below, this arrangement gives the letter what appears at first glance to be a normal layout.

- The makeup of sales letters differs somewhat from that of ordinary letters. For example, sales letters may use impersonal salutations, headlines for inside addresses, and attention-gaining devices.

IT'S GREAT FOR PENICILLIN,
BUT YOU CAN DO WITHOUT IT
ON YOUR ROOF . . . .

We're referring to roof fungus, which, like penicillin, is a moldlike growth. However, the similarity ends there. Unlike penicillin, roof fungus serves. . . .

Sales letters may use a variety of mechanical techniques to gain attention. Pictures, lines, diagrams, and cartoons are common. So is the use of different ink colors. Such devices as coins, stamps, sandpaper, rubber bands, pencils, and paper clips have been affixed to sales letters to gain interest and help put over the appeal. One letter, for example, was mailed on scorched pages to emphasize the theme of "some hot news about fire insurance." A letter with a small pencil glued to the page used the theme that "the point of the pencil is to make it easy to order" a certain magazine. As you can see, the imaginative possibilities in sales writing are boundless.

Gaining Attention in the Opening

The opening of the sales letter has one basic requirement. It must gain attention. If it does not, it fails. The reason is apparent. As sales letters are sent without invitation, they are not likely to be received favorably. In fact, they may even be unwanted. Unless the first words of a sales letter overcome the barrier and gain attention, the letter goes into the wastebasket.

- The basic requirement of the opening is to gain attention.

Your plan for gaining attention is a part of your creative effort. But the method you use should assist in presenting the sales message. That is, it should help set up your strategy. It should not just gain attention for attention's sake. Attention is easy to gain if nothing else is needed. A small explosion set off when the reader opens the envelope would gain attention. So would an electric shock or a miniature stink bomb. But these methods would not be likely to assist the selling.

One of the most effective attention-gaining techniques is a statement or question that introduces a need that the product will satisfy. For example, a rational-appeal letter to a retailer would clearly tap his or her strong needs with these opening words:

Here is a proven best-seller—and with a 12 percent greater profit.

Another rational-appeal beginning is the first sentence of a letter seeking to place metered personal computers in hotel lobbies:

Can you use an employee who not only works free of charge but also pays you for the privilege of serving your clientele 24 hours a day?

Yet another rational-appeal beginning is this opening device from a letter selling a trade publication to business executives:

How to move more products,
Win more customers,
And make more money
. . . for less than $1 a week

This paragraph of a letter selling a fishing vacation at a lake resort illustrates a need-fulfilling beginning of an emotional-appeal approach:

Your line hums as it whirs through the air. Your lure splashes and dances across the smooth surface of the clear water as you reel. From the depth you see the silver streak of a striking bass. You feel a sharp tug. And the battle is on!

As you can see, the paragraph casts an emotional spell, which is what emotional selling should do. It puts a rod in the reader's hand, and it takes the reader through the thrills of the sport. To a reader addicted to fishing, the need is clearly established. Now the reader will listen to see how the need can be fulfilled.

As was mentioned previously, gimmicks are sometimes used to gain attention. But a gimmick is effective only if it supports the theme of the letter. One company made effective use of a penny affixed to the top of a letter with these words:

Most pennies won't buy much today, but this penny can save you untold worry and money—and bring you new *peace of mind*.

A paper manufacturer fastened small samples of sandpaper, corrugated aluminum, and smooth glossy paper to the top of a letter that began with these words:

You've seen the ads—
you've heard the talk—
now feel for yourself what we mean by *level-smooth*.

The use of a story is another opening approach. Most people like to read stories, and if you can start one interestingly, your reader should want to read the rest of it. Here is the attention-catching beginning of a masterpiece used by Boys Town to sell sponsor memberships:

A knock at the door, a swirl of snow over the threshold—and standing in the warm glow of the hall light was little Joe. His thin jacket was drawn tightly around his small body. "I'm here, Father. I'm here for an education," he blurted out.

Thus far, the attention-gaining techniques illustrated have been short. But longer ones have been used—and used effectively. In fact, a technique currently popular in direct-mail selling is to place a digest of the sales message at the beginning—usually before the salutation. The strategy is to quickly communicate the full impact of the sales message before the reader loses interest. If any of the points presented arouse interest, the reader is likely to continue reading.

Illustrating this technique is the beginning of a letter selling subscriptions to *Change*. These lines appeared before the salutation, which was followed by four pages of text.

A quick way to determine whether you should read this letter:

If you are involved in or influenced by higher education—and you simply don't have the time to read copiously in order to "keep up"—this letter is important. Because it offers you a money-shortcut (plus a *free gift* and a money-back guarantee).

As a subscriber to *CHANGE*, the leading magazine of higher learning, you'll have facts and feelings at your fingertips—to help *you* form opinions. On today's topics: tenure, professors' unions, open admissions, the outlook for new PhDs . . . On just about any subject that concerns academe and you.

CHANGE has the largest readership of any journal among academic people. To find out why 100,000 people now read *CHANGE* every month, take three minutes to read the following letter.

Presenting the Sales Material

After your attention-gaining opening has set up your sales strategy, you develop that strategy. What you do in this part of the letter is the product of the thinking and planning that you did at the beginning. In general, however, you should show a need and present your product or service as fulfilling that need.

The plan of your sales message will vary with your imagination. But it is likely to follow certain general patterns determined by your choice of appeals. If you select an emotional appeal, for example, your opening has probably established an emotional atmosphere that you will continue to develop. Thus, you will sell your product based on its effects on your reader's senses. You will describe the appearance, texture, aroma, and taste of your product so vividly that your reader will mentally see it, feel it—and want it. In general, you will seek to create an emotional need for your product.

- Plans vary for presenting appeals. Emotional appeals usually involve creating an emotional need.

If you select a rational appeal, your sales description is likely to be based on factual material. You should describe your product based on what it can do for your reader rather than how it appeals to the senses. You should write matter-of-factly about such qualities as durability, savings, profits, and ease of operation. Differences in these two sharply contrasting types of appeals are shown in the illustrations near the end of the chapter.

- Rational appeals stress fact and logic.

The writing that carries your sales message can be quite different from your normal business writing. Sales writing usually is highly conversational, fast moving, and aggressive. It even uses techniques that are incorrect or inappropriate in other forms of business writing—sentence fragments, one-sentence paragraphs, folksy language, and such. It uses mechanical emphasis devices (underscore, capitalization, bolding, italics, exclamation marks, color) to a high degree. It uses all kinds of graphics and graphic devices as well as a variety of type sizes and fonts. Its paragraphing often appears choppy. Apparently, the direct-mail professionals believe that whatever will help sell is appropriate.

- Sales writing is not ordinary writing.

Stressing the You-Viewpoint

In no area of business communication is you-viewpoint writing more important than in sales writing. We human beings are selfish creatures. We are persuaded best through self-interest. Thus, in sales writing you should base your sales points on reader interest. You should liberally use and imply the pronoun *you* throughout the sales letter.

- You-viewpoint is important in sales writing. Use it.

The techniques of you-viewpoint writing in sales letters are best described through illustration. For example, assume you are writing a sales letter to a retailer. One point you want to make is that the manufacturer will help sell the product with an advertising campaign. You could write this information in a matter-of-fact way: "Star mixers will be advertised in *Ladies' Home Journal* for the next three issues." Or you could write it based on what the advertising means to the reader: "Your customers will read about the new Star mixer in the next three issues of *Ladies' Home Journal*." For another example, you could quote prices in routine words such as "a four-ounce bottle costs $2.25, and you can sell it for $3.50." But you would emphasize the readers' interest with words like these: "You can sell the four-ounce size for $3.50 and make a 55 percent profit on your $2.25 cost." Using the you-viewpoint along with an explicit interpretation of how the facts benefit the reader will strengthen the persuasiveness. The following examples further illustrate the value of this technique:

MATTER-OF-FACT STATEMENTS	YOU-VIEWPOINT STATEMENTS
We make Aristocrat hosiery in three colors.	You may choose from three lovely shades . . . .
The Regal has a touch as light as a feather.	You'll like Regal's featherlight touch.
Lime-Fizz tastes fresh and exciting.	You'll like the fresh, exciting taste of Lime-Fizz.
Baker's Dozen is packaged in a rectangular box with a bright bull's-eye design.	Baker's Dozen's new rectangular package fits compactly on your shelf, and its bright bull's-eye design is sure to catch the eyes of your customers.

Choosing Words Carefully

- Consider the effect of your words.

In persuasive messages, your attention to word choice is extremely important, for it can influence whether the reader acts on your request. Try putting yourself clearly in your reader's place as you select words for your message. Some words, while closely related in meaning, have clearly different effects on one's behavior. For example, the word *selection* implies a choice while the word *preference* implies a first choice. Here are some examples where a single adjective affects how one reacts to a sentence.

You'll enjoy the sensation our hot salsa gives you.
You'll enjoy the sensation our fiery salsa gives you.
You'll enjoy the sensation our burning salsa gives you.

Framing your requests in the positive is also a proven persuasive technique. Readers will clearly opt for solutions to problems that avoid negatives. Here are some examples.

ORIGINAL WORDING	POSITIVE WORDING
Reorganization Plan A will cause 10 percent of the staff to lose their jobs.	Reorganization Plan A will retain 90 percent of the work force.
Our new laser paper keeps the wasted paper from smudged copies to less than 5 percent.	Our new laser paper provides smudge-free copies more than 95 percent of the time.

Including All Necessary Information

- Give enough information to sell. Answer all questions; overcome all objections.

- Coordinate the sales letter with accompanying booklets, brochures, and leaflets. But make the letter carry the main sales message. Enclosures should serve as supplements.

Of course, the information you present and how you present it are matters for your best judgment. But you must make sure that you present enough information to complete the sale. You should leave none of your reader's questions unanswered. Nor should you fail to overcome any likely objections. You must work to include all such basic information in your letter, and you should make it clear and convincing.

In your effort to include all necessary information, you can choose from a variety of enclosures—booklets, brochures, leaflets, and the like. When you use such enclosures, you should take care to coordinate all the parts. In other words, all the parts in

the mailing should form a unified sales message. As a general rule, you should use the letter to carry your basic sales message. This means your letter should not shift a major portion of your sales effort to an enclosure. Instead, you should use enclosures mainly to supplement the letter. The enclosures might cover descriptions, price lists, diagrams, and pictures—in fact, all helpful information that does not fit easily into the letter. To ensure that all the parts in the mailing fit into a unified effort, you would be wise to direct your reader's attention to each of them. You can do this best through incidental references at appropriate places in the letter (for example, by saying "as shown on page 3 of the enclosed booklet" or "see page 7 of the enclosed brochure").

Driving for the Sale

After you have sold your reader on your product or service, the next logical step is to drive for the sale. After all, this is what you have been working for all along. It is a natural conclusion to the sales effort you have made.

- End with a drive for the sale.

How you should word your drive for the sale depends on your strategy. If your selling effort is strong, your drive for action may also be strong. It may even be worded as a command. ("Order your copy today—while it's on your mind.") If you use a milder selling effort, you could use a direct question. ("Won't you please send us your order today?") In any event, the drive for action should be specific and clear. In no way should it resemble a hint. For best effect, it should take the reader through the motions of whatever he or she must do. Here are some examples:

- In strong selling efforts, a command is effective. For milder efforts, a request is appropriate. Take the reader through the motions.

Just check your preferences on the enclosed stamped and addressed order form. Then drop it in the mail today!
Won't you please permit us to deliver your Tabor recorder on approval? The number is 1-800-348-8821. Order it now, while you're thinking about it.
Mail the enclosed card today—and see how right the *Atlantic* is for you!

Urging the Action

Because readers who have been persuaded sometimes put things off, you should urge immediate action. "Do it now" and "Act today" are versions of this technique. You can make the technique especially effective if you tie it in with a practical reason for doing it now. Here are some examples:

- Urge action now.

. . . to take advantage of this three-day offer.
. . . so that you can be ready for the Christmas rush.
. . . so that you will be the first in your community.

As in this National Geographic example, most sales mailings consist of a letter and a coordinated group of support pieces.

Recalling the Appeal

- Recalling the appeal in the final words is good technique.

Yet another effective technique for the close of a sales letter is to use a few words that recall the basic appeal. Associating the action with the benefits that the reader will gain by taking it adds strength to your sales effort. Illustrating this technique is a letter selling Maxell videotapes to retailers. After building its sales effort, the letter asks for action and then follows the action request with these words:

. . . and start taking your profits from the fast-selling Maxell videotape.

Another illustration is a letter selling a fishing resort vacation that follows its action words with a reminder of the joys described earlier.

It's your reservation for a week of battle with the fightingest bass in the Southland.

Adding a Postscript

Unlike other business letters where a postscript (P.S.) appears like an afterthought, a sales letter can use a postscript as a part of its design. It can be used effectively in a number of ways—to urge the reader to act, to emphasize the major appeal, to invite attention to other enclosures, to suggest that the reader pass along the sales message, and so on. Postscripts effectively used by professionals include the following:

• Postscripts are acceptable and effective.

PS: Don't forget! If ever you think that Action is not for you, we'll give you every cent of your money back. We are that confident that Action will become one of your favorite magazines.
PS: Hurry! Save while this special money-saving offer lasts.
PS: Our little magazine makes a distinctive and appreciated gift. Know someone who's having a birthday soon?

Evaluating Contrasting Examples

The following two letters show good and bad efforts to sell Killshaw's restaurant consulting services. Clearly the bad letter is the work of an amateur and the better one was written by a professional.

• Following are bad and good letters.

Weakness in an Illogical Plan. The amateur's letter begins with a dull statement about the consultant's services that is little more than an announcement of what the consultant does. Then, as a continuation of the opening, it offers the services to the reader. Such openings do little to gain attention or build desire. Next comes a routine, I-viewpoint review of the consultant's services. The explanation of the specific services offered is little better. Although the message tells what the consultant can do, it is dull. The drive for action is more a hint than a request. The closing words do suggest a benefit for the reader, but the effort is too little too late.

Dear Ms. Collins:

• The bad letter is amateurish. It does little more than announce that services are available.

  You have probably heard in the trade about the services I provide to restaurant management. I am now pleased to be able to offer these services to you.
  From 28 years of experience, I have learned the details of restaurant management. I know what food costs should be. I know how to find other cost problems, be they the buying end or the selling end. I know how to design menu offerings for the most profitability. I have studied kitchen operations and organization. And I know how the service must be conducted for best results.
  From all this knowledge, I have perfected a simple system for analyzing a restaurant and finding its weaknesses. This I do primarily from guest checks, invoices, and a few other records. As explained in the enclosed brochure, my system finds the trouble spots. It shows exactly where to correct all problems.
  I can provide you with the benefits of my system for only $800—$300 now and $500 when you receive my final report on your operations. If you will fill out and mail in the enclosed form, I will show you how to make more money.

Sincerely,

Skillful Presentation of a Rational Appeal. The better letter follows the conventional sales pattern described in the preceding pages. Its appeal is rational, which is justified in this case. The opening quotation attracts attention. It holds interest for a restaurant manager. Thus, the chances of getting the prospect to read further are good. The following sentences explain the service quickly—and interestingly. Then, in good you-viewpoint writing, the reader learns what he or she will get from the service. This part is loaded with reader benefit (profits, efficiency, cost cutting). Next, after the selling

CASE ILLUSTRATION   **Sales Letters.** (Using Emotional Appeal to Sell New Orleans)
Sent to a select group of young business and professional people, this letter takes the readers through the experiences
that they will enjoy if they accept the offer.

September 9, 1996

Ms. Kathy Pettit
71721 Boyce Street
Atlanta, GA 30329

Dear Ms. Pettit:

*Casts
emotional
spell—whets
interest*

You slide back in the deep, plush chair, champagne tickles your nose,
the hills of Georgia float swiftly away 30,000 feet below--and the
cares of the week are left far behind in the steady whine of the jets.

Three more glasses, a mouth-watering selection of hors d'oeuvres,
and suddenly you're deplaning and swept up in the never-ending
excitement of America's fun capital--New Orleans. As the uniformed
doorman of the world-famous Royal Orleans welcomes you to the
understated elegance of the hotel's crystal chandeliered and marbled
lobby, you understand why this "city that time forgot" is the perfect
place for a completely carefree adventure--and that's what you're
on--a fabulous Delta Jet-Set Weekend. Every detail is considered to
give you the ultimate in enjoyment. You'll savor New Orleans as it's
meant to be experienced--gracious living, unsurpassed cuisine, jazz-
tempo excitement.

*Good
emotional
description—
vivid and
exciting*

*Note
you-viewpoint
throughout*

After settling in your magnificent Royal Orleans "home," you're off
to dinner at Antoine's--spicy, bubbling Oysters Bienville, an exotic
salad, trout almondine, selected fromages, all mellowed with a wine
from one of the world's most famous cellars, and topped off with
spectacular cherries flambe. A memorable meal sets you up for the
night-spot tour of many-splendored delights--the spots where jazz
was born, the undulating strippers, Pete Fountain's chic club, and
the rollicking sing-along of Pat O'Brien's, where a tall, frosty Hurri-
cane signals the close of a perfect evening. Then, just before returning to the hotel, time for a steaming cup of dark, rich French Market cafe au lait and some extra-special doughnuts.

*Reviews
highlights of
trip quickly
yet thoroughly*

Saturday morning dawns bright and crisp--perfect for casual browsing through the "treasure" shops of the Quarter--the world of artists, antiques, and astonishing sights awaits you. From noon, you
are escorted through some of the famous areas of the city--the Garden District (where the elegance of the past lives on), the lake area,
and the most famous historical sights of the Quarter. Late afternoon
finds you approaching famed Commander's Palace for an exclusive
cocktail party and dinner. You'll practically hear the moan of ol'
river steamers on the mighty Mississippi as you dine.

110 South Barkay
Bell, FL 32619
407-444 6758
FAX: 407-444-6758

Ms. Kathy Pettit
September 9, 1996
Page 2

Night ends back in the Quarter--with the particular pleasure of your
choice. But don't sleep too late Sunday! Unforgettable "breakfast at
Brennan's" begins at 11 a.m., and two hours later you'll know why
it is the most famous breakfast in the world! Wrap up your relaxed
visit with shopping in the afternoon; then the mighty Delta jet
whisks you back to Atlanta by 7 p.m. This perfect weekend can be
yours for the very special price of only $375, which includes trans-
portation, lodging, and noted meals. For double occupancy, the price
per person is only $335. Such a special vacation will be more fun
with friends, so get them in on this bargain--you owe yourself the
pleasures of a Jet-Set Weekend in America's fun capital.

*Tells how
need can be
satisfied--
gives details*

*Perhaps the
action would
be more
effective if it
were more
direct, but it
is persuasive*

This Jet-Set Weekend to dream about becomes a reality starting
right now--a free call to the Delta Hostell at 800-491-6700 confirms
your reservation to escape to the fun, the food, and the fantasy of
New Orleans, city of excitement. The city is swinging--waiting for
you!

*The final
words link
the action
with the
main appeal*

Sincerely,

Mary Massey

Mary Massey
Travel Consultant

P.S. Check out our web site at http://www.sun_n_fun.com/ for some
sights and sounds you'll experience on this fabulous Jet-Set
Weekend.

This sales letter is noteworthy for its concise presentation of major sales points to support a special discount offer. The words are clear and the appeal is rational. The closing drive for action and the postscript re-emphasizing benefits are well done.

The main message is in the attention position.

OPTIONS YOU SHOULD CONSIDER. AN OFFER YOU CAN'T REFUSE.

Dear MIS Professional:

Although somewhat matter-of-fact, these words give urgency to the message

Now through September 30, 1994 you can take advantage of an important offer from IBM.

This discount offer tempts the reader to continue reading

To introduce you to the Options™ by IBM® product line, we're giving you a $100 Rapidpay® Check good towards a $500 purchase of the option(s) of your choice. Why are we doing this? Because we want Options by IBM to be the source for your organization's after-market computer product needs.

IBM is introducing Options by IBM—a new and broad line of peripherals, add-ons, add-ins and system enhancements for many non-IBM as well as IBM systems. No matter which option you choose, you get the quality, technology and reliability IBM is known for—without having to pay a premium.

• Whether your organization currently uses IBM computers or not, you can still get the advantage of IBM quality.

Note the selection of sales points

Options by IBM products are not just for IBM computers. In fact, they're tested for compatibility with a variety of industry-standard personal computers, as well as Micro Channel® IBM and many non-IBM personal computers.

• And you won't have to pay more for this quality.

Options by IBM are competitively priced with other leading brands on the market today. So it doesn't pay to settle for anything less than IBM quality.

Good you-viewpoint throughout the sales presentation

• In a job like yours, peace of mind is a valuable asset.

You've got a lot riding on your computer systems running properly. So it's reassuring to know that IBM will give you the assistance you need to keep them running that way, including 24-hour support by the IBM HelpCenter®, a 30-day, money-back guarantee, and an IBM warranty. (See enclosed brochure for more information.)

A COMPLETE LINE OF QUALITY PERIPHERALS AND OPTIONS FOR IBM AND MANY NON-IBM COMPUTERS

But don't take our word for it. See for yourself. Enclosed you'll find a $100 Rapidpay Check which is good on a $500 minimum order of any Options by IBM product(s). But you have to act now. This offer is only good through September 30, 1994.

The drive for action is strengthened with recall of the discount and time limitation

Sincerely yours,

Steve Starkey
Options by IBM, Brand Management

OPTIONS. by IBM

A postscript directs the reader to the enclosed brochure and re-emphasizes action

P.S. The enclosed brochure describes Options by IBM in detail. If you'd like more literature, please complete and return the enclosed business reply card, or call us at 1-800-426-4550. And, be sure to use the enclosed $100 Rapidpay Check before September 30, 1994.

has been done, the letter drives for action. The final words tie in the action with its main benefit—making money.

Dear Ms. Collins:

"Killshaw is adding $15,000 a year to my restaurant's profits!"

With these words, Bill Summers, owner of Boston's famed Pirate's Cove, joined the hundreds of restaurant owners who will point to proof in dollars in assuring you that I have a plan that can add to your profits.

My time-proven plan to help you add to your profits is a product of 28 years of intensive research, study, and consulting work with restaurants all over the nation. I found that where food costs exceed 40 percent, staggering amounts slip through restaurant managers' fingers. Then I tracked down the causes of these losses. I can find these trouble spots in your business—and I'll prove this to you in extra income dollars!

To make these extra profits, all you do is send me, for a 30-day period, your guest checks, bills, and a few other items I'll tell you about later. After these items have undergone my proven method of analysis, I will write you an eye-opening report that will tell you how much money your restaurant should make and how to make it.

From the report, you will learn in detail just what items are causing your higher food costs. And you will learn how to correct them. Even your menu will receive thorough treatment. You will know what "bestsellers" are paying their way—what "poor movers" are eating into your profits. All in all, you'll get practical suggestions that will show you how to cut costs, build volume, and pocket a net 10 to 20 percent of sales.

For a more detailed explanation of this service, you'll want to read the enclosed information sheet. Then won't you let me prove to you, as I have to so many others, that I can add money to your income this year? This added profit can be yours for the modest investment of $800 ($300 now and the other $500 when our profit plan report is submitted). Just fill out the enclosed form, and place it along with your check in the addressed and stamped envelope that is provided for your convenience.

That extra $15,000 or more will make you glad you did!

Sincerely,

<aside>• Following the conventional pattern, the better letter uses good strategy and technique.</aside>

Using a Second Letter in the Mailing

A currently popular way of adding strength to the sales effort is to use a second letter (or note or memorandum) as a part of the mailing. This second letter is usually headed with a boldly displayed message saying something like "Don't read this unless you've decided not to buy." Apparently, the technique is effective. At least, direct-mail professionals seem to think it is, for they use it widely. An example of such a message follows.

Accompanying a letter selling subscriptions to a magazine, *The Texas Fisherman*, this second message reviews the main sales message of the letter. As you can see, it is really another sales letter. It even ends with a drive for action, and it has a postscript that intensifies the drive. This mailing was highly successful. Perhaps the second message contributed to its success.

<aside>• A second letter is often a part of the mailing.</aside>

DON'T READ THIS UNLESS YOU HAVE DECIDED NOT TO CLAIM YOUR *FREE TEXAS SALTWATER BIG 3 BOOK.*

Frankly, I'm puzzled.

I just don't understand why every fisherman and boat owner in Texas doesn't run—not walk—to the nearest mailbox and return the enclosed FREE BOOK CERTIFICATE.

Here's a guidebook that will bring you better times and better catches each and every time you head for that big beautiful Gulf. PLUS, you get a money-saving bargain on a subscription to THE TEXAS FISHERMAN—the news monthly that Texas outdoorsmen swear by. Month after month you'll be in on all the latest tips about where the big ones are biting. Each issue sports super-big photographs of fishermen grinning their heads off, holding up the catch for the day.

And Dave Ellison is there each month telling you the latest there is about boating. Plus many other boating articles every month. Over 34,000 Texas boaters and fishermen are subscribing now. And the yearly renewal rate is just fantastic!

But those 34,000 aren't important this morning. The important person to me today is YOU. I want YOU as a new subscriber—because I know you'll find more helpful advice here than in any other publication in the state today.

<aside>• Here is an example of a second letter.</aside>

Do yourself a favor. Send off your FREE BOOK CERTIFICATE now, today, while you're thinking about it. Have more fun and catch more fish!

Sincerely for better fishing and boating,

Bob Gray, Publisher

P.S. Please hurry! We have only a limited supply of this FREE BOOK. Get yours now!

....

SUMMARY ▶ by Chapter Objectives

① Use imagination in writing skillful persuasive requests that begin indirectly, use convincing reasoning, and close with goodwill and action.

1. Requests that are likely to be resisted require an indirect, persuasive approach.
   - Such an approach involves developing a strategy—a plan for persuading.
   - Your opening words should set up this strategy and gain attention.
   - Follow with convincing persuasion.
   - Then make the request—clearly yet positively.
   - The request can end the letter, or more persuasion can follow (whichever you think is appropriate).

② Describe the choices available in determining the structure of a sales mailing.

2. Sales letters are a special type of persuasive request.
   - Typically, a sales mailing contains a number of pieces—brochures, reply forms, and such.
   - But our emphasis is on the sales letter, which usually is the main item in the mailing.

③ Describe the preliminary steps of studing the product or service and selecting the appeals to use in a sales letter.

3. Begin work on the sales letter by studying the product or service to be sold. Also, study your prospects, using marketing research information if available.
   - Then select an appropriate appeal (or appeals).
   - Appeals fall into two broad groups: emotional and rational.
     —Emotional appeals play on our senses (taste, hearing, and so on) and our feelings (love, anger, fear, and the like).
     —Rational appeals address the rational mind (thrift, durability, efficiency, and such).
   - Select the appeals that fit the product and prospects.

④ Discuss the choices of letter mechanics available to the sales writer.

4. Before beginning to write, you determine the mechanics of the mailing.
   - Sales letters may use impersonal salutations (Dear Student), headlines rather than inside addresses, pictures, lines, and such to gain attention.
   - Your imagination is the major limitation on what you can choose to do.

⑤ Compose sales letters that gain attention, persuasively present appeals, and effectively drive for action.

5. Although innovations are frequently used, most sales letters follow this traditional plan:
   - The opening seeks to gain attention and set up the sales presentation.
   - The sales message follows.
   - In emotional selling, the words establish an emotional atmosphere and build an emotional need for the product or service.
   - In rational selling, the appeal is to the thinking mind, using facts and logical reasoning.
   - Throughout the letter, emphasis is on good sales language and the you-viewpoint.
   - All the information necessary for a sale (prices, terms, choices, and the like) is included in the letter, though references are made to details in the enclosures (brochures, leaflets, and so on).
   - Next comes a drive for a sale.
     —It may be a strong drive, even a command, if a strong sales effort is used.
     —It may be a direct question if a milder effort is desired.
     —In either case, the action words are specific and clear, frequently urging action *now*.
     —Taking the action may be associated with the benefits to be gained.
     —Postscripts often are included to convey a final sales message.

CRITICAL THOUGHT QUESTIONS

1. Explain why a persuasive request letter is usually written in the indirect order. Could the direct order ever be used for such letters? Discuss.

2. What is the role of the you-viewpoint in persuasive request letters?

3. Discuss the relationship between a persuasive request letter and a sales letter.

4. What appeals would be appropriate for the following products when they are being sold to consumers?

   a. Shaving cream.
   b. Carpenter's tools.
   c. Fresh vegetables.
   d. Software.
   e. Lubricating oil.
   f. Ladies' dresses.
   g. Perfume.
   h. Fancy candy.
   i. CD players.
   j. Hand soap.

5. With what products would you use strong negative appeals? Positive appeals?

6. When could you justify addressing sales letters to "occupant"? When to each reader by name?

7. Rarely should a sales letter exceed a page in length. Discuss this statement.

8. Should the traditional sales-letter organization discussed in the text ever be altered? Discuss.

9. Discuss the relationship between the sales letter and its accompanying printed brochures, leaflets, and the like.

10. When do you think a strong drive for action is appropriate in a sales letter? When do you think a weak drive is appropriate?

CRITICAL THINKING EXERCISES

1. Criticize the persuasive request letter below. It was written by the membership chairperson of a chapter of the Small Business Advisory Service, a service organization consisting of retired executives who donate their managerial talents to small businesses in the area. The recipients of the letter are recently retired executives.

Dear Ms. Petersen:

As membership chair it is my privilege to invite you to join the Bay City chapter of the Small Business Advisory Service. We need you, and you need us.

We are a volunteer, not-for-profit organization. We are retired business executives who give free advice and assistance to struggling small businesses. There is a great demand for our services in Bay City, which is why we are conducting this special membership drive. As I said before, we need you. The work is hard and the hours can be long, but it is satisfying.

Please find enclosed a self-addressed envelope and a membership card. Fill out the card and return it to me in the envelope. We meet the first Monday of every month (8:30 at the Chamber of Commerce office). This is the fun part—strictly social. A lot of nice people belong.

I'll see you there Monday!

Sincerely yours,

2. Criticize the sales letter below. It was written to people on a mailing list of fishing enthusiasts. The writer, a professional game fisher, is selling his book by direct mail. The nature of the book is evident from the letter.

Have you ever thought
why the pros catch
fish and you can't?

They have secrets. I am a pro, and I know these secrets. I have written them and published them in my book, *The Bible of Fishing*.

This 240-page book sells for only $29.95, including shipping costs, and it is worth every penny of the price. It tells where to fish in all kinds of weather and how the seasons affect fishing. It tells about which lures to use under every

condition. I describe how to improve casting and how to set the hook and reel them in. There is even a chapter on night fishing.

I have personally fished just about every lake and stream in this area for over forty years and I tell the secrets of each. I have one chapter on how to find fish without expensive fish-finding equipment. In the book I also explain how to determine how deep to fish and how water temperature affects where the fish are. I also have a chapter on selecting the contents of your tackle box.

The book also has an extensive appendix. Included in it is a description of all the game fish in the area—with color photographs. Also in the appendix is a glossary which covers the most common lures, rods, reels, and other fishing equipment.

The book lives up to its name. It is a bible for fishing. You must have it! Fill out the enclosed card and send it to me in the enclosed stamped and addressed envelope. Include your check for $29.95 (no cash or credit cards, please). Do it today!

Sincerely yours,

3. Criticize each of the following parts of sales letters. The product or service being sold and the part identification are indicated in the headings.

Letter Openings

Product or service: a color fax machine

a. Now you can fax in color!

b. Here is a full-color fax that will revolutionize the industry.

c. If you are a manufacturer, ad agency, architect, designer, engineer, or anyone who works with color images, the Statz Color Fax can improve the way you do business.

Product or service: a financial consulting service

d. Would you hire yourself to manage your portfolio?

e. Are you satisfied with the income your portfolio earned last year?

f. Dimmitt-Hawes Financial Services has helped its clients make money for over a half century.

Parts of Sales Presentations

Product or service: a paging service

a. Span-Comm Messaging is the only paging service that provides service coast to coast.

b. Span-Comm Messaging is the only paging service that gives you the freedom to go coast to coast and still receive text messages.

c. Span-Comm Messaging gives you coast-to-coast service.

Product or service: a color fax machine

d. The Statz Color Fax is extraordinary. It produces copies that are indistinguishable from the originals.

e. The extraordinary Statz Color Fax produces copies identical to the originals.

f. Every image the Statz Color Fax produces is so extraordinary you may not be able to tell a fax from an original.

Product or service: Vermont smoked hams

g. You won't find a better-tasting ham than the old-fashioned Corncob Smoked Ham we make up here on the farm in Vermont.

h. Our Corncob Smoked Ham is tender and delicious.

i. You'll love this smoky-delicious Corncob Smoked Ham.

Product or service: a unique mattress

j. Control Comfort's unique air support system lets you control the feel and firmness of your bed simply by pushing a button.

k. The button control adjusts the feel and firmness of Control Comfort's air support system.

l. Just by pushing a button you can get your choice of feel and firmness in Control Comfort's air support system.

Action Endings

Product or service: an innovative writing instrument

a. To receive your personal Airflo pen you have but to sign the enclosed card and return it to us.

b. You can experience the writing satisfaction of this remarkable writing instrument by just filling out and returning the enclosed card.

c. Don't put it off! Now, while it's on your mind, sign and return the enclosed card.

Product or service: a news magazine

d. To begin receiving your copies of *Today's World*, simply fill out and return the enclosed card.

e. For your convenience, a subscription card is enclosed. It is your ticket to receiving *Today's World*.

f. If you agree that *Today's World* is the best of the news magazines, just sign and return the enclosed card.

CRITICAL THINKING PROBLEMS

PERSUASIVE REQUESTS

1. As a business communication instructor, [you supply a name], you teach both an undergraduate and a graduate course. The graduate course is an elective component of the executive MBA. These students are highly motivated, working full time while participating in the program. They devote every other weekend for two years to attending classes, which meet from 8 A.M. until 5 P.M. on Fridays and Saturdays. But unlike the enthusiastic undergrads you work with in the mornings, these afternoon students seem polite but somewhat detached. Since you know they recognize the importance that communicating effectively plays in their jobs on a daily basis, you suspect something else accounts for their dispassionate behavior.

   However, it was not until you were talking with a former MBA student, Nancy Eickelman, that you recognized the possible culprit—big lunches. She reported growing very sleepy in afternoon classes, "wiped out" as she put it. Furthermore, she brought your attention to an article in *The Wall Street Journal* that reported on a popular Execufit wellness program recently instigated at Baldwin-Wallace College in Berea, Ohio. Basically, this program included fitness walking, lectures on fitness and nutrition, and healthy lunches. She encouraged you to persuade the dean of the graduate program to start this kind of program at your school.

   Not only do you think it's a terrific idea, but you're also quite convinced the experts you need for the lectures are right on your campus. In fact, they'd probably be honored to work with both the business faculty and this highly select group of MBA students. In writing your letter to the dean, persuade him or her to start a pilot program now rather than wait until next semester.

2. For years environmentalists have been pressing businesses to become more sensitive to pollution problems. And many businesses have responded both in the ways they produce and package their products. However, one area of environmental pollution that has not received the attention it deserves is noise pollution.

   A story in *The Wall Street Journal* reported that more than 9 million workers a year are exposed to dangerous levels of noise. And dangers coming from low-frequency, low pitched sources are often underestimated or even unrecognized since sound-level meters do not always catch it.

   Excessive levels of noise can lead to several problems that could impair employee productivity. In addition to hearing loss, excessive noise can cause fatigue, absenteeism, and accidents. While many manufacturing plants have been checked for noise levels, offices have been widely ignored.

   You're convinced that a noise audit of your offices

would be very constructive. Not only would you be able to identify any possible sources of excessive noise and take steps to eliminate or correct it, but you also would be demonstrating to your employees your concern for their welfare.

As Matt Lenaghan, director of human resources, write a letter to the president of your company, Mariana Deftos, persuading her to conduct the audit and follow through with any corrective actions needed. Stress the benefits to both the company and the employees.

3. Communication technology is changing so rapidly that you believe your company should review its communication policy now rather than wait for the annual review. Your present policy prevents employees from using phones aboard airlines, which you believe needs to be reevaluated. Not only is the competition between Airone, Flightlink, and Genstar causing the prices to drop, but also the technology itself is improving. The better quality service includes less breaking up or cutting off of calls. This means your employees who want to fax an important document no longer have to wait a couple of hours to send it.

Another innovation that needs to be included in the communication policy is the assignment of 500 numbers, numbers that go where the employees go. Since all the major telephone companies are offering the service, the cost is relatively inexpensive for the increased flexibility it offers employees and the company. However, there is a limited quantity of these numbers, which may drive the price up and the availability down if they're seen as providing a major competitive advantage or even as just a major convenience. Furthermore, airline phones now have the ability to receive calls. The recipient merely swipes a credit card through the airline's phone, which registers the passenger. Then the passenger can be reached by those on the ground.

The use of these new technologies and other new developments should be reflected in your company's policy. Write a persuasive letter to the president of the company, requesting immediate review and updating of the communication policy. Stress the benefits to the company as well as to the individual. Give specific examples where the new developments would give the company an edge over the competition.

4. As vice president of Fidelity Investments, one of your jobs is reporting results to investors. In fact, you and your company realize that the statement is the most important document you send your customers. While brochures may or may not always be read, the statement will. In fact, when you revised it a few years ago, it gave you a major competitive advantage over your competition until their forms, too, were revised. But as you recall, the design process took nearly two years. Therefore, you think you need to persuade the board of directors to authorize another review.

As before, your objective will have two missions—adding information and making existing information easier to see and use. In the last redesign, two added elements that your investors reacted to positively were the cash flow summary box and information on unrealized gains or losses. Your customers reported that these elements helped them immensely in their tax planning. You are sure part of this success was due to the use of focus groups and one-on-one interviews with investors. You'd like to see this methodology included again in the next redesign. You also realize that as your company grows, it needs to present itself in a professional, polished form. Attention to the function and look of the statement is critical to make your image consistent with your company's objective.

Persuade the board of directors to authorize immediate action on planning for and implementing the new design.

5. Your travel business has been doing well since your company "downsized" or "right-sized" just a few years ago. However, for the last couple of years you've relied heavily on temporary workers for holding down overall wages. In fact, last summer when business was booming, you had a difficult time finding competent temps. Even some of the temporary agencies, such as Manpower, reported a short supply of temp workers.

In planning ahead for next summer, you've determined that temps will still fit your needs best. And since your needs for help vary widely by season, the costs for temps are reasonable, for you're only paying them when you actually need them. They earn modest pay, but they aren't in your health plan, and other benefits are limited. But you want to assure that good ones will be available, so you need to persuade the owner to get a contract now rather than wait until the last minute.

You've read in *The Wall Street Journal* that Manpower is putting intensive efforts into recruiting good temps. It's enticed teachers to join it with offers of summer pay and chances for scholarships and book money. This sounds ideal to you. And you expect that other agencies will be doing the same. Write the owner a persuasive request for permission to get bids for summer contracts now. Explain that early planning will both give you some pricing breaks and assure the quality temps your travel business demands are there when you need them.

6. Megaskrub Oil Company recently accepted responsibility for one of the worst oil spills in the nation's history. Due to the bad publicity the company has received, stock prices have dropped dramatically and profits at the end of next quarter are predicted to be far below the norm. Needless to say, recent board meetings of the company have been filled with conflict, and tempers have been quick to flare.

As an environmental expert recently hired by Megaskrub in response to shareholders' demands, you receive an e-mail message this morning from the board's secretary asking you to prepare a persuasive letter to each board member selling any requests or recommendations you have based on the study you have just completed. The study you conducted recommended that the company sharply curtail its drilling program in three environmentally endangered coastal areas and temporarily discontinue drilling in a fourth. Although you have been told by the chief engineer that each of these large fields is extremely lucrative, you firmly believe it is urgent that the company adopt a proactive stance on environmental issues—even to the extent that it would make less money. As you see it, Megaskrub cannot survive the negative publicity of another environmental catastrophe. Thus, the company has little choice but to forgo short-run profits for longer-run survival.

Your writing task will not be an easy one, to say the least. The board is committed to keeping stock prices as stable as possible, and short-run profit is a key factor in that equation. The board secretary believes that board members should have ample time to think about your suggestions before the board convenes in two weeks.

You will construct a convincing request letter based on logical ideas and concepts related to environmentally sensitive issues. You will likely have to take the stance of a good debater; that is, you will need to identify objections to your request and then counter each objection with a benefit. The benefits will become an interwoven set of appeals you will use to persuade the reader to comply with your request.

Write the letter for the Megaskrub board members.

7. Several months ago, Ms. Veronica LeMay lost her life as she tried to rescue an injured passenger from a severe car wreck. As she tried to free the passenger from the wreckage, the gasoline tank of the car exploded, killing her and the passenger and burning two other emergency personnel. As a single parent, she is survived by two small children, a boy and a girl, who have been placed with Veronica's parents.

She had worked as an emergency medical technician for three years. Because of her young age and family life-style, she left little wealth to the family—a small insurance policy and some minor investments. Indeed, her loss to the community was tragic, for Veronica was an outstanding public servant and an excellent human being. You wonder about the support that her parents can provide for the children, as they are retired with fixed income and not people of significant means by any sense of the imagination.

As a civic-minded citizen of your community, you have joined with others in an effort to raise a Veronica LeMay Fund to help the LeMay family. In fact, the members of the group elected you president of the effort. As president, it is now your job to plan and to carry out the first collection campaign.

You first want to tap some of the prominent citizens of your community. So you will attempt to persuade these readers to give heavily and generously to the fund. The letter you prepare will need to be based on the most convincing appeals you can conceive. These appeals will form the heart of the letter that will request donations to the Veronica LeMay Fund.

Construct the persuasive request letter to the town leaders on your list. Make it sell the long-term meaning of being a faithful and loyal citizen of your community.

8. Today's persuasive writing assignment projects you into the role of the director of the Wellington (or some community that your instructor chooses) Chamber of Commerce. Acting as the liaison between the business community and the general public, your organization strives to attract new business to the Wellington area.

A direct-mail advertising piece on your desk catches your eye as you begin to plan your daily activities. The letter promotes and offers the services of Tom Peters, co-author of the classic *In Search of Excellence,* to speak to your local business community. According to the mailing, Mr. Peters would make a one-hour formal presentation to a group and then be available for a two-hour discussion after that. His fee for the sessions (three hours) is $10,000. Indeed, you believe this is a wonderful opportunity for the business community and general citizens of Wellington.

As you view the possible Peters's visit, you see two specific benefits arising from it. First, his presentation and presence would be well covered by the press in the community as well as those in adjoining areas. Such media coverage would certainly give you good exposure as a dynamic and avant-garde business community, one that should attract other organizations that might be considering site relocations. Second, Mr. Peters would introduce innovative and proven management concepts used by businesses all over the globe in an interesting and entertaining way. He is, to be sure, a captivating speaker. Thus, your business community would be perceived to be on the "cutting edge" of uniqueness in management philosophy and procedure.

You put pen to paper and determine that Mr. Peters's total cost for the program would amount to $15,000 (airfare, hotel, food expenses, publicity, and professional fee). Raising that amount from the business contingent in your community is your goal for the moment. So you decide to map out a persuasive request letter that will collect the money you need for the event. Those businesspeople who contribute $500 or more will receive front-row seats at Mr. Peters's presentation. Anyone who contributes $200 or more will be mentioned in the program.

Prepare a letter persuading local businesspeople to contribute to your fund for the Peters presentation. Select an appeal or appeals that will sway the readers to your way of thinking about the presentation. But you will need to have more than reader thinking. You'll need tangible contributions to make your idea a reality.

(Note to instructor: This case may be adapted to other authors, dignitaries, or speakers as situations may arise in local, regional, or state circumstances.)

9. As regional sales representative of Western Oil

Company, you are responsible for maintaining good business relationships between the company and its 35 franchised gasoline retail outlets. The service station dealers are obligated by contract to sell exclusively Western gasoline. They are not obligated to Western brands of tires, batteries, and accessories, known as TBAs in the industry. A big part of your job is to sell Western TBA products to these service station dealers.

In the next three weeks, Ms. Melanie Wilson, Western's vice president of marketing, plans to tour and inspect the service stations in San Francisco, the central part of your sales region. Wilson's impression of the franchise outlets will have a direct impact on your current and future success as a regional sales representative. Through much hard work and good promotional efforts, many of the dealers stock generous quantities of Western TBA products. Your concern, though, is about the general appearance and cleanliness of the stations. If your products appear in a station that is untidy and ill-kept, you know the perception of Western will suffer and, more specifically, the sales volume of gasoline and TBA products will likely decline. Thus, you'd like to have Western stations in your region looking neat and clean so that sales of Western products will increase. Of course, both you and the dealers will benefit from these sales increases. But the dealers are independent, and they don't like anyone telling them what to do. So you are on the edge of a dilemma: On one hand, you want to remain an interested friend to the dealer; and on the other hand, you want Ms. Wilson to be impressed with the physical appearance of the dealers' premises.

To solve this problem, you decide to write a persuasive request letter to all the Western dealers in your region. The letter will "sell" the dealers on the value of a tidy and clean appearance of their service stations. In writing the letter, remember that you have no direct authority over the franchised dealers. So you will have to sell them on the idea of keeping the premises clean to help them—not you!

Think through the strategy and select an appeal that is appropriate for the situation. Then develop that appeal into specific you-viewpoint reasons. Use these reasons as the heart of your letter to Western Oil Company dealers.

10. The Bear Creek Intermediate School (grades 5 and 6) burned down four weeks ago. Faulty electrical wiring was the reason; and the reconstruction of the physical facilities was fully covered by insurance. Through an amazing effort by Key Construction Company, the school has been restored so that children may begin attending classes in their own building again. During the interim, they were farmed out to other schools in the Philmont Independent School District while restoration work was completed.

When classes were resumed today, many students and teachers became nauseous and dizzy from toxic fumes that were in the air at the school. As principal of the school, you immediately notified the central

administrators, who made a thorough inspection of the facilities. They, along with the fire chief, concluded the fumes were originating from soot and residue that still remained on library books, textbooks, file cabinets, bookcases, walls, and such from the fire. Although the construction company paid a hefty fee for cleanup crews to do this work, it would seem their effort was haphazard and superficial to say the least. The school district's lawyer will certainly pursue the matter with both the construction company and the insurer to determine liability. But that will take time. Right now your concern is to keep the continuity of the students' learning experience intact.

Some parents have proposed that you extend the school year by two weeks and bring in emergency crews to completely reclean the entire school. As principal, you believe that by continuing to bus children to other schools, using vacant facilities at other schools, and placing some students in already existing classes can only further disrupt the students' learning activities. It is not healthy and certainly not in the best interests of the students. Your opinion is to keep classes going at the school and to have volunteers work at night, on weekends, and during the days to do the cleanup activities while classes continue. But to get these volunteers, you will need to persuade them to commit their time.

Thus, you must prepare a persuasive request letter to parents of the children in your school asking them to volunteer to help with cleanup activities. In the letter, you will convince the parents that their children's education will benefit most by keeping the school open now and beginning cleanup operations immediately. Nationally normed achievement tests will be given as usual in mid-April, right before the end of the school year (yours is not a year-round district). And you want the scores to reflect the continued development of each student.

Write the persuasive letter that will get you the volunteer assistance you so desperately need at Bear Creek Intermediate School.

SALES LETTERS

11. As an editor for Trade Service Corporation in San Diego, you love your job. Not only do you get to dress casually and have rock posters and decals decorating your work area, but you also get copies of promotional CDs. You are assigned to edit *Phonolog,* a 2,000-page product directory of prerecorded music. The directory lists every pop music release being sold by about 2,500 U.S. labels, including mammoth companies such as Columbia and Warner as well as tiny independents. The releases are listed by song, record, and artist. Additionally, the directory has special sections listing children's, Christmas, and international releases.

The directory is designed to help people make buying decisions. The company sees the product as one that bridges the gap between manufacturers, retailers, and customers.

Subscribers pay $45 a month or $540 a year for the service. In addition to the directory, they receive weekly updates. While most receive the information in printed form, some request it on disks. This computerized version of the catalog has a user-friendly interface, making the information easily accessible.

Currently, you have approximately 5,800 subscribers, who are mostly record-store owners. However, your boss wants to expand this base business to radio station owners, primarily those with pop music formats. Since your job involves keeping the directory up to date, you understand how accurate and thorough it is. Therefore, you've been selected to write the sales letter to these radio station owners. You may want to stress the fact that their station will not only always be up to date on the music industry, but his product also will help them present themselves knowledgeably to their listeners. Feel free to add other facts that would persuade radio station owners to subscribe.

12. You work for Motorola, the world's largest pager manufacturer. Your boss told you that the board has decided to support its distributors with a direct sales letter campaign targeted at middle-income families with teenagers but without pagers. And you've been asked to draft the letter promoting the recreational or family-use theme. While you realize that long gone are the days where only professionals and drug dealers used pagers, you need to convince these potential customers that this is the case.

You might want to cite examples of ways other people use pagers. For example, some child care centers, such as Kids Klubhouse in Portland, Oregon, give pagers to parents when they drop off their kids. Some parents give the pagers to their children, and other parents keep pagers so their children can reach them. Restaurants, such as TGI Friday's, use them to let customers or the kitchen help page waiters. There are even reports of people putting them on their animals to summon them. One farmer apparently beeped his cows when he wanted them to eat; a dog owner trained his dog to come home when the pager vibrated. Clearly, there are numerous uses of pagers.

The recent technological enhancements to the basic pager have created even more new possibilities. Not only can people be paged nationwide, but also data can be sent to pagers over wireless networks. Everything from financial data such as stock quotes, currencies, and bond prices to sport news such as scores, pre- and post-event analysis, and injury updates can be transmitted to pagers. A pager could even be programmed to beep you if your house has been broken into.

Be sure to include in the sales letter a variable [a merge field] for the name of the store(s) where pagers can be bought in the reader's area.

13. Recent developments in improved braking systems for in-line skates give this sport the potential to grow rapidly. Being unable to stop was a major cause for many people's hesitation to participate in skating. But with today's new braking systems, you predict more young and old alike will join the ranks of regular skaters.

Skating is one of the best fitness tools around. A study at the University of Massachusetts showed in-line skating burned calories and worked the heart as well as running and better than step exercise. Furthermore, people of all ages can skate. Even the health clubs are realizing they need to add facilities for in-line skating to keep their members coming back. Of course, serious competition and leagues are sprouting everywhere. And in good weather, skaters can take in fresh air and the local beauty while getting their exercise.

According to the National Sports Goods Association, skating is about to surpass tennis as the nation's sixth most popular sport. And its 12.5 million participants cross all age groups. Therefore, as the manager of an all-purpose sporting goods store, you believe you should be able to sell more skates to people of all ages. You decide to write a sales letter promoting family skating and your wide selection of skates and accessories for the whole family. Your target reader is the head of the household for residents within a five-mile range of your store. Your letter should not only convince your readers of the value and enjoyment skating would bring them, but it should also bring them into your store.

14. As the promotions director of Mammoth Mountain Ski Resort in Southern California, you're responsible for getting the word out on your new attraction—mountain biking. You officially started using your lifts to carry bikers to the top of trails in 1990; but while the number keeps growing a bit each season, your 50-plus trails can accommodate many more. Therefore, you decide to write a sales letter using a mailing list compiled by local merchants of visitors during the ski season. Not only are these skiers usually active and fit, but many also would probably enjoy seeing how the mountains look in the summer.

Your letter can stress that like skiing, your mountain trails offer trails for all levels and types of bikers. For the hard-core bikers, you have trails with challenging turns, rocks, and tree stumps as obstacles. For those wanting "safer," less-challenging trails, you offer an abundance of gentle mountain roads and jeep paths. For both groups you have short and long trails.

You can also promote the idea as reasonably priced. The lift tickets in the summer are only $15 compared to $38 in the winter. Also, the local hotels offer off-season rates during the summer. And bikers will get to enjoy their favorite restaurants without the winter crowds. Convince them summer mountain biking at Mammouth Mountain should be a must on their summer to-do list.

15. As James Andrews, a distributor for a new product from Securicor Alarms Ltd., you've just acquired a new product you think would sell extremely well in

big cities and near university campuses. It's a pocket device that squirts dye on an assailant. The dye isn't harmful and it doesn't smell. Also, it doesn't wash off soon. However, it does show up under ultraviolet light. And because the dye in each device is uniquely formulated, it can identify the criminal as the particular one.

The cost is reasonable—$16. The device does need to be restored every six months if it hasn't been used. Statistics show that in areas where the device has been installed in homes, break-ins are down 75 percent.

You decide to write a sales letter to managers of campus bookstores, convincing them not only to stock the item but also to display it prominently in the store. Of course, you'll promote the ease of use and effectiveness of the product. You may even want to include profit figures. In addition, you may want to appeal to the need to reduce crime on the campus, to make students who carry them feel more secure, and perhaps to their responsibility to protect their students. Jarring statistics and quotes from crime victims are often effective attention-getters for this type of product. Feel free to appeal to both the reader's emotions and knowledge.

16. As administrative assistant to Mr. Frank Wolfenbager, CPA, you have been given the assignment of writing a sales letter to small businesses in your locale. Mr. Wolfenbager restricts his accounting practice to tax issues only. And a good 85 percent of this practice is devoted to personal income tax counseling, planning, and preparation.

In the past year, however, the small-business component of the tax practice has shown a significant surge. In doing an informal exit survey of clients as they leave the office after having their tax returns prepared, you determine that many of your independently successful clients have referred their friends—who own small businesses—to Mr. Wolfenbager. It's his feeling—and yours—that this segment of the accounting services market merits a closer look. If this market could be developed, a more diversified practice could ensue. Possibly, another practicing accountant would join the firm. For you, however, this means more pay because you receive 30 percent of all billings to small businesses for doing the legwork involved.

For $100 each tax quarter, Mr. Wolfenbager provides the quarterly tax return (social security/medicare funds), any unemployment forms, state sales tax forms, and such—all computed based on the information submitted by the business. The quarterly fee also includes "normal and usual" phone calls and contacts with the IRS, state employment commissions, state comptrollers, and the like. If there are situations requiring extra research and preparation, Mr. Wolfenbager will bill the company beyond the $100 quarterly fee but not without consulting the firm first to determine its preference.

Thus, Mr. Wolfenbager puts the problem squarely on your shoulders: "I want to cultivate this market. It makes good business sense to provide a tax service to small partnerships and proprietors. But we'll need to sell our services. Prepare a sales piece on our letterhead that will promote our services in the new market. We'll use a brochure as an enclosure, and we'll purchase a mailing list of all small businesses in the area."

As you begin to think about the sales letter you must write, you first consider the reader benefits of the accounting services you provide. Although the dividing line between emotional and rational appeals is thin at best, you decide the rational benefits are your best bet to use as strategy. Convenience, saving time and frustration by not having to deal with government bureaucracies, saving money from tax liabilities and interest, professional experience, and such all apply as benefits that will accrue to customers as a result of your service.

But you will have to do more than list these benefits. You will need to weave them together with persuasive techniques—the you-viewpoint, positive emphasis, concreteness of diction, conversational tone, etc.—to create the message effect you desire. And you will need to develop a good attention-getting opening to set up the appeals.

Write the letter in a "picture-promise-push" sequence. You want your letter to sell, not just sound good. So make it specific and results oriented.

17. As director of the library at your school, you must sell area businesses on paying for periodical subscriptions. Most institutions of higher learning, both public and private, have experienced budget cutbacks in all activities. Appropriations from legislatures and unstable interest rates for endowments are the main causes for the cutbacks, although there are others to be sure. The bottom line, however, is that you do not have enough money in your budget to pay for all the subscription services that provide periodicals for the research needs of your students and your faculty.

At yesterday's library committee meeting, you discussed the problem at length. After distributing a list of the total periodicals to which the library subscribes, the committee whittled away at the list to separate the absolutely necessary from those that were secondary—a separation of the wheat from the chaff, so to speak. Yet, when you tallied the absolutely necessary periodicals' prices, the sum still exceeded the amount budgeted for periodicals by $7,000. In further discussion of the committee, members brainstormed what might be done to solve the problem. One idea that seemed to have special merit involved selling area businesses on picking up the tab on a publication(s) of their choosing. Indeed, if the businesses wanted to pay for several publications, you would certainly accept the payment. On one score, you appear to be lucky—you don't have to make any major personnel cuts. So you can maintain the same library hours for professionals that you have over the years.

At the end of the committee meeting, the members asked you to prepare a sales letter that would woo periodical purchases from local and regional businesses. They requested that you have a finished copy ready for their OK at the next meeting, which is next week. Because of your tight schedule, you will need to do much of the work today. So you begin to think about the plan you will use in your sales strategy.

As you zero in on the appeals, you reflect on what a school means to a community or city. To be sure, it means better citizens in general, but it also means a better work force. Thus, you decide you will appeal to pride in the community, the value of education, and whatever other appeals you think might move the readers to buy your product. As an enclosure, you will include a list of the periodicals and their prices. Some are relatively inexpensive ($35 to $40) while others, such as those in the sciences, are out of sight ($300 or more). If someone picks up the subscription for your journal, you will place a sticker on the journal noting it is "compliments of (business)." Contributors will also receive recognition as a Friend of the (your school) Library.

Identification of the appeals in your sales strategy is just one step in the process. You must now complete the strategy by adapting the appeals to the readers' needs. Complete the letter that will sell area businesses on purchasing periodicals for your school library. If they purchase them, everyone will win—the businesses, the students, the school, and the community!

18. As director of educational development at Georgetown University, you have recently conceived of a new program for high schoolers who earned good grades, and you think you can use it to recruit talented students for the university.

Called the Congressional Scholar Program (CSP), the program will bring together junior and some sophomore students for a one-week conference composed of lectures, tours, and excitement in Washington, D.C. To be selected, students must be in the upper 20 of their class and have strong recommendations of leadership potential from their high school principal. Also, no more than two students may attend from any one high school. You will limit each group to 30 participants, and you plan to involve three groups in the program.

During the weeklong conference, students will hear lectures from your distinguished faculty in political science about how our democratic form of government works. Overall, it is your goal to encourage students to learn more about their government and to become better, more productive citizens. In addition, you plan a week full of sightseeing and observing. Along with the monuments, galleries, and institutions, you will include meetings with legislative, executive, and judicial dignitaries as well as a two-hour tour of the White House. In fact, the group will observe the Senate and House in session. The students will stay in

Jesuit House, a remodeled dormitory for executive seminars, workshops, and such. Breakfast and dinner are provided, but students will need to buy their own lunches. The five-day, six-night experience will conclude with a "mock Congress" with participants sitting in a simulated legislative session.

The cost for the program is $700 plus airfare. High school administrators might question whether students could get the same features if they went to Washington, D.C., alone. You believe the group experience, the lecturers, and the informative tours provide advantages that far outweigh an individual tour.

What you must do now is sell the program to the students. And you decide to do so through a direct-mail letter to individual students. You have purchased a mailing list of students who have 3.5 GPAs or better in large high schools in metropolitan areas. In your letter you will need to sell the "sizzle" of the program and the learning experience it represents. You will not begin with a "Congratulations, you have been selected . . ." type of opening because it would be misleading. The students—or more likely their parents—will have to pay for the trip. You will work hard to make the benefits of the CSP exceed the cost so that your three groups of 30 will fill up immediately.

Prepare the sales letter to the high schoolers on your list. You will include enrollment forms and forms for administrators to attest to class standing and potential. Make the letter sell to students as well as their parents.

19. As a direct-mail consultant, you have recently been contracted by Southeast Legal Services (SLS) to prepare a sales letter to corporate prospects about purchasing prepaid legal services. SLS promises subscriber/buyers instant access to attorneys, unlimited telephone consultations, and an array of free or discounted legal services for $15 or less per month. Last year, there were 58 million Americans covered by legal plans. And SLS wants to tap into the market for such services. But SLS expects tough competition from other vendors already established in the field. That's the reason it wants a personalized, direct sales message that only a letter can provide.

Some competitors concentrate on enrolling individuals and solicit credit card holders and bank customers with inserts in bills. You want to take the corporate route and sell to benefit packages for employees. Thus, SLS has purchased a mailing list of human resource managers to which you will direct your selling effort. If SLC is successful, it could sell also to unions.

SLS offers free drafting of wills, document review, and unlimited telephone consultations in its basic services. Also, the plan allows a 25 percent discount on most other legal services, with SLS monitoring fees carefully to make sure plan members receive true discounts. In addition, subscribers can obtain divorces, for example, at no extra charge and be represented in other cases such as drunken driving.

Operationally, SLS refers clients to a panel of participating attorneys who have two or more years of experience. These lawyers provide service to and consultation with subscribers. Also, SLS permits subscribers to work outside its lawyer network when special expertise is needed; but a group of three network lawyers would have to attest to the needed expertise.

Using these ideas, write the sales letter that SLS has contracted for. You will need to determine appeals before you actually construct the letter. Remember the letter is directed to human resource directors and not individual subscribers.

8

Pattern Variations in Other Business Messages

Upon completing this chapter, you will be able to write effective collection letters, claim letters, memorandums and order letters. To reach this goal, you should be able to

1 Design a series of collection letters according to the credit risk involved and standard practice in the field of business.

2 Write effective letters for each of the stages in the collection series: early, middle, and last-resort.

3 Write claim letters that explain the facts in a firm but courteous manner.

4 Explain the variations in the form of memorandum stationery.

5 Discuss the wide range of formality used in memorandums.

6 Describe the primary differences between memorandums and letters written for similar situations.

7 Write clear and effective memorandums for routine inquiries, routine responses, policies and directives, bad-news messages, persuasive messages, and messages to file.

8 Write orders that begin with a clear authorization; contain an orderly arrangement of units, descriptions, and prices; cover all shipping

DIFFERENCES AND SIMILARITIES IN OTHER LETTER SITUATIONS

As we have noted, if you know the techniques and patterns covered in previous chapters, you should be able to adapt them to other letter situations. In this chapter we cover some of the more important of these likely situations. Specifically, we cover collections, claims, memorandums, and orders. Much of this coverage will support what you have already learned, but you will find some exceptions.

- The techniques previously studied apply to other situations, with some exceptions.

I N T R O D U C T O R Y   S I T U A T I O N

▶ to Collection Letters

Play the role of credit manager of Loren's Department Store. Like most credit managers, you have the assignment of handling all credit accounts. Your department is responsible for approving (or disapproving) all credit requests. After a credit account has been established, you keep records of credit sales, send out statements of what is owed, and record payments as they come in. For the most part, your duties are routine and pleasant.

You have one duty, however, that is less routine and less pleasant. It is the duty of collecting money from credit customers who do not pay on time. Most customers pay regularly, of course, but there are always some who do not. Getting delinquent customers to pay usually involves contacting them by mail. First, you send notices, which serve mainly as reminders. Then, if the reminders do not work, you send letters. *Collection letters,* as they are called, are the subject of this discussion. ■

THE COLLECTION SERIES

When your customers do not pay their bills on time, you must try to collect. If you follow conventional business practice, you are likely to use letters in your efforts. You could use other ways—for example, the telephone, personal visits, or collection agencies. But letters are the most common way.

- Letters are used to collect past-due accounts.

Now, computers play a significant role in the collection effort. In addition to their use in maintaining purchase and payment records, they are used to flag delinquent accounts and to generate collection letters. How to write these letters is the subject of this discussion.

- Computers are used in the collection effort.

Collecting through a Series of Efforts

Before discussing techniques used in writing collection letters, you should know how businesses usually collect past-due bills. Typically, their collection efforts consist of a series of steps. Each step is a contact (usually by mail) with the delinquent customer. In a first step, the bill is sent with a due date specified. If this bill is not paid, a second bill may be sent—maybe even a third. Sometimes, for added strength, reminder words such as "Please," "May we remind you," or "You have probably forgotten" are added to a past-due bill. These reminders may be in various forms—printed enclosures, stickers, or stamped words.

- The typical collection procedure consists of a number of progressively stronger efforts. The first are reminders.

If the reminders fail to bring in the money, the efforts get stronger. Letters are sent—in series, each one progressively stronger. How may letters are sent depends on company policy. When the buildup of letters fails to bring in the money, a final letter ends the mail effort. Additional action through collection agencies or the courts may follow.

- Next comes a series of persuasive letters, ending with a final, threatening letter.

FIGURE 8–1   Diagram of the Collection Procedure

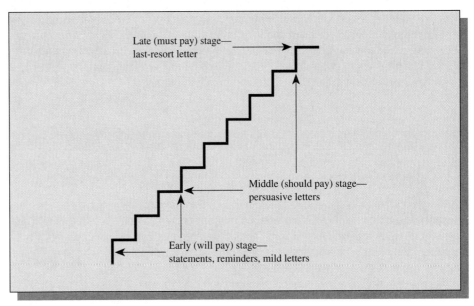

Late (must pay) stage—
last-resort letter

Middle (should pay) stage—
persuasive letters

Early (will pay) stage—
statements, reminders, mild letters

NOTE: The number of steps depends on the policy of the firm.

• The series resembles a stairway.

In a sense, the buildup of collection efforts resembles a stairway (see Figure 8–1). Each step represents a collection effort. The first steps are called *early-stage* collection efforts. These are mainly reminders. The assumption at this stage is that the debtors *will* pay and that the company need only remind them.

Following the early (will-pay) stage comes the middle stage of collection. Here the company's attitude is that debtors have to be convinced they *should* pay. This is truly a persuasion stage. The company's goal is to sell the debtors on the idea of paying, while retaining goodwill. This stage comprises the bulk of most collection series.

After all persuasive efforts to collect have failed, the letters must stop. Thus, a final stage must end the collection-letter series. In this stage the debtors have to be convinced that they *must* pay. This last-resort stage consists of just one letter. Because this letter is so different from the others, it justifies being treated as a stage in itself.

Determining the Collection Series

• The number of and time interval between letters are influenced by degree of risk and practice in the field.

The number of and time intervals between collection efforts vary by company. The choices made are influenced by two factors: the class of credit risk and standard practice in the field.

Typically, companies evaluate the degree of credit risk involved. They move slowly with good risks and fast with poor risks. Thus, a collection series for good risks might extend over several letters, only a few with poor risks. Businesses with a wide range of risks among their customers might classify them into groups and use different series of letters for each group.

• Collection efforts between businesses are usually short and fast.

Collection efforts between businesses illustrate how standard practice influences collection efforts. Businesses expect and generally receive payments from each other on time. Thus, when payment between businesses is slow, collection efforts typically move fast. Also, credit dealings between businesses are generally viewed as more impersonal than credit dealings between a business and an individual. As a result, collection efforts between businesses are more matter-of-fact and firm.

Careful screening of credit applicants can greatly reduce the need for collection letters.

Bill-paying time can be a frustrating experience for many people. Often the collection efforts of creditors compete for attention. Those that stand out from the rest are the ones most likely to bring in payment.

I N T R O D U C T O R Y   S I T U A T I O N

▷ to Reminder Letters

At the moment, your work at Loren's Department Store involves trying to collect from some good credit customers who are behind in paying their bills. All of them passed Loren's credit investigation at one time or another, but now they are delinquent. You must do something about it.

All the people in the group you are concerned about have open accounts. As is Loren's practice, you billed them on the due date and a month later. Another month later, you billed them a third

Before the United States had its current postal system, businesspeople placed collection messages in newspapers. Typical of these messages is the following, which appeared in the *Norwich (Conn.) Packet* in 1779:

BY AUTHORITY

To ALL those who are indebted as a subscriber for Newspapers, whose accounts are one or more years' standing—without even regarding the fashionable substitutes for payment, of IF's, AND's, & WAIT a few Days, VERILY, VERILY, I say unto you, that I have lately had loud and repeated calls for CASH!

Therefore, Nevertheless, Notwithstanding—I now inform all, great or small, young or old, rich or poor, male or female, that are indebted to me for the *Norwich Packet* that I must and will have my due, for this reason: "The Paper makers threaten the Printers, and the Printers threaten the Post." What is to be done? What steps can be taken! All debts must be paid, and I must pay mine;—of course you must pay me, before the expiration of one month from this date, if you wish to keep your accounts out of the hands of an Attorney.

Beriah Hartshorn
Franklin, August 1, 1779

time—this time with a printed reminder. Today you are ready to take a stronger step—to remind them in a letter.

Because Loren's has so many customers, you will use a form letter. You know that most large businesses do this, but you will work hard to make your form letter sound as individually tailored as possible. This means you will try to make it read like an individual letter and not like a form letter. You do not want to offend these customers. After all, they were at one time a very select group.   ∎

....

EARLY-STAGE COLLECTIONS

- The early stage of collection begins with reminders of the bill.

As long as you believe that your credit customers intend to pay, you should handle them tactfully. At first, you can simply send duplicates of the original bill, as suggested earlier. If these reminders do not bring in payment, you will need to write a first collection letter. This will usually be an early-stage letter. Although such letters vary in organization, most of them follow this plan:

- Most early-stage letters are written this way.

- Begin directly with a reminder of the past-due bill.

- Include some goodwill material—comments showing confidence that the debtor will pay.

- End with a friendly, forward-looking, goodwill comment.

Writing Reminder Letters

- Such letters remind directly and are short and courteous.

As noted previously, the most common early-stage letters are direct reminders of bills past due. Such letters are usually short—sometimes only two or three sentences. They remind the debtor forthrightly of the past-due account. They soften the force of the directness by conveying the underlying impression that the debtor will pay. They are courteous throughout, and they do not lecture or talk down. As the account is not long past due, they rarely use persuasive language urging payment.

Contrasting Reminder Letters

- Following are good and bad examples of an early-stage letter.

The following two form letters show bad and good ways of reminding Loren's delinquent customers of their debts. Both letters do the job of reminding, but the better one is more courteous.

Written for customers with good past records, this direct-style letter reminds about the past-due bill and subtly persuades the reader to pay.

Date

FIELD(Personal Title) FIELD(First Name) FIELD(Initial). FIELD() FIELD(Last Name)
FIELD (Street Address)
FIELD(City), FIELD(State) FIELD(Zip Code)

Dear FIELD(Personal Title) FIELD(Last Name):

Direct clear yet courteous

Your payment of the FIELD(Balance Due) now FIELD(Months Late) months past due on your account has not yet reached us. In view of your good record, we are confident you will want to clear your account by sending us your check right away. For your convenience, we are enclosing a return-addressed envelope.

Subtle persuasion

Goodwill close— a friendly forward look

We appreciate your past business, and we look forward to serving you again.

Sincerely,

Hilda Brand

Hilda Brand

enclosure

240 N. Berlin St.
Hamlin, TX 79520
915-676-5890
FAX: 915-676-5891

An Unnecessarily Harsh First Letter. The bad letter begins bluntly—and negatively. Its words are too harsh for this stage of the collection effort. The close contains the most positive wording in the letter, but such dangling expressions belong to the distant past.

Dear Mr. Beloit:

You have not responded to the last two statements we sent you and are now two months past due on your account. Thus, I am sending you yet another statement (enclosed). I urge you to pay immediately and protect your credit record.
Thanking you in advance for your payment.

Sincerely,

Enclosure

A Courteous Reminder to Pay. The better letter directly reminds the reader of the past-due bill, but it does so with courtesy and tact. It gives the reader a face-saving explanation (that he or she forgot). It includes the subtle suggestion that paying is something the reader will want to do. Appropriate goodwill comments end the letter.

Dear Mr. Beloit:

This is just a friendly reminder that your account with us shows $317.90 now two months past due. If you're like me, you'll appreciate my calling the matter to your attention.
Loren's genuinely appreciates your business. We look forward to serving you in the years ahead.

Sincerely,

INTRODUCTORY SITUATION

▶ to a Series of Persuasive Collection Letters

Back at your credit manager's desk at Loren's Department Store, you have analyzed the results of your reminder letters. On the whole, you are satisfied. Many of the delinquent customers came through. As you expected, however, some ignored your letter. Now you will have to take stronger measures.

Following a convention established by many companies over long years of experience, you will now write stronger letters. These letters will attempt to persuade—to show why the debtors *should pay*. Each letter will be stronger than the last. Of course, the collection letters stop when a debtor pays. But you will continue sending letters to debtors who do not pay. You will stop the buildup of letters when you think there is little chance that the debtor will respond to them.

The big task before you now is to write the letters that will bring in the money. Obviously, this is no routine letter-writing job. As the following pages show, it takes the very best in strategy and in persuasive writing. ■

MIDDLE-STAGE COLLECTIONS

If your reminders do not collect the money, you will need to write stronger letters to convince debtors that they *should* pay. Here your procedure is to select a basic appeal and then to present this appeal convincingly. That is, you persuade. Thus, you use the persuasion techniques described in Chapter 7.

Analyzing the Strategy

As in other cases requiring persuasion, the readers' wishes run contrary to yours. You want them to pay. They have shown by ignoring your reminders that at best they are not eager to pay. Thus, they are not likely to receive favorably your persuasive letter to collect. More than likely, they do not want to hear from you at all. In such situations, you must gain reader attention at the beginning. If you do not, the odds of getting your message across are slim.

In persuading debtors to pay, you should use strategy. As in other persuasion cases, you should begin by looking at the situation as the readers see it. Then you should select appeals that will work with your particular readers.

Although the available appeals are varied and may be applied with overlapping variations, they generally fall into the following categories:

- Pride—appeals to the reader's concern for self and what others think.

- Ethics—appeals to "doing the right thing."

- Self-interest—emphasizes why it is best for the reader to pay.

- Fear—stresses the bad things that could happen by not paying.

After selecting an appeal, you should develop it. That is, you should think out the reasoning that will persuade the reader to pay. Then you should present this reasoning in your letter with whatever strength is appropriate for the stage of your collection effort. Although such letters vary in organization, this is the most common plan for writing them:

- Begin with attention-gaining words that set up the appeal.

- Present the appeal using you-viewpoint adaptation and persuasive language.

- Request payment (you may end here).

- Consider ending with words recalling the appeal.

Gaining Attention in the Opening

This persuasion letter is not invited. It is probably not even wanted. Thus, your first words have a special need to gain attention. As your readers have received your reminders, they know that they owe you. More than likely, most of them intend to pay when it is convenient. They may quickly label your letter as just another dun and put it aside. If this letter is to have a chance of succeeding, it must gain attention right away.

To gain attention, you will need to find some interesting opening words. Whatever words you select, they should help set up your basic appeal. The possibilities are limited only by the imagination.

One successful late middle-stage letter began with the question, "When they ask about you, what should we tell them?" These personal words clearly gain attention, and they set up a discussion of the dire consequences of losing credit. Another beginning got the readers' attention with these words: "How would you write to a good friend on an embarrassing subject?" This personal and interesting question sets up a discussion of a topic that relates to friendship—to the reader's moral obligation to a friend.

Persuasively Presenting the Appeal

Following the persuasive strategy previously discussed, you next present the appeal your opening has set up. Because your opening words set up the appeal, the shift at this point should be smooth and natural.

- Debtors do not receive such letters favorably.

- Persuading debtors to pay requires strategy.

- First, select an appeal from these categories: pride, ethics, self-interest, fear.

- Then develop the appeal.

- Follow this plan.

- As the letter is not welcome, the opening should gain attention and should set up the strategy.

- Presentation of the appeal comes next.

Back in the 1870s, a little peddler arrived in a western mining town with little more than a mule, a wagon, and a wagonload of assorted merchandise. He had no sooner turned onto Main Street than the mule balked.

Calmly, the little peddler spoke: "This is once. Now giddap!" The mule didn't move.

Again the peddler spoke: "This is twice. Now giddap!" The mule didn't move.

A third time the peddler spoke: "This is the third time. Now giddap!" The mule didn't move.

The little peddler calmly walked to the back of the wagon, got his rifle, walked up to the mule, and in front of half the people in town shot the mule dead.

Without a mule, the little peddler could go no place, so he started a store in the town. It prospered, and in time people began to buy on credit. A few got a little behind in their payments. The little man just mailed them their bills. Across the bottom of each bill he wrote, "This is once."

He never had any trouble collecting.

- Persuade convincingly using just the right strength for this stage of collection.

As in all persuasive writing, your task here is to adapt to the reader's point of view. More specifically, you persuade—you sell—you convince. Your words should carry just the right degree of force for the particular stage of collection you are in. Early in the series you persuade mildly; toward the end you persuade forcefully. But do not forget that effective persuasion does not insult, talk down, lecture, or show anger. Instead, it is caring and friendly. Keep in mind also that throughout this stage of the collection series you hope to collect, to maintain cordial relations, and perhaps even to continue doing business with the debtor.

Closing with a Request for Payment

- End with a clear request for payment.

After you have made your persuasive appeal, the logical follow-up is to ask for the payment. You should ask directly, in words that do not merely hint at payment but form a clear question. "Will you please write a check for $77.88 today and mail it to us right away?" meets this requirement. "We would appreciate your writing and sending your check for $77.88" does not.

- Linking payment with a benefit to be gained is good.

In collection letters, as in sales letters, a closing reminder of a benefit resulting from the action strengthens the appeal. For example, a letter stressing the advantages of a prompt-pay record for a business could end with these words:

Will you please write out and mail a check for the $275.30 right now while you're thinking about it? It's your best insurance for keeping your invaluable prompt-pay record.

Contrasting Form Collection Letters

- Following are a series of good and a series of bad middle-stage letters.

The following examples are of contrasting series of middle-stage letters for the situation described at the beginning of this section. The letters, which include exact amounts owed, appear to be individually prepared; this is one benefit of today's word processing and database software's merge features. The letters in the first series are not very good. Those in the second series are much better.

Poor Writing and Weak Appeal in a Bad Series.   Letters like those in the first series are used all too often in business. Such letters have little appeal. What little they have does not form a logical buildup in strength throughout the series. In addition, these letters are all poorly written. Actual tests have shown them to be far less effective than the letters that follow the plan given in preceding pages.[1]

Flaws in the first letter are obvious. Its direct beginning is too harsh for this stage, and its I-viewpoint development of the appeal to the value of a good credit rating is hurried, lecturing, and generally ineffective. It includes also a second appeal—an appeal to shame. As you know, mixing appeals can be dangerous.

Dear Mr. Benoit:

I was very much disappointed to learn that you still have not paid your past-due account of $247.81 now 75 days past due. I have contacted you several times in regard to this matter and have endeavored in every way to persuade you to pay this honest obligation.

• This bad one has weak appeal and is harsh.

I had hoped to make you see that your credit depended on payment of your bills. However, it would appear that this phase of the matter does not interest you, and we are compelled to draw our own conclusions.

I am not in a position to devote much time to any one account, and your continued neglect will only cause us all a great deal of unpleasantness. I, therefore, urge you to give this matter your prompt attention.

Sincerely,

The second letter also is written with I-viewpoint emphasis. Its heavily negative words give the effect of directness, and they give away the objective before any persuading can be done. The tone is negative throughout.

Dear Mr. Benoit:

As you have ignored our last letter, I must insist that you pay the $247.81 now 60 days past due on your account.

I cannot understand why you are permitting your credit record to be ruined. Your credit record is valuable to you, and you should want to protect it. You can protect your credit record only by paying your bills on time.

• This bad one is typical of letters often used in business.

You will agree that we have made every effort to cooperate with you. We have been patient and have a right to expect you to meet your end of the bargain.

I will look forward to your immediate payment.

Sincerely,

The third letter attempts to shame the reader, and its negative language probably invites anger more than it persuades. Also, its negative review of last-resort action possibilities is premature for middle-stage collection letters.

Dear Mr. Benoit:

I have notified you on many previous occasions that your account with us is in arrears. Apparently, you have chosen to ignore all our notices. Once again, I appeal to your better judgment and request that you make payment. The amount owed is $247.81, now 90 days past due.

My time is valuable to this concern; therefore I cannot devote too much attention to any one account. Your continued failure to heed my requests will force me to take drastic action. I can do one of two things. I can report you to the Retailers Credit Bureau, in which event your credit would be severely injured. Or I can turn this matter over to our attorney for legal action.

• This harshly worded letter invites anger.

I am expecting payment by return mail.

Sincerely,

Buildup of Appeal in a Good Series.   The better series generally follows the instructions given in preceding pages. Each letter contains strong persuasion. Although each

• Gradual buildup of strength is evident in the following better series.

[1] The letters in these two series were tested through a Baton Rouge, Louisiana, department store. The second (good) series proved to be almost twice as effective as the first (bad) series.

September 17, 1996

Mr. Fulton M. Folts, President
Folts Furniture, Inc.
4217 Pemberton Road
North Attleboro, MA 02763

Dear Mr. Folts:

Good interest value

"Sure pay" as a credit record means sterling integrity, as you know.

"Prompt pay" means all that and more. It means alert business management.

Opening sets up discussion of appeal

You have both records, and we appreciate your account because you do. The record is worth a lot to you in the trade.

Appeal is strong-concise

The only way to keep a "prompt pay" standing is to pay promptly-- every time. And since your payment of $1,358.38, now 45 days overdue, is slipping over the margin, we'd like to see you send a check right away and clear it up. Then we could happily regard the lapse as a temporary matter and keep your card in the preferred file, where it belongs.

Good drive for payment recalls advantage reader gains by paying

Whether or not you have enjoyed much stove-selling weather, you were certainly foresighted in getting your stock early. Those Firefly Reflectors are worth more now than they were when you bought them. Definitely, it was a good deal for you.

Reference to goods bought and not paid for is subtle persuasion

Won't you make it a good deal for us, too? You can do so by sending us your check for $1,358.38 in the enclosed addressed envelope. Do it now and keep your "prompt pay" reputation.

Sincerely,

Shannon O Tatum

Shannon O. Tatum
Credit Manager

1380 Fulton Dr.
Madison, WI 53707
608-890-4567
FAX: 608-890-4556

The negativeness of this letter to a department store customer is justified because the customer has ignored two notices and three letters. The previous letters stressed the advantages of paying. Now it is time to stress the disadvantages of not paying.

Fultons Inc.

April 22, 1996

Ms. June I. Matson
1713 Penelope Lane
Baytown, TX 77520

Dear Ms. Matson:

Personal reference makes strong bid for attention

Introduce appeal— (negative effects of losing credit)

How much is it worth to you? It's your credit record I am referring to, and it's a most important question to you, now that it hangs in the balance.

Frank you-viewpoint language

Strong presentation of appeal

The good reports we got on you when you opened your account told us that you have successfully handled your promises to pay promptly for a long time. We know that you must want to maintain this good rating, for it means so much to you. Aside from the obvious advantages of credit buying, it is important to you personally. The community and your friends judge you by how you fulfill your promises. It is vital to your own peace of mind to know that you have fulfilled your promise to pay.

Shows way out—by paying

Request for payment follows logically

Direct request adds strength

Because your credit record means so much to you, it is hard to understand how you have permitted your account of $371.43 to run six months past due. Won't you please save your good credit record by sending us payment today?

Sincerely,

Frederick O. Calmes

Frederick O. Calmes
Credit Manager

3317 AVONDALE AVENUE • LIVONIA, MI 48151 • 313-678-9900 • FAX: 313-678-9954

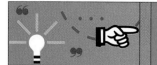
"What would your neighbors think if we repossessed your car?" the collection letter read.

"I have taken the matter up with them," the delinquent debtor responded. "They think it would be a lousy trick."

Crotchety old Mr. Crump received the following collection message from the big-city department store: "We are surprised that we haven't received any money from you."

The old gentleman responded, "No need to be surprised. I haven't sent any."

Obviously annoyed by strong collection letters, a retailer responded with these choice words: "I am doing the best I can. Every month I place my bills in a hat. Then I draw out bills and pay them until my money runs out. If you don't stop pestering me with your collection letters, you won't even get in the hat next month."

A retailer ordered a carload of refrigerators before paying for the last order. The manufacturer responded with a collection message saying that the goods could not be sent until payment was made for the last order.

"Unable to wait so long," the retailer replied. "Cancel order."

The collection letter was terse: "Please remit the amount you owe us right away."

The response was quick and equally terse: "The amount we owe you is $145.20."

letter in the series is stronger than the preceding one, no anger or lecturing tone is evident. The words are calm and reasonable throughout the series.

The first letter begins with an interesting question. The you-viewpoint of the question gives it extra attention value. The letter then moves into a presentation of the fair-play appeal, which it develops skillfully. The writing is strong yet positive. The closing request for money flows logically from the persuasion. Notice how the suggestion of urgency strengthens the request.

Dear Mr. Benoit:

- Good use of the fair-play appeal is shown here.

How would you write to a good friend on a somewhat embarrassing subject? That's the question we must answer now, and we're not sure that we know just how to go about it. You see, you are that friend; and the subject is your overdue account.

As you recall, some time ago you wanted something we had, and we were happy to let you have it simply on your promise to pay 30 days later. We are happy to have served you. But it's only fair, isn't it, that now you should fulfill your end of the agreement?

So, in all fairness, will you please send us your check for $247.81? As your account is 60 days past due, please do it right away. An addressed envelope is enclosed for your convenience.

Sincerely,

The second letter in the good series begins with an attention-gaining exclamation. The opening words set up an appeal to the reader's pride in having a prompt-pay record. Then the letter develops the appeal convincingly. The request for money logically follows the appeal. The final words link the action with the reward it will bring the reader.

- This letter skillfully uses an appeal to pride.

Dear Mr. Benoit:

You don't belong in that group!
Every day Loren's deals with hundreds of charge customers. More than

99 percent of them come through with their obligations to pay. We mark them as "prompt pay," and the doors to credit buying are opened to them all over town. Less than 1 percent don't pay right away. Of course, they sometimes have good reasons, and most of them explain their reasons to us. And we work something out. But a few allow their good credit records to tarnish.

Somehow, you have permitted your account to place your name in this last group. We don't think it belongs there. Won't you please remove it by writing us a check for $247.81, now 75 days past due? This would place you in the group in which you belong. You can use the addressed envelope or drop it by our store office. We're open 9–9, Monday–Saturday.

Sincerely,

The third letter in the series also has a strong attention-gaining opening. The following explanation builds the case convincingly. It is more negative than the explanation used in the two preceding letters. For the first time in the series, the message contains more talk about the consequences of not paying than the advantages of paying. But letters at this stage of the series can afford to be somewhat negative. After describing the consequences of not paying, the letter shows how paying can avoid them. The final words link the action with a benefit it will give the reader.

Dear Mr. Benoit:

What should we report about you?

As you may know, all members of the Capital Credit Bureau must report their long-past-due accounts for distribution to the members. At the moment, your own account hangs in the balance. And we are wondering whether we will be forced to report it. We are concerned because what we must say will mean so much to you personally.

A slow-pay record would just about ruin the good credit reputation you have built over the years. You wouldn't find it easy to buy on credit from Capital Bureau members (and this includes just about every credit-granting business in town). Your credit privileges would probably be cut off completely. It would take you long years to regain the good reputation you now enjoy.

So won't you please avoid all this by mailing a check for $247.81, now 90 days past due? It would stop the bad report and save your credit record.

Sincerely,

- Frankness and conviction make this letter effective.

I N T R O D U C T O R Y   S I T U A T I O N

▷ to Last-Resort Collection Letters

Assume now that the middle-stage collection letters you wrote for Loren's Department Store brought in money from most of the delinquent accounts. As is usually the case, however, they did not work with every debtor. Your problem now is to deal with these delinquents.

You think that you have given the delinquents every reasonable chance to pay, that the time has come to end the collection effort. So you will write a final letter. In it you will tell the debtors that unless they pay this time, you will turn the accounts over to a local collection agency. The agency will assist in collecting, and it will report the bad credit records to other businesses. You will also tell the debtors how this action will affect them. Then you will give them one last chance to pay. You do not like to do this, but the debtors have left you no other choice.

The letter will have to be strong, because it is the last one. The following section tells you how to write this letter. ■

LAST-RESORT LETTERS

Hard as you may try, your collection letters will not bring in all of the money. Some debtors will ignore your most persuasive efforts. Because you cannot continue your collection efforts indefinitely, you will need to take last-resort action with these

- Collection series end with a final (last-resort) letter.

CATHY © (Cathy Guisewite. Reprinted with permission of Universal Press Syndicate. All rights reserved.)

debtors. You will use the final letter in the collection series to inform them of this action.

A number of last-resort actions are available to you. One of the most common is to report the account to some credit interchange group, such as a local credit bureau. Another is to sell the account to a collection agency empowered with full authority to take legal steps if necessary. Yet another is to take the delinquent to court. You will need to decide what action is best in your case. In making your decision, you should consider the customs in your field of business, the nature and amount of the account, and the image of your firm.

In planning last-resort strategy, you should keep in mind that laws govern collection procedures and that more laws of this kind are likely to be enacted. Currently, a few states have debt-collection laws, and federal legislation controls some areas of debt. The state laws are numerous and varied, but they generally protect consumers from extreme abuses. The federal laws prohibit using language that threatens garnishment of wages, taking possession of property, and involving the consumer's employer and bank. As far as we can determine, the practices suggested in the following pages are in accord with current U.S. legislation.

Justifying Directness

Clearly, the final letter in the collection series conveys bad news. And usually indirectness is appropriate for such situations. This case, however, is an exception. We recommend directness for this letter, and for good reason.

As you have learned, directness lends strength. You have reached the point in the collection series where strength is justified. You did not use directness throughout the middle-stage because you were concerned with keeping goodwill. You wanted to salvage the account. Now you are more interested in collecting money. Thus, you can justify using the following time-tested direct plan for writing the last-resort letter:

- Begin by stating what you are doing, and why.
- Persuade by explaining the effects of this action—firmly, clearly, and without anger.
- Give the reader a last chance to pay by setting a deadline and urging that it be met.
- Perhaps end by associating paying with avoiding the effects of the action that will be taken if payment is not made.

Presenting the Action Directly

You begin the last-resort letter with a clear statement of your action. That is, you tell right away what you are going to do. Such direct openings are strong, and they gain

---

- They threaten some last-resort action (reporting to credit bureau, taking to court).

- You should know the laws governing collections.

- This bad-news letter logically is written in direct order.

- Directness adds strength, which is appropriate in this case.

- This time-tested plan is effective.

- Begin the letter with the threat of action. It is good to justify the action.

attention. In addition, you might consider bringing in facts that justify the action. Of course, the reader probably knows these facts very well. Even so, mentioning them may hold down a defensive reaction by the debtor. Something like this would do the job:

Your failure to pay the $378.40 now seven months past due on your account leaves us no choice but to report you to the Omaha Credit Bureau.

Interpreting the Action

Your explanation of the effects of the action on the debtor comes next. This is your last effort to persuade. In developing the persuasion, you should place yourself in the reader's position to see how last-resort action will affect him or her. It may, for example, mean the end of credit buying, court costs, loss of prestige, and personal embarrassment. Whatever the effects, you should select those most appropriate in the one case. Then you should decide how to present them convincingly.

• Then explain the effects of the action on the debtor. Use you-viewpoint.

Describing the effects of your action requires your best writing skills. You will especially need to watch the tone of your words. You need not be as tactful as you were in earlier letters, but you will need to avoid showing anger. As you know, anger invites resistance. So, instead of showing anger, let your words show concern for the debtor's problem. You wish things had not turned out this way, but the debtor's actions leave you no choice.

• The words should show concern, not anger.

Offering a Last Chance in the Close

After describing the effects of the last-resort action, you should give the debtor a last chance to pay. Thus, your close should set a deadline for payment or perhaps for other arrangements. You should urge the debtor to meet this deadline. As in other persuasive efforts, your final words might well recall what the debtor will gain (or avoid) by paying. The following close meets these requirements well:

• In the close, offer a deadline for paying before action is taken.

We will report you to the Capital Credit Bureau on the 15th. So won't you please help yourself by sending us your check for $129.90 by that date? It's the one way you can save your credit reputation.

• Recall the appeal.

Contrasting Last-Resort Letters

Both of the following last-resort letters are strong. For reasons explained below, the second one clearly is superior.

• Following are good and bad examples of last-resort letters.

Weakness in an Angry Letter. The indirect order in the first letter is the letter's greatest weakness. In addition, because they invite resistance, the angry words tend to

Sent after seven unsuccessful efforts to collect, this form letter was made to appear personally written by working in specific facts of the one case.

FANNINS
DEPARTMENT STORE

3423 S. Longfell Rd.   Jayess, MS 39641   601-565-4000   FAX: 601-565-4012

July 10, 1996

Mr. Tyrone H. Perry
409-87 Wicker Street
Bellsville, Ontario K8P 3Z1

Dear Mr. Perry:

Direct statement-gets attention —

Your failure to answer any of our seven requests for payment of the $3,317.10 now 10 months past due leaves us no choice but to take you to court for collection. We sincerely want to avoid this action for it would be unpleasant for both of us. It would be especially unpleasant for you.

Although strong, shows no anger— only concern for the reader —

For you it would mean that you would be forced to pay. You would pay not only the $3,317.10 you owe, but also court costs. In addition, you would pay attorneys' fees.

Also, legal action would be embarrassing to you. It produces the kind of information people talk about. Your friends would pick it up. So would other businesspeople. Results might well be an end to your credit buying. And your credit reputation would be injured permanently.

Explanation of effects of action is strong and convincing

Strong appeal for payment— in terms of reader benefit —

You can avoid the effects of court action only by paying before the 17th, the day we shall turn your account over to our attorney. Won't you please help yourself by mailing your check in the enclosed, self-addressed envelope by that date? It's the only way you can avoid the cost and embarrassment of going to court.

Links payment with benefits to be gained

Sincerely,

Crystal O. Charles

Crystal O. Charles
Credit Manager

Enclosure

reduce effectiveness. Also, the threat of action comes late—far from the beginning position of emphasis. Nowhere in the letter is there explanation of the effects of the action.

Dear Ms. Benoit:

We can no longer tolerate your complete disregard of your long-past-due account. We have written you repeatedly, but you have not shown the courtesy of an acknowledgment. Therefore, we must now turn over your account to the Capital Credit Bureau.

We will give you one week from the date of this letter to make payment of the $3,251.49, now 120 days past due. If payment is not received by May 3, we will take action.

Sincerely,

• This bad letter is mainly angry words.

Strength in a Calm and Firm Appeal.   The better letter gets right down to business with a clear statement of the action that will be taken. Then it moves into a convincing interpretation of this action. Notice the you-viewpoint—how the words emphasize the effects on the one reader. Although the message is negative, the overall tone is wholesome. There is no evidence of anger. The close, a final recall of the disadvantages of not paying, leaves the action in the reader's hands.

Dear Ms. Benoit:

Your failure to respond to our previous attempts to collect your 120-days overdue account of $3,251.49 leaves us no choice but to turn your account over to the Capital Credit Bureau for collection. This is an action we had hoped not to take, for it is unpleasant for both of us—particularly for you.

For you it means that you would be forced by the courts to pay the amount of your bill—plus court costs. In addition to being expensive, legal action may be embarrassing to you. Also, your credit record could be permanently injured.

Both of us want to avoid these bad effects of legal action. We'll do our part by holding off action for seven days after the date of this letter. To do your part, you must pay us before that date. It's all up to you, for only you can save your credit record and the embarrassment of court action.

Sincerely,

• This good letter is strong, yet shows concern.

I N T R O D U C T O R Y   S I T U A T I O N

▶ to Claim Letters

Occasionally something goes wrong with the goods and services that Pinnacle buys. When this happens in your area of responsibility, your job is to look after Pinnacle's interests. Today it happened. You received by motor freight an order for two dozen fire extinguishers. All of them were damaged. Leaking acid had ruined their finish. As Pinnacle cannot accept them, you must write the seller, explaining what happened, and getting the seller to correct the situation. In other words, you have to write a claim letter. Because the local fire marshal has ordered Pinnacle to have the fire extinguishers in place by next Monday, you must act fast.

The facts of the case tell you that this is not a routine letter. The news in claim letters is bad—bad for the writer and bad for the reader. How best to handle claim situations certainly requires careful thought. The following discussion should guide your thinking when you must handle claims.   ■

· · · · · · · · · ·
CLAIMS

When something goes wrong between a business and its customers, usually someone begins an effort to correct the situation. Typically, the offended party calls the matter to the attention of those responsible. In other words, he or she makes a claim. The

• Claim letters are written to correct for damages. They should follow this plan.

claim can be made in person, by telephone, or by letter. Our concern here is how to make it by letter. The following pages discuss a plan for handling claims by letter. In summary form, the plan is as follows:

- Begin directly. Tell what is wrong.
- Identify the situation (invoice number, product information, etc.) in the text or in a subject line.
- Present enough of the facts to permit a decision.
- Seek corrective action.
- End positively—friendly but firm.

Using Directness for Bad News

• Use directness for this bad-news because . . .

Claim situations are bad-news situations. Goods have been damaged or lost, a product has failed to perform, or service has been bad. The situation is unhappy for both writer and reader.

• (1) the reader wants to know and (2) it adds strength.

As you know, usually bad-news situations are handled in indirect order. But claims are exceptions—for two good reasons. First, businesspeople want to know when something is wrong with their products or services so they can correct the matter. Thus, there is no reason for delay or gentle treatment. Second, as we have noted, directness lends strength, and strength in a claim enhances the likelihood of success.

• Identify the transaction involved.

A claim letter concerns a particular transaction, item of merchandise, or service call. So that your reader will quickly know exactly what your claim is about, you will have to include the necessary identification information and place it somewhere near the beginning. What you include depends on what is needed in each case—invoice number, order number or date, serial number of product, and so on.

• Do this incidentally or in a subject line.

You can handle the identification information incidentally or in a subject line. By incidental handling we mean working it into the letter in a subordinate way. Handling it in a subject line involves using the mechanical device described and illustrated in Appendix B. Because a direct beginning is appropriate in the claim letter, the subject line may begin this directness, for it actually begins the message. The following example illustrates good wording and content for a subject line:

Subject: Damaged condition of fire extinguishers on arrival, your invoice No. C13144

Stating the Problem Directly

• Begin by stating the claim clearly, including all essential information.

A good claim letter is a combination of courtesy and firmness. You begin by stating the problem clearly. And you include all information necessary for judging it. Sometimes it lends strength to the claim if you explain the consequences of what happened. A broken machine, for example, may have stopped an entire assembly line; or damaged merchandise may have caused a loss in sales. The following beginning sentence illustrates this point:

The Model H freezer (Serial No. 713129) that we bought from you last September suddenly quit working, ruining $517 of frozen foods in the process.

Explaining the Facts

• Present the facts that justify the claim—objectively and without anger.

Your next logical step is to present the supporting facts. Do this in a straightforward manner. Include all the facts needed to judge the legitimacy of your claim. And do this frankly and respectfully, avoiding words that suggest anger or mistrust. Your goal is to present your case objectively, letting the facts justify your case.

Giving Choice in Correcting Error

• Next, handle the claim.

The facts you present should prove your claim. So your next step is to follow logically with the handling of the claim. How you handle the claim, however, is a matter for you to decide.

CASE ILLUSTRATION   Claim Letters. (Polite Firmness in a Claim about Defective Carpeting)

In this letter a hotel manager presents a claim about defective carpeting. She makes the claim directly and forcefully—yet politely. She explains the problem clearly and emphasizes the effect of the damage.

CHARLES HOTEL

September 17, 1996

Mr. Luther R. Ferguson, President
Rich Carpet, Inc.
13171 Industrial Boulevard
Seattle, WA 98107

Dear Mr. Ferguson:

Clearly states problem and identifies transaction

Direct statement of problem

Subject: Color fading of your Kota-Tuff carpeting, your invoice 3147 dated January 3, 1995.

Emphasis on effect

The Kota-Tuff carpeting you installed for us last January has faded badly and is an eyesore in our hotel pool area. As you can see in the enclosed photograph, the original forest green color now is spotted with rings of varying shades of white and green. The spotting is especially heavy in areas adjacent to the pool. Probably water has caused the damage. But your written warranty says that the color will "withstand the effects of sun and water."

Explains nature and extent of defect

Establishes case firmly

Suggests solution

As the product clearly has not lived up to the warranty, we ask that you replace the Kota-Tuff with a more suitable carpeting. If you are unable to find a satisfactory carpeting, we request a refund of the full purchase price, including installation.

Justifies claim

I will appreciate your usual promptness in correcting this problem.

Sincerely,

Luella E. Dabbs

Luella E. Dabbs
Manager

tos

Enclosure (photograph)

2-201 East 15th Street
North Vancouver, BC V7M 1S2
604-678-9080
FAX: 604-678-9076

One way of handling the claim is to state specifically the action you want taken— return of money, free repairs, new merchandise. Another is to leave the decision to the reader. As most businesspeople want to do the right thing for their customers, often this choice is the better one.

Overcoming Negativeness with a Friendly Close

Your final friendly words should remove all doubt about your cordial attitude. For added strength, when strength is needed to support a claim, you could express appreciation for what you seek. This suggestion does not support use of the timeworn "Thanking you in advance." Instead, say something like "I would be grateful if you could get the new merchandise to me in time for my Friday sale."

Contrasting Examples of Claim Letters

The following two letters show contrasting ways of handling Pinnacle's fire extinguisher problem. The first is slow and harsh. The second is courteous, yet to the point and firm.

A Slow and Harsh Letter.   The first letter starts slowly with a long explanation of the situation. Some of the details in the beginning sentence are helpful, but they do not deserve the emphasis that this position gives them. The problem is not described until the second paragraph. The wording here is clear but much too strong. The words are angry and insulting, and they talk down to the reader. Such words are more likely to produce resistance than acceptance. The negative writing continues into the close, leaving a bad final impression.

Dear Ms. Golby:

As your records will show, on December 7 we ordered 24 Fireboy extinguishers (our Order No. 7135). The units were shipped to us by Red Arrow Freight (your Invoice No. 715C) and arrived at our loading docks December 15.

At the time of delivery, our shipping and receiving supervisor noticed that all the boxes were soaked with fluid. Further inspection showed that your workers had been negligent in checking the cap screws. As a result of their negligence, acid leaked and destroyed the chrome finish on all the units.

It is hard for me to understand a shipping system that permits such errors to take place. Pinnacle does not accept these fire extinguishers. Further, we want these damaged units taken off our hands and replaced with good ones. Because we will be inspected by the fire marshal Monday, we further insist that the replacements reach us by that date.

Respectfully,

A Firm yet Courteous Letter.   The second letter follows the plan suggested in preceding paragraphs. A subject line quickly identifies the situation. The letter begins with a clear statement of the problem. Next, in a tone that shows firmness without anger, it tells what went wrong. Then it requests a specific remedy and asks what to do with the damaged goods. The ending uses subtle persuasion by implying confidence in the reader. The words used here leave no doubt about continued friendship.

Dear Ms. Golby:

Subject: Acid leakage of Fireboy extinguishers, your Invoice No. 715C

The condition of the 24 Fireboy extinguishers received today has affected their ability to function.

At the time of delivery, the condition of your shipment was called to the attention of the Red Arrow Freight Company driver by our shipping and receiving supervisor. Upon inspection, we found all the boxes thoroughly soaked with fluid. Further inspection revealed that at least six of the extinguishers had leaked acid from the cap screws. As a result, the chrome finish of all the units had been badly damaged.

As we are under orders from the fire marshal to have this equipment in our plant by Monday, please get the 24 replacement units to us by that date. Also, will you please instruct me what I should do with the defective units?

I am aware, of course, that situations like this will occur in spite of all precautions. And I am confident that you will replace the extinguishers with your usual courtesy.

Sincerely,

INTRODUCTORY SITUATION

▷ to Memorandums

To introduce yourself to memorandums, go back to your hypothetical position with Pinnacle. Much of your work involves communicating with fellow employees. Of course, oral communication serves your needs most of the time, for the bulk of your communicating is with people near you or easily reached by telephone. But sometimes you must communicate within the organization in writing, especially if the person you want to reach is unavailable or in another location or if you want a permanent record of your communication. Writing the formal letters discussed in preceding chapters hardly seems appropriate in intracompany communication, for such communication tends to be informal. In intracompany communication, instead of writing a letter, you would probably write an e-mail message or a memorandum, which is really an in-house letter. As you will see, the contents of these messages are much like those of letters except that these messages have a different physical arrangement and tend to be more informal. How to write them is the subject of this discussion. ■

THE NATURE OF MEMORANDUMS

The letter-writing instructions presented in the preceding chapters also apply to both printed and electronic memorandums (commonly called memos). Memorandums, of course, are letters written inside the organization, though a few companies use them in outside communication. Memorandums are primarily the written messages exchanged by employees in the daily conduct of their work. As you will see in Chapter 11, some memorandums communicate factual, problem-related information and are classified as reports. Those not classified as reports are the memorandums that concern us at this time. Nevertheless, much of the following discussion applies to both types.

- Memorandums are letters sent within the company.

Variations in Form

Most large companies have stationery printed especially for memorandums. Sometimes, the word *Memorandum* appears at the top in large, heavy type. But some companies prefer other titles, such as *Interoffice Correspondence, Office Memo,* or *Interoffice Communication.* Below this main heading come the specific headings common to all memorandums: *Date, To, From, Subject* (though not necessarily in this order). This simple arrangement is displayed in Figure 8–2. Because memorandums are often short, many companies use 5 × 8½-inch stationery for them as well as the conventional 8½ × 11-inch size. As Figure 8–3 shows, memorandums are usually initialed by the writer rather than signed.

Large organizations, especially those with a number of locations and departments, often include additional information on their memorandum stationery. *Department, Plant, Location, Territory, Store Number,* and *Copies to* are examples (see Figure 8–4). Since in some companies memorandums are often addressed to more than one reader, the heading *To* may be followed by enough space to list a number of names.

Not all companies use printed memorandum stationary for processing memorandums. In some the memorandums are individually typed. In others, memorandums are

- Most large companies use printed memorandum stationery with *Date, To, From,* and *Subject* headings.

- Some larger companies have additional headings (*Department, Plant, Territory, Store Number,* and such).

- Memorandums are processed in various ways: individual typing, templates or macros, e-mail.

FIGURE 8–2   A Typical Electronic Mail Memo

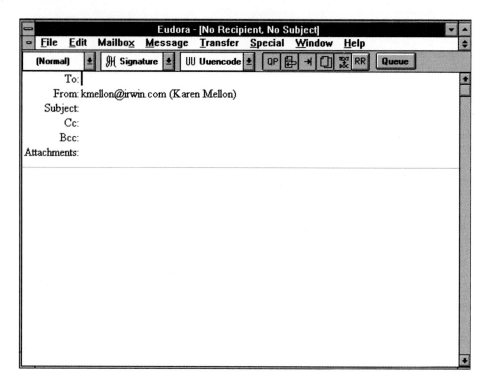

created through the use of template or macros (a word processing feature that prompts you for heading information and formats the document). In addition, many companies have memorandums structured in their e-mail system (see Figure 8–2).

Wide Range of Formality

• Memorandums vary widely in formality.

Because memorandums usually are messages among people who work with and know one another, they tend to be informal. Even so, their degree of formality ranges from one extreme to the other. At one end are the casual handwritten notes that workers exchange. At the other are the formal messages written by lower ranking workers to their top administrators. The typical memorandum falls somewhere between these extremes.

Similarities and Differences in Memorandums and Letters

• Because the situations involved are similar, the techniques for writing memos and letters are similar.

As we have noted, the order and techniques for writing memorandums are much the same as those for writing letters. The reason is that the situations for both are similar. Some memorandums ask for or give routine information; thus, they are appropriately written in the same order and use the same techniques as letters that do the same. And the same can be said about memorandums that communicate negative messages and memorandums that seek to persuade. The explanation, of course, is that in a very real sense memorandums are letters. They differ from letters primarily in that they are written to people within an organization rather than to people outside the organization.

• Memorandums differ from letters in two major ways: (1) They are more likely to be direct.

Although memorandums are internal letters, they differ from letters in two major ways. First, memorandum are more likely to be written in the direct order. Most letters also are direct, but an even greater percentage of memorandums are direct. Most memorandums are direct because they concern work information, and such information rarely requires preliminary explanation, justification, or persuasion strategies.

• (2) They are less likely to involve concern about word effect.

The second major difference is that usually the writers of memorandums have less need to be concerned about the effect of their words. That is, tactfulness, negativeness-positiveness, you-viewpoint, or such usually are not major concerns. This is not to say

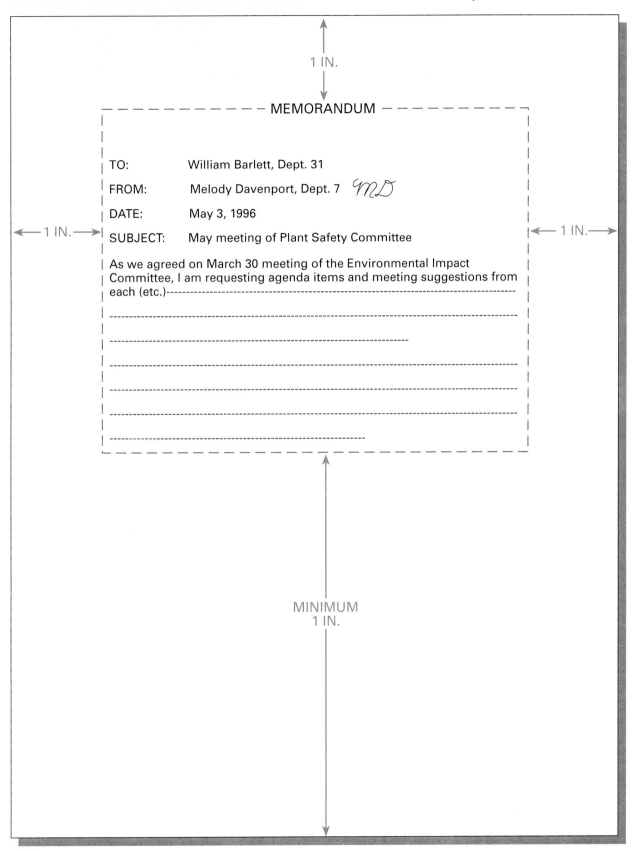

PENNY-WISE STORES, INC.

MEMORANDUM

To: **Date:**

                                           From:

Store: **Store:**

At: **At:**

Territory: **Territory:**

Copies to:

Subject: Form for in-house letters (memos)

This is an illustration of our memorandum stationery. It should be used for all written communications within the organization.

Notice that the memorandum uses no form of salutation. Neither does it have any form of complimentary close. The writer does not need to sign the message. He or she needs only to initial after the typed name in the heading.

Notice also that the message is single-spaced with double spacing between paragraphs.

that rudeness and harshness are acceptable. It simply means that people working together in business situations typically want and expect clear, straightforward communication. They are not personally involved in the message; so there is little need to be concerned about their sensitivity to the wording.

MEMORANDUMS ILLUSTRATED

The similarities and differences between memorandums and letters are clearly evident from examples. In the following pages, we present examples of the basic types of memorandums, and we make pertinent comments about each. First, we look at the direct-order forms—the direct inquiry and the direct response. Next, we review a policy memorandum (also called *directive*), which is a direct-order message that has no comparable letter type. We then inspect the less common indirect forms—those conveying negative messages. And finally we cover a unique message—the memorandum to file. Other forms of memorandums exist, buy they are rare.

- Look for the similarities and differences in the following examples.

Direct Memorandums—Routine Inquiries

The following direct-inquiry memorandum clearly follows the plan of a direct-inquiry letter. It begins directly. Then it systematically covers the vital bits of information. Note the logic of its organization and the straightforward and clear communication. Although its words are courteous, there is no need for delicacy to avoid offending the reader. Perhaps its close lacks the outgoing friendliness of a good letter, but it is courteous.

- The direct-inquiry memorandum follows the pattern of the direct-inquiry letter.

DATE: April 1, 1996
TO: Remigo Ruiz
FROM: Becky Pharr
SUBJECT: Request for cost information concerning meeting
           at Timber Creek Lodge

As we discussed in my office today, will you please get the necessary cost information for conducting our annual sales meeting at the Timber Creek Lodge, Timber Creek Village, Colorado. Our meeting will begin on the morning of Monday, June 5; so we should arrange to arrive on the 4th. We will leave after a brief morning session on June 9.
   Specifically, I want the following information:
- Travel costs for all 43 participants, including air travel to Denver and ground travel between the airport and the Lodge. I have listed the name and home stations of the 43 participants on the attached sheet.
- Room and board costs for the five-day period, including cost with and without dinner at the Lodge. As you know, we are considering the possibility of allowing participants to purchase dinners at nearby restaurants.
- Costs for recreational facilities at the Lodge.
- Costs for meeting rooms and meeting equipment (projectors, lecterns, and such). We will need a room large enough to accommodate our 43 participants.
   I'd like to have the information by April 15. If you need additional information, please call me.

- The memorandum begins directly—with the objective. The necessary explanation follows.

- Then the specific information needed is listed in logical order.

- The memorandum ends with courteous words.

Direct Memorandums—Routine Responses

The illustration selected for a routine-response memorandum is the answer to the preceding example. Like the comparable letter, this memorandum begins directly. Then it presents its contents in an orderly way, arranging them by general topics. As the situation involves no personal feelings on the part of the communicants, the emphasis is on clear and factual writing.

- This memorandum should be direct, orderly, and clearly worded.

Memos form a significant part of the communications used to coordinate the work in production units such as this.

DATE: April 14, 1996
TO: Becky Pharr
FROM: Remigo Ruiz
SUBJECT: Cost information for sales meeting at Timber Creek Lodge

- This example meets the requirements. It begins directly.

As you requested in your April 1 memo, here are the cost details for conducting our annual sales meeting at Timber Creek Lodge June 4–9.

Round-trip air transportation for our 43 representatives from their assignment stations to Denver would be $9,312 (see schedule attached). Ground transportation from Denver to Timber Creek Lodge could be by chartered bus or by rental car. The White Transport Company would provide round-trip bus transportation from the airport to the lodge for $25 per person, for a total of $1,075. Automobile rental costs for a midsize vehicle for the five-day meeting would be approximately $235 per vehicle, depending on the exact mileage. At one vehicle for every four people, we would need 11 automobiles, for a total cost of $2,585. The advantage of automobile rental is that the participants would have transportation throughout the week, although the Lodge provides limited shuttle service to Timber Creek Village.

- Then it presents the information—concisely and in good order.

Private room accommodations at the Lodge, including breakfast and lunch, would be $125 per day per person, or $625 for the entire meeting. The total for our 43 attendees would be $26,825. Dinners at the Lodge could be included for an additional $12 per person per day, making the per person total $685 and the total for all participants $29,405. However, several quality restaurants are in Timber Creek Village, which is less than a mile away. We would probably need to budget about $15 each for dinners away from the Lodge. The Lodge reports that its meeting room will easily accommodate our 43 participants. For a group the size of ours, the Lodge would provide the meeting room, projectors, lecterns, and such without additional charge. The Lodge recreational facilities (golf, tennis, swimming) would also be available without additional charge, except for equipment rentals.

- It ends courteously.

I have enclosed the Lodge's current descriptive brochure, which should answer other questions you may have. If you need additional information in making your decision, I'd be pleased to get it for you.

Enclosure

Direct Memorandums—Policy Memorandums and Directives

- Company policies and directives may be written in memorandum form.

Internal written messages giving work rules, procedures, instructions, and the like are common in most large organizations. Called *policies* and *directives*, these messages

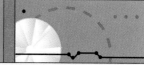
E-mail Etiquette: A Courtesy Guide for Business Writers

Some basic rules of etiquette must be followed for communicating with e-mail. Somehow, the impersonal nature and lack of face-to-face contact of e-mail tempt some writers to be rude, violating basic courtesies expected by other users. Here are some of the more important rules.

- Keep your line length under 80 characters—under 72 if possible.
- Don't use abusive or offensive language (flaming) you wouldn't use in person.
- Don't copy more than a few words from another source.
- Do give complete credit for others' ideas and words.
- Do ask for permission before you forward or post someone else's message to avoid breaking the writer's confidence.
- Avoid using all capital letters; it's called SHOUTING.
- Keep your signature concise.
- Check your e-mail regularly.
- Don't read others' messages waiting to be picked up at a printer.

* Adapted from David Angel and Brent Heslop, *The Elements of E-mail Style: Communicating Effectively via Electronic Mail* (Reading, MA: Addison-Wesley Publishing Company 1994).

from administrators to subordinates may be written as memorandums, though they sometimes take other forms. In general, such messages are formal documents and are more important than most internal communications. They are often compiled in policy manuals—perhaps kept in loose-leaf form in a notebook and updated as new memorandums are issued.

Policy memorandums and directives are more formally written than most internal communications because of their official nature. Typically, they follow the direct order. They begin with a topic (thesis) statement that repeats the subject-line information and includes the additional information needed to identify the specific situation. The remainder of the message consists of a logical, orderly arrangement of the rules and procedures covered. To make them stand out, the rules and procedures are often numbered or arranged in outline form.

- They should be somewhat formal, direct, clearly written, and well

The following example exemplifies the good qualities of a policy memorandum. It begins directly with words that tell the nature of the message. Then it clearly outlines the steps to be taken. It ends with an appeal for compliance. Although the wording lacks the warmth that would be appropriate in a letter, it conveys the firmness necessary in this situation. Even so, the words are respectful and cordial.

- The following example is direct, orderly, and firm.

DATE: June 10, 1996
TO: All Employees
FROM: Terry Boedeker, President
SUBJECT: Energy conservation

To help us through the current energy crisis, the following conservation measures are effective immediately.
- Thermostats will be set to maintain temperatures of 78 degrees Fahrenheit throughout the air-conditioning season.
- Air conditioners will be shut off in all buildings at 4 P.M. Monday through Friday.
- Air conditioners will be started as late as possible each morning so as to have the buildings at the appropriate temperature within 30 minutes after the start of the workday.
- Lighting levels will be reduced to approximately 50 to 60 footcandles in all work areas. Corridor lighting will be reduced to 5 to 10 footcandles.
- Outside lighting levels will be reduced as much as possible without compromising safety and security.

- The beginning is direct and immediately identifies the situation.

- Clear writing and listing result in good readability.

Businesses with multiple locations send many of their memos by fax or e-mail.

• Separate listing of other measures gives order and enhances understanding.

In addition, will each of you help in conservation areas under your control? Specifically, I ask that you do the following:
• Turn off lights not required in performing work.
• Keep windows closed when the cooling system is operating.
• Turn off all computer monitors and printers when not in use.
I am confident that these measures will reduce our energy use significantly. I will appreciate your efforts to follow them.

• Closing personal remarks add to effectiveness.

Indirect (Bad-News) Memorandums

• Although rare, memorandums refusing personal requests are occasionally written.

Memorandums that convey bad news are not rare in business. What is rare are bad-news memorandums that require indirect, diplomatic treatment. As we have noted, most memorandums communicate information of little personal concern to the people involved. Thus, most memorandums can be written in the direct order and with little or no concern for tactful handling. But there are exceptions—memorandums carrying bad news that concerns the reader personally. It is memorandums of this relatively rare type that we will now illustrate.

• They should be handled indirectly and tactfully.

Like the indirect-letter situations reviewed previously, such personal bad-news messages require tactful handling. This means treating them indirectly—paving the way for the bad news with explanation, justification, or such. It means watching words carefully, trying to emphasize the positive over the negative. It means writing from the reader's point of view with consideration for his or her best interests. These and other points discussed with respect to indirect letters also apply to this type of memorandum.

• The following memorandum illustrates such handling.

Illustrating this memorandum type is the following memorandum. It follows closely the plan and techniques recommended for bad-news letters. Note especially the concern for the reader's feelings and skillful use of strategy and words to soften the effect of the bad news.

• Subject line identifies without suggesting bad news.

• This example begins indirectly and pleasantly, leading to the explanation.

DATE: May 24, 1996
TO: Jerry Cunningham
FROM: Albert A. Morton
SUBJECT: Your request for change in vacation dates to July 8–21
    Your reasons for requesting a change in vacation dates are quite reasonable and certainly deserve consideration.
    In evaluating them, I must consider more than merit. I must also follow the rules carefully

specified in the contract agreement between the company and the union. These rules specify that no more than 10 percent of any department's workers can be on vacation at one time. This means a maximum of two for your department. The contract also specifies that seniority will determine vacation priorities.

In addition to you, both Rita Gann (18 years) and Beatrice Plachy (14 years) have requested vacations for July 8–21. Because both of them have more service than your 10 years, the best I can do for you is give you the July 22–August 4 period. These dates would permit you to do at least some of the things outlined in your request.

Please consider these dates. Then let me know whether they are satisfactory. I assure you that I'll do whatever I am permitted to help you with your vacation planning.

- The explanation is positively worded, clear, and convincing.
- The refusal follows, in the positive form of an alternative vacation time.
- The ending is positive and friendly.

Indirect (Persuasive) Memorandums

Although persuasive memorandums are rare, those that are written are likely to be highly important. Usually they concern a company project, proposal, or such that involves employee participation (a fund drive, company function, or safety campaign). In general, they follow the pattern of the persuasive letter. They present a persuasion strategy designed to move the reader to accept whatever is being promoted. Their pattern is indirect, beginning with attention-gaining words that set up the persuasion strategy. Then they present this persuasion strategy, leading to the request for action.

The following memorandum uses all these techniques, just as they would be used in a letter of the same type.

- Persuasive memos are rare. They follow the pattern of a persuasive letter.
- Following is such a memorandum.

DATE: August 22, 1996
TO: All Employees
FROM: Cindy VanVoorhes
                 Education Director
SUBJECT: Your professional development

Do you know any of these people—Monica Chavez, Hal Worley, Michael DuBoise, Pam Hawley, Stephanie Tomacek, Brad Benton?

They are your fellow employees, and they have two things in common. One, they were recently promoted to highly responsible positions. Two, they have all been participants in our Career Support Program.

As you may know, the Career Support Program is Gaston Petroleum's way of helping you develop professionally—completely at Gaston's expense. Through the program Gaston pays all costs (tuition, fees, and books) of your participation in the night program at City Tech.

All you need to do is follow an approved curriculum designed to help you professionally and satisfactorily meet course requirements (grade of C or better). It's as simple as that. You study. You learn. Gaston pays. And you benefit professionally—maybe through promotion.

I'd like to tell you more about how the Career Support Program can help you. Just drop by my office (20A, Personnel Suite) any time during work hours. I'll give you the details. Although I won't be able to promise you a promotion, I will promise to help you grow professionally.

- Use of familiar names gains attention and sets up the persuasion.
- Explanation of the program is persuasive.
- After the persuasion the readers are told what they must do to reap the benefits.
- The ending reemphasizes the major benefit.

The Memorandum to File

Memorandums are often written for the writer's file. Such *memorandums to file* are a means of making a record of events, activities, and such and of retaining this information for future use. For example, an executive who is having difficulties with an errant subordinate might record the subordinate's errors in memorandums as they occur and address the memorandums to file. Later, the executive could review these memorandums in building a case for disciplinary action. Or an executive who participates with other executives in a meeting at which no record is kept might record the events of the meeting in a memorandum addressed to file. The information would then be stored for future reference.

The following memorandum illustrates the second case. Here, copies might be routed to all the participants both for personal use and for confirmation of the events of the meeting.

- Executives write memorandums to their files as records and reminders.

DATE: October 19, 1996
TO: FILE
FROM: Cindy Boros
SUBJECT: Meeting on problems with in-house training program

- The direct beginning identifies the particulars.
- A concise summary of the event follows.

On October 17, 1996, Charles Davidson, Diane Kennedy, and Peter Dominguez met in my office to review the progress of our in-house management training program.

Diane and Peter reported that their employees expressed strong dissatisfaction with the first course conducted. Charles and I reported less negative (although not entirely positive) experiences from our employees. The evidence submitted clearly suggested that Dr. Warren Miles (the course instructor) talked "over the heads" of the participants. The subject matter, we concluded, was not too difficult for the employees involved.

- This part emphasizes the achievements.

We also agreed that in selecting the next instructor we will carefully consider the levels of subject matter and instruction. In addition, we agreed that I will monitor the instruction throughout the next course. Through counseling the instructor, I will make every effort to avoid the mistakes made in the past.

I N T R O D U C T O R Y   S I T U A T I O N

▶ to Order Letters

In your position at Pinnacle, you receive this month's *Business Administrator* in the morning mail. As usual, this professional journal is filled with articles useful to workers who want to advance into administration. One of the articles lists the 10 most valuable books for administrators. You are impressed. You want these books for your personal library.

You might be able to get the books by looking for them at local bookstores, but this procedure would take more time than you can spare. You decide instead to order them from the publishers. As you do not have these publishers' order forms, you will have to order by letter. The article gives publisher names along with the prices and necessary descriptions of the books. A business directory in the company library contains the publishers' addresses.

One of the order letters you write will be to Business Books, Inc., publisher of three of the books you want. You are ready to write the order. But how do you organize the letter? What information do you include? The answers to these questions appear in the following discussion. ■

ORDERS

- Rarely will you write an order letter.

As most orders are now either placed orally or made on order forms, order letters are not often written. When you must write an order letter, however, you would do well to follow the plan that the following pages discuss in detail:

- But when you write one, follow this plan.

- Begin directly—with clear authorization.

- Systematically and consistently arrange items with identifying facts (number, units, catalog number, name, description points, unit price, total price).

- Cover shipping instructions and manner of payment.

- End with goodwill comment.

Directly Authorizing the Order

- Begin order letters directly with a clear authorization.

The preceding plan follows the direct arrangement appropriate for good-news letters. Clearly, an order is good news to the reader. This good news is best presented in words that authorize, such as "Please send me . . ." Anything less direct, such as "I would like to have . . ." falls short of authorization.

Specifically Covering the Sale

- Identify the goods added clearly and in an orderly way.

The remainder of the letter is an exercise in clear, orderly, and complete coverage of the details the reader needs. There is no one best arrangement for these details, but you should be consistent in whatever you do. A good plan is to begin with the number and units needed and to follow with this arrangement of the remaining items:

- Identifying number (catalog number, ISBN number, model number)
- Basic name (including trade names and brands when helpful).
- Unit price
- Total price.

In finished form, the information might read like this:

3 dozen   No. 712AC, Woolsey Claw hammer,
           drop-forged head, hickory handle, 13
           inches overall length, 16 ounces, at
           $44.74 per dozen. $134.22

In addition to describing the items ordered, you need to include other vital information—shipping instructions, method of payment, and anything else necessary for filling the order. You may work some of this information into the beginning, following the authorization statement. You may include the remainder with your closing remarks.

• Cover all the information needed—shipping instructions, payment, and the like.

Closing with a Friendly Comment

As you would do in other direct-style letters, end this one with an appropriate friendly comment. If there is need for urgency, this information might well go with these good-will words. If possible, make them fit the one case, as in this example:

• Close with friendly words.

As we have promised to make our first delivery on the 17th, would you please get these supplies to us by the 13th at the latest. We will sincerely appreciate your promptness.

Contrasting Orders

The following contrasting letters for the case described earlier show good and bad ways of ordering books.

• The following two examples are of bad and good order letters.

A Slow and Disorderly Order.   The letter showing bad technique begins indirectly. The first sentence is useless and merely delays the main message. This message comes in the second sentence, but it is more a suggestion than an authorization. The information on the books is not orderly, and the format does not display it clearly. Neither the number of books wanted nor their prices stand out. One has to look for this information. The book titles are clear and will probably lead the reader to the right books. But edition numbers have been omitted, and this information could be important. Also, the items are ordered inconsistently. Payment details appear in the close, but they are vague and incomplete. The letter's abrupt ending will produce little good-will.

Dear Sales Manager:

Information I have indicates that your company is the publisher of three books I would like for my personal library. I would sincerely appreciate it if you would be so kind as to send them to me. They are as follows:
    Basic Management, price $26.95, by Alonzo Bevins, 1 copy.
    Clear Writing for Business, price $21.95, by Mildred Knauth, 1 copy.
    Managing Organizations, 2 copies, by Hugo W. Bass, price $25.95.
I have enclosed a check in the amount of $100.80. I will pay any additional charges.

                        Sincerely,

• This bad one is slow and disorderly.

A Direct and Orderly Order.   The second letter avoids the faults of the first. It begins with a direct authorization to ship goods. Then it lists the books wanted in an orderly

CASE ILLUSTRATION Order Letters. (An Involved Order for Supplies)

A business manager's small mail order for office supplies is illustrated in this letter. The items ordered require a detailed description, which the writer provided in an orderly way.

Pioneer Insurance Company

1717 West 17th St.
Stockton, CA 95202

202-552-8989
FAX: 209-552-8943

November 7, 1996

Ms. Viola Green, Sales Manager
The Office Warehouse
1735 Townsend Street
San Francisco, CA 94107

Dear Ms. Green:

Direct authorization

Please send me the office supplies listed below by prepaid parcel post at the address above. I am ordering from your September 7 price list.

Tells how to ship

Qualifies prices quoted

Items stand out

Orderly listing of details

10 reams	No. 321A, Scroll bond paper, white, 25%-rag, 8 1/2 by 11 inches, 20-pound, @ 3.25	$32.50
4 boxes	No. 106B, laser paper, 8 1/2 by 11 inches, 20-lb, @ $5.40	21.60
5 dozen	No. 1171A, printer cartridges, @ $10.50 . . .	52.50
5 each	No. 215H, copy stands, Luddell model K, 26 inches high, black, @ $9.60	48.00
	TOTAL	$154.60

Prices stand out

Courteous yet forceful urge for prompt action

Please charge the amount to me on the usual 2/10, n/60 terms. As our supplies of these items are nearly depleted, I will appreciate any rush service you can give this order.

Payment method covered

Sincerely,

Clovis S. Rosenbaum

Clovis S. Rosenbaum
Manager

eme

fashion. The numbers and units stand out. Clear identification information appears in the center position. Extensions in the right-hand column emphasize the price information, including the total cost. In the close, the remaining matter of additional charges is handled. Although the closing goodwill words are somewhat routine, they are appropriate for this routine situation.

Dear Sales Manager:

Please send me the following books:
1 copy Alonzo Bevins, *Basic Management,* 2nd ed., 1995,
@ $26.95 . . . . $26.95
1 copy Mildred Knauth, *Clear Writing for Business,* 1996,
@ $21.95 . . . . 21.95
2 copies Hugo W. Bass, *Managing Organizations,* 3rd ed., 1996,
@ $25.95 . . . . <u>51.90</u>
Total $100.80
The enclosed check for $100.80 covers your 1996 list prices for the books. If prices have increased and/or if I owe shipping charges or sales taxes, please bill me for the additional amount. Or, if you prefer, I will pay on delivery.
I will appreciate your promptness in handling this order.

Sincerely,

* This good order letter is fast and efficient.

....

SUMMARY ▶ by Chapter Objectives

1. Collection letters are usually sent in a series.
   - First comes a reminder, usually not a letter.
   - Next comes persuasive letters.
   - The series ends with a last-resort letter.
   - The number of letters in the series is influenced by credit risk and practice in the field.
     —Exclusive shops, for example, would be likely to use a longer, slower series than that used by stores catering to bad risks.
     —Some businesses classify customers into risk groups and treat each differently.
   - Typically, collection series between businesses are short and move fast.
   - Increased use of computer billings appears to have led to shorter collection efforts and harsher letters.

2. *Early.* Begin a collection series on the assumption that the reader *will* pay.
   - Your first letter should be a short, courteous reminder of the past-due bill.
   - Such letters are typically direct, though the indirect order is effective sometimes.
   - These letters usually contain appropriate goodwill talk.
   Middle. Write the middle-stage letters on the assumption that the reader *should* pay.
   - Thus, persuasion is needed.
   - Begin by selecting an appeal (fair play, pride, or such), and develop this appeal in words that convince.
   - Each succeeding letter in this stage is stronger than the preceding one.
   - Since letters in this stage are not invited, begin them with attention-gaining words.
   - These words should set up your strategy (the appeal selected).
   - Then present the appeal, taking care to make it convincing and at the right strength for the collection stage involved.
   - But keep the tone friendly (no anger).

① Design a series of collection letters according to the credit risk involved and standard practice in the field of business.

② Write effective letters for each of the stages in the collection series: early, middle, and last-resort.

- End with a request for payment, perhaps linking payment with a benefit to be gained by paying.

  Last-resort. After the buildup of middle-stage letters has failed, write a final letter (last resort). The assumption here is that the reader *must* pay.

- Begin by selecting a last-resort action (reporting to a credit bureau, going to court).
- Write the letter in direct order, telling what action you will take.

  —Use directness because it adds strength.

  —And make this last letter strong.
- Throughout, show concern rather than anger.
- Present the effects of this action in convincing words.
- Close with a last-chance offer of a deadline for paying before taking the action threatened.
- Consider a final recall of the appeal, associating it with the action.

3 Write claim letters that explain the facts in a firm but courteous manner.

3. Claim letters are a special case. Even though they carry bad news, they are best written in the direct order. The reason: the reader usually wants to correct the problem and requires only that the facts be presented; also, directness strengthens the claim. Follow this general plan:
   - Somewhere early in the letter (in a subject line or incidentally in the first sentence) identify the transaction.
   - Then state what went wrong, perhaps with some interpretation of the effects.
   - Follow with a clear review of the facts, without showing anger.
   - You may want to suggest a remedy.
   - End with cordial words.

4 Explain the variations in the form of memorandum stationery.

4. Memorandums (letters written inside a company) usually are processed on special stationery.
   - Typically, *Memorandum* appears at the top and *Date, To, From,* and *Subject* follow.
   - Large organizations often include more information (for example, *Department, Plant, Location, Copies to, Store Number*).

5 Discuss the wide range of formality used in memorandums.

5. Most memorandums are informal, but they can be formal.
   - Simple inquiries, responses, and such from and to employees are informal.
   - Messages from employees to higher authorities in the organization are likely to be formal.

6 Describe the primary differences between memorandums and letters written for similar situations.

6. The situations for writing memorandums and letters are much alike, but there are two differences.
   - Memorandums are more likely to be written in the direct order.
   - Memorandums frequently have less need for you-viewpoint and positive language.

7 Write clear and effective memorandums for routine inquiries, routine responses, policies and directives, bad-news messages, persuasive messages, and messages to file.

7. Generally, write memorandums as you would a comparable letter.
   - Use the direct pattern for routine inquiries and responses, policy memorandums, and directives.
   - Use the direct pattern even for some bad-news messages—those that do not involve the reader personally.
   - Use indirectness for bad-news memorandums that personally involve the reader.
   - Use the indirect pattern for persuasive memorandums.
   - Use clear summaries of events, activities, and such in memorandums to file, which are written to assist the writer's memory.

8 Write orders that begin with a clear authorization; contain an orderly arrangement of units, descriptions, and prices; cover all shipping information; and close with goodwill.

8. Order letters are best written in the direct order, as follows:
   - Begin with a direct authorization to ship.
   - Carefully and systematically identify the items you want (catalog number, basic name, descriptive points, unit price, total price, and so on).
   - Include all other information vital to the sale (shipping instructions, method of payment, time requirements).
   - End with friendly, appropriate words that fit the one case.

CRITICAL THOUGHT QUESTIONS

1. "Only one test is meaningful in determining how good a collection letter is: how well it brings in the money." Discuss.

2. Describe the collection-letter series you would recommend for a store selling inexpensive clothing to high-risk customers. Explain your selection.

3. Describe the collection series you would recommend for an exclusive clothing store selling mainly to low risks. Explain your selection.

4. Most first reminders are written in the direct order. Middle-stage letters tend to be written in the indirect order. Discuss the reasons for these practices.

5. This book recommends cordiality throughout the collection procedure. What is the logic of this practice?

6. If the last-resort collection letter is the strongest in the series and, therefore, the most likely to bring in the money, why not use it earlier?

7. Discuss the role of negative and positive wording and the you-viewpoint throughout the collection series.

8. Usually bad-news letters are appropriately written in the indirect order. Why should claim letters be exceptions.

9. Justify the use of negative words in claim letters. Can they be overused? Discuss.

10. Explain the logic of using negative words in memorandums that you would not use in letters carrying similar messages.

11. Although bad-news memorandums are not rare, indirect bad-news memorandums are. Explain.

12. Discuss and justify the wide range of formality used in memorandums.

13.` Memorandums differ much more than letters in their physical makeup. Explain and discuss.

14. Discuss the special need for clear writing and adaptation in policy memorandums and directives.

15. Discuss the relative directness of these beginnings of an order letter:
    a. "Please ship the following items . . ."
    b. "I would like to have the following . . ."
    c. "I need the following items . . ."
    d. "I would appreciate your sending me the following items . . ."
    e. "Can you send me the following items . . . ?"

CRITICAL THINKING EXERCISES

Criticize the following form collection letters. They were written for a large department store for middle- to upper-income customers with good credit records at the time they were granted credit. The series consists of five letters.

1. *First letter (60 days past due)*

Dear _____:

Please be informed that your account with us shows an unpaid balance of $327.48 now 60 days past due. Surely there must be some mistake. I know you will correct the matter right away by mailing in your check. If there is some problem, please call me to make arrangements.

Sincerely yours,

Alice Blumberg, Credit Manager

2. *Third letter (120 days past due)*

Dear _____:

Because you have ignored my previous efforts to collect the $327.48 now four months past due, I must firmly call this matter to your attention.

Perhaps you do not realize the seriousness of what you have done. Your credit rating is in jeopardy. You are in danger of losing a reputation that took a lifetime to build. And once your reputation is ruined, you will find it very difficult to regain it.

I know you do not want this to happen. So please send us the amount owed right away. If there is a problem, at least

call me or write me and explain so we can work out a payment plan. If we do not hear from you soon, we will take appropriate action.

Sincerely yours,

Alice Blumberg, Credit Manager

3. *Fifth letter (180 days past due)*

Dear _____:

I am extremely disappointed to find your name among our debtors who are a full six months past due in paying their honest obligations. In spite of the fact that I have repeatedly informed you of your obligation, you have completely ignored the matter. I will no longer be patient.

Unless you pay the $327.48 you owe, we will take drastic action. We will go to court; and we can and will collect. Either you pay us by November 16 or I'll see you in court.

Sincerely yours,

Alice Blumberg, Credit Manager

4. Criticize the following claim letter.

Dear Mr. Stanton:

For many years now I have bought your candies and have been pleased with them. However, last June 4 I ordered 48 boxes of your Swiss Decadance chocolates, and it appears you tried to push off some old stock on me. I have sold some of the boxes, and already three customers have returned the candy to me. The candy is rancid—obviously old. Probably the whole lot was bad and I now have a bunch of dissatisfied customers.

I have taken the remaining boxes off the shelves and will send them back to you—after I get my money back.

Sincerely,

5. Point out the weaknesses in this policy memorandum. The writer's objective is to establish a clear policy for hiring and terminating employment.

TO: All Administrators
FROM: Ada H. Horton, President
DATE: June 7, 1996
SUBJECT: Hiring and terminating policies

Since joining ElectroTech 16 years ago, I have witnessed every conceivable discrepancy in our employment policies, racism, sex discrimination, nepotism—you name it. It is time that you stop these practices. Henceforth you will rigidly adhere to the following rules.

Do not consider race, religion, sex, or nationality because they have no relationship to job performance. When selecting new employees, make sure that all qualifications are considered. Do not consider physical ability or age. However, when the job requires it, you can consider physical ability to perform. For similar reasons you can consider age. Use the doctor's report for these decisions and do not make these evaluations yourself. Always hire the best applicant for the job.

When you have to reduce your force, do not play favorites as has sometimes been done in the past. Always discharge first the less competent. Job performance appraisals should determine which employees to discharge. When you have two or more with equal performance ratings, seniority should be used. Job terminations based on poor performance or for disciplinary reasons must be supported by evidence and must be approved in advance by our Personnel Review Committee.

A personnel action memo is required every time we hire or fire. Send it to Personnel explaining what was done and why. Include all supporting evidence upon which the decision was based.

6. Criticize this memo informing an employee that she was not selected for promotion to a higher position in the organization.

TO: Alma DuPuis
FROM: Monty Duke
DATE: May 17, 1996
SUBJECT: Your application for position of personnel director

One of my most difficult assignments is having to tell a colleague that he or she did not get a promotion sought. But it is my duty to do so. Therefore I must report that you were not judged best qualified for the position of personnel director.

The committee recommended Don James. They considered Don to be best qualified because of his long and distinguished record with us. I am confident you would agree if you saw his credentials.

Although you were not selected, the committee wants you to know that they appreciate your interest in the position and your years of service to the company.

CRITICAL THINKING PROBLEMS ▶ Collections

▶ Quail Ridge Hunting Club Series

1. *(Early Stage).* The Quail Ridge Hunting Club was a dream of Jessie Lee Hampton five years ago. Today, it is a reality. In the three years of its actual existence, he has been increasing business and increasing profits as well. The club offers game hunting to those who want to do it without an ongoing camp lease type of situation. Initially, Jessie Lee wanted to cater to the individual hunter. But as things have developed, he now books groups of hunters, especially those from a business that wants to use the experience for developing executive morale and for entertaining existing and potentially profitable customers.

Quail Ridge, located 50 miles southwest of Amarillo, Texas, offers partridge, pheasant, turkey, and quail hunting on 10,000 acres of high-plains ranch country. Hunters receive guides, dogs, lodging, meals, bird cleaning, and all transportation with the $100 per day charge. It is highly unusual for hunters to leave after two or three days without their limit of game. The club has constructed bunkhouses to accommodate guests with each one limited to four persons. Although originally intended to cater only to male guests, QRHC has increasingly had couples and female guests whom it can easily accommodate. All

meals are served cafeteria style in the main lodge with an all-you-can-eat policy. Presently, the club can house 48 guests in the 12 cabins. Plans are to expand the capacity by five cabins in the off-season. Indeed, the owner is thrilled that his original idea has met with so much success.

But along with that success has come increasingly complex business issues. One of these deals with credit and collections. When Quail Ridge originally began business, things were informal. The club requested that all money for hunting reservations be paid in advance. If it did not receive such advance payment, it would drop the person's reservations and add another from a waiting list because more people wanted the product than could be accommodated. As the business has grown, however, the nature of the transactions has become more complex. As large corporate entities have become customers, Quail Ridge has had to adapt its credit policies. But collection procedures have not worked well. The owner believes they are too informal and need to be brought in line with current practice. Thus, he has retained Collection Plus, with you as the chief correspondent, to revamp his collection procedures so that they reflect more professional standards.

In your initial conference with Mr. Hampton, you

mapped out the following progressive collection procedure. First, he would require one-half payment when booking the reservations with the remaining one-half due in 30 days. If payment is not received in 30 days, Quail Ridge will send a second statement with a stamp of ",tis the season—past due" on the bill. Should customers not respond to this collection notice, Quail Ridge will then send a first-stage collection letter to the overdue account. It will be about 80 percent to 20 percent goodwill to collection effort in strategy; mostly the letter will emphasize that the customer will pay if reminded. Thereafter, middle-stage and last-resort collection letters will be sent to those not responding to the first collection attempts.

You realize that this series (three letters) is rather quick, but the nature of the business and the clientele demand it. Quite frankly, Quail Ridge needs the money for operations and for capital expansion. The seasonal nature of the business makes the need for ready cash even greater. In time, Quail Ridge might like to use its facilities for summer camping and retreats; but for now, it needs a steady financial foundation to survive without diversification. And the planned collection procedure will help the club with any cash flow problems.

Write the first-stage collection letter for Quail Ridge Hunting Club. You will include a brochure with the letter that will anticipate future reservations. This collection letter will be positive with an incidental "we know you will pay" request for payment.

2. *(Middle Stage).* The reminder letter you sent one month ago did not bring payment from your accounts. At this point, the amount is 60 days past due. So it is now time to step up the force of your collection series with a "must pay" middle-stage letter. This effort will emphasize "fair play" as a theme. In all sporting activities, there should be fair play. Just as hunting has its "game" rules, so, too, does credit extension. Payment is not a seasonal opportunity but a responsibility. You will work hard not to preach but to discuss the situation fairly and candidly with the customer. Your collection effort should be about 60 percent persuasive and 40 percent goodwill. Ask for payment of the account as a logical conclusion to your "fair play" appeal. Write this middle-stage letter for Quail Ridge Hunting Club.

3. *(Last Resort).* It is now 30 days since you sent the middle-stage letter. Still, you have not received payment. Because you have had no contact from your overdue accounts, you have no choice but to send a last-stage, customer "must pay' letter. If you do not receive payment from the debtors within 30 days of the date of the letter, you will turn the procedure over to Collection Plus for legal action.

This last-resort collection attempt will be about 90 percent collection effort and 10 percent goodwill. You would still prefer to have the money rather than to resort to legal means to collect. So give the person a chance; but leave no question in the reader's mind that this letter will be the club's last. It will spell out

the consequences of the legal action if you have to take it. And it will show the reader escaping this action with payment. Don't threaten but prepare a forceful letter for these long overdue accounts.

▶ Corporate Jet Service Series

4. *(Early Stage).* Corporate Jet Service (CJS), a young and growing business you started several years ago, is presently a stable enterprise on the move. When you began the business, you thought at best that you would act in a backup role to businesses that might have their own jets in maintenance or special needs that their own planes could not accommodate. From this modest beginning, CJS has grown beyond your highest expectation. You now fly executive personnel all over the globe because some corporations do not purchase their own planes. As you did not expect this market need to develop when you started the business, you currently have five jets with which to service corporate travel and transportation needs.

Along with your successful growth, however, has come increasingly more complex business issues— one of which involves credit and collection. You offer your executive jet services to the corporate world on a 24-hour advance notice basis. For $1,000 per flight hour, you can have a jet at any location ready to transport company personnel wherever they might want to go. The growth of your service had led you to believe that some businesses prefer not to own their own jets and to pay for flight services from specialized firms such as yours. As a technical point, you must comply with all FAA regulations to continue to operate your service.

Your services are not paid for in cash. It's general practice for you to bill companies on a monthly basis. If you do not receive payment in 30 days, you send a second notice with the amount owed printed in red and the words *"Please pay promptly"* on the statement. If accounts do not respond to this second notice, you write them a letter that is reminder oriented.

Because you are dissatisfied with the present letter you are sending (you think it is too direct, blunt, and tactless), you decide to construct a new one that will collect accounts more quickly and will retain goodwill as well. You have read that such early-stage letters are called "reminder letters" because they assume readers will pay if they are politely reminded of their payment obligations.

Prepare the new letter that you will send to your 30-day-old accounts. A personal letter after 30 days is somewhat quick in the collection chain; but businesses by tradition expect rapid payment from one another. You will try to apply the 75/25 rule to your letter—that is, 75 percent goodwill and 25 percent persuasion/collection effort.

5. *(Middle Stage).* The new friendly reminder letter you prepared and sent to your 30-day past-due accounts

must have fallen on deaf ears. It certainly didn't produce the results you expected; so you must now step up your efforts to collect accounts with a well-thought-out middle-stage letter. This one will discuss the reasons the account holder should pay. You will need to select an appropriate appeal and base your reasons for paying on this appeal. Self-interest or how a company could benefit from keeping a good credit rating might be ones you could use. There might be others.

Write the middle-stage letter that will be sent to overdue accounts if they have not responded to your reminder letter within 20 days. Your goodwill to collection ratio should be about 50:50.

6. *(Middle Stage).* Assume your first middle-stage letter did not collect the account and it is now 30 days later. Your "be reasonable nerve" says you should notify your attorney. But as you look at the situation more objectively, you value your goodwill. So, you will select another appeal—perhaps a stronger one—and write a second "should pay" letter. Your ratio here is going to be 35:65, goodwill to collection.

7. *(Last Resort).* Another 20 days have passed, and now you must exert full force at collecting the overdue account. Because your discussion letters have not brought results, you will spell out in detail the negative effects of your next steps to collect the amount owed you. You are going to turn the matter over to your lawyer, and there will be fees and court costs. She will seek payment to the full extent of the law.

Write this final letter to your "must pay" accounts. Picture them as escaping these negative effects if they pay the overdue account. Give them 10 days to do so, lest you will take the legal action you describe. Still, you would rather have the money than pursue legal force.

▶ **Coda's Tree Service Series**

8. *(Early Stage).* Barney Coda started Coda's Tree Service two years ago on a hope and a promise. Today, it is a thriving business due mainly to the hard work of the owner. His dedicated work, however, was helped along by the climate and the weather. Last winter, a severe ice storm hit the area, damaging power and utility lines as well as causing residential losses to homeowners. The entire area was without power and telephone service for one week, and parts of the area lacked service for two weeks. During that time, Coda subcontracted his three regular crews (five workers each) and three others he hired temporarily to clear broken limbs and trees so utility workers could restore service. After that, he had all the work he could handle with residential customers. His fees were paid by the utility companies and by insurers. These jobs gave Coda's Tree Service name recognition and built a reputation of reliable, dependable, quality service.

Throughout the spring, the business continued to prosper—so much so that Coda had to schedule appointments for tree service one week in advance. Moreover, he retained the three temporary work crews he hired during the ice storm cleanup. The business landed a three-year contract with the Parks and Recreation Department of the local community to prune, fertilize, trim, and shape trees in local parks and at the municipal golf course.

It is now summer and business continues to increase. Local residents are requesting tree service to assure their landscapes are manicured to perfection. Some residents might lose shrub and lawn growth because of excessive shade; so they will need trees thinned. Along with the expanding business, however, are other complicating factors that require attention to keep the business going. One of these factors is collection of past-due accounts. And in the role of Barney Coda, you are going to have to develop a collection plan for the business.

When you bill the city and insurers for payment, you allow 30 days for payment. To date, these debtors have complied with that billing cycle. But residents seem to be on a different page. Or at least you are not high on their payment priority list. In earlier days, you billed people once. If they didn't pay in 30 days, you called them by phone or you stopped to remind them at their homes if you were in their neighborhoods. These contacts usually brought payment. But conditions are different now.

As you look at your accounts receivable for the last three months, you find that the average account is paid in 75 days. The revenue from your industrial accounts just cannot provide you with the cash flow to cover your direct and indirect expenses. Thus, you are going to have to generate quicker payment from the accounts receivables than you have recently.

As you think about the collection strategy you will use for the residential accounts, you decide to continue mailing your monthly statements to them. If you do not receive payment in 30 days, you will send a second statement with a stamped reminder—"Please pay promptly—30 days past due." If this stamped notice does not bring payment, you will write a personal letter reminding the debtors that their accounts are 30 days past due. Indeed, you do not want to ruin the good image you have created in the last year. So your effort to collect will constitute only 20 percent of the letter; the 80 percent will be goodwill talk. Write this reminder letter for Coda's Tree Service.

9. *(Middle Stage).* Another 30 days have passed and you still have not received payment. Thus, you must now step up your efforts to collect with a discussion "should pay" letter. This middle effort will be built around the theme of pride. If homeowners take pride in the appearance of their home, they should take pride in their payment obligations as well. You will strike a 60:40 goodwill-to-persuasion ratio in your letter. Write this letter for the business.

10. *(Middle Stage).* If your first middle-stage letter does

not bring payment, you will send a second one. This second middle-stage letter will emphasize the theme of social acceptance and paying one's bills. It will be a stronger letter by the choice of the theme. You don't want to preach; so watch the wording. The letter should aim for a 50:50 mix of goodwill and persuasion. Write this second middle-stage letter.

11. *(Last Resort)*. Twenty days after you send your second middle-stage letter, you plan to send one last letter—a final attempt to collect. In this "must pay" letter, you are almost entirely (90 percent) interested in getting your money. But you would still rather have the money than take legal action to collect. If you do not receive payment in full within 15 days of the date of the letter, you will turn the account over to Allied Collection Agency. As with all good collection letters, you will tell how much is owed and how many days overdue the account is. Write this last-resort letter for CTS.

▶ Petmart Series

12. *(Early Stage)*. Buying a Petmart franchise was one of the best investments you've made. Not only do you enjoy helping people make life better for their pets, but you also enjoy running your own business. One aspect of it that's difficult for you to understand is those who don't keep their accounts up-to-date. However, you understand that managing these accounts effectively will make the financial side of the business strong. One regular customer, Dr. Stephen Nguyen, a prominent local veterinarian, hasn't paid anything on his account for 60 days. He owes you nearly $500 for items he purchased for use in his practice on small animals. You need to collect for these items.

    You know Dr. Nguyen is still in business because several of your customers have said he's referred them to your store. In the past, he's always taken care of his accounts promptly, never carrying a balance past 30 days. And the local credit bureau gives him the highest rating, showing he pays all his accounts promptly.

    While you believe in low-key collections, especially with good customers, you still need to write Dr. Nguyen a friendly letter asking for full payment of the $493.57 he owes you. Remind him of the good service he and his customers have received from you. Be sure to maintain his goodwill, for he had been continuing to refer customers to your store.

13. *(Middle Stage)*. Last month's friendly reminder apparently did not work. You received no response from it. Now you must write a bit stronger letter, persuading Dr. Nguyen to pay. Convince him to pay on the basis of fair play. You may wish to play on his understanding of providing a product or service and expecting to be paid for that exchange. You might want to do some resale, too. You can remind him of all the times you've placed special orders for him, even delivering emergency supplies to his office on occasion. You

might even give specific examples, including names of people and their pets, when you give his customers special services based on his recommendations for their pets' needs. Continue to stress goodwill while making it clear he needs to take care of his account immediately.

14. *(Middle Stage)*. Another month has gone by with no word from Dr. Nguyen. Therefore, you need to write him a stronger letter convincing him to pay. This time you'll try an economic appeal that encourages him to pay to maintain the outstanding credit record he's built up over the years. Stress the value of good credit to all aspects of his life, personal and business. In addition to discussing the importance of a good rating, discuss ways it might help him. These might include such things as loans for building an addition to his clinic, the ability to attract a good, competent partner one day, and the ability to sleep nights without unnecessary economic worries. You may suggest that he contact you to set up payment options if that would help him clear up this outstanding account. Be sure to be firm, yet work to retain his goodwill.

15. *(Last Resort)*. Dr. Stephen Nguyen is nearly nine months overdue on his account balance. While you've checked his mailing address and know he's still in business, your statements have not been paid; and your letters persuading him to take care of the account have gone unanswered. You really wonder why because he's been continuing to refer others to your business. And you saw his picture in the paper recently for directing a walk/run for the March of Dimes. You want to keep Dr. Nguyen's goodwill, but you do need to collect the $493.57 he owes you for pet supplies. Let him know that this is his last chance to pay before you turn the account over to a collection agency. You'll give him two weeks to contact you before you take any action, but you will act!

▶ Checks Unlimited Series

16. *(Early Stage)*. You and Linda Hittle operate a small but lucrative business, Checks Unlimited, that sells checks for personal use. Several years ago you identified a market niche, universities and clubs, to target for customers of your checks. The check forms you offer are the basic ones most people use—those traditionally used for handwritten checks and those used with computers in both the tractor-fed form and laser form. Also, your checks include the colors and logos of the universities and clubs that order them. And you split your profits with the sponsoring group.

    Since the sponsoring groups are interested in getting their share of the profits promptly, you've had no serious problem with collections. However, one of your newest accounts, Kuru State University, placed orders for $1,500 in checks. You delivered them nearly 90 days ago, but have not received payment, although the university has been billed three times. Because this is a new customer, you decided to give it a little longer than your normal 60 days to get its system in order. But since you've heard nothing from the customer, you have decided to write a friendly letter to let the university know it hasn't slipped through the collection process.

In your letter, you might remind it that the school benefits from your getting your payment promptly. Also, tell how the checks with the university's logo on it helps build school spirit. You might want to let the school know its potential revenue based on average figures for schools its size and student demographics. Stress the importance of taking care of the account as soon as possible.

Because this is a new customer, work hard to retain goodwill as well as encouraging it to pay promptly.

17. *(Middle Stage)*. Nearly four months have gone by since you delivered the checks to Kuru State University. You have not heard a word from anyone at the school, including receiving any new orders. According to your marketing plan, the alumni association should be advertising your checks this month in its publication. It's bound to bring in thousands of dollars in orders. So you decide to use a fair-play appeal.

Stress the goodwill Kuru would be building with you by making full, immediate payment on its outstanding account. Stress that you will return the gesture by giving full, immediate attention to alumni orders when they come in next month. Remind Kuru that it shares in the profits, making a timely payment in its best interest, too. Encourage it to pay while working to retain goodwill and future business.

18. *(Middle Stage)*. Another month has passed with no word from the people at Kuru State University. However, alumni orders are beginning to come in. So your next letter will appeal to its continued reputation as a respectable organization. Talk about the good response to your product and the image it helps create for the university, an image it might spoil by not keeping its account up-to-date. Appeal to the important role alumni can play both through their donations and their word-of-mouth advertising of the school. Remind Kuru that its actions could seriously tarnish the fine reputation the school has maintained in the business community. Stress the importance of paying now to clear up this past-due account and continue in business with your company.

19. *(Last Resort)*. You never thought it would come to this. Kuru State University is the first customer you have had to worry about defaulting on its debt to you. You are greatly disturbed because you know from reading the public reports on the financial condition of the school that it is in good shape. However, the lack of response to your statements and appeal letters has left you no alternative. You and your partner, Linda Hittle, decided from the start that you were in business to provide a service, not act as a bank for slow-paying customers. As much as you dread it, you must let Kuru know it must pay in full within two

weeks or you will turn the account over to a professional collection agency.

▶ Maid Clean Series

20: *(Early Stage)*. You are Matt Colby, administrative assistant and office manager for Maid Clean. Organized two years ago as a family business dedicated to residential cleaning, Maid Clean has been built into a solid business, even adding a few employees outside the family. You've been able to do this by providing a complete, competent, and dependable service. You've established your business by simple but important concerns, concerns for the customers and their property. Many of your new customers are acquired through referrals from current customers or are current customers with growing needs.

One of your original customers asked you to clean a residential rental property that belonged to a friend. When you agreed, the customer gave you the phone number of the friend. You called and arranged over the phone to clean the property, getting entrance to the property from a neighbor. While you couldn't state a price without first seeing the property, the owner did state your basic hourly rate of $40 was reasonable.

But what a mess! The tenant had trashed the home. It took your team of three employees over six hours. You thoroughly cleaned all the bathrooms and kitchen as well as vacuumed the rest of the house. Also, you hauled out nearly a dozen full yard-size garbage bags of trash. When you left, the house was in good enough condition to be shown to a potential renter. When you called the owner, he told you to send him a bill.

However, you've sent him two statements in the past 60 days and have not had a response. You hate to put your own customer in the middle, so you decide to write a friendly reminder letter asking for the full payment of the $240 for the cleaning immediately.

21. *(Middle Stage)*. You can't believe you haven't heard from your customer. You've driven by the house you cleaned for him and have noticed that it appears to be rented. In your next letter to him, you decide to use the fair-play appeal. You've provided a service that enabled him to rent the house and probably collect a damage deposit. Now it's his turn to send you a check for the $240 cleaning. You might even want to build goodwill by reminding him who referred you. Or you might want to do some resale of your quality, professional cleaning service. Be sure to state clearly that you expect to be paid in full and immediately.

22. *(Middle Stage)*. Another month has passed without a word from your customer. You've checked his credit rating and discovered it's a good one. In fact, you've noticed he's quite active in some of your community projects for a clean environment. So you've decided to write your next stronger appeal to him based on his good reputation for promoting a clean environment,

especially a clean house. Remind him that while a clean environment might be his avocation, it's your company's vocation. Urge him to pay immediately.

23. *(Last Resort).* Still no word from your customer—four months since you cleaned his property. You must remind him that you're in business to provide a quality service for pay and that you expect to be paid the full $240 within 15 days. If you don't receive payment, you will pursue a legal remedy through the small claims court.

Claims

24. While you have usually embraced new technologies for improving the quality of your life, your recent experience with a cutting-edge concept in custom-made jeans disappointed you. The concept sounded like a good one—custom-made Levis for only $10 more than the off-the-rack price. You only had to go to the local Levi's store, have your measurements taken, and try on some samples. Then your measurements, style, and material description were sent by computer to a factory in Tennessee where an automated cutting machine cut the fabric to your specifications. Having jeans that fit perfectly sounded wonderful.

    You were impressed when you learned your custom-made jeans were ready for you to pick up in less than a week. In fact, you had already been thinking about ordering a couple more pair. However, much to your dismay, the jeans were nearly six inches too long, and you know you haven't gotten in shorter this week.

    Write a claim letter to Thomas Jajeh, Director of Marketing, at Levi's corporate headquarters. While you want a pair of jeans that fits perfectly, you also want to be reassured this new mass customization really works. Tell him you think the concept is a good one but you were extremely disappointed in your first use of it. Ask for an explanation of the error.

25. As a student, you've found biking is not only a convenient way to get to and from campus, but it is also economical and nonpolluting. You make efforts and take great pride in doing what's best for the environment. In fact, last month when you bought new tires for your bike, you spent a bit extra for "green" tires.

    The new tires, manufactured by Green Tyre, are made from microcellular polyurethane. They have no inner tubes and are promoted as never going flat. They supposedly handle nails, broken glass, and even sharp stones with ease. Furthermore, this British-made tire is recyclable and lasts two to three times longer than standard tube tires.

    The tires seemed almost too good to be true. The fact that they are 30 percent lighter than standard tires also sounded like a plus. The $79 price per pair was within your budget, too. So you ordered them sight unseen by phone. The Shannon Group, which produces the Green Tyre, even gave you a $10 rebate for your worn tires and tubes.

    However, you've used them for nearly a week and are extremely dissatisfied with their performance. While on flat, straight surfaces they handle about the same as standard tires; on sharp cornering they made you feel very insecure. Because you make lots of turns and are concerned about your safety, you'd like to return them and get your money back (minus the $10 rebate).

    Write a letter that accomplishes your purpose while maintaining goodwill.

26. One of your favorite places to go is a local coffee-house, [you name it]. This business provides a wonderful atmosphere to relax with coffee and often a treat while you read. Normally, you stop by in the morning to enjoy an espresso and a breakfast pastry over the morning newspaper. Usually soft instrumental music is played; Kenny G's sax music is about as strong as it ever gets. You've been a regular customer for nearly two years, and you're familiar with most of those who work there as well as the manager/owner—Ken Weidmann.

    One day last week, you stopped in around 5 P.M. When you first walked in, it felt very different. Initially, you attributed it to the difference in the morning and afternoon crowd. However, neither Ken nor the other employees you know were there. And the environment was too loud and distracting to relax; alternative music blared throughout the restaurant. You ordered a decaffeinated espresso but must have received a double-strength caffeinated dose. Because of the "unfriendly" environment, you drank it quickly and were on your way. However, almost immediately your heart started racing rapidly, so rapidly you had a friend take you to the emergency room. The physician who treated you stated that the racing could have come from the extra caffeine.

    Not only are you out the time and money the mistake caused you, but you're also very disappointed you ran into this problem in one of your favorite places. Write Ken Weidmann a letter that not only states the problem and asks for reimbursement for your expenses but also asks for reassurance that the relaxing environment you value so highly will be restored to the restaurant.

27. Yesterday afternoon as you were leaving your office in downtown [a metropolitan city near your school], you witnessed a thief grab a woman's purse on a highly congested street corner and two men on the street catch and hold the thief until police officers

arrived. Because the incident happened right in front of you, you were a witness to the crime.

When the police arrived, they quickly handcuffed the suspect and placed him in a squad car. Also, they roped off the immediate area and used bullhorns to blare out that all pedestrians should clear the area and not linger or mill about. Because of your strong devotion to civic responsibility, you told one of the officers at the scene that you had seen everything that had happened. The officer abruptly responded that you would have to wait to give your statement and that you should not interfere with police business. When you asked her how long you would have to wait, she blurted loudly in your face, "You're disrupting police work, buddy; that's a crime. Now move on!"

As you drove home on the freeway, you thought specifically about the officer's conduct. It appeared enraged, overreactive, and out of control. You wonder how she might have handled a "deadly force" situation.

The next morning at the office, your thoughts get the best of you; and you decide to report the incident in writing to the captain of the local police precinct. As you think more specifically about the structure of the letter you will prepare, you decide to begin directly by stating what was wrong with the officer's handling of the situation. You will follow that opening with a concise, objective review of the facts that will explain what happened. You might want to suggest corrective action or ask the chief to do whatever is appropriate. The ending of your letter will reinforce with firmness your original conclusion.

You'll want to avoid two extremes as you write. First, you will not want to appear to be a loud-mouthed businessperson who was embarrassed in public. Yes, you are quite prominent in local affairs as president of your own financial services firm and in various leadership positions in the city. On the other hand, you will want to avoid giving the impression that this was an incident that just happened routinely. You will word your report professionally, uniquely, and sincerely.

Write the claim to the police captain that will give a clear idea of what happened in the purse theft situation.

28. Two weeks ago, immediately after the NFC and AFC division playoffs determined the Super Bowl teams, you ordered 100,000 T-shirts from Super Bowl Supplies to arrive two days after the Sunday championship game. You specified you wanted the picture of the winning team's quarterback (Young/Humphries) and San Francisco 49ers/San Diego Chargers, Superbowl Champions, at the top and bottom of the picture respectively on the front of the shirts. Over the years, you've found that these T-shirts have been big sellers and profit makers for your business, Down Memory Lane in Tampa, Florida.

Today, right on schedule, two days after the big game with San Francisco an overwhelming winner, the shipment of T-shirts arrives from Super Bowl Supplies. Because you have advertised the product in the local newspapers and in spot radio broadcasts on local hard rock music stations, you are eager to get the merchandise displayed to satisfy the demands of your clientele. As your order-receiving crews begin unpacking the boxes, however, they soon discover that Humphries' picture is on the shirts and that the San Diego Chargers rather than the San Francisco 49ers is printed as the Superbowl champion. To put things mildly, you are upset! More realistically, you are incensed at the obvious snafu, which is taking money out of your pocketbook on this seasonal product. After several minutes of deliberate self-talk, you ask the crew supervisor of shipment to return the wrong order to Super Bowl Supplies. Then you go directly to your office and sit down at your computer to begin writing a claim letter that you will fax to the Dallas-based supplier.

In the letter, you will begin directly with your statement of what went wrong to give the point emphasis. You will follow that with a presentation of the facts that will support your position. You will end with a firm statement about what you want the supplier to do about the situation. As angry as you are, your "cool hand" will prevail. You want the correct order—soon, right away, as soon as possible!

Be steady, reasonable, and firm as you prepare the claim letter to Super Bowl Supplies.

(Note to instructors: This case may be adapted to other sporting events [basketball, hockey, baseball, soccer, etc.] or to other situations that may arise locally, regionally, or nationally. Also, it may be updated to involve a current championship game.)

29. Early in the spring, you purchased eight 48-inch Hush ceiling fans for the offices of your Labor Ready employment business. You offer temporary personnel when and where it is needed—24 hours a day. You selected Hush mainly because of the claim that they were "the quietest operating fan on the market."

Today, you are convinced that they are not the quietest. In fact, they may well be the noisiest. Six of them make so much noise that the people whose desks are under them will not turn them on. Each of these six fans has its unique whining noise, and all create situations that are unproductive for your employees. You can't explain why, but two of the fans appear to be living up to the manufacturer's claim for quiet operation.

You plan to do something about the noisy fans. Specifically, you'll write directly to the manufacturer's sales office, which is the place from which you ordered them. You'll tell these people how noisy the fans are. And you'll ask for an adjustment—either your money back or replacement fans (quiet ones) at no cost to you. Your records show that you ordered the fans on March 3, received them on March 31, and paid for them April 1 (invoice no. 217A6, dated March 20). The price was $326 per fan, shipping charges included, plus sales tax. The installation cost was $45 per fan.

Prepare the claim letter with forthright directness.

Present in detail the facts that support your claim. Make the letter as task-specific as possible.

30. As Ms. Shannon Fox, president of the Dallas Dowagers Association, a group of 40 women in their 60s who like to travel, you have a matter to settle with Satisfaction Guaranteed Travels. And you are going to write a strongly worded letter to tell how unhappy you are with the service. You are enraged that you would be treated the way you were on your trip to the Grand Canyon, from which you returned only yesterday.

When you left last week, the flight to Flagstaff was excellent. And the first night's stay in the Imperial Hotel was truly elegant—wonderful meals, attentive service, lavish accommodations. On the second day of the tour, you and the other 39 in your tour group boarded buses for the anticipated trip to the Grand Canyon. But when the group arrived at the Grand Canyon Lodge and Resort, there were no confirmed reservations for them—at least so said the young tour guide, Timothy Fair, who was assigned to escort the group on the canyon expedition. When Mr. Fair was working with the sales manager of the GCL & R, he called to the central office of Satisfaction Guaranteed Travels to check the original files for the itinerary and confirmation of accommodations. But the central office reported no such overnight arrangements were ever made. You know that such accommodations existed because you signed a copy of the group's contract; and you reviewed it immediately upon your return home. The contract does indeed state that the meals and lodging are included in the flat rate per person charge.

Because all the area resorts and hotels were booked solid, the Dowagers had to spend the night in the bus—and it was horrible. First, the weather was cold in the Arizona high country, as it usually is. Also, the seats were not suitable for sleeping. And, finally, the one restroom on the bus was not adequate for 40 people. All told, your group had a miserable experience. They returned the next day to Flagstaff and flew home one day early.

On behalf of the group, you will steady your "be reasonable nerves" and prepare a claim to the Satisfaction Guaranteed Travels. You paid for something you didn't get. And that made 40 people totally dissatisfied and unhappy. You'll tell about the experience in your letter—properly written—to Satisfaction Guaranteed Travels.

....

CRITICAL THINKING PROBLEMS ▶ Memorandums

▶ **Direct Memorandums (Responses)**

31. As a middle manager, you've been receiving requests from your first-line managers for guidelines on hiring part-time workers or permitting full-time employees to work part time. Until now, you've been doing it on a case-by-case basis. As has Target Stores, you've found most part-time employees are very efficient. Not only do they take short coffee breaks, but they also usually prefer to work part time. And like many other companies, Target has always paid full benefits for part-timers working at least 20 hours.

However, some of your first-line managers report some employees want to reduce their hours to part-time to try other careers. In fact, one employee reported wanting her hours reduced in order to student teach, clearly with the intention of obtaining teaching credentials not needed in her present job. Another wanted time to write a novel. However, some just wanted a reduction in order to be home with young children.

You recognize the benefits and drawbacks of having part-time workers. However, you believe that a study that identifies the appropriate positions for part-time workers would help you establish some guidelines that will help you use them most effectively.

Tell your first-line managers that you plan to investigate the appropriate use of part-timers and develop the guidelines they requested. You might even want to solicit their ideas or help in compiling information and writing guidelines.

32. Today's e-mail brought a request from nine employees seeking use of company facilities immediately after the workday to take a telecourse from the local university [you name the school]. The course covers ways to use cutting-edge technology for competitive advantage in business. And its listed professor is one who is known to be well versed on the topic, not just an advocate for the newest and latest developments. By taking the course in the company's conference room, your employees will be able to work a full day rather than needing time off to travel to the site. Furthermore, they argue that by delaying their departure by 90 minutes, they'll actually be helping to relieve some of the rush-hour traffic congestion. Additionally, these employees want the company to pay all fees associated with the course.

You realize they've selected a good course from a good school. You've always encouraged employees to keep their skills and knowledge up to date. And this is a good time to test the use of telecourses for such a purpose. You think the convenience of being able to take the course at work is real plus, too. Therefore, you'll agree to the use of facilities. But you'll pay for all the associated fees, including books, only when an employee has successfully completed the course.

33. Today, you are Donald Wayne McElroy, assistant to the manager of human resources of Imprimis. As you log onto your e-mail today, you note you have a message from your boss, James Hemingway. He asks you to find the information that he wants about cultural

awareness training (see Problem 37, Direct Memorandums [Inquiries] for background details). Mr. Hemingway wants to see your response in two days. To continue to develop your always-ready, always-efficient image, you will work hard to meet his deadline.

First, you access the Internet and run a topic check through public and university libraries you have access to. Then you contact several professional organizations by e-mail (SHRM, ASTD, etc.) to determine their experience with the topic. Last, you make several phone calls to other firms in the industry to investigate how they handle relocation training. These efforts produce a sufficient amount of information for you to respond with confidence to Mr. Hemingway. The information is highly inconclusive and incomplete, however.

In answer to the question of program content, you found a variety of topics covered. It appears that companies prefer cultural relocation training to fit their own needs. Common topics include the role of culture, language differences, work and culture, laws, and things to avoid doing. But the list is not universal because each company prefers to add a special topic or two due to the uniqueness of its business. Thus, the topics vary by the competitive niche of the company/industry and not the part of the world in which the relocation occurs. In general, more formal programs cover more topics and cost more, although cost is far from standardized.

Yes, there are trainers who specialize in cultural awareness training, and there are private companies that provide it. But they are quite expensive. Perhaps the best programs are run by state universities. In fact, the University of (your state) conducts two-day seminars frequently throughout each year. Team taught by professors in history, law, anthropology, and business, the seminar can be tailor-made for a specific culture. Families to be relocated can travel to the campus on Friday and participate in the training on Saturday and Sunday. The price of the seminar is $100 per person, which includes lodging in a dormitory-type facility and six meals (Friday evening through Sunday noon) served in the dorm cafeteria. Considering the travel time, the lack of lost work time, and the money, the public university program appears to be ideal. The contact person is Dr. Kamal Fatehi. You will be glad to contact him for a proposal if Mr. Hemingway would like you to.

Your search through Internet and professional associations did generate some professional articles on the topic. You'll send the bibliography and abstracts you collected to Mr. Hemingway. Most of the literature appears to be descriptive and not scientific in the measurement sense. Thus, the topics of assessment and effectiveness are still open to questions. The state of the field (new) and the problem of what to measure and how are areas of concern to researchers. On the surface, those who receive cultural awareness training appear to adjust better in

relocations. But the matter of being more productive is far from resolved.

Write the response memo to Mr. Hemingway that will give him the information he wants about cultural awareness programs. After he reads your returned e-mail, he will likely want to discuss the topic with you.

34. Glenella Weimer, vice president of marketing for Veritech and your boss, makes two requests of you today. (See Problem 38, Direct Memorandums [Inquiries] for background information; you will prepare one or both as your instructor decides.) On the one hand, she wants you to think through an evaluation instrument to assess the recent annual sales meeting. On the other hand, she wants you to investigate several programs on effective presentation skills to be taken by sales managers to improve their presentation techniques.

On the matter of evaluation, you decide to use a combination of yes/no and open-ended questions. You'll begin with the simpler yes/no questions and move progressively to more complex issues that will involve open-ended questions. Some of the topics that you will cover at first are length of the individual sessions, physical arrangement of the facilities, timing of breaks, and such. Each of the topics will be asked as a question that can be answered by circling a yes or no on the form. You will ask for an explanation from those who circle no.

In addition, you will ask more difficult questions in an open-ended format. Even though these responses will be difficult to tally, the information they provide will give much insight into the perceived degree of effectiveness of the annual meeting. Among the topics you will cover in the open-ended format are the sessions that each sales representative liked most and least. For each question, you will ask why. Also, you will ask about presentation style, use of visual aids, voice quality, and overall effectiveness of the sessions. A final question will ask for any input for making the meetings more effective next year. Thus, you will design the instrument containing these questions for Ms. Weimer's review. But do not be confused by the assignment. Your message is a response to Ms. Weimer's inquiry. Even though your response is an evaluation form of questions, it is still a response memo, not an inquiry. Prepare it for transmittal to your boss, Ms. Glenella Weimer.

On the matter of training in effective presentation skills, you ask the local chapter of the American Society of Training and Development (ASTD) for information. The organization indicates that its central headquarters has brochures and course descriptions that will illustrate several different approaches to presentations. The first course, Basic Presentation Skills, impresses you most because it is fundamental and direct. The following list of topics is covered: Organizing and Conveying Information Effectively; Tailoring Your Message to the Audience; Understanding Players and Goals for Meetings;

Choosing Language and Structure; and Practicing Effective Speaking (eye contact, voice projections, use of gestures, interpretation). Designed for line and staff managers who desire constructive ideas on making better presentations, the course videotapes mock presentations from participants with the instructor and other participants critiquing each video performance. Cost of the course is $125 per person for eight hours of instruction. Classes are limited to 10 for high participation and individual feedback.

The course seems to fit the ideas that Ms. Weimer had in mind for the sales managers. Write her a response about the one-day skill development training.

▶ Direct Memorandums (Inquiries)

35. You work for Offsite, a local business whose major function is to help over 300 small businesses back up data. Recently your boss decided to switch your company's customer database to Microsoft Access.

    While most employees have adapted easily, you believe receiving the magazine *Access Adviser* would help them get the most from this tool. The magazine gives ideas for creating custom applications as well as custom forms, queries, and reports. It also reviews concepts of the Access Basic language, helping readers master it. Readers can also learn how to create and use Access Wizards. But most importantly, it shows readers how to embed powerful objects with OLE. You believe this is a low-cost way to provide training, developing your employees into power Access users. And for a small but growing business, getting the most out of the database can provide the competitive advantage it needs to dominate its market.

    Ask your boss, Ray Olson, to authorize purchasing three subscriptions at $24.95 each.

36. Last week you read a story in *The Wall Street Journal* about a trend in performance evaluations that is moving toward peer evaluations, spreading from the blue-collar to white-collar work force. Apparently, as work forces grow less hierarchical, gathering input from all levels is gaining popularity. The story you read told about a worker at Eastman Chemical Company who usually shrugged off her bosses' suggestions. However, when her teammates told her that her constant gossiping and pitting co-workers against one another was poisoning the work environment, she quit her job. While the result was a bit extreme, it did show she listened to her peers.

    However, not all workers know how to give effective evaluations. They need to understand both the technical side as well as the interpersonal aspects of delivering feedback on performance. Before implementing peer evaluations, both Honeywell's and Eastman's employees were given special training on such topics as listening, delivering constructive criti-

cism, and building self-esteem. In fact, some companies use consultants as screens for helping interpret criticisms and deliver them effectively. But while honest peer feedback can sting, it can also be both instructive and valuable to employees.

Write your boss a memo inquiring about the possibility of implementing a trial on peer evaluations coupled with either appropriate training or the use of consultants.

37. Today's assignment projects you into the role of human resources manager of Imprimis. With the expanding revenue from product sales on a global basis, the company has been sending more people to foreign countries to manage company affairs and to support business. All told, about 20 percent of your workforce is located in foreign countries with most employees relocating their families as well. With these relocations come adjustment problems. And one way to overcome such problems is to orient company personnel to the cultural differences they can expect in a different country.

    A Department of Labor study you read in *Forbes* gives the following guidelines:

    Selection criteria of U.S. staff for assignment in foreign countries should include technical abilities as required for the job as well as cultural awareness, and to the extent possible, language capability. Cultural awareness, at a minimum, should pertain to spouses and children. Pre-assignment cultural and language training is preferable.

    You admit that with the rapid sales growth, you have probably not given cultural orientation of relocated personnel the attention it deserves. From a human resources perspective, you have had prelocation meetings with people who have been selected for foreign assignment. But the meetings have been technically oriented—visas, compensation, benefits, and such. You have offered cultural awareness support—but only in the form of videos, books, and such. You have not offered formal orientation sessions. Now might be the time to consider more formal efforts at cultural awareness training. Thus, you will assign the task of investigating the subject to your most trusted assistant, Donald Wayne McElroy.

    First, you'd like to know what is involved in a complete cultural awareness program. Are there certain topics that are essential? And do these topics vary by the part of the world or country to which personnel are assigned? Also, you want to know how the training should be conducted. Are there programs you could purchase? And are there trainers who specialize in cultural awareness training?

    Perhaps of most importance is cost. How much do such programs cost? Is there any professional literature you can read to keep you current in the area? And then there is the matter of effectiveness. Is there any evidence that cultural awareness training for foreign-bound employees makes them more productive? Or do they just feel more informed?

These and other possible areas are what you want your assistant to explore for you to increase your knowledge of cultural awareness training for employees who plan to relocate in foreign countries. Prepare the direct-inquiry memo that you will send by e-mail to Mr. McElroy.

38. As you are returning from your annual sales meeting of Universal Instruments, producers of precision tools and parts, you reflect on the three-day occasion. Your sales managers and sales representatives showed enthusiasm and commitment. But you believe that annual sales meetings should be more than "rah-rah" affairs. They should be technical learning sessions as well. And it is in this part of the sales meetings that you felt the most disappointment.

More specifically, you thought the presenters at the product and strategy sessions knew their content very well. But their presentations stunk. The sales managers had done their homework and had prepared diligently, but you doubt the sales representatives came away with much of the technical information that had been presented to them. These ideas lead you to a two-part assignment for your assistant, Louise Tegarten.

The first part will be to design an inquiry memo to each sales representative (125 in all) asking them to evaluate the meeting they just attended. You will ask them specifically what they liked and what they didn't. And more importantly, you will ask them why. For the most part, you will avoid the simple yes-no type question and concentrate on those that are more probing. Also, you will focus on the formal sessions of the meetings and not the social affairs. Your memo will take the form of a direct-inquiry message that you will send by e-mail to each sales representative in your sales force. The reps can download the inquiry, answer the questions, and return them to you anonymously by regular mail. Or they can return their answers by e-mail to the human resources department, which will remove all names and identifying information before transmitting them to you.

In addition, you believe that much of the blame for the lack of understanding of the technical information at the meetings involved faulty presentation skills of the sales managers. Thus, you will ask your assistant to examine several training programs that teach effective presentation skills. You want a "hands-on" approach, for sure. And you want to know whether programs include how to organize information, how to develop presentation materials, how to adapt presentations to different audiences, and how to use effective speaking skills. No doubt, there are other ideas that you could think about to include in your assignment.

Prepare one or both of the assignments as your instructor designates. Both will be direct-inquiry memorandums.

▶ Direct Memorandums (Directives)

39. You've recently been bothered by the number of employees wearing Walkmans on the job in your business offices. They are appearing on the heads of employees of all ages, not just those in their 20s. While these workers appear to get the work done, they close others off by wearing these devices. This can be a particular problem where employees are working in teams and interaction is needed. Of course, you're also worried about the distraction the music could cause, leading to miscommunication, mistakes, and maybe even accidents.

You recognize some of the arguments workers will present. Some will claim the beat of the music speeds them up, making them more productive. Others will say it relieves stress and improves the quality of their work. And some may even say it helps them tolerate the boring work they're doing.

In writing your directive prohibiting the use of Walkmans on the job, you realize the need to overcome some of these objections. Use plenty of you-viewpoint, stressing reader benefits as much as possible.

40. As a manager for No Fear, a San Diego maker of casual wearing apparel, you get frustrated with knock-offs of your products. Not only can you cross the border to Tijuana and find copies of your newest designs, but you also even see them for sale locally.

Your designers work hard on designs even as simple as tank tops. To see their work copied a day or so after you've first presented it to buyers is upsetting. Since today's technology permits one to take a snapshot and the same day fax it to a manufacturer somewhere else in the world, you're having a difficult time keeping copies out of U.S. markets. In fact, some companies have found copies of their designs being sold within a week of their introduction.

Your products with your company's logo are protected by U.S. law, making it illegal to sell knockoffs or counterfeits. However, that hasn't stopped those wishing to cash in on your product quality and respected, popular name. While you've always dismissed the idea that spying is occurring within your company, you've recently become wary. To assure that leaks aren't coming from inside, you've decided to issue a directive to help curb this problem.

The directive you write will stress the importance of keeping all aspects of all products in development and production a secret until they are on store shelves. Remind your employees not to tell others anything about the new designs, including colors, fabrics, or new products. Offer a whistle-blower reward of $1,000 for both internal and external attempts at knockoffs. This strategy was effective for a New York manufacturer, Marisa Christina Inc. Its employees help the company successfully prosecute offenders and keep the illegal copies off store shelves.

41. Three years ago your company tested and established

a casual-dress day for the last Friday of each month. Results of the test revealed that employee morale improved dramatically while productivity remained the same as with standard business dress. Therefore, you decided to permanently designate the last Friday of each month as a casual-dress day.

Although you haven't measured employee morale recently, you have had customers complain about their dress. Three years ago your customers reacted positively to the relaxed look your employees projected. But as you recall, casual dress then was informally defined as khaki skirts or slacks and a polo shirt. While you realize styles change, you're not so sure that boots, crumpled shirts, and cutoffs are appropriate casual wear for the business environment. In fact, on the last casual day you sent an employee home to change. To your surprise the cutoffs were exchanged for wrinkled jeans and a ridiculous tie. Therefore, you've decided to bring in an image consultant to educate your employees on appropriate casual dress for your business.

Send employees a directive requiring them to attend one of the three sessions conducted by experts from Image One International of Houston. Let them know how important learning and applying appropriate professional dress is to the image your business conveys to its customers.

42. As director of your company's child care center, write a memorandum to the employees who use the facility explaining the policies that will become effective at the beginning of the year.

Since the center opened just nine months ago, several parents have complained about sick children being brought to the center. In addition, your staff members have complained several times about parents not picking up their children on time. This has caused your department to be over budget due to excess overtime expenses.

While the majority of these policies are the same, or slightly modified, several are new. Your company believes that these policies will benefit not only the staff at the center, but more importantly, the children and parents as well.

The policies you want to communicate to the parents include the following:

Children with a temperature of 100 degrees or higher will not be allowed to stay at the center. A listing of "sick child care centers" will be provided to each parent when requested.

If a child has been absent for four or more days due to illness, a note from a physician will be required for the child to return to the center.

Each parent must sign in and sign out his or her children each day. A sheet is located on the door of each room.

Parents must provide diapers, infant formula, and

bottles for those children who need them. (Note: Only disposable diapers will be allowed.)

For first-shift employees: Parents may bring their children to the center no earlier than 6:30 A.M. and must pick them up no later than 3:30 P.M.

For second-shift employees: Parents may bring their children to the center no earlier than 2:30 P.M. and must pick them up no later than 11:30 P.M.

Payment for each child is due on the first of the month. A late penalty of $1 per day will be assessed for each day the payment is received after the first.

Unless otherwise informed, only those individuals listed on the child's consent form will be allowed to pick him or her up from the center.

Use these items to prepare the policy directive for company employees.

43. As president of Tri State Utilities, you and your executive committee have been working for the last several weeks to develop a Cold Weather Program for customers. Because you are a public utility, you want to serve the public well. Over the years, however, you have received some bad press because you have discontinued service, rightly or wrongly, to poor, indigent, and elderly customers. From a personal and company perspective, you believe you should have a Cold Weather Program that will serve as a fair and equitable guide to your customers. Also, you want to use the policy as a public relations device as well.

Accordingly, your top management team has developed these policy guidelines for use during cold weather months. First, the Cold Weather Program, as it will be called, will be in effect between November 1 and March 31 of each year. During these months, service disconnections will not be made when the National Weather Service (NWS) forecasts the temperature to drop below 35 degrees or be in the mid-30s or colder within the following 48 hours.

To reconnect service regardless of temperature or to avoid disconnection when weather is above the stated temperatures, customers must take certain steps called the Good Faith Test. For instance, they must notify the company that they cannot pay their bill in full; and they must give Tri State information so that the company can place them on a 12-month payment plan. When they are placed on this plan, they must make an initial payment of $1/12$ of the total bill and enroll in the 12-month payment plan. Future monthly payments will be based on their current bill or average usage plus $1/12$ of the remaining balance in arrears. Last, customers should apply for local, state, federal, or other funds for which they are eligible. They should not take service illegally, and they should not default on the payment plan.

In case of any payment difficulties, Tri State will do whatever it can to help. Specifically, the company will inform customers of agencies with funds to assist with utility bills. It will also make personal or telephone contact with customers one day before terminations of service. In addition to providing customers with the telephone number of the Consumer Protection Agency in each state of service, it also will inform them of any other pay arrangements they may qualify for.

Your job now is to present these guidelines in a direct-order policy memorandum. You will use this order, even though the memo will be directed to customers and not employees. In writing the memo, you will want to personalize the points and make them easy to read by bulleting or itemizing them. Prepare the memorandum that will eventually be stuffed into monthly bills to each customer of Tri State Utilities. You will run the memo by the executive committee members for their critique before you print the final copy.

44. As assistant to the president of _____ Bank (a large metropolitan bank of your choice), the president has asked you to write a directive in memorandum form prescribing a dress code for bank employees. The president wants two separate directives—one for males and one for females. (For class purposes, write the one for your sex.)

While you prepare to write this directive, you recall the president's instructions: "For years we have had an unwritten code specifying conservative dress and grooming for all employees who are visible to the public. Recently, however, more and more employees have strayed from this unwritten code. Every day I see our employees wearing some pretty far-out clothes, and some of their hairstyles and their use of cosmetics don't project the image of a bank. The situation appears to be getting worse. I want you to work up an appropriate set of dress and grooming standards that we can live with. Don't make them too stringent, but certainly rule out anything that would project a wrong image. Work up a first draft. Then we'll talk about it before we send it out."

Now you will begin to jot down the dress and grooming rules that you think will meet the president's requirements. When you have finished, you'll write them up in the memorandum form that will convey them to the employees.

▶ Indirect Memorandums (Bad News)

45. You have been asked by your company's board of directors to let the employees know that the extended trial run of the four-day week ends this month. The directors have decided not to implement it as an alternative work schedule. You realize that many on this plan have gotten used to the extra day off and will view the news negatively. So you decide to present the facts collected by your staff before announcing the end of the trial.

Several negatives have been reported by people electing to be part of the trial. The shorter week causes stress in numerous ways. One is early hours; another is the extensive burden any overtime places

both mentally and physically on the worker. You are also concerned that the long day could induce more repetitive stress injuries such as carpal tunnel syndrome. In fact, productivity has dropped and errors increased in overtime work. Furthermore, the long day creates child care and other personal problems. In fact, one employee stated the long day caused her to eat more fast food, resulting in a gain of 15 pounds. Within the first year, nearly 10 percent of those in the trial returned to the standard five-day workweek.

Other concerns have led to dropping the schedule, too. While your site was designated as the test for this alternative, others in the company viewed it as an extra benefit. This caused much internal friction. Additionally, these employees often complained that when they tried to work with people at your site, the person they needed often was not there. This lack of flexibility was a major concern at the outset of the trial, but the cross-training implemented before the trial didn't seem to help alleviate the problem. Along this same line, customers often complained they couldn't get their business done.

However, the trial was not a complete failure. In fact, because you were able to accommodate longer production runs, your costs for production dropped measurably. Also, it did allow you to comply easily with new environmental regulations for reducing commuter air emissions. These two positives are worth holding onto in some way while going back to the full five-day week.

46. Eliminating an employee benefit is always bad news, and it's your job to report it to all employees. The benefit the company has decided to eliminate is tuition reimbursement.

Cost reduction was not the major reason for eliminating it; executives found it to be underused and misused. The costs amounted to only 1 percent of total benefits cost, and only 7 percent of the employees used it annually. The underuse was even evident during downsizing, a period where one might expect its use to increase in order to gain skills necessary to protect one's job. An informal evaluation showed only 25 percent of the courses taken were directly related to the work the employee was doing; the other 75 percent of courses taken were for work toward degrees, one-third of which were outside the nature of the business. Company executives believe the money spent on the program and administering it could better be spent on in-house training programs.

Let your employees know the tuition reimbursement program will stop at the end of the current academic year. Any work in progress that is completed with a C or better will be fully reimbursed as the present policy states.

47. Two requests on your desk today for additional full-time employees indicate that you need to prepare an indirect memorandum to respond to them. As director of human resources at Hirsig-Frazier Company, Inc., you will say no to the requests; but not until you have given the justification for the decision.

One month ago, the general staff of Hirsig-Frazier

decided to extend overtime to workers rather than hire new employees. This personnel policy was to remain in existence until such time that a true recovery in the general economy and for all product lines in the company could be determined. Thus, the overtime strategy was a cautious and short-run solution to increasing demand for products. When it could be determined that the economy was indeed on a steady upward trend rather than on short-run cyclical "peaks and valleys," then a hiring "thaw" could occur to meet the increased orders for Hirsig-Frazier products.

To justify the short-term freeze even more, the staff cited a Department of Labor study that showed U.S. workers put in 3.8 overtime hours per week in the first quarter of the year, about the same as a year ago but up from a five-year average of 3.3 hours per week. Most plants are using the overtime approach because they laid off so many workers during hard times several years ago. Coors, Chrysler, Vernitran, Lumex, and others are taking the same wait-and-see approach. Authorities estimate that nine months of increased overtime recovery exist. In addition, market analysis needs to reveal that sales are increasing for all lines of products and not just a few.

All of these reasons justify your refusing to hire new employees as requested. Your first thought is to refuse directly as a matter of employment policy. The more you think about the matter, however, the more you believe that an indirect memo would do the best job in the situation. You know, for instance, that the grapevine works quickly and accurately. Accordingly, you want as many of the company personnel as possible to know the staff's rationale and position. The indirect memo will give you the opportunity to present these reasons. If you write it skillfully enough, the memo could boost morale.

Write the memo as an ambassador of top management. You will refuse the requests from department heads. But you will tell why you must refuse using the you-viewpoint, positive emphasis, and other techniques of effect. Make the refusal specific and the memo goodwill oriented.

48. Over the years, Tycom, Inc., has developed a very liberal policy for "high-potential" managers and executives to attend off-site development courses ranging from specific functional areas (finance, marketing, global economy, etc.) to courses to keep people mentally inspired and to see the "whole world fits" (humanities and arts courses). Such a policy keeps your executive talent fresh and visionary; it also serves as an executive perk and motivator of behavior. You usually send people to well-established, prestige universities such as MIT, Harvard, Stanford, Northwestern, Wharton, Michigan, Virginia, and schools in Switzerland and France. In turn, these professional development programs have experienced a 25 percent increase in executive participation in the last 10 years.

But many companies—including yours—find that they no longer can spare executive time with such perks. Often executives schedule vacations immedi-

ately after the development sessions so that they are away from their jobs for three and four weeks at a time. During such absences, decisions are often made by less experienced personnel and operations frequently suffer because of it. After studying the matter for a month or so, the compensation and benefits committee of the board of directors has decided to cancel the policy of executives attending off-site seminars. In addition to the foregoing reasons about on-site presence and time, the committee believes that the policy is expensive and that a cutback in spending is needed to show better performance throughout the year. It plans to review the policy in one year.

For the present, however, the committee needs to convey the bad news to the management team at Tycom. Rather than having a blank statement of this-is-the-way-it-is policy, the committee believes that more tactful treatment is needed. Committee members do not want excessive turnover in management ranks because that could lead to decreased morale and a loss on human resource investment. Thus, they ask you, administrative assistant to the board, to draft an e-mail memo to all salaried personnel, excluding technical staff.

As you size up the situation, you will prepare the memo indirectly with reasons preceding the decision to cancel seminar attendance for a year. You will think specifically about how these reasons benefit both parties involved and how they could help managers in the long run. Write a draft copy for the committee that will say no to seminar attendance but will retain the goodwill of the managers. If the committee OKs the work, the memo will be distributed to the Tycom management team.

▶ Indirect Memorandums (Persuasive)

49. As sales manager of Carboloy, you have recently received letters and telephone calls about discourteous treatment by some of your office personnel. You expect a few complaints because you handle adjustment situations. But over the last two months, your hate mail/calls have increased about 20 percent. Although you do not have telephone training for your staff, per se, you do have a junior-senior arrangement whereby experienced workers sponsor newly hired personnel for the first three months of a new worker's employment. This arrangement has worked well over the years with experienced workers passing along tips for success, monitoring calls, and giving work advice as needed. In addition, all employees who apply for work in your sales office are given a paper and pencil stress tolerance test. Only those that score 90 or above are considered for employment. Of course, there are other job criteria that must be met for employment as well.

In the last year, turnover in your office personnel has increased about 25 percent. With one in four people being new, you wonder whether the buddy system is working as well as it should. At any rate, you decide that something must be done about the complaints. A quick call to the office of ATE, the telephone company that services your area, reveals that it has a two-hour course on telephone etiquette and techniques that it offers free to larger customers. The course, it appears on the surface, is just what the doctor ordered for your office personnel.

In terms of design, the course begins with *how* to use the telephone, the central part of telephone service. It provides hands-on training in using the ATE system—placing calls, transferring calls, putting callers on hold, setting up conference calls, and such. In addition, a short video titled "Irate Caller" by Carolyn Waters, The Telephone Doctor, is shown. The firm demonstrates how to handle the irate, angry, rude, and sometimes abrasive caller. Indeed, the two-hour package appears ideal to refresh the telephone habits of your office personnel. It is offered in two one-hour sessions with a limit of 10 people each session.

But the negative point associated with the program is that it will have to be offered after hours. You cannot do without 10 of your office staff of 50 and still maintain efficiency and good service. Besides, doing the training during regular work hours would be expensive. Thus, you decide to run the program Monday through Friday from 5:30 to 6:30 P.M. for two weeks. Although the program will be voluntary, you want everyone to attend. If you paid for the workers' attendance, you would be forced to pay overtime; and this would be even more expensive.

Thus, you decide to write a persuasive memo to your office workers selling them on the need to attend the after-hours training. As in all persuasive efforts, you will begin by identifying objections to your request. Then you will counter each objection with a benefit of attending. These benefits will become the appeals you will use in the body of your memo. What are they? Pride in work? Achievement? Being part of a productive team? You can possibly use these and others to sway your office personnel to attend the session. But work hard not to threaten them. They will become defensive.

Write the persuasive memo to your office staff at Carboloy.

50. In your 10 years as public relations director of Pawlick, Inc., you have been asked to sell many things. But the assignment you receive today from Vice President of Operations John Keliehor sends your creative mind reeling. Rather than an external writing piece, you are going to develop an internal memo selling "lunchtime lectures" to the employees of Pawlick. Keliehor suggests several examples of lecture topics in his e-mail message to you.

Most of the lecture topics stated in Keliehor's directive could be classified as life-cycle programs—lectures addressed to employees' everyday problems. For example, "AIDS and Adolescence," "Sibling Battle," and "Sharing the World of Deaf and Hard of Hearing People" are representative of the suggested topics. In addition, you can envision lectures dealing with terminal illness, personal finances, care of the elderly, and paying for a college education. A survey of companies recently indicated about 50 percent of employees use some life-cycle program or service.

The odds appear to be on your side to get the ball rolling for the lunchtime lectures; but the differences between the odds and actual attendance at the lectures is first a well-thought-out persuasive memo that will pull employees to attend the sessions. Here are the details. Lectures will begin promptly at 12:05 P.M. and end at 12:55 P.M. They will be held weekly on Wednesdays in the Pawlick Orientation Room, which seats 200 people. Employees should indicate their intention to attend by sending an e-mail message to your office. They should also bring a brown-bag lunch.

Ordinarily, you would simply announce to employees that the lunchtime lectures were available. But they are more important to management than to be taken casually. Thus, you will need to develop appeals that will sell the program to employees. To begin the process, you will start to identify appeals that will overcome any objections the employees might have to attending. These appeals will make good use of the you-viewpoint, conversational tone, and other techniques of effect that will persuade the employees to sign up right away. The company wants to grow its employees to the fullest, and the lunchtime series is a way to do just that.

Prepare the persuasive memo that will sell Pawlick employees on attending the life-cycle programs.

51. You volunteer for the local symphony, helping it in as many ways as you've been asked. You've ushered, helped at food booths, and even called for donations and ticket sales. Lately, most of your work has been in the symphony office; so the symphony's paid business director, Terrence Lenaghan, knows you personally.

When you read a story in *USA Today* about the University of San Francisco's new high-tech fund-raising tool, you immediately thought about its use for the symphony. It was simply a multimedia presentation on a disk mailed to potential donors. With the number of households having computers growing rapidly, this idea seems like a good way to "show and tell" the symphony's story. By combining text, sound, and photos, donors could work their way individually through a multimedia presentation with hypertext links. Those with an interest in the bottom-line numbers could follow the financial statements and explanations. Those with an interest in what the symphony has done could see and listen to excerpts of the best work. Also, the disk could showcase all the times the symphony performed for different audiences—children, businesspeople, and the community. A well-done presentation has the ability to increase donations, especially from the younger set. In fact, the market of potential donors can be easily segmented and sent variations of the presentation most appropriate to them.

Write the symphony's business director, Terrence Lenaghan, a memo persuading him to consider the multimedia presentation as a donation solicitation tool for this year's spring fund-raising drive.

52. As a student, you've been exposed repeatedly to the importance of exercise and diet. Yet, when you evaluate the food sold on and around campus, much of it is sugary, high-fat content food. In the past the director of campus programs told you that the university only provides what students want. Yes, it's another case of the bottom-line dollars driving decisions, not necessarily what's best for students. But now you've come across an idea that will meet both needs—a health-mex menu that tastes good and will sell.

   Write the director of your campus food program a persuasive memo pleading your case for health-mex cuisine. Let the director know that it is possible to have good-tasting, low-fat Mexican food. One Mexican food chain, La Salsa, reports that it uses vegetable oil and none of the lard that traditional Mexican dishes use. In fact, 9 out of 10 items on its menu meet the American Heart Association's recommendation for low fat and low salt. Other health-mex dishes offered by restaurants include vegetarian burritos in whole-wheat tortillas with only 10 percent fat, veggie tacos with 18 percent fat, and cheese quesadilla with only 34 percent fat. Furthermore, grocery stores now sell fat-free, good-tasting tortilla chips and salsa.

   Also, because people tend to shun food labeled "healthy," encourage the director not to label it that way. You believe that the campus food program can provide health-mex items that taste good for a reasonable price and still be profitable.

ORDERS

53. As Theresa Sanchez, office manager of a medical clinic, you've been given the honor of and responsibility for upgrading the image of the clinic in its upcoming remodeling. One way you've decided to do this is through choosing functional accessories for the clinic's waiting areas that are also decorative. You reason that patients will associate a contemporary yet functional environment with an up-to-date yet thrifty clinic. In discussing this idea with a co-worker, Mary McQuire, she gave you a catalog that was perfect. It was called *Attitudes: Style and Substance.* You found the three items below that you want.

- **Time flies.** An Italian pagliaccio (clown) dangles in black metal silhouette as he stretches the face of the clock. Is he trying to make time stand still? Or does time in its flight bear him aloft like a balloon? You decide! Delightful clock is the work of Massimo Tani of Florence, and is a splended example of fun-follows-function! In metal and glass, 8″ W × 20″ L. Powered by one AA size battery, not included. **#K1808 Pagliaccio Clock $125.**
- **Our light fantastic**. A statement of style and grace, our sconce adds a subtle accent of light to a room. Dark forest green finished wrought iron rods are gently curved, then topped with a white Kinwashi shade. The sconce attaches to the wall and just one

nail (not included). Because of the unique design, no pre-wiring is necessary and no unsightly wires show. Convenient on-off foot switch is included. Measures 75″ high. Uses up to a 75 watt bulb (not included). Please allow 5–7 weeks for delivery. **#K1917 Entwin'd Sconce $339.**

- **Let the sun shine**. A softly glowing, sun-shaped disk of light illuminates this beautiful table lamp. The frosted glass "sun" rises and sets over the cast resin hills at its base, or tilts to angle light wherever you like. Lit by low-voltage halogen bulb (included), this unique lamp provides a focal point for any environment and its wonderful mix of materials—cast resins, aluminum, and nickel-plated brass—makes it an outstanding piece of art as well. Available in gold or silver (not shown). Made in USA. Lamp stands 24½″ H. Base is 3″ W × 11½″ L. **#K13490 Sunlight Lamp $250.**

   From the descriptions, select the information your reader needs to fill your order accurately and completely. Also, let your reader know that you'd like the order to arrive on October 26, the scheduled completion date for the painting and carpet laying. And be sure to tell your reader how you'll pay for the items.

   Create an order letter that you'll fax to Attitudes at 408-734-8004. However, you'll address it to Attitudes, P.O. Box 61158, Sunnyvale, CA 94088-1148.

54. As a buyer for Sunglass Hut International, a retail chain, you want to keep your selection of sunglasses up to date. Because other retailers have discovered that sunglasses are high-margin items, competition is growing rapidly. In fact, it is the fastest growing segment of the eyeglass market. Not only are other specialty stores like SunGear and Sunglass World expanding, but also stores like Sears and the Gap are adding sunglasses to their product mix.

   You recently read a story in *The Wall Street Journal* about a technological advance in lenses that allows the wearer to discriminate better between reds, ambers, and greens of light because of a special filtering ability. The glasses are produced by Ray-Ban using a formula with neodymium, made by Bausch & Lomb. They sell for $133. While these glasses target a niche market, you do want to offer them to your customers.

   You reason that these glasses will be most popular with men, who suffer color blindness more than women, and those over 16 who drive. Therefore, you'll order styles and numbers for the store in your town to fit the demographics of your potential customers. Currently, the FDA is pushing for stricter standards on the type of protection glasses provide as well as the labeling. The agency wants glasses to allow in less than 1 percent of ultraviolet B rays and less than 50 percent of ultraviolet A rays. In addition, the FDA wants those promoting the glasses to use accurate labeling, not strictly celebrity appeal or fear of cataracts and retina damage appeals. You want your customers to know about the protection the glasses provide as well as the special qualities of the lenses. Therefore, you will specify in your order that the glasses be labeled appropriately.

As with other orders, tell how you expect to pay as well as where and how to ship the glasses.

55. As president of the Sedgwick County Medical Society, you need to construct an on-line Internet message to MEDLINE, Inc.

The doctors (65 in total) in the Sedgwick County Medical Society voted unanimously last night at their monthly meeting to subscribe to three of MEDLINE's network subscription services—MEDNET (general) PEDNET (pediatrics); and OBGYNET (obstetrics/gynecology). MEDLINE provides 10 years of database research in each of the medical areas specified by the net for a monthly charge. More specifically, physicians can research a database to confirm a diagnosis, to refer patients to a specialty area outside their own, or to determine what actual diagnosis to make if symptoms are unusual. What used to be done by conversation can now be completed by computer search and retrieval. The brochure you received from MEDLINE several weeks ago indicates the costs are $4,500 per month for MEDNET (general) and $4,000 per month for PEDNET and OBGYNET.

Along with your order for the network service, you will attach a list of the doctors who are authorized to receive the service and their Internet numbers. As the County Medical Society is the governing unit for medical doctors, you will assess all charges to practicing physicians for the on-line services and will attest to the accuracy of the list. If doctors should move in or out of the county, you will add or delete their names and determine appropriate charges for the services.

You want the network services to begin as soon as possible. Your doctors are clamoring to get the latest information at their fingertips to help them do their work. They will provide their own computers, printers, and such. But they cannot access the databases directly without your authorization. You must certify their specialties and their ability to practice medicine in the county.

Prepare this on-line order as you would any order letter by beginning directly with clear authorization, arranging the network services with identifying facts, covering transmission and manner of payment (you'd like 30 days), and ending with a goodwill comment. Send it to Medline@mdsm.mds.com.

56. As senior minister at St. Christopher's Church, you have been authorized by your Board of Elders (the governing board of the church) for $5,000 worth of

technical support services for your work for the forthcoming year. Indeed, you are most grateful for the budget allocation. For some time, you have been considering subscribing to several of the on-line computer services that are available to ministers.

You think back about what it must have been like in the early days of the church—monks working by candlelight with guills to provide handwritten documents for church leaders. "How things have changed," you muse to yourself. Using today's technology, you can pay a fee and have information at your fingertips that will help you improve the services you give to your congregation and your community. You are excited to be a part of organizational life today with its use of information technology in storage and retrieval. You will use the information services to promote better services to your "customers," and you will use the time savings to provide more service. You know that many organizations are tapping on-line information sources for similar results.

The latest issue of *Today's Minister* contains several advertisements about on-line database resources that are available in the market. As you peruse that issue, you note that on-line services exist for Sermon Topics, Quotes/Anecdotes for Sermons, Mission Ministries, and Tips for Church Administration. Subscription prices vary but they are not cheap. There is a connection fee for each one; and if you subscribe to more than three services, you get a 10 percent discount. Once you subscribe, prices are good for six months. You need to give 30 days' notice to cancel each of the services.

With these ideas in mind, you decide to subscribe to the subdirectory services of PREACHNET, the umbrella network owned by Network Ministries, Inc., Los Angeles, CA. The connection and subscription fees for the subnets are SERMONS—$500/150 per month; QUOTES—$350/125 per month; and ADMINISTRATION—$300/100 per month. You will provide last fiscal year's compilation report from your accountant as proof of the solvency of your church. You'd like to have a 30-day account. Also, you will provide your Federal Employee Identification Number (FEIN) to prove your tax-exempt status.

Prepare the order letter to be sent to PREACH-NET. Of course, you will send it on-line through Internet to Preach@pvssm.pcm.com.

57. Prepare an order letter for some on-line information service that your instructor designates. Many such services exist. Your instructor will specify the details of the assignment.

Strategies in the Job Search Process

9

Upon completing this chapter, you will be able to conduct an effective job search and compose effective job-application letters, résumés, and follow-up letters. To reach this goal, you should be able to

1 Develop and use a network of contacts in your job search.

2 Assemble and evaluate information that will help you select a career.

3 Describe the sources that can lead you to an employer.

4 Compile traditional and electronic résumés that are strong, complete, and well arranged.

5 Write letters of application that skillfully sell your abilities.

6 Explain how you should conduct yourself in an interview.

7 Write application follow-up letters that are appropriate, friendly, and positive.

8 Maintain your job-search skills.

▶ to the Job-Search Process

Introduce yourself to this chapter by assuming a role similar to one you are now playing. You are Jason Andrews, a student at Olympia University. In a few months, you will complete your studies for a career in labor relations.

You believe that it is time to begin seeking the job for which those studies have been preparing you. But how do you do this? Where do you look? What does the search involve? How should you conduct yourself for the best results? The answers to these and related questions are reviewed in the following pages. ■

. . . .

THE JOB SEARCH

Of all the things you do in life, few are more important than getting a job. Whether it involves your first job or one further down your career path, job seeking is directly related to your success and your happiness. It is vital that you conduct the job search properly—that you prepare wisely and carefully and proceed diligently. The following review of job-search strategies should help you succeed.

• For success in job seeking, use the following procedure.

Building a Network of Contacts

You can begin the job search long before you are ready to find employment. In fact, you can do it now by building a network of contacts. More specifically, you can build relationships with people who can help you find work when you need it. Such people include classmates, professors, and businesspeople.

• Begin the job search by building a network of contacts in this way:

At present, your classmates are not likely to be holding positions in which they make or influence hiring decisions. But in the future, when you may want to make a career change, they may hold such positions. Even right now, some of them may know people who can help you. The wider your circle of friends, the more likely you are to make employment contacts.

• (1) Broaden your circle of friends.

Knowing your professors and making sure that they know you can also lead to employment contacts. As professors often consult for business, they may know key executives and be able to help you contact them. Professors sometimes hear of position openings, and in such cases they can refer you to the hiring executives. Demonstrating your work ethic and your ability in the classroom is probably the best way to get your professors to know you and help you. Take advantage of opportunities to know your professors outside the classroom. Knowing the professors in your major field is especially beneficial.

• (2) Get to know your professors.

Obviously, knowing key business executives can also lead to employment contacts. You may already know some through family and friends. But broadening your relationships among businesspeople would be helpful. You can do this in various ways, but especially through college professional clubs such as the Data Processing Management Association, Delta Sigma Pi, and the Society for the Advancement of Management. By taking an active role in the organizations in your field of study, especially by working on program committees and by becoming an officer, you can get to know the executives who serve as guest speakers.

• (3) Meet executives.

If your school offers internships, you can make good career contacts through them. But you should find the one that is best for you, that offers you the best training for your career objective. And by all means, do not regard an internship as just a job. Regard it as a foundation step in your career plan. The experience you gain and the contacts you make in an internship might well lead to your first career position. In fact, if you perform well, your internship could turn into full-time employment.

• (4) Make contacts through internships.

In addition to the more common ways of making contacts discussed above, you can use some less common ones. By working in community organizations (charities, com-

• (5) Work with community organizations.

munity improvement groups, fund-raising groups), you can meet community leaders. By attending meetings of professional associations (every field has them), you can meet the leaders in your field. In fact, participation in virtually any activity that provides contacts with business leaders can open doors for you now and well into the future.

Identifying Appropriate Jobs

- Look at both your internal and external factors.

To find the right job, you need to investigate both internal and external factors. The best fit occurs when you have carefully looked at yourself—your education, personal qualities, experience, and any special qualifications. However, to be realistic, these internal qualities need to be analyzed in light of the external factors. Some of these factors may include the current and projected job market, economic needs, location preferences, and family needs.

- Begin with a self-analysis covering these background areas:

Analyzing Yourself. When you are ready to search for your career job, you should begin the effort by analyzing yourself. In a sense, you should look at yourself much as you would look at a product or service that is for sale. After all, when you seek employment, you are really selling your ability to work—to do things for an employer. A job is more than something that brings you money. It is something that gives equal benefits to both parties—you and your employer. Thus, you should think about the qualities you have that enable you to do the work that an employer needs to have done. This self-analysis should cover the following categories.

- (1) Education. For specialized curricula, the career path is clear.

Education.   The analysis might well begin with education. Perhaps you have already selected your career area, such as accounting, finance, information systems, management, or marketing. If you have, your task is simplified, for your specialized curriculum has prepared you for your goal. Even so, you may be able to note special points—for example, electives that have given you special skills or that show something special about you (such as psychology courses that have improved your human-relations skills, communication courses that have improved your writing and speaking skills, or foreign language courses that have prepared you for international assignments).

- For general curicula, a career choice must be made.

If you have pursued a more general curriculum (general business, liberal arts, or such), you will need to look at it closely to see what it has prepared you to do. Perhaps you will find an emphasis on computers, written communication, human relations, foreign languages—all of which are sorely needed by some businesses. Or perhaps you will conclude that your training has given you a strong general base from which to learn specific business skills.

- Consider quality of educational record (grades, honors, courses taken).

In analyzing your education, you should look at the quality of your record—grades,

Thanks for stopping by, and yes, you certainly are the aggressive, self-motivating sales applicant we're looking for. (From The Wall Street Journal, *with permission of Cartoon Features Syndicate.*)

honors, special recognitions. If your record is good, you can emphasize it. But what if your work was only mediocre? As we will point out later, you will need to shift the emphasis to your stronger sales points—your willingness to work, your personality, your experience. Or perhaps you can explain, for example, by noting that working your way through school limited your academic performance.

Personal Qualities.   Your self-analysis should also cover your personal qualities. Qualities that relate to working with people are especially important. Qualities that show leadership or teamwork ability are also important. And if you express yourself well in writing or speaking, note this, for good communication skills are valuable in most jobs.

- (2)Personal qualities (people skills, leadership, and such).

Of course, you may not be the best judge of your personal qualities, for we do not always see ourselves as others see us. You may need to check with friends to see whether they agree with your assessments. You may also need to check your record for evidence supporting your assessments. For example, organization membership and participation in community activities are evidence of people and teamwork skills. Election to organization offices is evidence of leadership ability. Participation on a debate team is evidence of communication skills.

Work Experience.   If you have work experience, you should analyze it. Work experience in your career path deserves major emphasis. In fact, such work experience becomes more and more important as you move along your career path. Work experience not related to the job you seek can also tell something important about you—even if the work was part-time and menial. Menial work can show willingness and determination, especially if you have done it to finance your education. And almost any work experience can help develop your skills in dealing with people.

- (3) Work experience (with interpretations).

Special Qualifications.   Your self-analysis should also include special qualifications that might be valuable to an employer. The ability to speak a foreign language can be very helpful for certain international businesses. Athletic participation, hobbies, and interests may also be helpful. To illustrate, athletic experience would be helpful for work for a sporting goods distributor, a hobby of automobile mechanics would be helpful for work with an automotive service company, and an interest in music would be helpful for work with a piano manufacturer.

- (4) Special qualities (languages, communication skills, and such).

Analyzing Outside Factors.   After you have analyzed yourself, you need to combine this information with the work needs of business and other external influences. Your goal in this process is to give realistic direction to your search for employment. Where is the kind of work you are seeking available? Are you willing to move? Is such a move compatible with others in your life—your partner, your children, your parents? Does the location meet with your approval for meeting life-style needs? Although the availability of work may drive the answer to some of these questions, you should answer them as well as you can on the basis of what you know now and then conduct your job search accordingly. Finding just the right job is one of the most important goals in your life.

- Combine internal and external factors.

Finding Your Employer

You can use a number of sources in your search for an employer with which you will begin or continue on your career path. Your choice of sources will probably be influenced by where you are in your career path.

- Search for potential employers by using these sources:

Placement Centers.   If you are just beginning your career, one good possibility is the placement center at your school. Most of the large schools have placement centers, and these attract employers that are looking for suitable applicants. Many placement centers offer excellent job-search counseling and maintain files on registrants con-

- (1) your school's placement center,

taining school records, résumés, and recommendation letters for review by prospective employers. Most have directories listing the major companies with contact names and addresses.

• (2) your network of personal contacts,

Network of Personal Contacts.   As has been noted, the personal contacts you make can be extremely helpful in your job search. In fact, according to one employment report, personal contacts are the leading means of finding employees. Obviously, personal contacts are more likely to be a source of employment opportunities later in your career path—when you may need to change jobs.

• (3) classified advertisements,

Classified Advertisements.   Help-wanted advertisements in newspapers, professional journals, and on-line provide good sources of employment opportunities for many kinds of work. Many are limited, however, in the opportunities they provide for new college graduates. They are good sources for experienced workers who are seeking to improve their positions, and they are especially good sources for people who are conducting a major search for high-level positions.

• (4) on-line databases,

On-line Databases.   In addition to finding opportunities in printed sources, you will also find them on-line. E-span, for example, lists jobs available throughout the country with new opportunities posted regularly. Some companies even have bulletin board systems where job openings are posted. While many of these are used internally, some companies open these systems to all interested job seekers. And, of course, there are some private on-line companies that will place your résumé and companies' jobs in databases that can be accessed for a fee. Furthermore, you could query users of local bulletin board systems about job openings they know exist. Be sure not to overlook on-line systems as a source for job opportunities.

• (5) career television network,

Career Television Network.   While relatively new, the career television network is still not prime-time material. But with the advent of 500 channels, it promises to be one with 24-hour programming.

• (6) employment agencies, and

Employment Agencies.   Companies that specialize in finding jobs for employees can be useful. Of course, such companies charge for their services. The employer sometimes pays the charges, usually if qualified applicants are scarce. While employment agencies are commonly used to place experienced people in executive positions, they can also help one gain temporary employment.

Temping can lead to permanent employment with a good fit. It allows the worker to get a feel for the company and the company to observe the worker before making a job commitment.

• (7) prospecting techniques.

Prospecting.   Some job seekers approach prospective employers directly, either by personal visit or by mail. Personal visits are effective if the company has an employment office or if a personal contact can set up a visit. Mail contacts typically include a résumé and an application letter. The construction of these messages is covered later in the chapter.

I N T R O D U C T O R Y   S I T U A T I O N

▶ to Résumés and Application Letters

In your role as Jason Andrews, you consider yourself well qualified for a career in labor relations. You know the field from both personal experience and classroom study. You grew up in a working-class neighborhood. From an early age, you worked at a variety of jobs, the most important of which was a job as a shipping and receiving clerk. You were a truck driver and a member of the Teamsters for two years. Your college studies were especially designed to prepare you for a career in labor relations. You studied Olympia University's curriculum in industrial relations, and you carefully chose the electives that would give you the best possible preparation for your career objective. As evidenced by your grades, your preparation was good.

Now it is time to begin your career. Over the past weeks you followed good procedures in looking for employment (as reviewed in the preceding pages). Unfortunately, you had no success with the recruiters who visited your campus. Now you will send written applications to a select group of companies that you think might use a person with your skills. You have obtained the names of the executives you should reach at these companies. You will mail them the conventional application package—résumé and application letter. The following discussion shows you how to prepare these documents for best results. ■

PREPARING THE APPLICATION DOCUMENTS

After your search has uncovered a job possibility, you pursue it. How you pursue it depends on the circumstances of the case. When it is convenient and appropriate to do so, you make contact in person. It is convenient when the distance is not great, and it is appropriate when the employer has invited such a contact. When a personal visit is not convenient and appropriate, you apply by mail, e-mail, or fax.

- Pursue job openings by personal visit or by mail.

Whether or not you apply in person, you are likely to use some written material. If you apply in person, probably you will take a résumé with you to leave as a record of your qualifications. If you do not apply in person, of course, the application is completely in writing. Typically, it consists of a résumé and a letter of application. At some point in your employment efforts, you are likely to use each of these documents.

- You are likely to use résumés and application letters in your job search.

Preparing résumés and application letters is much like preparing a sales mailing. Both situations involve selling. In one case, you are selling a product or service; in the other, you are selling your ability to do work. The résumé is much like the supporting material that accompanies the sales letter. The application letter is much like the sales letter. These similarities should become obvious to you as you read the following pages.

- Prepare them as you would prepare a sales mailing.

As in preparing a sales mailing, you begin work on a written application for a job by studying what you are selling. And what you are selling is you. Then you study the work. Studying yourself involves taking personal inventory—the self-analysis discussed earlier in the chapter. You should begin by listing all the information about you that you believe an employer would want to know. Studying the work means learning as much as you can about the company—its plans, it policies, its operations. It also means learning the requirements of the work that the company wants done. Sometimes you can get this information through personal investigation. More often, you will have to develop it through logical thinking.

- Study the product (you) and the work.

With this preliminary information assembled, you are ready to plan the application. First, you need to decide just what your application will consist of. Will it be just a letter, or will it be a letter and a résumé (also called a *vita, qualifications brief,* or *data sheet*)? The résumé is a summary of background facts in list form. You will probably select the combination of letter and résumé, for this arrangement is likely to do a better job. Some people prefer to use the letter alone. When this is done, the letter usually contains much detail for it must do the whole sales job.

- Next, decide on whether to send a letter alone or with a résumé.

After you've decided to use the résumé, you must decide whether to use the traditional, electronic, or hybrid form. The traditional is used in face-to-face interviews where you know it will be used exclusively there. If you have reason to believe the company will store your résumé electronically, you should use the electronic or hybrid format. Constructing these forms are similar, but they differ in some very important ways.

- Choose the traditional, electronic, or a hybrid form.

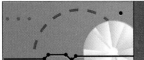

Résumé software programs are sold nearly everywhere. And résumé templates are included with most full-featured wordprocessing programs. Not only does their price vary widely but their quality varies widely as well. Your decision regarding résumé software may be twofold—should you use one? And which one?

Résumé programs have features that serve some very well. For example, if you don't know how to set up a résumé, most programs provide templates you fill in, and the program arranges the information. If you haven't thought out carefully what to include on a résumé, these programs will give you ideas through the questions they pose. Some of these programs include spell checkers and thesauruses to help you describe yourself accurately. Furthermore, some include useful manuals that give tips on topics ranging from résumé construction to interview techniques. A few of these programs have small databases for you to keep track of names and addresses of contacts. And a few even include a calendar feature, allowing you to keep track of interviews.

But these programs have drawbacks, too. Some lack basic features such as spell checkers. And some have only a limited number of arrangements to choose from, creating the possibility that your résumé will look very similar to someone else's résumé created with the same software. A few have limitations on the length of each category.

When making a decision on whether to use résumé-generating software and templates, you should carefully evaluate the features you intend to use. If you are competent with your full-featured word processing software and don't need the added features, you can probably manage without one. On the other hand, some of the well-done programs can make your entire job search process easier and more manageable. If the package you are evaluating serves you well, use it!

CONSTRUCTING THE TRADITIONAL RÉSUMÉ

- The résumé lists facts in some orderly way.

After deciding what your form will be, you construct the parts. Perhaps you will choose to begin with the résumé, for it is a logical next step from the personal inventory discussed above. In fact, the résumé is a formal arrangement of that inventory.

You will want to include in the résumé all background information you think the reader should have about you. This means including all the information that is reviewed in an accompanying letter plus supporting and incidental details. Designed for quick reading, the résumé lists facts that have been arranged for the best possible appearance. Rarely does it use sentences.

The arrangements of résumés differ widely, but the following procedure generally describes how most are written:

- Follow this plan in constructing a résumé.

- Logically arrange information on education (institutions, dates, degrees, major field), information on employment (dates, places, firms, duties, accomplishments), personal details (memberships, interests, achievements, and such—but not religion, race, and sex), special information derived from other information (achievements, qualifications, capabilities), and information on references (optional—authorities disagree).

- Construct a heading for the entire résumé and subheadings for the parts.

- Include other vital information, such as objectives and contact information.

- Arrange the data for best eye appeal, making it balanced, not crowded, and not strung out.

- Begin by reviewing the background facts you have assembled. Select the facts that will help the reader evaluate you.

Selecting the Background Facts. Your first step in writing the résumé is to review the background facts you have assembled about yourself and then to select the facts

Need to Standout?

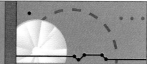

Sometimes a résumé gives you an opportunity to present yourself while showing your creativity and potential job skills as well. Preparing a unique résumé such as a video, a run-time presentation, or a home page on a web site can illustrate your skills and make you standout from the crowd. A video might be particularly effective for someone going into sales by illustrating the ability to sell a particular product; the picture shows oral communication, interpersonal, and persuasive skills. A run-time résumé presentation could show not only one's ability to fully utilize the software, but to use it creatively. Integrating video, sound, and text effectively is another talent it could show. The ability to put up a home page on a web site shows one's ability to organize and use hypertext. It probably implies one is familiar with the Internet, too. As technology moves us forward and as the appropriate situation presents itself, using the technology for unique, standout résumés can be quite effective.

that you think will help your reader evaluate you. You should include all the information covered in the accompanying letter, for this is the most important information. In addition, you should include significant supporting details not covered in the accompanying letter to avoid cluttering it.

Arranging the Facts into Groups.   After selecting the facts you want to include, you should sort them into logical groups. Many grouping arrangements are possible. The most conventional is the three-part grouping of *Education, Experience,* and *Skills* or *Personal Qualities.* Another possibility is a grouping by job functions or skills, such as *Selling, Communicating,* and *Managing.* Yet another is an arrangement by time—perhaps listing the information in reverse chronological order to show a progression of training and experience. You may be able to work out other logical arrangements.

- Sort the facts by conventional groups, job functions, time, or a combination.

You can also derive additional groups from the four conventional groups mentioned above. For example, you can have a group made up of your Achievements. Such a group would consist of special accomplishments taken from your experience and education information. Another possibility is to have a group made up of information highlighting your major qualifications. Here you would include information drawn from the areas of experience, education, and skills or personal qualities. Illustrations of and instructions for constructing groups such as these appear later in the chapter.

- Also, consider groups such as *Achievements* and *Highlights.*

Constructing the Headings.   With your information organized, a logical next step is to construct the headings (captions) for the résumé. Probably you will begin by constructing the main head—the one that covers the entire document.

- Write headings for the résumé and its parts.

The most widely used form of main head is the topic, which consists only of words that describe what follows. Your name is usually the main heading. It should be presented clearly; usually this means using larger and bolder type so that the name stands out from the rest of the résumé. If an employer remembers only one thing from your résumé, that fact should be your name. It can be presented in either all caps or caps and lower case.

- Topic heads are most common.

Terrence P. Lenaghan

The next level of headings might be *Objective, Education, Experience,* and *Skills.* These headings can be placed to the left or centered above the text that follows.

A second and less widely used form is the talking head. This form uses words that tell the nature of what follows. For example, instead of the topic head, *Education,* a talking head might read *Specialized Training in Accounting* or *Computer Software*

- Talking heads interpret for the reader.

Program Skills in Using. Obviously, these heads add to the information covered. They help the reader interpret the facts that follow.

As you can see from the illustrations in the chapter, the headings are distinguished from the other information in the résumé by the use of different sizes and styles of type. The main head should appear to be the most important of all (larger and heavier). Headings for the groups of information should appear to be more important than the information under them. You will want to choose heading forms carefully, making sure they are neither so heavy and large that they offend nor so light and small that they show no distinctions. Your goal is to choose forms that properly show the relative importance of the information and are pleasing to the eye.

Including Contact Information.   Your address and telephone number are the most likely means of contacting you. Thus you should display them prominently somewhere in the résumé. You may also want to display your fax number or e-mail address. The most common location for displaying contact information is at the top, under the main head.

When it is likely that your address or telephone number will change before the job search ends, you would be wise to include two addresses and numbers—one current and the other permanent. If you are a student, for example, your address at the time of applying for a job may change before the employer decides to contact you. Therefore, you may want to consider using an answering service or having 500 service. The 500 service assigns the number to you rather than to a place, so you can receive your messages wherever you go.

Including a Statement of Objective.   Although not a category of background information, a statement of your objective is appropriate in the résumé. Headings such as *Career Objective, Job Objective,* or just *Objective,* usually appear at the beginning.

Not all authorities agree on the value of including the objective, however. Recommending that they be omitted from today's résumés, one widely read author suggested that one should concentrate instead on skills, experience, and credentials.[1] Some experts argue that the objective includes only obvious information that is clearly suggested by the remainder of the résumé. They argue also that an objective limits the applicant to a single position and eliminates consideration for other jobs that may be available.

Those favoring the use of a statement of objective reason that it helps the recruiter see quickly where the applicant might fit into the company. As this argument appears to have greater support, at least for the moment, probably you should include the objective. But make an exception when your career goal is unclear and you are considering a variety of employment possibilities.

Primarily, your statement of objective should describe the work you seek. When you can, you should add to its effectiveness by including words that convey a long-term interest, as in this example:

Objective: A position in human resource management that will provide an opportunity for
            growth and advancement.

Another technique for enhancing the effectiveness of the objective statement is to include words that emphasize your major qualifications for the work, as in this example:

Objective: To apply 17 years of successful high-tech sales experience to selling quality
            products for an agile company.

Also, for a résumé tailored to fit a specific company, the wording can include the company name and exact job title the company uses:

---

[1] Bruce Neusbaum, "A Career Survival Kit" *Business Week,* October 7, 1991, p. 104.

- Distinguish the headings from the other information by font selection.

- Display your contact information prominently.

- Anticipate changes in contact information.

- Consider a statement of your objective.

- However, note that some authorities oppose it.

- Even so, probably you should use it.

- The statement should cover the job you seek and more, as in these examples.

Career Objective: Sales Representative for Johnson & Johnson leading to sales management.

Presenting the Information. The information you present under each heading will depend on your good judgment. You should list all the facts that you think are relevant. You will want to include enough information to enable the reader to judge your ability to do the work you seek.

• List the facts under the headings.

Your coverage of work experience should identify completely the jobs you have held. A minimum coverage would include dates, places, firms, and responsibilities. If the work was part-time, you should say so without demeaning the skills you developed on the job. In describing your duties, you should select words that highlight what you did, especially the parts of this experience that qualify you for the work you seek. For example, in describing a job as office manager, you could write "Office manager for Carson's, Inc., Chicago, Ill., 1996–98." But it would be more meaningful to give this fuller description: "Office manager for Carson's, Inc., Chicago, Ill., 1996–98, supervising a staff of seven in processing company records and communications."

• When covering work experience, at a minimum include dates, places, firms, and responsibilities.

If your performance on a job shows your ability to do the work you seek, you should consider emphasizing your accomplishments in your job description. For example, an experienced marketer might write this description: "Marketing specialist for Colgate-Palmolive, 1995–98. Served in advisory role to company management. Developed marketing plan that increased profits 24 percent in two years." Or a successful advertising account executive might write this description: "Phillips-Ramsey Agency, San Diego, 1996–98. As account executive, developed successful campaigns for nine accounts and led development team in increasing agency volume 18 percent."

• When appropriate, show achievements.

As you can see from the examples above, the job descriptions are strengthened by the use of action verbs. Verbs are the strongest of all words. If you choose them well, they will do much to sell your ability to do work. A list of the more widely used action verbs appears in Figure 9–1.

• Use action verbs to strengthen the appeal.

Because your education is likely to be your strongest selling point for your first job after college, you will probably cover it in some detail. (Education gets less and less emphasis in your applications as you gain experience.) At a minimum, your coverage of education should include institutions, dates, degrees, and areas of study. For some jobs, you may want to list specific courses, especially if you have little other information to present or if your coursework has uniquely prepared you for those jobs. If your GPA (grade point average) is good, you may want to include it. Remember, for your résumé, you can compute your GPA in a way that works best for you as long as you label it accurately. For example, you may want to select just those courses in your major, labeling it Major GPA. Or if your last few years were your best ones, you may want to present your GPA for just that period. In any case, include GPA when it works favorably for you.

• For education, include institutions, dates, degrees, and areas of study.

What personal information to list is a matter for your best judgment. In fact, the trend appears to be toward eliminating such information. If you do include personal information, you should probably omit race, religion, sex, age, and marital status because current laws prohibit hiring based on such information. But not everybody agrees on this matter. Some authorities believe that at least some of these items should be included. They argue that the law only prohibits employers from considering such information in hiring—that it does not prohibit applicants from presenting the information. They reason that if such information helps you, you should use it. The illustrations shown in this chapter support both viewpoints.

• For legal reasons, some personal information (on race, religion, sex) should probably not be listed.

Personal information that is generally appropriate includes all items that tell about your personal qualities. Information on your organization memberships, civic involvement, and social activities is evidence of experience and interest in working with people. Hobbies and athletic participation tell of your balance of interests. Such information can be quite useful to some employers, especially when personal qualities are important to the work involved.

• Information on activities and interests tells about one's personal qualities.

FIGURE 9–1 A List of Action Verbs* That Add Strength to Your Résumé

The underlined words are especially good for pointing out accomplishments.

Management Skills	interpreted	maintained	forecasted	guided
administered	lectured	operated	managed	motivated
analyzed	mediated	overhauled	marketed	referred
assigned	moderated	programmed	planned	rehabilitated
attained	negotiated	remodeled	projected	represented
chaired	persuaded	repaired	researched	
consolidated	promoted	solved		**Clerical or Detail Skills**
contracted	publicized	upgraded	**Creative Skills**	approved
coordinated	reconciled		acted	arranged
delegated	recruited	**Teaching Skills**	conceptualized	catalogued
developed	spoke	adapted	created	classified
directed	translated	advised	customized	collected
evaluated	wrote	clarified	designed	compiled
executed		coached	developed	dispatched
improved	**Research Skills**	communicated	directed	executed
increased	clarified	coordinated	established	generated
organized	collected	demystified	fashioned	implemented
oversaw	critiqued	developed	founded	inspected
planned	diagnosed	enabled	illustrated	monitored
prioritized	evaluated	encouraged	initiated	operated
produced	examined	evaluated	instituted	organized
recommended	extracted	explained	integrated	prepared
reviewed	identified	facilitated	introduced	processed
scheduled	inspected	guided	invented	purchased
strengthened	interpreted	informed	originated	recorded
supervised	interviewed	instructed	performed	retrieved
	investigated	persuaded	planned	screened
Communication Skills	organized	set goals	revitalized	specified
addressed	reviewed	stimulated	shaped	systematized
arbitrated	summarized	trained		tabulated
arranged	surveyed		**Helping Skills**	validated
authored	systematized	**Financial Skills**	assessed	
collaborated		administered	assisted	**More Verbs for Accomplishments**
convinced	**Technical Skills**	allocated	clarified	achieved
corresponded	assembled	analyzed	coached	expanded
developed	built	appraised	counseled	improved
directed	calculated	audited	demonstrated	pioneered
drafted	computed	balanced	diagnosed	reduced (losses)
edited	designed	budgeted	educated	resolved (problems)
enlisted	devised	calculated	expedited	restored
formulated	engineered	computed	facilitated	spearheaded
influenced	fabricated	developed	familiarized	transformed

* From *The Damn Good Resume Guide* © 1993 by Yana Parker. Reprinted by permission of Ten Speed Press, Berkeley, California.

• Consider listing references, but some authorities favor postponing using them.

Authorities disagree on whether to list references on the résumé. Some think that references should not be bothered with until negotiations are further along. Others think that references should be listed because some employers want to check them early in the screening process. One study[2] of major corporations found that 42 percent of the employers want references on or accompanying the résumé. The remaining 58 percent have other preferences. Clearly, both views have substantial support. You will have to make the choice based on your best knowledge of the situation.

• Consider using a separate sheet for references.

A commonly used tool is a separate reference sheet. When you use it, you close the résumé with a statement indicating references are available. Later, when the reader

[2] Lorraine A. Krajewski and Susan Wood, "The Use of Applicant-Provided References in the Selection Process: A Study of the Forbes 500," paper presented at meeting of the Association for Business Communication—Southwest, Houston, Texas, March 14, 1991.

wants to check references, you give her or him this sheet. The type size and style of the main heading of this sheet should match that used in your résumé. It will say something like "References for *your name*." Below this heading is a listing of your references, beginning with the strongest one. In addition to solving the reference dilemma, use of this separate reference sheet allows you to change both the references and the ordering of them for each job. A sample reference sheet is shown in the example on page 275.

Sometimes you may have good reason not to list references, as when you are employed and want to keep the job search secret. If you choose not to list them, you should explain their absence. You can do this in the accompanying letter; or you can do it on the résumé by following the heading "References" with an explanation, such as "Will be furnished on request."

How many and what kinds of references to include will depend on your background. If you have an employment record, you should include one for every major job you have held—at least for recent years. You should include references related to the work you seek. If you base your application heavily on your education or your personal qualities, or both, you should include references who can vouch for these areas—professors, clergy, community leaders, and the like. Your goal is to list those people who can verify the points on which your appeal for the job is based. At a minimum, you should list three references. Five is a good maximum.

Your list of references should include accurate mailing addresses, with appropriate job titles. Complete addresses are important because the reader is likely to write the references. Also useful are telephone and fax numbers as well as e-mail addresses. Job titles (officer manager, president, supervisor) are helpful because they show what the references are able to tell about you. As a matter of courtesy, you should use references only with their permission.

Handling the Special Groupings.
As noted previously, special groupings such as *Achievements* and *Highlights* present a summary of information usually drawn from the more conventional groupings. *Achievements,* for example, usually includes unusual performances in education or experience. Illustrating this arrangement is the following example:

Achievements
Successfully managed the Delgado store for two years in a period of economic decline with these results:
· increased profits 37 percent;
· reduced employee turnover 55 percent; and
· increased volume 12 percent.

Information covered under a *Highlights* heading may include information from the three conventional information groups—education, experience, and personal qualities. Typically, this arrangement emphasizes the applicant's most impressive background facts that pertain to the work sought, as in this example:

Highlights
· Experienced: three years of practical work as programmer/analyst in designing and developing financial software for the banking industry
· Highly trained: B.S. degree with honors in computer science
· Self-motivated: proven record of successful completion of independent work on major projects

Although such items may overlap others in the résumé, using them in a separate group emphasizes the applicant's strengths.

Writing Impersonally and Consistently.
As the résumé is a listing of information, you should write without personal pronouns (no *I*'s, *we*'s, *you*'s). You should also write all equal-level headings and the parts under each heading in the same grammatical form. For example, if one major heading in the résumé is a noun phrase, all the other major headings should be noun phrases. The following four headings illustrate the point. All

- Select references that cover your background.

- Include accurate mailing addresses and job titles.

- If you use an *Achievements* grouping, include unusual performances in education or experience.

- If you use a *Highlights* grouping, emphasize your most impressive background information.

- List the information without use of personal pronouns (*I, we, you*).

- Use the same grammatical form for all equal-level headings and for the parts listed under each heading.

but the third (an adjective form) are noun phrases. The error can be corrected by making the third a noun phrase, as in the examples to the right:

NOT PARALLEL	PARALLEL
Specialized study	Specialized study
Experience in promotion work	Experience in promotion work
Personal and physical	Personal and physical qualities
Qualified references	Qualified references

Illustrating grammatical inconsistency in the parts of a group are the following items:

Have good health
Active in sports
Ambitious

Inspection of these items shows that they do not fit the same understood words. The understood word for the first item is "I" and for the second and third, the understood words are "I am." Any changes that make all three items fit the same understood words would correct the error.

- Make the résumé attractive.

Making the Form Attractive.   The attractiveness of your résumé will say as much about you as the words. The appearance of the information that the reader sees plays a part in forming his or her judgment. A sloppy, poorly designed presentation may even ruin your chances of getting the job. Thus, you have no choice but to give your résumé and your application letter an attractive physical arrangement.

- Design it as a book designer would. Use balance and space for eye appeal.

Designing the résumé for eye appeal is no routine matter. There is no one best arrangement, but a good procedure is to approach the task as a book designer would. Your objective is to design an arrangement of type and space that appears good to the eye. You would do well to use the following general plan for arranging the résumé.

- Here are some suggestions on form.

Margins look better if at least an inch of space is left at the top of the page and on the left and right sides of the page and if at least 1½ inches of space are left at the bottom of the page. Your listing of items by rows (columns) appears best if the items are short and if they can be set up in two uncrowded rows, one on the left side of the page and one on the right side. Longer items of information are more appropriately set up in lines extending across the page. In any event, you would do well to avoid long and narrow columns of data with large sections of wasted space on either side. Arrangements that give a heavy crowded effect also offend the eye. Extra spacing between subdivisions and indented patterns for subparts and carryover lines are especially pleasing to the eye.

- Take care in choosing fonts.

While layout is important in showing your ability to organize and good spacing increases readability, design considerations such as font and paper selection affect attractiveness almost as much. Commercial artists currently recommend using sans serif fonts (without feet) for headings and serif fonts (with feet) for body text. They say that types for headings should be at least 14 points and for body text, 10–14 points. They also recommend using fewer than four font styles on a page. Most word processing software has a "best fit" feature that allows one to fit information on one page. It will automatically adjust font sizes to fit the page. Be sure the resulting type size is both appropriate and readable.

- Conservative paper usually is best.

Another factor affecting the appearance of your application documents is the paper you select. The paper should be appropriate for the job you seek. In business, erring on the conservative side is usually better; you do not want to be eliminated from consideration simply because the reader did not like the quality or color of the paper. The most traditional choice is white, 100 percent cotton, 20- to 24-lb. paper. Of course, reasonable variations can be appropriate.

- Figures 9–2 and 9–3 show bad and good form.

Contrasting Bad and Good Examples.   The résumés in Figures 9–2 and 9–3 are at opposing ends of the quality scale. The first one, scant in coverage and poorly

FIGURE 9–2   Incompleteness and Bad Arrangement in a Résumé

This résumé presents Jason Andrews' ineffectively (see "Introductory Situation to Résumés and Application Letters"). It is scant and poorly arranged.

RÉSUMÉ

JASON L. ANDREWS

3177 North Hawthorne Boulevard
Olympia, New York 12407

*Bad form –
Type heavily
weighted to
left*

Telephone?

Personal

Age: 27
Married
One child, age 1
5 ft. 11 in. tall
Interests: tennis, fishing, reading
Active in sports
Weight: 165 lbs.
Memberships: Delta Sigma Pi, Sigma Iota Epsilon, Methodist Church, Olympia
  Community League

*Not
parallel
and some
extraneous
information*

Experience

1990-94 Equipment repair, Davidson Electric, Olympia, NY
1988-90 Driver, Wayland Trucking Co., New York, NY
1986-88 Clerk, Kiawa Garment Co., New York, NY

*Scant
information
on work done*

Education

1990-94 Olympia University, Bachelor of Business Administration degree,
         major in labor relations, 24 semester hours in labor and management
         courses, a 3.7 grade-point average, 3.9 in major field.
1987-90 C.H. Aldridge High School, New York, NY

Not needed

References

Ms. June Rojas
Davidson Electric
Olympia, N.Y. 12509

Prof. Helen K. Robbins
Olympia University
Olympia, NY 12507

Mr. Todd Frankle
Wayland Trucking Co.
47723 Beecher
New York, NY 10029

Prof. Carl Cueno
Olympia University
Olympia, NY 12507

*Incomplete
addresses –
No job titles*

FIGURE 9–3 Thoroughness and Good Arrangement in a Résumé

This complete and attractively arranged résumé and reference sheet presents Jason Andrews's case effectively (see "Introductory Situation to Résumés and Application Letters").

Jason L. Andrews

Mailing Address
3177 North Hawthorne Boulevard
Olympia, NY 12407

Telephone
(500) 967-3117 (home)
(914) 938-4449 (work)

Objective

A position in labor relations that will lead to work as a labor-relations specialist

Education emphasized by position

Education

Bachelor of Business Administration, Olympia University, May 1996
Major in Labor Relations
Major grade-point average: 3.9/4.0   Overall grade-point average 3.7/4.0

Experience

Equipment repair technician, Davidson Electric Company, Olympia, NY, 1993-present

Driver, Wayland Trucking Company, New York, NY (was a member of Local 714, International Brotherhood of Teamsters, Chauffeurs, Warehousemen, and Helpers of America) 1992-93

Shipping and receiving clerk, Kiawa Garment Company, New York, NY (part-time) 1989-91

Decription shows quality of work done

Reverse chronological approach with position emphasized and date de-emphasized

Personal Qualities

Interests: tennis, fishing, reading, jogging
Memberships: Delta Sigma Pi (professional); Sigma Iota Epsilon (honorary), served as treasurer and president; Board of Stewards for church; League of Olympia, served as registration leader.

Trivial information omitted

References

Will gladly furnish personal and professional references upon request.

Statement tells reader that someone will speak for him

Jason L. Andrews

*Heading
stationery
match résumé*

Mailing Address	*Telephone*
3177 North Hawthorne Boulevard	(500) 967-3117 (home)
Olympia, NY 12407	(914) 938-4449 (work)

Ms. June Rojas, Service Manager
Davidson Electric Company
7114 East 71st Street
Olympia, NY 12509
Telephone: (518) 342-1171

Professor Helen K. Robbins
Department of Management
Olympia University
Olympia, NY 12507
Telephone: (518) 392-6673

Mr. Todd E. Frankle, Manager
Wayland Trucking Company
47723 Beecher Road
New York, NY 10029
Telephone: (718) 466-9101

Professor Carol A. Cueno
Department of Economics
Olympia University
Olympia, NY 12507
Telephone: (518) 392-0723

*Complete
and balanced
arrangement*

This form of résumé could be used both face to face and scanned. The computer skills section uses precise words often searched for; the experience section uses strong verbs.

Julie Smith
2019 Shadytree Lane
Encinitas, CA 92024-3121
(619) 753-5722

Name and contact information presented prominently

Precise terms here help scanned résumé get retrieved

Objective   A challenging position in the field of Information Technology.

Education   Bachelor of Science in Business Administration with an emphasis in
                  Information and Decision Systems, San Diego State University: May 1995
                  GPA: Major 3.8   Overall 3.6

Computer   **Applications:** Lotus 1-2-3, AmiPro, Microsoft Word, Powerpoint, MASS-11
Skills   **Languages:** COBOL, C, Visual Basic, LISP, PowerBuilder
                  Operating Systems: VAX/VMS, DOS, WINDOWS, UNIX

Experience   Andersen Consulting–Los Angeles, California
                  Staff Consultant (Intern) June - August 1994

                  ❑ Attended Andersen Consulting Student Leadership Conference.
                  ❑ Worked at client site with a consulting team to create a business application

Major job functions emphasized with parallel action verbs

                  Law Offices of Solomon, Ward, Seidenwurm & Smith–San Diego, California
                  Case Assistant/Administrative Assistant 1991-1992
                  Legal Secretary June-October 1993

                  ❑ Created and maintained client database using mainframe operating system
                  ❑ Reorganized law library database and maintained files and pleading indexes for
                     17 attorneys
                  ❑ Assisted in overall administration in operation of midsize law firm handling
                     corporate and civil litigation

Honors   Dean's List 1989-1994 (6 Times)
                  DPMA Certificate of Excellence
                  University Scholar Award (Twice)
                  Alvin Morrison Memorial Scholarship (Twice)
                  Pacific Corporate Group Scholarship
                  Andersen Consulting Outstanding Junior Scholarship

Activities   **President,** SDSU International Collegiate Business Games Team
                  President, Data Processing Management Association (DPMA)
                  Vice-President of Tours and Careers, (DPMA)
                  Volunteer, Serving Seniors
                  Lab Assistant, COBOL
                  Tutor, Business Communications

Activities presentation balanced and symmetrical format

References available

Casey Christopher Schroeder
5602 Bermuda Street, Apartment D
San Diego, CA 92112
(619) 252-0387
E-mail: infoc2331@ucsvax.sdsu.edu

Entire resume emphasizes tight organization through use of horizontal lines

Objective	Information Technology Consultant

Education *Degree and GPA emphasized through placement*	<u>Bachelor of Science</u>, San Diego State University, December 1994 Major: Business Administration Emphasis: Information Systems GPA. 3.42 with Honors

Readability increased through use of internal bullets in space-saving presentation form

<u>Computer Course Work</u>:
Applied Artificial Intelligence ✯ COBOL ✯ Comparative Programming Languages
Database Management Systems ✯ Data Communications ✯ Hardware and Software Organization
Information Systems Analysis ✯ Information Systems Design ✯ Introduction to Information Systems
Lotus 1-2-3 ✯ Management of Information Systems ✯ Systems Documentation

<u>Activities</u>:
Vice-President of Finance, Data Processing Management Association
Co-Chair of Membership, Data Processing Management Association
Member, Golden Key National Honors Society

<u>Honors</u>:
Chevron Scholarship

Skills Computer Skills	✪	Programmed in COBOL, C, and Visual Basic languages to create several class-related data processing applications.
	✪	Designed and implemented an Oracle 7 relational database for a class-related library network project.
Emphasizes key skills relevant to objective	✪	Used Windows, DOS, Macintosh, UNIX, and Vax VMS operating systems to run several applications.
	✪	Generated multiple Lotus Freelance Graphics presentations and presented them as computer slide shows on Sony projectors.
	✪	Used Lotus Ami Pro, WordPerfect 6.0 for Windows, and Aldus PageMaker 5.0a for documenting information systems projects.

Good use of a variety of action verbs

Business Communications Skills	✪	Prepared the College of Business Computer Lab Manual on Aldus PageMaker 5.0a with a team of documentation students.
	✪	Composed several business letters and reports for two business communication courses on WordPerfect 6.0 for Windows, Lotus Ami Pro, and Aldus PageMaker 5.0a.
	✪	Delivered several individual and team presentations on business cases, projects, and reports to business students.
Accounting Skills	✪	Prepared federal income tax returns for individuals on Arthur Andersen's A-Plus tax package.

Work History Computer Assistant	<u>Disabled Student Services High Tech. Center, San Diego State University</u> San Diego, CA Spring 1994. Spring 1993.
Tax Assistant	<u>Jerry Simms, Certified Public Accountant</u>. San Diego, CA 1994.

References available upon request

CLIFFORD A. SCHENKHUIZEN
1829 Oliver Avenue #3
San Diego, CA 92109
(619) 483-4874

Uses a forward looking objective

| **Objective** | Programmer, leading to a career as systems analyst in a growth-oriented consulting firm. |

Education

| Degree | Bachelor of Science in Business Administration, San Diego State University | June 1993 |

Major — Management Information Systems

GPA — In Major: 3.94   SDSU Cumulative: 3.76

Computer Skills — Experience with DEC VAX, IBM 360, and CYBER systems
VAX/VMS 5.2, TSO-ISPF/E, and MS-DOS/Windows operating systems
JCL, COBOL, C, Pascal, LISP, Forth, FORTRAN, and VAX Assembly
WordPerfect, MS Word, Lotus 123, and Paradox

Experience

Gives concise description of work experience

Data Processing Intern, *Teledyne Ryan Aeronautical*   January 1992-Present
Hands-on training on IBM 360. Financial systems maintenance writing in COBOL and JCL. Work with users updating older programs and developing new systems.

Emphasizes position held rather than place or date

Senior Operator, *HSN/Mistix Corporation*   October 1989 - May 1991
Supervised 20 phone operators processing merchandise orders for the Home Shopping Club. Aided in computer operations and remedied customer dissatisfaction. Also worked as Lifeway Product representative, marketing health product repurchases, and servicing customer complaints.

Assistant Manager, *Radio Shack*   October 1988 - August 1988
Sold retail electronics and managed customer service for store. Supervised installation of POS sales and inventory system. Responsible for tracking merchandise repairs through Tandy Service Center and responsible for bimonthly inventory count. Duties also include opening and closing store and processing nightly bookkeeping.

Also paying 75 percent of tuition costs through continuing employment at Sea World as foodserver since May 1991.

Special Awards and Interests

Scholarship, Electronic Data Systems - Spring 1992
Dean's List, Semester Honors. Fall 1989 - present
Vice President, SDSU Waterski Team
Instructor of the Year, West Coast Tae Kwon Do
Member, Data Processing Management Association

Hobbies include reading, martial arts, and collegiate tournament waterskiing.

References

References will gladly be furnished if requested. *Reference statement provides closure and says someone will speak for him*

(A Traditional Résumé that Effectively Presents the Applicant's Military Experience and Work History. Also Highlights Key Skills.)

Presents contact information clearly

George Español Oboza
10671 Penara Street • San Diego, California 92126 • (619) 689-2290 • 570-45-2209

Objective To secure an entry-level management position with Alamo's Los Angeles Management Team

Uses precise, targeted objectives

Education San Diego State University
Bachelor of Science in Business Administration -- Emphasis: Management
May 1993

Military Experience United States Naval Reserve
Hospital Corpsman (August 1985 to present)

Describes military experience in clear terms, avoiding military jargon

Prepared personnel evaluation reports ✦ Updated navy and marine medical records ✦ Inoculated personnel ✦ Assisted with the company's plan-of-the-month mailers ✦ Supplied medical assistance to marines during field-combat exercises

Operation Desert Storm
Served at Camp Pendleton, California (February 1991 -- August 1991)

Coordinated medical officer's physical readiness reports, lab reports, and other administrative paperwork in a clinic environment ✦ Supervised junior personnel in clinic protocol ✦ Administratively processed home-bound, Camp Pendleton marines from the Gulf War ✦ Medically supervised combat-training exercises ✦ Inventoried medical supplies and placed orders on needed medicines ✦ Dispensed drugs ✦ Tested marines for sexually-transmitted diseases ✦ Prepared agar-plate cultures for pathological confirmation ✦ Drew blood from patients

Work History San Diego Fire Department - Human Resources Division
Administrative Intern (January 1992 to October 1992)

Composed fire chief's public letters and commendation letters to fire fighters and administrative staff ✦ Served as liaison for fire fighters scheduled for respiratory-fitness examinations with Sharp Rees-Stealy clinics throughout San Diego ✦ Assisted the division secretary with various projects and reports. ✦ Updated and maintained division's manuals and logs

7-Eleven
Clerk (February 1990 to February 1991 and June 1988 to July 1989)

Processed cash, check, and credit card sales ✦ Trained new clerks in store's operating procedures ✦ Serviced customers' requests and inquiries ✦ Stocked inventory

Summary of Skills
➢ *Skilled in customer service*
➢ *Strong in written communication*
➢ *Experienced in supervisorial duties*
➢ *Proficient in Windows 3.1, Word for Windows 2.0, and DOS*

Emphasizes strongest points in special section with distinctive look

References Furnished upon request

CASE ILLUSTRATION   Résumés. (A Traditional Résumé Using Tight Organization with Highlights of Qualifications and Accomplishments Sections)

Kathleen M. Garcia
585 E Street #3
Chula Vista, CA 91910
(619) 426-3095

JOB TARGET   CONSULTANT

HIGHLIGHTS OF QUALIFICATIONS

Emphasizes those qualifications most relevant to position sought

• Experience programming in COBOL, Oracle's SQL*FORMS, C, FORTRAN, Lisp, Prolog, Forth, SQR, and BASIC.
• Enthusiastic team member / leader whose participation brings out the best in others.
• Excellent analytical ability.
• Skill in gathering and defining customer requirements.
• Bilingual -- English / Spanish.

EDUCATION

Presents the most important items here

DEGREE --   B.S., Business Administration - December 1993 - San Diego State University

MAJOR --   Information Systems   MAJOR GPA--3.87

HONORS --   Dean's List, each semester
             Chevron Information Technology Scholarship, Fall 1992

MEMBER --   Data Processing Management Association, S.D.S.U. Chapter
                  Vice-President of Membership, Fall 1992
                  Vice-President of Programs, Spring 1993, Fall 1993

EMPLOYMENT

QUALCOMM, INC.   SAN DIEGO GAS & ELECTRIC   *Identifies most significant places of work and de-emphasizes less important work*
Programmer Intern, June 1993 - Present Financial and Computer Services
                                        Intern, 1992

Several years experience in the restaurant business including supervisorial positions.

ACCOMPLISHMENTS

Presents only selected accomplishments from various work experience that relate to position sought

§ Developed model of a proposed system using an object-oriented methodology; completed working prototype based on model.
§ Managed hardware/software inventory database.
§ Coded new screens and reports; debugged and "tuned" old screens and reports for better performance.
§ Provided PC network-help desk service to over 100 Marketing personnel.
§ Designed a time-saving expert system using VP Expert system shell.

Will gladly furnish personal and professional references upon request

Samuel C. Reeves
4817 54th Street - San Diego, CA 92115-2225 - (619) 582-0257

Keyword Profile

Programmer/Analyst. System Manager. Accounts Payable. Product Manager Assistant. Inside Sales Representative. Field Sales Representative. UNIX. Business Basic. COBOL. WordPerfect. Lotus. VAX VMS.

Experience

Uses easily scanned font and style

Emphasize experience over education

January 1992 -- Present. Programmer/Analyst

In charge of the entire MIS department for Neumann Electronics, Inc., San Diego, CA. Design, develop, implement, and maintain custom business applications using Business Basic on a UNIX platform. Select and recommend for purchase new software and hardware for computer system. Train new and current employees on modifications and new software/hardware. Coordinate computer projects with consultants. Chair monthly MIS meetings with executive managers.

Avoids italics, under-lining, and unique bullets

June 1989 -- January 1992. UNIX System Manager/Accounts Payable

Assisted with computer conversion from Minicomputer to PC-based Unix system. Maintained and modified business applications and trained new and current employees on computer system. Processed weekly A/P check run and bi-weekly company payroll check run.

August 1988 -- June 1989. Product Manager Assistant

Organizes with placement, bolding, and white space

Purchased electronic components for annual contracts for major customers. Scheduled and rescheduled shipments with factories arriving for annual contracts.

August 1987 -- August 1988. Inside Sales Representative

Built rapport with customers via phone. Negotiated pricing, delivery, and contracts with customers. Customer support for assigned customer base.

February 1987 -- August 1987. Field Sales Representative

Built rapport with customers and engineers through personal contact. Negotiated pricing, delivery, and contracts with customers. Developed new sales territory.

Education

Bachelor of Science in Business Administration with an emphasis in Information Systems, San Diego State University, May 1994

Professional Affiliations

DPMA, Data Processing Management Association -- Student Chapter, SDSU

arranged, does little to help the applicant. Clearly the second one is more complete and better arranged.

Weakness in Incompleteness and Bad Arrangements.
Shortcomings in the first example (Figure 9–2) are obvious. First, the form is not pleasing to the eye. The weight of the type is heavy on the left side of the page. Failure to indent carryover lines makes reading difficult.

This résumé also contains numerous errors in wording. Information headings are not parallel in grammatical form. All are in topic form except the first one. The items listed under *Personal* are not parallel either. Throughout, the résumé coverage is scant, leaving out many of the details needed to present the best impression of the applicant. Under *Experience,* little is said about specific tasks and skills in each job; and under *Education,* high school work is listed needlessly. The references are incomplete, omitting street addresses and job titles.

Strength through Good Arrangement and Completeness.
The next résumé (Figure 9–3) appears better at first glance, and it gets even better as you read it. It is attractively arranged. The information is neither crowded nor strung out. The balance is good. The content is also superior to that of the other example. Additional words show the quality of Mr. Andrews' work experience and education. They emphasize points that make the man suited for the work he seeks. This résumé excludes trivial personal information and has only the facts that tell something about Andrews' personal qualities. Complete mailing addresses permit the reader to contact the references easily. Job titles tell how each is qualified to evaluate the subject.

Constructing the Electronic Résumé

- The electronic résumé should be constructed to be scanned accurately and retrieved when an appropriate position is being filled.

Although paper résumés are not obsolete, a recent addition to the job search process is the electronic résumé. Today's electronic résumé is simply one that can be scanned into a database and retrieved when a position is being filled. While OCR software and hardware are improving all the time, choosing a font with scanning in mind will help assure that one's résumé is scanned accurately. An accurately scanned résumé can then be retrieved when terms searched for are on the résumé. Since the objective is getting your résumé reviewed in order to be interviewed, there are some basic strategies you can use to improve your chances with the computer.

- Use keywords that describe precisely what you can do.

Including Keywords. One strategy, using keywords, is often recommended for use with database scanning software. These words can be put at the beginning of the résumé. They are usually nouns that describe skills and accomplishments precisely. Instead of listing a course in comparative programming, you would list the precise languages compared, such as Visual Basic, C++, and COBOL. Instead of saying you would like a job in information systems, you would name specific job titles such as systems analyst, customer support, or end-user support.

- Use keywords common to those an employer would use to retrieve your résumé.

One way to identify the keywords in your field is by reading ads, listening to recruiters, and listening to your professors. Start building a list of words you find used repeatedly. From this list, choose those words most appropriate for the kind of work you want to do. Amplify your use of abbreviations, acronyms, and jargon appropriate to the work you want to do. One maker of scanning software, Resumix, compiled a list of words most used by companies when looking for interpersonal traits (Figure 9–4). If some of these terms fit you, you will want to be sure you list the words exactly the way the employer is likely to look for them.

- Use precise nouns on the electronic résumé.

Choosing Words Carefully. Unlike the traditional résumé, the electronic résumé is strengthened not by the use of action verbs but rather by the use of nouns. Informal studies have shown that those retrieving résumés from these databases tend to use precise nouns.

FIGURE 9–4   Keywords for Interpersonal Traits

Ability to delegate	Ethic	Problem solving
Ability to implement	Flexible	Public speaking
Ability to plan	Follow instructions	Results oriented
Ability to train	Follow through	Risk taking
Accurate	Follow up	Safety conscious
Adaptable	High energy	Self accountable
Aggressive work	Industrious	Self managing
Analytical ability	Innovative	Sensitive
Assertive	Leadership	Setting priorities
Communication skills	Multitasking	Supportive
Competitive	Open communication	Takes initiative
Conceptual ability	Open minded	Team building
Creative	Oral communication	Team player
Customer oriented	Organizational skills	Tenacious
Detailed minded	Persuasive	Willing to travel
Empowering others		

Source: Joyce Lain Kennedy and Thomas J. Morrow, *Electronic Resume Revolution* (New York: John Wiley & Sons, Inc., 1994), p. 70.

For the hybrid résumé, one you use in face to face and scanning situations, you can combine the use of precise nouns with strong action verbs. The nouns will help ensure that the résumé gets pulled from the database, and the verbs help the face-to-face recruiter see the link to the kind of work you want to do.

- Use both precise nouns and action verbs in the hybrid résumé.

Presenting the Information.   Since you want your résumé to be read accurately, you will use a font most scanners can read without problem. Figure 9–5 shows some of these fonts. Most scanners can easily handle fonts between 10 and 14 points. Although many handle bold, when in doubt use all caps for emphasis rather than bolding. Also, because they often confuse scanners, avoid italics. Underlining is best left out as well. It creates trouble with descending letters such as g or y when the line cuts through the letter. In fact, you should use all lines sparingly. Also, avoid graphics and shading wherever possible; they just confuse the software. Also, use white paper to maximize the contrast and always print in the portrait mode. The Samuel C. Reeves Case Illustration is an electronic résumé; the one for Julie Smith is a hybrid form.

- Be sure the font you use can be read easily by scanners.

Writing the Application Letter

You should begin work on the application letter by fitting the facts from your background to the work you seek and arranging those facts in a logical order. Then you present them in much the same way that a sales writer would present the features of a product or service. Wherever logical, you adapt the points made to the reader's needs. Like those of sales letters, the organizational plans of application letters vary. However, the following procedure (discussed in detail below) is used in most successful efforts:

- Writing the application letter involves matching your qualifications with the job.

- Begin with words selected to gain attention appropriately and to set up the review of information.

- This plan for writing the letter has proved to be effective.

- Present your qualifications, keeping like information together and adapting to the company and the job.

FIGURE 9–5   10 Good Typefaces for Scannable Résumés

Helvetica	**Times**
Want a Job?	Want a Job?
Find a Job	Find a Job
In Ways You Never	In Ways You Never
Knew About Before . . .	Knew About Before . . .
The Technology is New	The Technology is New
The Technology is Now!	The Technology is Now!
Futura	**New Century Schoolbook**
Want a Job?	Want a Job?
Find a Job	Find a Job
In Ways You Never	In Ways You Never
Knew About Before . . .	Knew About Before . . .
The Technology is New	The Technology is New
The Technology is Now!	The Technology is Now!
Univers	**ITC Bookman**
Want a Job?	Want a Job?
Find a Job	Find a Job
In Ways You Never	In Ways You Never
Knew About Before . . .	Knew About Before . . .
The Technology is New	The Technology is New
The Technology is Now!	The Technology is Now!
Optima	**Palatino**
Want a Job?	Want a Job?
Find a Job	Find a Job
In Ways You Never	In Ways You Never
Knew About Before . . .	Knew About Before . . .
The Technology is New	The Technology is New
The Technology is Now!	The Technology is Now!
ITC Avante Garde Gothic	**Courier**
Want a Job?	Want a Job?
Find a Job	Find a Job
In Ways You Never	In Ways You Never
Knew About Before . . .	Knew About Before . . .
The Technology is New	The Technology is New
The Technology is Now!	The Technology is Now!

Source: Joyce Lain Kennedy and Thomas J. Morrow, *Electronic Resume Revolution* (New York: John Wiley & Sons, Inc., 1994), p. 76.

- Use good sales strategy, especially you-viewpoint and positive language.

- Drive for the appropriate action (request for interview, reference check, further correspondence).

Gaining Attention in the Opening.   As in sales writing, the opening of the application letter has two requirements: It must gain attention, and it must set up the review of information that follows.

Gaining attention is especially important in prospecting letters (application letters that are not invited). Such letters are likely to reach busy executives who have many things to do other than read application letters. Unless the letters gain favorable attention right away, the executives probably will not read them. Even invited letters must gain attention because they will compete with other invited letters. The invited letters that stand out favorably from the beginning have a competitive advantage.

As the application letter is a creative effort, you should use your imagination in writing the opening. But the work you seek should guide your imagination. Take, for example, work that requires an outgoing personality and a vivid imagination, such as

- Gain attention and set up the information review in the opening.

- Gaining attention in the opening makes the letter stand out.

- Use your imagination in writing the opening. Make the opening fit the job.

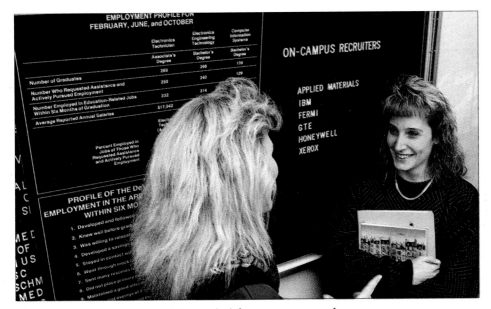

Job boards on campus are a good place to look for announcements of openings.

sales or public relations. In such cases, you would do well to show these qualities in your opening words. At the opposite extreme is work of a conservative nature, such as accounting or banking. Openings in such cases should normally be more restrained.

In choosing the best opening for your case, you should consider whether you are prospecting or writing an invited letter. If the letter has been invited, your opening words should begin qualifying you for the work to be done. They should also refer incidentally to the invitation, as in this example:

• An invited letter might refer to the job and the source of the invitation.

Will an honor graduate in accounting with experience in petroleum accounting qualify for the work you listed in today's *Times*?

In addition to fitting the work sought, your opening words should set up the review of qualifications. The preceding example meets this requirement well. It structures the review of qualifications around two areas—education and experience.

You can gain attention in the opening in many ways. One way is to use a topic that shows understanding of the reader's operation or of the work to be done. Employers are likely to be impressed by applicants who have made the effort to learn something about the company, as in this example:

• You can gain attention by showing an understanding of the reader's operations.

Now that Taggart, Inc., has expanded operations to Central America, can you use a broadly trained business administration graduate who knows the language and culture of the region?

Another way is to make a statement or ask a question that focuses attention on a need of the reader that the writer seeks to fill. The following opening illustrates this approach:

When was the last time you interviewed a young college graduate who wanted to sell and had successful sales experience?

• You can stress a need of the reader that you can fill.

If you seek more conservative work, you should use less imaginative openings. For example, a letter answering an advertisement for a beginning accountant might open with this sentence:

Because of my specialized training in accounting at State University and my practical experience in petroleum accounting, I believe I have the qualifications you described in your *Journal* advertisement.

• Use conservative openings for applications in a conservative field.

Sometimes one learns of a job possibility through a company employee. Mentioning the employee's name can gain attention, as in this opening sentence:

• Using an employee's name gains attention.

Effectiveness of a Salutation

After reading a student's application letter to the business communication class, Professor Sneer made this comment: "This is positively the worst letter submitted. It violates just about every writing principle I have emphasized in this course."

"That's my letter," an angry student responded. "I'll have you know that I copied it from one a friend wrote. And *it got the job* for my friend!"

"I was just getting to the letter's strong point," replied Professor Sneer. "The salutation overcomes all the letter's weaknesses. Can you imagine anything more effective than 'Dear Dad'!"

At the suggestion of Ms. Martha S. Hawkes of your staff, I am sending the following summary of my qualifications for work as your loan supervisor.

• Many opening possibilities exist, but avoid the old-style ones.

Many other possibilities exist. In the final analysis, you will have to use what you think will be best for the one case. But you should avoid the overworked beginnings that were popular a generation or two ago, such as "This is to apply for . . . ." and "Please consider this my application for . . . ." Although the direct application these words make may be effective in some cases (as when answering an advertisement), the words are timeworn and dull.

• Present your qualifications. Fit them to the job.

Selecting Content.   Following the opening, you should present the information that qualifies you to do the work. Begin this task by reviewing the job requirements. Then select the facts about you that qualify you for the job.

• You do this by studying the job. Use all available information sources.

If your letter has been invited, you may learn about the job requirements from the source of the invitation. If you are answering an advertisement, study it for the employer's requirements. If you are following up an interview, review the interview for information about job requirements. If you are prospecting, your research and your logical analysis should guide you.

• Include education, experience, personal qualities, references.

In any event, you are likely to present facts from three background areas: education, experience, and skills or personal details. You may also include a fourth—references. But references are not exactly background information. If you include references, they will probably go into the reference sheet.

• The emphasis each of these areas deserves varies by job. So consider the job in determining emphasis.

How much you include from each of these areas and how much you emphasize each area should depend on the job and on your background. Most of the jobs you will seek as a new college graduate will have strong educational requirements. Thus, you should stress your education. When you apply for work after you have accumulated experience, you will probably need to stress experience. As the years go by, experience becomes more and more important—education, less and less important. Your personal characteristics are of some importance for some jobs, especially jobs that involve working with people.

• Do not rely too heavily on the résumé. The application letter should carry all the major selling points.

If a résumé accompanies the application letter, you may rely on it too much. Remember that the letter does the selling and the résumé summarizes the significant details. Thus, the letter should contain the major points around which you build your case, and the résumé should include these points plus supporting details. As the two are parts of a team effort, somewhere in the letter you should refer the reader to the résumé.

• In organizing the background facts, select the best of these orders: logical grouping, time, job requirements.

Organizing for Conviction   You will want to present the information about yourself in the order that is best for you. In general, the plan you select is likely to follow one of three general orders. The most common order is a logical grouping of the information, such as education, skills or personal details, and experience. A second possibility is a

Choice Lines Gleaned from Application Letters

"I have no influential father, uncles, or friends. I have no political ties, no drag, no pull. The result: no job. I am just an ambitious and intelligent young man who will work hard."

"Actually, I am looking for a big desk and an upholstered chair with a position attached. The duties (if any) must be amusing or interesting."

"I am familiar with all phases of office procedure, including bowling, coffee-breaking, working crossword puzzles, doodling, personal letter writing, and collection taking."

"I have answered all the questions on your application form except 'Sex.' This I think is a very personal matter."

"For three years I worked for Ms. Helen Simmons, who I am sending to you as a reference on the attached data sheet."

time order. For example, you could present the information to show a year-by-year preparation for the work. A third possibility is an order based on the job requirements. For example, selling, communicating, and managing might be the requirements listed in an advertised job.

Merely presenting facts does not ensure conviction. You will also need to present the facts in words that make the most of your assets. You could say, for example, that you "held a position" as sales manager; but it is much more convincing to say that you "supervised a sales force of 14." Likewise, you do more for yourself by writing that you "earned a degree in business administration" than by writing that you "spent four years in college." And it is more effective to say that you "learned cost accounting" than to say that you "took a course in cost accounting."

• Use words that present your qualifications most favorably.

You can also help your case by presenting your facts in reader-viewpoint language wherever this is practical. More specifically, you should work to interpret the facts based on their meaning for your reader and for the work to be done. For example, you could present a cold recital like this one:

• Use the you-viewpoint wherever practical.

I am 21 years old and have an interest in mechanical operations and processes. Last summer I worked in the production department of a container plant.

Or you could interpret the facts, fitting them to the one job:

The interest I have held in things mechanical over most of my 21 years would help me fit into one of your technical manufacturing operations. And last summer's experience in the production department of Moyse Container Company is evidence that I can and will work hard.

Since you will be writing about yourself, you may find it difficult to avoid overusing I-references. But you should try. An overuse of *I*'s sounds egotistical and places too much attention on the often repeated word. Some *I*'s, however, should be used. The letter is personal. Stripping it of all I-references would rob it of its personal warmth. Thus, you should be concerned about the number of I-references. You want neither too many nor too few.

• Avoid the tendency to overuse *I*'s, but use some.

Driving for Action in the Close.
The presentation of your qualifications should lead logically to the action that the close of the letter proposes. You should drive for whatever action is appropriate in your case. It could be a request for an interview, an invitation to engage in further correspondence (perhaps to answer the reader's questions), or an invitation to write references. Rarely would you want to ask for the job in a first letter. You are concerned mainly with opening the door to further negotiations.

• In the close, drive for whatever action is appropriate.

Your action words should be clear and direct. Preferably, you should put them in

• Make the action words clear and direct.

question form. As in the sales letter, the request for action may be made more effective if it is followed by words recalling a benefit that the reader will get from taking the action. The following close illustrates this technique:

The highlights of my training and experience show that I have been preparing for a career in personnel. May I now discuss beginning this career with you? You can reach me at 500-921-4113 or by e-mail at ljdeftos@ucsd.edu to talk about how I can help in your personnel work.

• The following two letters show bad and good application techniques.

Contrasting Application Letters.   Illustrating bad and good techniques, the following two application letters present the qualifications of Jason L. Andrews, the job seeker described in the introductory situation at the beginning of the chapter. The first letter follows few of the suggestions given in the preceding pages, whereas the second letter is in general accord with these suggestions.

A Bland and Artless Presentation of Information.   The bad letter begins with an old-style opening. The first words stating that this is an application letter are of little interest. The following presentation of qualifications is a matter-of-fact, uninterpreted review of information. Little you-viewpoint is evident. In fact, most of the letter emphasizes the writer (note the *I*'s). The information presented is scant. The closing action is little more than an I-viewpoint statement of the writer's availability.

Dear Mr. Stark:

• This bad one is dull and poorly written.

    This is to apply for a position in labor relations with your company.
    At present, I am completing my studies in labor at Olympia University and will graduate with a Bachelor of Business Administration degree with a major in labor relations this May. I have taken all the courses in labor relations available to me as well as other helpful courses, such as statistics, law, and report writing.
    I have had good working experience as a shipping and receiving clerk, truck driver, and repairer. Please see details on the enclosed résumé. I believe that I am well qualified for a position in labor relations and am considering working for a company of your size and description.
    As I must make a decision on my career soon, I request that you write me soon. For your information, I will be available for an interview on March 17 and 18.

                                Sincerely,

Skillful Selling of One's Ability to Work.   The better letter begins with an interesting question that sets the stage for the following presentation. The review of experience is interpreted by showing how the experience would help in performing the job sought. The review of education is similarly covered. Notice how the interpretations show that the writer knows what the job requires. Notice also that reader-viewpoint is stressed throughout. Even so, a moderate use of *I*'s gives the letter a personal quality. The closing request for action is a clear, direct, and courteous question. The final words recall a main appeal of the letter.

Dear Mr. Stark:

• This better letter follows textbook instructions.

    Is there a place in your labor relations department for a person who is specially trained in the field and who knows working people and can talk with them on their level? My background, experience, and education have given me these unique qualifications.
    All my life I have lived and worked with working people. I was born and reared by working parents in a poor section of New York City. While in high school, I worked mornings and evenings in New York's garment district, primarily as a shipping and receiving clerk. For two years, between high school and college, I worked full-time as a truck driver for Wayland Trucking and belonged to the Teamsters. Throughout my four years of college, I worked half-time as an equipment repairer for Davidson Electric. From these experiences, I have learned to understand labor. I speak labor's language, and working people understand and trust me.

The job interview is the final examination of the application process. Appropriate grooming and relaxed, yet enthusiastic behavior are helpful to the applicant's success.

My college studies at Olympia University were specially planned to prepare me for a career in labor relations. Pursuing a major in human resources, I studied courses in labor relations, labor law, personnel administration, organizational behavior, administrative management, business policy, and collective bargaining. In addition, I studied a wide assortment of supporting subjects: economics, business communication, information systems, industrial psychology, human relations, and operations management. My studies have given me the foundation of knowledge on which to learn the practical side of labor relations work. I plan to begin the practical side of my development in June after I receive the Bachelor of Business Administration degree, with honors (3.7 grade-point average on a basis of 4.0).

These brief facts and the information in my résumé describe my diligent efforts to prepare for a career in labor relations. May I now talk with you about beginning that career? Please call 917-938-4449 to bring me to your office at your convenience to talk about how I could help in your labor relations work.

Sincerely,

Handling the Interview

Your initial contact with a prospective employer can be by mail or by a personal (face-to-face) visit. Even if you contact the employer by mail, a successful application will eventually involve a personal visit—or an *interview,* as we will call it. Much of the preceding parts of this chapter concerned the mail contact. Now our interest centers on the interview.

- Apply for the job—by mail or visit.

In a sense, the interview is the key to the success of the application—the "final examination," so to speak. You should carefully prepare for the interview, as the job may be lost or won in it. The following review of employment interview highlights should help you understand how to deal with the interview in your job search. You will find additional information about interviewing in Chapter 14.

- The interview is essential. For it, follow this procedure:

Investigating the Company. Before arriving for an interview, you should learn what you can about the company—its products or services, its personnel, its business practices, its current activities, its management. Such knowledge will help you talk knowingly with the interviewer. And perhaps more important, the interviewer is likely to be impressed by the fact that you took the time to investigate the company. That effort might even place you above your competitors.

- (1) Find out what you can about the employer.

Written by a recent college graduate seeking her first job, this letter was prepared for use with a number of different types of companies.

Mary O. Mahoney
1718 Cranford Avenue
Rockwell, MD 20854
Voice: 301-594-6942
Fax: 301-594-1573
May 17, 1996

Mr. Nevil S. Shannon
Director of Personnel
Snowdon Industries, Inc.
1103 Boswell Circle
Baltimore, MD 21202

Dear Mr. Shannon:

Question gets attention

Will you please review my qualifications for work in your administrative trainee program? I base my case on my training, work attitude, and personal skills.

Sets up organization plan

Good interpretation of education

My training for administration consists primarily of four years of business administration study at State University. The Bachelor of Business Administration degree I will receive in June has given me a broad foundation of business knowledge. As a general business major, I studied all the functional fields (management, marketing, information systems, finance, accounting) as well as the other core business subjects (communications, statistics, law, economics, production, and personnel). I have the knowledge base that will enable me to be productive now. And I can build upon this base through practical experience.

Skillfully handles lack of experience

As I am seeking my first full-time job, I must use means other than work experience to prove my work attitude. My grade point record at State is evidence that I took my studies seriously and that I worked hard. My 3.3 overall average (4.0 basis) placed me in the top 10 percent of the graduating class. I also worked diligently in student associations. My efforts were recognized by the special assignments and leadership roles given me. I assure you that I would bring these work habits with me to Snowdon Industries.

Individually adapted

Good use of fact to back up personal qualities

Throughout college, I devoted time to the development of my personal skills. As an active member of the student chapter of the Society for the Advancement of Management, I served as treasurer and program chairperson. I participated in intramural golf and volleyball. And I was an active worker in the Young Republicans, serving as publicity chairperson for three years. All this experience has helped me to have the balance you seek in your administrative trainees.

Clear request for action — flows logically from preceding presentation

Good ending message

These highlights and the additional evidence presented in the enclosed resume present my case for a career in administration. May I have an interview to continue my presentation? I could be in your office at your convenience to talk about working for Snowdon. You can reach me at 301-764-0017.

Sincerely,

Mary O Mahoney

Mary O. Mahoney

Enclosure

Using a company executive's name to gain attention, this letter is conservative in style and tone.

Mildred E. Culpepper
2707 Green Street
Lincoln, NE 68505
Message: 402-594-6942
Fax: 402-594-1573
April 17, 1996

Ms. Marlene O'Daniel
Vice President for Administration
Continental Insurance Company
3717 Donahue Street
Des Moines, IA 50316

Dear Ms. O'Daniel:

Interpretations of experience show the writer knows the work

On the suggestion of Mr. Victor O. Krause of your staff, here is a summary of my qualifications for work as your communications specialist.

Associate's name gains attention – opens door

Presently I am in my fifth year as communications specialist for Atlas Insurance. Primarily my work consists of writing letters to Atlas policyholders. This work has made me a convert of business writing. It has sharpened my writing skills. And more important, it has taught me how to gain and keep customers for my company through writing.

Conservative in style and tone

Additional experience working with businesspeople has given me an insight into the communication needs of business. This experience includes planning and presenting a communication improvement course for local civil service workers, a course in business writing for area business executives, and a course in bank communication for employees of Columbia National Bank.

Subtle you-viewpoint – implied from writer's understanding of work

My college training was certainly planned to prepare me for work in business writing. Advertising and public relations were my areas of concentration for my B.S. degree from Northern State University. As you will see in the enclosed resume, I studied all available writing courses in my degree plan. I also studied writing through English and journalism.

Brings review to a conclusion – fits qualification presented to the job

In summary, Ms. O'Daniel, my experience and my studies have equipped me for work as your communication specialist. I know business writing. I know how it should be practiced to benefit your company. May I have the privilege of discussing this matter with you personally? Please call me at 402-786-2575 so that I can arrange to be in your office at any time convenient to you.

An appropriate move for action

Sincerely,

Mildred E. Culpepper

Mildred E. Culpepper

Enc.

CASE ILLUSTRATION   **Application Letters.** (A Bland but Straightforward Prospecting Letter)

Some personnel specialists favor the matter-of-fact quality of this bland letter.

12713 Sanchez Drive
San Bernardino, CA 92405
July 10, 1996

Mr. Conrad W. Butler
Office Manager
Darden, Inc.
14316 Butterfield Road
San Francisco, CA 94129

Dear Mr. Butler:

Question gains attention

Can Darden, Inc., use a hardworking State University business major who wants a career in office administration? My experience, education, and personal qualities qualify me well for office administration work.

Justifies job search

My five years of work experience (see enclosed resume) have taught me to do all phases of office work. For the past two years I have been in charge of payrolls at Gynes Manufacturing Company. As the administrator of payrolls, I have had to handle all types of office operations, including records management and general correspondence. Although I am happy on this job, it does not offer the career opportunity I seek with Darden.

Review of experience brings out highlights

Complementing my work experience are my studies at Metropolitan Community College. In addition to studying the prescribed courses in my major field of business administration, I selected electives to help me in my career objective. And I believe I have succeeded. In spite of full-time employment through most of my time in college, I was awarded the Associate of Arts degree last May with a 3.3 grade-point average (4.0 basis). But most important of all, I learned from my studies how office work should be done.

Interprets positively

In addition, I have the personal qualities that would fit me harmoniously into your organization. I like people, and through experience I have learned how to work with them as both a team leader and a player.

Concluding statement sets up action

My preparation has been designed to prepare me for work in office administration, Mr. Butler. So may I talk to you about working for Darden? Please call me at 714-399-2569 to arrange an interview.

Clear and appropriate request for action

Sincerely,

Jimmy I. Goetz

Jimmy I. Goetz

Enc.

CASE ILLUSTRATION   **Application Letters.** (Interest and Good Organization in an Answer to an Advertisement)

Three job requirements listed in an advertisement determined the plan used in this letter.

4407 Sunflower Drive
Phoenix, AZ 85017
July 8, 1996

Ms. Anita O. Alderson, Manager
Tompkins-Oderon Agency, Inc.
7403 Tamaron Street
Los Angeles, CA 90022

Dear Ms. Alderson:

Good attention gainer – uses reader's words

Sound background in advertising. . . well trained. . . works well with others. . . .

Writing style shows ability to write advertising copy

These key words in your July 6 advertisement in the *Times* describe the person you want, and I believe I am that person.

Interpretation shows what writer can do on job

As summarized in the enclosed resume, I have gained experience in every phase of retail advertising while working for the *Lancer*, our college newspaper. I sold advertising, planned layouts, and wrote copy. During the last two summers, I got more firsthand experience working in the advertising department of Wunder & Son. I wrote a lot of copy for Wunder, some of which I am enclosing for your inspection; but I also did just about everything else there is to do in advertising work. I enjoyed it, and I learned from it. I am confident that this experience would help me fit in and contribute to the work in your office.

Good interpretation, shows strong determination

In my concentrated curriculum at the university, I studied marketing, with a specialization in advertising. I studied every course offered in advertising and related fields. My honor grades give some evidence that I worked hard and with sincerity. I am confident that upon my graduation in June I can bring to your organization the firm foundation of knowledge and imagination your work demands.

Understanding the importance of being able to get along well with people, I actively participated in Sigma Chi (social fraternity), the First Methodist Church, and Pi Tau Pi (honorary business fraternity). From the experience gained in these associations, I am confident that I can fit in harmoniously with the people in your advertising department.

Good evidence of social skills

Leads smoothly to action

The preceding review of my qualifications summarizes my case for a career in advertising. May I now meet with you to discuss the matter further? A call to 602-713-2199 would bring me to your office at any convenient time to talk about doing your advertising work.

Clear and strong drive for action

Sincerely,

Michael S. Janek

Michael S. Janek

Enc.

- (2) Make a good appearance (conservative dress and grooming).

Making a Good Appearance.   How you look to the interviewer is a part of your message. Thus, you should work to present just the right image. Interviewers differ to some extent on what that image is, but you would be wise to present a conservative appearance. This means avoiding faddish, offbeat styles, preferring the less flamboyant, conventional business colors such as browns, blues, blacks, and grays. Remember that the interviewer wants to know whether you fit into the role you are seeking. You should appear to fit the part.

Some may argue that such an insistence on conformity in dress and grooming infringes on one's personal freedom. Perhaps it does. We will even concede that employers should not force such biases on you. But you will have to be realistic if you want a successful career. If the people who can determine your future have fixed views on matters of dress and grooming, you will have to respect those views in order to succeed.

- (3) Anticipate the questions; plan the answers.

Anticipating Questions and Preparing Answers.   You should be able to anticipate some of the questions that the interviewer will ask. Questions about your education (courses, grades, honors, and such) are usually asked. So are questions about work experience, interests, career goals, location preferences, and activities in organizations. You should prepare answers to these questions in advance. Your answers will then be thorough and correct, and your words will display poise and confidence.

In addition to the general questions noted above, interviewers often ask more complicated ones. Some of these are designed to test you—to learn your views, your interests, and your ability to deal with difficult problems. Others seek more specific information about your ability to handle the job in question. Although such questions are more difficult to anticipate, you should be aware that they are likely to be asked. Following are questions of this kind that one experienced interviewer asks:

What can you do for us?

Would you be willing to relocate? To travel?

Do you prefer to work with people or alone?

How well has your performance in the classroom prepared you for this job?

What do you expect to be doing in 10 years? In 20 years?

What income goals do you have for those years (10 and 20 years ahead)?

Why should I rank you above the others I am interviewing?

Why did you choose _____ as your lifework?

How do you feel about working overtime? Nights? Weekends?

Did you do the best work you are capable of in college?

Is your college record a good measure of how you will perform on the job?

What are the qualities of the ideal boss?

What have you done that shows leadership potential?

What are your beginning salary expectations?

Sometimes interviewers will throw in tough or illegal questions to test your poise. These are naturally stressful, but being prepared for these kinds of questions will keep you cool and collected.[3] Here are some examples:

What is your greatest weakness?

With hindsight, how could you have improved your progress?

What kind of decisions are most difficult for you?

What is the worst thing you have heard about this company?

---

[3] Martin John Yate, *Knock 'em Dead* (Holbrook, MA: Bob Adams, 1994), pp. 170–84.

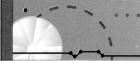
See this pen I'm holding. Sell it to me.

Tell me about a time when you put your foot in your mouth.

What kinds of people do you find it difficult to deal with?

What religion do you practice?

How old are you?

Are you married?

Do you plan to have children?

Putting Yourself at Ease.   Perhaps this is easier to say than to do, but you should be at ease throughout the interview. Remember that you are being inspected and that the interviewer should see a calm and collected person. How to appear calm and collected is not easy to explain. Certainly, it involves talking in a clear and strong voice. It also involves controlling your facial expressions and body movements. Developing such controls requires self-discipline—working at it. You may find it helpful to convince yourself that the stress experienced during an interview is normal. Or you may find it helpful to look at the situation realistically—as merely a conversation between two human beings. Other approaches may work better for you. Use whatever approaches work. Your goal is to control your emotions so that you present the best possible appearance to the interviewer.

• (4) Be at ease—calm, collected, confident.

Helping Control the Dialogue.   Just answering the questions asked is often not enough. Not only are you being evaluated, but you are evaluating others as well.[4] The questions you ask and the comments you play off them should bring up what you want the interviewer to know about you. Your self-analysis revealed the strong points in your background. Now you should make certain that those points come out in the interview.

• (5) Help bring out the questions that show your qualifications.

How to bring up points about you that the interviewer does not ask is a matter for your imagination. For example, a student seeking a job in advertising believed that a certain class project should be brought to the interviewer's attention. So she asked, "Do you attach any importance to advertising campaigns done as class projects in your evaluation?" The anticipated affirmative answer allowed her to show her successful project. For another example, a student who wanted to bring out his knowledge of the prospective employer's operations did so with this question: "Will your company's expansion at the Bakersfield plant create new job opportunities there?" How many questions of this sort you should ask will depend on your need to supplement your

• Here are some examples of how to do it.

---

[4] Kevin Collins and Patricia B. Carr, "A Short Course on Landing a Job," *The College Edition of the National Business Employment Weekly,* published by *The Wall Street Journal,* Fall 1988, p. 38.

interviewer's questioning. Your goal should be to make certain that the interviewer gets all the information you consider important.

Following Up and Ending the Application

- Follow up the interview with thank-you, status-inquiry, job-acceptance, and job-rejection messages.

The interview is only an early step in the application process. A variety of other steps can follow. Conveying a brief thank-you message by letter or telephone is an appropriate follow-up step. It shows interest, and because some of your competitors will not do this, it can give you an advantage. If you do not hear from the prospective employer within a reasonable time, it is appropriate to inquire by telephone or letter about the status of your application. You should certainly do this if you are under a time limit on another employer's offer. The application process may end with no offer (frequently with no notification at all—a most discourteous way of handling applicants), with a rejection notice, or with an offer. How to handle these steps in writing is reviewed in the following paragraphs.

· ·
OTHER JOB-SEARCH LETTERS

- Getting a job can involve writing more than letters and résumés.

Getting a job can involve writing more than application letters and résumés. You should follow up an interview with a thank-you letter. After much time has passed, you may want to write a letter inquiring about the status of your application. You may need to write a letter accepting a job, refusing one, or resigning one.

From the preceding instructions, you should be able to write such letters. For this reason, the following review of them is brief.

- You should write a thank-you letter following an interview.

Writing a Thank-You Letter.   After an interview you should write a thank-you letter. It is the courteous thing to do, whether or not you are interested in the job. If you are interested, the letter can help your case. It singles you out from the competition and shows your interest in the job.

- The typical order for such a letter is as follows: (1) expression of gratefulness, (2) appropriate comments fitting the situation, (3) any additional information needed, and (4) a goodwill close.

Such letters are usually short. They begin with an expression of gratefulness. They say something about the interview, the job, or such. They take care of any additional business (such as submitting information requested). And they end on a goodwill note—perhaps a hopeful look to the next step in the negotiations. The following letter does these things:

Dear Ms. Chubbuck:

   I genuinely appreciate the time you gave me yesterday. You were most helpful. And you did a first-rate job of selling me on Graystone-Brune, Inc.
   As you requested, I have enclosed samples of the advertising campaign I developed as a class project. If you need anything more, please let me know.
   I look forward to the possibility of discussing employment with you soon.

                    Sincerely,

- When employers do not respond, you may write a follow-up letter. It follows the order of the routine inquiry letter.

Constructing a Follow-Up to an Application.   When a prospective employer is late in responding to an application, you may need to write a follow-up letter. Employers are often just slow, but sometimes they lose the application. Whatever the explanation, a follow-up letter may help to produce action.

Such a letter is a form of routine inquiry. As a reason for writing, it can use the need to make a job decision, or some other good explanation. The following letter is an example:

Dear Mr. Lemon:

As the time is approaching when I must make a job decision, will you please tell me the status of my employment application with you.

You may recall that you interviewed me in your office November 7. You wrote me November 12 indicating that I was among those you had selected for further consideration.

Barrow, Inc. remains one of the organizations I would like to consider in making my career decision. I will very much appreciate hearing from you by December 3.

Sincerely,

Planning the Job Acceptance.   Job acceptances in writing are merely favorable response letters with an extra amount of goodwill. As the letter should begin directly, a yes answer in the beginning is appropriate. The remainder of the letter should contain a confirmation of the starting date and place and comments about the work, the company, the interview—whatever you would say if you were face to face with the reader. The letter need not be long. This one does the job well:

- You may need to write a letter accepting a job. Write it as you would a favorable response letter.

Dear Ms. Polansky:

I accept your offer of employment. After my first interview with you, I was convinced that Allison-Caldwell was the organization for me. It is good to know that you think I am right for Allison-Caldwell.

Following your instructions, I will be in your Toronto headquarters on May 28, ready to begin a career with you.

Sincerely,

Writing a Letter Refusing a Job.   Letters refusing a job offer follow the normal refusal pattern. One good technique is to begin with a friendly comment—perhaps something about past relations with the company. Next, explain and present the refusal in clear yet positive words. Then end with more friendly comment. This example illustrates the plan.

- To refuse a job offer, use the normal refusal pattern (indirect).

Dear Mr. Segura:

Meeting you and the other people at Northern was a genuine pleasure. All that I saw and heard impressed me most favorably. I was especially impressed to receive the generous job offer that followed.

In considering the offer, I naturally gave some weight to these favorable impressions. Even though I have accepted a job with another firm, they remain strong in my mind.

Thank you for the time and the courteous treatment you gave me.

Sincerely,

Writing a Letter of Resignation.   At some point in your career you are likely to resign from one job to take another. When this happens, probably you will inform your employer of your resignation orally. But when you find it more practical or comfortable, you may choose to resign in writing. In some cases, you may do it both ways. As a matter of policy, some companies require a written resignation even after an oral resignation has been made. Or you may prefer to leave a letter of resignation following your oral announcement of it.

- Job resignations are made in person, by letter, or both.

Your letter of resignation should be as positive as the circumstances permit. Even if your work experiences have not been pleasant, you will be wise to depart without a final display of anger. As an anonymous philosopher once explained, "When you write a resignation in anger, you write the best letter you will ever regret."

- Make the letter as positive as circumstances permit.

The best resignation letters are written in the indirect order. The situation is negative; and, as you know, indirectness usually is advisable in such cases. But many are

- Preferably use indirect order, for the situation is negative.

written in the direct order. They present the resignation right away, following it with expressions of gratitude, favorable comments about past working experiences, and the like. Either approach is acceptable. Even so, you would do well to use the indirect order, for it is more likely to build the goodwill and favorable thinking you want to leave behind you.

The example below shows the indirect order, which is well known to you. It begins with a positive point—one that sets up the negative message. The negative message follows, clearly yet positively stated. The ending returns to positive words chosen to build goodwill and fit the case.

Dear Ms. Knauth:

- This illustration letter begins and ends positively.

Working as your assistant for the past five years has been a genuinely rewarding experience. Under your direction I have grown as an administrator. And I know you have given me a practical education in retailing.

As you may recall from our past discussions, I have been pursuing the same career goals that you held early in your career. Thus I am sure you will understand why I now submit my resignation to accept a store management position with Lawson's in Belle River. I would like my employment to end on the 31st; but I could stay a week or two longer if needed to help train my replacement.

I leave with only good memories of you and the other people with whom I worked. Thanks to all of you for a valuable contribution to my career.

Sincerely,

Continuing Job-Search Activities

- Keeping your attention on the job market alerts you to changes and opportunities in the field.

Some authorities recommend continuing your job search two weeks into a new job. It provides insurance if you should discover the new job isn't what you expected. However, continuously keeping your finger on the pulse of the job market is a good idea. Not only does it provide you with information about the changes occurring in your field, but it also keeps you alert to better job opportunities as soon as they are announced.

- Update your résumé regularly to reflect new accomplishments and skills.

Maintaining Your Résumé   While many people intend to keep their résumés up to date, they just don't make it a priority. Some others make it easy by updating as changes occur. And a few update their résumés at regularly designated times such as one's birthday, New Year's Day, or even the anniversary of one's employment. No matter what works best for you, updating your résumé as you gain new accomplishments and skills is important.

- Keeping current in your professional reading brings many benefits.

Reading Job Ads/Professional Journals   Nearly as important as keeping your résumé updated is keeping up on your professional reading. Most trade or professional journals have job notices or bulletin boards you should check regularly. These ads give you insight into what skills are in demand, perhaps helping you choose assignments where you get the opportunity to develop new skills. Staying up to date in one's field can be stimulating; it can provide both challenges and opportunities.

· ·

SUMMARY ▶ by Chapter Objectives

1 Develop and use a network of contacts in your job search.

1. A good first step in your job search is to build a network of contacts.
   - Get to know people who might help you later—classmates, professors, business leaders, and such.
   - Use them to help you find a job.

2. When you are ready to find work, analyze yourself.
   - Look at your education, personal qualities, and work experience.
   - From this review, determine what work you are qualified to do.
   - Then select the career that is right for you.
3. When you are ready to find a job, use the contact sources available to you.
   - Check university placement centers, advertisements, career television network, on-line sources, employment agencies, and personal contacts.
   - If these do not produce results, prospect by mail.
4. In your application efforts, you are likely to use résumés and application letters. Prepare them as you would written sales material.
   - First, study your product—you.
   - Then study your prospect—the employer.
   - From the information gained, construct the résumé and letter.
   In writing the résumé (a listing of your major background facts), you can choose from two types.
   - The *traditional* type for face-to-face interviews.
   - The *electronic* type for scanned résumés.
   In preparing the traditional résumé, follow this procedure:
   - List all the facts about you that an employer might want to know.
   - Sort these facts into logical groups—*experience, education, personal qualities, references, achievements, highlights.*
   - Put these facts in writing. As a minimum, include job experience (dates, places, firms, duties) and education (degrees, dates, fields of study). Use some personal information, but omit race, religion, and sex, marital status, and age.
   - Authorities disagree on whether to list references. If you list them, use complete mailing addresses and have one for each major job.
   - Include other helpful information: address, telephone number, career objective.
   - Write headings for the résumé and for each group of information; use either topic or talking headings.
   - Preferably write the résumé without personal pronouns, make the parts parallel grammatically, and use words that help sell your abilities.
   - Present the information for good eye appeal, selecting fonts that show the importance of the headings and the information.
   In preparing the electronic résumé, follow these procedures
   - Include keywords.
   - Choose precise nouns over action verbs.
   - Present the information in a form read accurately by the computer.
5. As the application letter is a form of sales letter, plan it as you would a sales letter.
   - Study your product (you) and your prospect (the employer) and think out a strategy for presentation.
   - Begin with words that gain attention, begin applying for the job, and set up the presentation of your sales points.
   - Adapt the tone and content to the job you seek.
   - Present your qualifications, fitting them to the job you seek.
   - Choose words that enhance the information presented.
   - Drive for an appropriate action—an interview, further correspondence, reference checks.
6. Your major contact with a prospective employer is the interview. For best results, you should do the following:
   - Research the employer in advance so you can impress the interviewer.
   - Present a good appearance through appropriate dress and grooming.
   - Try to anticipate the interviewer's questions and to plan your answers.
   - Make a good impression by being at ease.
   - Help the interviewer establish a dialogue with questions and comments that enable you to present the best information about you.

2 Assemble and evaluate information that will help you select a career.

3 Describe the sources that can lead you to an employer.

4 Compile traditional and electronic résumés that are strong, complete, and well arranged.

5 Write letters of application that skillfully sell your abilities.

6 Explain how you should conduct yourself in an interview.

Write application follow-up letters that are appropriate, friendly, and positive.

7. You may need to write other letters in your search for a job.
   - Following the interview, a thank-you letter is appropriate.
   - Also appropriate is an inquiry about the status of an application.
   - You may also need to write letters accepting, rejecting, or resigning a job.
   - Write these letters much as you would the letters reviewed in preceding chapters: direct order for good news, indirect order for bad.

8 Maintain your job-search skills.

8. To learn information about the change occurring in their field and to be aware of better job opportunities, employees should
   - maintain their résumés, and
   - read both job ads and professional journals.

CRITICAL THOUGHT QUESTIONS

1. "Building a network of contacts to help one find jobs appears to be selfish. It involves acquiring friendships just to use them for one's personal benefit." Discuss this view.

2. Maryann Brennan followed a broad program of study in college and received a degree in general studies. She did her best work in English, especially in the writing courses. She also did well in history, sociology, and psychology. As much as she could, she avoided math and computer courses.

   Her overall grade-point average of 3.7 (4.0 basis) placed her in the top 10 percent of her class. What advice would you give her as she begins her search for a career job?

3. Discuss the value of each of the sources for finding jobs to a finance major (*a*) right after graduation and (*b*) after 20 years of work in his or her specialty.

4. Assume that in an interview for the job you want, you are asked the questions listed in the text under the heading "Anticipating Questions." Answer these questions.

5. The most popular arrangement of résumé information is the three-part grouping: education, experience, and personal details. Describe three other arrangements. When would each be used?

6. Distinguish between the traditional résumé and the electronic résumé. When would each be most appropriate?

7. What is meant by parallelism of headings?

8. Describe the application letter and résumé you would write (*a*) immediately after graduation, (*b*) 10 years later, and (*c*) 25 years later. Point out similarities and differences, and defend your decision.

9. What differences would you suggest in the writing of application letters for jobs in (*a*) accounting, (*b*) banking, (*c*) advertising copy writing, (*d*) administration, (*e*) sales, (*f*) consulting, and (*g*) information systems?

10. Discuss the logic of beginning an application letter with these words: "This is to apply for . . ." and "Please consider this my application for the position of . . ."

11. "In writing job-application letters, just present the facts clearly and without analysis and interpretation. The facts alone will tell the employer whether he or she wants you." Discuss this viewpoint.

12. When should the drive for action in an application letter (*a*) request the job, (*b*) request an interview, and (*c*) request a reference check?

CRITICAL THINKING EXERCISES

1. Criticize the following résumé parts. (They are not from the same résumé.)
   a. Work Experience

1993–96	Employed as sales rep for Lloyd-Shanks Tool Company
1990–93	Office manager, Drago Plumbing Supply, Toronto
1988–90	Matson's Super Stores. I worked part time as sales clerk while attending college.

   b. References
   Mr. Carl T. Whitesides
   Sunrise Insurance, Inc.
   317 Forrest Lane
   Dover, DE 19901

   Patricia Cullen
   Cullen and Cullen Realtors
   2001 Bowman Dr.
   Wilmington, DE 19804

   Rev. Troy A. Graham
   Asbury Methodist Church
   Hyattsville, MD 20783

   D. W. Boozer
   Boozer Industries
   Baltimore, MD 21202

   c. Education

1992	Graduated from Tippen H.S. (I was in top 10 percent of class.)
1996	B.S. from Brady University with major in marketing
1996 to present.	Enrolled part time in M.B.A. program at Waldon University

   d. Qualifications
   Know how to motivate a sales force. I have done it.
   Experienced in screening applicants and selecting salespeople.
   Know the pharmaceutical business from 11 years of experience.
   Knowledgeable of realistic quota setting and incentives.
   Proven leadership ability.

2. Criticize these sentences from application letters:
   Beginning Sentences
   a. Please consider this my application for any position for which my training and experience qualify me.
   b. Mr. Jerry Bono of your staff has told me about a vacancy in your loan department for which I would like to apply.
   c. I am that accountant you described in your advertisement in today's *Times-Record.*
   d. I want to work for you!
   Sentences Presenting Selling Points
   e. From 1992 to 1996 I attended Brady University where I took courses leading to a B.S. degreer with a major in finance.

f. I am highly skill in trading corporate bonds as a result of three years spent in the New York office of Collins, Bragg, and Weaver.

g. For three years (1993–96) I was in the loan department at Northwest Bank.

h. My two strongest qualifications for this job are my personality and gift of conversation.

<u>Sentences from Action Endings</u>

i. I will call you on the 12th to arrange an interview.

j. If my qualifications meet your requirements it would be greatly appreciated if you would schedule an interview for me.

k. Please call to set up an interview. Do it now—while it is on your mind.

CRITICAL THINKING PROBLEMS

▶ **Applications**

1. Move the date to the time you will complete your education. You have successfully prepared yourself for the career of your choice, but the visiting recruiters have not yet offered you a job. Now you must look on your own. So you find the best job for which you believe you are qualified in the "Classified Advertisements" sections of the area newspapers. Write the application letter that will present your qualifications for this job. Attach the advertisement to the letter. (Assume that a résumé accompanies the letter.)

2. Write the résumé to accompany the letter for Problem 1.

3. Project yourself five years past your graduation date. During those years, you have had good experience working for the company of your choice in the field of your choice. (Use your imagination to supply this information.)

   Unfortunately, your progress hasn't been what you had expected. You think that you must look around for a better opportunity. Your search through the classified advertisements in your area newspapers, online, and *The Wall Street Journal* turns up one promising possibility (you find it). Write an application letter that skillfully presents your qualifications for this job. (You may make logical assumptions about your experience over the five-year period.) For class purposes, clip the advertisement to your letter.

4. Write the résumé and reference sheet to accompany the letter in Problem 3.

5. Assume you are in your last term of school and graduation is just around the corner. Your greatest interest is in finding work that you like and that would enable you to support yourself now and to support a family as you win promotions.

   No job of your choice is revealed in the want ads of newspapers and trade magazines. No placement bureau has provided anything to your liking. So you decide to do what any good salesperson does: survey the product (yourself) and the market (companies that could use a person who can do what you are prepared to do) and then advertise (send each of these companies a résumé with an application letter). This procedure sometimes creates a job where none existed before; and sometimes it establishes a basis for negotiations for the "big job" two, three, or five years after graduation. And very frequently, it puts you on the list for the good job that is not filled through advertising or from the company staff. Write the application letter.

6. Write the résumé and reference sheet to accompany the letter for Problem 5.

7. Move the calendar to your graduation date so that you're now ready to sell your working ability in the job market for as much as you can get and still hold your own. Besides canvassing likely firms with the help of prospecting letters and diligently following up family contacts, you've decided to look into anything that appears especially good in the ad columns of newspapers, on-line services and magazines. The latest available issues of big-town publications and on-line services list the following jobs that you think you could handle. (You may change publication and place names to fit your section of the country.)

   a. *Office manager.* Insurance company seeks personable, college-trained person to manage office of five employees. People skills and good communication ability a must. Knowledge of office procedures and word processing essential. Send application material to Human Resource Office, P.O. Box 7197, __[your city]__ .

   b. *Private secretary.* Vice president of major manufacturing company seeks highly competent, personable, and dependable private secretary. College training preferred. Must have excellent word processing skills (IBM PC and WordPerfect) as well as knowledge of business writing. Apply to Human Resource, Box 739, __[your city]__ .

   c. *Management trainee.* Fast growing manufacturer in the food-processing industry has opening in its training program. Only high-energy, results-oriented people with good communication skills need apply. Opportunities for advancement to management positions based on performance. Applicants must demonstrate a professional image and possess skills in working with people. Computer literacy required. Apply to Human Resource Director, P.O. Box 9133, __[your city]__ .

   d. *Accounting majors.* International accounting firm seeks recent accounting graduates. Well-rounded study of accounting and computers essential. Some travel. Advancement based on performance. Communication and human-relations skills required. Must be a hard worker and willing to work long hours during peak periods. Excellent compensation and benefits. Apply to Accounting Director, P.O. Box 2985, __[your city]__ .

   e. *Desktop publishing graphics specialist.* A leader in developing and implementing custom software systems is seeking an individual to work with our team of publishing professionals in producing high-quality publications. Responsibilities for this position include producing camera-ready art for large documentation projects using Ventura desktop publishing software. This person will also prepare mechanicals, coordinate production, and maintain schedules. Knowledge of project management software is a plus. Qualified candidates will be detail oriented with experience in graphic design. A strong knowledge of DOS and WordPerfect is also required. We offer an excellent benefits package including generous vacation policy, medical/dental/vision plans, and tuition assistance. Please send résumé to HRD, 2501 Dallas Street,__[your city]_.

f. *Programmer analyst.* A large financial services company located in Los Angeles is looking for a programmer analyst to join its IS department. The job involves analyzing, designing, and programming applications in an advanced mainframe environment using COBOL II, CCS, DB, VRAM, and JCL. Fax résumé and cover letter to the director of professional recruitment at 310-772-6361.

g. *Technology analyst/consultant.* A fast-growing, highly regarded information technology assessment/consulting firm has a position for someone with expertise in client/server technology and object-oriented technology and/or related areas. Must have excellent written communications and interpersonal skills. Vendor or user organization experience is highly desirable. Position is in the Bay Area. Send or fax your résumé to director of human resources at 500 Airport Road, Suite 100, __[your city]__ or 415-579-1022.

h. *Financial analyst.* An eastern-based investment firm is seeking an analyst to help with the evaluation of potential private equity investments and marketing of an existing and new leveraged buyout fund. Should have a bachelor's degree from a good school and some experience in banking. Ideal candidates will have strong analytical capabilities and excellent PC skills, particularly spreadsheet and word processing. Please fax résumé and cover letter to 203-869-1022.

i. *Manager of corporate communications.* A Fortune 500, high-technology company seeks a well-rounded communication manager. Applicants should possess excellent writing skills and be able to think strategically, implement plans, and manage projects including those with budgets. The ability to use Windows programs such as Microsoft Word, Excel, and PowerPoint is highly desirable. The ideal candidate will thrive in a high-energy, highly challenging environment and be willing to travel occasionally. Send résumé to director of human resources, 7000 Hermes Blvd., __[your city]__.

j. *Sales representative.* An international company providing specialized products for flight and machinery components seeks to expand its client base in the West Coast, Central, Northeast, and Southeast regions. Successful candidates will be poised, persuasive "closers" with some technical knowledge. Sales experience or utility maintenance experience is desirable. Good knowledge of these new territories is desirable. Send résumé to Box 1022, __[your desirable city]_.

k. *Client/server programmer.* The largest supplier of curriculum and support services seeks to expand its staff. Desirable candidates will have experience with PowerBuilder, Visual Basic, or C^{++}; object-oriented analysis and design skills; GUI design experience; and a solid understanding of Windows 95 and OS/2. Applicants should be able to design, implement, and test systems, working on projects from inception to completion. Please send or fax résumé to the human relations coordinator at 825 Lincoln Blvd., __[your city]_, or 215-295-1022.

l. *Marketing professional.* An international, rapidly growing consumer and trade publisher is seeking a self-motivated individual to help us reach our goal of doubling revenues by the year 2000. Ideal candidate will be an innovative, results-oriented professional willing to take the challenge of developing new markets. Should be good at packaging and repackaging information products for a large and expanding customer base. We are looking for those with some experience, creative writing talent, leadership skills, good communications skills, and strong interpersonal skills. Sell yourself through your cover letter and résumé. Send to Thomas Jajeh, corporate vice president, 2411 Blackhawk Road, __[your city]_, or fax to 619-681-1022.

m. *Executive administrative assistant.* Vice president of a Fortune 500 manufacturing company seeks a highly competent, personable, organized and dependable executive assistant. College degree desired. Must have excellent communication skills and thorough command of word processing and graphics programs. In addition to basic business knowledge in accounting, finance, marketing, and management an understanding of manufacturing in a global market would be desirable. Apply to director of human resources, P.O. Box 3733, __[your city]_.

n. *Graphic artist.* An employee-owned systems integration firm has an immediate need for a graphic artist. A bachelor's degree or an associate's degree with some experience desired. Must be proficient in CorelDraw, preferably in a Windows environment. Will prepare presentation and curriculum support graphics for government customer. Knowledge of project management software is a plus. Must have a work portfolio. Send résumé to the attention of KML, P.O. Box 900, __[your city]_.

o. *MIS specialist.* A local medical clinic is seeking an individual to manage a multisite, multiplatform computer system. Will be responsible for troubleshooting and coordinating problems in a Unix/Novell environment and writing reports for management. A background in the health care/medical field combined with a good knowledge of computing is highly desirable. Send résumé to [your city's name] Community Clinic, 1113 Henderson, ___[your city]___.

p. *Data systems technician.* An innovative and progressive local company is seeking a data systems technician to generate and analyze reports for claims. Would also be responsible for maintaining operating systems and applications. Must also be willing to play a support role in installation of software and hardware. Position requires thorough knowledge of all aspects of telecommunications, including LANs and WANs. Send your résumé to the attention of HR/TECH, P.O. Box 12, ___[your city]___.

q. *Accountant.* A major real estate developer and property management company seeks an accountant. Must have a bachelor's degree in accounting. Will assist in financial reporting, tax preparation, cash flow projections, and year-end audit workpaper preparation. Mastery of Lotus 1-2-3 is required as are good communication skills. Some work experience in accounting is desirable; internship experience in an accounting or real estate environment is also desirable. Send your résumé and cover letter to TPL, P.O. Box 613, ___[your city]___.

r. *Accounting majors.* Multinational consumer electronics firm seeks entry-level accountant for work in its controller's division. This person must be knowledgeable in financial and cost accounting, internal auditing, budgeting, and capital investments. A multinational orientation, degree in accounting, and progress toward completion of CPA or CMA are a plus. Good communication skills (written and oral) and computer applications are required. Interested applicants should send letter and résumé to Box B.O. & L., ___[your city]___.

s. *Bank examiner.* Federal Reserve Bank (nearest to your location) seeks positions for career-oriented individuals. Persons hired will conduct on-site examinations of foreign banks operating in the U.S. in their lending activities, derivative products, bank operations, and financial information. Applicants must possess a bachelor's degree in accounting, finance, or economics. Evidence of cross-cultural sensitivity and foreign language proficiency are preferred. Travel 30–50 percent of the time. Excellent oral/written skills and U.S. citizenship required. Apply with letter and résumé to Federal Reserve Board, Human Resources Department, ___[your region]___.

t. *Proposal writer.* Global leader in high-technology asset management needs individual to prepare proposals for clients. Person selected must be a team player, thrive on high-tech challenges in fast-paced environment, and possess a state-of-the-art solution orientation. Excellent writing skills essential, along with BBA degree and experience with various hardware/software technologies. Job includes coordinating appropriate persons to define solutions and preparing program plans with cost estimation

for clients. Send letter and résumé to Department SAS, ___[your city]___.

u. *Assistant to operations manager.* Proven leader in the insurance industry seeks a highly motivated assistant to the operations manager of regional service center. Technical skills include proficiency in Microsoft Word, Excel, Powerpoint, Access, and other database applications. College training preferred with good people skills. Person selected must be able to develop and maintain effective working relationships with internal and external customers. Apply to H R Department, Box 7438, ___[your city]___.

v. *Safety and health assistant.* World leader in battery manufacturing is looking for an individual to work in safety and health area of production plant and distribution center. The successful candidate will need to have a business or related degree and possess excellent organizational and people skills. Job duties involve administering health/safety programs, conducting training, and working with governmental agencies and regulatory personnel. Excellent opportunity for results-oriented individual seeking to work for a safe, attractive, and sanitary environment. Send letter and résumé to Box SH, ___[your city]___.

w. *Account executive for display advertising.* State business journal invites applications for career-oriented individuals. Qualified candidates must be college graduates (business preferred) and have work background to demonstrate reliability and commitment. Job scope involves selling display advertising in creative ways for specialized business publications. Applicants should be of high energy, aggressive, and creative. Send applications to Drawer HBD, ___[your city]___.

x. *Financial services representative.* Major Wall Street investment firm with offices nationwide wants self-motivated, career-minded individuals for (your locale) to train as registered representatives of firm. Those selected will have future management opportunities. Business degree preferred with emphasis in finance and marketing. Investment services provided by firm include mutual funds, IRAs, pensions, tax-deferred programs, and insurance. Candidates must demonstrate adaptability to different people and good time management skills. Send applications to Box CSB, ___[your city]___.

y. *Accounts payable trainees.* National beverage company is looking for persons to oversee and manage all aspects of accounts payable processing in various regional locations. Applicants should know how to match and code invoices for payment, input data, and analyze vendor accounts. Business education with strong secretarial skills necessary (Lotus 1-2-3 and WP at a minimum). Individuals should be well organized and willing to blend into a busy office. Apply to Human Resources Department, P.O. Box 4665, ___[your city]___.

z. *Materials management trainee.* Progressive health

food producer with 11 state-of-the-art manufacturing facilities and participative work environment needs materials management trainee. The position will help to manage master scheduling functions, production control, customer service, product distribution, and capacity planning. Business degree with production/operations management concentration and progress toward APICS Certification preferred. Excellent analytical, communication, and people management skills. Interested applicants should send letter and résumé to Box 7801, [your city] .

aa. *Convention services marketer.* Major international hotel organization needs trainees to work in its convention services division. Job activities include prospecting for clients, selling hotel facilities and services, negotiating contracts, servicing client needs, coordinating with intermediaries, and performing other activities for marketing planning/control. Individuals with degrees in marketing and with job experience in service industries preferred. High-energy, good visionary applicants will join team of success-oriented professionals. Qualified applicants should apply to Box SRD, [your city] .

bb. *Marketing trainees.* International leader in precious gemstone mining and processing seeks qualified persons to help build marketing program. Candidates must have ability to analyze market opportunities; research and select target markets; design market strategies; plan market programs; and organize, implement, and control marketing effort. This position offers the right persons the opportunity to use education and skills in an exciting high-growth corporate environment. College education with emphasis in marketing plus career-minded orientation are essential. To be considered, send cover letter and résumé to Box 3355, [your city] .

cc. *Compensation analyst.* Large transportation company has an exciting and challenging opportunity for a junior-level compensation professional to support the corporate compensation program in the areas of job analysis, market pricing, merit/incentive programs, pay structures, and various compensation studies. The ideal candidate will have a college degree with demonstrated analytical skills in compensation analysis and job evaluation. Spreadsheet knowledge, strong communication/interpersonal skills, and ability to interact with

senior-level management are essential. Interested applicants should apply by sending letter and résumé to Drawer OWG, [your city] .

dd. *Instruction assistant.* Airline Training and Consulting Group is seeking individuals to assist with instructional design and development. Job responsibilities include training and development of new instructors, developing and enhancing training courses in instructional design, and maintaining classroom and associated equipment. A college degree and a thorough knowledge of state-of-the-art learning technologies are a must. Individuals should possess people-enhancing skills. Send letter and résumé to Box 5551, [your city] .

Concentrate on the ad describing the job you would like most or could do best—and then write an application letter that will get you that job. Your letter will first have to survive the siftings that eliminate dozens (sometimes hundreds) of applicants who lack the expected qualifications. Toward the end you'll be getting into strong competition in which small details may give you the little extra margin of superiority that will get you an interview and a chance to campaign further.

Study your ad for what it says and even more for what it implies. Weigh your own preparation even more thoroughly than you weigh the ad. You may imagine far enough ahead to assure completion of all the courses that are blocked out for your degree. You may build up your case a bit on what you actually have. Sort out the things that line you up for the *one* job, organize them strategically, and then present them. Assume that you've attached a résumé.

8. Write the résumé and reference sheet to accompany the letter for Problem 7.

9. You are looking ahead to your graduation soon. You've decided to begin to look for jobs on-line. Tap into a system that you know posts jobs in your major (such as E-span) or one where people on it may lead you to such a board. Browse through the jobs until you see one that appeals to you and for which you'll be qualified when you graduate. Print (or save) a copy of the ad so you'll have it handy when you write your résumé and letter of application. Address the points covered in the ad and tell them that you learned about the position from a particular on-line system. If you are transmitting your response on-line, be sure to chunk your documents with your strongest points on the first few screens.

PART FIVE

FUNDAMENTALS OF REPORT WRITING

10

Basics of Report Writing

Upon completing this chapter, you will be able to prepare well-organized, objective reports. To reach this goal, you should be able to

1 State a problem clearly in writing.

2 List the factors involved in a problem.

3 Explain the common errors in interpreting and the attitudes and practices conducive to good interpreting.

4 Organize information in outline form, using time, place, quantity, factor, or a combination of these as bases for division.

5 Construct topic or talking headings that outline reports logically and meaningfully.

6 Write reports that are clear, objective, consistent in time viewpoint, smoothly connected, and interesting.

7 Prepare reports collaboratively.

▶ to Report Writing

Introduce yourself to the subject of report writing by assuming the role of administrative assistant to the president of Technicraft, Inc. Much of your work at this large manufacturing company involves getting information for your boss. Yesterday, for example, you looked into the question of excessive time spent by office workers on coffee breaks. A few days earlier, you worked on an assignment to determine the causes of unrest in one of the production departments. Before that assignment you investigated a supervisor's recommendation to change a production process. You could continue the list indefinitely, for investigating problems is a part of your work.

So is report writing, for you must write a report on each of your investigations. You write these reports for good reasons. Written reports make permanent records. Thus, those who need the information contained in these reports can review and study them at their convenience. Written reports can also be routed to a number of readers with a minimum of effort. Unquestionably, such reports are convenient and efficient means of transmitting information. Your report-writing work is not unique in your company. In fact, report writing is common in virtually all operations of the company. Sometimes reports are written by individuals. Increasingly, however, they are prepared in collaboration with others. For example, the engineers often report on the technical problems they encounter. The accountants regularly report to management on the company's financial operations. From time to time, production people report on various aspects of operations. The salespeople regularly report on marketing matters. And so it is throughout the company. Such reporting is vital to your company's operations—as it is to the operations of all companies. Organizations require information for many reasons. In a sense, they feed on information. Reports supply them with a vital portion of the information they need.[1]

This chapter and the following two chapters describe the structure and writing of this vital form of business communication. ■

How often you write reports in the years ahead will depend on the size of the organization you work for. If you work for a very small organization (say, one with fewer than 10 employees), you will probably write only a few. But if you work for a midsize or larger organization, you are likely to write many. In fact, the larger the organization, the more reports you are likely to write. The explanation is obvious. The larger the organization, the greater is its complexity; and the greater the complexity, the greater is the need for information to manage the organization. As reports supply much of the information needed, the demand for them is great.

- • Reports are vital to larger organizations. You will probably write them.

DEFINING REPORTS

You probably have a good idea of what reports are. Even so, you would be likely to have a hard time defining them. Even scholars of the subject cannot agree, for their definitions range from one extreme to the other. Some define reports to include almost any presentation of information; others limit reports to only the most formal presentations. For our purposes, this middle-ground definition is best: *A business report is an orderly and objective communication of factual information that serves a business purpose.*

The key words in this definition deserve emphasis. As an *orderly* communication, a report is prepared carefully. Thus, care in preparation distinguishes reports from casual exchanges of information. The *objective* quality of a report is its unbiased approach. Reports seek truth. They avoid human biases. The word *communication* is broad in meaning. It covers all ways of transmitting meaning—speaking, writing,

- • A business report is an orderly and objective communication of factual information that serves a business purpose.

- • The key words are *orderly, objective, communication, factual information,* and *serves a business purpose.*

---

[1] The following review of report writing is condensed from Raymond V. Lesikar and John D. Pettit, Jr., *Report Writing for Business,* 9th ed. (Burr Ridge, Ill.: Richard D. Irwin, 1995).

Report writing requires hard work and clear thinking in every stage of the process. To determine the problem and to gather facts, you will need to consult many sources of information.

drawing. The basic ingredient of reports is *factual information.* Factual information is based on events, records, data, and the like. Not all reports are business reports. Research scientists, medical doctors, ministers, students, and many others write them. To be classified as a business report, a report must *serve a business purpose.*

This definition is specific enough to be meaningful, yet broad enough to take into account the variations in reports. For example, some reports (information reports) do nothing more than present facts. Others (analytical reports) go a step further by including interpretations, sometimes accompanied by conclusions and recommendations. There are reports that are highly formal both in writing style and in physical appearance. And there are reports that show a high degree of informality. Our definition permits all of these variations.

DETERMINING THE REPORT PURPOSE

- Work on a report begins with a business need (problem).

Your work on a report logically begins with a need, which we refer to generally as the *problem* in the following discussion. Someone or some group (usually your superiors) needs information for a business purpose. Perhaps the need is for information only; perhaps it is for information and analysis; or perhaps it is for information, analysis, and recommendations. Whatever the case, someone with a need (problem) will authorize you to do the work. Usually the work will be authorized orally. But it could be authorized in a letter or a memorandum.

- Your first task is to get the problem clearly in mind.

After you have been assigned a report problem, your first task should be to get your problem clearly in mind. Elementary and basic as this task may appear, all too often it is done haphazardly. And all too often a report fails to reach its goal because of such haphazardness.

The Preliminary Investigation

- To do this, you should begin by gathering all the information you need to understand the problem.

Getting your problem clearly in mind is largely a matter of gathering all the information needed to understand it and then applying your best logic to it. Gathering the right information involves many things, depending on the problem. It may mean gathering material from company files, talking over the problem with experts, searching through printed sources, and discussing the problem with those who authorized the report. In general, you should continue this preliminary investigation until you have the information you need to understand your problem.

Need for a Clear Statement of the Problem

After you understand your problem, your next step is to state it clearly. Writing the problem statement is good practice for several reasons. A written statement is preserved permanently. Thus, you may refer to it time and again. In addition, a written statement can be reviewed, approved, and evaluated by people whose assistance may be valuable. Most important of all, putting the problem in writing forces you to think it through.

- Then you should express the problem clearly, preferably in writing.

The problem statement normally takes one of three forms: infinitive phrase, question, or declarative statement. To illustrate each, we will use the problem of determining why sales at a certain store have declined:

- The problem statement may be (1) an infinitive phrase, (2) a question, or (3) a declarative statement.

1. *Infinitive phrase:* "To determine the causes of decreasing sales at Store X."

2. *Question:* "What are the causes of decreasing sales at Store X?"

3. *Declarative statement:* "Store X sales are decreasing, and management wants to know why."

DETERMINING THE FACTORS

After stating the problem, you determine what needs to be done to solve it. Specifically, you look for the factors of the problem. That is, you determine what subject areas you must look into to solve the problem.

- Next, you should determine the factors of the problem.

Problem factors may be of three types. First, they may be subtopics of the overall topic about which the report is concerned. Second, they may be hypotheses that must be tested. Third, in problems that involve comparisons, they may be the bases on which the comparisons are made.

- The factors may be subtopics of the overall topic, hypotheses, or bases for comparison.

Use of Subtopics in Information Reports

If the problem concerns a need for information, your mental effort should produce the main areas about which information is needed. Illustrating this type of situation is the problem of preparing a report that reviews Company X's activities during the past quarter. Clearly, this is an informational report problem—that is, it requires no analysis, no conclusion, no recommendation. It only requires that information be presented. The mental effort in this case is concerned simply with determining which subdivisions of the overall topic should be covered. After thoroughly evaluating the possibilities, you might come up with something like this analysis:

- Subtopics of the overall topic are the factors in information reports.

Problem statement: To review operations of Company X from January 1 through March 31.

Subtopics
1. Production.
2. Sales and promotion.
3. Financial status.
4. Plant and equipment.
5. Product development.
6. Personnel.

Hypotheses for Problems Requiring Solution

Some problems concern why something bad is happening and perhaps how to correct it. In analyzing problems of this kind, you should seek explanations or solutions. Such explanations or solutions are termed *hypotheses*. Once formulated, hypotheses are tested, and their applicability to the problem is either proved or disproved.

- Hypotheses (possible explanations of the problem) may be the factors in problems requiring solution.

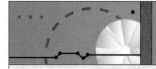

TECHNOLOGY IN BRIEF

Styles or Tags: A Useful Formatting Feature

Anytime you find a need to repeatedly use the same formatting codes, styles or tags is a feature you will want to use. Although the feature is called styles in word processing and tags in desktop publishing, the two do essentially the same thing. When writing reports is a regular part of your job, you can create styles or tags to help you format titles, heading levels, body text, bibliography items, and any other parts that you use repeatedly.

In addition, you can create a library of styles to use across all your documents. Not only will using these styles ensure consistency within your report, but also your reports will be consistent over time. And you will save yourself the time and effort of having to look up the formatting you used the last time you wrote a similar report. Furthermore, if you decide to change the look of your report, you can simply edit the style instead of having to search through your entire document for all the individual formatting codes. Or you could simply delete the current style and apply a new one.

Styles and tags are easy both to create and to use. Once you have set them up, you reap rewards every time you use them.

To illustrate, assume that you have the problem of determining why sales at a certain store have declined. In preparing this problem for investigation, you would think of the possible explanations (hypotheses) for the decline. Your task would be one of studying, weighing, and selecting, and you would come up with such explanations as these:

• For example, these hypotheses could be suggested to explain a store's loss in sales.

Problem statement: Why have sales declined at the Milltown store?

Hypotheses:
1. Activities of the competition have caused the decline.
2. Changes in the economy of the area have caused the decline.
3. Merchandising deficiencies have caused the decline.
4. Changes in the environment (population shifts, political actions, etc.) have caused the decline.

In the investigation that follows, you would test these hypotheses. You might find that one, two, or all apply. Or you might find that none is valid. If so, you would have to advance additional hypotheses for further evaluation.

Bases of Comparison in Evaluation Studies

• For evaluation problems, the bases for evaluating are the factors.

When the problem concerns evaluating something, either singularly or in comparison with other things, you should look for the bases for the evaluation. That is, you should determine what characteristics you will evaluate. In some cases, the procedure may concern more than naming the characteristics. It may also include the criteria to be used in evaluating them.

• This illustration shows the bases for comparing factory locations.

Illustrating this technique is the problem of a company that seeks to determine which of three cities would be best for a new factory. Such a problem obviously involves a comparison of the cities. The bases for comparison are the factors that determine success for the type of factory involved. After careful mental search for these factors, you might come up with a plan such as this:

Problem statement: To determine whether Y Company's new factory should be built in City A, City B, or City C.

Comparison bases:
1. Availability of labor.
2. Abundance of raw material.

3. Tax structure.
4. Transportation facilities.
5. Nearness to markets.
6. Power supply.
7. Community attitude.

Need for Subbreakdown

Each of the factors selected for investigation may have factors of its own. In the last illustration, for example, the comparison of transportation in the three cities may well be covered by such subdivisions as water, rail, truck, and air. Labor may be compared by using such categories as skilled labor and unskilled labor. Breakdowns of this kind may go still further. Skilled labor may be broken down by specific skills: machinists, plumbers, pipefitters, welders, and such. The subdivisions could go on and on. Make them as long as they are helpful.

* The factors sometimes have factors of their own. That is, they may also be broken down.

GATHERING THE INFORMATION NEEDED

For most business problems, you will need to conduct a personal investigation. A production problem, for example, might require gathering and reviewing the company's production records. A sales problem might require collecting information through discussions with customers and sales personnel. A computer problem might require talking to both end users and programmers. A purchasing problem might require getting sales literature, finding prices, compiling performance statistics, and so on. Such a personal investigation usually requires knowledge of your field of work, which is probably why you were assigned the problem.

* The next step is to conduct the research needed. A personal investigation is usually appropriate.

Some business problems require a more formal type of research, such as an experiment or a survey. The experiment is the basic technique of the sciences. Business uses experiments primarily in the laboratory, although experiments have some nonlaboratory applications in marketing. Surveys are more likely to be used in business, especially in marketing problems. If you are called on to use experiments or surveys, it will probably be because your training has prepared you to use them. If you should need these techniques in this course, you will find them summarized in Chapter 19.

* Experiments or surveys are sometimes needed.

In some cases, you may use library research to find the information you need. Perhaps you have a good, working knowledge of the techniques of library research. If you do not, you will find these techniques also summarized in Chapter 19. To present facts from library sources in reports, you will need to use still other techniques—constructing a bibliography, citing references, quoting, paraphrasing, etc. These techniques are covered in Appendix E.

* Sometimes library research is used.

With the computer, you can search for electronically stored information. By using the Internet, a worldwide collection of networks, you can connect to information sources throughout the world. For example, you can work with others at different locations, you can access databases, you can use larger computers to help in your research, or you can browse any number of library catalogs. As noted in Chapter 16, the Internet is a vital source for information gathering in business reports.

* Internet gives you access to many information sources.

In any event, your task is to apply whatever research techniques are required to get the information you need for your problem. When you have gathered that information, you are ready for the next step in report preparation.

* Apply the research techniques needed for the problem

INTERPRETING THE FINDINGS

With your research done, you are ready to prepare your findings for presentation. If your goal is merely to present information, you need only organize by subtopics of the subject. If you must analyze the information and apply it to a problem, you must do

* Next, apply the information collected to the problem. Interpret it.

Interpreting facts requires playing the role of a judge. To get to the truth, you must rise above the ordinary person and think without bias, prejudice, and emotion. You should consider all sides of a problem in your search for the truth.

* Interpreting is mental. You can profit from the following advice.

much more. You must interpret the information as it affects the problem. Applying and interpreting your findings is obviously a mental process. Thus, we can give you only limited advice on how to do it. But even though this advice is limited, you can profit by following it.

Advice for Avoiding Human Error

* Avoid human error by remembering these fundamentals:

The first advice is to avoid certain human tendencies that lead to error in interpretation. Foremost among these are the following:

* 1. Report the facts as they are.

1. Report the facts as they are. Do nothing to make them more or less exciting. Adding color to interpretations to make the report more interesting amounts to bias.

* 2. Do not think that conclusions are always necessary.

2. Do not think that conclusions are always necessary. When the facts do not support a conclusion, you should conclude that there is no conclusion. All too often report writers think that if they do not conclude, they have failed in their investigation.

* 3. Do not interpret a lack of evidence as proof to the contrary.

3. Do not interpret a lack of evidence as proof to the contrary. The fact that you cannot prove something is true does not mean that it is false.

* 4. Do not compare noncomparable data.

4. Do not compare noncomparable data. When you look for relationships between sets of data, make sure they have similarities—that you do not have apples and oranges.

* 5. Do not draw illogical cause-effect conclusions.

5. Do not draw illogical cause-effect conclusions. Just because two sets of data appear to affect each other does not mean they actually do. Use your good logic to determine whether a cause-effect relationship is likely.

* 6. Beware of unreliable and unrepresentative data.

6. Beware of unreliable and unrepresentative data. Much of the information to be found in secondary sources is incorrect to some extent. The causes are many: collection error, biased research, recording mistakes. Beware especially of data collected by groups that advocate a position (political organizations, groups supporting social issues, and other special interest groups). Make sure the sources you uncover are reliable. And remember that the interpretations you make are no better than the data you interpret.

* 7. Do not oversimplify.

7. Do not oversimplify. Most business problems are complex, and all too often we neglect some important parts of them.

You're right. This report does make you look like a fool.
Vietor's Funny Business

Appropriate Attitudes and Practices

In addition to being alert to the most likely causes of error, you can improve your interpretation of findings by adopting the following attitudes and practices:

1. Maintain a judicial attitude. Play the role of a judge as you interpret. Look at all sides of every issue without emotion or prejudice. Your primary objective is to uncover truth.

2. Consult with others. It is rare indeed when one mind is better than two or more. Thus, you can profit by talking over your interpretations with others.

3. Test your interpretations. Unfortunately, the means of testing are subjective and involve the thinking process. Even so, testing is helpful and can help you avoid major error. Two tests are available to you.

First is the test of experience. In applying this test, you use the underlying theme in all scientific methods—reason. You ponder each interpretation you make, asking yourself, "Does this appear reasonable in light of all I know or have experienced?"

Second is the negative test, which is an application of the critical viewpoint. You begin by making the interpretation that is directly opposite your initial one. Next, you examine the opposite interpretation carefully in light of all available evidence, perhaps even building a case for it. Then you compare the two interpretations and retain the one that is more strongly supported.

Statistical Tools in Interpretation

In most cases, the information you gather is quantitative—that is, expressed in numbers. Such data in their raw form usually are voluminous, consisting of tens, hundreds, even thousands of figures. To use these figures intelligently, you must first find ways of simplifying them so that your reader can grasp their general meaning. Statistical techniques provide many methods for analyzing data. By knowing them, you can improve your ability to interpret. Although a thorough review of statistical techniques is beyond the scope of this book, you should know the more commonly used methods described in the following paragraphs.

Possibly of greatest use to you in writing reports are *descriptive statistics*—measures of central tendency, dispersion, ratios and probability. Measures of central tendency—the mean, median, and mode—will help you find a common value of a series that appropriately describes a whole. The measures of dispersion—ranges, variances, and standard deviations—should help you describe the spread of a series. Ratios (which express one quantity as a multiple of another) and probabilities (which determine how

- Adopt the following attitudes and practices:
- 1. Maintain a judicial attitude.
- 2. Consult with others.
- 3. Test your interpretations.
- Use the test of your experience—reason.
- Use the negative test—question your interpretations.
- Statistics permit one to examine a set of facts.
- Descriptive statistics should help the most.

many times something will likely occur out of the total number of possibilities) can also help you convey common meaning in data analysis. Inferential and other statistical approaches are also useful but go beyond these basic elements. You will find descriptions of these and other useful techniques in any standard statistics textbook.

A word of caution, however: Your job as an analyst is to help your reader interpret the information. Sometimes unexplained statistical calculations—even if elementary to you—may confuse the reader. Thus, you must explain your statistical techniques explicitly. You must remember that statistics are a help to interpretation, not a replacement for it. Whatever you do to reduce the volume of data deserves careful explanation so that the reader will receive the proper meaning.

• Do not allow statistics to confuse the reader; they should help interpret.

••

ORGANIZING THE REPORT INFORMATION

When you have finished interpreting your information, you know the message of your report. Now you are ready to organize this message for presentation. Organizing the report message, of course, is the procedure of constructing the outline. As you know, an outline is the plan for the writing task that follows. It is to you, the writer, what the blueprint is to the construction engineer or what the pattern is to the dressmaker. Constructing an outline forces you to think before you write. When you do this, your writing is likely to benefit.

• After you know what your findings mean, you are ready to construct

Although your plan may be written or mental, using a written plan would be advisable for all but the shortest problems. In a longer report, the outline forms the basis for the table of contents. Also, in most long reports, and even in some short ones, the outline topics may be used as guides to the reader by placing them within the text as headings to the material they cover.

• Outlines should usually be written. They serve as tables of contents and captions.

In constructing your outline, you probably will use either the conventional or the decimal symbol system to mark the levels. The conventional system uses Roman numerals to show the major headings and letters of the alphabet and Arabic numbers to show the lesser headings, as illustrated here:

Conventional System

• This conventional symbol system is used in marking the levels of an outline.

I. First-level heading
   A. Second level, first part
   B. Second level, second part
      1. Third level, first part
      2. Third level, second part
         a. Fourth level
            (1) Fifth level
               (a) Sixth level
II. First-level heading
   A. Second level, first part
   B. Second level, second part
   Etc.

The decimal system uses whole numbers to show the major sections. Whole numbers followed by decimals and additional digits show subsections. That is, the digits to the right of the decimal show each successive step in the outline. Illustration best explains this system:

Decimal System

• This decimal system is also used.

1.0 First-level heading
   1.1 Second level, first part
   1.2 Second level, second part

        1.2.1 Third level, first part
        1.2.2 Third level, second part
                1.2.2.1 Fourth level
2.0 First-level heading
        2.1 Second level, first part
        2.2 Second level, second part
        Etc.

Whatever system you use, when you begin producing the final report you also will show differences in the levels of headings by placement and form (font, size, or style). The placement and form options available to you are reviewed in Appendix B.

The Nature and Extent of Outlining

In general, you should build the outline around the objective of the report and the information you have gathered to meet that objective. With the objective and your information in mind, you build the structure of the report mentally. In this process, you shift facts and ideas about until the most workable order becomes clear. That order is the one that presents the findings in the clearest and most meaningful way.

- The outline is designed to meet the objective of the report.

How much work you will have to do at this stage varies by problem. In some cases, you may have little to do, for you may have determined the order of the report in preceding steps. For example, the problem factors that you determined early in the investigation may also be the main heads of your outline. Or perhaps you worked out an order for presenting your research findings when you analyzed and interpreted them. In all likelihood, when you reach the stage of consciously constructing the outline, you will find that you have already done some of the work. Even so, there will probably be much to do. In doing it, you would be wise to use the general procedure described in the following paragraphs.

- When you reach the outlining stage, you have probably done some of the work.

Introductory and Concluding Parts

Outlining is concerned mainly with the part of the report commonly called the *body*. The body is the part of the report that presents the information gathered, with analyses and interpretations where needed. It is usually preceded by an introduction, which is common in all but the shortest reports. And it is usually followed by an ending section, which may be a summary, a conclusion, a recommendation, or some combination of the three. The introduction and the ending section are parts of the outline, of course, but the following discussion does not concern them. The structure and content of these parts are discussed where appropriate in following chapters.

- The following discussion of outlining deals with the body of the report. Assume that an introduction and a conclusion will be added.

Organization by Division

The outlining procedure described in the following pages is based on the idea that outlining is a process of dividing. The subject you are dividing is all the information (facts) you have gathered and interpreted. Thus, you begin the task of organizing by looking over that information for some logical way of dividing it into comparable parts. When you find a way, you divide it. This process gives you the major outline parts indicated in Figure 10–1 by the Roman numeral captions (I, II, III, and so on).

- You may view outlining as a process of division. First, you divide the whole into parts.

In short reports, one division may be enough. Long reports, however, may require that each part in the first division be divided. The parts in the second division are identified by capital letter headings (A, B, C). You may have to divide a third time (for the 1, 2, 3 outline parts). In fact, you may continue to subdivide as long as it is practical to do so. Each division makes a step in the outline.

- Then you divide the parts into subparts. You may subdivide further.

FIGURE 10–1   Procedure for Constructing an Outline by Process of Division

I Introduction	I A B C	I A B C

Step 1

Step 2

Step 3

etc.

Step 1

Divide the whole into comparable parts. This gives the Roman numbered parts of the outline. Usually an introduction begins the outline. Some combination of summary, conclusion, recommendation ends it.

Step 2

Divide each Roman section. This gives the A, B, C headings.

Step 3

Then divide each A, B, C heading. This gives the 1, 2, 3 headings.

etc.

Continue dividing as long as it is practical to do so.

Source: Raymond V. Lesikar and John D. Pettit, Jr., *Report Writing for Business,* 9th ed. (Burr Ridge, Ill.: Richard D. Irwin, Inc., 1995).

Division by Conventional Relationships

- Time, place, quantity, and factor are the bases for the process of division.

- When the information has a time basis, division by time is possible.

In dividing your information into subparts, you have to find a way of dividing that will produce approximately equal parts. Time, place, quantity, and factor are the general bases for these divisions.

Whenever the information you have to present has some time aspect, consider organizing it by *time.* In such an organization, the divisions are periods of time. These time periods usually follow a sequence. Although a past-to-present or present-to-past sequence is the rule, variations are possible. The periods you select need not be equal in duration, but they should be about equal in importance.

A report on the progress of a research committee illustrates this possibility. The period covered by this report might be broken down into the following comparable subperiods:

The period of orientation, May–July.
Planning the project, August.
Implementation of the research plan, September–November.

The happenings within each period might next be arranged in order of occurrence. Close inspection might reveal additional division possibilities.

If the information you have collected has some relation to geographic location, you may use a *place* division. Ideally, this division would be such that the areas are nearly equal in importance.

- When the information is related to geographic location, a place division is possible.

A report on the U.S. sales program of a national manufacturer illustrates a division by place. The information in this problem might be broken down by these major geographic areas:

New England.
Atlantic Seaboard.
South.
Southwest.
Midwest.
Rocky Mountains.
Pacific Coast.

Another illustration of organization by place is a report on the productivity of a company with a number of manufacturing plants. A major division of the report might be devoted to each of the plants. The information for each plant might be broken down further, this time by sections, departments, divisions, or the like.

Quantity divisions are possible for information that has quantitative values. To illustrate, an analysis of the buying habits of potential customers could be divided by such income groups as the following:

- Division based on quantity is possible when the information has a number base.

Under $10,000.
$10,000 to under $15,000.
$15,000 to under $20,000.
$20,000 to under $25,000.
$25,000 to under $30,000.
$30,000 and over.

Another example of division on a quantitative basis is a report of a survey of men's preferences for shoes, in which an organization by age groups might be used to show variations in preference by ages. Perhaps the following division would be appropriate:

Youths, under 18.
Young adults, 18–30.
Adults, 31–50.
Senior adults, 51–70.
Elder adults, over 70.

Factor breakdowns are less easily seen than the preceding three possibilities. Problems often have few or no time, place, or quantity aspects. Instead, they require that certain information areas be investigated. Such areas may consist of questions that must be answered in solving a problem, or of subjects that must be investigated and applied to the problem.

- Factors (areas to be investigated) are a fourth basis for dividing information.

An example of a division by factors is a report that seeks to determine which of three cities is the best as the location of a new office for property management. In arriving at this decision, one would need to compare the three cities based on the factors affecting the office location. Thus, the following organization of this problem would be a possibility:

Location accessibility.
Rent.
Parking.
Convenience to current customers.
Facilities.

Another illustration of organization by factors is a report advising a manufacturer whether to begin production of a new product. The solution of this problem will be reached by careful consideration of the factors involved. Among the more likely factors are these:

Production feasibility.
Financial considerations.
Strength of competition.
Consumer demand.
Marketing considerations.

Combination and Multiple Division Possibilities

- Combinations of time, place, quantity, and factor are sometimes logical.

Not all division possibilities are clearly time, place, quantity, or factor. In some instances, combinations of these bases of division are possible. In a report on the progress of a sales organization, for example, the information collected could be arranged by a combination of quantity and place:

Areas of high sales activity.
Areas of moderate sales activity.
Areas of low sales activity.

Although less logical, the following combination of time and quantity is also a possibility:

Periods of low sales.
Periods of moderate sales.
Periods of high sales.

- Multiple organization possibilities can occur.

Some problems can be organized in more than one way. For example, take the problem of determining the best of three towns for locating a new manufacturing plant. It could be organized by towns or by the bases of comparison. Organized by towns, the bases of comparison would probably be the second-level headings:

- This plant-location problem is organized by place.

   II. Town A
      A. Availability of workers.
      B. Transportation facilities.
      C. Public support and cooperation.
      D. Availability of raw materials.
      E. Taxation.
      F. Sources of power.
  III. Town B
      A. Availability of workers.
      B. And so on.
  IV. Town C
      A. Availability of workers.
      B. And so on.

Organized by bases of comparison, towns would probably be the second-level headings:

- Here, it is organized by factors (the bases of comparison).

   II. Availability of workers
      A. Town A.
      B. Town B.
      C. Town C.

III. Transportation facilities
   A. Town A.
   B. Town B.
   C. Town C.
IV. Public support and cooperation
   A. Town A.
   B. Town B.
   C. Town C.

At first glance, both plans appear logical. Close inspection, however, shows that organization by towns separates information that has to be compared. For example, three different parts of the report must be examined to find out which town has the best worker availability. In the second outline, the information that has to be compared is close together.

Nevertheless, these two plans show that some problems can be organized in more than one way. In such cases, you must compare the possibilities carefully to find the one that best presents the report information.

- The second plan is better because it makes comparison easy.

Wording of the Outline

The outline in its finished form is the table of contents. Its parts serve as headings to the sections of the report (which is why we refer to these parts as *headings* in the following discussion). Since the outline is an important part of the report, you should construct its final wording carefully. In this regard, you should consider the conventional principles of construction reviewed in the following pages.

- When the outline will appear in the report, take care in its wording.

Topic or Talking Headings.   In selecting the wording for outline headings, you have a choice of two general forms—topic headings and talking headings. *Topic headings* are short constructions, frequently consisting of one or two words. They merely identify the topic of discussion. Here is a segment of a topic-heading outline:

- You may use topic or talking headings. Topic headings give only the subject of discussion.

II. Present armor unit
   A. Description and output.
   B. Cost.
   C. Deficiencies.
III. Replacement effects
   A. Space.
   B. Boiler setting.
   C. Additional accessories.
   D. Fuel.

Like topic headings, *talking headings* (or *popular headings,* as they are sometimes called) identify the subject matter covered. But they go a step further. They also indicate what is said about the subject. In other words, talking headings summarize the material they cover, as in this illustration:

- Talking headings identify the subject and tell what is said about it.

II. Operation analyses of armor unit
   A. Recent lag in overall output.
   B. Increase in cost of operation.
   C. Inability to deliver necessary steam.
III. Consideration of replacement effects
   A. Greater space requirements.
   B. Need for higher boiler setting.
   C. Efficiency possibilities of accessories.
   D. Practicability of firing two fuels.

The following report outline is made up of headings that talk:

I. Orientation to the problem
  A. Authorization by board action
  B. Problem of locating a woolen mill
  C. Use of miscellaneous government data
  D. Factors as bases of problem solution
II. Community attitudes toward the woolen industry
  A. Favorable reaction of all towns to new mill
  B. Mixed attitudes of all towns toward labor policy
III. Labor supply and prevailing wage rates
  A. Lead of San Marcos in unskilled labor
  B. Concentration of skilled workers in San Marcos
  C. Generally confused pattern of wage rates
IV. Nearness to the raw wool supply
  A. Location of Ballinger, Coleman, and San Marcos in the wool area
  B. Relatively low production near Big Spring and Littlefield
V. Availability of utilities
  A. Inadequate water supply for all towns but San Marcos
  B. Unlimited supply of natural gas for all towns
  C. Electric rate advantage of San Marcos and Coleman
  D. General adequacy of all towns for waste disposal
VI. Adequacy of existing transportation systems
  A. Surface transportation advantages of San Marcos and Ballinger
  B. General equality of airway connections
VII. A final weighting of the factors
  A. Selection of San Marcos as first choice
  B. Recommendation of Ballinger as second choice
  C. Lack of advantages in Big Spring, Coleman, and Littlefield

This report outline is made up of topic headings:

I. Introduction
  A. Authorization
  B. Purpose
  C. Sources
  D. Preview
II. Community attitudes
  A. Plant location
  B. Labor policy
III. Factors of labor
  A. Unskilled workers
  B. Skilled workers
  C. Wage rates
IV. Raw wool supply
  A. Adequate areas
  B. Inadequate areas
V. Utilities
  A. Water
  B. Natural gas
  C. Electricity
  D. Waste disposal
VI. Transportation
  A. Surface
  B. Air

VII. Conclusions
    A. First choice
    B. Alternative choice
    C. Other possibilities

Parallelism of Construction.   As a general rule, you should write headings at each level of the outline in the same grammatical form. In other words, equal-level headings should be parallel in structure. For example, if the heading for Roman numeral I is a noun phrase, all other Roman numeral headings should be noun phrases. If the heading for A under I is a sentence, the A, B, C headings throughout the outline should be sentences. However, a few authorities permit varying the form from one part to another (example: sentences for A, B, and C under II and noun phrases for A, B, and C under III).

> • Headings making up a level of division should be parallel grammatically.

The following segment of an outline illustrates violations of parallelism:

A. Machine output is lagging (sentence).
B. Increase in cost of operations (noun phrase)
C. Unable to deliver necessary steam (decapitated sentence)

You may correct this violation in any of three ways—by making the headings all sentences, all noun phrases, or all decapitated sentences. If you desire all noun phrases, you could construct such headings as these:

A. Lag in machine output
B. Increase in cost of operations
C. Inability to deliver necessary steam

Or you could make all the headings sentences, like this:

A. Machine output is lagging.
B. Cost of operations is increasing.
C. Boiler cannot deliver necessary steam.

Variety of Expression.   In the report outline, as in all other forms of writing, you should use a variety of expressions. You should not overwork words, for repeating words too frequently makes for monotonous writing; and monotonous writing is not pleasing to the reader. The following outline excerpt illustrates this point:

> • Repeating words in headings can be monotonous.

A. Chemical production in Texas
B. Chemical production in California
C. Chemical production in Louisiana

As a rule, if you make the headings talk well, there is little chance of monotonous repetition. Since your successive sections would probably not be presenting similar or identical information, headings really descriptive of the material they cover would not be likely to use the same words. The headings in the preceding example can be improved simply by making them talk:

> • Talking headings are not likely to be monotonous.

A. Texas leads in chemical production.
B. California holds runner-up position.
C. Rapidly gaining Louisiana ranks third.

· ·
WRITING THE REPORT

After you have collected and organized your information, you are ready to begin writing. Much of what you should do in writing the report was covered in the review of clear writing techniques in Chapters 2 and 3. All of these techniques apply to report writing, and you would do well to keep them in mind as you write. In addition, you

> • In writing the report, follow the instructions in Chapters 2 and 3 as well as the following.

should be aware of some general characteristics of good report writing. These are objectivity, consistency of time viewpoint, transition, and interest.

Requirement of Objectivity

• Good report writing is objective.

Good report writing presents fact and logical interpretation of fact. It avoids presenting the writer's opinions, biases, and attitudes. In other words, it is objective.

• Keep out all bias. Seek truth.

You can make your report writing objective by putting aside your prejudices and biases, by approaching the problem with an open mind and looking at all sides of every issue, and by fairly reviewing and interpreting the information you have uncovered. Your role should be much like that of a fair-minded judge presiding over a court of law. You will leave no stone unturned in your search for truth.

• Objective writing is believable.

Objectivity as a Basis for Believability. An objective report has an ingredient that is essential to good report writing—believability. Biased writing in artfully deceptive language may at first glance be believable. But if bias is evident at any place in a report, the reader will be suspicious of the entire report. Painstaking objectivity is, therefore, the only sure way to make report writing believable.

• Historically, objective writing has meant writing impersonally (no *I*'s, *we*'s, *you*'s).

Objectivity and the Question of Impersonal versus Personal Writing. Recognizing the need for objectivity, the early report writers worked to develop an objective style of writing. Since the source of bias in reports was people, they reasoned objectivity was best attained by emphasizing facts rather than the people involved in writing and reading reports. So they tried to take the human beings out of their reports. The result was impersonal writing, that is, writing in the third person—without *I*'s, *we*'s, or *you*'s.

• Recently, some writers have argued that personal writing is more interesting than impersonal writing and just as objective.

In recent years, some writers have questioned impersonal report writing. They argue that personal writing is more forceful and direct than impersonal writing. They point out that writing is more conversational and, therefore, more interesting if it brings both the reader and the writer into the picture. They contend that objectivity is an attitude—not a matter of person—and that a report written in personal style can be just as objective as a report written in impersonal style. Frequently, these writers argue that impersonal writing leads to an overuse of the passive voice and a dull writing style. This last argument, however, lacks substance. The style of impersonal writing can and should be interesting. Any dullness that impersonal writing may have is the fault of the writer. As proof, one has only to look at the lively style of writers for newspapers, newsmagazines, and journals. Most of this writing is impersonal—but it is usually not dull.

• There is merit to both sides. You would be wise to do what is expected of you.

As in most controversies, the arguments of both sides have merit. In some situations, personal writing is better. In other situations, impersonal writing is better. And in still other situations, either type of writing is good.

• Good advice is to use personal style for routine reports and impersonal style for more formal reports.

Your decision should be based on the facts of each report situation. First, you should consider the expectations of those for whom you are preparing the report. More than likely, you will find a preference for impersonal writing, for businesspeople have been slow to break tradition. Then you should consider the formality of the situation. You should use personal writing for informal situations and impersonal writing for formal situations.

Perhaps the distinction between impersonal and personal writing is best made by illustration.

PERSONAL	IMPERSONAL
Having studied the advantages and disadvantages of using coupons, I conclude that your company should not adopt this practice. If you use the coupons, you would have to pay out money for them. You would also have to hire additional employees to take care of the increase in sales volume.	A study of the advantages and disadvantages of using coupons supports the conclusion that the Mills Company should not adopt this practice. The coupons themselves would cost extra money. Also, use of coupons would require additional personnel to take care of the increase in sales volume.

The story is told of the sea captain who once found his first mate drunk on duty. A man of the old school, the captain dutifully recorded the incident in his daily report to the ship's owners. He wrote: "Today First Mate Carlos E. Sperry was drunk on duty."

The first mate, unhappy about the incident, was determined to get revenge at the first opportunity. Some days later, his chance came. The captain was so ill that he could not leave his quarters, and First Mate Sperry was now in charge. At the end of the day it was Sperry's duty to write the daily report. This is what he wrote: "Today Captain Eli A. Dunn was sober."

The words were literally true, of course. But what a second meaning they carried!

Consistency in Time Viewpoint

Presenting information in the right place in time is a major problem in keeping order in a report. Not doing so confuses the reader and creates barriers to communication. Thus, it is important that you maintain a proper time viewpoint.

- Keep a consistent time viewpoint throughout the report.

You have two choices of time viewpoint—past and present. Although some authorities favor one or the other, either viewpoint can produce a good report. The important thing is to be consistent—to select one time viewpoint and stay with it. In other words, you should view all similar information in the report from the same position in time.

- There are two time viewpoints—past and present. Select one, and do not change.

If you adopt the past time viewpoint, you treat the research, the findings, and the writing of the report as past. Thus, you would report the results of a recent survey in past tense: "Twenty-two percent of the managers *favored* a change." You would write a reference to another part of the report this way: "In Part III, this conclusion *was reached*." Your use of the past time viewpoint would have no effect on references to future happenings. It would be proper to write a sentence like this: "If the current trend continues, 30 percent *will favor* a change by 2000." Prevailing concepts and proven conclusions are also exceptions. You would present them in present tense. For examples, take the sentences: "Solar energy *is* a major potential source of energy" and "The findings show conclusively that managers are not adequately trained."

- The past time viewpoint views the research and the findings as past, and prevailing concepts and proven conclusions as present.

Writing in the present time viewpoint presents as current all information that can logically be assumed to be current at the time of writing. All other information is presented in its proper place in the past or future. Thus, you would report the results of a recent survey in these words: "Twenty-two percent of the managers *favor* a change." You would refer to another part of the text like this: "In Part III, this conclusion *is* reached." In referring to an old survey, you would write: "In 1994 only 12 percent *held* this opinion." And in making a future reference, you would write: "If this trend continues, 30 percent *will hold* this opinion by 2000."

- The present time viewpoint presents as current all information that can be assumed to be current at the time of writing.

Need for Transition

A well-written report reads as one continuous story. The parts connect smoothly. Much of this smoothness is the result of good, logical organization. But more than logical order is needed in long reports. As you will see in Chapter 12, a coherence plan may be needed in such reports. In all reports, however, lesser transitional techniques are useful to connect information.

- You should use transitions to connect the parts of the report.

By *transition* we mean a "bridging across." Transitions are made by means of words or sentences that show the relationships of succeeding parts. They may appear at the beginning of a part as a way of relating this part to the preceding part. They may appear at the end of a part as a forward look. Or they may appear within a part as words or phrases that help move the flow of information.

- *Transition* means a "bridging across."

Whether you use transitional words or a transitional sentence in a particular place depends on need. If there is need to relate parts, you should use a transition. Because good, logical organization frequently makes clear the relationships of the parts in a short report, such reports may need only a few transitional words or sentences. Longer and more involved reports, on the other hand, usually require more.

Before we comment more specifically on transitions, we should make one point clear. You should not use transitions mechanically. You should use them only when they are needed—when leaving them out would produce abruptness. Transitions should not appear to be stuck in. They should blend naturally with the surrounding writing. For example, avoid transitions of this mechanical form: "The last section discussed Topic X. In the next section, Y will be analyzed."

Sentence Transitions.   Throughout the report you can improve the connecting network of thought by the wise use of sentence transitions. You can use them especially to connect parts of the report. The following example shows how a sentence can explain the relationship between Sections A and B of a report. Note that the first words draw a conclusion for Section B. Then, with smooth tie-in, the next words introduce Section C and relate this part to the report plan. The words in brackets explain the pattern of the thought connections.

[Section B, concluded] . . . Thus, the data show only negligible differences in the cost for oil consumption [subject of Section B] for the three brands of cars.

[Section C] Even though the costs of gasoline [subject of Section A] and oil [subject of Section B] are the more consistent factors of operation expense, the picture is not complete until the costs of repairs and maintenance [subject of Section C] are considered.

In the following examples, succeeding parts are connected by sentences that make a forward-looking reference and thus set up the next subject. As a result, the shift of subject matter is smooth and logical.

These data show clearly that Edmond's machines are the most economical. Unquestionably, their operation by low-cost gas and their record for low-cost maintenance give them a decided edge over competing brands. *Before a definite conclusion about their merit is reached, however, one more vital comparison should be made.*

(The final sentence clearly introduces the subsequent discussion of an additional comparison.)

. . . *At first glance the data appear convincing, but a closer observation reveals a number of discrepancies.*

(Discussion of the discrepancies is logically set up by this sentence.)

Placing topic sentences at key points of emphasis is another way of using sentences to link the various parts of the report. Usually the topic sentence is best placed at the paragraph beginning. Note, in the following example, how topic sentences maintain the flow of thought by emphasizing key information.

Brand C accelerates faster than the other two brands, both on a level road and on a 9 percent grade. According to a test conducted by Consumption Research, Brand C reaches a speed of 60 miles per hour in 13.2 seconds. To reach the same speed, Brand A requires 13.6 seconds, and Brand B requires 14.4 seconds. On a 9 percent grade, Brand C reaches the 60-miles-per-hour speed in 29.4 seconds, and Brand A reaches it in 43.3 seconds. Brand B is unable to reach this speed. *Because it carries more weight on its rear wheels than the others, Brand C has the best traction of the three.* Traction, which means a minimum of sliding on wet or icy roads, is important to safe driving, particularly during the cold, wet winter months. As traction is directly related to the weight carried by the rear wheels, a comparison of these weights should give some measure of the safety of the three cars. According to data released by the Automobile Bureau of Standards, Brand C carries 47 percent of its weight on its rear wheels. Brands B and A carry 44 and 42 percent, respectively.

Choice Lines Gleaned from Accident Reports Submitted to Insurance Companies

- Coming home, I drove into the wrong house and collided with a tree I don't have.
- The other car collided with mine without giving warning of its intentions.
- I thought my window was down, but found it was up when I put my hand through it.
- I collided with a stationary truck coming the other way.
- A pedestrian hit me and went under my car.
- The guy was all over the road. I had to swerve a number of times before I hit him.
- I pulled away from the side of the road, glanced at my mother-in-law, and headed over the embankment.
- I was having rear-end trouble when my universal joint gave way, causing me to have this accident.
- My car was legally parked as it backed in to the other car.
- I told police that I was not injured, but on removing my hat, I found that I had a fractured skull.
- I was sure the old fellow would never make it to the other side of the road when I struck him.
- The pedestrian had no idea which direction to run, so I ran over him.
- The indirect cause of this accident was a little guy in a small car with a big mouth.
- The telephone pole was approaching. I was attempting to swerve out of the way when it struck my front end.
- I saw the slow-moving, sad-faced old gentleman as he bounced off the hood of my car.

Transitional Words.   Although the major transition problems concern connection between the major parts of the report, transitions are needed between the lesser parts. If the writing is to flow smoothly, you will need to connect clause to clause, sentence to sentence, and paragraph to paragraph. Transitional words and phrases generally serve to make such connections.

- Transitional words show relationships between lesser parts.

Numerous transitional words are available. The following list shows such words and how you can use them. With a little imagination to supply the context, you can easily see how these words relate ideas. For better understanding, the words are grouped by the relationships they show between what comes before and what follows.

RELATIONSHIP	WORD EXAMPLES
Listing or enumeration of subjects	In addition First, second, and so on Besides Moreover
Contrast	On the contrary In spite of On the other hand In contrast However
Likeness	In a like manner Likewise Similarly
Cause-result	Thus Because of Therefore Consequently For this reason

- This partial list shows how words explain relationships.

RELATIONSHIP	WORD EXAMPLES
Explanation or elaboration	For example
	To illustrate
	For instance
	Also
	Too

Maintaining Interest

- Report writing should be interesting. Interesting writing is necessary for good communication.

Like any other form of writing, report writing should be interesting. Actually, interest is as important as the facts of the report, for communication is not likely to occur without interest. Readers cannot help missing parts of the message if their interest is not held—if their minds are allowed to stray. Interest in the subject is not enough to ensure communication. The writing must be interesting. This should be evident to you if you have ever tried to read dull writing in studying for an examination. How desperately you wanted to learn the subject, but how often your mind strayed!

- Interesting writing is the result of careful word choice, rhythm, concreteness—in fact, all the good writing techniques.

Perhaps writing interestingly is an art. But if so, it is an art in which you can develop ability by working at it. To develop this ability, you need to avoid the rubber-stamp jargon so often used in business and instead work to make your words build concrete pictures. You need to cultivate a feeling for the rhythmic flow of words and sentences. You need to remember that back of every fact and figure there is life—people doing things, machines operating, a commodity being marketed. A technique of good report writing is to bring that life to the surface by using concrete words and active-voice verbs as much as possible. You should also work to achieve interest without using more words than are necessary.

- But efforts to make writing interesting can be overdone. The writing style should never draw attention away from the information.

Here a word of caution should be injected. You can overdo efforts to make report writing interesting. Such is the case whenever your reader's attention is attracted to how something has been said rather than to what has been said. Effective report writing simply presents information in a clear, concise, and interesting manner. Perhaps the purpose and definition of report-writing style are best summarized in this way: Report-writing style is at its best when the readers are prompted to say "Here are some interesting facts" rather than "Here is some beautiful writing."

COLLABORATIVE REPORT WRITING

- Collaborative report preparation is common for good reasons.

In your business career, you are likely to participate in collaborative writing projects. That is, you will work on a report with others. Group involvement in report preparation is becoming increasingly significant for a number of reasons. For one, the specialized knowledge of different people can improve the quality of the work. For another, the combined talents of the members are likely to produce a document better than could be done by any one of the members. A third reason is that dividing the work reduces the time needed for the project.

Determination of Group Makeup

- Groups should have five or fewer members and include all pertinent specialization areas.

As a beginning step, the membership of the group should be determined. In this determination, the availability and competencies of the people in the work situation involved are likely to be the major considerations. As a minimum, the group will consist of two. The maximum will depend on the number actually needed to do the project. As a practical matter, however, a maximum of five is a good rule, for larger groups tend to lose efficiency. More important than size, however, is the need to include all major areas of specialization involved in the work to be done.

- Preferably, the group has a leader, but there are exceptions.

In most business situations the highest ranking administrator in the group serves as leader. In groups made up of equals, a leader usually is appointed or elected. When no leader is so designated, the group works together informally. In such cases, however, an informal leader usually emerges.

Some reports written in business are produced in collaboration with others. Although you will do some work individually, you can expect to plan, organize, and revise the report as a group.

Techniques of Participation

The group's work should be conducted much the way a meeting should be conducted. As described in Chapter 14, leaders and members of meetings have clear roles and duties. Leaders must plan the sessions and follow the plan. They must move the work along. They must control the discussion, limiting those who talk too much and encouraging input from those who are reluctant to participate. Group members should actively participate, taking care not to monopolize. They should be both cooperative and courteous in their work with the group.

* Leaders and participants have clear duties to make the procedure work.

Procedure of the Work

As a general rule, groups working together on report projects need a minimum of two meetings with a work period between meetings. But the number of meetings required will vary with the needs of the project. For a project in which data gathering and other preliminary work must be done, additional meetings may be necessary. On the other hand, if only the writing of the report is needed, two may be adequate.

* At least two meetings and a work period are needed.

Activities Involved

Whatever number of meetings are scheduled, the following activities typically occur, usually in the sequence shown. As you review them, it should be apparent that because of the differences in report projects, these activities vary in their implementation.

* The following activities normally occur, usually in this sequence.

Determine the purpose.   As in all report projects, the participants must determine just what the report must do. Thus, the group should follow the preliminary steps of problem determination discussed previously.

* First, determine the report purpose.

Derive the factors.   The group next determines what is needed to achieve the purpose. This step involves determining the factors of the problem, as described earlier in the chapter.

* Next, derive the factors involved.

Gather the information needed.   Before the group can begin work on the report document, it must get the information needed. This activity could involve conducting any

* If necessary, make a plan for gathering the information needed.

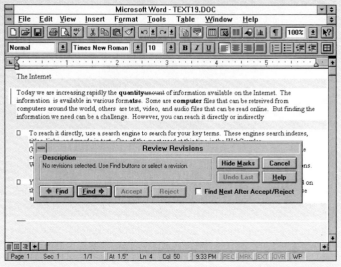
of the research designs mentioned earlier in the chapter. In some cases, group work begins after the information has been assembled, thus eliminating this step.

• The members interpret the information, applying it to the problem.

Interpret the information.   Determining the meaning of the information gathered is the next logical step for the group. In this step, the participants apply the findings to the problem, thereby selecting the information to be used in the report.

• They organize the information for presentation in the report.

Organize the material.   Just as in any other report-writing project, the group next organizes the material selected for presentation.

• They plan the writing of the report.

Plan the writing.   A next logical step is that of planning the makeup of the report. In this step the formality of the situation and the audience involved determine the decision. In addition, matters of writing such as tone, style, and formality are addressed.

• They assign themselves report parts to write.

Assign parts to be written.   After the prewriting work has been done, the group next turns its attention to the work of writing. The usual practice is to assign each person a part of the report.

• The members then write their parts.

Write parts assigned.   Following comes a period of individual work. Each participant writes his or her part.

• The group members collaboratively review the writing.

Revise collaboratively.   The group meets and reviews each person's contribution. This should be a give-and-take session with each person actively participating. It requires that every person gives keen attention to the work of each participant, making constructive suggestions wherever appropriate. It requires courteous but meaningful criticisms. It also requires that the participants be thick-skinned, keeping in mind that the goal is to construct the best possible document. In no case should the group merely give rubber-stamp approval to the work submitted. In cases of controversy, the majority views of the group should prevail.

• A selected member edits the final draft.

Edit the final draft.   After the group has done its work, one member usually is assigned the task of editing the final draft. This gives the document consistency. In addition, the editor serves as a final proofreader. Probably the editor should be the most competent writer in the group.

If all the work has been done with care and diligence, this final draft should be a report better than anyone in the group could have prepared alone.

··

SUMMARY ▶ by Chapter Objectives

1. Your work on a report begins with a problem (purpose, goal, objective).
   - Get the problem in mind by gathering all the information you need about it.
   - Then develop a problem statement from the information.
   - Phrase this statement as an infinitive, a question, or a declarative statement.

   (1) State a problem clearly in writing.

2. From the problem statement, determine the factors involved.
   - These may be subtopics in information reports.
   - They may be hypotheses (possible explanations) in problems requiring a solution.
   - They may be bases of comparison in problems requiring evaluations.

   (2) List the factors involved in a problem.

3. After you have gathered the information needed, interpret it as it applies to the problem.
   - Interpreting is mental and thus difficult to describe.
   - Heed this advice for avoiding human error:
     —Report the facts as they are.
     —Do not think that conclusions are always necessary.
     —Do not interpret a lack of evidence as proof to the contrary.
     —Do not compare noncomparable data.
     —Do not draw illogical cause-effect conclusions.
     —Beware of unreliable and unrepresentative data.
     —Do not oversimplify.
   - Adopt these attitudes and practices:
     —Maintain a judicial attitude.
     —Consult with others.
     —Test your interpretations by applying the test of experience (reason) or the negative test (question them).

   (3) Explain the common errors in interpreting and the attitudes and practices conducive to good interpreting.

4. Next, organize the information (construct an outline).
   - Probably you will use the conventional outline symbols (I, A, 1, a) or numeric symbols (1.0, 1.1, 1.11, 1.111) in structuring the outline.
   - Probably you will begin with an introduction and end with a summary, conclusion, or recommendation.
   - Organize the report body (the part between the introduction and the ending section) by a process of division.
     —Look over the findings for ways of dividing on the basis of time, place, quantity, or factor.
     —Then divide, forming the major parts of the report (Roman numeral headings).
     —Next, look at these divisions for ways of dividing them (making the capital letter headings).
     —Continue to subdivide as far as necessary.
     —The end result is your outline.

   (4) Organize information in outline form, using time, place, quantity, factor, or a combination of these as bases for division.

5. Construct headings for each part in the outline.
   - Use the topic form (identifies topic).
   - Or use the talking form (identifies topic and says something about it).
   - Make the wording of comparable parts parallel grammatically.
   - Avoid excessive repetition of words.

   (5) Construct topic or talking headings that outline reports logically and meaningfully.

6. From the outline, write the report.
   - Follow the rules of clarity discussed previously in the book.
   - Maintain objectivity (no bias).

   (6) Write reports that are clear, objective, consistent in time viewpoint, smoothly connected, and interesting.

—Impersonal writing style (third person) has long been associated with objectivity.

—But some authorities question this style, saying personal style is more interesting.

—The argument continues, although most formal reports are written in impersonal style.

· Be consistent in time viewpoint—either past or present.

—Past time viewpoint views the research and findings as past and prevailing concepts and conclusions as present.

—Present time viewpoint presents as current all that is current at the time of writing.

· Use transitions to make the report parts flow smoothly.

—Between large parts, you may need to use full sentences to make connections.

—Topic sentences also can help the flow of thought.

—Use transitional words and phrases to connect the lesser parts.

· Work to make the writing interesting.

—Select words carefully for best effect.

—Follow techniques of good writing (correctness, rhythmic flow of words, vigorous words, and such).

—Do not overdo these efforts by drawing attention to how you write rather than what you say.

 Prepare reports collaboratively.

7. Expect that you will sometimes prepare reports collaboratively in groups.

· Groups (two to five members) may produce better reports than individuals if all things go well.

· Members of groups (leaders and participants) should have clear roles.

· Groups should plan two or more meetings with a work period.

· Groups should follow this procedure in writing reports collaboratively:

—Determine report purpose.

—Derive factors.

—Collect facts for the report.

—Interpret the facts.

—Organize the facts.

—Plan for writing.

—Assign parts to members.

—Write assigned parts.

—Revise members' contributions collaboratively.

—Edit the final draft.

CRITICAL THOUGHT QUESTIONS

1. Collaborative reports are better than reports written by an individual because they use many minds rather than one. Discuss.
2. Explain the concept of outlining as a division process.
3. You are writing a report on the progress of your regional Bell Company's efforts to increase sales of five of its products through extensive advertising in newspapers, on television or radio, and in magazines. Discuss the possibilities for major headings. Evaluate each possibility.
4. Not all business reports are written objectively. In fact, many are deliberately biased. Why, then, should we stress objectivity in a college course that includes report writing?
5. Explain how the question of personal and impersonal writing is related to objectivity.
6. Explain the differences between the present time viewpoint and the past time viewpoint.
7. Is it incorrect to have present, past, and future tense in the same report? In the same paragraph? In the same sentence? Discuss.
8. "Transitional sentences are unnecessary. They merely add length to a report and thus are contrary to the established rules of conciseness." Discuss.
9. "Reports are written for business executives who want them. Thus, you don't have to be concerned about holding your reader's interest." Discuss.

CRITICAL THINKING EXERCISES

1. For each of the following problem situations, write a clear statement of the problem and list the factors involved. When necessary, you may use your imagination logically to supply any additional information needed.
   a. A manufacturer of breakfast cereals wants to determine the characteristics of its consumers.
   b. The manufacturer of a toothpaste wants to learn what the buying public thinks of its product in relation to competing products.
   c. Southwestern Oil Company wants to give its stockholders a summary of its operations for the past calendar year.
   d. A building contractor engaged to build a new factory for Company X submits a report summarizing its monthly progress.
   e. The Able Wholesale Company must prepare a report on its credit relations with the Crystal City Hardware Company.
   f. The supervisor of Department X must prepare a report evaluating the performance of his secretary.
   g. Baker, Inc., wants a study made to determine why its employee turnover is high.
   h. An executive must rank three of her subordinates on the basis of their suitability for promotion to a particular job.
   i. The supervisor of production must compare three competing machines that are being considered for use in a particular production job.
   j. An investment consultant must advise a client on whether to invest in the development of a lake resort.
   k. A consultant seeks to learn how a restaurant can improve its profits.
2. Select a hypothetical problem with a time division possibility. What other division possibilities does it have? Compare the two possibilities as the main bases for organizing the report.

3. Assume that you are writing the results of a survey conducted to determine what styles of shoes are worn throughout the country on various occasions by women of all ages. What division possibilities exist here? Which would you recommend?
4. For the problem described in the preceding exercise, use your imagination to construct topic headings for the outline.
5. Point out any violations of grammatical parallelism in these headings:
   a. Region I sales lagging.
   b. Moderate increase seen for Region II.
   c. Region III sales remain strong.
6. Point out any error in grammatical parallelism in these headings:
   a. High cost of operation.
   b. Slight improvement in production efficiency.
   c. Maintenance cost is low.
7. Which of the following headings is logically inconsistent with the others?
   a. Agricultural production continues to increase.
   b. Slight increase is made by manufacturing.
   c. Salaries remain high.
   d. Service industries show no change.
8. Select an editorial, feature article, book chapter, or the like that has no headings. Write talking headings for it.
9. Assume that you are writing a report that summarizes a survey you have conducted. Write a paragraph of the report using the present time viewpoint; then write the paragraph using the past time viewpoint. The paragraph will be based on the following information:

   Answers to the question about how students view the proposed Aid to Education Bill in this survey and in a survey taken a year earlier (in parentheses).

   For, 39 percent (21); Against, 17 percent (43).

   No answer, undecided, etc., 44 percent (36).

11

Report Structure: The Shorter Forms

Upon completing this chapter, you will be able to write well-structured short reports. To reach this goal, you should be able to

1 Explain the structure of reports relative to length and formality.

2 Discuss the three major differences involved in writing short and long reports.

3 Write clear and well-organized short reports.

4 Write clear and well-organized letter and memorandum reports.

5 Adapt the procedures for writing short reports to such special reports as staff, audit, progress, and technical reports.

6 Write complete, well-organized, and effective proposals.

▶ to the Structure of Short Reports

Assume again the position of assistant to the president of Technicraft and the report-writing work necessary in this position. Most of the time, your assignments concern routine, everyday problems—personnel policies, administrative procedures, work flow, and the like. Following what appears to be established company practice, you write the reports on these problems in simple memorandum form.

Occasionally, however, you have a more involved assignment. Last week, for example, you investigated a union charge that favoritism was shown to the nonunion workers on certain production jobs. As your report on this very formal investigation was written for the benefit of ranking company administrators as well as union leaders, you dressed it up.

Then there was the report you had helped prepare for the board of directors last fall. That report summarized pressing needs for capital improvements. A number of plant administrators contributed to this project, but you were the coordinator. Because the report was important and was written for the board, you made it as formal as possible.

Clearly, reports vary widely in structure. How report structures vary is the first topic of this chapter. Because the shorter reports are more important to you, they are discussed next. ■

Before you can put your report in finished form, you will need to decide on its structure. Will it be a simple memorandum? Will it be a long, complex, and formal report? Or will it fall between these extremes?

AN OVERVIEW OF REPORT STRUCTURE

Your decision as to report structure will be based on the needs of your situation. Those needs are related to report length and the formality of the situation. The longer the problem and the more formal the situation, the more involved the report structure is likely to be. The shorter the problem and the more informal the situation, the less involved the report structure is likely to be.

- Length and formality determine report structure.

So that you may understand the various report structures, we will review the possibilities. The following classification plan provides a very general picture of how reports are structured. This plan does not account for all the possible variations, but it does acquaint you with the general structure of reports. It should help you construct reports that fit your specific need.

- The following classification plan provides a general picture of report structure.

The classification plan arranges all business reports as a stairway, as illustrated by the diagram in Figure 11–1. At the top of the stairway are the most formal, full-dress reports. Such reports have a number of pages that come before the text material, just as this book has pages that come before the first chapter. These pages serve useful purposes, but they also dress up the report. Typically, these *prefatory pages,* as they are called, are included when the problem situation is formal and the report is long. The exact makeup of the prefatory pages may vary, but the most common arrangement includes these parts: the title fly, title page, letter of transmittal, table of contents, and executive summary. Flyleaves (blank pages at the beginning and end that protect the report) may also be included.

- It pictures report structure as a stairway (Figure 11–1). Long, formal reports are at the top. Prefatory pages dress up these reports.

These parts are explained in the following chapter, but a brief description of them at this point should help you understand their roles. The first two pages (the title fly and title page) contain identification information. The *title fly* carries only the report title. The *title page* typically contains the title, identification of the writer and reader, and sometimes the date. As the words imply, the *letter of transmittal* is a letter that transmits the report. It is a personal message from the writer to the reader. The *table of contents,* of course, is a listing of the report contents. It is the report outline in finished form, with page numbers to indicate where the parts begin. It may also include

- Prefatory pages consist of the title fly, title page, letter of transmittal, table of contents, and executive summary.

FIGURE 11–1   Progression of Change in Report Makeup as Formality Requirements and Length of the Problem Decrease

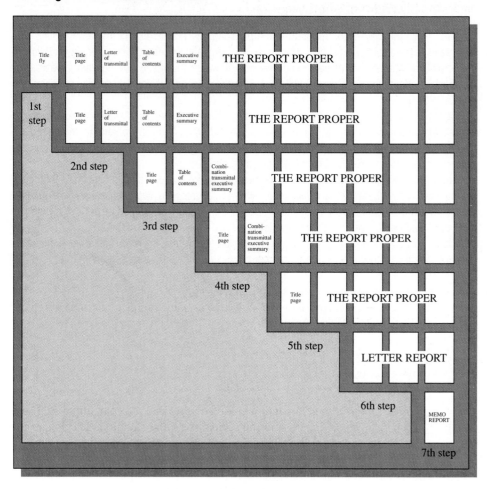

a list of illustrations (tables, figures, diagrams), which may be a separate part. The *executive summary* summarizes whatever is important in the report—the major facts and analyses, conclusions, and recommendations.

As the need for formality decreases and the problem becomes smaller, the makeup of the report changes. The changes primarily occur in the prefatory pages. As we have noted, these pages give the report a formal appearance. So it is not surprising that they change as the report situation becomes less formal.

Although the changes that occur are far from standardized, they follow a general order. First, the title fly drops out. This page contains only the report title, which also appears on the next page. Obviously, the title fly is used primarily for reasons of formality.

Next in the progression, the executive summary and the letter of transmittal are combined. When this stage is reached, the report problem is short enough to be summarized in a short space. As shown in Figure 11–1, the report at this stage has three prefatory parts: title page, table of contents, and combination transmittal letter and executive summary.

A third step down, the table of contents drops out. The table of contents is a guide to the report text, and a guide has little value in a short report. Certainly, a guide to a 100-page report is necessary. But a guide to a one-page report is not. Somewhere between these extremes a dividing point exists. You should follow the general guide of including a table of contents whenever it appears to be of some value to the reader.

• As reports become shorter and less formal, changes occur in this general order.

• The title fly drops out.

• The executive summary and the letter of transmittal are combined.

• Next, the table of contents is omitted.

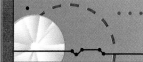
Another step down, as formality and length requirements continue to decrease, the combined letter of transmittal and executive summary drops out. Thus, the report commonly called the *short report* now has only a title page and the report text. The title page remains to the last because it serves as a very useful cover page. In addition, it contains the most important identifying information. The short report is a popular form in business.

Below the short-report form is a form that reinstates the letter of transmittal and summary and presents the entire report as a letter—thus, the *letter report.* And finally, for short problems of more informality, the *memorandum* (informal letter) form is used.

As mentioned earlier, this is a general analysis of report change; it probably over-simplifies the structure of reports. Few actual reports coincide with the steps in the diagram. Most reports, however, fit generally within the framework of the diagram. Knowledge of the general relationship of formality and length to report makeup should help you understand and plan reports.

- The combined letter of transmittal and executive summary drops out, and what is left forms the popular short report.

- The next step is the letter report, and the step after that is the memorandum report.

- This progression of structure is general.

CHARACTERISTICS OF THE SHORTER REPORTS

The shorter report forms (those at the bottom of the stairway) are by far the most common in business. These are the everyday working reports—those used for the routine information reporting that is vital to an organization's communication. Because these reports are so common, our study of report types begins with them.

The techniques for organizing discussed in the preceding chapter cover all forms of reports. But there the emphasis was on organizing the information gathered—on the body of the report. As we noted, introductory and concluding parts would be attached when needed. Thus, the following discussion relates to how these parts are used in the shorter reports.

- The shorter report forms are the most common in business.

- Their need for introductions and conclusions varies.

Little Need for Introductory Information

Most of the shorter, more informal reports require little (sometimes no) introductory material. These reports typically concern day-to-day problems. Their lives are short; that is, they are not likely to be kept on file for future readers. They are intended for only a few readers, and these readers know the problem. They are likely to need little introduction to it.

This is not to say that all shorter reports have no need for introductory material. Some do need it. In general, however, the need is likely to be small.

Determining what introductory material is needed is simply a matter of answering one question: What does my reader need to know before receiving this report? In very short reports, sufficient introductory material is provided by an incidental reference to

- Shorter reports have little need for introductory material.

- Some shorter reports need introductory material. Include as much introductory material as is needed to prepare the reader for the report.

Most short reports are personal, direct, and without formal introductions. Although exceptions exist, they provide everyday working information to organizations that is essential to survival.

the problem, authorization of the investigation, or the like. In extreme cases, however, you may need a detailed introduction comparable to that of the more formal reports.

Reports need no introductory material if their very nature explains their purpose. This holds true for personnel actions. It also holds true for weekly sales reports, inventory reports, and some progress reports.

Predominance of the Direct Order

- The shorter reports usually begin directly—with conclusions and recommendations.

Because the shorter reports usually solve routine problems, they are likely to be written in the direct order. By *direct order* we mean that the report begins with its most important information—usually the conclusion and perhaps a recommendation. Business writers use this order because they know that their readers' main concern is to get the information needed to make a decision. So they present this information right away.

- Sometimes, but not often, longer reports are written in the direct order.

As you will see in the following chapter, the longer report forms may also use the direct order. Many longer reports do, but most do not. Most follow the traditional logical (introduction, body, conclusion) order. As one moves down the structural ladder toward the more informal and shorter reports, however, the need for the direct order increases. At the bottom of the ladder, the direct order is more the rule than the exception.

- Use the direct order when the conclusion or recommendation will serve as a basis for action.

Deciding whether to use the direct order is best based on a consideration of your readers' likely use of the report. If your readers need the report conclusion or recommendation as a basis for an action that they must take, directness will speed their effort by enabling them to quickly receive the most important information. If they have confidence in your work, they may choose not to read beyond this point and to quickly take the action that the report supports. Should they desire to question any part of the report, however, the material is there for their inspection.

- Use the indirect order when you need to take the readers through the analysis.

On the other hand, if there is reason to believe that your readers will want to arrive at the conclusion or recommendation only after a logical review of the analysis, you should organize your report in the indirect (logical) order. This arrangement is especially preferable when your readers do not have reason to place their full confidence in your work. If you are a novice working on a new assignment, for example, you would be wise to lead them to your recommendation or conclusion by using the indirect order.

Because order is so vital a part of constructing the shorter reports, let us be certain that the difference between the direct arrangement and the indirect arrangement is clear. To make it clear, we will go through each, step by step.

The direct arrangement presents right away the most important part of the report. This is the answer—the achievement of the report's goal. Depending on the problem, the direct beginning could consist of a summary of facts, a conclusion, a recommendation, or some combination of summary, conclusion, and recommendation.

• The direct order gives the main message first.

Whatever introductory material is needed usually follows the direct opening. As noted previously, sometimes little or none is needed in the everyday, routine reports. Next come the report findings, organized in good order (as described in the last chapter). From these facts and analyses comes the conclusion, and perhaps a recommendation.

• Then it covers introductory material (if any), findings and analyses, conclusions, and recommendations.

Illustrating this arrangement is the following report of a short and simple personnel problem. For reasons of space economy, only the key parts of the report are shown.

Clifford A. Knudson, draftsman, tool design department, should be fired. This conclusion has been reached after a thorough investigation brought about by numerous incidents during the past two months . . .
The recommended action is supported by this information from his work record for the past two months:
• He has been late to work seven times.
• He has been absent without acceptable excuse for seven days.
• Twice he reported to work in a drunken and disorderly condition.
• And so on.

The indirect arrangement begins with whatever introductory material is needed to prepare the reader for the report. Then comes the presentation of facts, with analyses when needed. Next comes the part that accomplishes the goal of the report. If the goal is to present information, this part summarizes the information. If the goal is to reach a conclusion, this part reviews the analyses and draws a conclusion from them. And if the goal is to recommend an action, this part reviews the analyses, draws a conclusion, and, on the basis of the conclusion, makes a recommendation.

• The indirect order has this sequence: introduction, facts and analyses, conclusions, and recommendations.

Using the simple personnel problem from the last example, the indirect arrangement would appear like this:

FRANK & ERNEST® by Bob Thaves

Numerous incidents during the past two months appear to justify an investigation of the work record of Clifford A. Knudson, draftsman, tool design department.
The investigation of his work record for the past two months reveals these points:
• He has been late to work seven times.
• He has been absent without acceptable excuse for seven days.
• Twice he reported to work in a drunken and disorderly condition.
• And so on to the conclusion that Knudson should be fired.

More Personal Writing Style

• Personal writing is common in the shorter reports.

Although the writing for all reports has much in common, that in the shorter reports tends to be more personal. That is, the shorter reports are likely to use the personal pronouns *I, we,* and *you* rather than only the third person.

• The reasons are that the shorter reports usually (1) involve personal relationships, (2) concern a personal investigation, and (3) are routine.

The reasons for this tendency toward personal writing in the shorter reports should be obvious. In the first place, short-report situations usually involve personal relationships. Such reports tend to be from and to people who know each other and who normally address each other informally when they meet. In addition, the shorter reports are apt to involve personal investigations and to represent the observations, evaluations, and analyses of their writers. Finally, the shorter reports tend to deal with day-to-day, routine problems. These problems are by their very nature informal. It is logical to report them informally, and personal writing tends to produce this informal effect.

• Write impersonally (1) when your reader prefers it and (2) when the situation is formal.

As explained in Chapter 10, your decision about whether to write a report in personal or impersonal style should be based on the situation. You should consider the expectations of those who will receive the report. If they expect formality, you should write impersonally. If they expect informality, you should write personally. If you do not know their preferences, you should consider the formality of the situation. Convention favors impersonal writing for the most formal situations.

From this analysis, it should be clear that either personal or impersonal writing can be appropriate for reports ranging from the shortest to the longest types. The point is, however, the short-report situations are most likely to justify personal writing.

Constructing short reports requires many of the same organization skills used to develop longer, more formal reports.

FORMS OF SHORTER REPORTS

As was noted earlier, the shorter report forms are by far the most numerous and important in business. In fact, the three forms represented by the bottom three steps of the stairway (Figure 11–1) make up the bulk of the reports written. Thus, a review of each of these three types is in order.

• Following is a review of the more popular shorter reports.

The Short Report

One of the more popular of the less formal report forms is the short report. Representing the fifth step in the diagram of report progression, this report consists of only a title page and text. Its popularity may be explained by the middle-ground impression of formality that it conveys. Including the most important prefatory part gives the report at least some appearance of formality. And it does this without the tedious work of preparing the other prefatory pages. The short report is ideally suited for the short but somewhat formal problem.

• The short report consists of a title page and the report text.

   Like most of the less formal report forms, the short report may be organized in either the direct or indirect order. But the direct order is far more common. As illustrated by Figure 11–2, this plan begins with a quick summary of the report, including and emphasizing conclusions and recommendations. Such a beginning serves much the same function as the executive summary (described in Chapter 12) of a long, formal report.

• It is usually in the direct order, beginning with the conclusion.

FIGURE 11–2   Illustration of a Short Report

Designed for the busy reader who wants the main message quickly, this report begins with recommendations and summary. Then it presents the report in logical order, following a brief introduction with a comparison of three methods of depreciation for delivery trucks (the subject of the investigation). The somewhat formal style is appropriate for reports of this nature.

RECOMMENDATIONS FOR DEPRECIATING DELIVERY TRUCKS

BASED ON AN ANALYSIS OF THREE PLANS

PROPOSED FOR THE BAGGET LAUNDRY COMPANY

Submitted to

Mr. Ralph P. Bagget, President
Bagget Laundry Company
312 Dauphine Street
New Orleans, Louisiana 70102

Prepared by

Charles W. Brewington, C.P.A.
Brewington and Karnes, Certified Public Accountants
743 Beaux Avenue, New Orleans, Louisiana 70118

April 16, 19—

FIGURE 11–2   (Continued)

RECOMMENDATION FOR DEPRECIATING DELIVERY TRUCKS

BASED ON AN ANALYSIS OF THREE PLANS

PROPOSED FOR THE BAGGET LAUNDRY COMPANY

I. Recommendations and Summary of Analysis

The Reducing Charge method appears to be the best method to depreciate Bagget Laundry Company delivery trucks. The relative equality of cost allocation for depreciation and maintenance over the useful life of the trucks is the prime advantage under this method. Computation of depreciation charges is relatively simple by the Reducing Charge plan but not quite so simple as computation under the second best method considered.

The second best method considered is the Straight-Line depreciation plan. It is the simplest to compute of the plans considered, and it results in yearly charges equal to those under the Reducing Charge method. The unequal cost allocation resulting from increasing maintenance costs in successive years, however, is a disadvantage that far outweighs the method's ease of computation.

Third among the plans considered is the Service Hours method. This plan is not satisfactory for depreciating delivery trucks primarily because it combines a number of undesirable features. Prime among these is the complexity and cost of computing yearly charges under the plan. Also significant is the likelihood of poor cost allocation under this plan. An additional drawback is the possibility of variations in the estimates of the service life of company trucks.

II. Background of the Problem

Authorization of the Study. This report on depreciation methods for delivery trucks of the Bagget Laundry Company is submitted on April 16, 19—, to Mr. Ralph P. Bagget, President of the Company. Mr. Bagget orally authorized Brewington and Karnes, Certified Public Accountants, to conduct the study on March 15, 19—.

Statement of the Problem. Having decided to establish branch agencies, the Bagget Laundry Company has purchased delivery trucks to transport laundry back and forth from the central cleaning plant in downtown New Orleans. The Company's problem is to select from three alternatives the most advantageous method to depreciate the trucks. The three methods concerned are Reducing Charge, Straight-Line, and Service-Hours. The trucks have an original cost of $7,500, a five-year life, and trade-in value of $1,500.

Method of Solving the Problem. In seeking an optimum solution to the Company's problem, we studied Company records and reviewed authoritative literature on the subject. We also applied our best judgment and our experience in analyzing the alternative methods. We based all conclusions on the generally accepted business principles in the field. Clearly, studies such as this involve subjective judgment, and this one is no exception.

1

FIGURE 11–2   (Continued)

2

Steps in Analyzing the Problem. In the following analysis, our evaluations of the three depreciation methods appear in the order in which we rank the methods. Since each method involves different factors, direct comparison by factors is meaningless. Thus our plan is that we evaluate each method in the light of our best judgment.

III. Marked Advantages of the Reducing Charge Method

Sometimes called Sum-of-the-Digits, the Reducing Charge method consists of applying a series of decreasing fractions over the life of the property. To determine the fraction, first compute the sum of years of use for the property. This number becomes the denominator. Then determine the position number (first, second, etc.) of the year. This number is the numerator. Then apply the resulting fractions to the depreciable values for the life of the property. In the case of the trucks, the depreciable value is $6,000 ($7,500 - $1,500).

As shown in Table I, this method results in large depreciation costs for the early years and decreasing costs in later years. But since maintenance and repair costs for trucks are higher in the later years, this method provides a relatively stable charge over the life of the property. In actual practice, however, the sums will not be as stable as illustrated, for maintenance and repair costs will vary from those used in the computation.

Table I

DEPRECIATION AND MAINTENANCE COSTS FOR
DELIVERY TRUCKS OF BAGGET LAUNDRY FOR 19X2-19X6
USING REDUCING CHARGE DEPRECIATION

End of Year	Depreciation	Maintenance	Sum
1	5/15 ($6,000) = $2,000	$ 100	$ 2,100
2	4/15 ($6,000) = 1,600	500	2,100
3	3/15 ($6,000) = 1,200	900	2,100
4	2/15 ($6,000) = 800	1,300	2,100
5	1/15 ($6,000) = 400	1,700	2,100
	$6,000	$4,500	$10,500

In summary, the Reducing Charge method uses the most desirable combination of factors to depreciate trucks. It equalizes periodic charges, and it is easy to compute. It is our first choice for Bagget Laundry Company.

FIGURE 11-2 (Continued)

IV. <u>Runner-up Position of Straight-Line Method</u>

The Straight-Line depreciation method is easiest of all to compute. It involves merely taking the depreciable value of the trucks ($6,000) and dividing it by the life of the trucks (5 years). The depreciation in this case is $1,200 for each year.

As shown in Table II, however, the increase in maintenance costs in later years results in much greater periodic charges in later years. The method is not usually recommended in cases such as this.

Table II

DEPRECIATION AND MAINTENANCE COSTS FOR DELIVERY TRUCKS OF BAGGET LAUNDRY FOR 19X2-19X6 USING STRAIGHT-LINE DEPRECIATION

End of Year	Depreciation	Maintenance	Sum
1	1/5 ($6,000) = $1,200	$ 100	$1,300
2	1/5 ($6,000) = 1,200	500	1,700
3	1/5 ($6,000) = 1,200	800	2,100
4	1/5 ($6,000) = 1,200	1,300	2,500
5	1/5 ($6,000) = 1,200	1,700	2,900
	Totals $6,000	$4,500	$10,500

In addition, the Straight-Line method generally is best when the properties involved are accumulated over a period of years. When this is done, the total of depreciation and maintenance costs will be about even. But Bagget Company has not purchased its trucks over a period of years. Nor is it likely to do so in the years ahead. Thus, Straight-Line depreciation will not result in equal periodic charges for maintenance and depreciation over the long run.

FIGURE 11–2   (Continued)

4

V. <u>Poor Rank of Service-Hours Depreciation</u>

The Service-Hours method of depreciation combines the major disadvantages of the other ways discussed. It is based on the principle that a truck is bought for the direct hours of service that it will give. The estimated number of hours that a delivery truck can be used efficiently according to automotive engineers is computed from a service total of one-hundred thousand miles. The depreciable cost ($6,000) for each truck is allocated pro rata according to the number of service hours used.

The difficulty and expense of maintaining additional records of service hours is a major disadvantage of this method. The depreciation cost for the delivery trucks under this method will fluctuate widely between first and last years. It is reasonable to assume that as the trucks get older more time will be spent on maintenance. Consequently, the larger depreciation costs will occur in the initial years. As can be seen by Table III, the periodic charges for depreciation and maintenance hover between the two previously discussed methods.

The periodic charge for depreciation and maintenance increases in the later years of ownership. Another difficulty encountered is the possibility of a variance between estimated service hours and the actual service hours. The wide fluctuation possible makes it impractical to use this method for depreciating the delivery truck.

The difficulty of maintaining adequate records and increasing costs in the later years are the major disadvantages of this method. Since it combines the major disadvantages of both the Reducing Charge and Straight-Line methods, it is not satisfactory for depreciating the delivery trucks.

Table III

DEPRECIATION AND MAINTENANCE COSTS FOR
DELIVERY TRUCKS OF BAGGET LAUNDRY FOR 19XX-19XX
USING SERVICE-HOURS DEPRECIATION

End of Year	Estimated Service-Miles	Depreciation	Maintenance	Sum
1	30,000	$1,800	$ 100	$1,900
2	25,000	1,500	500	2,000
3	20,000	1,200	900	2,100
4	15,000	900	1,300	2,200
5	10,000	600	1,700	2,300
	100,000	$6,000	$4,500	$10,500

Following the summary come whatever introductory remarks are needed. (See Chapter 12 for a more detailed discussion of the introduction.) Sometimes this part is not needed. Usually, however, a single paragraph covers the facts of authorization and a brief statement of the problem and its scope. After the introductory words come the findings of the investigation. As in the longer report forms, the findings are presented, analyzed, and applied to the problem. From all this comes a conclusion and, if needed, a recommendation. These last two elements—conclusions and recommendations—may come at the end even though they also appear in the beginning summary. Omitting a summary or a conclusion would sometimes end the report abruptly. It would stop the flow of reasoning before reaching the logical goal.

• The introduction comes next, then the findings and analyses, and finally the conclusions.

The mechanics of constructing the short report are much the same as the mechanics of constructing the more formal, longer types. The short report uses the same form of title page and page layout. Like the longer reports, it uses headings. But because of the short report's brevity, the headings rarely go beyond the two-division level. In fact, one level of division is most common. Like any other report, the short report uses graphics, an appendix, and a bibliography when these are needed.

• See Figure 11–2 for this report form.

Letter Reports

The second of the more common shorter report forms is the letter report, that is, a report in letter form. Letter reports are used primarily to present information to persons outside the organization, especially when the information is to be sent by mail or fax. For example, a company's written evaluation of a credit customer may be presented in letter form and sent to the person who requests it. An outside consultant may write a report of analyses and recommendations in letter form. Or the officer of an organization may report certain information to the membership in a letter.

• Letter reports are reports in letter form.

Typically, the length of letter reports is three or four pages or less. But no hard-and-fast rule exists on this point. Long letter reports (10 pages and more) are not unusual.

• They usually cover short problems.

As a general rule, letter reports are written personally, using *I, you,* and *we* references. (Exceptions exist, of course, such as letter reports for very important readers—for example, a company's board of directors.) Otherwise, the writing style recommended for letter reports is much the same as that recommended for any other reports. Certainly, clear and meaningful expression is a requirement for all reports (see Figure 11–3).

• They are usually written in personal style.

Letter reports may be in either the direct order or the indirect order. If such a report is to be mailed, there is some justification for using the indirect order. As such reports arrive unannounced, it is logical to begin with a reminder of what they are, how they originated, and the like. A letter report written to the membership of an organization, for example, might appropriately begin as follows:

• Most of them begin indirectly.

As authorized by your board of directors last January 6, this report reviews member company expenditures for direct-mail selling.

If a letter report is begun in the direct order, a subject line is appropriate. The subject line consists of identifying words appearing at the top of the letter, usually right after the salutation. Another common practice is to omit the word *subject* and the colon and to type the entire subject description in capital letters. Although subject lines may be formed in many ways, one acceptable version begins with the word *subject* and follows it with words that identify the situation. As the following example illustrates, this identifying device helps overcome any confusion that the direct beginning might otherwise create.

• Subject lines are appropriate to begin them.

Subject: Direct-mail expenditures of Association members, authorized by board of directors, January 1994.
Association members are spending 8 percent more on direct-mail advertising this year than they did the year before. Current plans call for a 10 percent increase for next year.

FIGURE 11–3   Illustration of a Letter Report

This direct-order letter report compares two hotels for a meeting site. Organized by the bases used in determining the choice, it evaluates the pertinent information and reaches a decision. The personal style is appropriate. Note the merge variables that form the inside address.

INTERNATIONAL COMMUNICATION ASSOCIATION

3141 Girard Street • Washington, D.C.

January 28, 19—

FIELD(Personal Title) FIELD(First Name) FIELD(Second Name) FIELD(Last Name)
Board of Directors
International Communication Association
FIELD(School or Company)
FIELD(Address)
FIELD(City), FIELD(State) FIELD(Zip)

Dear FIELD(Personal Title) FIELD(Last Name):

Subject: Recommendation of Convention Hotel for the 19— Meeting

RECOMMENDATION OF THE LAMONT

The Lamont Hotel is my recommendation for the International Communication Association meeting next January. My decision is based on the following summary of the evidence I collected. First, the Lamont has a definite downtown location advantage, and this is important to convention goers and their spouses. Second, accommodations, including meeting rooms, are adequate in both places, although the Blackwell's rooms are more modern. Third, Lamont room costs are approximately 15% lower than those at the Blackwell. The Lamont, however, would charge $400 for a room for the assembly meeting. Although both hotels are adequate, because of location and cost advantages the Lamont appears to be the better choice from the members' viewpoint.

ORIGIN AND PLAN OF THE INVESTIGATION

In investigating these two hotels, as was my charge from you at our January 7th meeting, I collected information on what I believed to be the three major factors of consideration in the problem. First is location. Second is adequacy of accommodations. And third is cost. The following findings and evaluations form the basis of my recommendations.

THE LAMONT'S FAVORABLE DOWNTOWN LOCATION

The older of the two hotels, the Lamont is located in the heart of the downtown business district. Thus it is convenient to the area's two major department stores as well as the other downtown shops. The Blackwell, on the other hand, is approximately nine blocks from the major shopping area. Located in the periphery of the business and residential area, it provides little location advantage for those wanting to shop. It does, however, have shops within its walls which provide virtually all of the guest's normal needs. Because many members will bring spouses, however, the downtown location does give the Lamont an advantage.

FIGURE 11-3 (Concluded)

Board of Directors   -2-   January 28, 19—

ADEQUATE ACCOMMODATIONS AT BOTH HOTELS

Both hotels can guarantee the 600 rooms we will require. As the Blackwell is newer (since 1982), its rooms are more modern and therefore more appealing. The 69-year-old Lamont, however, is well preserved and comfortable. Its rooms are all in good repair, and the equipment is modern.

The Blackwell has 11 small meeting rooms and the Lamont has 13. All are adequate for our purposes. Both hotels can provide the 10 we need. For our general assembly meeting, the Lamont would make available its Capri Ballroom, which can easily seat our membership. It would also serve as the site of our inaugural dinner. The assembly facilities at the Blackwell appear to be somewhat crowded, although the management assures me that it can hold 600. Pillars in the room, however, would make some seats undesirable. In spite of the limitations mentioned, both hotels appear to have adequate facilities for our meeting.

LOWER COSTS AT THE LAMONT

Both the Lamont and the Blackwell would provide nine rooms for meetings on a complimentary basis. Both would provide complimentary suites for our president and our secretary. The Lamont, however, would charge $400 for use of the room for the assembly meeting. The Blackwell would provide this room without charge.

Convention rates at the Lamont are $80-$90 for singles, $90-$100 for double-bedded rooms, and $88-$110 for twin-bedded rooms. Comparable rates of the Blackwell are $90-$100, $100-$110, and $100-$120. Thus, the savings at the Lamont would be approximately 15% per member.

Cost of the dinner selected would be $18.00 per person, including gratuities, at the Lamont. The Blackwell would meet this price if we would guarantee 600 plates. Otherwise, they would charge $20.00. Considering all of these figures, the total cost picture at the Lamont is the more favorable one.

Respectfully,

Willard K Mitchell

Willard K. Mitchell
Executive Secretary

A successful businessman fell in love with a woman who he felt might not meet the requirements of a person in his position. So he hired a detective agency to investigate her background. After weeks of intensive checking, the detective agency submitted this report:

Ms. Stoner has an excellent reputation. She has high morals, lives within her means, and is well respected in the community. The only blemish on her record is that in recent months she has been seen repeatedly in the company of a business executive of doubtful repute.

- The organizational plans of letter reports are much like those of longer reports.

Regardless of which type of beginning is used, the organizational plans for letter reports correspond to those of the longer, more formal types. Thus, the indirect-order letter report follows its introduction with a logical presentation and analysis of the information gathered. From this presentation, it develops a conclusion or recommendation, or both, in the end. The direct-order letter report follows the initial summary-conclusion-recommendation section with whatever introduction is appropriate. For example, the direct beginning illustrated above could be followed with these introductory sentences:

These are the primary findings of a study authorized by your board of directors last January. As they concern information vital to all of us in the Association, they are presented here for your confidential use.

- Supporting facts and analyses follow an appropriate introduction.

Following such an introduction, the report would present the supporting facts and their analyses. The writer would systematically build up the case supporting the opening comment. With either the direct or indirect order, a letter report may close with whatever friendly, goodwill comment fits the occasion.

Memorandum Reports

- Memorandums (internal written messages) are widely used.

As we noted in Chapter 8, memorandums (commonly called *memos*) are the most widely used form of written communication in business. Although sometimes used for correspondence with outside parties, memorandums are primarily internal messages. That is, they are written by and to people in an organization. Figure 11–4 illustrates a memorandum report.

- Most of them are written informally.

Because memorandums are primarily communications between people who know each other, they are usually informal. In fact, many are hurried, handwritten messages. Some memorandums, however, are formal, especially those directed to readers high in the administration of the organization.

- Some resemble letters and follow letter form.

- Some are reports. Such memorandums tend to be formal and problem related.

Most memorandums are forms of letters. Some, however, are more appropriately classified as reports. The distinction between internal letters and internal reports is not always clear, though the reports tend to be more formal. In fact, some memorandum reports rival the longer report forms in formality. Like the longer forms, they may use captions to display content and graphics to support the text. Memorandum reports tend to be problem related.

SPECIAL REPORT FORMS

- Some special report forms deserve review.

As noted previously, this review describes only generally the report forms used in business. Many variations exist, a few of which deserve emphasis.

FIGURE 11-4   Illustration of a Progress Report in Memorandum Form

This memorandum report summarizes a sales manager's progress in opening a new district. It begins with highlight information—all a busy reader may need to know. Organized by three categories of activity, the factual information follows. The writer-reader relationship justifies personal style.

MEMORANDUM

THE MURCHISON CO. INC.

To: William T. Chysler
               Director of Sales

From: James C. Calvin, Manager
               Millville Sales District

Date: July 21, 19—

Subject: Quarterly Report for Millville Sales District

SUMMARY HIGHLIGHTS

After three months of operation, I have secured office facilities, hired and developed three salespeople, and cultivated about half the customers available in the Millville Sales District. Although the district is not yet showing a profit, at the current rate of development it will do so this month. Prospects for the district are unusually bright.

OFFICE OPERATION

In April I opened the Millville Sales District as authorized by action of the Board of Directors last February 7. Initially I set up office in the Three Coins Inn, a motel on the outskirts of town, and remained there three weeks while looking for permanent quarters. These I found in the Wingate Building, a downtown office structure. The office suite rents for $940 per month. It has four executive offices, each opening into a single secretarial office, which is large enough for two secretaries. Although this arrangement is adequate for the staff now anticipated, additional space is available in the building if needed.

PERSONNEL

In the first week of operation, I hired an office secretary, Ms. Catherine Kruch. Ms. Kruch has good experience and has excellent credentials. She has proved to be very effective. In early April I hired two salespeople—Mr. Charles E. Clark and Ms. Alice E. Knapper. Both were experienced in sales, although neither had worked in apparel sales. Three weeks later I hired Mr. Otto Strelski, a proven salesperson whom I managed to attract from the Hammond Company. I still am searching for someone for the fourth subdistrict. Currently I am investigating two good prospects and hope to hire one of them within the next week.

FIGURE 11–4 (Concluded)

William T. Chysler
Page 2
July 21, 19—

PERFORMANCE

After brief training sessions, which I conducted personally, the salespeople were assigned the territories previously marked. They were instructed to call on the accounts listed on the sheets supplied by Mr. Henderson's office. During the first month, Knapper's sales totaled $17,431 and Clark's reached $13,490, for a total of $30,921. With three salespeople working the next month, total sales reached $121,605. Of the total, Knapper accounted for $37,345, Clark $31,690, and Strelski $52,570. Although these monthly totals are below the $145,000 break-even point for the three subdistricts, current progress indicates that we will exceed this volume this month. As we have made contact with only about one half of the prospects in the area, the potential for the district appears to be unusually good.

The Staff Report

One of the more popular forms of reports used in business is the staff report. Usually written in memorandum form, it can be adapted to any structural type, including the long, formal report.

The staff report differs from other forms of reports primarily in the organization of its contents. It arranges contents in a fixed plan, similar to that used in technical writing. The plan remains the same for all problems. As this arrangement leads systematically to conclusions and recommendations, it is especially useful for business problems.

Although the organization of staff reports varies by company, this plan used by a major metals manufacturer is typical:

Identifying information: As the company's staff reports are written on intracompany communication stationery, the conventional identification information (*To, From, Subject, Date*) appears at the beginning.
Summary: For the busy executive who wants the facts fast, the report begins with a summary. Some executives will read no further. Others will want to trace the report content in detail.
The problem (or objective): As with all good problem-solving procedures, the report text logically begins with a clear description of the problem—what it is, what it is not, what its limitations are, and the like.
Facts: Next comes the information gathered in the attempt to solve the problem.
Discussion: This is followed by analyses of the facts and applications of the facts and the analyses to the problem. (The statement and discussion of the facts can often be combined.)
Conclusions: From the preceding discussion of the facts come the final meanings as they apply to the problem.
Recommendation: If the problem's objective allows for it, a course of action may be recommended on the basis of the conclusions.

Perhaps the major users of staff reports are the branches of the Armed Forces, all of which use a standardized form. As shown in Figure 11–5, the military version of the staff report differs somewhat from the plan just described.

Of course, anytime you use a standardized form, you will want to consider developing a template macro or merge document with your word processing software. A macro would fill in all the standard parts for you, pausing to let you enter the variable information. It would be most suitable for periodic reports, such as progress reports or quarterly sales reports. A template merge document would prompt you for the variables first, merging them with the primary document later. You'll find this feature most useful when you are repeatedly having to write several reports at the same time. For example, personnel evaluations or client reports are good applications of the merge.

The Progress Report

As its name implies, a progress report presents a review of progress made on an activity. For example, a fund-raising organization might prepare weekly summaries of its efforts to achieve its goal. Or a building contractor might prepare for a customer a report on progress toward completing a building. Typically, the contents of these reports concern progress made, but they may also include such related topics as problems encountered or anticipated and projections of future progress.

Progress reports follow no set form. They can be quite formal, as when a contractor building a large manufacturing plant reports to the company for whom the plant is being built. Or they can be very informal, as in the case of a worker reporting by memorandum to his or her supervisor on the progress of a task being performed. Some progress reports are quite routine and structured, sometimes involving filling in blanks on forms devised for the purpose. Most, however, are informal, narrative reports, as illustrated by the example in Figure 11–4.

- One is the staff report.

- Staff reports follow a fixed organization plan that leads to a conclusion.

- A typical plan for staff reports has these parts:

- Identifying information.

- Summary.

- Problem (or objective).

- Facts.
- Discussion.

- Conclusions.

- Recommendation.

- See Figure 11–5 for the military form of staff reports.

- Progress reports review progress on an activity.

- Most are informal and narrative; some are formal.

FIGURE 11-5   Military Form of Staff Study Report

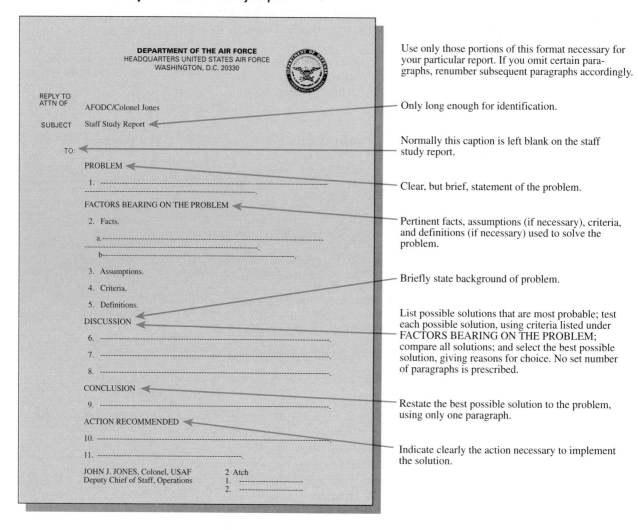

DEPARTMENT OF THE AIR FORCE
HEADQUARTERS UNITED STATES AIR FORCE
WASHINGTON, D.C. 20330

REPLY TO
ATTN OF   AFODC/Colonel Jones

SUBJECT   Staff Study Report

TO:

PROBLEM

　1. --
---.

FACTORS BEARING ON THE PROBLEM

　2. Facts.

　　a.--
---.

　　b--.

　3. Assumptions.

　4. Criteria.

　5. Definitions.

DISCUSSION

　6. ---.

　7. ---.

　8. ---.

CONCLUSION

　9. ---.

ACTION RECOMMENDED

　10. --

　11. --.

JOHN J. JONES, Colonel, USAF   2 Atch
Deputy Chief of Staff, Operations   1. -------------------
                                       2. -------------------

Use only those portions of this format necessary for your particular report. If you omit certain paragraphs, renumber subsequent paragraphs accordingly.

Only long enough for identification.

Normally this caption is left blank on the staff study report.

Clear, but brief, statement of the problem.

Pertinent facts, assumptions (if necessary), criteria, and definitions (if necessary) used to solve the problem.

Briefly state background of problem.

List possible solutions that are most probable; test each possible solution, using criteria listed under FACTORS BEARING ON THE PROBLEM; compare all solutions; and select the best possible solution, giving reasons for choice. No set number of paragraphs is prescribed.

Restate the best possible solution to the problem, using only one paragraph.

Indicate clearly the action necessary to implement the solution.

The Audit Report

- Short- and long-form audit reports are well known in business.

Short-form and long-form audit reports are well known in business. The short-form audit report is perhaps the most standardized of all reports—if, indeed, it can be classified as a report. Actually, it is a standardized statement verifying an accountant's inspection of a firm's financial records. Its wording seldom varies. Illustrations of this standard form are found in almost any corporate annual report.

- Long-form audit reports vary in their makeup.

Long-form audit reports vary greatly in their makeup. In fact, a national accounting association that studied the subject exhaustively found the makeup of these reports to be so varied that it concluded that no typical form existed.

The Technical Report

- Technical reports differ from other reports primarily in their subject matter.
- This arrangement of prefatory parts is typical: title pages, letter of transmittal, table of contents, summary parts (findings, conclusions, recommendations, objectives, acknowledgments).

Although often treated as a highly specialized form, the technical report differs from other reports primarily in its subject matter. As you can see from Figure 11–6, a technical report can be much like the memorandum reports we have described. The longer technical reports, however, tend to follow a somewhat standardized arrangement.

This arrangement begins much like that of the traditional formal report. First come the title pages, although a routing or distribution form for intracompany use is frequently worked in. A letter of transmittal is likely to come next, followed by a table of

Whether invited or prospecting, proposals must do an effective job of presenting a complete picture of what is being proposed. You must work hard to meet readers' needs so they can make decisions in your favor.

contents and illustrations. From this point on, however, the technical report is different. Its differences lie mainly in two places: (1) beginning summary and (2) text organization.

Instead of having a standard summary, the long technical report often presents the summary information in a number of prefatory sections. There may be, for example, separate sections covering findings, conclusions, and recommendations. Parts of the conventional introduction, especially objectives and acknowledgments, sometimes appear as prefatory sections.

• The text of the long technical report is typically organized in a fixed order like this one: introduction, methodology, facts, discussion, conclusion, recommendation.

The long technical report usually follows a standard order similar to that of the staff report. The most common order is the following:

Introduction.
Methodology (or methods and materials).
Facts.
Discussion.
Conclusion.
Recommendation.

The Proposal

Whether proposals belong in a discussion of the shorter reports is debatable, for they are not always short. In fact, they range in length from just a few pages to several volumes. We discuss them here primarily as a matter of convenience.

• Proposals vary in length.

Proposals Defined.   By definition, a *proposal* is a presentation for consideration of something. In actual practice, some proposals fit this definition well—for example, one company's proposal to merge with another company, an advertising agency's proposal to promote a product, or a city's proposal to induce a business to locate within its boundaries. But other proposals are more precisely described as appeals or bids for grants, donations, or sales of products or services. To illustrate, a college professor submits a request for research funds to a government agency, a community organization submits a request to a philanthropic foundation for help in establishing a drug rehabilitation facility, or a company submits a bid for the sale of its products or services.

• A proposal is a presentation for consideration of something.

FIGURE 11–6   Illustration of a Technical Memorandum Report

This memorandum report presents an investigation of a technical process the writer was asked to make. It begins with a brief introduction. Then comes a narrative summary of the investigation, organized by the major areas inspected. Note the use of graphics to help present somewhat difficult concepts.

MEMORANDUM

the CROWELL COMPANY, inc.

To: Charles E. Groom   May 3, 19—

From: Edmund S. Posner ESP

Subject: Graff Lining Company's use of Kynar pipe lining

Following is the report you requested January 9 on the Graff Lining Company's process of using Kynar for lining pipe. My comments are based on my inspection of the facilities at the Graff plant and my conversations with their engineers.

<u>Dimension limitations</u>

Graff's ability to line the smaller pipe sizes appears to be limited. To date, the smallest diameter pipe they have lined in 10-foot spool lengths is 2 inches. They believe they can handle 1 1/2-inch pipe in 10-foot spools, but they have not attempted this size. They question their ability to handle smaller pipe in 10-foot lengths.

This limitation, however, does not apply to fittings. They can line 1 1/2-inch and 1-inch fittings easily. Although they can handle smaller sizes than these, they prefer to limit minimum nipple size to 1 inch by 4 inches long.

Maximum spool dimensions for the coating process are best explained by illustration:

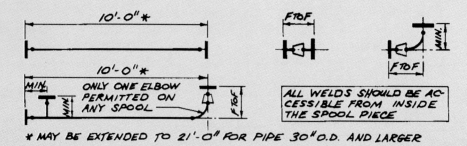

Source: Raymond V. Lesikar and John D. Pettit, *Report Writing for Business*, 9th ed. (Burr Ridge, Ill. Richard D. Irwin, 1995).

FIGURE 11-6 (Continued)

Charles E. Groom   2   May 3, 19—

Graff corrects defects found. If the defect is small, they correct by retouching with sprayer or brush. If the defect is major, they remove all the coating by turning and reline the pipe.

Recommendations for piping

Should we be interested in using their services, Graff engineers made the following recommendations. First, they recommend that we use forged steel fittings rather than cast fittings. Cast fittings, they point out, have excessive porosity. They noted, though, that cast fittings can be used and are less expensive. For large jobs, this factor could be significant.

Second, they suggest that we make all small connections, such as those required for instruments, in a prescribed manner. This manner is best described by diagram:

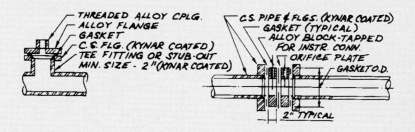

Graff engineers emphasized this point further by illustrating a common form of small connections that will not work. Such connections are most difficult to coat. Pinhole breaks are likely to occur on them, and a pinhole break can cause the entire coating to disbond. A typical unacceptable connection is the following:

FIGURE 11–6 (Continued)

Charles E. Groom   3   May 3, 19—

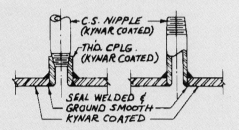

Preparation of pipe for lining

Graff requires that all pipe to be lined be ready for the coating process. Specifically, they require that all welds be ground smooth (to avoid pitting and assure penetration.) Because welds are inaccessible in small pipe, they require forged tees in all piping smaller than 4 inches. In addition, they require that all attachments to the pipe (clips, base ells, etc.) be welded to the pipe prior to coating.

The lining procedure

The procedure Graff uses in lining the pipe begins with cleaning the pipe and inspecting it for cracked fittings, bad welds, etc. When necessary, they do minor retouching and grinding of welds. Then they apply the Kynar in three forms: primer, building, sealer. They apply the building coat in as many layers as is necessary to obtain a finished thickness of 25 mils. They oven bake each coat at a temperature and for a time determined by the phase of the coating and the piping material.

Inspection technique

Following the coating, Graff inspectors use a spark testing method to detect possible pinholes or other defects. This method is best explained by illustration:

FIGURE 11–6   (Concluded)

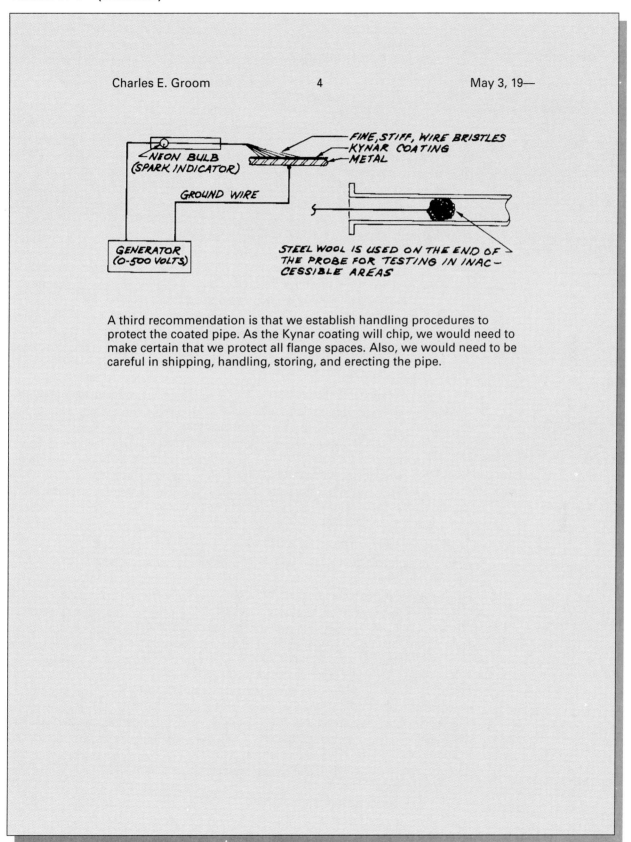

A third recommendation is that we establish handling procedures to protect the coated pipe. As the Kynar coating will chip, we would need to make certain that we protect all flange spaces. Also, we would need to be careful in shipping, handling, storing, and erecting the pipe.

Proposals are usually written, but they can be oral presentations or a combination of both. They may be made by individuals or organizations, including business organizations, and they may be made to any of a variety of individuals or organizations such as government agencies, foundations, businesses. They can even be made internally—by one part of a business to another part or to the management of the business. For example, a department might outline its needs for new equipment in a proposal to management.

- Proposals are made by individuals or organizations to individuals or organizations.

Invited or Prospecting. Proposals may be invited or prospecting. By *invited* we mean that the awarding organization announces to interested parties that it will make an award and that it is soliciting proposals. To illustrate, a government agency might have funds to award for research projects, a foundation might wish to make grants for educational innovations, or a business might want competing suppliers to bid on a product or service that it needs. In their announcements, the awarding organizations typically describe their needs and specify the unique requirements that the proposals should cover.

- They may be invited or prospecting.

In business situations, invited proposals usually follow preliminary meetings between the parties involved. For example, if a business has a need for certain production equipment, its representatives might initiate meetings with likely suppliers of this equipment. At these meetings the representatives would discuss the need with suppliers. Each supplier would then be invited to submit a proposal for fulfilling the need with its equipment. In a sense, such a proposal is a bid supported by the documentation and explanation needed for conviction.

- In business, invited proposals usually follow meetings.

Prospecting proposals are much like rational sales letters. They amount to descriptions of what the writer or the writer's organization could do if given an award by the reader's organization. For example, a university department that wishes to seek funding for the development of a new curriculum in international management might then write proposals to philanthropic foundations describing the curriculum, outlining its financial needs for instituting the curriculum, and proposing that the foundation award the funds needed. Or a business supplying unique services might submit an unsolicited description of the services to a business that might use them. Such proposals differ from rational sales letters primarily in their physical form (they are in report form, not letter form). When products or services are being proposed, such proposals may also differ from rational sales letters by being specifically adapted to the reader's business.

- Prospecting proposals are like sales letters.

Format and Organization. The physical arrangement and organization of proposals vary widely. The simplest proposals resemble formal memorandums. Internal proposals (those written for and by people in the same organization) usually fall into this category, though exceptions exist. The more complex proposals may take the form of full-dress, long reports, including prefatory pages (title pages, letter of transmittal, table of contents, executive summary), text, and an assortment of appended parts. Most proposals have arrangements that fall somewhere between these extremes.

- Their formats vary from memorandums to long-report forms.

Because of the wide variations in the makeup of proposals, you would be wise to investigate carefully before designing a particular proposal. In your investigation, try to determine what format is conventional among those who will read it. Look to see what others have done in similar situations. In the case of an invited proposal, review the announcement thoroughly, looking for clues concerning the preferences of the inviting organization. If you are unable to follow any of these courses, design a format based on your knowledge of report structure. Your design should be the one that you think is best for the one situation.

- Select the format appropriate for your one case.

Formality Requirements. The formality requirements of proposals vary. In some cases (a university's proposal for a research grant, for example), strict formality is expected. In other cases (such as a manufacturing department's proposal that the plant

- The formality requirements of proposals vary. Do what is appropriate.

manager change a production procedure), informality is in order. As with other reports, the decision should be based primarily on the relationship between the parties involved. If the parties are acquainted with each other, informality is appropriate. If they are not, a formal report is usually expected. An exception would be made in any case in which formality is expected regardless of the relationship of the parties.

Content. You should consider the needs of the individual case in determining the content of a proposal. In the case of an invited (solicited) proposal, review the proposal announcement (if the proposal is in writing). If the proposal results from a meeting, review your announcement of the meeting or the notes you took at the meeting. Such a review will usually tell you what is wanted. In fact, some written invitations even give a suggested plan for the proposal. It is highly important that you follow such guidelines, for in competitive situations the selection procedure frequently involves a checkoff and rating for each point stated in the invitation.

If you are making an uninvited proposal, you will have to determine what your readers need to know. As each case will involve different needs, you will have to use your best judgment in making that determination.

Although the number of content possibilities is great, you should consider including the eight topics listed below. They are broad and general, and you can combine or subdivide them as needed to fit the facts of your case. (See Figure 11–7 for one logical application.)

1. Writer's purpose and the reader's need. An appropriate beginning is a statement of the writer's purpose (to present a proposal) and the reader's need (to reduce turnover of field representatives). If the report is in response to an invitation, that statement should tie in with the invitation (as described in the July 10 announcement). The problem should be stated clearly, in the way described in Chapter 10. This proposal beginning illustrates these recommendations:

> As requested at the July 10 meeting with Alice Burton, Thomas Cheny, and Victor Petrui in your Calgary office, the following pages present Murchison and Associates' proposal for reducing turnover of field representatives. Following guidelines established at the meeting, the proposal involves determining the job satisfaction of the current sales force, analyzing exit interview records, and comparing company compensation and personnel practices with industry norms.

If a proposal is submitted without invitation, its beginning has an additional requirement: it must gain attention. As noted previously, uninvited proposals are much like sales letters. Their intended readers are not likely to be eager to read them. Thus, their beginnings must overcome the readers' reluctance. An effective way of doing this is to begin by briefly summarizing the highlights of the proposal, with emphasis on its benefits. This technique is illustrated by the beginning of an unsolicited proposal that a restaurant consultant sent to prospective clients:

> The following pages present a proven plan for operations review that will (1) reduce food costs, (2) evaluate menu offerings for maximum profitability, (3) increase kitchen efficiency, (4) improve service, and (5) increase profits. Mattox and Associates proposes to achieve these results through its highly successful procedures, which involve analysis of guest checks and invoices and observational studies of kitchen and service work.

Your clear statement of the purpose and problem may be the most important aspect of the proposal. In order to win a contract, you must convince your reader that you have a clear understanding of what needs to be done.

2. Background. A review of background information promotes an understanding of the problem. Thus, a college's proposal for an educational grant might benefit from a review of the college's involvement in the area to which the grant would be applied. A company's proposal of a merger with another company might review industry developments that make the merger desirable. Or a chief executive officer's proposal to the board of directors that a company's administration be reorganized might present the background information that justifies the proposal.

- Determine the content of a proposal by reviewing the needs of the case. If the proposal has been invited, review the invitation.

- If the proposal is uninvited, use judgment in determining the readers' needs.
- Consider including these eight topics:

- 1. Writer's purpose and the reader's need (good beginning topics).

- Uninvited proposals must gain attention.

- 2. Background.

FIGURE 11–7   Illustration of a Short Proposal

This simple proposal seeks organization membership for its writer. It begins with a quick introduction that ties in with the reader's invitation for the proposal. Then it presents the case, logically proceeding from background information to advantages of membership, to costs. It concludes with the recommendation to sponsor membership.

TO: Helen S. Hobson

DATE: May 19, 19—

FROM: Ross H. Jefferson   *RHJ*

SUBJECT: Sponsored membership in the Association for Business Communication

As you requested May 17, following is my proposal for Stoner to sponsor my membership in the Association for Business Communication (ABC).

Description of ABC

The primary professional organization in business communication, ABC is dedicated to keeping its members informed of the latest developments in business communication practice and theory. It informs its members through two quarterly publications: The Journal of Business Communication (research and theory) and The ABC Bulletin (practice). In addition, the Association holds an annual meeting as well as regional meetings throughout the United States and Canada. Papers presented at these meetings cover both the current theoretical and practical topics in business communication.

Founded in 1936, ABC now has 2,401 members, including 850 institutions. Of the individual memberships, most (1,182) are academics from the United States and Canada. But 148 are business professionals. Companies represented include IBM, AT&T, Exxon, Imperial Oil, State Farm Insurance, McDonnell Douglas, and Aetna Insurance. ABC's diverse membership provides an effective exchange of experience and knowledge.

Benefits of Membership

Membership in ABC would benefit Stoner as well as me personally. The meetings and the publications would enable me to bring the latest communication knowledge to my editorial work. ABC would be especially helpful in my assignments involving teaching communication to our employees, for much of its emphasis is on teaching techniques. Also, membership in ABC would enhance Stoner's image. ABC is a prestigious organization, and its members include the corporate elite. In addition, meeting with the members of other companies and exchanging ideas would help me do a better job of directing Stoner's communication activities.

FIGURE 11–7 (Concluded)

Helen S. Hobson, 2, May 19, 19—

Costs of Membership

ABC annual dues are $40, which includes subscriptions to the Journal and the Bulletin. The costs of attending the meetings would vary with the meeting sites. For this year, the approximate costs for the international meeting in Chicago would be $700 (registration, $80; transportation, $330; hotel, $180; meals, $90; miscellaneous, $20). For the regional meeting in Dallas it would be $570 (registration, $70; transportation, $150; hotel, $200; meals, $120; miscellaneous, $30). The total cost for this year would be $1,310.

Recommended Action

Based on the preceding information, I believe that membership in ABC offers us benefits well worth the cost. Thus, I recommend that Stoner sponsor my membership on a one-year trial basis. At the end of this year, I would review actual benefits received and recommend whether or not to continue membership.

3. Need. Closely related to the background information is the need for what is being proposed. In fact, background information may well be used to establish need. But because need can be presented without such support, we list it separately.

4. Description of plan. The heart of a proposal is the description of what the writer proposes to do. This is the primary message of the proposal. It should be concisely presented in a clear and orderly manner.

5. Particulars. Although the particulars of the proposal are a part of the plan description, they are discussed separately for reasons of emphasis. By *particulars* we mean the specifics—time schedules, costs, performance standards, means of appraising performance, equipment and supplies needed, guarantees, personnel requirements, and such. What is needed in a given case depends on its unique requirements. But in any event, the particulars should anticipate and answer the readers' questions.

6. Evidence of ability to deliver. The proposing organization must sometimes establish its ability to perform. This means presenting information on such matters as the qualifications of personnel, success in similar cases, the adequacy of equipment and facilities, operating procedures, and financial status. Whatever information will serve as evidence of the organization's ability to carry out what it proposes should be used.

7. Benefits of the proposal. The proposal might also describe good things that it would bring about, especially if a need exists to convince the readers. Reader benefits were what we stressed in sales writing, but as we have noted, proposals can be much like sales presentations. The greater the need to persuade, the more you should stress benefits. As will be noted in a later chapter, however, the writing in proposals is more objective and less flamboyant than the writing in sales literature.

As an example of benefits logically covered in proposals, a college's request for funding to establish a program for minorities could point to the bright futures that such funding would give disadvantaged students. And a proposal offering a consulting service to restaurants could stress such benefits as improved work efficiency, reduced employee theft, savings in food costs, and increased profits.

8. Concluding comments. The proposal should end with words directed to the next step—acting on the proposal. One possibility is to present a summary review of the highlights. Another is to offer additional information that might be needed. Yet another is to urge (or suggest) action on the proposal.

· ·

SUMMARY ▶ by Chapter Objectives

(1) Explain the structure of reports relative to length and formality.

1. Length and formality determine the following general progression of report structure:
   - The very long ones have prefatory pages (title fly, title page, letter of transmittal, table of contents, executive summary).
   - As reports become shorter and less formal, the composition of the prefatory parts section changes, generally in this order:
     —First, the title fly drops out.
     —Then, in succession, the executive summary and letter of transmittal are combined.
     —The table of contents is omitted, and
     —The combined letter of transmittal and executive summary is dropped.
   - Below these steps are the letter report and the memorandum report.

(2) Discuss the three major differences involved in writing short and long reports.

2. The shorter and by far the most common reports are much like the longer ones except for these three differences:
   - They have less need for introductory material.
   - They are more likely to begin directly (conclusion and recommendation first).
   - They are more likely to use personal style.

3. One of the more popular forms of less formal reports is the short report.
   - It consists of a title page and report text.
   - Usually it begins with a summary or conclusion.
   - Then it presents findings and analyses.
4. Letter reports are another popular short form.
   - Usually they are written in the indirect order.
   - They are organized much like the longer reports.
   Memorandum reports are like letter reports.
   - They are written for and by people within an organization.
   - They are the most common report form.
5. Among the various special reports, four stand out.
   - The staff report follows a fixed organization plan (for example, identifying information, summary, problem, facts, discussion, conclusions, recommendation).
   - A progress report reviews the progress on an activity and follows no set form.
   - The audit report presents the results of an audit and follows a variety of forms.
   - The technical report differs primarily in its subject matter.
     —The longer ones may follow a specified order.
     —One such order is introduction, methodology, facts, discussion, conclusion, recommendation.
6. A proposal is a presentation for the consideration of something—a merger, a bid for an account, a research grant, and so on.
   - Individuals and organizations make them to other individuals and organizations.
   - Some are made internally, from one department to another.
   - They may be invited or prospecting. They range from the very short to the very long.
   - They vary in form, from simple memorandums to full-dress reports.
   - They may be formal or informal.
   The contents of proposals vary with need, but one should consider these topics:
   - writer's purpose and reader's need,
   - background,
   - need,
   - plan description,
   - particulars (time, schedule, costs, performance standards, and such),
   - ability to deliver,
   - benefits, and
   - concluding comments.

---

3 Write clear and well-organized short reports.

4 Write clear and well-organized letter and memorandum reports.

5 Adapt the procedures for writing short reports to such special reports as staff, audit, progress, and technical reports.

6 Write complete, well-organized, and effective proposals.

CRITICAL THOUGHT QUESTIONS

1. Discuss the effects of formality and problem length on the model of report makeup described in the chapter.
2. Which of the prefatory pages of reports appear to be related primarily to the length of the report? Which to the need for formality?
3. Explain why some routine report problems require little or no introduction.
4. Why is the direct order generally used in the shorter reports? When is the indirect order desirable for such reports?
5. Give examples of short report forms that are appropriately written in personal style. Do the same for impersonal style.
6. Describe the organization of the conventional short report.
7. What types of problems are written up as letter reports? As memorandum reports? Explain the differences.
8. Why is the order of the staff report said to be a problem-solving order?
9. Discuss the differences between technical reports and the other business reports.
10. "To be successful, a proposal must be persuasive. This quality makes the proposal different from most short reports (which stress objectivity)." Discuss.

CRITICAL THINKING EXERCISES

1. Review the following report situations and determine for each the makeup of the report you would recommend for it:
   a. A professional research organization has completed a survey of consumer attitudes toward the Alto Company. The survey results will be presented to the Alto president in a 28-page report, including seven charts and three tables.
   b. Eva Campbell was asked by her department head to inspect the work area and report on safety conditions. Her report is two pages long and written in personal style.
   c. Chad Benton has an idea for improving a work procedure in his department at Dorner Manufacturing Company. His department head suggested that Chad present his idea in a report to the production superintendent. The report is almost five pages long, including a full-page diagram. It is written in the personal style.
   d. Karen Canady, a worker in the supply room of Edmunds & Sons Plumbing Contractors, was asked by Doug Edmunds, its president, for current inventory information on a number of basic products. Her report is less than a full page and consists mostly of a list of items and numbers.
   e. Bryan Toups, a sales manager for the Batla Chemical Company, was asked by the vice president of marketing to prepare an analysis of the results of a promotional campaign conducted in Toups' district. The report is six pages long (including one chart) and is written in the personal style.
2. Following is a report that was written for the manager of a large furniture retail store by the manager's assistant. The manager was concerned about customer complaints of late deliveries of furniture purchased and wanted to know the cause of the delays. Criticize this report.

11-17-95

TO: Martina Kalavoda
FROM: Anthony Dudrow
SUBJECT: Investigation requested 11-17-95

This morning at staff meeting it was requested that an investigation be made of the status of home deliveries and of the causes of the delays that have occurred. The investigation has been made with findings as follows.

Now that a new driver's helper, Morris Tunney, has been hired, there should be no more delays. This was the cause of the problem.

Over the past two weeks (10 working days), a total of 143 deliveries were made, and of these, 107 were made on or before the date promised, but some of the deliveries were late because of the departure two weeks ago of the driver's helper, Sean Toulouse, who had to be fired because of dishonesty and could not be replaced quickly with a permanent, qualified helper. Now that a permanent, qualified helper has been hired, there should be no more delays in delivery as this was the cause of the problem.

The driver was able to find a temporary helper, a man by name of Rusty Sellers, for some help in the unloading work, but he got behind and couldn't seem to catch up. He could have caught up by working overtime, in the opinion of the writer, but he refused to do so. Of the 36 deliveries that were late, all were completed within two days. The problem is over now that the driver has a helper, so there should be no additional delays.

▶ Short Length: Memorandum and Letter Reports

1. *Assessing results of a program to combat gang violence.* Assume the role of administrative assistant to the city manager of Metroville. Like most large cities, Metroville has suffered in recent years from problems related to gang violence. The problems became so bad that five months ago the city council decided to take remedial steps. Council members developed a comprehensive plan consisting of the establishment of neighborhood youth centers and police-sponsored athletic clubs. In addition, they provided additional funds for increased police patrols in problem areas.

   Perhaps it is too early to assess the value of the program. Even so, the council has asked for a first report on results. You were assigned the task of reporting.

   You began by going to the Metroville Police Department and extracting the pertinent information from files. Specifically, for each of the past four months you got the actual numbers of gang-related offenses, arrests of juveniles, drive-by shootings, and total arrests. You can't be certain that all drive-by shootings are gang related, but past evidence suggests that almost all are. And you got the total of all arrests to give you a basis for comparing gang-related crime with the total of all crime in the city. In summary form, your findings are as follows:

	4 Months Ago	3 Months Ago	2 Months Ago	Last Month
Gang-related offenses	97	122	81	74
Arrests of gang members	52	52	31	27
Drive-by-shootings	7	7	4	2
Total of all arrests	239	277	266	277

   Now you must present this information to the council in a memorandum report.

2. *Reporting supervisors' viewpoints on AIDS to management.* The main topic of discussion at last month's meeting of the executive staff of EZ Electronics, Inc., was the question of how to deal with employees who have AIDS. As viewpoints were mixed, no consensus was reached. Group members concluded they needed more information before continuing.

   They asked you, administrative assistant to the plant manager, to get some of the information they think they need. Specifically, they want the viewpoints of the company's supervisors. Such information, they believe, should be considered in working out any comprehensive policy on the matter. After all, the supervisors are the ones who will have to implement whatever policies are worked out.

   You began your task by going directly to the supervisors with the basic question of how a supervisor should react upon learning that an employee has AIDS. You got their reactions to eight likely responses. You were able to interview all but five of EZ's 62 supervisors (These five were unavailable for various reasons.) Following is a summary of the responses obtained:

Basic question: How should a supervisor respond to the knowledge that an employee has AIDS?

Responses	Yes	No	Don't know
Dismiss employee	5	24	28
Educate yourself on AIDS	35	5	17
Provide support to the victim	37	3	17
Encourage victim to resign	8	15	34
Provide victim with AIDS information	36	6	15
Inform the co-workers	29	10	18
Meet with experts to answer employee questions	23	13	21
Keep AIDS worker from contact with others	16	8	33

   Now you will present this information to the staff in a memorandum report. The report will not merely present the facts, but will also include implications for any policies on the matter devised by the staff.

3. *Determining the meaning of sexual harassment for a committee.* You are an administrative assistant to the director of human resources at Gifford-Belino Manufacturing Company, Inc. Your boss has been assigned to a committee charged with developing guidelines that will crystallize company policies on sexual harassment. At its first meeting, the committee members found that they could not agree on just what defines sexual harassment. They decided to get the answer from those directly involved—the women workers. And your boss volunteered you for the assignment.

   To get the information you need, you designed a simple survey. You randomly selected 100 female workers, and you asked them to either agree or disagree on whether eight specific types of attention constituted sexual harassment. You inquired further as to whether they had actually experienced each of these types of attention. The answers should provide a practical answer to the committee's question.

   Now the information is before you in the form of the following simple table. Analyze these results and present your findings to the committee in a memorandum report.

Types of Sexual Attention	Considered Sexual Harassment	Personally Experienced
Staring	7	57
Flirting	8	71
Suggestive gestures	46	27
Sexual remarks	51	61
Touching, grabbing, brushing	69	41
Sexual propositions	81	26
Sexual relations	46	8
Other	3	4

4. *Helping Protecto Inc.'s clients control their shoplifting problem.* Today's assignment finds you as assistant manager of Protecto, Inc., a service company that assists retailers in keeping their merchandise secure. Originally founded as a security patrol business, Protecto has expanded its product mix to include laser surveillance, crime prevention, and loss detection. It is in this last area of service—loss detection—that you have your writing assignment.

Several months ago, you were talking with one of your store manager clients when the subject of shoplifting arose. The client mentioned she believed losses from shoplifting had risen in the past year. She didn't know exactly how to approach the problem or its solution. She did know, however, that missing merchandise—unaccounted for in her inventory control system—was eating away at her already low profit margin. In other words, her problem was causing her losses at the bank.

Informally, you checked out the shoplifting problem with several other clients and they confirmed its existence, although the magnitude of the problem varied. All the clients you contacted, however, indicated the problem was real and created significant losses.

With these informal contacts in mind, you decided to determine in more detail the extent of the shoplifting problem in retail establishments. You designed a short questionnaire that emphasized the who, when, and how of the problem. Specifically, you emphasized the how of the problem because of the practical and preventative nature of the services you offer to customers. After you designed and pretested the questionnaire, you sent it to 100 retailers in the trading area that you serve. You stratified your sample to include supermarkets, drugstores, and discount stores, because these outlets represent 70 percent of your clients and because you believe that shoplifting occurs more frequently in these types of marketing institutions.

Today, four weeks after your initial mailing of the questionnaire, you have received 65 usable responses. After tallying them, you determine some definite patterns of the trading area shoplifting problem. First,

Fridays and Saturdays are more common for shoplifting than other days of the week. Second, more shoplifting seems to occur between 4:00 and 7:00 P.M. than at other times. Third, the methods used by shoplifters vary by type of outlet as follows:

Methods Used to Shoplift	Drug-store	Super-market	Discount Store
Pocket	28.2%	25.4%	28.3%
Under clothing	28.3	24.3	20.9
Purse	23.1	28.8	27.7
Shopping bag	3.1	2.7	2.9
Label switching	2.1	0.9	1.8
Accomplice	3.0	3.8	3.1
Other bag	4.3	4.9	2.8
Other method	7.9	9.2	12.5

It's this last area of information that you think will benefit your customers the most. So you will use it as the basis of a memo you will prepare for all store managers served by Protecto, Inc.

In the memo, you will present and interpret the findings—specifically the ways used by shoplifters to steal—to the store managers. Perhaps they can use these findings to alert their employees to detect those who might be likely suspects—especially at key times of the day and week. In time, you might develop your own training program for store managers on the subject. But for now your purpose is to help your existing clientele with a problem that affects them.

Write the memo to the store managers to give them your findings, tell them what the findings mean, and help them solve one of their merchandising problems.

5. *Using survey results to increase Compumart's sales.* As assistant manager of Compumart, a chain of computer retail stores, you have an interesting and important assignment for the moment. Your boss, Mr. Warren Bottoroff, tells you this way: "It's always been my philosophy that we compete best on service not price. We do our best job when we relate our product knowledge to an individual customer's needs. So send these facts to our store managers and tell them how to use them. It will mean increased sales for all of them, I'm sure."

The "facts" that Mr. Bottoroff refers to are those you collected from sales prospects of Compumart stores across the country. You designed a short questionnaire listing possible ways people could use a personal computer. You sent the questionnaire to all Compumart store managers and asked them to make it available to people who entered their businesses—whether they purchased anything or not. A postage paid return envelope was provided.

Although you did not control for demographics or

seasonal factors, you feel that the number of returns you have received gives you reasonably reliable results. Also, the percentages by category appear to have stabilized as you have tallied the results. Thus, you are confident that the results are not random and show a certain preference/profile for using a personal computer. The results are as follows:

Uses for a Personal Computer	% Response*
Budgeting/paying bills	28.2
Keeping books/household records/rent/utility bills/taxes	18.8
Schooling/help with school work/homework	17.5
Finances/checkbook balancing/bank statements	16.9
Entertainment/games	14.5
Business	10.4
Writing	9.6
Math	6.4
Store addresses/phone numbers/special events	5.8
Real estate purchases	2.1
Set up office at home	2.1
Hook up to a bank	0.8
Resumes	0.8
Communication purposes	0.8
Other	0.8
No use/no need for one	2.9

* Totals are more than 100% because of multiple responses.

Your job now is to send this information to Compumart store managers. For this purpose, you will use your standard e-mail format. As your boss has instructed you, however, you will need to do more than present the facts. You will need to comment on them, showing how floor sales personnel can use them to increase sales. Thus, you will need to relate the facts to the sales work of the employees—and that's a process of interpretation.

Write the e-mail memo report for the Compumart store managers.

6. *Developing a nonsmoking campaign at Avant Gentry.* Avant Gentry, a large office supply company, is considering banning smoking at work. To implement such a policy successfully, the company will need to be strategic in its efforts to establish the behavior change program. As assistant to the owner, you have been selected to help with the nonsmoking program.

Susan Scallan, the owner of Avant Gentry, reasons that a nonsmoking personnel policy is best for the company at this stage of its growth for several reasons. First, it will reflect society's values about good health. In fact, Avant Gentry may even be behind the times, as most companies have already banned smoking from company premesis. Second, the company will save in insurance claims and premiums. For both

these reasons and perhaps others, it makes good sense for Avant Gentry to pursue its nonsmoking program.

And this is where you enter the picture. Ms. Scallan gives you the problem in this manner: "We'll need to approach this nonsmoking problem systematically and scientifically. Before we do anything, I need to know the attitudes of our people. Find out what our workers think about this smoking issue. Then we can accurately diagnose the problem and design an effective strategy."

With these words still ringing in your ears, you return to your desk, trying to clear your thoughts about how you can collect the data Ms. Scallan wants. You conclude generally that a survey would be best. Using your own logic and the ideas of several colleagues, you derive reasons for quitting and not quitting smoking. Then you arrange them on paper for easy checking by respondents. This instrument will be the one you use to collect the facts.

Next, you duplicate the form and distribute it through paycheck envelopes and paycheck receipts (for those who use electronic transfers to financial institutions) to all employees. The questionnaire asks for several demographics—age, gender, smoker vs. nonsmoker, and such; but it does not ask for the names of the respondents. Today you have received 225 returns—135 who are smokers and 90 who are not. Thus, you believe the results below represent reliably the sentiments of your employees.

Reasons for Quitting Smoking	Yes	No
Fear of losing job	23%	77%
Peer pressure	16	84
Information provided in a quit-smoking program	17	83
Pressure from family members	38	62
Personal concern for health	86	14
Increased restriction on smoking in public	21	79
Pressure from clients	1	99
Increased social view of smoking as a dirty habit	43	57

7. *Investigating the glass ceiling issue of women's participation in executive education programs.* Last week's board meeting of the Association of Women Executives was a spirited one, to say the least. The issue of women's involvement in executive training programs arose, and many viewpoints were presented. Most of the board believed that few women were selected for these programs.

The rationale for this opinion seemed to be that the lack of women in these programs mirrored the dearth of women in the upper echelons of corporate America. Typically, according to most of the board, male managers identify rising stars; and they often

TABLE 1 Enrollment in Five Leading Executive Education Programs

Course/Institution	Women	Total Enrollment	% Women
Advanced Management Program/ Harvard Business School	13	275	5%
Advanced Management Program/ INSEAD	7	307	2
Stanford Executive Program/ Stanford University	13	168	8
Leadership at the Peak/ Center for Creative Leadership	15	163	9
Executive Program/ University of Michigan	7	113	6

exclude women. Thus, executive training programs become men-only affairs. At the end of the session, the board members acknowledged that they had no factual information to support their majority position. Thus, they asked you, the executive director, to get this information for them.

You begin by collecting the information by contacting five of the leading programs in executive education. Specifically, you asked for enrollment data for the last year. Based on your collection efforts, you assemble the facts as shown in Table 1. Although your procedure was not totally scientific, you believe the information is indicative of most other executive education programs. You will use the facts as the basis for a memorandum report.

Using the facts in the table, prepare this memo report to the board of the Association of Women Executives. Interpret the facts in terms of the participation issue in executive education programs.

8. *Reporting communication activities of ICA business members.* The International Communication Association is a professional organization of business communication professors and business executives. Its purpose is to study and research areas of interest in the teaching and practice of communication in business. You are the executive director of the ICA with a staff of two full-time employees.

From time to time, you send information memos to ICA members on topics of interest to them. Recently, your office surveyed the 120 business executive members to determine the communication activities they engage in at work. Your purpose was to get information that will tell the communication professors the importance of each activity in the real world of business. You believe the survey results will enable the professors to plan their instruction for better results.

In time, a full-scale report will be written. But for now, you have assembled the highlights (Table 2) based on 42 business executive members who returned your questionnaire. Based on the response rate (35 percent) and the industry diversification of

the questionnaire returns, you believe the results are both reliable and representative.

Now you must prepare a memo report to the professor members presenting and interpreting these highlights. You will not just refer to the data and let it go at that. You will tell what the data mean by comparing and analyzing them. Write the report in memo form to the professor members of the ICA.

9. *Evaluating fund-raisers' compensation for members of a professional association.* The National Association of Development Executives recently conducted a salary survey of its members. The results, shown in Table 3, reveal that salaries differ—sometimes markedly and sometimes slightly—by type of institution employing development officers. You believe that the salary figures tell a story about the status of the profession; thus, as executive director of NADE, you decide to present your finding to the membership in a memorandum.

Development officers (or fund-raisers as they are sometimes called) have reaped the benefits of several societal occurrences. Social program cuts by the federal government in the early 1980s gave the profession visibility as gifts became critical for organizations. More recently, many fund-raisers' jobs have become stepping-stones to an organizations's presidency or chief executive position. These events, along with the cyclical nature of the economy, have propelled fund-raisers to center stage in most organizations.

Prepare the memo to NADE's members that will show them the reward side of the professional picture. You will do more than merely report the information in Table 3. You will interpret the facts so that the members will get the true meaning of the information for the profession. Write the memo with a conclusion-first beginning.

10. *Reporting on vehicle thefts to association members in selected cities.* As executive director of the National Automobile Club, part of your job is to present timely tidbits of information that will benefit the 120,000 members of your organization. One way you do this is

TABLE 2 Communication Activities

Activity	Percent of Time Spent Daily				
	0–20	20–40	40–60	60–80	80–100
Letter writing	34	8			
Report writing	12	9	12	7	2
Memo writing	27	9	4	2	
Talking to others on phone or in person	9	22	5	5	1
Listening	14	15	9	2	2
Other (Proposals, procedures, etc.)		2	9	2	

TABLE 3 Development Officers' Salaries by Type of Institution

	Under $18,000	$18,000 to $33,000	$33,001 to $50,000	$50,001 to $75,000	$75,001 to $90,000	Over $90,000
Educational	1.1%	19.4%	39.2%	29.6%	6.6%	4.4%
National Health	3.7	24.7	38.2	24.7	6.2	2.5
Nat'l Social Service	2.2	26.1	37.0	23.9	2.2	8.7
Youth Organization	2.0	23.8	40.6	24.8	5.9	2.0
Conservation-Wildlife	0.0	30.0	60.0	0.0	10.0	0.0
Environmental	0.0	20.0	60.0	0.0	13.3	6.7
Cultural	3.4	33.3	31.7	23.1	4.3	4.3
Retirement	0.0	8.7	60.9	17.3	13.0	0.0
Hospital-Medical Center	1.0	14.7	26.2	36.7	12.4	9.2
Religious	5.1	8.5	42.3	33.9	5.1	5.1

through a "Tips for Travelers" memo, which you prepare as the need arises for it. You distribute the memo electronically and by regular mail.

Recently, a tabular array of information caught your eye (Table 4) in the *Automobile News,* a trade publication. Prepared by the American Crime Bureau, the table compared vehicle thefts for 1994 with 1993 for selected cities with populations over 100,000. As you think about the information, you decide to share it with your members through a "Tips for Travelers" memo. First, you will want to point out cities that have changed for the good (a minus percentage change) and those that have changed for the bad (a plus percentage change). You will not want to degrade the high theft locations. But you do want to alert NAC members about high-risk contingencies that might affect their travel.

Second, you will want to suggest actions members should take to protect themselves. Probably, these suggestions will evolve out of the data analysis you

present initially; they could be conclusions derived from the data. As members travel to vacation sites, to visit with family members, to conduct work, etc., they should check their insurance coverage, park safely in well-lighted areas, and such. On these points, you will not take a hard-sell, persuasive approach. You are still preparing a report—an orderly, objective communication of factual information that serves some business purpose.

Write the "Tips for Travelers" memo that will present the facts, interpret them, and derive key points for members to consider about vehicle thefts.

11. *Presenting an attendance analysis for a professional baseball team.* The Tri City Cats, a professional baseball team, wants to continue to be a major sports attraction for fans and potential fans in the Tri City metro area. Three years ago, you were hired as director of sales and promotion to ensure that the Cats continued to exist as a visible and viable sports entertainment outlet.

TABLE 4   Percentage Change from 1993 to 1994 in Number of Vehicle Thefts for Selected Cities over 100,000 Population

City	Percentage Change	City	Percentage Change
Atlanta	−24.70%	Beaumont, Texas	54.54%
Houston	−24.31	Baton Rouge, La	35.04
Boston	−15.25	Fort Lauderdale, Fla.	27.88
New York	− 9.61	Tampa, Fla.	22.38
Philadelphia	− 8.22	Buffalo, N.Y.	23.15
Chicago	− 5.80	Portland, Ore.	21.04
Detroit	− 5.58	Jackson, Miss.	20.43
Los Angeles	− 2.54	Inglewood, Calif.	15.92
Miami	− 1.24	Fresno, Calif.	11.25
Newark, N.J.	− 0.59	Pittsburgh	8.23

TABLE 5   Comparison of Attendance at Tri City Cats' Baseball

Attendance Category	No. of Fans in Category		Percent Increase 2 Years Ago/Last Season	Average No. of Games Attended		Percent Increase 2 Years Ago/Last Season	Total Attendance		Percent Increase 2 Years Ago/Last Season
	2 Years Ago	Last Season		2 Years Ago	Last Season		2 Years Ago	Last Season	
Heavy (mostly season-ticket holders)	10,000	11,000	10	20	24	20	200,000	264,000	32
Medium	16,500	17,250	4.5	13	16	23	214,500	276,000	28.7
Light	235,000	278,000	18.2	2.5	3.75	50	587,500	1,042,500	77.4
Total	261,500	306,250	17.1	3.83	5.17	35	1,002,000	1,582,500	57.9

When you assumed your job, you designed a questionnaire that was distributed at selected games both by hand and inserted into game programs. On the questionnaire, you asked that people return the completed form at boxes in Cat Stadium or mail it in a pre-addressed envelope. The public address announcer reinforced your requests several times during the game. You repeated the procedure this past season to get comparisons. These figures, plus those about actual attendance from your own records, are shown in Table 5. You believe that these tangible results of who attends Cats games tell much about the team's success at the gate. Moreover, they will prove useful in planning for forthcoming seasons.

Because these facts are so revealing, you decide to share them in a memo with the club's owner, Craig Beytien. If presented and analyzed properly, they should tell a good story about the Cats' following. One point revealed by the data concerns the myth of "new customers." More existing fans attending more games seems to be one trend in the data. This

occurred even though the win/loss record was about the same. Of course, the idea assumes that fans two years ago returned for games last season. There are other trends as well.

Write the memo to Mr. Beytien that will give him a clear picture of the Cats' attendance. You will present the conclusions first in your memo followed by supporting facts and analyses. Also, you will use captions to show good organization of the data.

12. *Presenting trends in coffee consumption.* As assistant to the sales manager of Imperial Coffee Company, you have just returned from the annual meeting of the International Coffee Institute (growers and exporters of coffee) in New Orleans. You were sent to the meeting as Imperial's delegate.

At the meeting, you heard many informative presentations on the status of coffee consumption; and you also mixed and mingled with other delegates in the industry at breaks and at social functions. In all of your contacts, you learned much about the goings-on of the coffee business—inside and out! One of the more interesting formal sessions was on trends in coffee consumption and was conducted by Carlos Lopez, the institute's research director. Things certainly have changed over the years, you discovered; and Lopez has hard data to support his points. Thus, you will prepare a memo to your boss, Jeremiah Walsh, highlighting the major findings of the trends in coffee consumption. You believe this information can help in planning and market penetration for Imperial in forthcoming years.

The basis of your report is the material Lopez distributed at the meeting (Tables 6, 7, and 8). As noted in the handouts, consumption by time of day, by cups per drinker, and by comparison with other beverages—all over time—should tell much about the competitive niche for coffee as a beverage of choice by the American consumer.

Write the memo to Mr. Walsh in direct order. Also, use first-level captions to show good organization of your thinking and to help readability.

13. *Examining consumer attitudes about importance of country of origin in purchasing decisions.* At its meeting last year in Detroit, the National Association of Retailers experienced controversy among members about promoting consumer goods with a "made in North America" appeal. On the one hand, some members voiced concern that the appeal would hinder product quality, brand name, price, and such that retailers would consider in promoting their products. On the other, some members felt that the homemade appeal made little difference to customers in their purchasing decisions. As the issue was debated, it became evident that there were many opinions but few facts to support any side of the issue. Thus, the

TABLE 6   The American Coffee Drinker

	20 Years Ago	5 Years Ago	4 Years Ago	3 Years Ago	2 Years Ago	Last Year
Cups per drinker per day	4.17	3.41	3.38	3.36	3.48	3.33
Percentage drinking	74.7	56.4	56.3	55.2	57.3	54.9

TABLE 7   Consumption by Time of the Day

	Percentage Share					Change	
	20 Years Ago	4 Years Ago	3 Years Ago	2 Years Ago	Last Year	20 Years Ago to Last Year	2–4 Years to Last Year*
Breakfast	38	46	48	46	48	+10	+1
Other meals	31	19	19	18	16	−15	−3
Between meals	33	35	34	36	36	+3	+1
Total	100	100	100	100	100		

* These figures represent the change of data between last year and the average of 4–2 years ago.

TABLE 8   Consumption of Coffee and Other Beverages

	Percentage Drinking					Change	
	20 Years Ago	4 Years Ago	3 Years Ago	2 Years Ago	Last Year	20 Years Ago to Last Year	2–4 Years to Last Year*
Coffee	74.7	56.3	55.2	57.3	54.9	−19.8	−1.4
Tea	24.7	31.6	31.8	30.9	30.9	+6.2	−0.5
Milk	53.6	48.9	48.8	47.7	47.4	−6.2	−1.1
Soft drinks	32.6	52.9	55.1	57.1	59.4	+26.8	+4.4
Juices	41.4	44.5	44.8	45.7	45.5	+4.1	+0.5

association's board charged the research department to investigate the matter and to report to it and the members whenever there were meaningful results.

As a member of the research department, you have been appointed to complete the charge from the board. To do so, you designed a questionnaire and sent it to a randomly selected sample of consumers who were diversified by income, locale, age, and other demographics. The questionnaire was detailed; although the returns are still coming in irregularly and in smaller numbers than earlier, you believe it is time to tally the results.

Because you are interested in the "homemade" issue, you tally this part of the questionnaire first (Table 9). And you decide the issue is significant enough to the NAR membership for you to write a memo emphasizing the meaning of the findings. A full-scale report of all the results will be written eventually, but the issue of made in North America is hot enough for you to give a glimpse of the entire report now. Besides, it can demonstrate that you are earnestly and consistently working to benefit NAR members. And for the first time, you have facts to support your case.

Write the memo in direct order to the members. It will be an analytical one consisting of facts, interpretations, and conclusions. You will use captions to show good organization of thought, and you will write impersonally.

14. *Recommending a pager watch for your sales representatives.* As the regional manager for a major pharmaceutical company, you work to continuously improve the way you and your staff get your work done. In fact, a few years ago you gave your sales representatives portable computers to help them communicate with both you and their customers. That technology initially gave you some competitive advantage, enabling you to give your customers quickly the information they needed. Today a new technology—a pager watch—looks like a candidate for granting some competitive advantage.

While sales representatives can check their e-mail at any time to communicate with you and their customers as well as to gather information for their customers, you often wish you could reach them with new information rather than having to wait for them to check in. With a nonintrusive pager that also functions as a watch, you could develop a code to use with pagers. The code could signal the representative about the nature and urgency of the page.

Both Seiko and Swatch offer these pager watches. While the Swatch only pages, its cost is $175, or $95 more than the Seiko, priced at $80. The Swatch's paging costs run approximately $9 per month. On the other hand, the Seiko offers both paging and information services. Some services offered in addition to basic paging include voice mail alerts, weather updates, and basic and deluxe information services. While the basic paging and weather update service costs $8.95/month, the voice mail feature adds $5 or more to the cost. At the moment, the basic and deluxe information packages include such items as market closing prices, lottery numbers, ski conditions, sport scores, UV index, and pollution count. This type of information service is likely to vary by location and change due to demand of its users. These packages add another $2.98 to the monthly cost.

Recommend and justify purchasing one of these watches for your sales representatives. Be sure to include in your recommendation a method for training the reps on the use of this new communication tool as well as a way to evaluate its effectiveness.

15. *Presenting and recommending a ticketing system for a ski resort.* As Michael Deftos, accountant for one of Utah's most beautiful ski resorts [you choose one], you have been asked by your client, the manager of the ski resort, to review three methods of ticketing systems and recommend one. The goal of these methods is to shorten lines, but they each have other potential advantages and disadvantages. The methods you have been asked to evaluate are electronic ticketing, pay-per-run, and kiosks.

Electronic ticketing, already in use at the Northstar resort in Lake Tahoe, California, allows scanners to read microchips embedded in wristbands or plastic cards. Some of these are read as skiers pass through electronic gates, and others are read by lift operators with handheld bar code readers. Like credit cards, this system would enable resorts to keep track of various factors relating to each skier. For example, you would know who were your frequent skiers, perhaps helping you set up some type of frequent skier program. You could find out other information such as days and dates preferred, rental and lesson purchases, and other information. This kind of information can help you in planning your staffing and purchasing decisions to enable you to serve your customer better.

The pay-per-run system appears fairest; those who

TABLE 9   Ratings of Country of Origin by Product Category

Category	Importance of Country of Origin		
	High	Middle	Low
Adult clothing/shoes	4.7%	37.9%	57.4%
Home electronics/camera	6.5	39.1	54.4
Housewares	8.0	36.3	55.7
Furniture	2.7	37.3	60.0
Major appliances	7.8	39.2	53.0
Hardware/lawn & garden	15.4	43.6	41.0
Children's clothing	5.0	40.0	55.0
Home textiles	—	33.3	66.7
Sporting goods/recreation	33.3	33.3	33.3
Other	3.7	51.9	44.4

ski more pay more. However, most of the European resorts that have used this system have sliding scales, allowing those who purchase more runs to pay less per run. This is like buying the large, economy-size package. It rewards those with high volume use through discounts. The tickets are transferable and do not need to be used in a day, which is often a popular feature with families and groups. Two U.S. resorts—Mt. Bachelor in Oregon, and Snow Valley in Southern California—use a similar system with points. Points are charged on a pay-per-use basis.

Kiosks placed in sporting goods stores are beginning to be used in Southern California. The skier gets up-to-date information on costs for lift tickets, lodging, and weather. The kiosks allow the skier to purchase the tickets in advance, some are for specific dates, and others are open-ended so the skier can have some flexibility.

In presenting the report to management, be sure to include how each system might affect accounting for revenues as well as for generating revenues.

16. *Educating grocers on the changing methods in food production.* As the world population expands, the food industry is being pushed hard to change to keep up with demand. Your job as public relations agent for the Food Marketing Institute is to keep grocers informed of these changes as well as when to expect them. In a short, readable report, explain the five methods of "farming" being experimented with today to meet some of the growing demand—indoor hydroponics, superpreservatives, aquaculture, food tablets, and genetic engineering.

Hydroponics uses a nutrient rich water bath rather than soil to grow plants. While this technology has been around for over 20 years, it still costs much more than using the nutrients already in the ground. However, it does enable supermarkets to offer out-of-season products year round. Superpreservatives are still simply a concept. While it would be nice to have ripe, delicious peaches in mid-winter, no preservative yet has been able to retain taste and consistency while retarding spoilage.

Aquaculture, the farming of fish in undersea cages or land-based cages, is likely to become a reality. Not only would consumers benefit from the availability of a wide variety of fish, but they also would welcome the product knowing the breeding areas would be regulated for safety. They would be reassured that they were protected from both bacteria and pollution. Food tablets are not likely to become a reality. While technically possible to produce them, the public is not ready to accept them. As a culture we've come to use food as a socializing tool, going out to eat more often and eating a wider variety of foods.

Only genetically engineered foods seem to hold a near-term, viable solution. By making every product "perfect," none is lost to insect infestations or disease. Breeding heartier plants and animals spreads what we do have.

Five experts in food science were recently surveyed for their forecasts on when consumers might expect to see some of these products in the stores. Table 10 shows the year they expect the technology to be evident to the consumer.

17. *Recommending ways of financing a child's college education.* (Requires research) As Julie Jahn, a certified financial planner, several of your clients recently have been asking you for ideas on ways to finance their child's education. You think it might be wise to create a document that would both answer your clients' questions as well as help promote your financial planning business.

Since your immediate clients' needs are for financing the education now, rather than in 18 years, the report you prepare will cover immediate funding. Also, you realize that while a few of their children are superstar scholars, most are average to above-average scholars. Most want to go to public or reasonably priced private schools, not pricey private schools. Also, your clients' philosophies differ widely on the role of their child in funding the education. Some believe firmly in having the student pick up a good share of the expenses. However, some want the children to get the education now and pay later. Others don't want their child to graduate in debt, believing the student should work to meet expenses while going to school. Others believe that their responsibility as parents includes giving their child as much education as needed. Therefore, your report should include a variety of options to meet a variety of situations.

TABLE 10   Expectations of Experts

Expert	Hydroponic	Superpreservative	Aquaculture	Food Tablet	Genetically Engineered
Mahamoud El-Begearmi	2000	Never	1997	Never	1998
Manfred Kroger	2085	Never	2025	1995	1960
Pam Marrone	2020	2050	2050	2040	2020
Ellen Martin	2100	Never	2000	Never	2015
Jim McCamant	Never	Never	2030	2010	2030

Source: David Pescovitz, "The Future of Food," *Wired*, January 1995, p. 52.

This report should include both primary and secondary sources. Interviews with counselors, bankers, and parents who have recently financed a child's education will give a variety of perspectives. Also, secondary information from the Institute of Financial Planners and other financial planning literature will give you an objective view. Write a report to address the needs of most parents in searching for ideas for ways to fund their child's education. In addition to your immediate clients, the report will be sent to anyone responding to advertising used to promote your services.

18. *Recommending training for computer end users.* As the director of MIS, you received a request this week from Nancy Bray, a vice president in your company, for training on the use of the new e-mail program your division recently installed. This request prompted you to investigate informally the need for end-user training on e-mail. Your investigation revealed an immediate, swelling need for formal training for end users.

An inspection of your user support technicians' logs revealed a steep increase in the number of calls about the new e-mail package. Furthermore, your technicians report that they believe this may be just the beginning since questions are coming in on the "easy-to-use" features of the package. Some fear the nature and number of calls on the more advanced features; however, others forecast that users will not go beyond the basics, not fully employing the tool or employing it appropriately. Clearly, the information you have gathered from the support technicians indicates an immediate need for training.

However, you decided to walk around and ask users at various levels and in various jobs about the new e-mail software. While most report they like the look of the user interface, the terms used in it are often confused with different terms from the old system. One user reported high frustration when trying to upload a file. He reported reviewing the on-line help as well as checking the full documentation out of the company library to no avail before contacting the support technicians. When he learned the answer was simply one of using the term *import* rather than *upload,* he was frustrated. He reported others in his division were having similar frustrations. When you asked your power end users about the advanced features, you were surprised that even these users report not using them. You heard this "It's nice but . . ." comment often enough to realize that hands-on training is needed at all levels. Furthermore, you believe you need both basic and advanced training to garner full advantage from the tool.

Therefore, the report you write to your boss, CIO Thomas McLaughlin, will recommend training. Send a copy to Nancy Bray so she will learn that you have followed through on her request. Recommend basic training at all levels and all sites on a voluntary attendance basis. Recommend use of the distance learning lab as well as videotaping sessions for individual checkout from the corporate library. Stress the imme-

diacy and importance of this training.

19. *Encouraging employee fitness.* Your company has finally taken formal steps to encourage employee fitness by appointing you the official organizer of company-sponsored activities. For several years the company has declared its support of the importance of fitness; it has even helped sponsor local run/walk events. However, those efforts only gave fitness verbal or financial support; they left individual employee participation to chance.

Now with evidence that fit employees con contribute to the bottom line through improved productivity, fewer accidents, less absenteeism, and less use of health care services, it's time to do more than leave fitness to chance. Companies such as Du Pont, General Motors, and Control Data have all reported savings in the millions of dollars in medical expenses that are directly attributable to their fitness programs. Furthermore, there are many accounts of improved fitness providing intangible benefits such as increased alertness, higher morale, and generally better spirits.

To create an environment where fitness is both supported and encouraged, you have been put in charge of organizing regular fitness programs and special events. To encourage regular fitness, the company will now pay half the initiation fee of any fitness club the employee joins. That will allow employees to choose one near work or near home, participating in the one that meets their needs. Additionally, for those employees wanting to work regular fitness into the lunch hour, you will now allow employees up to an hour and half break. Of course, you still expect them to work a full eight-hour day.

The first special event you have decided to promote is company participation in the 10K walk for the March of Dimes. You will set up a practice training schedule of walks each weekend for the next six weeks, and all employees participating will get a special T-shirt with company logo. To show you are serious about preparing for the walk, your plan will include arranging for alternative indoor training to eliminate bad weather as an excuse.

Write a report to employees outlining the new, committed emphasis on fitness. Talk about both the importance of regular fitness as well as the sense of camaraderie they'll develop by participating in the special event. Your report will convey the information while showing the company is now committing its time and resources to support the fitness objective.

20. *Reporting and interpreting new EEOC guidelines for conducting interviews.* As a human resource specialist, one of your jobs is coordinating interviewing with employees in departments that participate in the interviewing process. While your office does most of the initial screening of job candidates, employees in the department where the new hires will work interview candidates as well. Part of your job is to keep these employees up to date on the legal issues related to hiring practices. Write a report that will help them conduct interviews without violating federal

TABLE 11 Discriminating Questions

Legal	Illegal
• Do you have 20/20 corrected vision?	• What is your corrected vision?
• How well can you handle stress?	• Does stress ever affect your ability to be productive?
• Can you perform this function with or without reasonable accommodation?	• Would you need reasonable accommodation in this job?
• How many days were you absent from work last year?	• How many days were you sick last year?
• Are you currently illegally using drugs?	• What medications are you currently taking?
• Do you regularly eat three meals per day?	• Do you need to eat a number of small snacks at regular intervals throughout the day in order to maintain your energy level?
• Do you drink alcohol?	• How much alcohol do you drink per week?

SOURCE: EEOC's "Enforcement Guidance on Pre-Employment Disability-Related Inquiries," May 1994.

disability-discrimination laws and avoid costly, time-consuming lawsuits.

While many of the regulations seem stupid to some employment specialists, you still need to comply. The Disabilities Act is an attempt to protect a disabled worker from discrimination where accommodating the worker would not cause undue hardship on the employer. However, employers need to know what accommodations are needed, but they need to know how to ask the questions in ways that comply with the law. Recently, the EEOC issued some guidelines. In your report, you may want to use some of the illustrations shown in Table 11. Point out the importance of the work choice and perhaps the distinctions between the similar questions. You may want to give examples that illustrate what kinds of responses the questions elicit in order to illustrate the differences.

▶ **Intermediate-Length Reports**

21. *Presenting survey results on a convention center to council members.* Two years ago, the Metroville Convention Center opened its doors. At the time, enthusiasm for this costly structure ran high, especially with the mayor and the other civic leaders who were instrumental in promoting the project. In short time, however, the enthusiasm waned. Operational problems cropped up, and patrons increasingly voiced discontent with the center.

In fact, concerns about the center and its operations became so great that after 15 months of operation, the council fired the convention center manager and hired a new one. After of few months of operation under the new manager, however, complaints again surfaced. They increased steadily until they appeared to be as negative as before. They had become so negative the council placed the matter on the agenda for its first meeting this month.

At this meeting, the subject was thoroughly discussed, Accusations and strong statements flowed

freely, and temper flared. After two hours of heated discussion, council member Albert J. Cobb suggested that much of what had been said was more rumor and opinion than fact. He further suggested that the council get first-hand information from the users of the convention facilities. "These are the ones who count," Cobb said. "They are the ones who will determine the success of the center. Why not conduct a survey of them? Ask them the pertinent questions. Then we'll have something substantive to work with."

The council members quickly bought Cobb's suggestion. They agreed to ask city manager Otis A. Patton to conduct a survey of convention users. Since you are Patton's assistant, in turn you got the assignment. Of course, you will do the bulk of the work, but Patton will look over your shoulder and will be designated as coauthor of the report (if he approves your work).

After the meeting, you began the task by designing a comprehensive but simple questionnaire covering all the problem areas discussed at the meeting. It simply asked the respondents to rank on a 1-to-5 scale their views on the various facilities and activities at the center. Next, using attendance rolls from a variety of conventions held at the center, you built a sample of people to be interviewed. Because many on the list are out-of-towners, you elected to mail the questionnaires, with return-postage-paid envelopes. (For class purposes, you may create any other specific methodology information you may need.)

Now you have your returns, and you have computed scale averages for each question (Table 12). Next you must review these findings to see what they tell you about the center—and perhaps more important, what they tell you about how to improve things. With your analyses done, you will then organize your information in the best possible order for presentation. Then you will supply the words that will convey your message in a fast-moving, readable report.

Probably you will use conventional short-report form (title page and text). Since the council members

TABLE 12 (PROBLEM 21)   Satisfaction of Respondents with Metroville Convention Center Facilities and Operations*

	All Events	Events Held before Management Change	Events Held on or after Management Change	One-Day Events	Two-Day Events	Three-Day Events	Longer than Three-Day Events	Less than 1,000 Attendees	1,000 to 10,000 Attendees	More than 10,000 Attendees
Overall experience at center	2.16	2.50	1.93	2.40	2.33	1.90	2.00	2.22	2.33	2.33
Functionality of meeting space	1.79	1.86	1.75	1.87	1.83	1.50	2.33	1.83	2.08	1.00
Functionality of loading area	2.39	2.40	2.39	3.50	2.71	1.83	1.67	2.80	2.42	2.25
Functionality of overall building	2.06	2.00	2.10	1.92	2.43	1.92	2.25	1.91	2.25	2.25
Cooperation of sales staff	1.61	1.65	1.57	1.73	1.57	1.58	1.25	1.75	1.58	1.50
Honesty and integrity of center staff	1.61	1.71	1.52	1.93	1.86	1.25	1.00	1.58	1.67	1.25
Cooperation of center staff during the event	1.47	1.59	1.38	1.60	1.57	1.42	1.00	1.42	1.42	1.75
Cooperation of center top management	1.87	2.00	1.75	2.17	2.00	1.58	1.67	1.78	1.73	2.25
Fairness of overall price	2.50	2.41	2.57	2.67	2.86	2.25	2.00	2.58	2.33	3.00
Quality of food	2.61	2.41	2.79	1.93	3.43	2.75	3.33	1.90	2.92	3.25
Affordability of food	3.00	2.69	3.29	2.75	3.50	2.92	3.33	3.00	3.08	3.50
Availability of parking	4.13	4.06	4.19	4.13	4.29	4.00	4.25	4.17	4.33	4.00
Building location	2.65	2.50	2.76	2.71	2.86	2.33	3.00	2.55	3.25	2.25
Availability of hotel space	2.18	1.86	2.33	2.50	2.50	1.80	2.50	2.00	2.36	1.00
Quality of hotel space	2.00	1.86	2.07	2.25	1.83	1.90	2.50	1.75	2.27	1.00
Proximity of hotels	2.09	1.75	2.27	2.00	2.17	1.90	3.00	2.00	2.27	1.00
Assistance from City Convention and Visitors Bureau	2.24	1.83	2.40	3.00	2.20	1.90	2.50	3.00	1.90	1.00

* Ranking System   1: excellent   2: good   3: average   4: bad   5: very poor

will want the highlights fast, you will begin with a summary. You may use graphics—wherever they help tell the report story. Address the report to the city council, listing all seven of its members.

22. *Reporting on employee viewpoints about stealing from their employer.* For this problem, assume the role of executive trainee in the Human Resources Department of Electronco, Inc., a major manufacturer of electronic products. Today, you were called into the office of the director, Helen O. Cortez. Ms. Cortez explained to you that at the staff meeting she attended earlier in the day the discussion centered on employee theft. Apparently, the various executives believe that some

of their workers are stealing and they support their views with evidence such as inventory records, personal observations, and employee admissions.

As Ms. Cortez explained it, some of the pilferage involves little things like paper and pencils; but much of it concerns big items like work tools, manufactured products in inventory, and telephone answering machines. In fact, one department has discovered that one of its computers has disappeared.

The staff agreed to begin work on policy changes designed to reduce the stealing. But so the administrators will fully understand the problem they face, they have asked your department to conduct a survey of company employees. The objective of this survey will

TABLE 13 (Problem 22)   Tabulations of Questions Involving Yes-No Responses

Question	Employees Admitting Stealing (96)			Employees Denying Stealing (116)		
	Yes	No	No Response	Yes	No	No Response
Would you report a fellow worker whom you saw stealing?	16	76	4	44	52	20
Should your employer provide an incentive for reporting stealing?	8	81	7	31	69	8

TABLE 14 (Problem 22)   Responses to Question on Why Employee Thinks Other Employees Steal from Their Employer*

Explanation	Employees Admitting Stealing (96)	Employees Denying Stealing (116)
Believe underpaid	24	11
Has grudge against employer	21	6
Easy to do	9	36
Doesn't see it as stealing	67	38
Thinks he/she can get away with it	11	39
Thinks he/she deserves it	36	5
Personal or financial problems	6	4
Other	21	19

* Responses exceed number interviewed because some respondents gave more than one explanation.

be generally to get a measure of employee opinions toward stealing—who steals, what they think about stealing, what should be done about the matter, and such. Ms. Cortez assigned you the task of conducting this survey.

You began the task by designing a questionnaire that will get the information the administrative staff needs. You included what you believe to be all the questions necessary. You concluded that you would like to report the views separately of those who have stolen and those who have not; so you took elaborate pains to make the responses anonymous. Then you conducted the survey (for class purposes, you may create any additional logical information about methodology you may need).

After conducting the survey, you first tabulated responses to the question concerning whether the employee ever had stolen from his or her employer. Surprisingly, of the 212 responses you received, 96 admitted having stolen and 116 denied stealing. Because you suspect these two groups differ in their

views on the subject, you tabulated the responses to the other questions separately (Tables 13 and 14).

Now you have completed the tabulations and have begun to analyze findings. You will present your analyses and the data uncovered to the administrative staff in conventional short report form (title page plus text). Whether you will use graphics will depend on the need for them. Probably you will begin with a quick summary of highlights.

23. *Comparing retail data of selected cities for the RMA.* In your capacity as research associate for the Ableburg Retail Merchants Association, you have been assigned the task of comparing the retailing activity of your city with five other cities. As explained by Eva Barton, chair of the association's board, you are to present a current report on just how Ableburg ranks with comparable cities in other areas. Ms. Barton's instructions were both simple and clear: "We'd like to know how our market compares with others of about the same size. And most important, we want to know how we're performing relative to these markets."

Ms. Barton didn't say more. She didn't even suggest which other cities to use in the comparisons. Apparently, she trusts your good judgment on this important matter.

So you began your assignment by carefully selecting the five cities. Your choices come from all major regions of the country; and although they are not precisely comparable (no cities are), they appear to serve your purposes well. Next, from the most recent *National Research Bureau Shopping Directory,* you gathered the pertinent data. First, you gathered the data that generally present a market overview of the cities—data such as population, number of households, income, and shopping centers (Table 15). Then you got the sales data. These data you recorded by general category of retail operations—food, furniture, apparel, and such (Table 16).

Now you are ready to organize your findings and present them to the association. For the most part, your presentation will be informational—an orderly and clear presentation of data. But you will make conclusions concerning Ableburg's ranking with the other cities. Perhaps you will be able to make an overall conclusion about Ableburg's relative status.

TABLE 15 (Problem 23)   Market Overview of Cities Used in Study

Market Overview	Metropolitan Areas					
	Ableburg	Bakerville	Charleston	Danfield	Eaton	Fall City
Population	909,600	974,400	913,400	1.04 million	970,000	1.54 million
Median age	30 years	31.5 years	32.3 years	31.7 years	34.1 years	32.3 years
Number of households	351,800	347,400	359,500	377,400	372,000	525,900
Median household pre-tax incomes	$32,487	$35,546	$35,493	$31,379	$33,662	$50,296
Number of shopping centers*	216	47	168	180	153	234
Leasable shopping center space per capita	21.4 sq. ft.	7.79 sq. ft.	25.18 sq. ft.	22.2 sq. ft.	20.3 sq. ft.	17.6 sq. ft.

* Shopping centers are defined as buildings that contain at least three retail stores. Single-standing retail locations are not reflected in these figures.

TABLE 16 (Problem 23)   Retail Spending for Cities Used in Study

Retail Spending	Metropolitan Areas					
	Ableburg	Bakerville	Charleston	Danfield	Eaton	Fall City
Total retail sales	$7.48 billion	$7.6 billion	$7.7 billion	$7.7 billion	$7.51 billion	$13 billion
Total food store sales	$1.59 billion	$1.1 billion	$1.41 billion	$1.48 billion	$1.25 billion	$1.9 billion
General merchandise sales	$877 million	$1.28 billion	$788 million	$1.2 billion	$1.26 billion	$1.75 billion
Furniture, appliances sales	$480 million	$446 million	$463 million	$478 million	$319 million	$1.16 billion
Automotive sales	$1.54 billion	$1.87 billion	$1.6 billion	$1.7 billion	$1.87 billion	$2.62 billion
Apparel sales	$411 million	$366 million	$369 million	$363 million	$234 million	$946 million

You will present the report in conventional short report form (title page and text). And you will use graphics wherever they help to tell the report story. Probably, you will begin with a brief summary. Eventually, the report information will be distributed to the membership in the form of a newsletter, but the current report will be addressed to the Board of Directors, Ableburg Retail Merchants Association, Eva Barton, Chair.

24. *Analyzing sales data for Chock-O-Let.* Today's report-writing assignment casts you into the role of assistant to the executive vice president of the Chock-O-Let Company. Your job is to prepare the annual sales report for your boss, Thomas H. Mongon. As in the past, you will present sales data for your company and compare them with the two leading competitors, showing changes from the preceding year.

The sales data assembled in Tables 17 and 18 will provide the facts for your report. Your report will show the progress made (if any) for Chock-O-Let's major candy. Also, it will present a picture of sales for the major sales seasons for candy (Easter, Halloween, Christmas, and Valentine's Day), as shown in Table 18.

The report will be informational to some extent, but it will need to include an analysis of any changes observed. The company is especially sensitive to its competitive position even though it might be slight.

Thus, you will need to be alert to major patterns as well as minor variations in sales that could affect the company's position. You will submit the report in the typical short report format—title page and report proper in direct order; and you will need to include graphics to tell the sales story to Mr. Mongan. You will word the report without personal references.

25. *Examining topic issues for next year's CEO Symposium.* You are the executive secretary of the CEO Symposium, which is conducted at Crescent View University. This two-day conference focuses on issues of concern to chief executives each year. It draws key executives from all types of industries throughout the United States and Canada.

You have recently completed the current year's annual conference and it was total success—in attendance and in the eyes of the executives who attended and participated. But your experience tells you that you must begin now to plan for a successful conference for next year. In fact, the CEO Symposium Board of Directors instructed you to determine the most pressing executive issues that currently exist. These issues will be the topics for coverage and discussion at next year's symposium.

To determine what these issues are, you asked three groups—executives, professors, and executives of small-business organizations—to give you their

TABLE 17 (Problem 24)   Top-Selling Candy in Past 52 Weeks (Regular-sized items)

Product Name	Manufacturer	Sales $ (Millions)	% Change from Last Year
Sniders	Chock-O-Let	$62.4	11.3%
Russell's Peanut Butter Cups	Russell's	42.2	9.3
Chip Chat	Russell's	37.5	15.9
O & A's Plain	Chock-O-Let	32.4	−1.3
Magnabar	Haven	31.5	15.7
O & A's Peanut	Chock-O-Let	29.3	−2.6
Munch	Haven	27.0	9.0
Russell's Milk Chocolate	Russell's	24.5	16.4
Russell's Almond	Russell's	23.0	12.3
Anchors Away	Chock-O-Let	19.9	7.8

TABLE 18 (Problem 24)   Seasonal _____ ales

Season and Product	$	% Change from Last Year	Share of Seasonal Category Sales
Easter Candy		31.5%	100.0%
Russell's	.3	30.4	26.9
Chock-O-Let	.3	24.6	12.4
Haven	4.6	88.1	3.5
Halloween Candy	420.5	14.6	100.0
Russell's	127.6	7.8	32.2
Chock-O-Let	133.8	14.5	33.7
Haven	62.1	16.9	13.6
Christmas Candy	370.2	13.4	100.0
Russell's	133.3	9.4	36.1
Chock-O-Let	74.5	8.6	19.3
Haven	5.5	67.7	1.7
Valentine's Day	195.3	17.9	100.0
Russell's	27.7	48.9	13.1
Chock-O	23.9	55.3	12.2
Haven	8.4	4.6	3.7

perceptions of the most pressing business issues. You surveyed by mail 1,100 professors, 1,025 executives, and 675 executives of small-business organizations. (You may assume whatever research design details you prefer as long as they are in keeping with standards of sound research methodology.) Today, two months after your initial mailing, you have the returns tallied as shown in Table 19. Now you will present them to the directors for their review.

You will use the short report form (title page plus text) for your report. Because it is an internal document, you will use a four-spot title page as the only prefatory element. The report proper will begin with recommendations based on the facts you have assembled. You will do more than present the facts in the report body, however, You will need to analyze the facts, comparing responses among the groups, before a final picture emerges. It's likely, too, that you will need graphics to help your analysis as well.

Construct the report that will present and discuss the significant business issues for next year's CEO Symposium.

26. *Evaluating selection criteria for store managers at Electronic Super Stores.* Electronic Super Stores, a major chain of computer hardware and software, believes that the key to its future is leadership. Toward that end, top management is committed to attracting and selecting good leadership talent—especially at the store manager level. This is where your report situation begins.

In order to remain competitive and to be a significant player in the market, ESS management must select and retain talented store managers for the 125 stores it owns. To do that, management hired you—a human resource consultant—to develop criteria to use in selecting store managers.

Accordingly, you interviewed 100 successful high-tech store managers to determine their views on desir-

TABLE 19 (Problem 25) Significant Business Issues as Viewed by Professors, Executives, and Executives of Small-Business Organizations

Groups and Issues	Number	Percent
Professors		
Competing globally	157	29.35%
Productivity	61	11.40
Quality products/services	47	8.79
Incorporating new technology	46	8.60
Short-term/long-term	45	8.41
LBOs	44	8.22
Managing better	43	8.04
R & D/innovation	34	6.36
Motivating employees	31	5.79
Change	27	5.04
Total	535	100.00
Executives		
Regulations and paperwork	118	21.85
Competing globally	88	16.30
Motivating employees	46	8.52
Attracting quality workers	46	8.52
Quality products/services	40	7.41
Taxes/tax laws	40	7.41
Education of the workforce	36	6.67
Short-term/long-term	34	6.30
Productivity	32	5.93
Budget deficit	30	5.56
Cost of health insurance/care	30	5.56
Total	540	100.00
E/SBOs		
Regulation and paperwork	76	20.11
Competing globally	54	14.29
Attracting quality workers	32	8.47
Taxes/tax laws	32	8.47
Motivating employees	30	7.94
Education of the workforce	26	6.88
Quality products/services	26	6.88
Mandated benefits	22	5.82
Cost control	20	5.29
Cost of health insurance/care	20	5.29
Short-term/long-term	20	5.29
Productivity	20	5.29
Total	378	100.00

vant, and necessary for the work of managing store operation. Because you needed more specificity in the "necessary" category, you had the 100 respondents further differentiate these characteristics as below average, average, above average, and highly developed.

Now, you must analyze these responses and report them to ESS. Your final report will include recommendations, as well as facts and analyses. Prepare the formally worded report (in short report form—indirect with three-spot title page) for the ESS top management team. You will need to include graphics to help the words tell the story of the successful store manager at ESS.

27. *Explaining sources of job information for a recruiting plan.* The Worsham Company wants to improve its recruiting of college students. Its logic is that the company's future will be much brighter if it attracts and keeps good young talent.

Your boss has been appointed recruiting coordinator with instructions to develop a recruiting plan. Part of this plan will involve publicizing the company and its employment opportunities. To do this activity well will involve determining how students get information about jobs. Being an effective manager, your boss delegates this task to you.

To obtain facts about student job information sources, you decide to visit your friend, Diane Hignight, director of career planning and placement, at San Saba University. When you explain to her what you need, she tells you she has been keeping data on sources of job information reported by students over the past three years. She even volunteered to assemble and tabulate the information for you (Table 21).

You must report this information to your boss, Ms. Pollyann Garris. You will need to analyze the facts in terms of how they will be used by the company. Put differently, you will need to tell what the facts mean to Worsham Company's recruiting program. Using the typical short form report, prepare the analysis for Ms. Garris.

28. *Interpreting information about selection of and expectations for franchisees.* The International Franchising Association consists of franchisors, franchisees, and others who are involved in franchising operations. A practitioners' organization, it services members with special publications, a quarterly *Journal of Franchising,* an annual convention, and other professional services. You are the executive director of the IFA.

Periodically, you and your staff conduct research for the membership on areas of special interest. The project that currently has your concern involves gathering information that will be helpful in selecting successful franchisees. In addition to information about recruiting and selecting, you believe that information about the extent of involvement expected from franchisees would also be helpful.

To gather this information, you and your staff pulled the names of directors of franchising for 200

able characteristics for effective leadership in computer sales and service at the retail level. As shown in Table 20, you asked the 100 managers to rate 19 characteristics of a store manager as detrimental, irrele-

TABLE 20 (Problem 26)   Evaluation of Characteristics of Store Managers in Computer Retail Sales and Service

Characteristic	Detrimental	Irrelevant	Necessary			
			Below Average	Average	Above Average	Highly Developed
High achievement motivation (i.e. strong desire to succeed)	0%	0%	0%	8%	37%	55%
Enthusiastic about product and business	0	1	0	11	39	49
Persevering	0	0	2	17	36	45
Creative	0	1	4	9	45	41
Highly competitive	4	8	1	15	50	22
Unable to work well with others	92	6	1	0	0	1
Does not freely communicate information ("plays cards close to chest")	75	11	2	8	2	2
Disruptive	73	9	9	7	2	0
Does not delegate well	67	21	4	6	2	0
Obstinate	66	14	4	13	3	0
Strong ego	6	22	5	15	43	9
Personal charisma	0	20	5	43	25	7
Makes decisions rapidly	12	17	5	33	30	3
Makes decisions intuitively	23	20	10	16	25	6
A good organization person	12	29	12	33	7	7
Willing to take large but calculated risks	3	4	5	31	39	18
Compulsive	61	17	1	11	7	3
Physically strong	1	50	6	27	10	6
A zealot	41	21	6	13	19	0

franchisors from your membership database. You sorted them by type of franchisor—fast food, non-food, etc. Then you randomly selected 50 of them in proportion to their existence in each subcategory to be interviewed. These 50 franchising directors became the sample for your study.

Because you wanted accurate results and because you wanted them rather quickly, you decided to gather the facts by telephone. After two weeks of diligent work, you now have the information summarized in Tables 22–26. You will use these facts as the underpinning of the report you must prepare for the IFA members.

In your report, you will make good use of graphics to tell the report story. But you will need to remember that graphics are a supplement to words in a report. Moreover, you will do more than merely repeat the facts; you will interpret the facts to tell what they mean. You will use the traditional short form report (title page and report text written in direct order). And you will write the report impersonally (without I, we, and you) so that its wording will match the formality of the report situation. You will make the report available to those who ask for it as long as they are current members in good standing of IFA.

Write the report that will tell the story of how fran-

chisees are selected and what is expected from them.

29. *Analyzing morale and employee problems at Bayco Company.* At its executive committee meeting yesterday, the top administrative officers of Bayco Company discussed the possibility of morale problems at work. Some top managers suspected that the problem might reside in various employee situations. Moreover, they wanted to know how the company thought its programs, supervisors, and activities could help.

As an administrative assistant to the director of the Human Resources Department at Bayco, you have been asked to get information on the perceived problems and report it to the executive committee. To comply with this request, you conducted a survey (supply any details needed about methodology). The results of your work are tallied in Tables 27 and 28. Now you must organize the data, relate them to the problem, and determine whether problems do exist for the company.

Write the report on employee morale and problems for the executive committee. You will use graphics to help your words tell the report story. Also, you will select an appropriate format for this middle-length report.

TABLE 21 (Problem 27) Useful Sources of Job Information for Students

A. Which two or three of these sources have you found most useful in determining the *type of career field* you are interested in?

B. Which two or three of these sources have you found most useful for evaluating *where there are jobs* within your chosen career field?

C. And which of these sources have you found most useful in finding more detailed information on specific employers? Which others?

	A	B	C
Work experience/vacation work	32%	8%	6%
Talks with people who work in your chosen field	29	17	13
Talking with fellow students	25	9	5
Advice from parents and family	18	4	3
Talking with careers officer	17	16	12
Talking with academic staff	14	12	6
Recruitment brochures	12	13	26
Literature written by own careers office	12	15	14
Career directories (DOG,GO, GET,ROGET, etc.)	11	18	11
Presentations/talks given by employers	11	8	3
Career fairs	11	8	5
Articles/features in the press/on TV	9	8	3
Interviews with employers' recruiters	6	3	6
Visits to employers' offices/plants etc.	6	2	4
Job advertisements in the press/on TV	5	9	2
Career advertisements in the press/on TV	4	8	2
Forward vacancies/Current vacancies	3	7	2
Advice from school	3	1	*
Orientation courses (i.e., CRAC Insight)	2	*	1
AIESEC/Industrial Society	*	1	1
Video cassettes	1	*	1
Other	2	2	1

Sample: 1,015 students = 100%

30. *Preparing a report on purchasing patterns of consumers.* The research department of the National Marketing Council conducts research designed to keep its membership informed on general marketing matters. You are a research associate with the NMC.

   Your assignment is to gather information on purchasing patterns of consumers across the nation. After conducting this research (you may supply any methodology details needed), you now have the data in tabular form (Table 29).

   Your next task is to present the information in good report form. You will need to analyze it for any meaning it may have for the membership. Such data are often useful in production planning and promoting goods and services. Perhaps there are other useful purposes you could imagine.

TABLE 22 (Problem 28) How Franchisees Are Recruited

	Total Respondents (N = 50)
Advertisements in major newspapers	50%
Personal contact/word of mouth	48
Response to unsolicited inquiries	26
Advertisements in trade papers	24
Information/cards at stores	18
Advertisements in magazines	12
Franchise/trade shows	10
Listings in franchise directories	8
Local newspapers	2
National advertisements	2
Miscellaneous	16

TABLE 23 (Problem 28) Desirable Personal Characteristics

	Total Respondents (N = 50)
Net worth/adequate money/ financial stability	30%
Business skills/business sense	30
Track record/background/history of success	24
Motivation/enthusiasm/determination/ ambition	24
Educational background for this business	22
Experience in this business	22
Personal commitment to business	16
Honesty/character	16
Work ethic/hard worker/energy	14
Ability to work with people	12
Aggressive/outgoing	10
Good communicator	10
Active involvement in the business	8
Management ability/leadership	8
Intelligence	6
Maturity	4
Hands-on type	2
Operate clean shop	2
Do not look for personal characteristics	8

Write the report in proper form for the membership of the National Marketing Council.

31. *Investigating a new compensation plan.* (Requires research) A few years ago your company along with

TABLE 24 (Problem 28)   Involvement of Franchisees

	Total Respondents (N = 50)
All of them work personally in their stores	2%
Most of them work personally in their stores	66
Some work in their stores and some are absentee owners	26
Most of them are absentee owners	6
All of them are absentee owners	0

TABLE 25 (Problem 28)   Reasons for Personal Involvement

	Respondents Saying Very/ Somewhat Important (N = 47)
Hands-on policy/watch the business/ control/right on top of it/most failures had multi-units	62%
One with money at risk does better job/requires full commitment	49
Understands customers better/know what public wants/know the town/ be a community member	36
Sensitivity is heightened/can relate to problems/more involved	25
At beginning it's important until they get good people/depends on number of units/with multiples can use time better in development and management	21

TABLE 26 (Problem 28)   Factors Important to Success

	Total Respondents (N = 50)
Skill and background for business	32%
Capital\having it properly financed	30
Willingness and staying power to put in hard work, time, and money	26
Location of unit	24
Franchisor support/franchisor who has the "bugs" worked out/ quality of the franchise	18
Cleanliness/quality of store, personnel, service	12
Character/attitude/cooperation with operational rules	14
All important factors were previously cited	12

many others in its industry went through some major downsizing, eliminating many managerial-level positions. As a result, your company now has a much flatter organization, which leaves little room for promotions. With the incentives of higher status and higher pay positions diminished, many workers have lost their enthusiasm for work. Therefore, you are looking for some ways to lessen their apathy toward work.

One idea that you got from an article in *Beyond Computing*[1] was using skill-based or competency-based compensation. This system rewards with higher pay employees who learn more skills. When workers are multiskilled, they become more valuable employees and more flexible, too. They are more valuable in your company's attempts to restructure or reengineer itself to become the more agile company needed in the next century; you will need workers who are cross-trained to give your company the flexibility it needs to adapt to rapidly changing business environments.

The article you read reported that organizations using skill- or competency-based compensation plans reaped many benefits. Not only were there measurable productivity gains as well as lower costs, but there were also boosts in job satisfaction. Most also reported improvements in product and service quality.

But the article was just a teaser. It presented no details and did not mention any drawbacks to such plans. So while it sounded good initially, you want to do a more thorough investigation. Not only do you want to gather more details of this type of compensation plan, but you also decide to gather some first-hand information by interviewing those managers and employees who have used this plan in the past five years. You are searching for information on where this strategy is most effective—which industries, management styles, and employees can this plan be applied to effectively.

Write a report to your boss that highlights your major findings and recommends the next action that is needed.

32. *Evaluating CASE (computer-assisted engineering software) tools.* (Requires research) Your boss, Tami Hilbert, has asked you to compare and evaluate the newest CASE tools on the market. These tools are purported to help in the specifying, designing, and constructing of software. She wants to know whether any of them offer features that would save your company money and/or offer some competitive advantage.

Will the software allow you to work faster or better? Will it support collaborative efforts? Will it support the coordination of activities and schedules of a group? Will you be able to do jobs you couldn't handle before either because of their complexity or length? What kind and extent of training is needed to

[1] E. R. McCoy Jr., "Competence Pays Off," *Beyond Computing,* May/June 1994, p. 13.

TABLE 27 (Problem 29)   Employee Satisfaction

Questions		Choices	Responses
1.	Considering everything, how would you rate your overall satisfaction in the company at the present time?	Satisfied Dissatisfied Neither	58.3% 26.0 15.7
2.	How do you feel about the amount of work you do?	Too much Right amount Too little	27.2% 62.3 10.5
3.	How do you like your job—the kind of work you do?	Good Average Poor	61.8% 25.2 13.0
4.	I feel my job makes the best use of my abilities.	Yes No	47.4% 52.6
5.	How do you feel about the quality of supervision you get?	Good Average Poor	50.4% 29.6 20.0
6.	Do you feel the company is concerned about your performance?	Yes No	75.2% 24.8

TABLE 28 (Problem 29)   Employee Perceptions of Problems

Questions	Responses					
	Alcohol Habit	Drug Habit	Marital	Over-weight	Psycho-logical	Smoking
1. Do you know of anyone in your unit who has missed work because of any of the following problems? Yes *26.1%* No *73.9%* Which problem?	8.7	1.7	14.8	6.1	12.2	2.6
2. In your opinion, has anyone in your organization hindered everyday business of the company because of a problem? Yes *27%* No *73%* Which problem?	10.4	3.5	12.2	3.5	13.9	3.5
3. Do you feel the company should provide private, personal assistance with a professional counselor in any of the following areas?	30.4	29.6	25.2	24.3	42.6	27.8
4. I think that programs such as these are a good idea and should be implemented. (Yes responses)	74.8	71.0	55.7	47.6	71.9	49.5
5. Would you seek information from one of these counselors if they were available on a confidential basis?	30.4	31.9	26.4	35.0	45.5	33.3
6. If you needed help in any of the above areas (alcohol, drug, etc.), would you feel free to speak to your supervisor about the problem? Yes *33.3%* No *66.7%*						
7. Should the supervisor be made aware if any of the employees in his or her unit has sought help in the following areas? (Yes responses)	43.6	40.9	21.7	19.8	33.3	19.4
8. The programs should take place inside the company. Inside *58.4%* Outside *41.6%*						
9. Should the company pay for the program? Company *46.8%* Employee *12.6%* Split *36.0%*						

TABLE 29 (Problem 30)   Expenditures by Age of Primary Provider (Family of Four)

	Percentage Distribution of Expenditures of Consumption						
	Under 25	25–34	35–44	45–54	55–64	65–74	75 and Over
Food	21.6	23.2	24.8	24.0	24.9	25.7	26.7
Tobacco and liquor	3.3	3.5	3.6	3.7	3.3	2.9	1.7
Housing	30.7	31.3	28.5	27.2	28.8	32.6	35.9
Clothing	9.5	10.0	11.3	11.4	9.8	7.7	6.4
Personal care	2.8	2.8	2.9	2.9	2.9	2.8	2.7
Medical care	5.7	6.0	5.8	6.0	7.4	9.4	12.0
Recreation	4.6	4.5	4.4	4.1	3.5	2.7	1.7
Reading	.8	.9	.9	.9	1.0	1.1	1.2
Education	1.1	.8	1.2	1.9	.8	.4	.2
Transportation	18.8	15.6	14.4	15.1	14.6	12.5	8.7
Other expenditures	1.0	1.4	2.1	2.8	2.9	2.4	2.7

become proficient enough with the tool to use it effectively? Will the new products (or versions) create new job opportunities? In other words, she is not looking for merely a feature-by-feature comparison but a more in-depth analysis of both the nature and value of the features. Your report should contain some accounts of first-hand users of the technology, whether favorable or unfavorable. She, of course, wants you to identify particular products in the PC and Macintosh environments. Be sure your report addresses her major concerns and the technical aspects of the tools.

33. *Choosing which sport watches to stock in your sporting goods store.* (Requires research) As the buyer for watches in a sporting goods store located in the local mall, you are trying to select two to four different sports watches in the $30 to $60 range for your inventory. You'd like the sport watches not only to serve your current customers but also to draw in some new ones. Your sales data help you profile your regular customers, and the mall data give you the demographics of the average mall shopper. You want to combine these statistics to find an inventory mix that serves both groups.

You can identify at least five manufacturers of sport watches—Casio, Lorus, FreeStyle, Sportline, and Timex—but you realize there may be more. Your regular customers cover the full range of athletic types from weekend athlete to supertrained athlete. These groups would probably use sport watches in some similar ways and some very diverse ways. Most probably they would like an alarm, hourly signal, and a stopwatch. In addition, other uses might include lap counters and/or splits, miles walked, blood pressure

monitors, pacers, countdown timers, and even calorie counters.

Create a report for your boss, Mark Federighi, that profiles sport watches available today. So that the information is easy to compare, include a graphic that presents the name of the watches and compares them by feature. Then match this information to your store data and local mall demographics to identify the two or four watches you plan to sell. Recommend both an inventory mix and level based on your projected sales gathered from historical data and your best professional judgment.

34. *Determining which types of cross-cultural training to use in expanding markets.* (Requires research) As your consumer products company [you choose one] is seriously considering expanding into new markets in China, India, and Vietnam, you recognize that without experience there you need to outsource your training of these new expatriate employees. Unlike Europe and Japan where a lot is known about the culture and workplace environments, much less is known about the cultures of these new markets. However, you do know that you want to provide these employees with cross-culture training. Therefore, you've decided to gather information on the types and effectiveness of cross-cultural training for these countries before you put out a RFP (request for proposals).

Not only do you want your report to your boss to present an awareness and knowledge of the training content, but you also want it to recommend the goals you want to accomplish through your training program. These new markets are important to your company's growth, and recommending the most effective form of cross-cultural training program for the employees who will be working there is critical to success.

▷ Proposals

35. *Proposing the hiring of summer interns to cover for vacationing employees.* During the summer, nearly everyone in your division takes some vacation days. While some use it to extend weekends, others use it in blocks of one to three weeks. In the past, the work simply accumulated until the vacationing employee returned. This clearly violates your new emphasis on serving your customers. Both your internal and external customers had to wait until the employee returned. And it often took the returning worker days to determine just where to begin working again much less get any new work done.

    One solution to this dilemma is to hire summer interns as revolving replacements for your vacationing employees. A highly talented pool of college business students would benefit both from the pay and the experience while your company benefited, too. Junior- and senior-level students will bring with them a set of up-to-date knowledge and skills. They are likely to be good at thinking critically and at problem solving. Their generally optimistic attitudes and creative energies could have a very positive effect on your employees, too. Additionally, not only would the internal and external customers continue to be served, but your employees also could return from vacations refreshed from a change of pace and ready to do new work. Furthermore, your company would get a chance to observe these future business graduates in action; you might even find a few good ones you'd like to hire. And by working closely with the local colleges and universities, you'll be building some bridges between business and education.

    You're convinced that hiring summer interns is a good short- and long-term investment. Write a persuasive proposal to your division manager calling for the temporary positions for this coming summer.

36. *Proposing pay raises for those getting certifications in their specialties.* As Julie Smith, director of MIS, you have long been concerned about turnover. While your company now offers competitive salaries for attracting new employees, you often lose your most talented and hardworking current employees. On exit interviews, these employees often cite disappointment with "having to leave." While most haven't been asked to leave, they feel their current pay is not in line with the pay the market rewards others with the same skills. This usually occurs when an employee has independently or even through company-sponsored programs acquired new skills.

    In recent years your company's organizational structure has become much flatter, lessening an employee's opportunity for advances in pay.

However, your better employees are continuously acquiring new skills, keeping up with the rapidly changing field. In fact, they are making themselves more valuable to your company as they become more knowledgeable, skilled, and flexible. These are the very employees you want to keep.

Today there are numerous authentic certifications in different aspects of MIS. Professional organizations offer certifications as systems analysts and managers, and software companies certify competency in networks, word processing, and other programs. Most of these certifications require studying the subject in-depth and passing rigorous exams. Some have additional requirements, too.

Write a proposal to the CIO of your company requesting automatic raises for those achieving these recognized certifications.

37. *Proposing the purchase of video desktop conferencing equipment.* As Lee McLaughlin, public relations director for Beeline Company, you want your company to purchase new computer systems for video desktop conferencing use within corporate headquarters. This hardware lets you conference with others in the company and see them at the same time.

    You realize that being able to see another person isn't always necessary to get the job done, but it does add an important dimension to interpersonal communications. As the public relations expert for the company, it's important that you have a good relationship with employees in other divisions throughout the company. Whether you're dealing with a simple new product introduction or with a crisis communication situation, relating effectively and quickly with others within the company will help you do your job better.

    You realize the technology is in its infancy and that its most effective business uses haven't been documented yet. However, you firmly believe that this technology is one that will give your company an edge in working with the public. It will improve internal communication, thereby helping you get your message out to your publics faster and more accurately.

38. *Proposing to establish an adopt-a-school program.* As a member of the underwriting department of Metro Insurance Co., Inc., you and several others in the department believe you could perform a significant public service for the community by establishing an adopt-a-school program. This program would send volunteers from the department to a sponsored, "adopted" public school for two hours each week on company time. The volunteers would perform support work for the school and the classroom teachers. They would not be expected to do menial work or teacher/curriculum evaluation.

    The volunteers could counsel students, tutor, assist with classroom activities, and in general help with teaching activities in whatever ways they were needed. Operationally, participating employees would work for two hours at a designated school with travel time of 30 minutes to get to and from the school. You believe a morning time of two and one-half hours would be best for the company and school.

After talking these ideas through with colleagues, you schedule a meeting with the department head, Mr. Ralph Haynes, to get his feedback on the matter. As things develop in the meeting, Mr. Haynes is receptive to the idea but wants you to present it to him formally in a written proposal. He notes, "I'll have to sell this thing to the top boss at our executive committee meeting. So be sure to include benefits and costs to the company in your proposal. If we're going to be good citizens, we'll need to know how much it will cost us."

As you ponder these words on the way back to your desk, you think more specifically about benefits to the company. In general, the publicity for Metro is a definite plus. Also, the program could attract good young talent to the business profession. On the other hand, the school would reap the benefit of having "free assistance" from college-trained, dedicated employees. As you think more about it, you will prepare the proposal for a local high school.

Think through the areas of coverage you will need to include in the proposal. Then prepare the proposal as Mr. Haynes requested.

(Note: This proposal situation could be adapted to a marketing, accounting, or public relations department. It could also be prepared for an elementary, middle, or junior high school).

39. *Proposing a center for cultural awareness training at a university.* As a professor of international business at Marble Falls State University, you have developed quite a consulting business over the last two years. It began when Multiproducts, Inc., asked you to prepare an orientation program in cultural awareness for employees and their families who were being transferred to other countries. You designed an eight-hour program and offered it on Saturdays at the company facilities.

Since that first program, you have expanded the content of your coverage and increased the contact hours to 16. Also, your clients have increased, making it necessary for you to add colleagues in foreign languages and cultural anthropology to your teaching team. You have a backlog of programs that will take you two months to complete. And you still have organizations asking for programs.

With the demand for your services and your track record, you believe the time is right to establish a Center for Cultural Awareness Training at MFSU. Toward that end, you schedule a meeting with your dean in the college of business to discuss the matter. At the meeting, the dean is receptive and enthusiastic about your idea. But she puts the responsibility squarely on your shoulders with this charge: "I like your ideas. But I'd prefer to see them on paper. Write

your plan up for me and submit it in proposal form."

As you reflect on the charge, you envision a weekend program. Employees and their families would arrive on Friday afternoon and check into a specially designated dormitory. After dinner, you will conduct your first session and the program will continue all day Saturday and Sunday morning. Families will pay for two nights and six meals per person.

There could be many benefits to the university for the program; so you will need to include them in the proposal. Also, you will team teach the program with three professors—an anthropologist, a foreign language professor in the language of the country where employees will be located, and you in international business. You may assume whatever content details are logical for the situation.

You will need to cover other necessary details in the proposal. Think through these details; then prepare the proposal for a Center for Cultural Awareness Training for the dean.

40. *Presenting a low-fat menu for the company cafeteria.* Several years ago, you were diagnosed in your annual physical exam as having borderline high cholesterol. Your physician did not prescribe medication but did suggest that you watch your diet closely. In fact, she gave you an American Heart Association publication that showed high- and low-fat food items. Also, she suggested that you exercise moderately to supplement your low-fat diet.

To comply with these suggestions and to maintain your career goals as a business professional, you prepare your own lunches and take them with you to work, storing them in the departmental refrigerator and using a microwave to heat items as needed. You have found that other employees do the same thing, although not always for diet reasons. Most of the employees who prepare their own meals huddle together for informal conversation during allotted times for lunch. The company does maintain a cafeteria for its employees. And most of them frequent it regularly. But the selections are primarily fast-food items and entrées that are high in fat. Moreover, the quantities served are more than some prefer to eat and then continue working in the afternoons.

At one of your regular bring-own-lunch sessions, someone suggested the group ask the "powers that be" to offer a low-fat menu selection in the company cafeteria. Much discussion followed for the next couple of days about the possibility—food items to offer, costs, number of people who would select the option, benefits for the company, the need for the selection, and the like. After this discussion, the group asked you to meet with the director of employee services—the person in charge of cafeteria operation—to see if your low-fat food menu suggestion had possibilities of being implemented. You arranged for a meeting the next day, telling your immediate boss the reason for your forthcoming meeting.

At the meeting, you found the director to be most receptive to your ideas. But he asked you to follow up on the meeting by preparing a written proposal that would give him details of your ideas. Said he: "I like your ideas. But I deal in tangible realities—specifics! Write up your thoughts in a proposal I can use to make my decision. It's likely that I'll have to show the proposal to the general plant manager as well."

With this charge still fresh in your mind, you report back to the group about the meeting. They will help you prepare the report and will offer support. But it will be submitted in your name.

Now you must create the proposal. Write it concisely, clearly, and completely for the director of employee services.

▶ Procedures

41. *Developing procedures for setting up a flextime schedule.* To increase morale and job satisfaction, which may lead to increased productivity, your company's officers recently approved a move to flextime scheduling. In order to implement this scheduling system in an orderly manner, the officers decided to let the first-line managers in each section set up procedures for applying for a flextime schedule.

While employees will still work 40 hours a week, managers in each section will identify various schedules from which employees can select. Because the needs and workloads vary by section, first-line managers are in the best position to know what will work for their sections. Realizing that there are various reasons for flex schedules including child care, fitness training, elder care, petcare, traffic, car pools, spouse's employment, and bus and train schedules, the procedures will not ask employees to give a reason for their requests.

Since the policy is new, the board agreed to implement it for a one-year trial. After one year, it will be evaluated and changes to the policy may be implemented. At the moment, the flextime schedules will be available on a first-come, first-serve basis. However, needs of the section will drive the decisions made by the first-line managers.

As the first-line manager employees in your section [you determine its function], write a clear set of procedures that all employees can follow easily. The procedure should be such that you get the data you need in a timely fashion to set up the schedules.

42. *Writing procedures to implement a casual dress policy.* In recent years, casual dress has been expanding its presence in the workplace. In fact, your company recently designated the last Friday of every month as a "casual" day and announced employees can petition for other casual days.

While the policy created by management clearly defines what is meant by casual dress, it does not include the procedures for applying for additional casual days. Furthermore, neither the policy nor management has indicated what an acceptable reason for additional casual days might include. Therefore, you have some leeway to design and interpret this part of the policy as your best judgment guides you. However, you expect that vague procedures could lead to abuse of this new policy, causing management to revoke it. Therefore, you want to write clear procedures that enable you to collect the information that will help you make good decisions.

43. *Preparing procedures for reporting ethics violations.* Your company recently endorsed an ethics policy that stated the company was committed to ethical values and conduct in all its activities. But the policy will have little meaning unless someone puts teeth into it. Thus, the executive committee of the company has assigned you, as administrative assistant, the task of preparing procedures for reporting ethical situations, problems, and such (especially theft).

The procedures you develop will need to be complete, clear, and logical. As you think more specifically about the matter, you will consider the following points at a minimum: to whom will people report violations; how will reports be investigated; what efforts will be made to keep reports anonymous; would a telephone hot line be in order; and should training in ethics be considered. No doubt there are other areas you will need to include as you begin to prepare the procedures.

Write the procedures for the executive committee of the company about reporting ethical violations. The procedures you identify should permit the company to control its ethical issues smoothly.

44. *Developing procedures for filing travel expenses.* As an accountant in the comptroller's department of your company, you have handled the filing and reimbursing of travel expenses for several years. During that time, you have noticed employees sometimes fail to file expenses in a timely manner, don't include receipts for expenses, file follow-up expenses because they were overlooked initially, and the like. All these matters affect the smooth functioning of your job personally. But more than that, they affect the balancing of accounts and make the control function for the department ineffective.

In a budget meeting of the department, you mention the problem to your boss and several other workers. After much discussion, the group decides to have you develop a set of procedures that would reconcile some of these matters. Your boss gives you the directive as the meeting ends: "Write up these procedures and let met see them in a couple of days. I'll be out of town tomorrow, but I'd like to review them when I return."

As you go back to your desk, you begin to think specifically about the procedures you need to develop. Among the ideas that race through your mind are these: the types of receipts and documentation to include, a three-day time limit to file expenses upon returning from travel, when to expect reimbursement, what items to exclude, and checkpoints for accuracy of the amount submitted. Perhaps others will evolve as you get deeper into the project.

Your task now is to write the procedures. You will be orderly, complete, and logical. The procedures will likely become a part of the company operating manual. So you will work hard to make them clear and distinct.

45. *Preparing procedures to establish reasonable accommodation at a company.* The Americans with Disabilities Act (ADA) covers employees with disabilities at most organizations. And yours is no exception. Since passage of the act, you think your company has done a good job of meeting the needs of disabled workers. But most of the efforts have been conducted on individual and situational basis. It's your feeling—and more importantly the feeling of your boss—that you should establish standard procedures for establishing "reasonable accommodation" for workers with disabilities. An an administrative assistant to the director of human resources, you draw the assignment of developing procedures for all to follow to meet the reasonable accommodation rule.

You will write to the department heads through-out the company to get their ideas on the subject and how they have handled accommodating situations on their own. From these reports, you will construct a universal document, one that all supervisors can follow for completeness and consistency.

Assume that you have received the reports and opinions from the department heads. As you scan them, you notice several commonalities for compliance: validating the disability with a physician, meeting with the person to work out a plan, keeping records of work incidents, implementing and controlling the plan, and being open and receptive to unique needs. No doubt there will be others as you study the reports in more detail. You wonder whether it would be appropriate to have a meeting on compliance periodically—perhaps even a training session. Moreover, you wonder about consulting other companies to see how they have complied with the act. Most likely, these efforts will follow what you prepare as company procedure. You must now write the procedures for your boss so that management personnel will be consistent in their efforts to establish reasonable accommodation for disabled workers.

Remember that you are complying with federal law; so it is likely that your work will be reviewed by federal compliance officers.

TOPICS FOR REPORT PROBLEMS

Following are topics that may be developed into reports of varying length and difficulty. In each case, the facts of the situation will need to be created through the student's (or the instructor's) imagination before a business-type problem exists. The information needed in most cases should be available in the library.

1. Recommend for X Company a city and hotel for holding its annual meeting of sales representatives.

2. Determine the problem areas and develop a set of rules for employees who work at home during business hours for X Company.

3. For an investment service, determine which mutual funds do better: those that invest for the long run or those that emphasize market timing.

4. What can X Company (you choose the name and industry) do to improve the quality of its product or service?

5. Investigate the problem of worker theft and recommend ways to decrease it.

6. Evaluate the impact of the European Community on X Company (you choose the name and industry) profits.

7. Determine the problems of recycling and recommend ways to overcome them.

8. Investigate the advantages and disadvantages of requiring workers to wear uniforms and recommend whether X Company should require them.

9. Advise X Company on the advantages and disadvantages of hiring student interns from the local college.

10. Evaluate and compare the economic forecasts of three leading forecasters over the past five years.

11. Advise Company X on the desirability of establishing a child care center for the children of its employees.

12. Report to Company X management what other leading companies are doing to increase ethics consciousness among employees.

13. Report to a large chain of department stores on current means of reducing shoplifting.

14. Determine the effects of smoking on worker health and/or productivity.

15. Determine whether Company X should ban smoking in the workplace.

16. Evaluate the status of affirmative action in _____ (company, industry, country).

17. Report on the office design of the future for Company X.

18. What can Company X (you choose the type of company) do to improve productivity?

19. Determine how Company X should cope with the problem of an aging work force.

20. Evaluate the advantages and disadvantages of flex-time.

21. Determine the advantages and disadvantages of fixed-rate and variable-rate mortgages.

22. Study the benefits and problems of a two-career marriage, and draw conclusions on the matter.

23. Study and report on the more popular forms of creative financing being used in real estate today.

24. Review the literature to determine the nature and causes of executive burnout and remedies for it.

25. What should Company X do about employees who have been made obsolete by technological change?

26. Your company (to be specified by your instructor) is considering the purchase of _____ (number) laptop computers for its sales representatives. Evaluate three brands, and recommend one for purchase.

27. Evaluate _____ (city of your choice) as a site for the annual meeting of a large professional association (your choice), ending with a recommendation.

28. Advise Company X (a national grocery chain) on whether to use double coupons.

29. Investigate and report on the demand for college-trained people in the coming years.

30. Determine the status and progress of women's rights in business for _____ (association).

31. Determine the recent developments in, current status of, and outlook for _____ industry.

32. Investigate and report on the criminal liability of corporate executives.

33. Investigate whether hiring physically challenged workers is charity or good business for Company X.

34. Assess the status of pollution control in _____ industry for an association of firms in that industry.

35. Review the status of consumer protection laws, and recommend policies for Company X.

36. For the International Association of Secretaries, review current developments in word processing and determine whether we are truly moving toward the "paperless office."

37. Advise Company X (your choice of a specific manufacturer) on the problems and procedures involved in exporting its products to _____ (country or countries of your choice).

38. Report to Company X on the quality of life in your city. The company may open a factory there and would move some executives to it.

39. Report to Company X on the ethics and effectiveness of subliminal advertising.

40. Compare the costs, services, and other relevant factors of the major automobile rental firms, and recommend which of these firms Company X should use.

41. Survey the franchise possibilities for _____ (fast foods, automotive services, or such), and select one of these possibilities for a business client.

42. Advise Company X on developing a wellness (preventive health) program.

Additional topics are listed at the end of the long-length problem section following Chapter 12. Many of these topics are suitable for intermediate-length reports, just as some of the above topics are suitable for long reports.

12

Long, Formal Reports

Upon completing this chapter, you will be able to construct long, formal reports for important projects. To reach this goal, you should be able to

(1) Describe the roles and contents and construct the prefatory parts of a long, formal report.

(2) Organize each introduction by considering all the likely readers and selecting the appropriate contents.

(3) Determine, based on the goal, the most effective way to end a report—a summary, a conclusion, a recommendation, or a combination of the three.

(4) Describe the role and content of the appendix and bibliography of a report.

(5) Write a long, formal report using a structural coherence plan.

▶ to Long, Formal Reports

Assume the role of associate director of research, Midwestern Research, Inc. As your title indicates, research is your business. Perhaps it would be more accurate to say that research and reports are your business. Research is your primary activity, of course. But you must present your findings to your customers. The most efficient way of doing so is through reports.

Typical of your work is your current assignment with Armor Motors, a manufacturer of automobiles. The sales division of Armor wants information that will help to improve the effectiveness of its salespeople. Specifically, it wants answers to the question of what its salespeople can do to improve their performance. The information gathered will be used in revising the curriculum of Armor's sales training program.

To find the answer to the basic question, you plan to investigate three areas of sales activities: how salespeople use their time, how they find prospects, and how they make sales presentations. You will get this information for two groups of Armor salespeople: the successful and the unsuccessful. Next, you will compare the information you get from these two groups. The differences you detect in these comparisons should identify the effective and the ineffective sales practices.

Your next task will be to determine what your findings mean. When you have done this, you will present your findings, analyses, conclusions, and recommendations in a report to Armor Motors. Because Armor executives will see the report as evidence of the work you did for the company, you will dress the report up. You know that what Armor sees will affect what it thinks of your work.

So you will use the formal arrangement that is traditional for reports of this importance. You will include the conventional prefatory pages. You will use headings to guide the readers through the text. And you will use graphics liberally to help tell the report story. If the situation calls for them, you may use appended parts. In other words, you will construct a report that matches the formality and importance of the situation. How to construct such reports is the subject of this chapter. ■

Although not numerous, long, formal reports are highly important in business. They usually concern major investigations, which explains their length. They are usually prepared for high-level administrators, which explains their formality.

• Long, formal reports are important but not numerous in business.

ORGANIZATION AND CONTENT OF THE LONGER REPORTS

In determining the structure of the longer, more formal reports, you should view your work much as architects view theirs. You have a number of parts to work with. Your task is to design from those parts a report that meets your reader's needs.

• Needs should determine the structure of long, formal reports.

The first parts in your case are the prefatory pages. As noted in Chapter 11, the longest, most formal reports contain all of these. As the length of the report and the formality of the situation decrease, certain changes occur. As the report architect, you must decide which arrangement of prefatory parts meets the length and formality requirements of your situation.

• The need for the prefatory parts decreases as reports become shorter and less formal.

To make this decision, you need to know these parts. Thus, we will describe them in the following pages. In addition, we will describe the remaining structure of the longest, most formal report. As you proceed through these descriptions, it will be helpful to trace the parts through the illustration report at the end of this chapter. In addition, it will help to consult Appendix B for illustrations of page form.

• In determining which prefatory parts to include, you should know their roles and contents.

For convenience in the following discussion, the report parts are organized by groups. The first group comprises the prefatory parts, the parts that are most closely related to the formality and length of the report. Then comes the report proper, which, of course, is the meat of all reports. It is the report story. The final group comprises the appended parts. These parts contain supplementary materials, information that is not essential to the report but may be helpful to some readers. In summary, the presentation follows this pattern:

• Thus, they are reviewed in the following pages.

Introduction to long reports greet readers and prepare them for the facts and interpretations which will follow. You should be complete in long report introductions to prepare readers to accept the report findings.

Prefatory parts: Title fly. Title page. Letter of authorization. Letter of transmittal, preface, or foreword. Table of contents and list of illustrations. Executive summary.

The report proper: Introduction. The report findings (presented in two or more divisions). Summary, conclusion, or recommendation.

Appended parts: Bibliography. Appendix.

· ·

THE PREFATORY PARTS

As you know from preceding discussion, there may be many variations in the prefatory parts of a formal report. Even so, the six parts covered in the following pages are generally included in the longer reports.

Title Fly

- The title fly contains only the report title.

The first of the possible prefatory report pages is the title fly (see page 409). It contains only the report title, and it is included solely for reasons of formality. As the title appears again on the following page, the title fly is somewhat repetitive. But most books have one, and so do most formal reports.

- Construct titles to make them describe the report precisely.

Although constructing the title fly is simple, composing the title is not. In fact, on a per word basis, the title requires more time than any other part of the report. This is as it should be, for titles should be carefully worded. Their goal is to tell at a glance what the report does and does not cover. A good title fits the report like a glove. It covers all the report information snugly.

- As a checklist, use who, what, where, when, why, and sometimes how.

For completeness of coverage, you should build your titles around the five Ws: *who, what, where, when, why.* Sometimes *how* may be important. In some problems, you will not need to use all the Ws. Nevertheless, they serve as a good checklist for completeness. For example, you might construct a title for the report described at the chapter beginning as follows:

Who: Armor Motors
What: Sales training recommendations
Where: Implied (Armor dealerships)

When: 1995
Why: Understood (to improve sales training)
How: Based on a 1995 study of company sales activities

From this analysis comes this title: "Sales Training Recommendations for Armor Motors Based on a 1995 Study of Company Sales Activities."

For another example, take a report analyzing the Lane Company's 1995 advertising campaigns. This analysis would be appropriate:

Who: Lane Company
What: Analysis of advertising campaigns
Where: Not essential
When: 1995
Why: Implied
How: Not essential

Thus, this title emerges: "Analysis of Lane Company's 1995 Advertising Campaigns."

Obviously, you cannot write a completely descriptive title in a word or two. Extremely short titles tend to be broad and general. They cover everything; they touch nothing. Even so, your goal is to be concise as well as complete. So you must seek the most economical word pattern consistent with completeness. In your effort to be concise and complete, you may want to use subtitles. Here is an example: "A 1995 Measure of Employee Morale at Pfeifer's Mossback Plant: A Study Based on a Survey Using the Semantic Differential."

• One- or two-word titles are too broad. Subtitles can help conciseness.

Title Page

Like the title fly, the title page presents the report title. In addition, it displays information essential to identification of the report. In constructing your title page, you should include your complete identification and that of the authorizer or recipient of the report. You may also include the date of writing, particularly if the date is not in

• The title page displays the title, identification of the writer and authorizer, and the date.

the title. The construction of this page is illustrated in Appendix B and in the report at the end of the chapter.

Letter of Authorization

- Include the letter of authorization if the report was authorized in writing.

Although not illustrated in the diagram of report structure in Chapter 11 or in the report at the end of this chapter, a letter of authorization can be a prefatory part. It was not shown in the diagram (Figure 11–1) because its presence in a report is not determined by formality or length but by whether the report was authorized in writing. A report authorized in writing should include a copy of the written authorization. This part usually follows the title page.

- Write the letter of authorization in the direct order: authorization, information about the problem, goodwill close.

As the report writer, you would not write the letter (or memorandum) of authorization. But if you ever have to write one, handle it as you would a direct-order letter. In the opening, authorize the research. Then cover the specific information that the reader needs to conduct it. This might include a clear description of the problem, time and money limitations, special instructions, and the due date. Close the letter with appropriate goodwill comment.

Letter of Transmittal, Foreword, Preface

- The letter of transmittal is a personal message from the writer to the reader.

Most formal reports contain a personal message of some kind from the writer to the reader. In most business reports, the letter of transmittal performs this function. In some cases, particularly where the report is written for a group of readers, a foreword or preface is used instead.

- It substitutes for a face to face meeting.

The letter of transmittal transmits the report to the reader. In less formal situations, the report is transmitted personally (orally). In more formal situations, a letter usually does the job. But keep in mind that the letter merely substitutes for a face-to-face meeting. What you write in it is much like what you would say if you were face to face with the reader.

- Its main goal is to transmit the report.

As the goal of transmitting the report is positive, you should begin the letter of transmittal directly, without explanation or other delaying information. Your opening words should say, in effect, "Here is the report." Tied to or following the transmittal of the report, you should briefly identify the report goal, and you can refer to the authorization (who assigned the report, when, why).

- In addition, it includes helpful comments about the report. The close is goodwill.

What else you include in the letter of transmittal depends on the situation. In general, you should include anything that would be appropriate in a face-to-face presentation. What would you say if you were handing the report to the reader? It would probably be something about the report—how to understand, use, or appreciate it. You might make suggestions about follow-up studies, warnings about limitations of the report, or comments about side issues. In fact, you might include anything that helps the reader understand and value the report. Typically, the letter of transmittal ends with appropriate goodwill comment. An expression of gratefulness for the assignment or an offer to do additional research if necessary makes good closing material.

- A summary follows the opening when the executive summary and the letter of transmittal are combined.

When you combine the letter of transmittal with the executive summary (an acceptable arrangement), you follow the opening transmittal statement with a summary of the report highlights. In general, you follow the procedure for summarizing described in the discussion of the executive summary. Following the summary, you include appropriate talk about the report. Then you end with a goodwill comment.

- The letter of transmittal is usually in personal style.

Because the letter of transmittal is a personal note to the reader, you may write in a personal style. In other words, you may use personal pronouns (*you, I, we*). In addition, you may write the letter in conversational language that reflects the warmth and vigor of your personality. You may not want to use the personal style in very formal cases. For example, if you were writing a report for a committee of senators or for other high-ranking dignitaries, you might elect to write the letter of transmittal impersonally. But such instances are rare.

As noted previously, you may transmit reports to broad audiences in a foreword or a preface. Minor distinctions are sometimes drawn between forewords and prefaces. But for all practical purposes, they are the same. Both are preliminary messages from the writer to the reader. Although forewords and prefaces usually do not formally transmit the report, they do many of the other things done by letters of transmittal. Like letters of transmittal, they seek to help the reader appreciate and understand the report. They may, for example, include helpful comments about the report—its use, interpretation, follow-up, and the like. In addition, they frequently contain expressions of indebtedness to those helpful in the research. Like letters of transmittal, they are usually written in the first person. But they are seldom as informal as some letters of transmittal. There is no established pattern for arranging the contents of forewords and prefaces.

- For broad audiences, a foreword (or preface) is used. Forewords do not transmit the report—they comment about it.

Table of Contents, List of Illustrations

If your report is long enough to need a guide to its contents, you should include a table of contents. This table is the report outline in finished form with page numbers. As noted in the discussion of outlining in Chapter 10, the outline headings appear in the text of the report as headings of the various parts. Thus, a listing showing the pages where the headings appear helps the reader find the parts of the report. A table of contents is especially helpful to the reader who wants to see only a few selected parts of the report.

- Include a table of contents when the report is long enough to need a guide to its contents.

In addition to listing the text contents, the table of contents lists the parts of the report that appear before and after the report proper. Thus, it lists the prefatory parts, but usually only those that follow the table of contents. It also lists the appended parts (bibliography, appendix) and the figures and tables that illustrate the report. Typically, the figures and tables appear as separate listings following the listings reviewed above. More detailed instructions for constructing the table of contents appear in Appendix B.

- The table of contents lists text headings, prefatory parts, appended parts, and figures and tables. It gives page numbers.

Executive Summary

The executive summary (also called *synopsis, abstract, epitome, précis, digest*) is the report in miniature. It concisely summarizes whatever is important in the report. For some readers, the executive summary serves as a preview to the report. But it is written primarily for busy executives who may not have time to read the whole report.

- The executive summary summarizes the report.

Playing possum doesn't work anymore, Stephmeyer! I want that report by 5 p.m. or else!
(Reprinted by permission: Tribune Media Services.)

"How could I have hired this fellow Glutz?" the sales manager moaned as he read this first report from his new salesperson: "I have arrive in Detroit. Tomorry I will try to sell them companys here what ain't never bought nothing from us."

Before the sales manager could fire this stupid fellow, Glutz's second report arrived: "I done good here. Sold them bout haff a millun dollars wirth. Tomorry I try to sell to them there Smith Company folks what threw out that last feller what sold for us."

Imagine how the sales manager's viewpoint changed when he read Glutz's third report: "Today I seen them Smith folks and sole them bout a millun dollars wirth. Also after dinner I got too little sails mountin to bout half a millun dollars. Tomorry I going to do better."

The sales manager was so moved that he tacked Glutz's reports on the company bulletin board. Below them he posted his note to all the salespeople: "I want all you should reed these reports wrote by Glutz who are on the road doin a grate job. Then you should go out and do like he done.

Perhaps they can get all they need to know by reading the executive summary. If they need to know more about any part, they can find that part through the table of contents. Thus, they can find out whatever they need to know quickly and easily.

- It includes highlights of the facts, analyses, and conclusions—in proportion.

You construct the executive summary simply by reducing the parts of the report in order and in proportion. More specifically, you go through the report, selecting whatever is essential. You should include all the major items of information—the facts of the report. You should include all the major analyses of the information presented. And you should include all the conclusions and recommendations derived from these analyses. The finished product should be a miniature of the whole, with all the important ingredients. As a general rule, the executive summary is less than an eighth as long as the writing it summarizes.

- Work on writing style in this part.

As your goal is to cut the report to a fraction of its length, much of your success will depend on your skill in word economy. Loose writing is costly. But in your efforts to be concise, you are more likely to write in a dull style. You will need to avoid this tendency.

- Either direct or indirect order is appropriate.

The traditional executive summary reviews the report in the indirect order (introduction, body, conclusion). In recent years, however, the direct order has gained in popularity. This order shifts the conclusions and/or recommendations (as the case may be) to the major position of emphasis at the beginning. From this direct beginning, the summary moves to the introductory parts and then through the major highlights of the report in normal order. One good reason for the growing popularity of the direct order is the fact that information technology retrieves information on screens limited in size. Most readers expect the key information to appear on the first screen or two.

Diagrams of both arrangements appear in Figure 12–1. Whichever arrangement you choose, you will write the executive summary after the report proper is complete.

THE REPORT PROPER

- Arrangements of the report proper may vary, but the following review of the indirect order should be helpful.

As noted in Chapter 11, the contents of most longer reports are written in the indirect order (introduction, body, conclusion). But there are exceptions. Some longer reports are in the direct order—with summaries, conclusions, or recommendations at the beginning. And some are in a prescribed order similar to that of the technical and staff

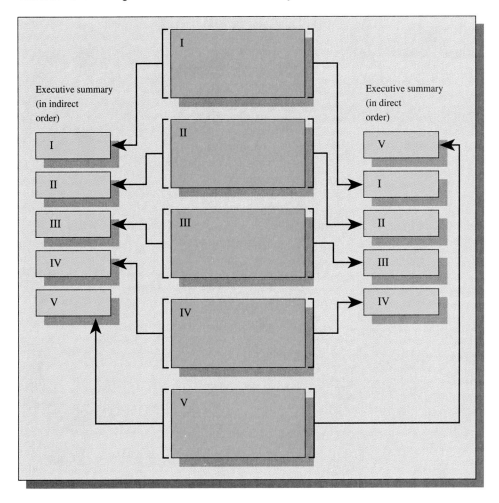

reports described in Chapter 11. Even though the orders of longer reports may vary, the ingredients of all these reports are similar. Thus, the following review of the makeup of a report in the indirect order should help you in writing any report.

Introduction

The purpose of the introduction of a report is simply to prepare the readers to receive the report. Whatever will help achieve this goal is appropriate content.

In determining what content is appropriate, consider all the likely readers of your report. As we noted earlier, the readers of many of the shorter reports are likely to know the problem well and have little or no need for an introduction. But such is not often the case for the longer reports. Many of these reports are prepared for a large number of readers, some of whom know little about the problem. These reports often have long lives and are kept on file to be read in future years. Clearly, they require some introductory explanation to prepare the readers.

Determining what should be included is a matter of judgment. You should ask yourself what you would need or want to know about the problem if you were in your readers' shoes. In selecting the appropriate information, you would do well to use the following checklist of likely introduction contents. Remember, though, that it is only a checklist. Rarely would you include all the items.

* The introduction should prepare the readers.

* In deciding what to include, consider all likely readers.

* Then determine what those readers need to know. Use the following checklist.

Origin of the Report.
• 1. Origin—the facts of authorization.

The first part of your introduction might well include a review of the facts of authorization. Some writers, however, leave this part out. If you decide to include it, you should present such facts as when, how, and by whom the report was authorized; who wrote the report; and when the report was submitted. Information of this kind is particularly useful in reports that have no letter of transmittal.

Problem and Purpose.

A vital part of almost every report is a statement of its problem. The *problem* is whatever the report seeks to do. It is the satisfaction of the need that prompted the investigation.

• 2. Problem—what the report seeks to do.

• The problem is commonly stated in infinitive or question form.

You may state the problem of your report in different ways. A very common way is to word it in the infinitive form: "To determine standards for corporate annual reports." Another common way is to word it as a question: "What retail advertising practices do Centerville consumers disapprove of?" Whatever does the best job of explaining what your report seeks to do is what you want.

• The purpose is the reason for the report.

Closely related to *what* you are doing is *why* you are doing it. The *purpose* (often called by other names such as *objective, aim, goal*) tells the reason of the report. For example, you might be determining standards for the corporate annual report *in order to streamline the production process.*

Scope.

• 3. Scope—the boundaries of the problem.

If the scope of the problem is not clearly covered in any of the other introductory parts, you may need to include it in a separate part. By *scope* we mean the boundaries of the problem. In this part of the introduction—in plain, clear language—you should describe what is included in the problem. You should also identify the delimitations—what you have not included.

Limitations.

• 4. Limitations—anything that impairs the quality of the report.

In some reports, you will need to explain limitations. By *limitations* we mean things that impair the quality of your report. For example, you may not have been given enough time to do the work right. Or perhaps a short budget prevented you from doing everything that should have been done. And there are other limitations—unavoidable conditions, restrictions within the problem, absence of historical information. In general, this part of the introduction should include whatever you think might explain possible shortcomings in your report.

Historical Background.

• 5. History—how the problem developed and what is known about it.

Knowledge of the history of the problem is sometimes essential to understanding the report. Thus, you may need to cover that history in your introduction. Your general aim in this part is to acquaint the readers with how the problem developed and what has been done about it. Your discussion here should bring out the main issues. It should review what past investigations have determined about the problem, and it should lead to what still needs to be done.

Sources and Methods of Collecting Information.

• 6. Sources and methods—how you got the information.

You usually need to tell the readers how you collected the information in the report. That is, you explain your research methodology. You tell whether you used library research, survey, experiment, or what not. And you describe the steps you followed. In general, you describe your work in enough detail to allow your readers to judge it. You tell them enough to convince them that your work was done competently.

• Sometimes it is necessary to cite sources.

In a simple case in which you conducted library research, you need to say little. If most of your findings came from a source or two, you could name the sources. If you used a large number of sources, you would be wise to note that you used library research and refer to the bibliography in the report appendix.

• More complex research requires thorough description.

More complex research usually requires a more detailed description. If you conducted a survey, for example, you would probably need to explain all parts of the investigation. You would cover sample determination, construction of the questionnaire, interview procedure, and checking techniques. In fact, you would include as much detail as is needed to gain the readers' confidence in your work.

Definitions, Initialisms, and Acronyms.   If you use words, initialisms, or acronyms that are likely to be unfamiliar to readers of the report, you should define these words and initials. You can do this in either of two ways: you can define each term in the text or as a footnote when it is first used in the report, or you can define all unfamiliar terms in a separate part of the introduction. This part begins with an introductory statement and then lists the terms with their definitions. If the list is long, you may choose to arrange the terms alphabetically.

• 7. Definitions of unfamiliar words, acronyms, or initialisms used.

Report Preview.   In very long reports, a final part of the introduction should preview the report presentation. In this part you tell the readers how the report will be presented—what topics will be taken up first, second, third, and so on. Of even greater importance, you give your reasons for following this plan. That is, you explain the *strategy* of your report. In short, you give your readers a clear picture of the road ahead. As you will see later in the chapter, this part of the introduction is a basic ingredient of the coherence plan of the long report. Illustrations of report previews appear in the discussion of this plan (page 405) and in the report at the end of the chapter (page 416).

• 8. Preview—a description of the route ahead.

The Report Body

In the report body, the information collected is presented and related to the problem. Normally, this part of the report comprises most of its content. In a sense, the report body is the report. With the exception of the conclusion or recommendation part, the other parts of the report are attached parts.

• The report body presents and analyzes the information gathered.

Although the body makes up most of the report, practically all that we need to say about it has already been said. Its organization was discussed extensively in Chapter 10. It is written in accord with the instructions on clear writing presented in Chapters 2 and 3 and the writing techniques covered in Chapter 10. It uses good presentation form, with figures, tables, and caption display, discussed and illustrated at various places in this book. In fact, most of our discussion of report writing has concerned this major part of the report.

• Writing this part involves instruction covered elsewhere in the book.

The Ending of the Report

You can end your report in any of a number of ways: with a summary, a conclusion, a recommendation, or a combination of the three. Your choice should depend on the goal of your report. You should choose the way that enables you to satisfy that goal.

• Reports can end in various ways.

Ending Summary.   When the goal of the report is to present information, the ending is logically a summary of the major findings. Such reports usually have minor summaries at the end of the major sections. When this arrangement is followed, the ending summary recapitulates these summaries.

• Informational reports usually end with a summary of the major findings.

You should not confuse the ending summary with the executive summary. The executive summary is a prefatory part of the report; the ending summary is a part of the report text. Also, the executive summary is more complete than the ending summary. The executive summary reviews the entire report, usually from the beginning to the end. The ending summary reviews only the highlights of the report.

• The ending summary is not as complete as the executive summary.

Conclusions.   Some reports must do more than just present information. They must analyze the information in light of the problem; and from this analysis, they must reach a conclusion. Such reports typically end with this conclusion.

• Reports that seek an answer end with a conclusion.

The makeup of the conclusion section varies from case to case. In problems for which a single answer is sought, the conclusion section normally reviews the preceding information and analyses and, from this review, arrives at the answer. In problems with more than one goal, the report plan may treat each goal in a separate section and

• The structure of the conclusion varies by problem.

Technical Writer's Report on Humpty Dumpty

A 72-gram brown Rhode Island Red country-fresh candled egg was secured and washed free of feathers, blood, dirt, and grit. Held between thumb and index finger, about 3 ft. or more from an electric fan (GE Model No. MC-2404, Serial No. JC23023, nonoscillating, rotating on "Hi" speed at approximately 1045.23 plus or minus 0.02 rpm), the egg was suspended on a pendulum (string) so that it arrived at the fan with essentially zero velocity normal to the fan rotation plane. The product adhered strongly to the walls and ceiling and was difficult to recover. However, using putty knives a total of 13 grams was obtained and put in a skillet with 11.2 grams of hickory-smoked Armour's old-style bacon and heated over a low Bunsen flame for 7 min. 32 sec. What there was of it was of excellent quality.

"The DP Report," Du Pont Explosive's Department, Atomic Energy Division, Savannah River Laboratories, July 12, 1954.

---

draw conclusions in each section. The conclusion section of such a report might well summarize the conclusions previously drawn. There are other arrangements. In fact, almost any plan that brings the analyses together to reach the goals of the report is appropriate.

- Include recommendations when the readers want or expect them.

Recommendations.   When the goal of the report is not only to draw conclusions but also to present a course of action, a recommendation is in order. You may organize it as a separate section following the conclusion section. Or you may include it in the conclusion section. In some problems, the conclusion is the recommendation—or at least a logical interpretation of it. Whether you include a recommendation should be determined by whether the readers want or expect one.

Appended Parts

- Add an appendix or a bibliography when needed.

Sometimes you will need to include an appendix or a bibliography, or both, at the end of the report. Whether you include these parts should be determined by need.

- The appendix contains information that indirectly supports the report.

- Information that directly supports the report belongs in the text of the report.

Appendix.   The appendix, as its name implies, is a tacked-on part. You use it for supplementary information that supports the body of the report but has no logical place within the body. Possible appendix contents are questionnaires, working papers, summary tables, additional references, and other reports.

As a rule, the appendix should not include the charts, graphs, sketches, and tables that directly support the report. These should be placed in the body of the report, where they support the findings. Reports should be designed for the convenience of the readers. Obviously, it is not convenient for readers to look for appendix illustrations of the facts they read in the report body.

- Include a bibliography if you make heavy use of printed sources.

Bibliography.   When your investigation makes heavy use of printed sources, you normally include a bibliography (a list of the publications used). The construction of this list is described in Appendix E of this book.

. . . .
STRUCTURAL COHERENCE HELPERS

- Longer reports need structural coherence helpers.

As we have noted, the writing in the longer reports is much like the writing in the shorter ones. In general, the instructions given in earlier chapters apply to the longer

FIGURE 12–2   Diagram of the Structural Coherence Plan of a Long, Formal Report

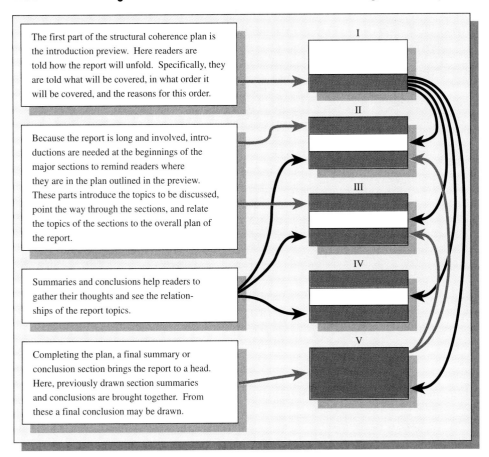

The first part of the structural coherence plan is the introduction preview. Here readers are told how the report will unfold. Specifically, they are told what will be covered, in what order it will be covered, and the reasons for this order.

Because the report is long and involved, introductions are needed at the beginnings of the major sections to remind readers where they are in the plan outlined in the preview. These parts introduce the topics to be discussed, point the way through the sections, and relate the topics of the sections to the overall plan of the report.

Summaries and conclusions help readers to gather their thoughts and see the relationships of the report topics.

Completing the plan, a final summary or conclusion section brings the report to a head. Here, previously drawn section summaries and conclusions are brought together. From these a final conclusion may be drawn.

reports. But the longer reports have one writing need that is not present in the shorter ones—the need for structural coherence helpers.

By *structural coherence helpers* we mean a network of explanations, introductions, summaries, and conclusions that guide the reader through the report. You should use these helpers wherever they will help relate the parts of the report or move the message along. Although you should not use them mechanically, you will find that they are likely to follow the general plan described in Figure 12–2.

• These are a network of explanations, introductions, summaries, and conclusions.

The coherence plan begins with the report preview in the introduction. As you will recall, the preview tells the readers what lies ahead. It covers three things: the topics to be discussed, their order, and the logic of that order. With this information in mind, the readers know how the parts of the report relate to one another. They know the overall strategy of the presentation. The following paragraphs do a good job of previewing a report comparing four automobiles to determine which is the best for a company's sales fleet.

• The coherence plan begins with the preview, which describes the route ahead.

The decision as to which light car Allied Distributors should buy is reached by comparing the cars on the basis of three factors: cost, safety, and performance. Each of these factors is broken down into its component parts, which are applied to the specific makes being considered.

Because cost is the most tangible factor, it is examined in the first major section. In this section, the four makes are compared for initial and trade-in values. Then they are compared for operating costs, as determined by gasoline mileage, oil use, repair expense, and the like. In the second major section, the safety of the four makes is compared. Driver visibility, special safety features, brakes, steering quality, acceleration rate, and traction are the

Structural coherence helpers provide a network of explanations to guide readers through the report. Helpers are similar to freeway connections. Readers can see clearly where they have been, where they are, and where they will go next. By constructing paragraphs, sentences, and words at important positions throughout the report, readers can be guided skillfully to the report's ending.

main considerations here. In the third major section, the dependability of the four makes is compared on the basis of repair records and salespersons' time lost because of automobile failure. In the final major section, weights are assigned to the foregoing comparisons, and the automobile brand that is best suited to the company's needs is recommended.

• Introductions to and summaries of the report sections keep readers informed of where they are in the report.

In addition to the preview in the introduction, the plan uses introductory and summary sections at convenient places throughout the report. Typically, these sections are at the beginning and end of major divisions, but you should use them wherever they are needed. Such sections remind the readers where they are in the report. They tell the readers where they have been and where they are going. Illustrating this technique is the following paragraph, which introduces a major section of a report. Note how the paragraph ties in with the preceding discussion, which concerned industrial activity in three geographic areas. Note also how it justifies covering secondary areas.

Although the great bulk of industry is concentrated in three areas (Grand City, Milltown, and Port Starr), a thorough industrial survey needs to consider the secondary, but nevertheless important, areas of the state. In the rank of their current industrial potential, these areas are the Southeast, with Hartsburg as its center; the Central West, dominated by Parrington; and the North Central, where Pineview is the center of activities.

The following summary-conclusion paragraph is a good ending to a major section. The paragraph brings to a head the findings presented in the section and points the way to the subject of the next section.

These findings and those pointed out in preceding paragraphs all lead to one obvious conclusion. The small-business executives are concerned primarily with subject matter that will aid them directly in their work. That is, they favor a curriculum slanted in favor of the practical subjects. They insist, however, on some coverage of the liberal arts, and they are also convinced of the value of studying business administration. On all these points, they are clearly out of tune with the bulk of the big-business leaders who have voiced their positions on this question. Even the most dedicated business administration professors would find it difficult to support such an extremely practical concept. Nevertheless, these are the opinions of the small-business executives. As they are the consumers of the business-education product, their opinions should at least be considered. Likewise, their specific recommendations on courses (the subject of the following section) deserve careful review.

Completing the coherence plan is the final major section of the report. In this section, you achieve the goal of the report. Here you recall from the preceding section summaries all the major findings and analyses. Then you apply them to the problem and present the conclusion. Thus, you complete the strategy explained in the introduction preview and recalled at convenient places throughout the report.

• The final major section of the report brings together the preceding information and applies it to the goal.

Wise use of coherence helpers can form a network of connections throughout the report. You should keep in mind, however, that these helpers should be used only when they are needed. That is, you should use them when your readers need help in seeing relationships and in knowing where they are and where they are going. If you use them well, they will appear as natural parts of the report story. They should never appear to be mechanical additions.

• Use coherence helpers naturally—when they are needed.

THE LONG ANALYTICAL REPORT ILLUSTRATED

Illustrating the long analytical report is the report presented at the end of this chapter (Figure 12–3). The report's structure parallels that of the formal type described in the preceding pages.

• Figure 12–3 is an illustration of a long, formal report.

SUMMARY ▶ by Chapter Objectives

1. The prefatory section of the long, formal report consists of these conventional parts:
   • Title fly—a page displaying only the title.
     —As a checklist for constructing the title, use the 5 Ws (*who, what, where, when, why*).
     —Sometimes *how* is important.
   • Title page—a page displaying the title, identification of writer and recipient, and date.
   • Letter of authorization—included only when a letter (or memorandum) authorized the report.
   • Letter of transmittal—a letter (or memorandum) transmitting the report (a *foreword* or *preface* in very long and highly formal papers).
     —This part takes the place of a face-to-face presentation.
     —Begin it with a presentation of the report.
     —Include comments about the report you would have made in a face-to-face presentation.
     —In some cases you may combine it with the executive summary.
     —Write the letter in personal style (first and second person).
   • Table of contents—a listing of the report parts with page numbers.
   • Executive summary—the report in miniature.
     —Include, in proportion, everything that is important—all the major facts, analyses, and conclusions.
     —Write it in either direct or indirect order.

① Describe the roles and contents and construct the prefatory parts of a long, formal report.

2. The report introduction prepares the readers to receive the report.
   • Include whatever helps reach this goal.
   • Use these items as a checklist for content: purpose, scope, limitations, problem history, methodology, definitions, preview.
   • A preview telling the order and reasoning for the order is useful in longer, more involved reports.

② Organize each introduction by considering all the likely readers and selecting the appropriate contents.

3. The ending of the report achieves the report goal.
   • Use a summary if the goal is to review information.
   • Use a conclusion if the goal is to reach an answer.
   • Use a recommendation if the goal is to determine a desirable action.

③ Determine, based on the goal, the most effective way to end a report—a summary, a conclusion, a recommendation, or a combination of the three.

4 Describe the role and content of the appendix and bibliography of a report.

4. An appendix and/or bibliography can follow the report text.
   - The appendix contains items that support the text but have no specific place in the text (such as questionnaires, working papers, summary tables).
   - The bibliography is a descriptive list of the printed sources that were used in the investigation.

5 Write a long, formal report using a structural coherence plan.

5. The longer reports need various structural helpers to give them coherence.
   - These helpers consist of a network of explanations, introductions, summaries, and conclusions that guide the reader through the report.
   - Begin the coherence plan with the introduction preview, which tells the structure of the report.
   - Then use the introductions and summaries in following parts to tell readers where they are in this structure.
   - At the end, bring together the preceding information, analyses, and conclusions to reach the report goal.
   - Make these coherence helpers inconspicuous—that is, make them appear to be a natural part of the message.

FIGURE 12–3   Illustration of a Long, Formal Report

This long, formal report presents the findings of an observational study of successful and unsuccessful salespeople to determine the differences in how each group works. The results will be used to revise the content of the company's sales training program. Because the report is extensive and the situation formal, the report has all the major prefatory parts. The significant statistical findings are effectively emphasized by graphics.

Title fly

*The title includes
the essentials
of the 5 W's.*

SALES TRAINING RECOMMENDATIONS FOR ARMOR MOTORS

BASED ON A 1995 STUDY OF COMPANY SALES ACTIVITIES

FIGURE 12–3   (Continued)

Title page

SALES TRAINING RECOMMENDATIONS FOR ARMOR MOTORS

BASED ON A 1995 STUDY OF COMPANY SALES ACTIVITIES

Prepared for

Here the essential
facts of
authorization are
provided.

Mr. Peter R. Simpson, Vice President for Sales
Armor Motors, Inc.
72117 North Musselman Road
Dearborn, MI 48126

Prepared by

Ashlee P. Callahan
Callahan and Hebert Research Associates
Suite D, Brownfield Towers
212 North Bedford Avenue
Detroit, MI 48219

November 17, 1995

FIGURE 12–3   **(Continued)**

Callahan and Herbert Research Associates
Suite D, Brownfield Towers
212 North Bedford Avenue
Detroit, MI 48219

November 17, 1995

Letter of transmittal

Mr. Peter R. Simpson
Vice President for Sales
Armor Motors, Inc.
72117 North Musselman Road
Dearborn, MI 48126

Dear Mr. Simpson:

The letter begins directly, with the authorization.

Here is the report on the observational study of your salespeople you asked us to conduct last August 17.

Pertinent comments help the reader understand and appreciate the research.

As you will see, our observations pointed to some specific needs for sales training. Following the procedure we agreed to, we will prepare an outline of these needs in a revised curriculum plan that we will submit to your training director December 4. We are confident that this curriculum plan will aid in correcting the shortcomings in your sales force.

A goodwill comment ends the letter.

We at Callahan and Hebert appreciate having this assignment. If you should need any assistance in interpreting this report or in implementing our recommendations, please call on us.

Sincerely yours,

Ashlee P. Callahan

Ashlee P. Callahan
Senior Research Associate

FIGURE 12–3   (Continued)

TABLE OF CONTENTS

Table of contents

A review of the problem facts prepares the reader to receive the report.

The three areas of sales work investigated logically form the main headings.

Subfactors of the work areas make logical second-level headings.

Note the parallel wording of the headings.

Note also the talking quality of the second-level headings.

FIGURE 12–3 (Continued)

List of charts (a continuation of the table of contents)

A list of the graphics in the report appears here, with complete titles that describe content.

LIST OF CHARTS

FIGURE 12–3 (Continued)

Executive
summary

Following the direct-order plan, this executive summary places the recommendations first. Highlights of the supporting findings follow.

Executive Summary

Conclusions drawn from this study suggest that these topics be added to Armor's sales training program:

1. Negative effects of idle time
2. Techniques of cultivating prospects
3. Development of bird dog networks
4. Cultivating repeat sales
5. Projection of integrity image
6. Use of moderate persuasion
7. Value of product knowledge

Supporting these recommendations are the following findings and conclusions drawn from an observational study comparing sales activities of productive and marginal salespeople.

The remaining paragraphs summarize the major findings in the order presented in the report.

The data show that the productive salespeople used their time more effectively than did the marginal salespeople. As compared with marginal salespeople, the productive salespeople spent less time in idleness (28% vs. 53%). They also spent more time in contact with prospects (31.3% vs. 19.8%) and more time developing prospects (10.4% vs. 4.4%).

Note that the important facts and figures are present.

Investigation of how the salespeople got their prospects showed that because floor assignments were about equal, both groups profited about the same from walk-ins. The productive group got 282; the marginal group got 274. The productive group used bird dogs more extensively, having 64 contacts derived from this source during the observation period. The marginal group had 8. Productive salespeople also were more successful in turning these contacts into sales.

The significant comparisons and conclusions are emphasized throughout.

Observations of sales presentations revealed that productive salespeople displayed higher integrity, used pressure more reasonably, and knew the product better than marginal salespeople. Of the 20 productive salespeople, 16 displayed images of moderately high integrity (Group II). Marginal group members ranged widely with 7 in Group III (questionable) and 5 each in Group II (moderately high integrity) and Group IV (deceitful). Most (15) of the productive salespeople used moderate pressure, whereas the marginal salespeople tended toward extremes (10 high pressure, 7 low pressure). On the product knowledge test, 17 of the productive salespeople scored excellent and 3 fair. Of the marginal members, 5 scored excellent, 6 fair, and 9 inadequate.

vi

FIGURE 12–3   (Continued)

SALES TRAINING RECOMMENDATIONS FOR ARMOR MOTORS
BASED ON A 1995 STUDY OF COMPANY SALES ACTIVITIES

THE PROBLEM AND THE PLAN

Incidentals of Authorization and Submittal

This study of Armor salespeople's sales activities is submitted to Mr. Peter R. Simpson, Vice President for Sales, on November 17, 1995. As specified by written agreement dated August 28, the investigation was conducted under the direction of Ashlee P. Callahan of Callahan and Hebert Research Associates.

Objective of Sales Training Improvement

The objective of the study was to find means of improving the effectiveness of Armor salespeople. The plan for achieving this objective involved first determining the techniques and characteristics of effective selling. This information then will be used in improving Armor's sales training program.

Use of Observational Techniques

The methodology used in this investigation was an observational study of Armor salespeople. Specifically, the study employed the time-duty technique, which is a unique means of observing work performance under real conditions. A detailed description of this technique is a part of the proposal approved at the August meeting and is not repeated here. Specific items relative to the application of this method in this case are summarized below.

Two groups of 20 Armor salespeople were selected for the observation—a productive and a marginal group. The productive group was made up of the company's top producers for the past year; the marginal group comprised the lowest producers. Only salespeople with three years or more of experience were eligible.

A team of two highly trained observers observed each of the salespeople selected for a continuous period of five working days. Using specially designed forms, the observers recorded the work activities of the salespeople. At the end of the observation period, the observers conducted an exit interview, recording certain demographic data and administering a test of the salesperson's knowledge of Armor's automobiles.

1

FIGURE 12–3   (Continued)

2

A Preview of the Presentation

In the following pages, the findings and analysis appear in the arrangement discussed at the August meeting. First comes a comparison of how the productive and the marginal salespeople spend their work time. Second is an analysis of how the productive and the marginal salespeople find their prospects. Third is a comparative analysis of the observable differences in sales presentations of the two groups. Conclusions drawn from these comparisons form the bases for recommendations of content emphasis in Armor's sales training program.

ANALYSIS OF WORK TIME USE

The time-duty observation records were examined to determine whether differences exist between the productive and marginal salespeople in their use of work time. Activities were grouped into four general categories: (1) idleness, (2) contacting prospects, (3) finding prospects, and (4) miscellaneous activities. This examination revealed the following results.

Negative Effect of Idle Time

As shown in Chart 1, the productive salespeople spent less work time in idleness (28%) than did the marginal salespeople (53%). Further

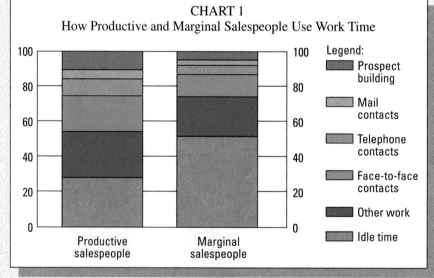

CHART 1
How Productive and Marginal Salespeople Use Work Time

FIGURE 12–3 **(Continued)**

3

examination of the observations reveals that the top five of the 20 productive salespeople spent even less time in idleness (13%); and the bottom five of the marginal salespeople spent more time in idleness (67%). Clearly, these observations suggest the predictable conclusion that successful salespeople work more than their less productive counterparts.

Correlation of Prospect Contacting and Success

Productive salespeople spent more time contacting prospects face to face, by telephone, and by mail (31.3%) than did marginal salespeople (19.8%). The specific means of making these contacts show similar differences. Productive and marginal salespeople spent their work time, respectively, 23.2% and 13.5% in face-to-face contacts, 4.8% and 2.0% in mail contacts, and 8.3% and 4.6% in telephone contacts. These data lend additional support to the conclusion that work explains sales success.

The text presents the data thoroughly yet concisely — and with appropriate comparisons.

Vital Role of Prospect Building

During the observation period, productive salespeople spent more than twice as much time (10.5%) as marginal salespeople (4.4%) in building prospects. Activities observed in this category include contacting bird dogs and other lead sources and mailing literature to established and prospective customers.

Necessity of Miscellaneous Activities

Both productive and marginal salespeople spent about a fourth of their work time in miscellaneous activities (tending to personal affairs, studying sales literature, attending sales meetings, and such). The productive group averaged 25.2%; the marginal group averaged 22.5%. As some of this time is related to automobile sales, productive salespeople would be expected to spend more time in this category.

A section summary helps the reader identify and remember the major findings.

Summary-Conclusions.

The preceding data reveal that the way salespeople spend their time affects their productivity. Productive salespeople work at selling. In sharp contrast with the marginal salespeople, they spend little time in idleness. They work hard to contact prospects and to build prospect lists. Like all automobile salespeople, they spend some time in performing miscellaneous duties.

This and the other major sections begin with helpful introductory comment.

DIFFERENCES IN FINDING PROSPECTS

A comparison of how productive and marginal salespeople find prospects and measurement of the productivity of these methods was a second area of investigation. For this study, the observations were classified by the four

FIGURE 12–3   (Continued)

4

primary sources of prospects: (1) walk-ins, (2) bird dogs and other referrals, (3) repeat customers, and (4) other. Only prospects that were contacted in person or by telephone during the observation period were included. Prospects were counted only once, even though some were contacted more than once.

<u>Near Equal Distribution of Walk-ins</u>

As expected, most of the contacts of both productive and marginal salespeople were walk-ins. Because both groups had about equal floor assignments, they got about the same number of prospects from this source. As illustrated in Chart 2, productive members got 282 (an average of 14.1 each), and marginal members got 274 (an average of 13.7 each)

Note how the use of color adds interest as well as helps the reader visualize the comparisons in the graphics.

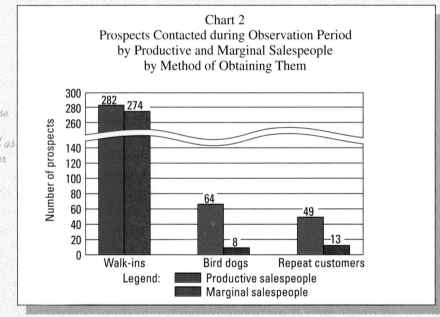

Although both groups got about the same number of prospects from walk-ins, productive salespeople got better results. A review of sales records shows that productive salespeople averaged 2.6 sales per week from walk-ins; marginal salespeople averaged 2.2. The difference, although appearing slight, represents roughly 16 automobiles per year.

<u>Value of Cultivating Long-standing Customers</u>

Returning long-standing customers and friends referred by them constitute the second most productive source of prospects. During the observation period,

FIGURE 12–3   (Continued)

5

productive salespeople had contacts with 49 such prospects; marginal salespeople had 13. Productive salespeople also had better sales success with these prospects, turning 40 of them into sales — an average of two per week. Marginal group members made sales to seven of these prospects — an average of .35 per person. These differences appear to be a direct result of effort (or lack of it) in maintaining contacts with customers after the sale.

Limited Effectiveness of Using Bird Dogs

Contacts from bird dogs comprise the third largest group, producing 64 total contacts for the productive and 8 for the marginal salespeople. Sales from this source totaled 9 for productive salespeople and 2 for marginal salespeople — an average of .45 and .1 sales per person, respectively. Although not large in terms of volume, these data explain much of the difference between the two groups. The use of bird dogs involves work, and the willingness to work varies sharply between the two groups.

Note how talking headings help emphasize the major findings.

Scant Use of Other Techniques

Other prospect gaining techniques were little used among the salespeople observed. Techniques long discussed in industry sales literature such as cold-spearing, placing written messages on automobile windshields, and random telephoning produced no prospects for either group during the observation period. All of the salespeople observed noted that they had used these techniques in the past, but with little success. The lack of evidence in this study leaves unanswered the question of the effectiveness of these techniques.

Summary–Conclusions.

The obvious conclusion drawn from the preceding review of how prospects are found is that the productive salespeople work harder to get them. Although both groups get about the same number of walk-ins, the successful ones work harder at maintaining contacts with past customers and at getting contacts from a network of bird dogs and friends.

OBSERVABLE VARIATIONS IN PRESENTATIONS

Differences in the sales presentations used constituted the third area of study. Criteria used in this investigation were (1) integrity, (2) pressure, and (3) product knowledge. Obviously, the first two of these criteria had to be evaluated subjectively. Even so, the evaluations were made by highly trained observers who used comprehensive guidelines. These guidelines are described in detail in the approved observation plan.

FIGURE 12–3   (Continued)

6

<u>Positive Effect of Integrity</u>

Evaluations of the salespeople's integrity primarily measured the apparent degree of truthfulness of the sales presentations. The observers classified the images of integrity they perceived during the sales presentations into four groups: Group I — Impeccable (displayed the highest degree of truthfulness), Group II — Moderately High (generally truthful, some exaggeration), Group III — Questionable (mildly deceitful and tricky); and Group IV — Deceitful (untruthful and tricky).

Here and elsewhere, text references tell the reader when to observe the charts.

Of the 20 productive salespeople observed, 16 were classified in Group II as shown in Chart 3. Of the remaining four, 2 were in Group I and 2 in Group III.

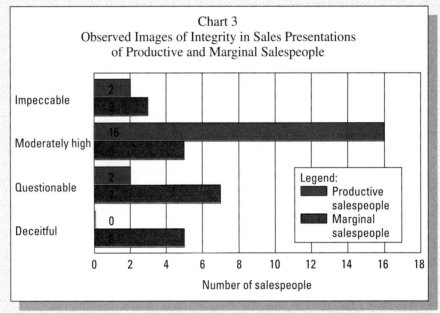

Chart 3
Observed Images of Integrity in Sales Presentations
of Productive and Marginal Salespeople

Distribution of the marginal salespeople was markedly different: 3 in Group I, 5 in Group II, 7 in Group III, and 5 in Group IV. Clearly, integrity was more apparent among the productive salespeople.

<u>Apparent Value of Moderate Pressure</u>

Measurements (by observation) of pressure used in the sales presentations were made in order to determine the relationship of pressure to sales success. Using the guidelines approved at the August meeting, the observers classified

FIGURE 12–3   (Continued)

7

each salesperson's presentations into three categories: (1) high pressure, (2) moderate pressure, and (3) low pressure. Observers reported difficulties in making some borderline decisions, but they felt that most of the presentations were easily classified.

Of the 20 productive salespeople, 15 used moderate pressure, 3 used low pressure, and 2 used high pressure as depicted in Chart 4. The 20 marginal

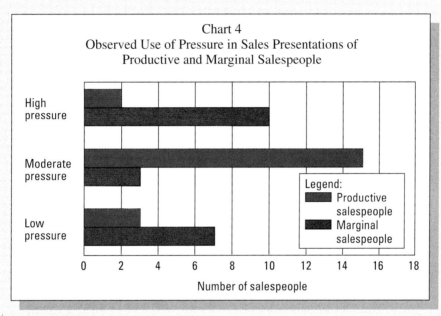

Chart 4
Observed Use of Pressure in Sales Presentations of
Productive and Marginal Salespeople

The facts are not just presented. They are compared and conclusions are drawn from them.

salespeople presented a different picture. Only 3 of them used moderate pressure. Of the remainder, 10 used high pressure and 7 used low pressure. The evidence suggests that moderate pressure is most effective.

Necessity of Product Knowledge

Product knowledge, a generally accepted requirement for successful selling, was determined during the exit interview. Using the 30 basic questions developed by Armor management from sales literature, observers measured the salespeople's product knowledge. Correct responses to 27 or more of the questions was determined to be excellent, 24 through 26 was fair, and below 24 was classified as inadequate.

Productive salespeople displayed superior knowledge of the product with 17 of the 20 scoring excellent. As shown in Chart 5, the remaining 3 scored fair.

FIGURE 12–3   (Continued)

8

Scores for product knowledge were sharply different in the marginal salesperson group. Although 5 of them scored excellent, 6 scored fair, and 9 scored inadequate.

Note how text and charts work closely together to present the information.

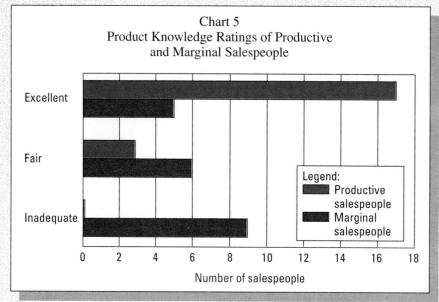

Chart 5
Product Knowledge Ratings of Productive
and Marginal Salespeople

Legend:
■ Productive salespeople
■ Marginal salespeople

Number of salespeople

These data point to an apparent weakness in training or a lack of individual preparation.

Summary-Conclusions

Another summary-conclusion brings the section to a close.

The preceding presentation reveals some basic differences in the sales presentations of the productive and marginal salespeople. The productive salespeople displayed higher integrity (though not the highest). They used moderate pressure, whereas the marginal people tended toward high or low extremes. Also, the productive people knew their products better.

RECOMMENDATIONS FOR TRAINING

The conclusions reached in preceding sections suggest certain actions that Armor Motors should take in training its sales force. Specifically, the instruction should be altered to include the following topics:

From the summary-conclusions of the preceding three sections the recommendations are derived.

1. Importance of minimizing idle time.

2. Sales rewards from productive work (mailing literature, telephoning, cultivating prospects, etc.).

FIGURE 12–3 **(Continued)**

9

3. Significance of creating a network of bird dogs and friends in building prospects.

Numbering makes the recommendations stand out.

4. Value of maintaining contacts with past customers.

5. Need for integrity, within reasonable limits.

6. Use of moderate pressure, avoiding extremes in either direction.

7. Need for a thorough knowledge of the product.

CRITICAL THOUGHT QUESTIONS

1. Long, formal reports are not often written in business. So why should you know how to write them?

2. A good title should be complete and concise. Are not these requirements contradictory? Explain.

3. Discuss the relative importance of the title fly and the title page in a report.

4. Distinguish among the letter of transmittal, the foreword, and the preface.

5. Describe the role and content of a letter of transmittal.

6. Why is personal style typically used in the letter of transmittal?

7. What is the basis for determining whether a report should have a table of contents?

8. Discuss the construction of the executive summary.

9. Why does the executive summary include the facts and figures in addition to the analyses and conclusions drawn from them?

10. Some reports need little or no introduction; others need a very long introduction. Why is this so?

11. Give examples of report problems that require introductory coverage of methods of collecting data, historical background, and limitations.

12. Give examples of report problems that require, respectively, (a) an ending summary, (b) an ending conclusion, and (c) an ending recommendation.

13. Using as a guide the diagram in Figure 12–2, summarize the coherence plan of the long, formal report.

CRITICAL THINKING EXERCISES

1. Making any assumptions needed, construct complete yet concise titles for the reports described below:
   a. A report writer reviewed records of exit interviews of employees at Marvel-Floyd Manufacturing Company who quit their jobs voluntarily. The objective of the investigation was to determine the reasons for leaving.
   b. A researcher studied data from employee personnel records at Magna-Tech, Inc., to determine whether permanent (long-term) employees differ from short-term employees. Any differences found would be used in hiring employees in the future. The data studied included age, education, experience, sex, marital status, test scores, and such.
   c. A report writer compared historical financial records (1935 to the present) of Super Saver Foods to determine whether this grocery chain should own or rent store buildings. In the past it did both.

2. Criticize the following beginning sentences of letters of transmittal:
   a. "In your hands is the report you requested January 7 concerning. . . ."
   b. "As you will recall, last January 7 you requested a report on. . . ."
   c. "That we should open a new outlet in Bragg City is the conclusion of this report, which you authorized January 7."

3. In a report comparing four automobiles (Alpha, Beta, Gamma, and Delta) to determine which one is the best buy for a company, section II of the report body covered cost data ((a) initial costs; (b) trade-in values; and (c) operating expenses). Section III presented a comparison of the safety features of the automobiles ((a) stan-

dard safety features; (b) acceleration data; (c) weight distribution; and (d) breaking quality).
   a. Criticize this introductory paragraph at the beginning of section III:
   In the preceding section was presented a thorough analysis of the cost data. Now safety of the cars will be compared. Although costs are important, Warren-Burke also is concerned about the safety of its salespeople, who spend almost half their work time driving.
   b. Write a more appropriate introductory paragraph.

4. The next section of the report (section IV) covered these topics: (a) handling; (b) quality of ride; and (c) durability.
   a. Criticize this introductory paragraph for the section:
   This section of the report presents a comparison of the overall construction of the four automobiles. These considerations also are important because they affect how a car rides, and this is important. Thus, we will take up in this order: handling, general riding quality, and construction qualities.
   b. Write a more appropriate introductory paragraph.

5. Criticize this final paragraph (a preview) of the introduction of the report described above:
   This report compares the automobiles by three factors. These are costs, safety, and comfort and construction, in that order. Costs include initial expenditure, trade-in value, and operating expense. Safety covers safety devices, acceleration, weight distribution, and braking. Comfort and construction includes handling, ride quality, and durability. A ranking is derived from this comparison.

CRITICAL THINKING EXERCISES

▶ **Long Reports**

1. *Reporting community viewpoints relating to a company's policy on same-sex partners.* For the past

week, the citizens of Flat Rock City have been in an uproar over a decision made by their city council. For some months, Starr Computer Company, Inc., has been negotiating with the council for a tax break as an inducement to locate a major customer service center in the city. The center would employ 800 initially. In time the number would increase to 1,700—quite an addition to a community of less than 100,000 population.

All appeared to be going well for Starr until a week ago when the matter came up for a vote. The council voted no—with two members supporting and three opposing. The reason was Starr's policy of extending insurance and other benefits to same-sex domestic partners. In the words of one of the council members opposing Starr, "To have voted otherwise would have been tantamount to endorsing immoral behavior." Following the vote, Starr officials announced they would locate elsewhere unless the council reconsidered its stand.

Immediately following Starr's announcement, loud cries of protest were heard throughout the community. The local newspaper was especially critical, and some local politicians loudly took the city council to task. But strong support for the council's decision also was heard. Led by a coalition of local ministers, the supporters vigorously defended the council action as a "move that would preserve the morality of our community." Quickly the citizens took sides, with neighbors against neighbors and friends against friends.

In the wake of this controversy, the city council called an emergency meeting. "Maybe we made a mistake," said Sam P. Wasson, leader of the council members opposing Starr. "Maybe we misjudged community attitudes. But I don't want to just give in to the extremists who are making most of the noise. I think we should find out what the community really thinks. Why not have a survey done on the matter. And we should do more than just find out what the majority want. We need to know where the opposition comes from—their ages, sex, incomes—even their political leanings. Their religions commitments are significant, too. I thought I knew our citizens, but with so many new families moving in, maybe things have changed."

Wasson's suggestion was quickly accepted by the other members, and in short order you, the assistant to the city manager, were given the task of conducting the survey. "You have all the city government resources at your disposal," they told you. "But work fast. You may have to sacrifice scientific correctness because of the time problem. But get for us information that will help us do the thing that is right for our community. We've told Starr that we will reconsider our decision. We have promised them a final decision by Friday of next week."

Quickly you constructed a simple questionnaire, building it around five basic questions that appear to be the keys to the problem. And to bring in information about just who thinks what, you worked in the demographics Wasson suggested (age, politics, income, etc.). Then, using personnel from the city manager's office, you conducted a telephone survey of voters. You randomly selected the people to be interviewed and think your final sample is fairly rep-

resentative of the citizens of Flat Rock City. (For class purposes, you may create any additional information about methodology you may need.)

Now you have tabulated the responses and have them neatly arranged before you (Table 1). You will present them as objectively as you can even though you may have your own bias on the matter. You will present your findings and analyses in appropriate form, which means you will include all the trappings of formality the situation justifies. Wherever it will help in communicating the report message, you will use graphics. Address the report to the city council, listing the five members by name.

2. *Reporting information on how to organize and operate a recycling program to a city manager.* As a research associate for Probst-Stecher Research, Inc., you have been given an interesting assignment by one of the leaders of your city. That leader is Rene Duby, city manager. Duby explained to you that the city is considering starting a recycling program in response to widespread demands expressed by the citizenry. The problem is that no one in city government knows much about recycling. So the city wants you to help.

As Duby explained the city's need, "We don't think we should proceed with something as important as this without knowing what we're doing. So we'd like for you to help us. We think we can learn from the experiences of other cities. As you know, many have such programs. So we'd like you to get the information we need from them—perhaps through a survey. Find out what they're doing—especially what items they recycle. Find out how they promote their programs—what incentives they use, if any. And if they have encountered any special problems, have them point them out for us. It would help, too, if you determined whether their programs are mandatory or voluntary. Some of my council members are wary of anything mandatory."

With Duby's words in mind, you began to plan the project. First, you constructed a simple questionnaire—one designed to get the information Duby outlined for you. Then you built a mailing list of city managers from a directory that Duby had given you. Next you mailed the questionnaires to the people on the list. To improve responses, you used a cover letter with Duby's signature on it, and you included return envelopes with Duby's office address on them. (Of course, you did this with Duby's approval.)

After a reasonable passage of time, you collected the returned questionnaires from the city manager's office. You are pleased with the returns. Of the 320 questionnaires you mailed, 264 were returned. Then you tabulated the responses and arranged the totals neatly in tabular form (Tables 2–6).

Now with the tables before you, you are ready to begin the really important part of the assignment—organizing, analyzing, and presenting the findings in meaningful report form. You will use a report form appropriate for the occasion—perhaps with all the formal prefatory trappings. And you will use attractive graphics wherever they help communicate the

TABLE 1 (Problem 1)   Responses to Questions Relating to City Council's Decision to Deny Tax Abatement to Starr Computer

Responses shown by various categories of demographics: political party affiliation, church attendance, age, income and residence of respondents. (For complete wording of question, see the box below.) All figures in percent.

	QUESTION 1				QUESTION 2				
	Approve	Mixed Feelings	Disapprove	Don't Know/ No Opinion	Oppose Tax Abatements	Oppose Domestic Partners	Oppose Both	Other Reason	Don'1 Know
All respondents	37	5	50	7	15	57	23	3	1
Political party identification									
Republican	47	8	39	6	12	64	17	3	2
Democrat	23	5	65	7	28	52	16	0	4
Independent/other	39	3	51	8	13	52	32	3	0
Church attendance									
Regular	45	4	43	8	10	62	24	2	1
Occasional	32	8	55	5	20	53	23	0	3
Rarely	25	3	64	8	25	50	12	6	0
Not at all	35	0	53	12	27	47	20	7	0
Sex									
Male	42	4	46	9	15	51	28	4	1
Female	33	6	55	6	16	64	16	1	1
Age									
18 to 34	27	4	56	13	16	74	11	0	0
35 to 44	37	5	53	6	15	51	23	6	4
45 to 64	39	4	49	8	15	56	25	2	0
65 and older	43	9	42	6	18	57	25	0	0
Years in Flat Rock City									
Less than 5	20	2	60	18	11	67	0	11	11
5 to 9	42	3	53	2	12	63	20	5	0
10 to 19	32	8	52	7	16	58	22	2	2
20 or more	48	3	40	9	18	49	31	0	0
Household income									
Less than $30,000	38	5	44	14	15	58	21	6	0
$30–40,000	44	9	40	7	10	71	19	0	0
$40–50,000	39	2	55	4	9	73	14	0	5
More than $50,000	30	6	57	7	26	38	26	5	2

Questions asked:
1. Do you approve or disapprove of the city council's decision to deny tax abatements to Starr Computer because Starr has a policy of extending benefits to domestic partners of their employees?

2. (If approve:) Do you approve that decision because you oppose tax abatements or because you oppose policies that recognize domestic partners?

report information. Although you suspect the report will be read by the council members and other dignitaries at city hall, you will address it to Duby. (For class purposes, if you need additional information on methodology, you may create it as long as it is logical and consistent with the information given in the assignment.)

3. *Reporting evaluation practices of sales managers to ASM directors.* At the annual meeting of the Association for Sales Managers (ASM), the directors discussed various projects that could be undertaken to benefit the membership. They selected one: "current practices of sales managers in evaluating performance

of their salespeople." It would be helpful, they agreed, if the membership knew how their fellow members do this important work. From the discussion, it became evident that opinions and practices concerning evaluation procedures vary widely. The directors agreed it would be good if the membership knew the extent of these variations. Such information should enable most of them to do a better job.

You, the executive secretary of ASM, are the person responsible for conducting the projects the directors select. Of course, you have easy access to the membership and usually have their good cooperation. So you decided to get the information needed through

QUESTION 3				QUESTION 4					QUESTION 5				
Yes	Maybe/ Depends	No	Don't Know/ No Opinion	Approve	Disapprove	No Strong Feelings	Depends	Don't Know/ No Opinion	Approve	Disapprove	No Strong Feelings	Depends	Don't Know/ No Opinion
51	14	28	6	9	42	43	1	5	5	47	42	1	4
42	16	33	7	4	51	37	1	6	4	58	35	1	8
63	12	21	4	11	39	46	0	5	7	39	49	0	5
51	14	29	6	12	36	47	1	4	4	44	45	2	5
48	17	29	5	4	59	33	1	4	2	63	30	1	4
53	9	34	4	14	37	45	1	3	6	41	45	2	5
61	8	22	9	11	12	70	2	5	9	20	67	0	3
49	21	23	7	19	21	47	0	14	9	33	51	0	7
49	12	33	6	9	43	44	1	4	4	51	41	1	4
54	16	24	6	9	41	43	1	6	6	44	44	1	5
54	17	23	7	23	27	39	1	10	11	35	48	0	6
51	11	32	5	10	32	50	2	5	5	43	47	3	2
55	16	27	2	5	49	43	0	3	4	52	41	0	4
40	15	29	15	2	63	32	0	3	2	65	26	0	8
58	18	16	7	11	27	58	2	2	7	38	56	0	0
51	14	30	5	8	39	47	1	5	4	46	45	2	3
59	10	28	2	12	42	41	1	4	6	48	41	1	3
36	19	32	13	6	51	36	0	7	3	52	36	0	9
43	18	31	8	11	41	42	0	6	6	49	40	0	6
53	16	29	3	10	54	30	0	6	6	56	33	0	6
57	9	30	4	2	43	52	0	4	2	48	46	0	4
54	16	24	6	10	33	51	1	5	6	41	49	1	3

3. Do you feel that the Council's decision will deter other businesses from relocating to Flat Rock City?

4. Do you personally approve or disapprove or have no strong feelings either way about heterosexual couples who live together outside of marriage?

5. Do you personally approve or disapprove or have no strong feelings either way about gay or lesbian couples who live together?

a random sample of the organization's 2,877 members. You began by constructing a questionnaire designed to get the information needed. Most of what you requested in it was suggested by the directors in their discussion, but you filled in a few voids. You are confident you have the subject covered thoroughly.

Next you mailed the questionnaires to a randomly selected sample of 500 members. Using a follow-up "prodding" letter to those slow in responding, you got what you believe is an excellent response of 416.

With the returned questionnaires in hand, you then began tabulating the information reported. From the demographic data you requested, you constructed a profile of respondents (Table 7). This information clearly shows that your sample is representative of the makeup of the membership.

You then recorded the information indicating how many used each of the conventional bases for evaluating performance, including both output (Table 8) and input (Table 9). These data show which of the salespeople's work activities the sales managers consider meaningful.

Next you recorded the qualitative bases the executives reported they use (Table 10). Based on perception and subjective evaluation, these bases nevertheless play a vital role in evaluating

TABLE 2 (Problem 2)   Materials Included in Municipal Recycling Programs

Material	Cities Reporting	Percent
Newspaper	254	96.2
Glass	248	93.9
Aluminum	233	88.3
Plastic bottles/jugs	177	67.0
Corrugated paper/cardboard	160	60.6
Scrap metals	138	52.3
Leaves, wood, brush, yard wastes	125	47.3
Waste oil	122	46.2
High grade paper	109	41.3
Mixed paper	85	32.2
Other (batteries, tin)	40	15.2
All rigid plastics	29	11.0
Chip board	17	6.4

TABLE 3 (Problem 2)   Importance of Problems in Municipal Recycling Programs (N = 264)

Problem	Mean Score*	Rank
Finding markets for recyclables	4.15	1
Getting residents to participate in the program	3.70	2
Lack of sufficient state grants or other financial assistance	3.50	3
Securing adequate local government financial support	3.40	4
Obtaining information/technical assistance for recycling	2.83	5
Theft of recyclables	1.76	6

* 1 = Not important. 5 = Very important.

TABLE 4 (Problem 2)   Use of Incentives to Increase Citizen Participation in Recycling (N = 264)

Incentives	Number	Percent
Official recognition of recycling efforts	89	34.5
Contests with prizes	66	25.6
Campaigns by local scouts to encourage citizens to recycle	44	17.1
Discounts or rebates on disposal fees	30	11.7
Cash awards	26	10.1
Tax credits	2	0.8
Tax exemptions	2	0.8
Incentives Listed by Respondents:		
Peer pressure by neighbors	20	
Increasing solid waste disposal fees for the use of more than one garbage can	11	
Having school age kids encourage their parents to recycle	11	
Fines for failure to recycle	6	

them for presentation. Then you will present the findings in clear and precise language. Although in time your findings will be sent to the membership in a newsletter, you will present the information to the directors in a formal report. The report will include the conventional prefatory parts appropriate for this relatively formal situation. It will use graphics wherever their appearance will help to communicate the report story. Address the report to the 11 directors, listing them by name. Tanya Krall is the chair.

4. *Determining reasons for weak survey response rates.*
Touch Screen Surveys, a marketing research group, is quite concerned about the weak responses it has been receiving recently to its mail surveys. Hearsay comments and anonymous notes on returned but uncompleted questionnaires indicate that most organizations never complete the deluge of questionnaires they receive—from you or anyone else—other than the local, state, and federal questionnaires industrial companies are legally obligated to answer. Too, most organizations find little value in academic questionnaires, as they are perceived to serve the publish-or-perish atmosphere of the university world.

Symptoms such as these have created a need for the agency to conduct a survey to find out more precisely why responses have been low. The objective is to learn how to get better results for clients.

As a research associate for Touch Screen, you have been assigned the task of conducting the survey. Thus, you selected 450 corporations for the sample—200 chosen at random from Fortune 500, and 50 each from Fortune's retailing, transportation, utility,

salespeople. Then you compiled the data relating to the mechanics of evaluating—specifically the sources of information used (Table 11) and the frequency of evaluations (Table 12).

Although it is not actually a part of the evaluation procedure, the question of how sales objectives are set was included in your questionnaire. So you tabulated the responses to this question (Table 13). You believe the topic belongs in the report. Sales objectives serve as a guide to performance measurement. How they are developed and their fairness is a highly controversial matter with sales managers and their salespeople.

With these data recorded and reduced to percentages, you are ready to begin analyzing and organizing

TABLE 5 (Problem 2)   Use of Public Information and Education Strategies (N = 264)

Strategy	Number	Percent
Pamphlets, brochures, or bumper stickers	220	84.6
Speeches by officials to schools or local groups about recycling	179	68.8
Special educational programs about recycling in the public schools	169	65.0
Free newspaper public service notices	134	51.7
Paid newspaper advertisements	121	46.7
Neighborhood or community information meetings	121	46.5
Free radio public service announcements	82	31.5
Free television public service ads	77	29.6
Window displays or posted notices in neightborhoods	75	28.8
Paid radio commercials	40	15.4
Billboard advertisements	29	11.2
Contract with advertising firm(s) for multimedia promotion campaign	21	8.1
Paid television commercials	17	6.6
No educational or promotional materials are used	7	2.7
Publicity Strategies Listed by Respondents as Being Successful		
Mail-outs about recycling with utility bills	20	
Public school programs that get kids to pressure their parents to recycle	11	
Block-leader programs	6	

TABLE 6 (Problem 2)   Participation and Diversion Rates by Program Type (N = 264)

Program Type	Mean Participation Rate	Mean Diversion Rate
Mandatory	74.3	21.6
All voluntary	39.7	12.2
With curbside pickup	48.6	12.3
With drop-off facilities only	24.6	10.8

TABLE 7 (Problem 3)   Profile of Respondents

Type of Business	Percentage
Manufacturer of industrial goods	44
Manufacturer of consumer goods	16
Wholesaler	9
Retailer	4
Services	27
Total	100

Annual Dollar Sales Volume (in 000)	Percentage
Over $100,000	46
$51,000–$100,000	12
$11,000–$50,999	27
Under $11,000	15
Total	100

Sales Management Position	Percentage
Vice president sales	3
National sales manager	4
Regional sales manager	34
Zone sales manager	6
Field sales manager	37
Other sales management titles	16
Total	100

banking, and insurance lists. Next you designed a questionnaire instrument to focus on what you think are the central issues in the study—increase in number of questionnaires, policies about answering surveys, benefits of questionnaires, number of questionnaires answered, reasons for not answering them, and preferences for questionnaire length. In the questionnaire, you asked respondents to assume that any changes you referred to were changes that had occurred in the last six years.

It has been two months since you mailed the questionnaire to the 450 corporations. To date, you have received 175 returned questionnaires (a 38.9 percent return rate), and you have tallied the results as shown in Tables 14–21. Not everyone responded to all questions in the survey; so not all of your totals equal 175. By looking at the returns by corporate type and by total numbers, however, you believe you have reliable and representative answers.

With the data assembled, you need to present them in a meaningful report. You will word the report on the impersonal side of the formality continuum—without I, you, and we. Also, you will use graphics where needed to help readers picture the results and their meaning. Because the report is considered formal, you will dress it up with prefatory parts—a

TABLE 8 (Problem 3) Output Bases Used in Performance Evaluation

Base	Percent Using
Sales	
Sales volume in dollars	81
Sales volume to previous year's sales	78
Sales volume by product or product line	68
Amount of new account sales	58
Sales volume in units	54
Sales volume to dollar quota	54
Sales volume by customer	49
Sales volume to market potential	34
Sales volume to physical unit quota	24
Sales volume per order	13
Sales volume by outlet type	11
Sales volume per call	10
Percentage of sales made by telephone or mail	8
Market share	
Market share per quota	19
Accounts	
Number of new accounts	71
Number of accounts lost	43
Number of accounts on which payment is over-due	22
Number of accounts buying in the full line	16
Profit	
Net profit dollars	26
Return on investment	16
Net profit contribution	14
Gross margin	14
Gross margin per sales	14
New profit as a % of sales	23
Orders	
Order-call ratio	29
Net orders per repeat order	17
Number of canceled orders per orders booked	14

TABLE 9 (Problem 3) Input Bases Used in Performance Evaluation

Base	Percent Using
Calls	
Calls per period	57
Number of calls per number of customers (by product class)	17
Selling Expense	
Selling expense to sales	41
Selling expense to quota	22
Average cost per call	13
Ancillary Activities	
Number of required reports turned in	44
Number of customer complaints	31
Training meetings conducted	28
Number of letters/phone calls to prospects	25
Number of demonstrations conducted	25
Number of service calls made	24
Number of dealer meetings held	15
Advertising displays set up	12

TABLE 10 (Problem 3) Qualitative Bases Used in Performance Evaluation

Base	Percent Using
Attitude	90
Product knowledge	89
Selling skills	85
Appearance and manner	82
Communication skills	81
Initiative and aggressiveness	80
Planning ability	78
Time management	73
Knowledge of competition	72
Judgment	69
Creativity	61
Knowledge of company policies	59
Report preparation and submission	59
Customer goodwill generated	50
Degree of respect from trade and competition	34
Good citizenship	23

four-spot title page, a table of contents, and a combination transmittal letter and executive summary.

Write the report that will present the facts, interpret them, and recommend actions that will help Touch Screen Surveys increase the responses to its questionnaires. Address the report to Staton P. Calhoun, president.

5. *Determining the profile of bank customers using questionnaire sources.* Communiquest, Inc., an advertising agency, has been retained by the Board of Directors of Guarantee Bank to do a study of the profile of the bank's customers. The board would like to use the profile data in its planning activities to serve the customers and the community more effectively. They also would use the study to promote bank services to various market segments.

As a research associate for Communiquest, you have drawn the assignment of conducting the research. To obtain the information you need, you

TABLE 11 (Problem 3)   Frequency of Performance Review

Frequency of Review	Percentage of Respondents
Weekly	5
Monthly	8
Quarterly	28
Semiannually	26
Annually	33

TABLE 12 (Problem 3)   Sources of Information Used in Salesperson Evaluation

Source	Percent Using
Printed form for performance evaluation	56
Analysis of computer printouts for each territory	50
Analysis of call reports	48
Other (supervisory calls, feedback from clients)	44

TABLE 13 (Problem 3)   Participation of Salespeople in Setting Standards or Objectives

Participation	Percent Using
Salespeople set their own objectives with no inputs from management	0
Salespeople set their own objectives with some inputs from management	3
Salespeople and management jointly set objectives	55
Management sets objectives with some inputs from salespeople	23
Management sets objectives with no inputs from salespeople	8
No response	11

TABLE 14 (Problem 4)   Increase in Percentage of Questionnaires Received

Percentage Increase	Number of Responses	Percentage of Total
0–29	26	17
30–59	49	32
60–99	17	11
100–149	29	19
150–200	10	7
200+	22	14
Total	153	100

TABLE 15 (Problem 4)   Degree of Restrictiveness of Corporate Policy about Answering Questionnaires

More Restrictive	Number of Responses	Percentage of Total
Very definitely	56	33
Moderately	38	23
Slightly	28	17
Not at all	46	27
Total	168	100

design a questionnaire asking for certain sets of data you will need to complete the profile. For example, you ask for certain demographics such as age, education, income, etc. Two of the items on your list— amount of deposit and percentage of total savings in the bank—are keys to your study as you see them; so you decide to cross-reference these items with other demographics after you receive the returned questionnaires.

To save on cost, you decide to insert the questionnaire with a cover letter in the monthly bank statements sent out to each depositor. You ask that depositors complete the questionnaire and return it in a postage-paid envelope. Or they may return it whenever they are at the bank. To get increased returns, you decide to insert the mailing into the next month's statement as well. You believe both of these mailings should give you the information you need for the study.

It is now two and one-half months since you began the mailings and 75 percent of the Guarantee depositors have returned their questionnaires. You assemble this information by item and tabulate your work as shown in Tables 22–24. You will use these tables to prepare the report to the board of directors.

Your report will address the issue of the profile of

TABLE 16 (Problem 4)   Benefits Received from Responding to Questionnaire

Benefit Received	Number of Responses	Percentage of Total
Very definite	2	1
Moderate	32	19
Slight	94	56
Not at all	41	24
Total	169	100

TABLE 17 (Problem 4)   Percentage of Questionnaires Answered

Percentage of Questionnaires Answered	Number of Responses	Percentage of Total
0–19	24	14
20–39	22	13
40–59	40	24
60–79	38	22
80–100	46	27
Total	170	100

TABLE 18 (Problem 4)   Sources of Questionnaires Received

Sources of Questionnaires	Composite Score
University personnel	271
University students	198
Trade organizations	149
Professional associations	116
Federal government	101
State government	50
Other businesses	39
Other	25
Total	949

* Respondents were asked to rank the three most numerous sources from 1–3, with 1 as most important. A rating of 1 was scored with 3 points, 2 with 2, and 3 with 1. Points were summed for all sources and presented as a composite score.

TABLE 19 (Problem 4)   Likelihood of Responding to a Questionnaire by Source*

Least Likely to be Answered	Composite Score
University students	360
Other businesses	328
University personnel	210
Professional associations	127
Trade organizations	115
State government	18
Federal government	0
Other	57
Total	1,215

* Respondents were asked to rank their likelihood on a 1–4 scale, with the least likely receiving a rating of 1. A rating of 1 was scored with a 4, a 2 with a 3, etc. Points were summed and presented as a total score.

TABLE 20 (Problem 4)   Reasons for Not Answering Questionnaires

Major Reasons for Not Answering	Number of Responses	Percentage of 171 Respondents
Too long	103	60
Too complex	94	55
Too academic	84	49
Too costly	80	47
Proprietary information	77	45
Lack of questionnaire focus	62	36
Sensitive information	61	36
Timing	55	32
Too many subject areas	39	23
Unimportant information	38	22
Responses may not be confidential	37	22
Answered a similar questionnaire	17	10
Cannot determine who will answer	15	9
Form letter enclosed	10	6
Other	51	30

TABLE 21 (Problem 4)   Preferences about Page Length of Questionnaires

Length in Pages	Too Long (%)	Acceptable (%)
6	99	1
5	96	4
4	83	17
3	56	44
2	9	91

TABLE 22 (Problem 5)   Characteristics of Depositors in the Survey

Characteristics	Percent
A. Age	
18–25	3.3
26–40	11.0
41–55	15.5
56–65	35.6
Over 65	34.6
B. Education (completed)	
Less than high school	9.5
High school	57.4
College	21.3
Graduate school	11.8
C. Approximate gross income (last year)	
$0–19,999	33.6
20,000–29,999	29.7
30,000–39,999	17.4
40,000–59,999	15.4
60,000 and over	3.9
D. Retirement	
Yes	56.6
No	43.4
E. Amount on deposit at Guarantee Bank	
$0–499	0.9
500–999	0.9
1,000–4,999	8.1
5,000–9,999	8.8
10,000–19,999	22.2
20,000–49,999	31.5
50,000–99,999	20.1
100,000 and over	7.5
F. Percent of total savings in Guarantee Bank	
Less than 10	7.5
11–25	15.8
26–50	20.4
51–75	22.2
76–100	34.1

Guarantee's depositors. In it, you will use graphics to convey the report message. Your report format will include a four-spot title page and a combination transmittal and executive summary. You will word the report formally—without I, you, and we.

Write the report that will give the board members of Guarantee Bank the depositors' profile they can use in their planning and promotion work.

6. *Determining whether gifts/entertainment will stimulate sales at Leander Industries.* Today's assignment finds you working as research specialist for Solution Research, Inc. After working with the company for five years, you know that hard work and clear thinking are the keys to producing good results for clients. And these characteristics are the underpinnings of effective reports, too. You will need them both in the long report you are going to prepare for Leander Industries.

Solution Research has been retained to conduct a survey for Leander, which is considering using gifts and entertainment to stimulate lagging sales. This client is convinced that a strong connection exists between these two variables—sales and gifts/entertainment expense. Moreover, Leander executives believe that more aggressive giving and entertaining behavior will produce a more aggressive sales effort for potential customers. Before they move operationally on these ideas, however, they need more facts about gifts and entertainments so that they can design appropriate policies to guide promotion strategy. And that's where you enter the picture.

To get the necessary facts, you designed a questionnaire and pretested it. The instrument itself contained gift/entertainment activities and a five-point rating scale asking respondents to assess each one of the activities based on how important the activity was in successful selling. Also, you asked for selected demographics of respondents.

After making adjustments based on the pretest, you mailed the questionnaire to 850 salespersons drawn from a larger list of 4,500 names that you purchased from a mailing list broker. Both the 4,500 and 850 names were randomly selected and represented different industries throughout the United States.

From the initial mailing, you have received 210 returned usable questionnaires—a 24.71 percent response. Of these 210 returns, 147 (70 percent) were from industrial salespersons and 63 (30 percent) from consumer salespersons. For the study, you defined industrial salespeople as those who sold to other businesses for business purposes and consumer salespeople as those who sold to consumers for personal use.

After tallying and editing the results, you now have them arranged for your analysis and interpretations. As shown in Tables 25, 26, and 27, the demographics of the respondents should tell you specifics about their background, customers, and selling efforts in general. More important to your study, however,

TABLE 23 (Problem 5) Comparison of Selected Characteristics and Diversification, Percent Distribution

A. Percent of total savings in Guarantee Bank	Age				
	18–25	26–40	41–55	56–65	over 65
Less than 10	5.56	8.62	5.88	8.90	7.57
11–25	5.56	10.34	11.76	14.14	21.62
26–50	11.11	13.79	27.06	18.32	21.62
51–75	5.56	22.41	24.71	26.70	18.38
76–100	72.22	44.83	30.59	31.94	30.81

B. Percent of total savings in Guarantee Bank	Gross Income (in thousands of dollars)				
	0–19.9	20–29.9	30–39.9	40–59.9	60 and over
Less than 10	8.38	3.92	4.60	16.46	10.00
11–25	16.17	16.99	14.94	15.19	10.00
26–50	17.96	22.22	20.69	18.99	25.00
51–75	13.17	27.45	27.59	18.99	35.00
76–100	44.31	29.41	32.18	30.38	20.00

C. Percent of total savings in Guarantee Bank	Retirement Status	
	Retired	Not Retired
Less than 10	7.67	6.81
11–25	19.33	11.49
26–50	20.67	20.00
51–75	22.00	22.13
76–100	30.33	39.57

D. Percent of total savings in Guarantee Bank	Amount on Deposit (in thousands of dollars)							
	$0–.49	.5–.99	1–4.9	5–9.9	10–19.9	20–49.9	50–100	over 100
Less than 10	60	0	25.0	23.1	11.0	1.2	0	2.6
11–25	20	20	25.0	21.2	22.9	13.0	11.2	0
26–50	0	20	9.1	19.2	25.4	25.4	18.7	5.1
51–75	20	20	6.8	5.8	13.6	28.9	32.7	33.3
76–100	0	40	34.1	30.8	27.1	31.4	37.4	58.9

are those facts shown in Table 28. Here you have the ratings the respondents gave to the entertainment/gift activities. These facts will provide the meat of your analysis.

Now you must analyze the data and present them in a meaningful report to Leander Industries. Your report will be on the long side of the physical format continuum—title fly, title page, table of contents, executive summary plus report proper. Also, you will need graphics to help tell the report story. Your report will include recommendations for the use of gifts/entertainment at Leander.

Address the report to Ms. Tracey Hebranson at Leander Industries. You will write the report formally without first- and second-person pronouns.

7. *Constructing a patient profile for Addicare.* As an independent researcher specializing in survey research, you have been hired by Addicare, a drug treatment facility. Addicare offers inpatient treatment to substance abuse clients for 60 days. The program is holistic in that it treats the total person—physically, emotionally, psychologically, socially, etc. Located in a large metropolitan area, the facility handles referrals from area hospitals, physicians, and businesses

TABLE 24 (Problem 5) Comparison of Income, Age, and Deposit Size, Percent Distribution

A. Amount on deposit at Guarantee Bank	Gross Income (in thousands of dollars)				
	$0–19.9	20–29.9	30–39.9	40–59.9	over 60
$0–499	2.38	0	1.15	0	0
500–999	1.79	0.66	0	0	0
1,000–4,999	14.88	4.64	2.30	7.59	5.00
5,000–9,999	11.90	8.61	11.49	7.59	0
10,000–19,999	22.63	25.17	21.84	12.66	20.00
20,000–49,999	29.17	27.15	36.78	41.77	30.00
50,000–99,999	13.69	25.83	20.69	18.99	15.00
100,000 and over	3.57	7.95	5.75	11.39	30.00

B. Amount on deposit at Guarantee Bank	Age				
	18–25	26–40	41–55	56–65	over 65
50–499	11.11	0	0	1.05	0.55
500–999	0	0	1.16	0.52	1.65
1,000–4,999	44.44	16.67	9.30	3.66	4.95
5,000–9,999	16.67	18.33	13.95	6.28	7.69
10,000–19,999	22.22	23.33	29.07	17.28	25.27
20,000–49,999	5.56	31.67	31.40	36.65	27.47
50,000–99,999	0	3.33	12.79	23.56	25.82
100,000 and over	0	6.67	2.33	10.99	6.59

C. Gross income	Age				
	18–25	26–40	41–55	56–65	over 65
$0–19,999	88.24	15.00	17.65	24.02	51.76
20,000–29,999	5.88	36.67	30.59	32.93	26.47
30,000–39,999	0	20.00	29.41	20.67	8.82
40,000–59,999	0	23.33	16.47	18.44	10.59
60,000 and over	5.88	5.00	5.88	3.91	2.35

through employee assistance programs.

Erwin Schweers, the chief administrator at Addicare, wants to know how successful the drug rehabilitation product that Addicare offers truly is. On the surface, you have enough patients entering the program to make operations profitable. And referrals seem to be continuing at consistent to slightly increasing rates. From a short run and tactical view, the facility seems to be effective.

But from a longer-run behavior change vantage point, Addicare wants to know the success of the facility in terms of rehabilitation (i.e., do people quit their drug habits after treatment, for how long, at what price, and such.) To help answer these questions about program effectiveness, you were retained to construct a profile of drug patients to serve as a guide to the facility's staff. The guide could be used for training other staff members, identifying program strengths and weaknesses, improving on services offered, pinpointing needed treatment areas, and the like. It is a logical follow-up to the usual financial and market data that often are used to assess organizational success.

To address these longer-run issues of treatment

TABLE 25 (Problem 6) Products Sold by Respondents

Product	Frequency	Product	Frequency
Consumer products	23	Fire apparatus	3
Automotive	20	Shipping containers	3
Real estate	19	Telecommunications	3
Business supplies	15	Men's apparel	3
Food products	14	Insurance	3
Industrial products	13	Transportation	3
Electrical supplies	10	Graphic arts	2
Pharmaceuticals/medical	8	Sporting goods	2
Advertising	7	Printing	2
Paper products	7	Trucking	2
Building materials	6	Storage	2
Agricultural chemicals	6	Tobacco	1
Women's apparel	6	Home improvement	1
Computers	5	Scientific	1
Petroleum products	5	Cable TV	1
Investments	5	Educational careers	1
Hardware	4	Total	210
Alcoholic beverages	4		

TABLE 26 (Problem 6) Years of Selling Experience

Years	Number	%
1	62	29.5
2–4	24	11.4
5–9	18	8.6
10 or more	99	47.2
No answer	7	3.3
Total	210	100.0

TABLE 27 (Problem 6) Primary Customers

Type	Number	%
Final consumers	63	30.0
Business manufacturers	4	1.9
Business wholesalers	2	1.0
Industrial distributors	2	1.0
Businesses	135	64.2
No answer	4	1.9
Total	210	100.0

success, you prepared an extensive questionnaire and sent it to 725 patients whom Addicare had served over the past five years. Your cover letter to the questionnaire invited the patients to participate in the study on an anonymous basis. The questionnaire that accompanied the letter was designed to capture patients' perceptions of different dimensions of the program's success. More specifically, you wanted to know how often patients used drugs at the beginning of their treatment, after one year from the program, and between one and two years. These before—after measures you hoped would give you the long-term measures of program success you needed.

In addition, you asked questions about various patient symptoms before and after treatment. And you asked about patient attitudes about drug use and changes in quality of life. These specific parts of success formed the basis of your approach to determining the long-run effectiveness of Addicare's problem.

Today you have received 350 usable returns (48.38 percent). To assure that the returns were representative, you telephoned selectively some of the nonresponding patients. A majority of them could not be located—a typical expectancy given the nature of the problem. The ones you did contact, however, indicated they had forgotten to respond. When questioned by phone, they confirmed generally the results you obtained through the usable returns. These official results, presented in Tables 29–41, will provide the facts for a long formal report you will prepare for

TABLE 28 (Problem 6) General Importance and Differences between Consumer and Industrial Salespeople Concerning Gift/Entertainment Activities

Gift/Entertainment Item	Overall Average*	Consumer Average*	Industrial Average*
Taking a client to lunch	3.51	2.86	3.57
Taking a client to dinner (evening)	3.30	2.91	3.30
Taking a client to breakfast	2.96	2.68	3.11
Giving a client free product samples for personal use	2.85	2.74	2.85
Playing golf with a client and paying the client's way	2.84	2.70	2.91
Paying a client's travel expenses to visit a product demonstration	2.74	2.62	2.80
Giving a client a work-related gift (i.e., desk pen set)	2.55	2.47	2.61
Buying a client alcoholic beverages at a cocktail lounge	2.51	2.21	2.64
Playing tennis with a client and paying the client's way	2.50	2.54	2.48
Inviting a client to your home for entertainment purposes	2.35	2.26	2.31
Taking a client to a sporting event	2.28	1.94	2.39
Playing handball with a client and paying the client's way	2.22	2.15	2.22
Taking a client to a nightclub show	2.13	1.99	2.13
Inviting a client to a private party	2.10	2.29	1.99
Taking a client to a cultural event (i.e., theater)	1.97	1.99	1.95
Giving a client a nonwork-related gift (i.e., golf bag)	1.95	1.67	2.00
Providing a client with lodging	1.94	2.04	1.88
Giving a client a recreational trip	1.77	1.66	1.74
Providing a client with social companionship	1.75	1.77	1.70
Providing a client with a car to use	1.53	1.95	1.33
Taking client to a movie	1.46	1.64	1.35
Giving a client a monetary gift	1.37	1.44	1.31

* 1 = Not Important and 5= Very Important

Addicare. Because the results are extensive, you will need to organize them logically before you interpret them. Also, you will need to use graphics to convey the findings. Prepare the report for Addicare. It will include the prefatory dressings of title fly, title page, table of contents, and executive summary before the actual report. You will write the report in third person to give it a tone of formality that the situation demands. Your report should do more than recite the facts. It should relate the facts to the evaluation of the treatment program of Addicare.

8. *Preparing a compensation picture of practicing human resource professionals.* As director of

research for the Americomp, Inc., a consulting group dealing with compensation theory and practice, you receive an interesting request from the National Association of Human Resource Professionals today. They want your firm to conduct a nationwide survey of compensation issues and practices of human resource professionals for their organization. As a partner in Americomp, you accept the assignment and agree to submit a written report to the group in four months.

To get the facts you need for the report, you decide to conduct a survey of human resource professionals, some of whom are managers and some of whom are

TABLE 29 (Problem 7)   Drug Usage at Beginning of Program Treatment

Usage	Cocaine	Alcohol	Marijuana
More than once a day	34.4%	17.6%	14.6%
Once a day	14.6	19.2	12.3
2–6 days/week	30.3	33.4	15.5
Once a week	10.1	12.8	13.1
2–3 times/month	3.5	4.4	6.2
Once a month	1.8	3.3	10.6
Less than once a month	1.7	2.7	8.5
Never (not using now)	3.6	6.6	19.2

TABLE 30 (Problem 7)   Cocaine Usage at Three Time Periods

Usage	Beginning of Treatment	Within 1 Year	1 to 2 Years
More than once a day	34.4%	2.4%	.5%
Once a day	14.6	.2	.4
2–6 days/weeks	30.3	4.1	4.0
Once a week	10.1	1.9	.3
2–3 times/month	3.5	2.8	.3
Once a month	1.8	3.2	.3
Less than once a month	1.7	11.0	6.8
Never (not using now)	3.6	74.4	87.4

TABLE 31 (Problem 7)   Alcohol Usage at Three Time Periods

Usage	Beginning of Treatment	Within 1 Year	1 to 2 Years
More than once a day	17.0%	2.7%	2.3%
Once a day	19.2	5.9	2.2
2–6 days/week	33.4	9.1	17.0
Once a week	12.8	8.4	10.3
2–3 times/month	4.4	17.4	6.6
Once a month	3.3	5.9	15.3
Less than once a month	2.7	7.5	14.1
Never (not using now)	6.6	43.3	32.2

TABLE 32 (Problem 7)   Marijuana Usage at Three Time Periods

Usage	Beginning of Treatment	Within 1 Year	1 to 2 Years
More than once a day	14.6%	2.3%	1.9%
Once a day	12.3	3.6	.5
2–6 days/week	15.5	5.2	2.6
Once a week	13.1	5.6	2.1
2–3 times/month	6.2	3.6	4.1
Once a month	10.6	2.7	2.2
Less than once a month	8.5	10.5	6.3
Never (not using now)	19.2	66.5	80.3

TABLE 33 (Problem 7)   Caffeinated Coffee Usage at Three Time Periods

Usage	Beginning of Treatment	Within 1 Year	1 to 2 Years
More than once a day	35.2%	23.1%	26.8%
Once a day	23.6	10.8	20.2
2–6 days/week	12.5	7.7	8.9
Once a week	7.7	5.6	4.1
2–3 times/month	3.5	4.0	.3
Once a month	2.6	.5	0.0
Less than once a month	2.9	2.7	2.2
Never	12.0	45.6	37.5

TABLE 34 (Problem 7)   Nicotine Usage at Three Time Periods

Usage	Beginning of Treatment	Within 1 Year	1 to 2 Years
More than once a day	46.2%	54.1%	43.8%
Once a day	16.0	.7	2.2
2–6 days/week	5.5	2.6	2.2
Once a week	1.8	.9	.2
2–3 times/month	.9	1.9	4.3
Once a month	1.6	.2	.1
Less than once a month	1.3	.5	0.0
Never	26.7	39.1	47.2

TABLE 35 (Problem 7)   Physical Symptoms at Three Time Periods

Symptoms	Beginning of Treatment	Within 1 Year	1 to 2 Years
Loss of energy	37.6%	13.8%	4.6%
Physical deterioration	31.2	9.6	2.5
Sinus problems	24.1	13.1	12.1
Insommnia	21.8	10.8	2.8
Headaches	20.9	8.3	6.1
General health failure	16.3	6.8	2.5
Heart palpitations	13.8	6.5	2.3
Lost sex drive	13.5	6.2	4.5
Sore throat	13.1	7.6	4.2
Shaking	13.0	4.3	2.2

TABLE 36 (Problem 7)   General Psychological Symptoms at Three Time Periods

Symptoms	Beginning of Treatment	Within 1 Year	1 to 2 Years
Depression	40.0%	25.6%	14.3%
Irritability	38.3	22.1	16.2
Anxiety	37.8	26.3	8.8
Fears	28.1	16.8	6.5
Paranoia	26.6	8.1	4.2
Concentration problems	27.3	12.2	6.3
Loss of interest in friends	26.1	5.8	6.2
Loss of interest in nondrug activities	25.6	3.3	4.4
Memory problems	24.4	14.8	10.4
Suspiciousness	21.8	7.8	4.4

TABLE 37 (Problem 7)   State of Mind about Drug Use at Three Time Periods

State of Mind	Beginning of Treatment	Within 1 Year	1 to 2 Years
Think I am Addicted	43.5%	31.6%	9.8%
Feel I cannot refuse drug/s of choice	39.9	9.8	8.1
Feel loss of control over drug use	38.5	8.1	6.5
Feel like binge using	34.2	4.0	4.3
Feel unable to stop	33.6	7.3	8.2
Using drugs			
Prefer drugs to food	30.5	7.5	4.1
Feel a real need for drug/s	29.5	11.5	4.7
Prefer drugs to family activities	28.3	5.7	2.2
Fear of being discovered as a user	28.0	8.6	2.2
Feel depressed when using	27.2	8.5	2.1

Social Symptom	Beginning of Treatment	Within 1 Year	1 to 2 Years
I miss work due to my drug use	41.9%	9.1%	.5%
I make excuses due to my drug use	39.9	7.5	2.6
Other people object to my drug use	33.3	9.6	4.7
There is fighting or arguing due to my drug use	31.5	9.5	4.5
My spouse objects to my drug use	30.5	9.3	4.1
I borrow money due to my drug use	28.2	4.0	.5
I have used 50% or more of my savings due to my drug use	26.3	7.6	2.2
I am in debt due to my drug use	25.4	12.8	6.1
Breakup of my family is threatened due to drug use	24.2	8.8	4.3
I have no money left due to my drug use	22.2	4.4	4.2

TABLE 39 (Problem 7)   Goals about Future Drug Use at Three Time Periods

Social Symptom	Beginning of Treatment	Within 1 Year	1 to 2 Years
Don't know	2.2%	1.2%	2.8%
100% clean	67.1	75.4	70.2
Continue alcohol, cocaine, and/or marijuana	6.4	1.8	0.0

TABLE 40 (Problem 7)   Long-Term Attitude Changes about Drug Use at Two Time Periods

Changes in Attitudes	Within 1 Year	1 to 2 Years
No change	3.1%	.3%
Yes change:		
Want more drugs	1.2	0.0
Want less	11.5	4.8
Don't want	27.1	59.7
Other specific changes (Increased awareness of negative effects of drugs; lowered tolerance of other drug users; increased awareness of one's own addiction)	57.1	35.2

resource specialists. As you think about the problem more specifically, you believe that a comparison of current compensation practices with those five years ago would give NAHRP the best compensation picture. Your comparison study could serve as a prelude to the remaining part of the 20th century as well.

As a compensation researcher, you realize that salary is one part of the job satisfaction picture of most jobs; but it is a significant one, to be sure. A study of human resource professionals' pay package should reveal the nature, role, and scope of the job of human resource personnel in today's organizations. Accordingly, you decide to study human resource compensation from several vantage points—through base and total compensation and through bonuses, benefit plans, and pay for new jobs. You design each area into the questionnaire that you will send to your survey sample.

After designing and pretesting the questionnaire, you mail it along with a cover letter to a list of practicing human resource professionals provided by NAHRP. The list includes 12,000 people in 45 jobs in human resource work in 960 U.S. organizations. The

TABLE 41 (Problem 7)   Changes in Quality of Life Measures at Two Time Periods

Changes	Within 1 Year		1 to 2 Years	
	Better	Much Better	Better	Much Better
In emotions	12.7%	62.1%	22.0%	66.7%
In social life	11.9	52.2	22.1	46.7
In family life	12.9	55.1	26.6	61.3
In energy level	17.8	58.1	7.9	89.1
In eating habits	15.5	56.0	28.8	46.7
In sleep patterns	7.7	67.7	12.5	71.2

TABLE 42 (Problem 8)   Base Salary in Large Organizations (>10,000 Employees)

Job Title	5 Years Ago	This Year	% Change
Top HR	$131,600	$179,200	+36%
Top labor relations	$94,000	$115,900	+23%
Top compensation and benefits	$89,000	$111,000	+25%
Top organizational development	$79,800	$99,600	+25%
Top employee relations	$67,100	$87,800	+31%
Total	**$461,500**	**$593,500**	**+29%**

TABLE 43 (Problem 8)   Total Cash Compensation in Large Organizations (>10,000 employees)

Job Title	5 Years Ago	This Year	% Change
Top HR	$168,600	$270,000	+60%
Top labor relations	$110,700	$158,200	+43%
Top compensation and benefits	$105,400	$146,800	+39%
Top organizational development	$91,500	$120,100	+31%
Top employee relations	$71,800	$109,400	+52%
Total	**$548,000**	**$804,500**	**+47%**

returns you have received in the past two months appear to have stabilized, and you have tallied the results in Tables 42–46. Now it is your job to interpret the data and prepare a meaningful report for your client.

As you think about the report structure, you decide that it will be a long formal one—title fly, title page, letter of transmittal, table of contents, executive summary, and report proper. You will word the report impersonally, and you will use graphics to assist the words in conveying the meaning of the facts. Put differently, your report will have all of the conventions

of formality that the situation dictates.

Prepare the report about human resource compensation for the NAHRP. You will address it to Kamal Fatehi, chair of the board of directors.

9. *Selecting a radio station to air your advertising.* (Requires research)   As Theresa Sanchez, office manager for the Eye and Ear Clinic, your job has been to manage all business aspects of the clinic. This includes the medical practice as well as the retail sales of eyewear and hearing aids. Recently, management hired a technician experienced in the design and assembly of hearing aids. With this expertise in-

TABLE 44 (Problem 8) Bonus Eligibility for Selected Nonmanagement Jobs

Job Title	5 Years Ago	This Year	% Change
Training specialist	12%	25%	+108%
Labor relations generalist	15%	31%	+106%
Recruiter	16%	29%	+81%
Benefits planning analyst	17%	30%	+77%
Compensation analyst	16%	26%	+63%

TABLE 45 (Problem 8) Benefits Plan Prevalence

Plan Type	5 Years Ago	This Year	% Change
Preferred provider organization (PPO)	31%	66%	+113%
401(k)	49%	86%	+76%
Vision coverage	31%	49%	+58%
Flextime	33%	49%	+49%
Flexible benefits	33%	47%	+42%

TABLE 46 (Problem 8) Current Pay Levels for New Jobs (Added in last 5 years)

Job Title	Average Base Salary	% Eligible for Incentive	Average Total Cash
Top total quality executive	$103,300	77%	$122,000
Total quality manager	$65,900	57%	$70,300
Work/family program manager	$55,000	49%	$56,800
Workers' compensation supervisor	$49,700	27%	$50,700
Wellness program manager	$44,900	32%	$45,900

house, management decided to expand the hearing-aid side of the business by opening an office in the local major indoor shopping mall. The mall is conveniently located, has easy access and extended hours your clinic doesn't have, and draws customers from a wide, two-state area.

The hearing-aid business, EarSound, will open after the current tenant has vacated and the space has been remodeled. You expect that to be in about three months. Therefore, you're beginning to get your "Open for Business" advertising lined up. In addition to the traditional newspaper advertising, you think other media should be used as well to reach as many potential customers as possible.

You have observed that the majority of hearing-aid patients at the clinic are brought in by a hearing person. This hearing person can be a parent or the adult child of an elderly parent. Therefore, you think that

using radio to target the hearing person rather than the patient is an appropriate choice of media. Also, radio advertising is much more within your budget than television advertising.

You have gathered the following demographic information on radio usage by place (Table 47), length (Table 48), and format (Table 49). Based on your analysis of these data, identify the stations in your area that would be most appropriate for your target audience. Collect cost data from these stations for similar time and length advertising spots.

Present your analysis and recommendation to the management in a clear, well-written report. Use tables or other graphic devices as you think appropriate. Also, you may wish to include any nice-to-know information you collect in the appendixes.

10. *Determining whether to publish in print or electronic format your school's computer lab guides. (Requires*

TABLE 47 (Problem 9)   Radio Audience by Location of Listening (% of all radio reach)*

	Men 18+	Women 18+	Teens 12–17
At home	74.3	80.1	93.0
In car	84.3	77.2	78.2
Other	46.7	39.8	48.5

SOURCE: Radio Fact Book/LNA Arbitron/RER 1992 Report.
* Seth Godin, ed. *The 1995 Information Please Business Almanac and Sourcebook* (Boston: Houghton Mifflin Company, 1994), p. 507.

TABLE 48 (Problem 9)   Radio Usage (Average daily time spent listening)*

By Age	Men (hr:min)	Women (hr:min)
18–	3:05	2:53
18–24	3:03	2:45
25–34	3:26	2:57
35–49	3:19	2:54
50+	2:35	2:52

SOURCE: Calculated from RADAR®, copyrighted© by Statistical Research, Inc., Spring, 1993.
* Seth Godin, ed. *The 1995 Information Please Business Almanac and Sourcebook* (Boston: Houghton Mifflin Company, 1994), p. 507.

research)   You work for your school in the computer support area that handles a wide variety of requests from faculty and staff. One project your area recently acquired was production of the computer lab manual. You've been assigned the task of determining whether the manual should continue to be published in print or whether you should move to electronic format. You will research the problem and present the findings and recommendation in a formal report to the dean.

While you have not read the manual from cover to cover, you know it is thorough, well written and well illustrated. The manuscript is about 150 pages with good illustrations and screen shots. You know this to be about a 100 page book in printed form. You could distribute this same manuscript on one floppy disk in electronic book form.

This dilemma is not unusual; today many organizations are making major decisions on which medium to use. Students are familiar with using print manuals. It might ease the technophobia fears some students have, easing them into the lab comfortably. However, it is bulky to carry in backpacks, so many may leave it behind and not have it available when they need to reference it. The print manual also costs the student more than twice the cost of the book distributed on a floppy.

The electronic book form could be published in cross platform versions with products like Envoy or Acrobat, allowing users with Macs or Windows to run it. This form allows writers to create links to various parts of the text so that the reader can skip around rather than reading through it in a solely linear fashion. Also, the electronic form allows the user to highlight important facts as well as annotate the manuscript as one might do when writing notes in the margin of printed material. Its small size would encourage students to carry it with them. However, its format might also encourage students to violate copyright laws by making illegal copies, a situation your school would like to discourage. On the other hand, the digital format is easy to update as configurations change in the lab, making the electronic version up to date when purchased.

Your task is to gather objective information on all aspects, recommending the best decision for the college. Try collecting information from students as well as from the campus bookstore or nearby copy centers. Present both the financial aspects to the student and the college as well as the use advantages and disadvantages for both formats. The computer lab manual contains important information that helps students use the lab efficiently. You want to be sure that it is distributed in a format that gets good use.

11. *Comparing and recommending a source of outdoor advertising.* (Requires research)   As the campus coordinator for a concert by Kenny G [or any entertainer you choose] to be held on your campus, you are in charge of evaluating and recommending the type of promotion the event needs to sell all the seats. The concert will be held the week school resumes next fall. It is scheduled to be held outdoors since the weather should be good then.

The last time Kenny G was on your campus the performance was a sellout. Therefore, this year he will give three concerts in two days, a challenge you think you can handle. To sell three times as many tickets as the last time means you need more promotion. One of the most cost-effective ways of reaching potential customers is outdoor advertising. While one might first think of billboards (unless you live in

TABLE 49 (Problem 9)   Profile of Daily Listeners of Radio Stations by Format*

Format	% Male	% Female	Median Age	Median Income ($ thousands)	% 1+ Years of College
Adult contemporary	41	59	37.3	39,100	29
All news	62	38	49.0	45,100	24
Album-oriented rock	63	37	30.4	40,500	32
Black/R&B	50	50	39.4	26,400	33
Classic rock	64	36	30.9	41,800	32
CHR/rock	44	56	30.6	36,600	27
Classical	56	44	46.4	44,400	22
Country	48	52	40.0	33,500	26
Beautiful	55	45	50.3	43,500	30
Golden oldies	49	51	40.3	42,200	27
MOR/nostalgia	49	51	59.8	37,500	23
News/talk	60	40	49.2	40,300	23
Religious	41	59	41.5	31,200	22
Urban contemporary	43	57	33.8	25,500	26

SOURCE: Simmons, Study of Media Markets, 1993.
* Seth Godin, ed. *The 1995 Information Please Business Almanac and Sourcebook* (Boston: Houghton Mifflin Company, 1994), p. 508.

TABLE 50 (Problem 11)   Billboard Reach (Frequency): Women*

Age	#100 Showing	#50 Showing	#25 Showing
18–24	90.6 (23.98)	85.8 (12.53)	74.2 (7.05)
18–34	89.0 (26.45)	84.3 (13.84)	75.3 (7.56)
18–49	90.4 (27.87)	86.1 (14.49)	78.6 (7.82)
25–34	88.1 (27.89)	83.5 (14.61)	76.0 (7.84)
35–44	92.7 (29.71)	88.4 (15.53)	82.6 (8.24)
45–54	90.7 (28.19)	87.6 (14.14)	80.7 (7.65)
55–64	87.4 (24.31)	80.4 (13.08)	73.2 (7.30)
65+	80.1 (18.65)	70.1 (10.13)	58.0 (6.15)

SOURCE: Simmons Market Research Bureau.
* Seth Godin, ed. *The 1995 Information Please Business Almanac and Sourcebook* (Boston: Houghton Mifflin Company, 1994), p. 516.

Maine, Vermont, Hawaii, and Alaska where they are illegal), there are many forms of outdoor advertising. Some of these include:

- Billboards
- Bus/train exteriors
- Mall displays
- Painted walls/murals
- Taxi/truck tops and backs
- Telephone booths

- Transit platforms/terminals

The previous Kenny G concert attracted an interesting mix of concertgoers. While nearly half were college age, the other half were composed of parents, younger sisters and brothers, and even some grandparents. In fact, the concert attracted widely from the community at large, not just students. You know you need to continue and perhaps extend this draw if you expect to fill seats for three concerts. Outdoor

TABLE 51 (Problem 11)   Billboard Reach (Frequency): Men*

Age	#100 Showing	#50 Showing	#25 Showing
18–24	91.0 (33.79)	86.8 (17.66)	84.0 (9.27)
18–34	90.8 (32.77)	87.2 (17.07)	83.5 (9.01)
18–49	90.4 (33.71)	87.5 (17.52)	83.3 (9.19)
25–34	90.6 (32.21)	87.5 (16.75)	83.2 (8.86)
35–44	89.7 (34.78)	88.1 (17.87)	83.2 (9.39)
45–54	90.8 (34.82)	87.0 (18.33)	82.5 (9.54)
55–64	85.8 (33.99)	83.2 (17.76)	79.8 (9.30)
65+	85.9 (24.01)	80.6 (12.57)	71.1 (7.02)

SOURCE: Simmons Market Research Bureau.
* Seth Godin, ed. *The 1995 Information Please Business Almanac and Sourcebook* (Boston: Houghton Mifflin Company, 1994), p. 516.

advertising seems a good way to reach the community.

Most agencies that place outdoor advertising will be able to give you statistics that will help you place the advertising effectively. They can usually tell you how many times a particular ad will be seen by what percentage of the area's population. Tables 50 and 51 show you reaches for women and men. In Table 50, a #50 showing to 18-to-24-year-old women would be seen an average of 12.53 times by 85.8 percent of the area's population.

Select two or three of the outdoor advertising methods that would be appropriate for your area. Gather the cost data, analyze them, and present them clearly along with your recommendation to your student government's executive committee.

12. *Identifying computer-related illnesses and recommending ways to prevent them.* (Requires research) As Melissa McGraw, director of end-user computing support for your company, you have been asked to prepare a report for all employees using computer technology. Because that means your audience will include those with a broad range of ages, experience, and education, you want to be sure it is extremely well organized and readable. Using graphics freely as well as including checklists will help emphasize key ideas.

The report should cover eyestrain, fatigue and musculoskeletal problems, and repetitive stress syndrome. It should explain thoroughly the potential problems and ways to prevent them. It should stress the newest findings as well as OSHA recommendations. What have studies revealed on those using ergonomic keyboards, such as the natural keyboard introduced by Microsoft in 1994? What are the newest findings on the effects of electromagnetic radiation on vision? Are the eye exercises, stretches, and breaks recommended when problems first started occurring effective preventative strategies? Therefore,

the secondary literature you collect should be current. It should cover the technology used in today's workplace, not yesterday's. Be sure you review any laws or regulations passed in the last five years that relate to computer use. If your research identifies some new technology on the near horizon that will eliminate or reduce the occurrences of any of these problems, be sure to include it in your report. Also, gather some first-hand research. Perhaps include accounts of changes workers have made in their work areas that have improved their ability to work effectively with the technology.

Your primary objective is to make your workers aware of potential problems and actions to take now to prevent problems.

13. *Investigating the outlook for investments.* (Requires research)   Assume you are employed in the Investments Research Department of the Whitmore Foundation, a philanthropic trust with over $300 million of invested funds. You have been assigned the task of determining the general outlook for investments in the _____ industry (choose one from list below).

Specifically, you will review past and present status of the industry's profits, sales, production, and the like. From these reviews you may be able to detect trends that may continue into the immediate future. Too, you will gather all facts and authoritative opinion relating to future growth. From all of this you hope to be able to make a somewhat specific recommendation about investments in the industry in general.

Although your report will concern the industry rather than a specific company (or companies), you are likely to refer frequently to the major firms in the industry. And your recommendation might point out the industry leaders. Write your report in a form appropriate for the formality of this situation. Submit it to the Investment Board, Whitmore Building, 317

Parkhurst Avenue, New York City.

Industries to choose from:

Aircraft	Tobacco
Electronics	Paper
Chemicals	Food processing
Aluminum	Automotive
Steel	Petroleum
Textile	Publishing
Shoes	Clothing (men's, women's, or
Pharmaceuticals	children's)

(You may limit your report to a subsection of the industry whenever appropriate.)

14. *Determining the possibility of international distribution for Engco.* (Requires research)   Engco Chemicals, Inc., a large producer of diversified chemical products for industrial and consumer uses, is investigating the possibility of international distribution for its products. As it produces a full line of products in both New Orleans and San Diego plants, it is interested in the expanding markets of the Orient and those of the Common Market.

To determine the most apparent and immediate implications of going into foreign markets, the president of Engco assigns several small reports to be developed and presented to the board of directors. The major decision on expansion is a long way off, but these small reports will be vital in determining whether more studies will be made.

You, as a staff specialist for Engco, are assigned *one* of these specific areas of interest:

a. Legal—licensing, government roles, etc.
b. Transportation—methods of shipping, ports' roles, etc.
c. Marketing—branding, advertising, sales, etc.
d. Finance—role of banks, trade payments, etc.
e. Management—multinational management, control, etc.

Develop a short report (1,500–2,500 words) that will highlight the positive and negative aspects of your chosen area of interest. Make your report thorough, but cover only the broader aspects of the issues involved.

15. *Solving a problem on your campus.* (Requires research)   Certain problems exist on many college campuses. At least, they exist in the minds of many of the faculty, students, and staff. From the following list of such problems, select one that you think needs attention at your college:

Library operation
Computer access from off-campus
Campus security
Policies on sales of tickets to athletic events
Regulation of social activities
Student government
Registration procedure
Faculty–student relations
Orientation program for freshmen
Curriculum improvement
Increasing enrollments
Scholastic honesty
Campus crime
Improving cultural atmosphere on campus
Class attendance policies
Scholastic probation policies
Parking, traffic control
Grade inflation
Student government
Emphasis on athletics
Campus beautification
Fire prevention
Food facilities
Computer facilities
Bookstore operation

You will first gather all the significant facts regarding the problem you select. When you are thoroughly acquainted with them, you will gather authoritative opinions concerning the solution. Obtaining such information may involve looking through bibliographic sources to find out what has been done on other campuses. It may involve interviewing people on campus who are attempting to deal with the problem. Next you will carefully analyze your problem in light of all you have learned about it. Then you will develop a solution to the problem.

To make the situation appear realistic, place yourself in the proper role at your school. Write a formal report, with all the conventional prefatory parts. Address the report to the appropriate administrator.

16. *Determining what business will be like in the months ahead.* (Requires research)   Roland A. Anderson, president of _____ (company of your choice), has assigned you, his assistant, to write a consensus business forecast for presentation at next Wednesday's meeting of the board of directors. The company does not employ an economist; Anderson does not believe in such frills. "Why should we pay for one," he says, "when the current business periodicals give us free forecasts by all the leading economists?"

Since Anderson's instructions were—as usual—quite vague, much of what you do will depend on your good judgment. All Anderson said was that he wanted you to survey the predictions of the leading economic forecasters for the months ahead and to present your findings in a clear and meaningful report to the board. And he wanted the forecasts consolidated—that is, he did not want a mere succession of individual forecasts. Your report, covering the entire economy, will, of course, be largely general in nature. But you will give special emphasis to forecasts pertaining to your industry.

The report will be in a form appropriate for the board. Because the board members will want to get at the most important material quickly, be sure to include a fast-moving executive summary. Address the report to President Anderson, who also chairs the board.

Following are suggestions for additional report problems ranging from the simple to the highly complex. You can convert them into realistic business problems by supplying details and/or adapting them to real-life business situations. For most of these problems, you can obtain the needed information through library research. The topics are arranged by business field, although many of them cross fields.

▶ Accounting

1. Report on current depreciation accounting practices and recommend depreciation accounting procedures for Company X.

2. Design an inventory control system for X Company.

3. Report to Company X executives on how tax court decisions handed down over the past six months will affect their firm.

4. What security measures should Company X take with access to its accounting data?

5. Advise the managers of X Company on the accounting problems that they can anticipate when the company begins overseas operations.

6. Analyze break-even analysis as a decision-making tool for X Company.

7. Explain to potential investors which sections in Company X's most recent annual report they should review most carefully.

8. Analyze the relative effects on income of the FIFO and LIFO methods of inventory valuation during a prolonged period of inflation.

9. Write a report for the American Accounting Association on the demand for accountants with computer systems training.

10. Develop for accounting students at your college information that will help them choose between careers in public accounting and careers in private accounting.

11. Advise the management of X Company on the validity of return on investment as a measure of performance.

12. Report on operations research as a decision-making tool for accountants and managers.

13. Report to the management of X Company on trends in the content and design of corporate annual reports.

14. Report to an association of accountants the status of professional ethics in accounting.

15. Report to management of X Company on the communication skills important to accounting.

16. Advise the founders of new Company X on income tax considerations in the selection of a form of business organization.

17. Review for Company X the pros and cons of installing a computerized accounting system.

▶ General Business

18. Evaluate the adequacy of current college programs for developing business leadership.

19. Which business skills should schools and colleges teach, and which should companies teach?

20. What should be the role of business leaders in developing courses and curricula for business schools?

21. Report on ways to build and use good teams in the workplace.

22. Identify the criteria Company X should use in selecting a public relations firm.

23. Report on the advisability of including business internships in a business degree program.

24. What images of business and businesspersons do current business textbooks convey?

25. How does today's business community regard the Master of Business Administration degree?

26. Evaluate the contribution that campus business and professional clubs make to business education.

27. How effective is computer-based training in education for business?

28. Should education for business be specialized, or should it provide a generalized, well-rounded education?

29. Determine the how to get and use permissions for music added to business presentations.

▶ Labor

30. For the executives of the National Association of Manufacturers (or some such group), report on the outlook for labor–management relations in the next 12 months.

31. For the officers of a major labor union, research and report progress toward decreasing job discrimination against minorities.

32. For X Union, project the effects that technology will have on traditionally unionized industries by the year 20XX.

33. Advise the management of X Company on how to deal with Y Union, which is attempting to organize the employees of X Company.

34. Evaluate the effectiveness of mediation in resolving labor–management disputes.

35. Interpret the change in the number of union members over the past _____ years.

36. Report on the successes and failures of employee-run businesses.

37. Report on the status and effects of "right to work" laws.

38. Evaluate the effects of a particular strike (your choice) on the union, the company, the stockholders,

and the public. Write the report for a government investigating committee.

39. For Union X, prepare an objective report on union leadership in the nation during the past decade.

40. Layoffs based on seniority are causing a disproportionate reduction in the number of women and minority workers at Company X. Investigate alternatives that the company can present to the union.

41. Investigate recent trends relative to the older worker and the stands that unions have taken in this area.

42. Review the appropriateness of unionizing government workers, and recommend to a body of government leaders the stand they should take on this issue.

43. Report on the role of unions (or managements) in politics, and recommend a course for them to follow.

▶ **Finance**

44. As a financial consultant, evaluate a specific form of tax shelter for a client.

45. Review the customer-relations practices of banks, and recommend customer relations procedures for Bank X.

46. Review current employee loan practices and recommend whether Company X should make employee loans.

47. Report on what Company X needs to know about financial matters in doing business with _____ (foreign country).

48. Give estate planning advice to a client with a unique personal situation.

49. Advise X Company on whether it should lease capital equipment or buy it.

50. Advise Company X on whether it should engage in a joint venture with a company overseas or establish a wholly owned foreign subsidiary.

51. Compare the costs for X Company of offering its workers child care or elder care benefits.

52. Should Company X accept national credit cards or set up its own credit card system?

53. Advise Company X on how to avoid a hostile takeover.

54. Advise Company X on whether it should list its stock on a major stock exchange.

55. Advise Company X, which is having problems with liquidity, on the pros and cons of factoring accounts receivable.

56. Recommend the most feasible way to finance newly formed X Company.

▶ **Management**

57. Develop for Company X a guide to ethics in its highly competitive business situation.

58. After reviewing pertinent literature and experiences of other companies, develop a plan for selecting and training administrators for an overseas operation on Company X.

59. Survey the current literature and advise Company X on whether its management should become politically active.

60. After reviewing the pros and cons, advise X Company on whether it should begin a program of hiring the handicapped or disadvantaged.

61. Report on the behavioral and psychological effects of introducing wellness programs to Company X.

62. The executives of X Company (a manufacturer of automobile and truck tires) want a report on recent court decisions relating to warranties. Include any recommendations that your report justifies.

63. Report on the problems involved in moving Company X headquarters from _____ (city) to (city). _____

64. After reviewing current practices with regard to worker participation in management, advise Company X on whether it should permit such participation.

65. Should Company X contract for _____ (service) or establish its own department?

66. Review the advantages and disadvantages of rotating executive jobs at Company X, and then make a recommendation.

67. What should be Company X's policy on office romances?

68. Develop an energy conservation or recycling plan for X Company.

69. Evaluate internal communications in the X Company and make specific suggestions for improvement.

70. Design a security system for preventing computer espionage at Company X, a leader in the highly competitive _____ industry.

71. Evaluate the various methods for determining corporate performance and select the one most appropriate for Company X.

72. Advise X Company on the procedures for incorporating in _____ (state or province).

73. Survey the literature to find meaningful criteria for selecting executives for foreign service for X Company.

74. Report to Company X on the civil and criminal liabilities of its corporate executives.

75. Report on the quality awards being given to businesses.

76. Determine for a legislative committee the extent of minority recruiting, hiring, and training in the industry.

77. As a consultant for an association of farmers, evaluate the recent past and project the future of growing or raising _____ (your choice—cattle, poultry, wheat, soybeans, or the like).

78. Develop a plan for reducing employee turnover for Company X.

79. Report to a labor union on recent evidence of sexual harassment, and recommend steps that the union should take to correct any problems you find.

80. Investigate the feasibility of hiring older workers for part-time work for X Company.

▶ Personnel/Human Resources Administration

81. Report on and interpret for X Company the effects of recent court decisions on the testing and hiring of employees.

82. Survey company retirement practices and recommend retirement policies for Company X.

83. Report on practices in compensating key personnel in overseas assignments and recommend for X Company policies for the compensation of such personnel.

84. Report on what personnel executives look for in application letters and résumés.

85. Report on the advantages and disadvantages of Company X's providing on-site day care for children of employees.

86. After reviewing the legal and ethical questions involved, make a recommendation concerning the use of honesty tests in employee hiring.

87. Review what other companies are doing about employees suffering from drug or alcohol abuse, and recommend a policy on the matter for Company X.

88. Report on effective interviewing techniques used to identify the best people to hire.

▶ Marketing

89. Review the available literature and advise Company X on whether it should franchise its _____ business.

90. Select a recent national marketing program and analyze why it succeeded or failed.

91. Advise the advertising vice president of Company X on whether the company should respond to or ignore a competitor's direct attack on the quality of its product.

92. Review the ethical considerations involved in advertising directed to children and advise X Company on the matter.

93. Determine for Company X the social and ethical aspects of pricing for the market.

94. Explore the possibilities of trade with _____ (a foreign country) for X Company.

95. Determine for a national department store chain changing trends in the services that customers expect.

96. Prepare a report to help a contingent of your legislature decide whether current regulation of advertising should be reduced.

97. Determine the problems X Company will encounter in introducing a new product to its line.

98. Report on the success of rebates as a sales stimulator and advise Company X on whether it should use rebates.

99. Should Company X rent or lease trucks for distributing its products?

100. Determine the trends in packaging in the _____ industry.

101. Should X Company establish its own sales force, use manufacturers' agents, or use selling agents?

102. How should Company X evaluate the performance of its salespeople?

103. Determine for X Company how it can evaluate the effectiveness of its advertising.

104. Select the best channel of distribution for new product Y and justify your choice.

105. Should X Company establish its own advertising department or use an advertising agency?

106. Make a market study of _____ (city) to determine whether it is a suitable location for _____ (a type of business).

107. Report to X Company on telemarketing and recommend whether it should use telemarketing to increase sales.

108. Determine whether any of the products of Company X are good candidates for infomercials.

▶ Computer Applications

109. Recommend a laptop computer for use by the salespeople of Company X when they are traveling.

110. Advise Company X about the steps it can take to protect its computerized files from sabotage.

111. Determine whether Company X should purchase or lease its computer equipment.

112. Report to the president of Company X the copyright and contract laws that apply to the use of computer programs.

113. What are the potential applications of artificial intelligence in the _____ industry?

114. Determine which positions Company X should designate as possible telecommuting candidates.

115. Report on the effectiveness of encryption as a means of data protection.

116. Report on the future developments of robotics in the industry.

117. Review and rank for possible adoption three software packages that Company X might use for its _____ work (name the field of operations).

118. Determine for Company X the factors it should consider in selecting computer insurance.

119. Report on the types of training available to X Company for its staff when upgrading its current word processing software.

▶ Business Education

120. Evaluate the effect of remodeling your new office site to take on a more homey look.

121. Report on why office romances still result in job losses.

122. Analyze the possibility of instituting companywide training on etiquette, covering everything from handling telephone calls, to sexual harassment, to dining out.

123. Advise management on the importance of the air quality in the offices.

124. Investigate ways to improve the retrieval time and accuracy of information at X Company.

125. Evaluate the reprographic services and practices at your school from an environmental perspective.

126. Report on ways to hire and keep the best employees in the word processing center.

127. Report on ways to combat illiteracy in the workplace.

13

Graphics

Upon completing this chapter, you will be able to use graphics effectively in business reports. To reach this goal, you should be able to

1 Determine which parts of your report should be communicated by graphics and where in the report the graphics should appear.

2 Explain the general mechanics of constructing graphics—size, layout, type, rules and borders, color and cross-hatching, clip art, numbering, titles, title placement, and footnotes and acknowledgments.

3 Construct textual graphics such as tables, in-text displays, and flow and process charts.

4 Construct and use visual graphics such as bar charts, pie charts, line charts, pictograms, and combination charts.

▶ to Graphics

In your job in the Cory, Inc., word processing section, your assignment today is to proofread reports prepared by your coworkers. As Cory manufactures electronic equipment, many of the reports are highly technical and complex. Many others, especially those coming from finance and sales, are filled with facts and figures. In your judgment, most of the reports you have proofread are hard to understand.

The one you are looking at now is packed with page after page of sales statistics. Your mind quickly gets lost in the mass of details. Why didn't the writer take the time to summarize the more important figures in a chart? And why didn't the writer put some of the details in tables? Many of the other reports you have been reading, especially the technical ones, are in equal need of graphics. Diagrams, pictures, and drawings would certainly help explain some of the concepts discussed. If only report writers would understand that words alone sometimes cannot communicate clearly—that words sometimes need to be supplemented with visual communication techniques. If the writers of your reports studied the following review of graphics, your job would be easier and more enjoyable. So would the jobs of the readers of those reports. ■

In many of your reports you will need to use graphics to help convey information quickly and accurately. By *graphics* we mean any form of illustration: charts, pictures, diagrams, maps. Although tables and bulleted lists are not truly graphic, they are included in this definition. In fact, most computer presentation software includes them.

• A graphic is any form of illustration.

PLANNING THE GRAPHICS

You should plan the graphics for a report soon after you make and organize your findings. Your planning of graphics should be based on the need to communicate. Graphics serve one purpose—to communicate—and you should use them primarily for that purpose. Graphics can clarify complex or difficult information, emphasize facts, add coherence, summarize, and add interest. Of course, well-constructed graphics also enhance the appearance of a report.

• You should plan the use of graphics.

In selecting graphics, you should review the information that your report will contain, looking for any possibility of improving communication of the report through the use of graphics. Specifically, you should look for complex information that visual presentation can make clear, for information too detailed to be covered in words, and for information that deserves special emphasis.

• In planning their use, look for parts that they should communicate.

Of course, you will want to plan with your reader in mind. You will choose graphics appropriate to both the content and context where they are presented. The time and money you spend on gathering or creating a graphic should be balanced in terms of the importance of the message you want to convey.

• Plan graphics with your reader in mind.

As you plan the graphics, remember that, as a general rule, they should supplement the writing—not take its place. They should help the writing by covering the more difficult parts, emphasizing the important points, and presenting details. But the words should carry the main message—all of it.

• But remember that graphics supplement and do not replace the writing.

PLACING THE GRAPHICS IN THE REPORT

For the best communication effect, you should place each graphic near the place where it is covered in writing. Exactly where on the page you should place it, however, should be determined by its size. If the graphic is small, you should place it

• Place the graphics near the first place in the text in which you refer to them.

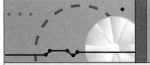

As today's word processors become more document-centric, writers can create their graphics at the point they want to use them. For example, if you needed a drawing or special effects on lettering, you simply click on a button within your word processor. When you have finished, the software allows you to place your creation in your document. Furthermore, with clip art you no longer need to be an artist to use good art and illustrations. Clip art often comes bundled with your software, is sold through retail outlets, and is available as shareware. Using the Internet, you can even get it from various computer sites around the world. Photographs can be either brought in from digital files or scanned in for easy use in documents. Specialized programs even allow you to edit photographs. Enhancing your documents with good graphics is easy but demands care in selection and presentation.

within the text that covers it. If it is a full page, you should place it on the page following the first reference to the information it covers.

- Placing graphics at the end of the report does not help the readers.

Some writers like to place all graphics at the end of the report, usually in the appendix. This arrangement may save time in preparing the report, but it does not help the readers. They have to flip through pages every time they want to see a graphic.

- Graphics not discussed in the report belong in the appendix.

Sometimes you may need to include graphics that do not fit a specific part of the report. For example, you may have a graphic that is necessary for completeness but is not discussed in the report. Or you may have summary charts or tables that apply to the entire report but to no specific place in it. When such graphics are appropriate, you should place them in the appendix.

- At the right place, incidentally invite the readers to look at the graphics.

Graphics communicate most effectively when the readers see them at the right place in the report. Thus, you should refer the readers to them at the right place. That is, you should tell the readers when to look at a graphic and what to see. You can do this best through an incidental reference to the information in the graphic. Of the many wordings used for this purpose, these are the most common:

. . . , as shown in Figure 4, ...
. . . , indicated in Figure 4, ...
. . . , as a glance at Figure 4 reveals, ...
. . . (see Figure 4) . . . .

DETERMINING THE GENERAL MECHANICS OF CONSTRUCTION

In constructing graphics, you will be concerned with various mechanical matters. The most common are summarized in the following paragraphs.

Size Determination

- Make each graphic the size its contents justify.

One of the first decisions you must make in constructing a graphic is determining its size. This decision should not be arbitrary, and it should not be based on convenience. You should give the graphic the size its contents justify. If a graphic is simple (with only two or three quantities), a quarter page might be more than enough and a full page would be too much. But if a graphic must display complex or detailed information, a full page might be justified.

- Graphics larger than a page are justified if they contain enough information.

With extremely complex, involved information, you may need to use more than a full page. When you do, make certain that this large page is inserted and folded so that the readers can open it easily. The fold you select will be determined by the size of the page. You simply have to experiment until you find a convenient fold.

Can he call you back? He's creating graphics.
Vietor's *Funny Business*

Layout Arrangement

You should determine the layout (shape) of the graphic by size and content requirements. Sometimes a tall, narrow rectangle (portrait) is the answer; sometimes the answer is a short, wide rectangle or a full-page rectangle (landscape). You simply consider the logical possibilities and select the one that appears best.

• Size and contents determine the shape of graphics.

Type

Type used in graphics throughout a report is generally consistent in both style and font. Style refers to the look of the type such as bold or italics; font refers to the look of the letters such as with or without feet, *serif* or *san serif*. Occasionally you may want to vary the type, but do so by design for some special reason. Be aware that even the design of the font you choose will convey a message, a message that should work with the text content and design.

• Choose a type to help convey the message clearly.

Size is another variable to watch. Major headings will be larger than subheads. Subheads will be larger than text in labels and legends. The size you choose should look appropriate in the context you use it. Your top priority in choosing type style, font, and size should be readability.

• Choose a type size that is readable.

Rules and Borders

You should use rules and borders when they help the appearance of the graphic. Rules help distinguish one section or graphic from another while borders help separate graphics from the text. As a general rule, you should place borders around graphics that occupy less than a full page. You can also place borders around full-page graphics, but such borders serve little practical value. Except in cases in which graphics simply will not fit into the normal page layout, you should not extend the borders of graphics beyond the normal page margins.

• Use rules and borders when they help appearance.

Color and Cross-Hatching

Color and/or cross-hatching, appropriately used, help readers see comparisons and distinctions. In fact, research has found that color in graphics improves the compre-

• Color and cross-hatching can improve graphics.

hension, retention, and ease of extracting information.[1] Also, both color and cross-hatching add to the attractiveness of the report. As color is especially effective for this purpose, you should use it whenever practical.

Clip Art

- Use clip art to help your reader understand your message.

Today you can get good looking clip art easily—so easily in fact that some writers often overuse it. While clip art can add interest and bring the reader into a graphic effectively, it can also overpower and distract the reader. The general rule is to keep in mind the purpose your clip art is serving—to help the reader understand the content. It should be appropriate in both its nature and size. Furthermore, if it is copyrighted, you need permission to use it. Today's court rulings seem to be strictly enforcing our copyright laws. So while it's easier than ever to scan or capture an illustration and reuse it, if the illustration is copyrighted you must have permission to use it.

Numbering

- Number graphics consecutively by type.

Except for minor tabular displays that are actually a part of the text, you should number all the graphics in the report. Many schemes of numbering are available to you, depending on the makeup of the graphics.

If you have many graphics that fall into two or more categories, you may number each of the categories consecutively. For example, if your report is illustrated by six tables, five charts, and six maps, you may number these graphics Table 1, Table 2, . . . Table 6; Chart 1, Chart 2, . . . Chart 5; and Map 1, Map 2, . . . Map 6.

- Figures are a miscellaneous grouping of types. Number tables separately.

But if your graphics comprise a wide mixture of types, you may number them in two groups: tables and figures. Figures, a miscellaneous grouping, may include all types other than tables. To illustrate, consider a report containing three tables, two maps, three charts, one diagram, and one photograph. You could number these graphics Table 1, Table 2, and Table 3 and Figure 1, Figure 2, . . . Figure 7. By convention, tables are not grouped with other types of graphics. But it would not be wrong to group and number as figures all graphics other than tables even if the group contained sufficient subgroups (charts, maps, and the like) to permit separate numbering of each of them.

Construction of Titles

- The titles should describe content clearly (consider the five Ws—who, what, where, when, why).

Every graphic should have a title that adequately describes its contents. Like the headings used in other parts of the report, the title of the graphic has the objective of concisely covering the contents. As a check of content coverage, you might well use the journalist's five W's—*who, what, where, when, why,* and sometimes you might also use *how* (the classification principle). But as conciseness is also desired, it is not always necessary to include all the W's in the title. A title of a chart comparing the annual sales volume of the Texas and California branches of the Brill Company for the years 1994–95 might be constructed as follows:

Who: Brill Company
What: Annual sales
Where: Texas and California branches
When: 1994–95
Why: For comparison

---

[1] Ellen D. Hoadley, "Investigating the Effects of Color," *Communications of the ACM,* 33, no. 2 (February 1990), p. 121.

The title might read, "Comparative Annual Sales of Texas and California Branches of the Brill Company, 1994–95. For even more conciseness, you could use a major title and subtitle. The major title might read, "A Texas and California Sales Comparison"; the subtitle might read, "Brill Company 1994–95".

Placement of Titles

Titles of tables conventionally appear above the tabular display; titles of all other types of graphics conventionally appear below it. It is also conventional to use a larger type for table titles than for the titles of other graphics. There has been a trend toward the use of lowercase type for all illustration titles and to place the titles of both tables and figures at the top. In fact, most presentation software defaults to the top. These practices are simple and logical; yet you should follow the conventional practices for the more formal reports.

• The conventional placement of titles is at the top for tables and at the bottom for charts. But many place all titles at the top.

Footnotes and Acknowledgments

Parts of a graphic sometimes require special explanation or elaboration. When this happens, as when similar situations arise in connection with the text of the report, you should use footnotes. Such footnotes are concise explanations placed below the illustration and keyed to the part explained by means of a superscript (raised) number or symbol (asterisk, dagger, double dagger, and so on). Footnotes for tables are best placed immediately below the graphic presentation. Footnotes for other graphic forms follow the illustration when the title is placed at the bottom of the page.

• Use footnotes to explain or elaborate.

Usually, a source acknowledgment is the bottom entry made on the page. By *source acknowledgment* we mean a reference to the body or authority that deserves the credit for gathering the data used in the illustration. The entry consists simply of the word *Source* followed by a colon and the source name. A source note for data based on information gathered by the United States Department of Commerce might read like this:

• Acknowledge source of data with note below.

Source: United States Department of Commerce.

If you or your staff collected the data, you may either omit the source note or give the source as "Primary," in which case the note would read:

• "Source: Primary" is the proper note for data you gathered.

Source: Primary.

Graphics for communicating report information fall into two general categories: those that communicate primarily by their textual content (words and numerals) and those that communicate primarily by some form of visual picture. Included in the textual group are tables, in-text displays, and a variety of flow and process charts (Gantt, flow, organization, and such).

- Graphics fall into two general categories: (1) textual (words and numerals) and (2) visual (pictures).

Tables

- A table is an orderly arrangement of information.

A *table* is an orderly arrangement of information in rows and columns. As we have noted, tables are not truly graphic (not really pictures). But they communicate like graphics, and they have many of the characteristics of graphics.

- You may use general-purpose tables (those containing broad information).

Two basic types of tables are available to you—the general-purpose table and the special-purpose table. General-purpose tables cover a broad area of information. For example, a table reviewing the answers to all the questions in a survey is a general-purpose table. Such tables usually belong in the appendix.

- Or you may use special-purpose tables (those covering a specific area of information).

Special-purpose tables are prepared for one special purpose—to illustrate a particular part of the report. They contain information that could be included with related information in a general-purpose table. For example, a table presenting the answer to one of the questions in a survey is a special-purpose table. Such tables belong in the report text near the discussion of their contents.

- See Figure 13–1 for details of table arrangement.

Aside from the title, footnotes, and source designation previously discussed, a table contains stubs, heads, and columns and rows of data, as shown in Figure 13–1. Stubs are the titles of the rows of data, and heads are the titles of the columns. The heads, however, may be divided into subheads—or column heads, as they are sometimes called.

FIGURE 13–1   Good Arrangement of the Parts of a Typical Table

	TABLE NO. Table Title			
	Spanner Head			
Stub Head	**Column Head**	**Column Head**	**Column Head**	**Column Head**
Stub	XXX	XXX	XXX	XXX
Stub	XXX	XXX	XXX	XXX
Stub	XXX	XXX	XXX	XXX
Stub	XXX	XXX	XXX	XXX
"	"	"	"	"
"	"	"	"	"
"	"	"	"	"
"	"	"	"	"
"	"	"	"	"
"	"	"	"	"
Total	XXX	XXX	XXX	XXX

FOOTNOTES

SOURCE:

The construction of text tables is largely influenced by their purpose. Nevertheless, a few general construction rules may be listed:

- If rows are long, the stubs may be repeated at the right.
- The dash (—) or the abbreviation "n.a. (N.A. or NA)," but not the zero, is used to indicate data not available.
- Footnote references to numbers in the table should be keyed with asterisks, daggers, double daggers, and such. Numbers followed by footnote reference numbers may cause confusion, but numbers may be necessary when many references must be made.
- Totals and subtotals should appear whenever they help the purpose of the table. The totals may be for each column and sometimes for each row. Row totals are usually placed at the right; but when they need emphasis, they may be placed at the left. Likewise, column totals are generally placed at the bottom of the column, but they may be placed at the top when the writer wants to emphasize them. A ruled line (usually a double one) separates the totals from their components.
- The units in which the data are recorded must be clear. Unit descriptions (bushels, acres, pounds, and the like) appropriately appear above the columns, as part of the headings or sub-headings. If the data are in dollars, however, placing the dollar mark ($) before the first entry in each column is sufficient.

In-Text Displays

Tabular information need not always be presented in formal tables. In fact, short arrangements of data may be presented more effectively as parts of the text. Such arrangements are generally made as either leaderwork or text tabulations.

Leaderwork is the presentation of tabular material in the text without titles or rules. (Leaders are the repeated dots.) Typically, a colon precedes the tabulation, as in this illustration:

- Tabular information can also be presented as (1) leaderwork (as illustrated here),

The August sales of the representatives in the Western Region were as follows:

Charles B. Brown $13,517
Thelma Capp   19,703
Bill E. Knauth   18,198

Text tabulations are simple tables, usually with column heads and some rules. But they are not numbered, and they have no titles. They are made to read with the text, as in this example:

- (2) text tabulations (as illustrated here), and

In August the sales of the representatives in the Western Region increased sharply from those for the preceding month, as these figures show:

Representative	July Sales	August Sales	Increase
Charles B. Brown	$12,819	$13,517	$ 698
Thelma Capp	17,225	19,703	2,478
Bill E. Knauth	16,838	18,198	1,360

Bullet lists are listings of points arranged with bullets (•) to set them off. These lists can have a title that covers all the points, or they can appear without titles, as they appear at various places in this book. When you use this arrangement, make the points grammatically parallel. If the points have subparts, use sub-bullets for them. Make the sub-bullets different by color, size, shape, or weight. The filled circle is commonly used for the primary bullets and darts, check marks, squares, or triangles for the secondary ones.

- (3) bullet lists.

FIGURE 13–2   An Organization Chart with Employee Names

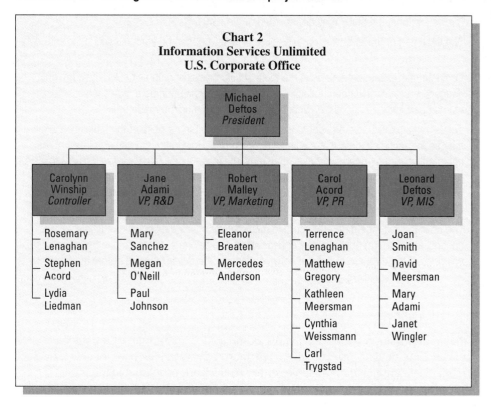

Chart 2
Information Services Unlimited
U.S. Corporate Office

Michael
Deftos
President

| Carolynn Winship *Controller* | Jane Adami *VP, R&D* | Robert Malley *VP, Marketing* | Carol Acord *VP, PR* | Leonard Deftos *VP, MIS* |

- Rosemary Lenaghan
- Stephen Acord
- Lydia Liedman

- Mary Sanchez
- Megan O'Neill
- Paul Johnson

- Eleanor Breaten
- Mercedes Anderson

- Terrence Lenaghan
- Matthew Gregory
- Kathleen Meersman
- Cynthia Weissmann
- Carl Trygstad

- Joan Smith
- David Meersman
- Mary Adami
- Janet Wingler

Principles of Graphicical Excellence[2]

- Graphical excellence in the presentation of intersting data—a matter of substance, of *statistics,* and of *design.*
- Graphical excellence consists of complex ideas communicated with clarity, precision, and efficiency.
- Graphical excellence is that which gives the viewer the greatest number of ideas in the shortest time with the least ink in the smallest space.
- Graphical excellence requires telling the truth about data.

Flow and Process Charts

• Various specialized management charts are useful in reports—for example, organization charts, Gantt charts, and flowcharts.

If you have studied business management, you know that administrators use a variety of specialized charts in their work. Often these charts are a part of the information presented in reports. Perhaps the most common of these is the *organization chart* (see Figure 13–2). These charts show hierarchy of positions, divisions, departments, and such in an organization. *Gantt charts* are graphic presentations that show planning and scheduling activities. As the words imply, a *flowchart* (see Figure 13–3) shows the sequence of activities in a process. Traditionally, flowcharts use specific designs and symbols to show process variations. A variation of the flowchart is the *decision tree.* This chart helps one follow a path to an appropriate decision. You can easily construct these charts with presentation and drawing software.

2Edward R.Tuttle, The Visual Display of Quantitative Information (Cheshire, Connecticut: Graphics Press, 1983), p. 51.

FIGURE 13–3 A Flowchart

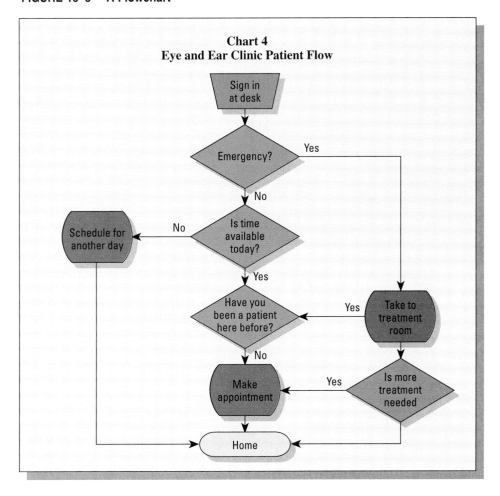

Chart 4
Eye and Ear Clinic Patient Flow

CONSTRUCTING VISUAL GRAPHICS

The truly visual types of graphics include a variety of forms—data-generated charts as well as artwork and photographs. Data-generated charts are ones built with raw data and include bar, pie, and line charts and all their variations and combinations. Artwork includes maps, diagrams, drawings, cartoons, and such.

Bar Charts

Simple bar charts compare differences in quantities by differences in the lengths of the bars representing those quantities. You should use them primarily to show quantity changes over time or over geographic distances.

As shown in Figure 13–4, the main parts of the bar chart are the bars and the grid (the field on which the bars are placed). The bars, which may be arranged horizontally or vertically, should be of equal width. You should identify each bar, usually with a caption at the left. The grid (field) on which the bars are placed is usually needed to show the magnitudes of the bars, and the units (dollars, pounds, miles, and such) are identified by the scale caption below.

When you need to compare two or three different kinds of quantities in one chart, you can use a *multiple* (or *clustered*) *bar chart.* In such a chart, bars show the values of the quantities compared. Cross-hatching, colors, or the like on the bars distinguish

• Visual graphics include data-generated charts, photographs, and artwork.

• Simple bar charts compare differences in quantities by varying bar lengths.

• Multiple bar charts are useful in comparing two or three kinds of quantities.

FIGURE 13–4   Illustration of Good Arrangement of the Parts of a Simple Horizontal Bar Chart

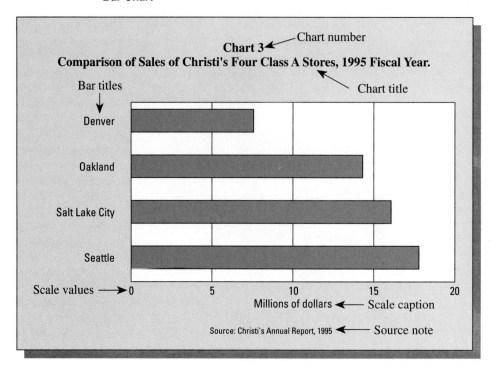

the different kinds of information (see Figure 13–5). Somewhere within the chart, a legend (explanation) gives a key to the differences in the bars. Because multiple bar charts can become cluttered, usually you should not compare more than three kinds of information on one of them.

> • When you need to show plus and minus differences, bilateral bar charts are useful.

When you need to show plus and minus differences, you can use *bilateral bar charts*. The bars of these charts begin at a central point of reference and may go either up or down, as illustrated in Figure 13–6. Bar titles appear either within, above, or below the bars, depending on which placement fits best. Bilateral bar charts are especially good for showing percentage changes, but you may use them for any series in which plus and minus quantities are present.

> • To compare subdivisions of bars, use a subdivided bar chart.

If you need to compare subdivisions of bars, you can use a *stacked (subdivided) bar chart*. As shown in Figure 13–7, such a chart divides each bar into its parts. It distinguishes these parts by color, cross-hatching, or the like; and it explains these differences in a legend. This stacked bar may be difficult for your reader to interpret since both the beginning and ending points need to be found. Then the reader has to subtract to find the size of the bar component. Multiple bar charts or pie charts do not introduce such errors.

> • Two-dimensional bars on two-dimensional axes are easiest for readers to use.

Another feature that can lead to reader error in interpreting bar chart data is the use of three dimensions. A recent study evaluated the speed and accuracy of readers' interpretation of two-dimensional bars on two-dimensional axes with three-dimensional bars on two-dimensional axes and three-dimensional bars on three-dimensional axes. The results showed that readers were able to extract information from the bar chart fastest and most accurately when it was presented in the simple two-dimensional bar on the two-dimensional axis.[3]

---

[3] Theophilus B. A. Addo, "The Effects of Dimensionality in Computer Graphics," *The Journal of Business Communication* 31, no. 4 (1994), p. 253.

FIGURE 13–5   Multiple Bar Chart

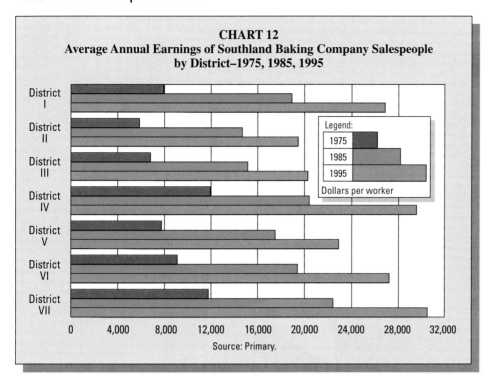

CHART 12
Average Annual Earnings of Southland Baking Company Salespeople
by District–1975, 1985, 1995

Legend:
1975
1985
1995
Dollars per worker

Source: Primary.

FIGURE 13–6   Bilateral Bar Chart

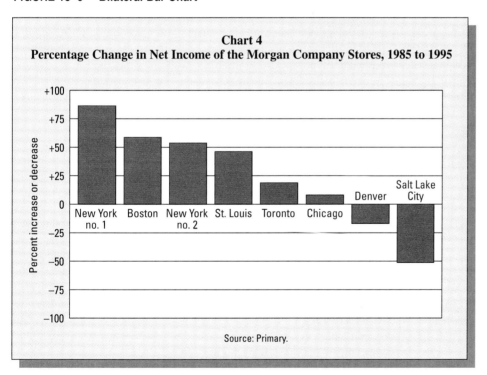

Chart 4
Percentage Change in Net Income of the Morgan Company Stores, 1985 to 1995

Source: Primary.

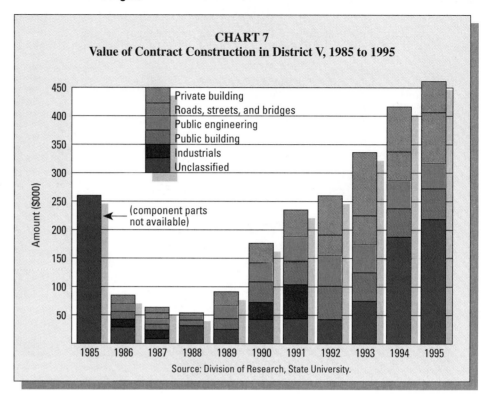

CHART 7
Value of Contract Construction in District V, 1985 to 1995

A special form of stacked (subdivided) bar chart is used to compare the subdivisions of percentages. In this form, all the bars are equal in length, for each represents 100 percent. Only the subdivisions within the bars vary. The objective of this form is to compare differences in how wholes are divided. The component parts may be labeled, as shown in Figure 13–8, but they may also be explained in a legend.

• You can also use such a chart for comparing subdivisions of percentages.

Pie Charts

• Pie charts show subdivisions of a whole.

Also important in comparing the subdivisions of wholes is the *pie chart* (see Figure 13–9). As the name implies, pie charts show the whole of the information being studied as a pie (circle), and the parts of this whole as slices of the pie. The slices may be distinguished by labeling and color or cross-hatching. A single slice can be emphasized by exploding—pulling out—a piece. As it is hard to judge the values of the slices with the naked eye, it is good to include the percentage values within or near each slice. A good rule to follow is to begin slicing the pie at the 12 o'clock position and then to move around clockwise. It is also good to arrange the slices in descending order from largest to smallest.

• But do not vary sizes of the pies.

In using pie charts to compare two or more wholes, you should never vary the sizes of the pies. Such comparisons are almost meaningless. The human eye simply cannot judge circle sizes accurately.

Line Charts

• Line charts show changes over time.

Line charts are useful to show changes of information over time. For example, changes in prices, sales totals, employment, or production over a period of years can be shown well in a line chart.

FIGURE 13–8   Illustration of a Subdivided Bar Chart with Bars of Equal Lengths

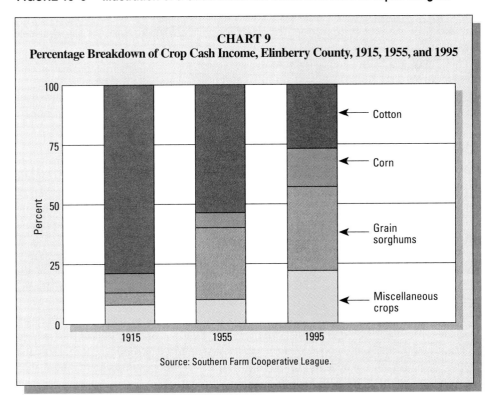

CHART 9
Percentage Breakdown of Crop Cash Income, Elinberry County, 1915, 1955, and 1995

Source: Southern Farm Cooperative League.

FIGURE 13–9   Illustration of a Pie Chart

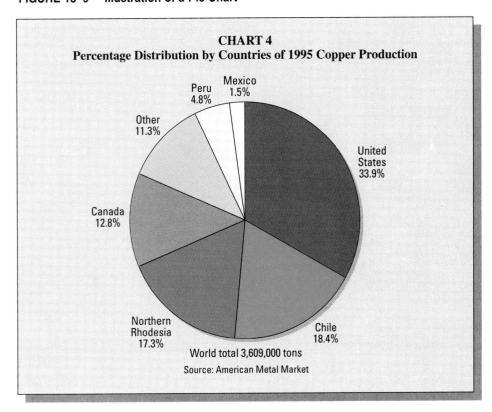

CHART 4
Percentage Distribution by Countries of 1995 Copper Production

World total 3,609,000 tons
Source: American Metal Market

- The line appears on a grid (a scaled area) and is continuous.

- Two or more lines may appear on one chart.

- Area charts show the makeup of a series.

- Variance charts show high and low points—sometimes more.

- But avoid these errors: (1) failure to start at zero (you can show scale breaks),

In constructing a line chart, you draw the information to be illustrated as a continuous line on a grid (see Figure 13–10). The grid is the area in which the line is displayed. It is scaled to show time changes from left to right across the chart (X-axis) and quantity changes from bottom to top (Y-axis). You should mark clearly the scale values and the time periods.

You may also compare two or more series on the same line chart (see Figure 13–11). In such a comparison, you should clearly distinguish the lines by color or form (dots, dashes, dots and dashes, and the like). You should clearly label them by a legend somewhere in the chart. But the number of series that you may compare on one line chart is limited. As a practical rule, the maximum number is four or five.

It is also possible to show parts of a series by use of an *area* chart—sometimes called a *surface* chart. Such a chart, however, can show only one series. You should construct this type of chart, as shown in Figure 13–12, with a top line representing the total of the series. Then, starting from the base, you should cumulate the parts, beginning with the largest and ending with the smallest. You may use cross-hatching or coloring to distinguish the parts.

Another variation of the line chart is the *scatter diagram.* Like the line chart, points are plotted on two axes; however, they are not joined by a line. The location of the individual points on the axes give the reader the information needed (see Figure 13–13).

Line charts that show a range of data for particular times are called *variance* or *hi-lo* charts (see Figure 13–14). Some variance charts show high and low points as well as the mean, median, or mode. When used to chart daily stock prices, they typically include closing price in addition to the high and low. When you use points other than high and low, be sure to make it clear what these points are.

Line charts are simple to construct, but you should guard against three common errors in their construction. The first is the error of violating the zero beginning of the series. For accuracy, you should begin the scale at zero. But when all the information shown in the chart has high values, it is awkward to show the entire scale from zero to the highest value. For example, if the quantities compared range from 1,320 to 1,350 and the chart shows the entire area from zero to 1,350, the line showing these quantities would be almost straight and very high on the chart. Your solution in this case is not to begin the scale at a high number (say, 1,300), for this would distort the information, but to begin at zero and show a scale break. Realize, however, that while this makes the differences easier to see, it does exaggerate the differences. The following two ways of showing scale breaks are recommended:

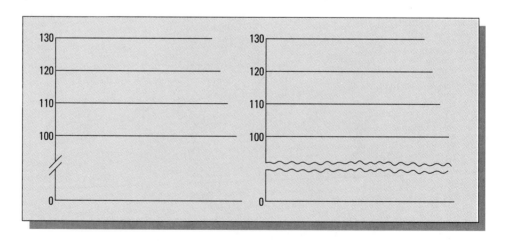

- (2) failure to keep scales uniform,

A second error in constructing line charts is failing to keep the chart scales uniform.

FIGURE 13–10   A Line Chart with One Series

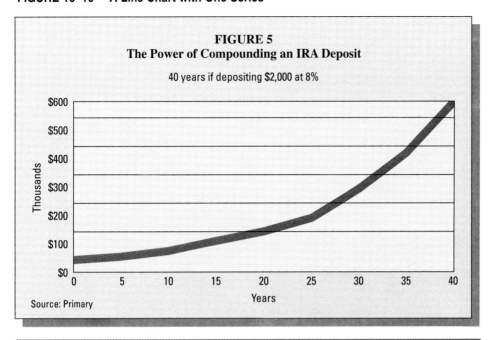

FIGURE 5
The Power of Compounding an IRA Deposit

40 years if depositing $2,000 at 8%

Source: Primary

FIGURE 13–11   A Line Chart Comparing More than One Series

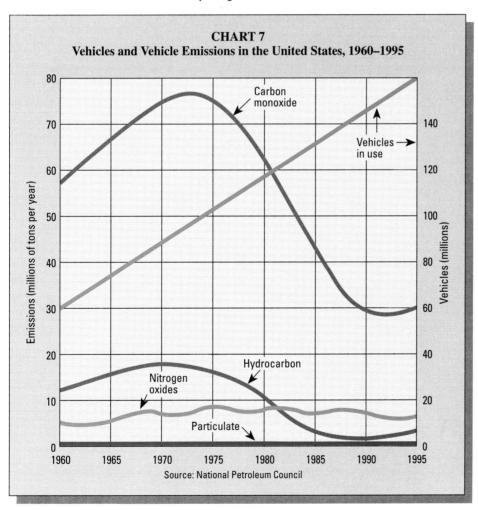

CHART 7
Vehicles and Vehicle Emissions in the United States, 1960–1995

Source: National Petroleum Council

FIGURE 13–12   Illustration of an Area Line Chart

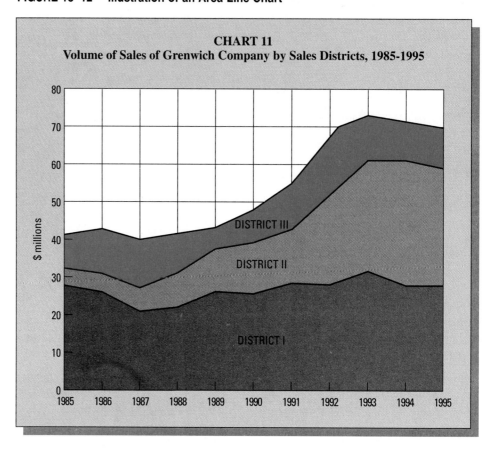

CHART 11
Volume of Sales of Grenwich Company by Sales Districts, 1985-1995

FIGURE 13–13   A Variance (Hi-Lo) Chart

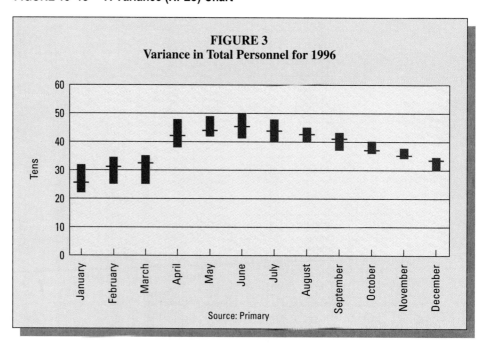

FIGURE 3
Variance in Total Personnel for 1996

FIGURE 13–14   A Scatter Diagram

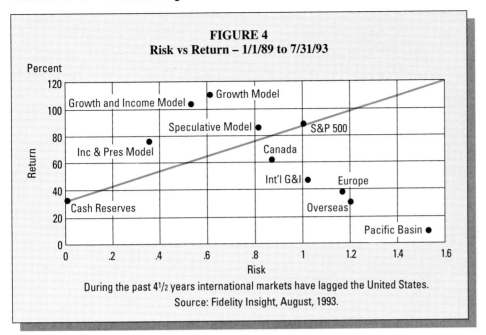

FIGURE 4
Risk vs Return – 1/1/89 to 7/31/93

During the past 4½ years international markets have lagged the United States.
Source: Fidelity Insight, August, 1993.

All the dimensions from left to right (X-axis) and from bottom to top (Y-axis) should be equal. Otherwise, an incorrect picture would be shown.

A third error is using grid distances that do not give a true picture of the information. Expanding a scale can change the appearance of the line. For example, if the values on a chart are plotted ½ inch apart instead of ¹⁄₁₆ inch apart, changes appear much more suddenly. Determining the distances that present the most accurate picture is a matter of judgment.

• (3) use of distances on the grid that do not show the true picture.

Statistical Maps

You may also use *statistical maps* to communicate quantitative as well as geographic information. They are useful primarily when quantitative information is to be compared by geographic areas. On such maps, the geographic areas are clearly outlined and some graphic technique is used to show the differences between areas. Of the numerous techniques available to you, these are the most common:

• You can show quantitative information for geographic areas in a statistical map.

• Here are some specific instructions for statistical maps.

■ Showing quantitative differences of areas by color, shading, or cross-hatching is perhaps the most popular technique (see Figure 13–15). Of course, maps using this technique must have a legend to explain the quantitative meanings of the various colors, cross-hatchings, and so forth.

■ Some form of chart may be placed within each geographic area to depict the quantity for that area, as illustrated in Figure 13–16. Bar charts and pie charts are commonly used in such statistical maps.

■ Placing the quantities in numerical form within each geographic area, as shown in Figure 13–17, is another widely used technique.

■ Dots, each representing a definite quantity (see Figure 13–18), may be placed within the geographic areas in proportion to the quantities for those areas.

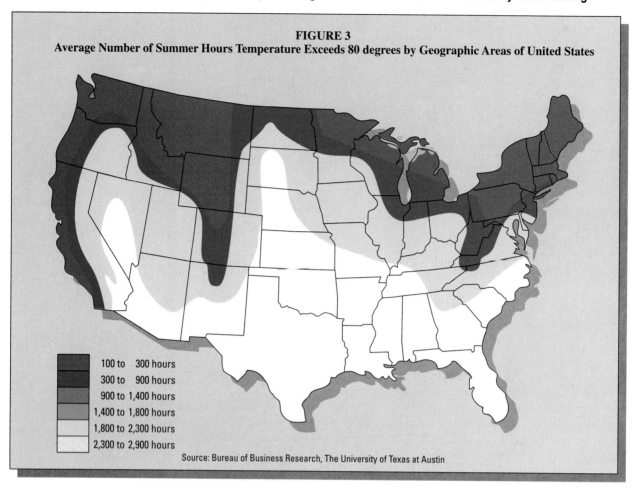

FIGURE 3
Average Number of Summer Hours Temperature Exceeds 80 degrees by Geographic Areas of United States

100 to   300 hours
300 to   900 hours
900 to 1,400 hours
1,400 to 1,800 hours
1,800 to 2,300 hours
2,300 to 2,900 hours

Source: Bureau of Business Research, The University of Texas at Austin

Pictograms

- Pictograms are bar charts made with pictures.

- In constructing pictograms, follow the procedure for making bar charts.

A *pictogram* is a bar chart that uses bars made of pictures. The pictures are typically drawings of the items being compared. For example, a company's profits over a period of years, instead of being shown by ordinary bars (formed by straight lines), could be shown by bar drawings of stacks of coins. This type of bar chart is a pictogram (see Figure 13–19).

In constructing a pictogram, you should follow the procedures you used in constructing bar charts and two special rules. First, you must make all the picture units equal in size. That is, you must base the comparisons wholly on the number of picture units used and never on variation in the areas of the units. The reason for this rule is obvious. The human eye is grossly inadequate in comparing geometric designs that vary in more than one dimension. Second, you should select pictures or symbols that fit the information to be illustrated. In comparing the cruise lines of the world, for example, you might use ships. In comparing computers used in the world's major countries, you might use computers. The meaning of the drawings you use must be immediately clear to the readers.

FIGURE 13–16 Statistical Map Showing Comparisons by Charts within Geographic Areas

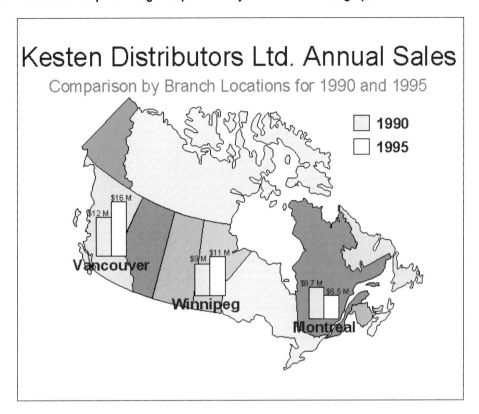

FIGURE 13–17 Statistical Map Showing Quantitative Differences by Means of Numbers Placed within Geographic Areas

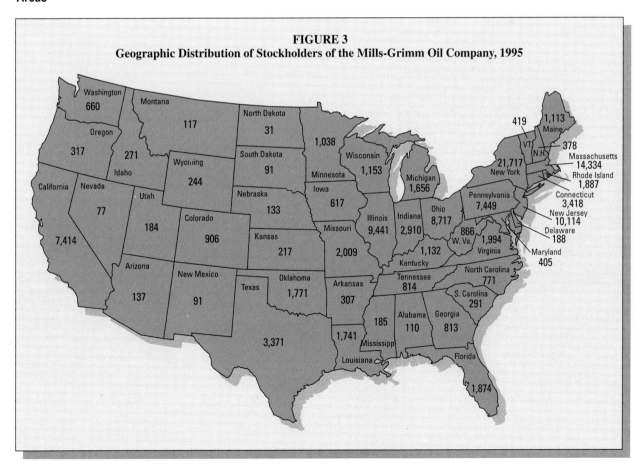

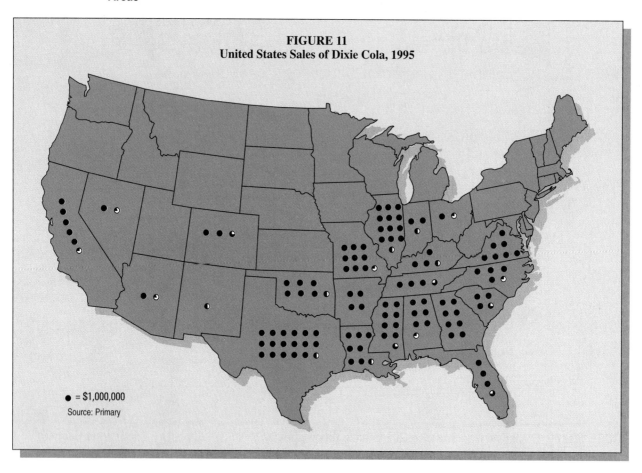

FIGURE 11
United States Sales of Dixie Cola, 1995

● = $1,000,000
Source: Primary

Combination Charts

• Sometimes a combination of chart types is effective.

Combination charts often serve readers extremely well by allowing them to see relationships of different kinds of data. The example shown in Figure 13–20 shows the reader the price of stock over time (the trend) as well as the volume of sales over time (comparisons). It allows the reader to detect whether the change in volume affects the price of the stock. This kind of information would be difficult to get from raw data.

Other Graphics

• Other graphics available to you are diagrams, drawings, and photographs—even cartoons.

The types of graphics discussed thus far are the ones most commonly used. Other types also may be helpful. *Photographs* may serve a useful communication purpose. *Diagrams* (see Figure 13–21), and drawings (see Figure 13–22) may help simplify a complicated explanation or description. *Icons* are another useful type of graphic. You can create new icons and use them consistently, or you can draw from an existing body of icons with easily recognized meanings ⬡ . Even carefully selected *cartoons* can be used effectively. Soon *video clips* and *animation* may become common graphics used in electronic documents. For all practical purposes, any graphic is acceptable as long as it helps communicate the true story. The possibilities are almost unlimited.

FIGURE 13–19   A Pictogram

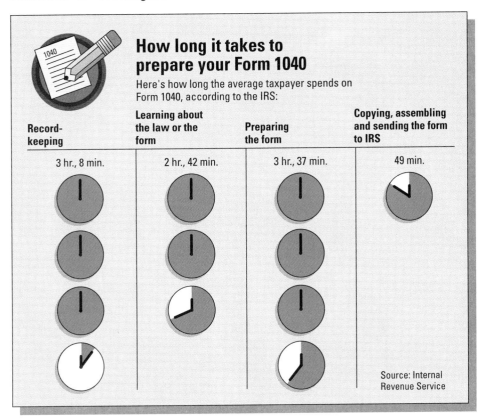

How long it takes to prepare your Form 1040

Here's how long the average taxpayer spends on Form 1040, according to the IRS:

Record-keeping	Learning about the law or the form	Preparing the form	Copying, assembling and sending the form to IRS
3 hr., 8 min.	2 hr., 42 min.	3 hr., 37 min.	49 min.

Source: Internal Revenue Service

FIGURE 13–20   A Combination Chart (Line, Variance, Bar)

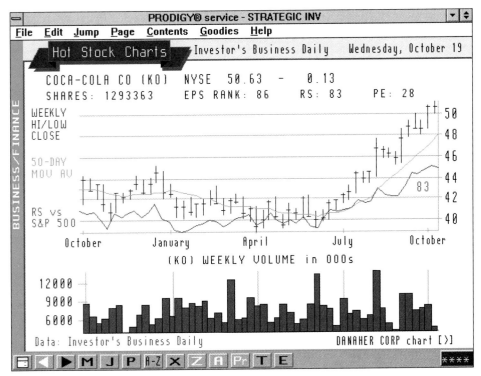

FIGURE 13–21   Illustration of a Diagram Tree

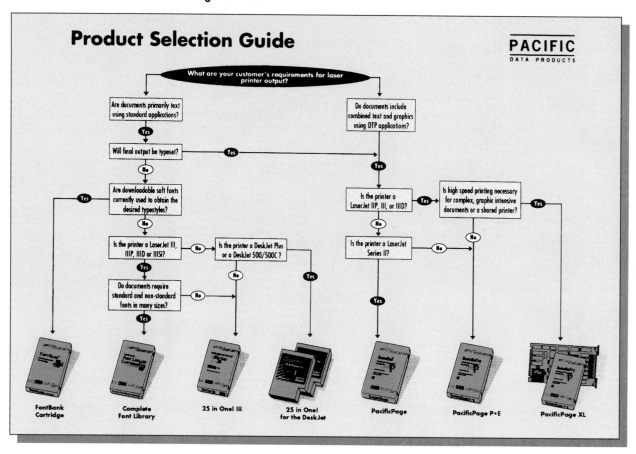

FIGURE 13–22   Illustration of a Drawing

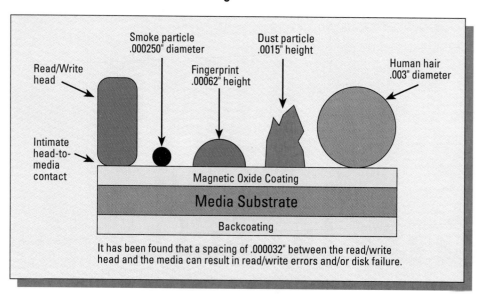

FIGURE 13–23 A Report Page Enhanced by Color Graphics

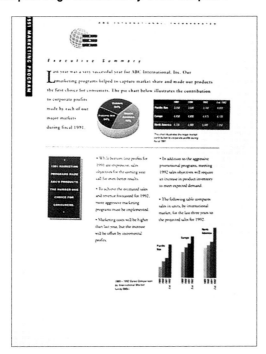

· ·

USING COMPUTER GRAPHICS

If you have access to the appropriate computer, printer, and software, you can use them to prepare graphics quickly and easily. Unlike the earlier versions, today's computer graphics software programs are simple and easy to use. With some of them, you need only choose the form of graph you want and then, using simple English instructions, supply the information the program requests. For example, when using one popular program to construct a bar chart, you simply respond "Bar" to the initial request for chart type. Then you supply plain English answers to a series of questions covering number of bars, names of bars, values of bars, and the like. As you supply the answers, the results appear on the screen. After producing the bar chart on the screen, you can manipulate its design until it meets your ideal requirements. When you are satisfied with the design you see on the screen, you print the chart in black and white or in color, depending on your equipment.

- Easy-to-use computer graphics are available.

Because computer graphics are easy to make and can be exciting and colorful, you may be tempted to overuse them. Keep in mind that the one requirement for including a graphic in a report is usefulness in communicating the report message. Too many charts can clutter the report and cause confusion.

- But do not overuse them.

Also keep in mind that clarity is a major requirement of graphics and that even computer-generated graphics can be unclear. The possibilities for changing and enhancing graphics can lead to interesting, beautiful, exciting, but confusing results. Thus, the purpose of graphics—to communicate instantly clear messages—is defeated. Even though the software package will do much of the planning and thinking for you, you should take care to follow the guidelines presented in this chapter as you construct graphics by computer.

- Make sure the graphics you use help to communicate.

Currently available software packages are capable of producing all the common forms of graphics, and more.

SUMMARY ▶ by Chapter Objectives

1 Determine which parts of your report should be communicated by graphics and where in the report the graphics should appear.

1. As graphics are a part of the communication in a report, you should plan for them.
   - But remember that they supplement the writing; they do not replace it.
   - Use them wherever they help communicate the report information.
   - Place them near the text part they illustrate.
   - Invite the readers to look at them at the appropriate place.
   - Place in the appendix those that you do not discuss in the text.

2 Explain the general mechanics of constructing graphics—size, layout, type, rules and borders, color and cross-hatching, clip art, numbering, titles, title placement, and footnotes and acknowledgments.

2. Construct each graphic carefully, following these general instructions:
   - Give each the size and arrangement its contents justify.
   - Choose a readable type.
   - Use rules, borders, and color when they help.
   - Use clip art appropriately.
   - Number the graphics consecutively by type.
   - Construct titles for them using the five Ws (*who, what, where, when, why*) as a checklist.
   - Use footnotes and acknowledgments when needed, placing them below the graphic.

3 Construct textual graphics such as tables, in-text displays, and flow and process charts.

3. Construct tables to display the larger groups of data.
   - Use general-purpose tables for information that is broad in scope.
   - Use special-purpose tables for information that is specific in scope.
   - See Figure 13–1 for the details of table construction.
   - Use in-text displays for less formal presentations.
     —You can do this as leaderwork.
     —You can do it as text tabulations or you can do it as bullet lists.
   - Use flow and process charts to show activity sequences.

4 Construct and use visual graphics such as bar charts, pie charts, line charts, pictograms, and combination charts.

4. In selecting a graphic, consider these primary uses of each:
   - *Simple bar chart*—shows quantity changes over time or over geographic distances.
   - *Multiple bar chart*—shows two or three kinds of quantities on one chart.

- *Bilateral bar chart*—shows plus and minus differences and is especially good for showing percentage changes.
- *Stacked (subdivided) bar chart*—used to compare differences in the division of wholes.
- *Pie chart*—used to show how wholes are divided.
- *Line chart*—useful in showing changes over time. Variations include surface charts, variance charts, and scatter diagrams.
- *Statistical map*—shows quantitative differences by geographic areas.
- *Pictogram*—shows quantitative differences in picture form.

For instructions on preparing each, review the text illustrations.

Apply other graphics to serve special needs:
- photographs
- diagrams and drawings
- icons
- cartoons
- video clips and animation

1. For the past 20 years, Professor Kupenheimer has required that his students include five graphics in the long, formal report he requires them to prepare. Evaluate this requirement.

2. Because it was easier to do, a report writer prepared each of his graphics on a full page. Some of these graphics were extremely complex; some were very simple. Comment on this policy.

3. "I have placed every chart near the place I write about it. The reader can see the chart without any *additional* help from me. It just doesn't make sense to direct the reader's attention to the charts with words." Evaluate this comment.

4. A report has five maps, four tables, one chart, one dia-

gram, and one photograph. How would you number these graphics?

5. How would you number these graphics in a report: seven tables, six charts, nine maps?

6. Discuss the logic of showing scale breaks in a chart.

7. Discuss the dangers of using illogical proportions in constructing a chart grid.

8. Discuss the techniques that may be used to show quantitative differences by area on a statistical map.

9. Select data that are ideally suited for presentation in a pictogram. Explain why use of a pictogram is good for this case.

10. Discuss the dangers of using pictograms.

1. Construct a complete, concise title for a bar chart showing annual attendance at home football (or basketball, hockey) games at your school from 1985 to the present.

2. The table prepared in Question 1 requires an explanation for the years 1990 to the present. In each of those years, one extra home game was played. Explain how you would provide the necessary explanation.

3. For each of the areas of information described below, which form of graphic would you use? Explain your decision.

   a. Record of annual sales for the Kenyon Company for the past 20 years.

   b. Comparison of Kenyon Company sales, by product, for this year and last year.

   c. Monthly production of the automobile industry in units.

   d. Breakdown of how the average middle-income family in your state (or province) disposes of its income dollar.

   e. How middle-income families spend their income dollar as compared with how low-income families spend their income dollar.

   f. Comparison of sales for the past two years for each of the B&B Company's 14 sales districts. The districts cover all 50 states, Canada, and Puerto Rico.

   g. National production of automobiles from 1930 to present, broken down by manufacturer.

4. For each of the following sets of facts, (*a*) determine the graphic (or graphics) that would be best, (*b*) defend your choice, and (*c*) construct the graphic.

   a. Average (mean) amount of life insurance owned by Fidelity Life Insurance Company policyholders. Classification is by annual income.

Income	Average Life Insurance
Under $10,000	$ 5,245
$10,000–14,999	14,460
$15,000–19,999	26,680
$20,000–24,999	39,875
$25,000–29,999	51,440
$30,000 and over	76,390

   b. Profits and losses for D and H Food Stores, by store, 1991–95, in dollars.

Year	Store Able City	Baker	Charleston	Total
1991	13,421	3,241	9,766	26,428
1992	12,911	−1,173	11,847	23,585
1993	13,843	−2,241	11,606	23,208
1994	12,673	2,865	13,551	29,089
1995	13,008	7,145	15,482	35,635

   c. Share of real estate tax payments by ward for Bigg City, 1990 and 1995, in thousands of dollars.

	1990	1995
Ward 1	17.1	21.3
Ward 2	10.2	31.8
Ward 3	19.5	21.1
Ward 4	7.8	18.2
City total	54.6	92.4

d. Percentage change in sales by employee, 1994–1995, District IV, Abbott, Inc.

Employee	Percentage Change
Joan Abraham	+ 7.3
Helen Calmes	+ 2.1
Edward Sanchez	− 7.5
Clifton Nevers	+41.6
Wilson Platt	+ 7.4
Clara Ruiz	+11.5
David Schlimmer	− 4.8
Phil Wirks	− 3.6

5. The basic blood types are O, A, B, and AB. These can be either positive or negative. With some basic research, determine what percentage of each type people in the United States have. Choose an appropriate graph type and create it to convey the data.

6. Through your research, find the approximate milligrams of caffeine in the following items and create an appropriate graphic to illustrate your findings.
   5-oz. cup of coffee (drip brewed)
   7-oz. glass of iced tea
   6-oz. glass of soda with caffeine
   1-oz. dark chocolate, semi-sweet

7. Choose five or six outdoor summer sport activities. In a graphic identify the activity and whether it affects cardiovascular, arms, legs, back, or abdominals. You can assume these activities can affect more than one fitness zone.

OTHER FORMS
OF BUSINESS
COMMUNICATION

14

Informal Oral Communication

Upon completing this chapter, you will be able to understand and use good speaking and listening techniques, conduct interviews, lead and participate in meetings, communicate by telephone, and dictate messages. To reach this goal, you should be able to

1 Discuss talking and its key elements.

2 Explain the listening problem and how to solve it.

3 Describe the nature and role of nonverbal communication.

4 Practice good interviewing and listening techniques.

5 Discuss the techniques for conducting and participating in meetings.

6 Describe good telephone and voice mail techniques.

7 Dictate letters and reports in an organized and effective manner.

▶ to Informal Oral Communication on the Job

Your job as assistant director in the Public Relations Department, Mastadon Chemicals, Inc., seems somewhat different from what you expected. It makes full use of your specialized college training, as you expected; but it also involves duties for which you did not train because you did not expect them. Most of these duties seem to involve some form of oral communication. In fact, you probably spend more of your work time in talking and listening than in any other activity.

To illustrate, take today's activities. Early this morning, your boss asked you to interview a prospective employee. After that, you conducted a meeting of the special committee to plan the department's annual picnic. As chairperson, you ran the meeting. It was a disaster, you felt—everybody talking at once, interrupting, arguing. It was a wonder that the committee made any progress. It seemed that everybody wanted to talk but nobody wanted to listen.

In the afternoon, you had other job duties involving oral communication. After you returned from lunch, you must have had a telephone conversation every 20 minutes or so. You felt comfortable with most of these calls, but you thought some of the callers needed a lesson or two in telephone etiquette. Also, you dictated a few letters between telephone calls.

You most certainly do a lot of talking (and listening) on your job, as do most of the people at Mastadon (and just about everywhere else). Oral communication is a vital part of your work. Perhaps you can become better at it by studying the following review of oral communication techniques. ■

As you know, your work will involve oral as well as written communication. The written communication will probably give you more problems, but the oral communication will take up more of your time. In fact, you are likely to spend more time in oral communication than in any other work activity.

- You will spend more time talking than writing in business.

Much of the oral communication that goes on in business is the informal, person-to-person communication that occurs whenever people get together. Obviously, we all have experience with this form of communication, and most of us do it reasonably well. But all of us can improve our informal speaking and listening with practice.

- Most of your oral communication will be informal.

In addition to informal talking and listening, various kinds of other more formal oral communication take place in business. Sometimes businesspeople interview job applicants, departing workers, and workers being evaluated. Sometimes they conduct and participate in committee meetings, conferences, and group discussions. Often they call one another on the telephone. Even their letters and reports are usually begun orally as spoken dictation. And frequently, they are called upon to make formal presentations—speeches, lectures, oral reports, and the like. All of these kinds of oral communication are a part of the work that businesspeople do.

- But some of it will be formal, as in interviews, meetings, telephone calls, dictation, speeches, and oral reports.

This and the following chapter cover these kinds of oral communication. This chapter reviews the somewhat less formal kinds: informal talking, listening, conducting interviews, participating in meetings, talking by telephone, and dictating. The following chapter presents the two most formal kinds: public speaking and oral reporting. Together, the two chapters should give you an understanding of the types of oral communication situations you will encounter in business.

- This and the following chapter cover these types of oral communication.

INFORMAL TALKING

As indicated previously, most of us do a reasonably good job of informal talking. In fact, we do such a good job that we often take talking for granted, and we overlook the possibility for improving our talking ability. To improve our talking, we need to be aware of its nature and qualities. As we become aware of these features, we can then improve our informal talking efforts. And when we improve them, other types of talk-

- Most people talk reasonably well. But all of us can improve if we know the nature of talking and its qualities.

ing (interviewing, telephoning, and such) will improve as well. The following paragraphs review the basics of talking.

Definition of Talking

• Think about having no words to speak. If you try to express yourself, you probably become frustrated.

Imagine for a few moments what it would be like to have no words to express your ideas. Trying as hard as you can, you have no words to utter to express the meanings in your mind. All that you have to express your thoughts are grunts, groans, and other such utterances. Of course, you have various nonverbal symbols such as pointing your fingers, nodding your head, and the like. As you find yourself increasingly in need of expressing yourself, you probably become more and more emotional and frustrated— to the point of exaggerating the nonverbal symbols and experiencing many physical symptoms such as redness of the face, heavy breathing, and an increased heartbeat.

• Thus, we learn words to control ourselves and the world about us.

More than likely, the foregoing analogy describes the way you learned to talk. As a dependent child, you expressed yourself with screams, cries, and nonverbal symbols. But as you matured, you learned words, and the words greatly reduced the frustrations of the past. They enabled you to communicate with others more exactly. They enabled you to relate better to the world about you and to some extent to control it.

• Talking, then, is the oral expression of knowledge, viewpoints, and emotions through words.

The foregoing review of how you learned to talk gives us the basis for defining talking. From it we can derive this definition: *talking* is the oral expression of knowledge, viewpoints, and emotions through words. Also, from this review we can see that talking replaces many of the body movements we made before we were able to talk. And as we will see, it is supplemented by various body movements we have acquired as we learned to talk—gestures, facial expressions, body positions, and such.

• Think about the best and worst speakers you can imagine. This contrast should give you the qualities of good talking—voice quality, speaking style, word choice, adaptation.

As a first step in improving your talking ability, think for a moment about the qualities you like in a good talker—one whom you would enjoy talking with in ordinary conversation. Then think about the opposite—the worst conversationalist you can imagine. If you will get these two images in mind, you will have a good picture of the characteristics of good talking. Probably this mental picture includes good voice quality, excellence in talking style, accuracy of word choice, and adaptation. As these elements control the overall quality of oral expression, we will now review them.

Elements of Good Talking

• Qualities of good talking help you communicate your message better.

Although the four qualities of good talking are important individually, you should remember that it is their purpose—to communicate better—that is of primary significance. Put differently, you want each of the following four qualities to help you deliver your message better to your listener. It is with that point in mind that we examine them.

• (1) Good voice quality means varying the pitch, changing delivery speed, and alternating volume.

Voice Quality.   It should be obvious that a good voice is central to good talking. But this obvious point needs underscoring as we concentrate on developing qualities of effective talking. Good voice quality means vocal expressions that vary in pitch, change in delivery speed, and alternate in volume. Because we will say more about these three qualities in our discussion of formal speeches in Chapter 15, we need only to recognize their importance to effective informal talking at this point.

• Imagine an unpleasant voice. It probably is monotone, spoken at the same speed, constant in volume.

To illustrate their importance, imagine meeting someone who has an unpleasant voice. Probably, this person talks in a monotone, a quality of voice that needs pitch variety. Moreover, the person delivers words at the same rate of speed. And the volume of speaking remains constant throughout. After several minutes of hearing such a voice, you probably will conclude that the person is unenthusiastic or disinterested.

• To correct unpleasant voice quality, do two things: (a) be aware of the unpleasantness and (b) practice.

To correct such unpleasant qualities, we must first be aware of them. We must remember that all of us need to improve our voice quality from time to time. After we become aware of the need to change, we can then practice, which is the second step to correcting unpleasant voice quality. The story is told about a visitor to New York City who wanted to attend a concert at Carnegie Hall. Not knowing the local subway

Good talking is the foundation for other types of discourse—interviewing, conducting meetings, telephoning, etc. You should develop good voice quality, perfect effective style, and select words that fit the mind of a listener.

system, she asked a native New Yorker on the street, "How do I get to Carnegie Hall?" The New Yorker's response: "Practice, lady, practice!"

That advice is also sound for those wanting to improve voice quality. Concentrate on words and their pronunciation. Note the range of your voice in speaking. And vary the volume from loud to soft. If you will practice these and other variations, you will find that you can indeed improve your voice quality. Like good actors, good speakers can select from a number of alternatives in their attempts to express orally their thoughts and feelings to others.

• Especially practice word pronunciation, voice range, and volume.

Talking Style.   Talking style refers to how the three parts of voice quality—pitch, speed, and volume—blend together. But it also means more. It means how well talkers project their personalities through their oral expression. As such, style refers to a set of behaviors of an individual that give uniqueness to that person.

• (2) Talking style means pitch, speed, and volume—plus personality.

When we refer to a talker as one who has a sharp, smooth, or polished style, we usually mean one whose pitch, volume, and speed are consistent with certain attitudes we infer—attitudes such as sincerity, kindness, understanding, etc. When these attitudes produce certain behaviors and blend with voice quality, we can say that a talker has a style. While it is beyond our purpose to analyze style in detail, we must note that it does exist; and it is a vital part of talking. But remember that as we noted about writing style, *what* you speak is more important than *how* you speak it. The best that a listener can say after hearing you speak is "These are interesting ideas" rather than "You have a beautiful voice."

• Good style implies that voice quality is consistent with positive attitudes.

Word Choice and Vocabulary. Still another quality of effective talking is word choice. By selecting the right word or words that create clear pictures in a listener's mind, good talkers are able to communicate better and more quickly. They do so because they have more choices available to them. Thus, vocabulary is a critical factor for good talking. The larger the vocabulary, the more selections that are available for creating pictures in the listener's mind.

As discussed in Chapter 2, there are a number of suggestions to use in choosing words that do a good job of communicating. These suggestions are just as important to talking as they are to writing. Because we have already covered them, we will not repeat them here. Nonetheless, they are important. In fact, using them in speaking requires quicker judgment because of the shorter time involved in selecting words. This shorter time cycle should underscore again the need to practice in selecting different words for different effects.

Central Role of Adaptation. Adaptation, a fourth quality of good talking, in effect sums up the previous three qualities of voice quality, style, and word choice. As discussed in Chapter 2, adaptation means fitting a message to a specific receiver. In our speaking efforts, all that we do is for adaptation. That is, we select the right words and use the right voice pitch, speed, volume, and style for the one intended listener.

To illustrate, assume that you must report to your boss about a specific project you are working on. Your boss has a master's degree and 15 years of experience with your organization. In speaking to her, you choose certain words to fit her education and experience; and you deliver them with a style and quality to accomplish the purpose you seek. But contrast that situation with another: that of instructing your subordinates. These subordinates have a high school education and less than one year on the job. The words, style, and voice quality of your oral direction probably would be quite different. Yet both messages would fit the minds of the listeners.

. . . .
LISTENING

Up to this point, our review of oral communication has been about sending information (talking). Certainly, this is an area in which businesspeople need help. But evidence shows that the receiving side (listening) causes more problems.

The Importance of Listening

Listening is important to us in our study of communication for at least three reasons. Foremost is the fact that listening is the first of the verbal skills we acquire as we develop the ability to use language, followed in sequence by speaking, reading, and writing. Second, listening accounts for about 45 percent of our verbal communication time—more than any other skill area—according to most authorities. Third, listening is an important area to business. When workers are asked what they like about supervisors, "They listen to me!" ranks atop or near the top of responses. But listening well requires patience and hard work as we will see. Too, it involves more than just hearing.

The Nature of Listening

When listening is mentioned, we think primarily of the act of sensing sounds. In human communication, of course, the sounds are mainly spoken words. Viewed from a communication standpoint, however, the listening process involves the additional activities of filtering and remembering.

• (3) Word choice allows speakers to communicate better and more quickly by giving more selections.

• The suggestions for word choice in Chapter 2 apply to speaking as well. Use them, and practice.

• (4) Adaptation is fitting a message to a specific listener.

• For example, your message would differ for people with great differences in education and experience.

• Poor listening is a major cause of miscommunication.

• Listening is important—in language skill development, in time spent communicating, and in business relations.

• Listening involves sensing, filtering, and remembering.

Sensing.   How well we sense the words spoken around us is determined by two factors. One factor is our ability to sense sounds—how well our ears can pick them up. As you know, we do not all hear equally well, although mechanical devices (hearing aids) can reduce our differences in this respect.

The other factor is our attentiveness to listening. More specifically, this is our mental concentration—our will to listen. As was noted in Chapter 1, our mental concentration on the communication symbols that our senses can detect varies from moment to moment. It can range from almost totally blocking out those symbols to concentrating on them very intensely. From your own experience, you can recall moments when you were oblivious to the words spoken around you and moments when you listened with all the intensity you could muster. Most of the time, your listening fell somewhere between these extremes.

Filtering.   From your study of the communication process in Chapter 1, you know that the filtering process enables you to give meanings to the symbols you sense. In this process, the contents of your mind serve as a sort of filter through which you give meaning to incoming messages. This filter is formed by the unique contents of your mind—your knowledge, emotions, beliefs, biases, experiences, expectations, and such. Thus, you sometimes give messages meanings different from the meanings that others give them.

Remembering.   Remembering what we hear is the third activity involved in listening. Unfortunately, we retain little of what we hear. We remember many of the comments we hear in casual conversation for only a short time—perhaps for only a few minutes or hours. Some we forget almost as we hear them. According to authorities, we even quickly forget most of the message in formal oral communications (such as speeches), remembering only a fourth after two days.

Improving Your Listening Ability

Improving your listening is largely a matter of mental conditioning—of concentrating on the activity of sensing. You have to want to improve it, for listening is a willful act. If you are like most of us, you are often tempted not to listen or you just find it easier not to listen. We human beings tend to avoid work; and listening may be work.

After you have decided that you want to listen better, you must make an effort to pay attention. How you do this will depend on your mental makeup, for the effort requires disciplining the mind. You must force yourself to be alert, to pay attention to the words spoken.

In addition to working on the improvement of your sensing, you should work on the accuracy of your filtering. To do this, you will need to think in terms of what words mean to the speakers who use them rather than what the dictionary says they mean or what they mean in your mind. You must try to think as the speaker thinks—judging the speaker's words by the speaker's knowledge, experiences, viewpoints, and such. Like improving your sensing, improving your filtering requires conscious effort.

One way to be more conscious and deliberate in your filtering effort is to realize that you can think (filter) much faster than others can talk—about three to four times as fast. Thus, you should caution yourself about jumping to quick conclusions, interrupting, rehearsing what you are going to say when the other person quits talking, and other nonproductive activity. Instead, you should use the extra mental time to determine the true meaning that the speaker intends.

For example, you should realize that 90 percent or more of the meaning we receive from a speaker comes from nonword symbols—gestures, the speed/pitch/volume of the voice, facial expressions, and such. As you sense the words of a speaker, you should sense the nonword symbols also. You should be aware that what speakers com-

- How well we sense spoken words is determined by (1) our ability to sense sounds, and

- (2) our attentiveness.

- Filtering is the process of giving symbols meanings through the unique contents of each person's mind.

- Remembering what we hear is a part of listening.

- To improve your listening, you must want to improve it.

- Be alert. Force yourself to pay attention.

- Concentrate on improving your mental filtering.

- Think from the speaker's viewpoint.

- Use your faster filtering time in listening to determine the total meaning the speaker is sending.

- Listen actively by focusing on word and nonword symbols.

Listening Error in a Chain of Communication

Colonel to the executive officer: "As the general feels the soldiers are unaware of the danger of drinking impure water, he wishes to explain the matter to them. Have all personnel fall out in fatigues at 1400 hours in the battalion area, where the general will address them. In the event of rain, assemble them in the theater."

Executive officer to company commander: "By order of the colonel, tomorrow at 1400 hours all personnel will fall out in fatigues in the battalion area if it rains to march to the theater. There the general will talk about their unawareness of the dangers of drinking."

Company commander to lieutenant: "By order of the colonel, in fatigues the personnel will assemble at the theater at 1400 hours. The general will appear if it rains to talk about the dangers of the unawareness of drinking."

Lieutenant to sergeant: "Tomorrow at 1400 hours the troops will assemble at the theater to hear the general talk about unawareness of drinking dangerously."

Sergeant to the enlisted personnel: "Tomorrow at 1400 hours the drunken general will be at the theater in his underwear talking dangerously. We have to go and hear him."

municate mirrors the meaning in their minds. So you need to sense and observe the word and nonword symbols being sent. If you focus on the total message the speaker conveys, you are practicing "active" listening; that is, you are mentally active in attempting to determine the meaning conveyed in a message.

- Consciously try to remember.

Remembering what you hear also requires conscious effort. Certainly, there are limits to what the mind can retain; but authorities agree that few of us come close to them. By taking care to hear what is said and by working to make your filtering process give you more accurate meanings to the words you hear, you add strength to the messages you receive. The result should be improved retention.

- In addition, follow these practical guidelines (summarized in italics).

In addition to the foregoing advice, various practical steps may prove helpful. Assembled in a classic document titled "The Ten Commandments of Listening,"[1] the following list summarizes the most useful of them:

1. *Stop talking.* Unfortunately, most of us prefer talking to listening. Even when we are not talking, we are inclined to concentrate on what to say next rather than on listening to others. So you must stop talking before you can listen.

2. *Put the talker at ease.* If you make the talker feel at ease, he or she will do a better job of talking. Then you will have better input to work with.

3. *Show the talker you want to listen.* If you can convince the talker that you are listening to understand rather than oppose, you will help create a climate for information exchange. You should look and act interested. Doing things like reading, looking at your watch, and looking away distracts the talker.

4. *Remove distractions.* The things you do can also distract the talker. So don't doodle, tap with your pencil, shuffle papers, or the like.

5. *Empathize with the talker.* If you place yourself in the talker's position and look at things from the talker's point of view, you will help create a climate of understanding that can result in a true exchange of information.

6. *Be patient.* You will need to allow the talker plenty of time. Remember that not

---

[1] To some anonymous author goes a debt of gratitude for these classic and often quoted comments about listening.

Some Sound Advice on Listening

Living in a competitive culture, most of us are most of the time chiefly concerned with getting our own views across, and we tend to find other people's speeches a tedious interruption of the flow of our own ideas. Hence, it is necessary to emphasize that listening does not mean simply maintaining a polite silence while you are rehearsing in your mind the speech you are going to make the next time you can grab a conversational opening. Nor does listening mean waiting alertly for the flaws in the other fellow's arguments so that later you can mow him down. Listening means trying to see the problem the way the speaker sees it—which means not sympathy, which is *feeling* for him, but empathy, which is *experiencing* with him. Listening requires entering actively and imaginatively into the other fellow's situation and trying to understand a frame of reference different from your own. This is not always an easy task.

S. I. Hayakawa

everyone can get to the point as quickly and clearly as you. And do not interrupt. Interruptions are barriers to the exchange of information.

7. *Hold your temper.* From our knowledge of the workings of our minds, we know that anger impedes communication. Angry people build walls between each other. They harden their positions and block their minds to the words of others.

8. *Go easy on argument and criticism.* Argument and criticism tend to put the talker on the defensive. He or she then tends to "clam up" or get angry. Thus, even if you win the argument, you lose. Rarely does either party benefit from argument and criticism.

9. *Ask questions.* By frequently asking questions, you display an open mind and show that you are listening. And you assist the talker in developing his or her message and in improving the correctness of meaning.

10. *Stop talking!* The last commandment is to stop talking. It was also the first. All the other commandments depend on it.

From the preceding review it should be clear that to improve your listening ability, you must set your mind to the task. Poor listening habits are ingrained in our makeup. We can alter these habits only through conscious effort.

THE REINFORCING ROLE OF NONVERBAL COMMUNICATION

In either your role of speaker or listener in oral communication, you will need to be aware of the nonverbal—nonword—part of your communication. In both roles, nonverbal communication accounts for a larger part of the total message than do the words you send or receive. Usually, we use nonverbal communication to supplement and reinforce our words. Sometimes, nonverbal communication communicates by itself. Because it is so important to both sides of the oral communication equation, we will look at the nature of nonverbal communication and some types of it.

• Nonverbal communication accounts for more of a total message than words do.

Nature of Nonverbal Communication

Nonverbal or nonword communication means all communication that occurs without words. As you can see, the subject is a broad one. And because it is so broad,

• Nonverbal (nonword) communication means all communication without words. It is broad and imprecise.

FRANK & ERNEST reprinted by permission of NEA, Inc.

nonverbal communication is quite vague and imprecise. For instance, a frown on someone's forehead is sometimes interpreted to mean worry. But could it be that the person has a headache? Or is the person in deep thought? No doubt, there could be numerous meanings given to the facial expression.

• Cross-cultural aspects give many meanings to nonverbal communication.

The number of possible meanings is multiplied even more when we consider the cross-cultural side of communication. As noted in Chapter 17, culture teaches us about body positions, movements, and various factors that affect human relationships (intimacy, space, time, and such). Thus, the meanings we give to nonverbal symbols will vary depending on how our culture has conditioned us.

• Be sensitive to intended nonverbal meanings. Go beyond the obvious.

Because of these numerous meanings, you need to be sensitive to what others intend with nonverbal communication. And you need to make some allowance for error in the meanings you receive from nonverbal symbols. As a listener, you need to go beyond the obvious to determine what nonword symbols mean. As we have said about word symbols, you need to see what people intend with their nonverbal symbols as well. Perhaps one good way to grasp the intent of this suggestion is to look at the intended meanings you have for the nonverbal symbols you use.

• Realize that nonverbal symbols can have many meanings.

Think for a few moments about the smile on your face, a gesture, or such. What do you mean by it? What could it mean to others? Is it exactly as you intend? Could it be interpreted differently? Could someone from a different culture give a different meaning to it? Only if you look at nonverbal symbols through the prism of self-analysis and realize their multiple meaning potential can you get some idea of how they might be interpreted differently. And when you become aware of the many differences, you then can become sensitive to the meaning intended by the nonverbal communication.

In order to become sensitive to the myriad of nonverbal symbols, we will look at some types of nonverbal communication. Specifically, we will study three types of communication that occur without words.

Types of Nonverbal Communication

• We will look at three common types of nonverbal communication: (1) body language, (2) space, (3) time.

Although there are many ways to classify nonverbal communication, we will examine three of the more common types—body language, space, and time. These three types are especially important to our discussion of speaking and listening.

Body Language. Much of what we send to others without using words is sent through the physical movements of our bodies. When we wave our arms and fingers, wrinkle our foreheads, stand erect, smile, gaze at another, wear a coat and tie, etc., we convey certain meanings; and others convey meanings to us in return. In particular, the face and eyes, gestures, posture, and physical appearance reflect the inner workings of emotions in our bodies.

* Our bodies send nonword messages—through arms, fingers, expressions, posture, etc.

The face and eyes are by far the most important features of body language. We look to the face and eyes to determine much of the meaning behind body language and nonverbal communication. For example, happiness, surprise, fear, anger, and sadness usually require definite facial expressions and eye patterns. Thus, you should be aware of these two aspects of body language as you speak and listen to others.

* The face and eyes are the most important.

In addition, gestures are another way we send nonword messages through our body parts. *Gestures* are physical movements of our arms, legs, hands, torsos, and heads. Through the movement of each of these body parts, we can accent and reinforce our verbal messages. And we can observe how others punctuate their verbal efforts with gestures. For example, observe the hand movements of another person while he or she is talking. Consider whether this person is fluid or sporadic with such hand movements. As you observe these gestures, you will get a good picture of the internal emotional state of the person. Moreover, speaking and gestures appear to be linked. In general, the louder someone speaks, the greater the gestures used, and vice versa.

* Gestures (physical movements of the arms, legs, torso, and head) send nonword messages.

Another area of body language is physical appearance—our clothing, hair, and adornments (jewelry, cosmetics, and such). The appearance of our bodies indicates how our body movements are seen. Consider, for example, how you might perceive a speaker at a formal banquet dressed in faded blue jeans. No doubt, the speaker's gestures, facial features, posture, and such would be perceived in relation to attire. Accordingly, you want to make sure that your appearance fits the expectancies of the one situation. And you want to make sure that you know that appearance is an important part of the body messages that are sent and received in oral communication.

* Physical appearance—clothing, hair, jewelry, cosmetics, etc.—also communicates.

Space. Another type of nonverbal communication involves space and how it communicates meaning in speaking and listening. How we use space and what we do in certain spaces we create tell much about us. Thus, each of us has a space language just as we do a body language. And this space language is crafted by our culture.

* Space is another type of nonverbal language.

Authorities tell us that we create four different types of space: intimate (physical contact to 18 inches); personal (18 inches to 4 feet); social (4 to 12 feet); and public (12 feet to range of seeing and hearing). In each of these spaces, our communication behaviors differ and convey different meanings. For example, consider the volume of your voice when someone is 18 inches from you. Do you shout? Whisper? Now contrast the tone of your voice when someone is 12 feet away. Unquestionably, there is a difference, just because of the distance involved.

* Four types of space exist: (1) intimate, (2) personal, (3) social, and (4) public. Communication behavior differs in each.

Also, our behaviors in each type of space are learned from our cultures. Thus, you will need to be sensitive to the spaces of others—especially those from different cultures. As noted in Chapter 17, when people's attitudes toward space are different, their actions are likely to be misinterpreted.

* Communication behaviors are learned from cultures.

Time. A third type of nonverbal communication involves time. Just as there is a body and space language, there is also a time language. That is, how we give meaning to time communicates to others. To illustrate, think about how you manage your daily schedule. Do you arrive early for most appointments? Do you prioritize telephone calls? Do you prepare agendas for meetings? How you respond to time communicates to others. And, of course, others' use of time communicates to you. In terms of nonverbal communication, you should recognize that time orientations are not always the same—especially in the cross-cultural arena—but they do communicate. As such, they become parts of the messages we send to and receive from one another.

* Time is a third type of nonverbal communication.

INTERVIEWING PEOPLE

- Interviews are conducted in business for employment purposes, to get information, and to give information.

In your work in business, you may need to participate in a variety of types of interviews. Perhaps the best-known type is the employment interview discussed in Chapter 9. But there are others. Interviews are often involved in the periodic evaluations that some companies make of their workers. These interviews are primarily a means of communicating the evaluations. When workers leave a company, they may be interviewed to determine their reasons for leaving. Interviews are sometimes conducted to gather information on such matters as worker attitudes, working conditions, managerial effectiveness, and worker plans.

- Although interviewing is not a precise activity, the following guidelines will help you.

As interviewing is a form of personal communication, usually between two people, it is not a precise activity—that is, no hard-and-fast rules exist. Rather, interviewing is a flexible activity that requires the good judgment of the people involved. Nevertheless, well-established guidelines exist, and you should follow them. In the following pages they are presented from the side of both the interviewer and the interviewee.

Guidelines for the Interviewer

- Here are some guidelines for the interviewer:

As the interviewer is in charge, the success of the interview is in his or her hands. Thus, it is especially important that the interviewer know and follow these general guidelines.

- (1) plan (determine what information is needed),

Plan the Interview.   You conduct most interviews because you need information. So as a starting point you should determine your information needs. You can usually express these needs in a list of specific questions. You should make such a list and use it as the outline for the interview.

- (2) put the interviewee at ease (using your social skills),

Put the Interviewee at Ease.   The chances are that the interviewee will be nervous. As nervous people are not good subjects for interviewing, you should try to put the interviewee at ease. How you should do this varies with the person involved and with your social skills. You could, for example, begin with some friendly talk on a point of common interest. Or you could begin with comments or questions about the interviewee—hometown, sports interests, hobbies, and the like.

- (3) explain the purpose when it is not apparent,

Make the Purpose Clear.   The interviewee should know the purpose of the interview from the beginning. Of course, the interviewee sometimes knows the purpose from the nature of the interview, as in an employment interview. But if she or he does not know the purpose, you should explain it clearly and honestly.

- (4) allow the interviewee to do the talking.

Let the Interviewee Do Most of the Talking.   You can get the information you seek only when the interviewee talks. Thus, you should let the interviewee do most of the talking. You should talk only to guide the course of the interview—to carry the discussion through the specific questions you want to cover. As some interviewees are reluctant to talk, you will sometimes need to work to get them to talk. But you should never put words in their mouths.

- (5) guide the interview through the plan (ask questions and end answers),

Guide the Interview.   Even though the interviewee does most of the talking, your task is to guide the interview so as to obtain the needed information. That is, you follow the plan you set up in the beginning. You ask specific questions, and you end answers when you have the information you need. In guiding the interview, you will need to handle moments of silence. Brief periods of silence are all right, for additional information sometimes comes after them. But too much silence can be awkward for all concerned.

Employment interviews are the most widely recognized type. There are others—performance appraisals, exit interviews, and research situations. For interviews to be successful, both parties must plan for them.

Listen.   You should listen carefully to all that the interviewee says. The purpose of an interview is to get certain information—by listening. You will need to practice the techniques of good listening presented previously in this chapter. And you will need to be aware of the reinforcing role of nonverbal communication, too.

In addition to listening, you should give the appearance of listening. Your interviewees will be more relaxed and will talk more if they believe they have your undivided attention.

- (6) listen and make it apparent that you are listening,

Keep a Record.   As you conduct interviews to get information, you will need to make a record of the information. How you record the information may vary with the situation. When you need much detailed information, you may have to take notes during the interview. Because your writing may be disturbing to the interviewee, you should explain at the beginning of the interview why you must take notes. Even after explaining, you should write as quickly and briefly as possible.

When you can remember the information you seek, you need not write during the interview. But you should record that information soon after the interview is over. As you know, not many of us can remember such information for very long.

- (7) record information either during the interview or soon after, and

End the Interview.   As you are in charge of the interview, you should end it. If the situation justifies it, some friendly talk can follow the questioning. But you should avoid letting the conversation trail off to meaningless talk. One good way of ending interviews is to ask a finalizing question—one that tells the interviewee that the interview is over. This one does the job well: "Is there anything else you would like to tell me? If not, thanks for giving me your time."

- (8) end the interview, perhaps with a finalizing question.

Guidelines for the Interviewee

When you are the person being interviewed, you may have little control over the situation. Nevertheless, you can help make the interview successful. The following guidelines tell you how.

- Here are some guidelines for the interviewee:

Prepare for the Interview.   When you know the nature of the interview, prepare for it. Your preparation should consist mainly of thinking about the questions you are likely to be asked and formulating answers to them. It may also include gathering additional information. In a job interview, for example, you would be wise to learn what you can about the company—its history, its current activities, its plans. By showing your knowledge of the company during the interview, you can impress the interviewer with your interest in it. Even if you prepare diligently, you are not likely to cover all that will be asked. So be prepared for the unexpected.

Make an Appropriate Appearance.   What the interviewer sees is a part of the message that he or she receives. So you should do what you can to make an appropriate appearance. As what is appropriate varies with the situation, you should consider the situation. You will find that the conventional standards of neatness and dress are desirable in most cases. In addition, you will usually want your posture, facial expressions, and physical movements to give favorable impressions. You will especially want to avoid the appearance of nervousness.

Show Interest.   You can improve the impression you make in most interview situations by showing interest. How you should show interest varies with the occasion. But you always help your case by looking at the interviewer and by giving her or him your undivided attention.

Answer Correctly and Completely.   If the interview serves a good purpose, it deserves correct and complete answers. You should give them. Dishonest answers benefit no one.

Practice Courtesy.   You probably know very well the value of courtesy in business. You know that it is a major part of the impression you make in every human contact. The interview is no exception.

CONDUCTING AND PARTICIPATING IN MEETINGS

From time to time, you will participate in business meetings. They will range from extreme formality to extreme informality. On the formal end will be conferences and committee meetings. On the informal end will be discussions with groups of fellow workers. Whether formal or informal, the meetings will involve communication. In fact, the quality of the communication will determine their success. As noted in Chapter 10, collaborative report-writing groups should use the suggestions for conducting effective meetings.

   Your role in a meeting will be that of either leader or participant. Of course, the leader's role is the primary one, but good participation is also vital. The following paragraphs review the techniques of performing well in either role.

Techniques of Conducting Meetings

How you conduct a meeting depends on the formality of the occasion. Meetings of such groups as formal committees, boards of directors, and professional organizations usually follow generally accepted rules of conduct called *parliamentary procedure.* These very specific rules are too detailed for review here. When you are involved in a formal meeting, you would do well to study one of the many books covering parliamentary procedure before the meeting. In addition, you should know and practice the following techniques. For less formal meetings, you can depart somewhat from parliamentary procedure and those techniques. But you should keep in mind that every meeting has goals and that such departures should never hinder reaching them.

Electronic Meeting System (EMS): A Tool for Facilitating the Effectiveness of Meetings

Technology is making its way into meetings, assisting in numerous ways and changing the basic structure of meetings a bit. Electronic meeting systems (EMS) software runs on a network, linking people together electronically. When these meetings are held at the same time and place, the technology is usually used in combination with oral communication. Research has shown that various components of the EMS toolkit are appropriate for different tasks. When used appropriately, EMS software helps meeting participants improve their performance and accomplish their goals in half the time of the traditional meeting.

The tool also changes the nature of meetings. Most EMS software elicits equal participation, which prevents the meeting from being dominated by one person. Additionally, some systems allow participants to maintain anonymity, entering their ideas through the network without others knowing whose idea it is. This removes the status and much of the personal biases people hold. Many people claim this feature alone improves quality by allowing participants to respond to the idea, not to who said it or how it was delivered. Others attribute the increased quality to the ability of the system to force an agenda and keep people focused on the task at hand. These systems are also different from face-to-face meetings because everyone is communicating simultaneously through the system rather than taking turns, as required by the traditional meeting. All participants are active. EMS software also provides a record of all ideas entered. This prevents thoughts from being lost as they often are in traditional meetings.

Plan the Meeting.   A key to conducting a successful meeting is to plan it thoroughly. That is, you develop an agenda (a list of topics to be covered) by selecting the items that need to be covered to achieve the goals of the meeting. Then arrange these items in the most logical order. Items that explain or lead to other items should come before the items that they explain or lead to. After preparing the agenda, if the meeting is formal, make it available to those who will attend. For informal meetings, you may find keeping the agenda in mind satisfactory.

* In addition, you should do the following: (1) plan the items to be covered (the agenda),

Follow the Plan.   You should follow the plan for the meeting item by item. In most meetings the discussion tends to stray and new items tend to come up. As leader, you

* (2) follow the plan item by item,

should keep the discussion on track. If new items come up during the meeting, you can take them up at the end—or perhaps postpone them to a future meeting.

• (3) move the discussion along,

Move the Discussion Along.   As leader, you should control the agenda. When one item has been covered, bring up the next item. When the discussion moves off subject, move it back on subject. In general, do what is needed to proceed through the items efficiently. But you should not cut off discussion before all the important points have been made. Thus, you will have to use your good judgment. Your goal is to permit complete discussion on the one hand and to avoid repetition, excessive details, and useless comments on the other.

• (4) allow no one to talk too much,

Control Those Who Talk Too Much.   Keeping certain people from talking too much is likely to be one of your harder tasks. A few people usually tend to dominate the discussion. Your task as leader is to control them. Of course, you want the meeting to be democratic, so you will need to let these people talk as long as they are contributing to the goals of the meeting. However, when they begin to stray, duplicate, or bring in useless matter, you should step in. You can do this tactfully by asking for other viewpoints or by summarizing the discussion and moving on to the next topic.

• (5) encourage everybody to take part,

Encourage Participation from Those Who Talk Too Little.   Just as some people talk too much, some talk too little. In business groups, those who say little are often in positions lower than those of other group members. Your job as leader is to encourage these people to participate by asking them for their viewpoints and by showing respect for the comments they make, even though the comments may be illogical.

• (6) control time when time is limited, and

Control Time.   When your meeting time is limited, you need to determine in advance how much time will be needed to cover each item. Then, at the appropriate times, you should end discussion of the items. You may find it helpful to announce the time goals at the beginning of the meeting and to remind the group members of the time status during the meeting.

• (7) at appropriate places, summarize what the group has covered and concluded.

Summarize at Appropriate Places.   After a key item has been discussed, you should summarize what the group has covered and concluded. If a group decision is needed, the group's vote will be the conclusion. In any event, you should formally conclude each point and then move on to the next one. At the end of the meeting, you can summarize the progress made. You should also summarize whenever a review will help the group members understand their accomplishments. For some formal meetings, minutes kept by a secretary provide this summary.

Techniques for Participating in a Meeting

• As a participant in a meeting you should

From the preceding discussion of the techniques that a leader should use, you know something about the things that a participant should do. The following review emphasizes them for you.

• (1) follow the agenda,

Follow the Agenda.   When an agenda exists, you should follow it. Specifically, you should not bring up items not on the agenda or comment on such items if others bring them up. When there is no agenda, you should stay within the general limits of the goal for the meeting.

• (2) participate in the meeting,

Participate.   The purpose of meetings is to get the input of everybody concerned. Thus, you should participate. Your participation, however, should be meaningful. You should talk only when you have something to contribute, and you should talk whenever you have something to contribute.

Do Not Talk Too Much. As you participate in the meeting, be aware that other people are attending. You should speak up whenever you have something to say, but do not get carried away. Always respect the rights of others. As you speak, ask yourself whether what you are saying really contributes to the discussion.

• (3) avoid talking too much,

Cooperate. A meeting by its very nature requires cooperation from all the participants. So keep this in mind as you participate. Respect the leader and her or his efforts to make progress. Respect the other participants, and work with them in every practical way.

• (4) cooperate with all concerned, and

Be Courteous. Perhaps being courteous is a part of being cooperative. In any event, you should be courteous to the other group members. Specifically, you should respect their rights and opinions, and you should permit them to speak.

• (5) practice courtesy.

USING THE TELEPHONE

A discussion of business telephone techniques may appear trivial at first thought. After all, most of us have had long experience in using the telephone and may feel that we have little to learn about it. No doubt, some of us have excellent telephone skills. But you have only to call a few randomly selected businesses to learn that not all users of the telephone are proficient in its use. You will get some gruff, cold greetings, and you will be subjected to a variety of discourtesies. And you will find instances of inefficient use of time (which, of course, is costly). This is not to say that the problem is major, for most progressive businesses are aware of the need for good telephone habits and do something about it. But poor telephone techniques are found often enough to justify reviewing the subject of telephone use in a business communication textbook.

• Many businesspeople are discourteous and inefficient in telephone communication.

Need for Favorable Voice Quality

In reviewing good telephone techniques, keep in mind that a telephone conversation is a unique form of oral communication. Only voices are heard; the speakers are not seen. Impressions are received only from the words and the quality of the voices. Thus, when speaking by telephone, it is extremely important that you work to make your voice sound cheerful and friendly.

• Because only sound is involved, friendly voices are important.

One often-suggested way of improving your telephone voice is to talk as if you were face to face with the other person—even smiling and gesturing as you talk, if this helps you be more natural. In addition, you would do well to put into practice the suggestions given earlier in this chapter concerning the use of the voice in speaking (voice quality, variation in pitch, and speed). Perhaps the best instructional device for this problem is to record one of your telephone conversations. Then judge for yourself how you come across and what you need to do to improve.

• So talk as if you were in face-to-face conversation.

Techniques of Courtesy

If you have worked in business for any length of time, you have probably experienced most of the common telephone discourtesies. You probably know that most of them are not intended as discourtesies but result from ignorance or unconcern. The following review should help you avoid them.

• Be courteous.

The recommended procedure when you are calling is to introduce yourself immediately and then to ask for the person with whom you want to talk:

• When calling, immediately introduce yourself and ask for the person you want (or explain your purpose).

"This is Wanda Tidwell of Tioga Milling Company. May I speak with Mr. José Martinez?"

Cellular telephones allow people to communicate throughout the world instantly. To use telephones effectively, you need good voice quality, courtesy, effective procedures, and sound techniques.

If you are not certain with whom you should talk, explain the purpose of your call:

"This is Wanda Tidwell of Tioga Milling Company. We have a question about your service warranty. May I talk with the proper executive about it?"

• When receiving a call, identify your company or office; then offer assistance.

When a secretary or someone else who is screening calls answers the telephone, the recommended procedure is to first identify the company or office and then to make a cheerful offer of assistance:

"Rowan Insurance Company. May I help you?"
"Ms. Santo's office. May I help you?"

When a call goes directly into the office of the executive, the procedure is much the same, except that the executive identifies herself or himself:

"Bartosh Realty. Toby Bartosh speaking. May I help you?"

• Secretaries should avoid offending callers by asking misleading questions, by making misleading comments, or

When a secretary answers for an executive (the usual case), special care should be taken not to offend the caller. Following a question like "Who is calling?" by "I am sorry, but Mr. Gordon is not in" leaves the impression that Gordon may be in but does not want to talk with this particular caller. A better procedure would be to state directly "Mr. Gordon is not in right now. May I ask him to return your call?" Or perhaps "May I tell him who called?" or "Can someone else help you?" could be substituted for the latter sentence.

• by being inconsiderate in placing callers on hold. Let the callers choose, and check on the hold status continually.

Especially irritating to callers is being put on hold for unreasonable periods of time. If the person being called is on another line or involved in some other activity, it may be desirable to place the caller on hold. But the choice should be the caller's. If the

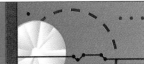
hold continues for a period longer than anticipated, the secretary should check back with the caller periodically, showing concern and offering assistance. Equally irritating is the practice of having a secretary place a call for an executive and then put the person called on hold until the executive is free to talk. While it may be efficient to use secretaries for such work, as a matter of courtesy the executive should be ready to talk the moment the call goes through.

Secretaries to busy executives often screen incoming calls. In doing so, they should courteously ask the purpose of the calls. The response might prompt the secretary to refer the caller to a more appropriate person in the company. It might also reveal that the executive has no interest in the subject of the call, in which case the secretary should courteously yet clearly explain this to the caller. If the executive is busy at the moment, the secretary should explain this and either suggest a more appropriate time for a call or promise a callback by the executive. But in no case should the secretary promise a callback that will not be made.

- Secretaries often screen calls. They should do this courteously and honestly.

Effective Telephone Procedures

At the beginning of a telephone conversation that you have initiated, it is good practice to state the purpose of the call. Then you should cover systematically all the points involved. For really important calls, you should plan your call, even to the point of making notes of the points to cover. Then you should follow your notes to make certain you cover them all.

- When calling, state your purpose early. Then cover your points systematically. Plan important calls.

Courteous procedure is much the same in a telephone conversation as in a face-to-face conversation. You listen when the other person is talking. You refrain from interrupting. You avoid dominating the conversation. And perhaps most important of all, you cover your message quickly, saving time (and money) for all concerned.

- Be considerate, listen, and do not dominate. Use time efficiently.

Effective Voice Mail Techniques

Sometimes when the person you are calling is not available, you will be able to leave a voice message in an electronic voice mailbox. Not only does this save you the time involved in calling back the person you are trying to reach, but it also allows you to leave a more detailed message than you might leave with a secretary. However, you need to be prepared for this to be sure your message is both complete and concise.

- Voice mail is becoming common in business.

You begin the message nearly the same way you would a telephone call. Be as courteous as you would on the telephone and speak as clearly and distinctly as you can. Tell the listener in a natural way your name and affiliation. Begin with an

- Use it much as you would any other telephone call,

overview of the message and continue with details. If you want the listener to take action, call for it at the end. If you want the listener to return your call, state that precisely, including when you can be reached. Slowly give the number where your call can be returned. Close with a brief goodwill message. For example, as a volunteer for your local symphony, you might leave this message in the voice mailbox of one of your sponsors:

• as in this example.

This is Linda Wingler from the Quad-City Symphony. I'm calling to remind you about the Summer Pops special concert for sponsors. The concert will be on Friday, June 25, at 7:30 P.M. It'll be held at Meersman Park on 34th Street and 24th Avenue in Moline. Fireworks will begin immediately after the concert. If you plan to attend, call the symphony office between 10:00 A.M. and 4:00 P.M. Monday through Friday for your tickets. You can reach us at 764-0017. We look forward to hearing from you.

DICTATING LETTERS AND REPORTS

• You will probably dictate most letters and some reports.

The odds are that you will dictate many of the letters you write in business. You may even dictate reports—especially the shorter, more informal ones. Developing good dictation skills offers many advantages. First, it is much faster than handwriting at around 15 words per minute or even keying at 80 words per minute. The average person speaks at around 160 words per minute. Second, if you use dictation equipment, you can dictate when you are ready. In some companies, you can even call in your dictation from remote locations and often at any time of the day or night. Finally, activated systems are currently being developed for personal computers. Also, some word processing packages already handle voice input. No doubt, these features will increase more quickly than we can imagine. In the future, you may have the option of dictating to your computer rather than keying. Thus, the following summary of the techniques of dictating should be useful to you.

Techniques of Dictating

• You should (1) get all the information you need, to avoid interruptions later;

Gather the Facts.   Your first logical step in dictating is to get all the information you need for the message. This step involves such activities as getting past correspondence from the files, consulting with other employees, and ascertaining company policy. Unless you get all the information you need, you will be unable to work without interruption.

• (2) plan the message (following procedures described in preceding chapters);

Plan the Message.   With the facts of the case before you, you next plan the message. You may prefer to do this step in your mind or to jot down a few notes or an outline. Whatever your preference, your goal in this step is to decide what your message will be and how you will present it. In this step you apply the procedures covered in our earlier review of letter and report writing.

• (3) dictate instructions, such as form, enclosures, inside address, and subject line;

Give Preliminary Information and Instructions.   Your first step in the actual process of dictating is to give the transcriptionist specific instructions. These include instructions about special handling, enclosures, form, and page layout. They also include all the necessary additional information about the message—such information as the mailing address, subject line, attention line, and salutation. When this information is easily available, you need only refer to the source (for example, "Get their address from their letter").

• (4) talk through the message,

Make the Words Flow.   Your next step is to talk through the message. Simple as this step appears, you are likely to have problems with it. Thinking out loud to a secretary or dictation equipment frightens most of us at first. The result is likely to be slow and awkward dictation.

Overcoming this problem requires self-discipline and practice. You should force yourself to concentrate and to make the words flow. Your goal should be to get the words out—to talk through the message. You need not be concerned with producing polished work on the first effort. You will probably need to revise, perhaps many times. After you have forced your way through enough messages, your need to revise will decrease and the speed and quality of your dictation will improve.

- forcing the words to flow if necessary (you can revise later);

Speak in a Strong, Clear Voice. As your dictation must be heard, you should dictate in a strong, clear voice. Speak at a speed slow enough to clearly separate the words. Words that do not stand out clearly can cause delays in work as well as errors in the message. Be especially careful when using dictation equipment, for it sometimes does not reproduce voices well.

- (5) speak so that the transcriptionist can understand each word;

Give Paragraphing, Punctuation, and Other Mechanics as Needed. How much of the paragraphing, spelling, punctuation, and other mechanics you should include in your dictation depends on your transcriptionist's ability. You may leave these matters to a transcriptionist who is competent in writing correctness and form. On most occasions, however, it would be wise to dictate most such information. Your dictation might well sound like this: "Dear Ms. Mott *colon paragraph* On Friday *comma* November 12 *comma* your order for 18 cases Bug-Nix *comma* 12 *hyphen* ounce packages *comma* should reach your loading docks *period*." (The instructions are indicated by italics.) It is also a good idea to spell out difficult, confusing, and unusual words such as *cyberpunk, suite* instead of *sweet,* and *Browne* instead of *Brown.*

- (6) give as much instruction on paragraphing, punctuation, and mechanics as is needed, and

Avoid Asides. Asides (side comments not intended to be a part of the message) should be avoided. They tend to confuse the transcriptionist, who must determine which words are part of the message and which are not. As proof, imagine the transcriptionist's difficulty in handling the following dictation (asides in italics):

- (7) avoid asides (side comments).

Dear Mr. Dobbs: *Well, let's see. How about this?* The attached check for $19.45 . . . *Is that the right figure? . . .* is our way of showing you that your good faith in us is appreciated. *That should make him happy.* Our satisfaction-or-money-back policy means much to us.

Read Back Intelligently. Although you should try to talk through the message without interruption, you will sometimes need to stop and get a read-back of what you have dictated. But do this only when necessary. More than likely, the need for a read-back results from confused thinking. When you are learning to dictate, however, some confused thinking is normal. Until you gain experience, you may profit from read-backs. You will find a read-back especially helpful at the end of the message to give you a check on the overall effect of your words.

- Read back when this helps you.

Letter Dictation Illustrated

Many of the foregoing techniques are illustrated in the following example of the dictation of a routine letter. This example shows all the dictator's words, with instructions and asides in italics. Note that the dictator does not give some of the more obvious punctuation (such as a colon after the salutation). Also note that the dictation gives unusual spelling.

- Here is an illustration of the dictation of a letter.

Let's acknowledge the Key Grocery Company order next. Get the address from the order. It's No. 9. Dear Mr. Key: Three crates of orchard *hyphen* fresh Texacates should be in your store sometime Wednesday morning as they were shipped today by Greene *that's G-R-E-E-N-E* Motor Freight *period.* As you requested in your August 29 order *comma* the $61.60 *parenthesis* Invoice 14721 *parenthesis* was credited to your account *period. Paragraph* Your customers will go for these large, tasty avocados *comma* I am sure *period.* They are the best we have handled in months *period. Paragraph* Thanks *comma* Mr. Key *comma* for another opportunity to serve you *period.* Sincerely *Type it for my signature.*

Your ability to communicate aloud is one of the most important factors contributing to your success on the job. Your attention to the skills discussed in this chapter and your continual efforts to get a bit better at each one will be worth the effort.

···

SUMMARY ▶ by Chapter Objectives

1 Discuss talking and its key elements.

1. Talking is the oral expression of our knowledge, viewpoints, and emotions. It depends on four critical factors:
   - Voice quality—talking that varies in pitch, delivery, and volume.
   - Speaking style—blending voice quality and personality.
   - Word choice—finding the right word or words for the listener.
   - Adaptation—fitting a message to the mind of a unique listener.

2 Explain the listening problem and how to solve it.

2. Listening is just as important as talking in oral communication; but it causes more problems.
   - Listening involves how we sense, filter, and retain incoming messages.
   - Most of us do not listen well because we tend to avoid the hard work that good listening requires.
   - You can improve your listening with effort.
   - Put your mind to it and discipline yourself to be attentive.
   - Make a conscious effort to improve your mental filtering of incoming messages; strive to retain what you hear.
   - And follow the practical suggestions offered in "The Ten Commandments of Listening."

3 Describe the nature and role of nonverbal communication.

3. Nonverbal (nonword) communication is the communication that occurs without words.
   - One major type is body language—the movements of our arms, fingers, facial muscles, and such.
     —Our face and eyes are the most expressive parts of body language.
     —Gestures also send messages.
     —Our physical appearance (clothing, cosmetics, jewelry, hairstyle) communicate about us.
   - Space is a second major type of nonverbal communication.
     —We create four unique types of spaces: (1) intimate, (2) physical, (3) social, and (4) public.
     —We communicate differently in each space, as determined by our culture.
   - How we give meaning to time is a third type of nonverbal communication.
   - In our speaking, we should use nonverbal communication to accent our words.
   - In listening, we need to "hear" the nonverbal communication of others.

4 Practice good interviewing and listening techniques.

4. In conducting the various types of interviews in business (employment, evaluation, and job exit), follow these guidelines:
   - Plan the interview to get the information you need.
   - Begin by putting the interviewee at ease.
   - Make certain the interviewee knows the purpose.
   - Let the interviewee do most of the talking.
   - Guide the interview, making sure you get what you need.
   - Listen carefully and give the appearance of listening.
   - Keep a record (take notes).
   - End the interview, perhaps with a finalizing question.

5 Discuss the techniques for conducting and participating in meetings.

5. In business, you are likely to participate in meetings, some formal and some informal.
   - If you are in charge of a meeting, follow these guidelines.
     —Know parliamentary procedure for formal meetings.
     —Plan the meeting; develop an agenda and circulate it in advance.
     —Follow the plan.

—Keep the discussion moving.

—Control those who talk too much.

—Encourage participation from those who talk too little.

—Control time, making sure the agenda is covered.

—Summarize at appropriate times.

- If you are a participant at a meeting, follow these guidelines:

—Stay with the agenda; do not stray.

—Participate fully.

—But do not talk too much.

—Cooperate.

—Be courteous.

6. To improve your telephone and voice mail techniques, consider the following:

Describe good telephone and voice mail techniques.

- Cultivate a pleasant voice.

- Talk as if in face-to-face conversation.

- Follow courteous procedures.

—When calling, introduce yourself and ask for the person you want.

—State your purpose early.

—Cover points systematically.

—When receiving, identify your company or office and offer assistance.

—When answering for the boss, do not offend by asking questions or making comments that might give a wrong impression; and do not neglect callers placed on hold.

—When screening calls for the boss, be courteous and honest.

—Listen when the other person is talking.

—Do not interrupt or dominate.

—Plan long conversations; and follow the plan.

- For good communication using voice mail, follow these suggestions:

—Identify yourself by name and affiliation.

—Deliver a complete and accurate message.

—Speak naturally and clearly.

—Give important information slowly.

—Close with a brief goodwill message.

7. In dictating letters and reports, follow these suggestions.

Dictate letters and reports in an organized and effective manner.

- First, gather all the information you will need so you will not have to interrupt your dictating to get it.

- Next, plan (think through) the message.

- Begin the dictation by giving the transcriptionist any special information or instructions needed (enclosures, forms, address, and the like).

- Then talk through the message.

- Until you are experienced, force the words—then revise.

- Remember, also, to speak in a strong, clear voice.

- And give punctuation and paragraphing in the dictation.

- Avoid asides (side comments not intended to be a part of the message).

- Read back only when necessary.

CRITICAL THOUGHT QUESTIONS

1. Talking is a natural occurrence, so we should give it little attention. Discuss.

2. How do the elements of talking help us communicate better?

3. Explain how each type of nonverbal communication relates to speaking and to listening.

4. Discuss why we have difficulty in listening.

5. What can you do to improve your listening?

6. Assume that you are being interviewed for the job of _____ (your choice) with _____ (company of your choice). What questions would you anticipate? How would you answer them?

7. Assume that you are the interviewer for the interview in Question 6 (above). Discuss specific ways in which you would put the interviewee at ease.

8. The people attending a meeting—not the leader—should determine the agenda. Discuss.

9. As meetings should be democratic, everyone present should be permitted to talk as much as he or she wants without interference from the leader. Discuss.

10. Describe an annoying telephone practice that you have experienced or know about (other than the ones discussed in the chapter). Explain and/or demonstrate how it should be corrected.

11. Describe the strengths and weaknesses of voice mail systems with which you are familiar.

12. Justify each of the dictating techniques suggested in the chapter.

CRITICAL THINKING EXERCISES

▶ Listening

After the class has been divided into two (or more) teams, the instructor reads some factual information (newspaper article, short story, or the like) to only one member of each team. Each of these team members tells what he or she has heard to a second team member, who in turn tells it to a third team member—and so on until the last member of each team has heard the information. The last person receiving the information reports what she or he has heard to the instructor, who checks it against the original message. The team able to report the information with the greatest accuracy wins.

▶ Interviewing

Working with a classmate, assume that you are an interviewer visiting your campus. Interview your classmate for a job in his or her field of specialization. Before beginning, explain any significant facts of the situation (nature of company, job requirements, applicant's limitations, and such). After finishing the interview, exchange your roles.

▶ Meetings

Because group meetings are meaningful only when they concern problems that the participants know about and understand, the following topics for meetings involve campus situations. For one of these topics, develop a specific problem that would warrant a group meeting. (Example:

For student government, the problem might be "To determine the weaknesses of student government on this campus and what should be done to correct them.") Then lead the class (or participate) in a meeting on the topic. Class discussion following the meeting should reinforce the text material and bring out the good and bad of the meeting.

a. Student discipline
b. Scholastic dishonesty
c. Housing regulations
d. Student–faculty relations
e. Student government
f. Library
g. Grading standards
h. Attendance policies
i. Varsity athletics
j. Intramural athletics
k. Degree requirements
l. Parking
m. Examination scheduling
n. Administrative policies
o. University calendar
p. Homework requirements
q. Tuition and fees
r. Student evaluation of faculty
s. Community-college relations
t. Maintenance of files of old examinations for students

▶ Telephoning

Make a list of bad telephone practices that you have experienced or heard about. With a classmate, first demonstrate the bad practice and then demonstrate how you would handle it. Some possibilities: putting a caller on hold tactlessly, harsh greeting, unfriendly voice quality, insulting comments (unintended), attitude of unconcern, cold and formal treatment.

▶ **Dictating**

Working with a classmate, select a letter problem from the problems following the letters chapters. Then dictate the letter to your classmate. Because your classmate will probably take your dictation in longhand, you may need to dictate slowly. After you have finished your dictation, exchange roles with your classmate.

15

Public Speaking and Oral Reporting

Upon completing this chapter, you will be able to use good speaking and oral reporting techniques. To reach this goal, you should be able to

(1) Select and organize a subject for effective formal presentation to a specific audience.

(2) Describe how personal aspects and audience analysis contribute to formal presentations.

(3) Explain the use of voice quality and physical aspects such as posture, walking, facial expression, and gestures in effective oral communication.

(4) Plan for visuals to support speeches and oral reports.

(5) Work effectively with a group in preparing and making a team presentation.

(6) Define oral reports and differentiate between them and written reports on the basis of their advantages, disadvantages, and organization.

▶ to Formal Speaking

In addition to your informal speaking and listening activities at Mastadon Chemicals, you have more formal ones involving oral communication.

Take last week, for example. Malra Cody (your boss) asked you to do something very special for the company. It seems that each year Mastadon Chemicals awards a $5,000 scholarship to a deserving business student at State University. The award is presented at the business school's annual Honors Day Convocation, usually by Ms. Cody. To show the business school's appreciation for the award, its administration requested that Ms. Cody be the speaker at this year's convocation. But Ms. Cody has a conflicting engagement, so you got the assignment. You responded to the challenge as well as you could, but you were not pleased with the results.

Then, at last month's meeting, Mastadon's executive committee asked you for a special oral report from your department for about the fifth time. This time the report concerned the results of a survey that your department conducted to determine local opinions about a dispute between Mastadon and its union. You did your best, but you felt uneasy about what you were doing.

Such assignments are becoming more and more a part of your work as you move up the administrative ladder at Mastadon. You must try to do them better, for your future promotions are involved. The following review of formal oral presentations (speeches and reports) should help you in this effort. ■

MAKING FORMAL SPEECHES

The most difficult kind of oral communication for most of us is a formal speech. Most of us do not feel comfortable speaking before others, and we generally do a poor job of it. But it need not be this way. With effort, we can improve our speaking. We can do this by learning what good speaking techniques are and then putting those techniques into practice.

• Speeches are difficult for most of us. The following techniques should help you.

Selection of the Topic

Your first step in formal speechmaking is to determine the topic of your presentation. In some cases, you will be assigned a topic, usually one within your area of specialization. In fact, when you are asked to make a speech on a specified topic, it is likely to be because of your knowledge of the topic. In some cases, your choice of topic will be determined by the purpose of your assignment, as when you are asked to welcome a group or introduce a speaker.

• Your topic may be assigned.

If you are not assigned a topic, then you must find one on your own. In your search for a suitable topic, you should be guided by three basic factors. The first is your background and knowledge. Any topic you select should be one with which you are comfortable—one within your areas of proficiency. The second basic factor is the interests of your audience. Selecting a topic that your audience can appreciate and understand is vital to the success of your speech. The third basic factor is the occasion of the speech. Is the occasion a meeting commemorating a historic event? A monthly meeting of an executives' club? An annual meeting of a hairstylists' association? Whatever topic you select should fit the occasion. A speech about Japanese management practices might be quite appropriate for the members of the executives' club, but not for the hairstylists. Your selection should be justified by all three factors.

• If you must select a topic, consider (1) your knowledge, (2) your audience, and (3) the occasion.

Preparation of the Presentation

After you have decided what to talk about, you should gather the information you need for your speech. This step may involve searching through your mind for experiences

• Conduct research to get the information you need.

I see that our next speaker needs no introduction.
(© 1975 William P. Hoest and Saturday Review Magazine.)

or ideas, conducting research in a library or in company files, gathering information on-line, or consulting people in your own company or other companies. In short, you do whatever is necessary to get the information you need.

- Then organize the information.

When you have that information, you are ready to begin organizing your speech. Although variations are sometimes appropriate, you should usually follow the time-honored order of a speech: *introduction, body, conclusion*. This is the order described in the following paragraphs.

- The greeting usually comes first.

Although not really a part of the speech, the first words usually spoken are the greeting. Your greeting, of course, should fit the audience. "Ladies and gentlemen" is appropriate for a mixed audience; "gentlemen" fits an all-male audience; and "my fellow Rotarians" fits an audience of Rotary Club members. Some speakers eliminate the greeting and begin with the speech, especially in more informal and technical presentations.

- Gain attention in the opening.

Introduction.   The introduction of a speech has much the same goal as the introduction of a written report: to prepare the listeners (or readers) to receive the message. But it usually has the additional goal of arousing interest. Unless you can arouse interest at the beginning, your presentation is likely to fail. The situation is somewhat like that of the sales letter. At least some of the people with whom you want to communicate are not likely to be interested in receiving your message. As you will recall from your study of listening, it is easy for a speaker to lose the audience's attention. To prove the point, ask yourself how many times your mind has drifted away from the speaker's words when you have been part of an audience. There is no question about it: you, the speaker, will have to work to gain and hold the attention of your audience.

- There are many opening possibilities—human interest,

The techniques of arousing interest are limited only by the imagination. One possibility is a human interest story, for storytelling has strong appeal. For example, a speaker presenting a message about the opportunities available to people with original ideas might open this way: "Nearly 150 years ago, an immigrant boy of 17 walked the streets of our town. He had no food, no money, no belongings except the shabby clothes he wore. He had only a strong will to work—and an idea."

- humor,

Humor, another possibility, is probably the most widely used technique. To illustrate, an investment broker might begin a speech on investment strategy as follows: "What you want me to give you today is some 'tried and trusted' advice on how to make money in the stock market. This reminds me of the proverbial 'tried and trusted' bank teller. He was trusted; and when they caught him, he was tried." Humor works best and is safest when it is closely related to the subject of your presentation.

Other effective ways for gaining attention at the opening are by using quotations and questions. By quoting someone the audience would know and view as credible, you build interest in your topic. You can also ask questions. One kind of question is the rhetorical question—the one everyone answers the same, such as "Who wants to be freed of burdensome financial responsibilities?" Another kind of question gives you background information on how much to talk about different aspects of your subject. With this kind of question, you must follow through your presentation based on the response. If you had asked "How many of you have IRAs?" and nearly everyone put their hand up, you wouldn't want to talk about the importance of IRAs. You could skip that part of your presentation, spending more time on another aspect, such as managing your IRA effectively.

• quotations, questions, and so on.

Yet another possibility is the startling statement, which presents facts and ideas that awaken the mind. Illustrating this possibility is the beginning of a speech to an audience of merchants on a plan to reduce shoplifting: "Last year, right here in our city, in your stores, shoplifters stole over $3.5 million of your merchandise! And most of you did nothing about it."

In addition to arousing interest, your opening should lead into the theme of your speech. In other words, it should set up your message as the above examples do.

• The opening should set up your subject.

Following the attention-gaining opening, it is appropriate to tell your audience the subject (theme) for your speech. In fact, in cases where your audience already has an interest in what you have to say, you can begin here and skip the attention-gaining opening. Presentations of technical topics to technical audiences typically begin this way. Whether you lead into a statement of your topic or begin with it, that statement should be clear and complete.

• Tell the subject of your speech . . .

Because of the nature of your subject, you may find it undesirable to reveal a position early. In such cases, you may prefer to move into your subject indirectly—to build up your case before revealing your position. This inductive pattern may be especially desirable when your goal is to persuade—when you need to move the views of your audience from one position to another. But in most business-related presentations you should make a direct statement of your theme early in the speech.

• unless you have reason not to, as when you must persuade.

Body.   Organizing the body of your speech is much like organizing the body of a report (see Chapter 10). You take the whole and divide it into comparable parts. Then you take those parts and divide them. And you continue to divide as far as it is practical to do so. In speeches, however, you are more likely to use factors other than time, place, or quantity as the basis of division because in most speeches your presentation is likely to be built around issues and questions that are subtopics of the subject. Even so, time, place, and quantity subdivisions are possibilities.

• Organize most speeches by factors, as you would a report.

You need to emphasize the transitions between the divisions because, unlike the reader who can see them, the listener may miss them if they are not stressed adequately. Without clear transitions, you may be talking about one point and your listener may be relating those ideas to your previous point.

• Emphasize transitions between parts.

Conclusion.   Like most reports, the speech usually ends by drawing a conclusion. Here you bring all that you have presented to a head and achieve whatever goal the speech has. You should consider including these three elements in your close: (1) a restatement of the subject, (2) a summary of the key points developed in the presentation, and (3) a statement of the conclusion (or main message). Bringing the speech to a climactic close—that is, making the conclusion the high point of the speech—is usually effective. Present the concluding message in strong language—in words that gain attention and will be remembered. In addition to concluding with a summary, you can give an appropriate quote, use humor, and call for action. The following close of a speech comparing Japanese and American management techniques illustrates this point: "These facts make my conclusion crystal clear. We are not Japanese. We do not have the Japanese culture. Most Japanese management methods have not worked—cannot work—will not work in our society."

• The ending usually (1) restates the subject, (2) summarizes key points, and (3) draws a conclusion.

The speaker had covered his subject carefully and thoroughly. But his conclusion, which followed logically from his presentation, was greeted with loud hisses by some members of his audience. Because hisses leave little trace of their origin, the speaker did not know who the dissenters were and could not respond directly to them. So he skillfully handled the situation by saying: "I know of only three creatures that hiss—snakes, geese, and fools. I will leave it to you to determine which of the three we have here."

Determination of the Presentation Method

• Choose one of these presentation methods.

With the speech organized, you are ready to prepare its presentation. At this time, you need to decide on your method of presentation—that is, whether to present the speech extemporaneously, to memorize it, or to read it.

• (1) extemporaneous presentation (thorough preparation, uses notes, rehearsed),

Presenting Extemporaneously.   Extemporaneous presentation is by far the most popular and effective method. With this method, you first thoroughly prepare your speech, as outlined above. Then you prepare notes and present the speech from them. You usually rehearse, making sure you have all the parts clearly in mind, but you make no attempt to memorize. Extemporaneous presentations generally sound natural to the listeners, yet they are (or should be) the product of careful planning and practice.

• (2) memorizing, or

Memorizing.   The most difficult method is memorizing. If you are like most people, you find it hard to memorize a long succession of words. And when you do memorize, you are likely to memorize words rather than meanings. Thus, when you make the speech, if you miss a word or two, you become confused—and so does your speech. You may even become panic-stricken.

Probably few of the speakers who use this method memorize the entire speech. Instead, they memorize key passages and use notes to help them through the speech. A delivery of this kind is a cross between an extemporaneous presentation and a memorized presentation.

• (3) reading.

Reading.   The third presentation method is reading. Unfortunately, most of us tend to read aloud in a dull monotone. We also miss punctuation marks, fumble over words, lose our place, and so on. Of course, many speakers overcome these problems, and with effort you can too. One effective way is to practice with a recorder and listen to yourself. Then you can be your own judge of what you must do to improve your delivery. You would be wise not to read speeches until you have mastered this presentation method. In most settings, it is not appropriate to read. Your audience is likely to be insulted, and reading is unlikely to be as well received as an extemporaneous delivery. However, when you are in a position where you will be quoted widely, such as president of the United States or the CEO of a major company, reading from a carefully prepared speech is recommended.

Consideration of Personal Aspects

• A logical preliminary to speechmaking is to analyze yourself as a speaker. You are a part of the message.

A preliminary to good speechmaking is to analyze yourself as a speaker. In oral presentations you, the speaker, are a very real part of the message. The members of your audience take in not only the words you communicate but also what they see in you. And what they see in you can significantly affect the meanings that develop in their

Good speakers project their personal qualities—confidence, sincerity, friendliness, enthusiasm, and interest.

minds. Thus, you should carefully evaluate your personal effect on your message. You should do whatever you can to detect and overcome your shortcomings and to sharpen your strengths.

The following summary of characteristics that should help you as a speaker may prove useful, but you probably already know what they are. To some extent, the problem is recognizing whether you lack these characteristics. To a greater extent, it is doing something about acquiring them. The following review should help you pinpoint and deal with your problem areas.

• You should seek the following four characteristics:

Confidence.   A primary characteristic of effective oral reporting is confidence—your confidence in yourself and the confidence of your audience in you. The two are complementary, for your confidence in yourself tends to produce an image that gives your audience confidence in you; and your audience's confidence in you can give you a sense of security that increases your confidence in yourself.

• (1) Having confidence in yourself is important. So is having the confidence of your audience.

Typically, you earn your audience's confidence over periods of association. But there are things you can do to project an image that builds confidence. For example, preparing your presentation diligently and practicing it thoroughly gives you confidence in yourself. That confidence leads to more effective communication, which increases your listeners' confidence in you. Another confidence-building technique is an appropriate physical appearance. Unfair and illogical as it may seem, certain types of dress and hairstyles create strong images in people's minds, ranging from highly favorable to highly unfavorable. Thus, if you want to communicate effectively, you should analyze the audience you seek to reach. And you should work to develop the physical appearance that projects an image in which that audience can have confidence. Yet another confidence-building technique is simply to talk in strong, clear tones. Such tones do much to project an image of confidence. Although most people can do little to change their natural voice, they can use sufficient volume.

• You must earn the confidence of your audience, project the right image, and talk in a strong, clear voice.

Sincerity.   Your listeners are quick to detect insincerity. And if they detect it in you, they are likely to give little weight to what you say. On the other hand, sincerity is valuable to conviction, especially if the audience has confidence in your ability. The way to project an image of sincerity is clear and simple: You must *be* sincere. Pretense of sincerity is rarely successful.

• (2) Sincerity is vital. You convey an image of sincerity by being sincere.

Thoroughness. Generally, a thorough presentation is better received than a scanty or hurried presentation. Thorough coverage gives the impression that time and care have been taken, and this tends to make the presentation believable. But thoroughness can be overdone. Too much detail can drown your listeners in a sea of information. The secret is to leave out unimportant information. This, of course, requires good judgment. You must ask yourself just what your listeners need to know and what they do not need to know.

• (3) Thoroughness—giving your listeners all they need—helps your image.

Friendliness. A speaker who projects an image of friendliness has a significant advantage in communicating. People simply like friendly people, and they are more receptive to what such people say. Like sincerity, friendliness is hard to feign and must be honest to be effective. But most people are genuinely friendly. Some, however, are just not able to project a genuinely friendly image. With a little self-analysis and a little mirror watching as you practice speaking, you can find ways of improving your projection of your friendliness.

• (4) Projecting an image of friendliness helps your communication effort.

These are but a few of the characteristics that should assist you as a speaker. There are others—*interest, enthusiasm, originality, flexibility,* and so on. But the ones discussed are the most significant and the ones that most speakers need to work on. Through self-analysis and dedicated effort, you can improve your speaking ability.

Audience Analysis

• You should know your audience.

One requirement of good speechmaking is to know your audience. You should study your audience both before and during the presentation.

• Size up the audience in advance. Look for audience characteristics that will affect your speech—things like the size, sex, age, education, and knowledge of the audience.

Preliminary Analysis. Analyzing your audience before the presentation requires that you size it up—that you search for audience characteristics that could affect how you should present your speech.

For example, the size of your audience is likely to influence how formal or informal your speech should be. As a rule, large audiences require more formality. Personal characteristics of your audience, such as age, sex, education, experience, and knowledge of subject matter, should also influence how you make your speech. They should affect the words, illustrations, and level of detail you use. Like writing, speeches should be adapted to the audience. And the more you know about the audience, the better you will adapt your presentation to them.

• Analyze audience reactions during the speech (called feedback). Facial expressions, movements, and noises give you feedback information that helps you adapt to the audience.

Analysis during Presentation. Your audience analysis should continue as you make the speech. *Feedback* is information about how your listeners are receiving your words. Armed with this information, you can adjust your presentation to improve the communication result.

Your eyes and ears will give you feedback information. For example, facial expressions will tell you how your listeners are reacting to your message. Smiles, blank stares, and movements will give you an indication of whether they understand, agree with, or accept it. You can detect from sounds coming (or not coming) from them whether they are listening. If questions are in order, you can learn directly how your message is coming across. In general, you can learn much from your audience by being alert; and what you learn can help you make a better speech.

Appearance and Physical Actions

• Your audience forms impressions from these six factors:

As your listeners hear your words, they are looking at you. What they see is a part of the message and can affect the success of your speech. What they see, of course, is you and what surrounds you. In your efforts to improve the effects of your oral presentations, you should understand the communication effects of what your listeners see. Some of the effects that were mentioned in Chapter 14 are expanded upon here because they are particularly important to speeches and oral reports.

Oral presentations to large audiences usually require formality and thorough preparation.

The Communication Environment.   Much of what your audience sees is the physical things that surround you as you speak—the stage, lighting, background, and so on. These things tend to create a general impression. Although not visual, outside noises have a related influence. For the best communication results, the factors in your communication environment should contribute to your message, not detract from it. Your own experience as a listener will tell you what factors are important.

• (1) all that surrounds you (stage, lighting, and the like),

Personal Appearance.   Your personal appearance is a part of the message your audience receives. Of course, you have to accept the physical traits you have, but most of us do not need to be at a disadvantage in appearance. All that is necessary is to use what you have appropriately. Specifically, you should dress in a manner appropriate for the audience and the occasion. Be clean and well groomed. Use facial expressions and physical movements to your advantage. Just how you should use facial expressions and physical movements is described in the following paragraphs.

• (2) your personal appearance,

Posture.   Posture is likely to be the most obvious of the things that your audience sees in you. Even listeners not close enough to detect such things as facial expressions and eye movements can see the general form of the body.

• (3) your posture,

You probably think that no one needs to tell you about good posture. You know it when you see it. The trouble is that you are not likely to see it in yourself. One solution is to have others tell you whether your posture needs improvement. Another is to practice speaking before a mirror or watch yourself on videotape.

In your efforts to improve your posture, keep in mind what must go on within your body to form a good posture. Your body weight must be distributed in a way consistent with the impression you want to make. You should keep your body erect without appearing stiff and comfortable without appearing limp. You should maintain a poised, alert, and communicative bearing. And you should do all this naturally. The great danger with posture is an appearance of artificiality.

Walking.   Your audience also forms an impression from the way you walk before it. A strong, sure walk to the speaker's position conveys an impression of confidence. Hesitant, awkward steps convey the opposite impression. Walking during the presentation can be good or bad, depending on how you do it. Some speakers use steps forward and to the side to emphasize points. Too much walking, however, attracts

• (4) your manner of walking,

attention and detracts from the message. You would be wise to walk only when you are reasonably sure that this will have the effect you want.

- (5) facial expressions (smiles, frowns), and

Facial Expression.

As noted in Chapter 14, probably the most apparent and communicative physical movements are facial expressions. The problem, however, is that you may unconsciously use facial expressions that convey unintended meanings. For example, if a frightened speaker tightens the jaw unconsciously and begins to grin, the effect may be an ambiguous image that detracts from the entire communication effort. A smile, a grimace, and a puzzled frown all convey clear messages. Without question, you should use these effective communication devices.

Eye contact is important. The eyes, which have long been considered "mirrors of the soul," provide most listeners with information about your sincerity, goodwill, and flexibility. Some listeners tend to shun speakers who do not look at them. On the other hand, discriminate eye contact tends to show that you have a genuine interest in your audience.

- (6) gestures.

Gestures.

Like posture, gestures contribute to the message you communicate. Just what they contribute, however, is hard to say, for they have no definite or clear-cut meanings. A clenched fist, for example, certainly adds emphasis to a strong point. But it can also be used to show defiance, make a threat, or signify respect for a cause. And so it is with other gestures. They register vague meanings, as discussed in Chapter 14.

- Gestures have vague meanings, but they communicate.

Even though gestures have vague meanings, they are strong, natural helps to speaking. It appears natural, for example, to emphasize a plea with palms up and to show disagreement with palms down. Raising first one hand and then the other reinforces a division of points. Slicing the air with the hand shows several divisions. Although such gestures are generally clear, we do not all use them in exactly the same way.

- In summary, your physical movements help your speaking.

In summary, it should be clear that physical movements can help your speaking. Just which physical movements you should use, however, is hard to say. The appropriateness of physical movements is related to personality, physical makeup, and the size and nature of the audience. A speaker appearing before a formal group should generally use relatively few physical movements. A speaker appearing before an informal group should use more. Which physical movements you should use on a given occasion is a matter for your best judgment.

Use of Voice

- Good voice is a requirement of good speaking. Four faults affect voice:

Good voice is an obvious requirement of good speaking. Like physical movements, the voice should not hinder the listener's concentration on the message. More specifically, it should not detract attention from the message. Voices that cause such difficulties generally fall into these areas of fault: (1) lack of pitch variation, (2) lack of variation in speed, (3) lack of vocal emphasis, and (4) unpleasant voice quality. Although these areas are mentioned in Chapter 14, we will examine them here because of their key significance to formal oral communication.

- (1) lack of variation in pitch (usually a matter of habit),

Lack of Pitch Variation.

Speakers who talk in monotones are not likely to hold the interest of their listeners for long. As most voices are capable of wide variations in pitch, the problem can usually be corrected. The failure to vary pitch generally is a matter of habit—of voice patterns developed over years of talking without being aware of their effect.

- (2) lack of variation in speed (cover the simple quickly, the hard slowly),

Lack of Variation in Speaking Speed.

Determining how fast to talk is a major problem. As a general rule, you should present the easy parts of your message at a fairly fast rate and the hard parts and the parts you want to emphasize at a slower rate. The reason for varying the speed of presentation should be apparent; it is more interesting. A slow presentation of easy information is irritating; hard information presented fast may be difficult to understand.

A problem related to the pace of speaking is the incorrect use of pauses. Properly used, pauses emphasize upcoming subject matter and are effective means of gaining attention. But frequent pauses for no reason are irritating and break the listeners' concentration. Pauses become even more irritating when the speaker fills them in with distracting nonwords such as *uh's*, *you know's*, and *OK's*.

Lack of Vocal Emphasis.   A secret of good speaking is to give words their proper emphasis by varying the manner of speaking. You can do this by (1) varying the pitch of your voice, (2) varying the pace of your presentation, and (3) varying the volume of your voice. As the first two techniques have already been discussed, only the use of voice volume requires comment here.

• (3) lack of vocal emphasis (gain emphasis by varying pitch, pace, and volume), and

You must talk loudly enough for your entire audience to hear you, but not too loudly. Thus, the loudness—voice volume—for a large audience should be greater than that for a small audience. Regardless of audience size, however, variety in voice volume is good for interest and emphasis. It produces contrast, which is one way of emphasizing the subject matter. Some speakers incorrectly believe that the only way to show emphasis is to get louder and louder. But you can also show emphasis by going from loud to soft. The contrast with what has gone on earlier provides the emphasis. Again, variety is the key to making the voice more effective.

Unpleasant Voice Quality.   It is a hard fact of communication that some voices are more pleasant than others. Fortunately, most voices are reasonably pleasant. But some are raspy, nasal, or unpleasant in another way. Although therapy can often improve such voices, some speakers must live with them. But concentrating on variations in pitch, speed of delivery, and volume can make even the most unpleasant voice acceptable.

• (4) unpleasant voice (improvement is often possible).

Improvement through Self-Analysis and Imitation.   You can overcome any of the foregoing voice faults through self-analysis. In this day of tape recorders, it is easy to hear yourself talk. Since you know good speaking when you hear it, you should be able to improve your vocal presentation. One of the best ways to improve your presentation skills is through watching others. Watch your instructors, your peers, television personnel, professional speakers, and anyone else who gives you an opportunity. Analyze these speakers to determine what works for them and what does not. Imitate those good techniques that you think would help you and avoid the bad ones. Take advantage of any opportunity you have to practice speaking.

• You can correct the foregoing faults through self-analysis and work.

Use of Visuals

The spoken word is severely limited in communicating. Sound is here briefly and then gone. A listener who misses the vocal message may not have a chance to hear it again. Because of this limitation, speeches often need strong visual support—charts, tables, boards, film, and the like. Visuals may be as vital to the success of a speech as the words themselves.

• Visuals can sometimes help overcome the limitations of spoken words.

Proper Use of Design.   Effective visuals are drawn from the message. They fit the one speech and the one audience.

• Use visuals for the hard parts of the message.

In selecting visuals you should search through your presentation for topics that appear vague or confusing. Whenever a visual of some kind will help eliminate vagueness or confusion, you should use it. You should use visuals to simplify complex information and improve cohesiveness, as well as to emphasize or add interest. Visuals are truly a part of your message, and you should look at them as such.

After deciding that a topic deserves visual help, you determine what form that help should take. That is, should the visual be a chart, a diagram, a picture, or what? You should select your visuals primarily on the basis of their ability to communicate. Simple and obvious as this injunction may appear, people violate it all too often.

• Use the type of visual (chart, diagram, picture) that communicates the information best.

These words by Mark Twain carry a vital message for windy speakers:

"Some years ago in Hartford, we all went to church one hot sweltering night to hear the annual report of Mr. Hawley, a city missionary who went around finding people who needed help and didn't want to ask for it. He told of the life in cellars, where poverty resided; he gave instances of the heroism and devotion of the poor. 'When a man with millions gives,' he said, 'we make a great deal of noise. It's noise in the wrong place, for it's the widow's mite that counts.' Well, Hawley worked me up to a great pitch. I could hardly wait for him to get through. I had $400 in my pocket. I wanted to give that and borrow more to give. You could see greenbacks in every eye. But instead of passing the plate then, he kept on talking and talking, and as he talked it grew hotter and hotter, and we grew sleepier and sleepier. My enthusiasm went down, down, down, down—$100 at a clip—until finally, when the plate did come around, I stole ten cents out of it. It all goes to show how a little thing like this can lead to crime."

They select visuals more for appearance and dramatic effect than for communication effect.

• Select from the various available types of visuals.

Types to Consider.   Because no one type of visual is best for all occasions, you should have a flexible attitude toward visuals. You should know the strengths and weaknesses of each type, and you should know how to use each type effectively.

In selecting visuals, you should keep in mind the available types. You will mainly consider the various types of graphics—the charts, graphs, tables, diagrams, and pictures discussed in Chapter 13. Each of these types has its strengths and weaknesses and can be displayed in various ways—for example, by slide, overhead, or opaque projector; by flip chart; by easel display; on a presentation board; or on a felt board. And each of these display methods has its strengths and weaknesses. In addition to using graphics to support your speech, you can support it with videotapes, photographs, models, samples, demonstrations, and the like.

Audience Size, Cost, and Ease of Preparation Considerations.   Your choice of visuals should also be influenced by the audience size and formality, the cost of preparing and using the media (visuals), and the ease and time of preparation. The table below illustrates how the different media fare on these dimensions.

Presentation Media Comparison*

Media	Image Quality	Audience Size	Cost	Ease of Preparation
Photos	Good–very good	2–20	Low	Easy
Slides	Very good	20–200	Low	Very easy
Overhead transparency	Good–very good	2–200	Low	Very easy
Video monitors	Good	2–50	Medium	Easy–fair
HiRes television	Very good	2–100	High	Fair
LCD screens	Poor	2–20	Medium	Easy
Video projection	Good	20–200	High	Fair
Film	Very good	2–200	High	Difficult
Computer graphics	Very good	2–200	High	Easy–fair

* Adapted from G.A. Marken, "Visual Aids Strengthen In-House Presentations," *Office Systems*, February 1990, p. 34.

Techniques in Using Visuals. Visuals usually carry key parts of the message. Thus, they are points of emphasis in your presentation. You blend them in with your words to communicate the message. How you do this is to some extent an individual matter, for techniques vary. They vary so much, in fact, that it would be hard to present a meaningful summary of them. It is more meaningful to present a list of dos and don'ts. Such a list follows:

- Make certain that everyone in the audience can see the visuals. Too many or too-light lines on a chart, for example, can be hard to see. An illustration that is too small can be meaningless to people far from the speaker.

- Explain the visual if there is any likelihood that it will be misunderstood.

- Organize the visuals as a part of the presentation. Fit them into the presentation plan.

- Emphasize the visuals. Point to them with physical action and words.

- Talk to the audience—not to the visuals. Look at the visuals only when the audience should look at them.

- Avoid blocking the listeners' view of the visuals. Make certain that the listeners' views are not blocked by lecterns, pillars, chairs, and such. Take care not to stand in anyone's line of vision.

- Make the visuals points of interest in your presentation.

- Here are specific suggestions for using visuals.

A Summary List of Speaking Practices

The foregoing review of business speaking has been selective, for the subject is broad. In fact, entire books have been devoted to it. But this review has covered the high points, especially those that you can easily transfer into practice. Perhaps even more practical is the following list of what to do and not to do in speaking.

- Organize the speech so that it leads the listeners' thoughts logically to the conclusion.

- Move surely and quickly to the conclusion. Do not leave a conclusion dangling, repeat unnecessarily, or appear unable to close.

- Use language specifically adapted to the audience.

- Articulate clearly, pleasantly, and with proper emphasis. Avoid mumbling and the use of non-words such as *ah, er, uh,* and so forth.

- Speak correctly, using accepted grammar and pronunciation.

- Maintain an attitude of alertness, displaying appropriate enthusiasm and confidence.

- Employ body language to best advantage. Use it to emphasize points and to assist in communicating concepts and ideas.

- Be relaxed and natural. Avoid stiffness or rigidity of physical action.

- Look the listeners in the eye and talk directly to them.

- Keep still. Avoid excessive movements, fidgeting, and other signs of nervousness.

- Punctuate the presentation with reference to visuals. Make them a part of the speech text.

- Even when faced with hostile questions or remarks, keep your temper. To lose your temper is to lose control of the presentation.

- This review has covered the high points of speaking.

- This summary checklist of good and bad speaking practices should prove helpful.

TEAM (COLLABORATIVE) PRESENTATIONS

Another type of presentation you may be asked to give is a group or team presentation. To give this type of presentation, you will need to use all you have learned about giving individual speeches. Also, you will need to use many of the topics discussed in Chapter 10 on collaborative writing groups. But you will need to adapt the ideas to an oral presentation setting. Some of the adaptations should be obvious. We will mention others that you should give special thought to in your team presentation.

- Group presentations require individual speaking skills plus planning for collaboration. Adapt the ideas on collaborative writing in Chapter 10 to team presentations.

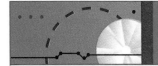
Spotlight: A Presentation Delivery Tool

While you must prepare and deliver the oral presentation, technology can help you do a better job. One tool, Spotlight, helps you prepare, practice, and deliver good presentations. In preparing your presentation, you can annotate, sort, time, and add special effects to screen shows created with a variety of presentation packages with this tool. Its timing feature helps you practice the delivery pace, giving you feedback on a gauge that shows whether you're ahead or behind your schedule. The navigation buttons shown in the middle of the screen give you some flexibility in delivering the presentation. For example, you may want to draw attention away from the visual and back to yourself, so you simply click the blank screen button. Or you may want to emphasize an item on the presentation; the program allows you to draw chalk annotations for emphasis. In addition to going forward and backward, you can pause a timed presentation, perhaps to answer a question. And you can click the navigation button with the tiny binoculars on it to locate quickly a particular slide that you want to reference, perhaps in a question-and-answer session. This tool is clearly one that can give a professional polish to presentations.

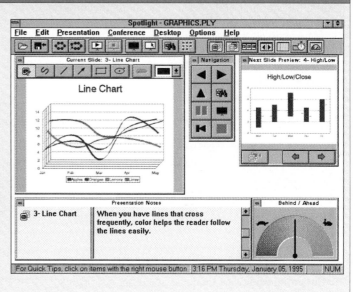

- Plan for the order of the presentation and each member's part.

- Plan for the physical factors.

- Plan for the physical staging.

- Plan for the close.

- Plan to rehearse the presentation.

First, you will need to take special care to plan the presentation—to determine the sequence of the presentation as well as the content of each team member's part. You will also need to select carefully supporting examples to build continuity from one part of the presentation to the next.

Groups should plan for the physical aspects of the presentation, too. You should coordinate the type of delivery, use of notes, graphics, and styles and colors of attire to present a good image of competence and professionalism. And you should plan transitions so that the team will look coordinated.

Another presentation aspect—physical staging—is important as well. Team members should know where to sit or stand, how visuals will be handled, and how to change or adjust microphones.

Attention to the close of the presentation is especially strategic. Teams need to decide who will present the close and what will be said. If a summary is used, the member who presents it should attribute key points to appropriate team members. If there is to be a question-and-answer session, the team should plan how it will be conducted. For example, will one member take the questions and direct them to a specific team member? Or will the audience be permitted to ask questions to specific members? Some type of final note of appreciation or thanks needs to be planned with all the team nodding in agreement or acknowledging the final comment in some way.

In all of their extra planning activities, teams should not overlook the need to plan for rehearsal time. Teams should consider practicing the presentation in its entirety several times as a group before the actual presentation. During these rehearsals, individual members should critique thoroughly each other's contributions, offering specific ways to improve. After first rehearsal sessions, outsiders (nonteam members) might be asked to view the team's presentation and critique the group. Moreover, the team might consider videotaping the presentation so that all members can evaluate it. In addition to a more effective presentation, the team can enjoy the by-products of group cohesion and *esprit de corps* by rehearsing the presentation. Successful teams know the value of rehearsing and will build such activity into their presentation planning schedules.

These points may appear minor. But careful attention to them will result in a polished, coordinated team presentation.

REPORTING ORALLY

A special form of speech is the oral report. You are more likely to make oral reports than speeches in business, and the oral reports you make are likely to be important to you. Unfortunately, most of us have had little experience and even less instruction in oral reporting. Thus, the following review should be valuable to you.

- The oral report is a form of speech.

A Definition of Oral Reports

In its broadest sense, an oral report is any presentation of factual information using the spoken word. A business oral report would logically limit coverage to factual business information. By this definition, oral business reports cover much of the information exchanged daily in the conduct of business. They vary widely in formality. At one extreme, they cover the most routine and informal reporting situations. At the other, they include highly formal and proper presentations. As the more informal oral exchanges are little more than routine conversations, the emphasis in the following pages is on the more formal ones. Clearly, these are the oral reports that require the most care and skill and are the most deserving of study.

- An *oral report* is defined as an oral presentation of factual information.

Differences between Oral and Written Reports

Oral reports are much like written reports, so there is little need to repeat much of the previously presented material on reports. Instead, we will focus on the most significant differences between oral and written reports. Three in particular stand out.

- Oral reports differ from written reports in these ways:

Visual Advantages of the Written Word. The first significant difference between oral and written reports is that writing permits greater use of visuals to communication than does speaking. With writing, you can use paragraphing to show readers the structure of the message and to make the thought units stand out. In addition, you can use punctuation to show relationships, subordination, and qualification. These techniques improve the communication effect of the entire message.

- (1) writing and speaking each have special advantages and disadvantages;

On the other hand, when you make an oral presentation, you cannot use any of these techniques. However, you can use techniques peculiar to oral communication. For example, you can use inflection, pauses, volume emphasis, and changes in the rate of delivery. Depending on the situation, the techniques used in both oral and written reports are effective in assisting communication. But the point is that the techniques are different.

Reader Control of Written Presentation. A second significant difference between oral and written reports is that the readers of a written report, unlike the listeners to an oral report, control the pace of the communication. They can pause, reread, change their rate of reading, or stop as they choose. Since the readers set the pace, writing can be complex and still communicate. On the other hand, since the listeners to an oral report cannot control the pace of the presentation, they must grasp the intended meaning as the speaker presents the words. Because of this limiting factor, good oral reporting must be relatively simple.

- (2) the speaker controls the pace of an oral report, and the reader controls the pace of a written report; and

In oral reports as well as formal speeches, visuals are effective in communicating important parts of the message.

- (3) written reports place more stress on correctness.

Emphasis on Correctness in Writing.   A third significant difference between oral and written reports is the different degrees of correctness that they require. Because written reports are likely to be inspected carefully, you are likely to work for a high degree of correctness when you prepare them. That is, you are likely to follow carefully the recognized rules of grammar, punctuation, sentence structure, and so on. When you present oral reports, on the other hand, you may be more lax about following these rules. One reason is that usually oral reports are not recorded for others to inspect at their leisure. Another is that oral communication standards of correctness are less rigid than written communication standards.

Planning the Oral Report

- Planning is the first step in preparing oral reports.

As with written reports, planning is the logical first step in your work on oral reports. For short, informal oral reports, planning may be minimal. But for the more formal oral reports, particularly those involving audiences of more than one, proper planning is likely to be as involved as that for a comparable written report.

- First determine the objective and what must be done to reach it.

Determination of Report Objective.   Logically, your first task in planning an oral report is to determine your objective. Just as was described for the written report in Chapter 10, you should state the report objective in clear, concise language. Then you should clearly state the factors involved in achieving this objective. Doing these things gives you a guide to the information you must gather and to the framework around which you will build your presentation.

In determining your report objective, you must be aware of your general objective. That is, you must decide on your general purpose in making the presentation. Is it to persuade? To inform? To recommend? This decision will have a major influence on your development of material for presentation and perhaps even on the presentation itself.

Organization of Content.   The procedure for organizing oral reports is similar to that for organizing written reports. You have the choice of using either the direct or indirect order. Even so, the same information is not necessarily presented in the same way orally and in writing. Time pressure, for example, might justify direct presentation for an oral report on a problem that, presented in writing, might be better arranged in the indirect order. Readers in a hurry can always skip to the conclusion or ending of the report. Listeners do not have this choice.

- Next organize content. Either the indirect or direct order is all right,

Although oral reports may use either the direct or indirect order, the indirect is the most logical order and by far the most widely used order. Because your audience is not likely to know the problem well, introductory remarks are needed to prepare it to receive your message. In addition, you may need such remarks to arouse interest, stimulate curiosity, or impress the audience with the importance of the subject. The main goal of the introductory remarks is to state the purpose, define unfamiliar terms, explain limitations, describe scope, and generally cover all the necessary introductory subjects (see discussion of introduction, Chapter 11).

- but the indirect order is more common.

In the body of the oral report, you should work toward the objective you have set. Here, too, the oral report closely resembles the written report. Division of subject matter into comparable parts, logical order, introductory paragraphs, concluding paragraphs, and the like are equally important to both forms.

- The organization of oral and written reports is much the same, except that oral reports usually have a closing summary.

The major difference in the organization of the written and oral report is in the ending. Both forms may end with a conclusion, a recommendation, a summary, or a combination of the three. But the oral report is likely to have a final summary, whether or not it has a conclusion or a recommendation. In a sense, this final summary serves the purpose of an executive summary by bringing together all the really important information, analyses, conclusions, and recommendations in the report. It also assists the memory by emphasizing the points that should stand out.

SUMMARY ▶ by Chapter Objectives

1. Consider the following suggestions in selecting and organizing a speech.
   - Begin by selecting an appropriate topic—perhaps one in your area of specialization and of interest to your audience.
   - Organize the message (probably by introduction, body, conclusion).
   - Consider an appropriate greeting ("Ladies and Gentlemen," "Friends").
   - Design the introduction to meet these goals:
     —Arouse interest—a story, humor, or such.
     —Introduce the subject (theme).
     —Prepare the reader to receive the message.
   - Use indirect order presentation to persuade and direct order for other cases.
   - Organize like a report—divide and subdivide, usually by factors.
   - Select the most appropriate ending, usually restating the subject and summarizing.
   - Consider using a climactic close.
   - Choose the best manner of presentation.
     —Extemporaneous is usually best.
     —Memorizing is risky.
     —Reading is difficult unless you are skilled.

1 Select and organize a subject for effective formal presentation to a specific audience.

Describe how personal aspects and audience analysis contribute to formal presentations.

②. To improve your speaking, take these steps:
- Work on these characteristics of a good speaker:
  —Confidence,
  —Sincerity,
  —Thoroughness, and
  —Friendliness.
- Know your audience.
  —Before the presentation, size them up—looking for characteristics that affect your presentation (sex, age, education).
  —During the presentation, continue to analyze them, looking at facial expressions, listening to noises, and such—and adapt to them.

③ Explain the use of voice quality and physical aspects such as posture, walking, facial expression, and gestures in effective oral communication.

3. What the listeners see and hear affects the communication.
- They see the environment (stage, lighting, background), personal appearance, posture, walking, facial expressions, gestures, and such.
- They hear your voice.
  —For best effect, vary the pitch and speed.
  —Give appropriate vocal emphasis.
  —Cultivate a pleasant quality.

④ Plan for visuals to support oral reports and speeches.

4. Use visuals whenever they help communicate.
- Select the types that do the best job.
- Blend the visuals into your speech, making certain that the audience sees and understands them.
- Organize your visuals as a part of your message.
- Emphasize the visuals by pointing to them.
- Talk to the audience, not the visuals.
- Do not block your audience's view of the visuals.

⑤ Work effectively with a group in preparing and making a team presentation.

5. Group presentations have special problems.
- They require all the skills of individual presentation.
- In addition, they require extra planning.
  —to reduce overlap and provide continuity,
  —to improve transition between presentations, and
  —to coordinate questions and answers.

⑥ Define oral reports and differentiate between them and written reports on the basis of their advantages, disadvantages, and organization.

6. Business oral reports are spoken communications of factual business information.
- Written and oral reports differ in three significant ways.
  —Written reports permit more use of visual helps to communication (paragraphing, punctuation, and such); oral reports allow voice inflection, pauses, and the like.
  —Oral reports permit the speaker to exercise greater control over the pace of the presentation; readers of a written report control the pace.
  —Written reports place more emphasis on writing correctness (grammar, punctuation, etc.).
- Plan oral reports just as you do written ones.
  —First, determine your objective and state its factors.
  —Next, organize the report, using either indirect or direct order.
  —Divide the body based on your purpose, keeping the divisions comparable and using introductory/concluding paragraphs, logical order, and the like.
  —End the report with a final summary—a sort of ending executive summary.

CRITICAL THOUGHT QUESTIONS

1. Assume that you must prepare a speech on the importance of making good grades for an audience of college students. Develop some attention-gaining ideas for the introduction of this speech. Do the same for a climactic close for the speech.

2. When is an extemporaneous presentation desirable? When should a speech be read? Discuss.

3. Explain how a speaker's personal characteristics influence the meanings of his or her spoken words.

4. An employee presented an oral report to an audience of 27 middle- and upper-level administrators. Then she presented the same information to three top executives. Note some of the probable differences between the two presentations.

5. Explain how feedback can be used in making a speech.

6. One's manner of dress, choice of hairstyle, physical characteristics, and the like are personal. They should have no influence on any form of oral communication. Discuss.

7. By description (or perhaps by example), identify good and bad postures and walking practices for speaking.

8. Explain how facial expressions can miscommunicate.

9. Give some illustrations of gestures that can be used to communicate more than one meaning. Demonstrate them.

10. "We are born with voices—some good, some bad, and some in between. We have no choice but to accept what we have been given." Comment.

11. What should be the determining factors in the use of visuals?

12. Discuss (or demonstrate) some good and bad techniques of using visuals.

13. In presenting an oral report to a group composed of fellow workers as well as some bosses, a worker is harassed by the questions of a fellow worker who is trying to embarrass him. What advice would you give the worker? Would your advice be different if the critic were one of the bosses? What if the speaker were a boss and the critic a worker? Discuss.

14. Give examples of ways a team could provide continuity between members through the use of supporting examples. Be specific.

15. Explain the principal differences between written and oral reports.

16. Compare the typical organization plans of oral and written reports. Note the major differences between the two kinds of plans.

CRITICAL THINKING EXERCISES

▶ Speeches

Since a speech can be made on almost any topic, it is not practical to list topics for speeches. You or your instructor can generate any number of interesting and timely topics in a short time. Whatever topic you select, you will need to determine the goals clearly, to work out the facts of the situation, and to set a time limit.

▶ Oral Reports

Most of the written report problems presented in the problem section following Chapter 11 can also serve as oral report problems. The following problems, however, are especially suitable for oral presentation.

1. Survey the major business publications for information about the outlook for the national (or world) economy for the coming year. Then present a summary report to the directors of Allied Department Stores, Inc.

2. As a student leader on your campus, you have been asked by the faculty senate (or a comparable faculty group) to report to its members on the status of faculty–student relations. You will include recommendations on what can be done to improve those relations.

3. Report to a meeting of a wildlife-protection organization on the status of an endangered species in your area. You will need to gather the facts through research, probably in wildlife publications.

4. A national chain of _____ (your choice) is opening an outlet in your city. You have been assigned the task of reviewing site possibilities. Gather the pertinent information, and make an oral recommendation to the board of directors.

5. The Future Business Leaders Club at your old high school has asked you to report to it on the nature and quality of business study at your college. You will cover all the factors that you think high school students need to know. Include a visual in your presentation.

6. As representative of a travel agency, present a travel package on _____ (place or places of your choice) to the members of the Adventurer Travel Club. You will describe places to be visited, and you will cover all the essential details—dates, hotels, guide service, meals, costs, manner of travel, and so on.

7. Report to a meeting of Consumers' Alliance (a consumer-protection organization) on the economics of renting telephones from the telephone company versus buying telephones. You will need to gather facts through research.

8. Look through current newspapers, magazines, and so on, and get the best available information on the job outlook for this year's college graduates. You will want to look at each major field separately. You may also want to show variations by geographic area, degree, and schools. Present your findings in a well-organized and illustrated oral report.

9. Present a plan for improving some phase of operation on your campus (registration, scholastic honesty, housing, grade appeals, library, cafeteria, traffic, curricula, athletics, and so on).

10. Present an objective report on some legislation of importance to business (right-to-work laws, environmental controls, taxes, and the like). Take care to present evidence and reasoning from all the major viewpoints. Support your presentation with facts, figures, and so on whenever they will help. Prepare visual supports.

11. Assume that you are being considered by a company of your choice for a job of your choice. Your prospective employer has asked you to make a _____-minute (your instructor will specify) report on your qualifications. You may project your education to the date you will be in the job market, making assumptions that are consistent with your record to date.

12. Prepare and present an informative report on how individuals may reduce their federal or state income tax payments. You will probably want to emphasize the most likely sources of tax savings—such as tax sheltering and avoiding common errors.

13. Make a presentation to a hypothetical group of investors that will get you the investment money you need for a purpose of your choice. Your purpose could be to begin a new business, to construct a building, to develop land—whatever interests you. Make your presentation as real (or realistic) as you can. And support your appeal with visuals.

14. As chairperson of the site-selection committee of the National Federation of Business Executives, present a report on your committee's recommendation. The committee has selected a city and a convention hotel (you may choose each). Your report will give your recommendation and the reasons that support it. For class purposes, you may make up whatever facts you may need about the organization and its convention requirements and about the hotel. But use real facts about the city.

15. As a buyer of men's (or women's) clothing, report to the sales personnel of your store on the fashions for the coming season. You may get the necessary information from publications in the field.

16. The top administrators of your company have asked you to look into the matter of whether the company should own automobiles, rent automobiles, or pay mileage costs on employee-owned automobiles. (Automobiles are used by sales personnel.) Gather the best available information on the matter, and report it to the top administrators. You may make up any company facts you need; but make them realistic.

17. In a group designated or approved by your instructor, present a persuasive presentation proposing that your school make more computing equipment available for student use. Be sure to cover all aspects of such a decision including cost, access, security, etc.

18. Choose a graphics package most of your classmates could use to prepare visuals for oral reports. Report on the features, documentation, and cost. Feel free to use visuals to support your report.

SPECIAL TOPICS IN BUSINESS COMMUNICATION

16

Technology-Enabled Communication

CHAPTER OBJECTIVES

Upon completing this chapter, you will be able to describe the role of technology in business communication. To reach this goal, you should be able to

(1) Explain how technology helps in constructing messages.

(2) Identify appropriate software tools for different stages in the writing process.

(3) Discuss how technology helps in the presentation of messages.

(4) Explain basic concepts of document layout and design.

(5) Discuss various ways to transmit messages and the hardware currently used.

(6) Describe how technology assists in collaboration.

(7) Discuss what impact future developments in technology might have on business communication.

▷ to Using Technology in Communication Tasks

The company that hired you after your recent graduation is looking into ways the MIS department can empower its employees with technological support. Your new boss has asked you to be on the team proposing new ideas. The boss has told you that this team, composed of employees from a variety of divisions, will discuss both hardware and software. One of the main focuses will be on identifying ways to help employees improve their day-to-day communication.

This chapter is designed to help you—to give you a picture of where we are now and where we may be going. It provides a structure for continuing to build your understanding on how future technology will assist in communication tasks. ■

Technological tools can enhance the uniquely human ability to communicate. But as with any set of tools, how one uses them determines their degree of effectiveness. By using your mind both to create messages and to focus the technology appropriately, you can improve the quality of your communication.

Appropriately used, technology can assist individuals and groups with both the routine work related to writing as well as the creative, thinking aspects. William Zinsser, author of *On Writing Well,* compares one tool—the word processor—to a dishwasher. He describes it as liberating one from a chore that's not creative and saps one's energy. As you'll learn, several technological tools assist you in this fashion. Bill Gates, CEO of Microsoft, predicts in *Information at Your Fingertips 2005* that technology will bring us enhanced sharing or collaboration. Technology assists the communicator in many ways and in various aspects of communication.

> • Technology assists with both the tedious and creative writing tasks.

When you think of enhancing the communication process with technology, you probably first think of using word processing software on a personal computer. While that is one important tool, there are numerous hardware and software tools that can help improve your messages. These tools help with the construction, presentation, and transmission of messages as well as with collaborative writing.

TOOLS FOR CONSTRUCTING MESSAGES

Computer tools for constructing written messages can be associated with the different stages of the writing process—planning, gathering and collecting information, analyzing and organizing information, and writing and rewriting. In the past, many of these tools were discrete tools. But today as we move toward greater document-centricity, they often work seamlessly with each other. And, of course, many of the formerly discrete tools have become integral parts of today's word processors. The more skilled you become with each of these tools, the better they serve you.

> • Computer tools can be used throughout the writing process.

Computer Tools for Planning

Whether you are writing a short letter or long report, you can use a computer to help you plan both the document and the writing project. In planning the content of the document, *outlining* or *brainstorming* tools are useful. You can brainstorm, listing your ideas as they occur to you. Later you tag related ideas, asking the computer to group them. Outlining tools are included in most word processors. One way to use an outliner is with a split screen as shown in Figure 16–1. In one part of the screen you'll see your outline and in another part the document you are writing. Another way you can use an outliner is as a separate document. In this case your outline is held in memory; you can toggle back and forth to view it and put it away when you're done.

> • Outlining software helps in planning the content of a message.

When you are working on a long writing project, several projects, or one carried over a long time, *project management software* is an excellent tool for planning the

> • Project management software assists in identifying tasks and allocating resources.

FIGURE 16–1   Illustration of a Planning Tool

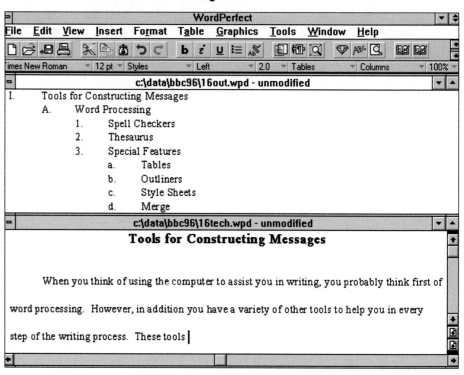

project. It allows you to identify all the tasks needed to complete the project, to determine how much time each task might take, and to generate a time and task chart (commonly called a Gantt chart). Also, it helps you to keep track of your progress and to determine how to reallocate your resources to complete the project on time or within budget. You can see a Gantt chart in Figure 16–2.

- Personal information management software assists with time management.

Finding time for writing, of course, is one of the major challenges for businesspeople. By using *personal information management (PIM) software,* you can plan time for completing writing projects. These time-management tools are merely annotated electronic calendars. However, using them to schedule your writing tasks is an excellent planning tool. They'll remind you of tasks to complete and days remaining before a document needs to be completed. Electronic calendar software is readily available. One simple but widely available calendar is the desktop accessory tool that is a part of Windows, WinPad. You can choose from a slew of other time-management tools. These offer a variety of ways to help you plan time for writing tasks from the day-to-day scheduling to longer-term planning. Figure 16–3 shows the way one tool looks. The bell icon in front of the time shows that this writer set an alarm to let the computer remind him or her when it was time to write. The alarm sounds and the window opens at the designated time with a precise message of what needs to be done.

Some research identifies planning as the primary step that separates good writers from others. However, few writers have discovered the power of electronic planning tools. Using the powerful features that both project management and PIM tools provide will give you the potential to produce high-quality work in a timely fashion.

Computer Tools for Gathering and Collecting Information

- When you need information for a writing task, consider conducting an electronic search.

Before you can write, you have to have something to say. Sometimes you may be writing about your own ideas, but often you will supplement them with facts. Gathering facts or data is one of the most important jobs of the writer. Today you will want to combine your manual search for facts with electronic searches. The computer can help

FIGURE 16–2   Illustration of a Planning Tool

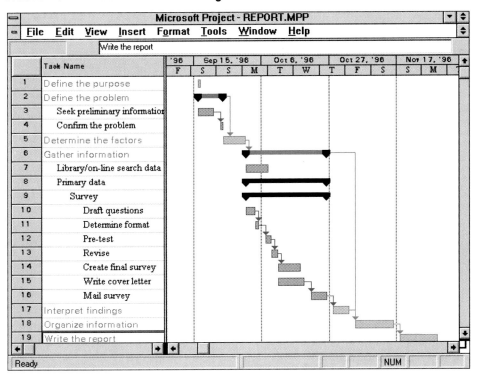

FIGURE 16–3   Illustration of a Planning Tool

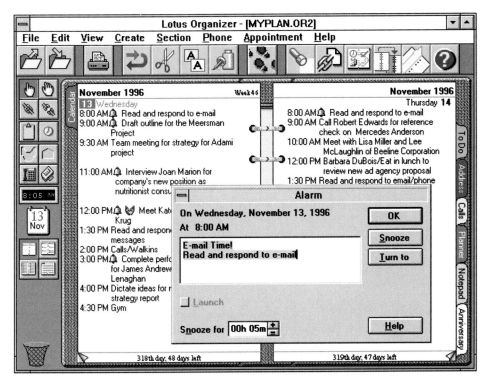

While technology makes constructing documents with graphics easy, writers still need to carefully review the messages they send.

you find a variety of information quickly and accurately because today much of our printed information is available electronically. In fact, some kinds of information are only available electronically.

From the numerous headlines about hackers and computer viruses, you are probably well aware that computers can connect with other computers all over the world. While the way physical connections are made is interesting to some, as a writer you only need to know that it can be done so you can take advantage of it.

- Data can be gathered from internal or external computers.

What you are looking for are facts. These facts can be stored in databases, which can either be internal or external. Your report due today at 1:00 P.M. might be on the current inventory of your on-site manufacturing product line. You could simply connect to your company's computer at noon and download (copy to your computer system) the most recent data before completing your report. However, if you need to project the number of completed units by the end of the month, you may also need to connect to your supplier's computer to check the inventory of the parts you will need to complete your units. In this case, you will be using your computer to find facts both internally from within your company and externally from your suppliers.

- Communications software connects over the telephone lines to external computers.

Most libraries are now allowing their on-line catalogs and databases to be accessed both internally and externally. This means you can use the on-line catalog from terminals within the library or with a computer with *communications ability* (and with a modem if you need to change signals from analog to digital) from anywhere outside the library. Many college networks also allow you to connect to the library resources from campus computer labs and offices.

With communications ability, you can also gather facts through the Internet. This expands your resources immensely beyond your local library. Not only can you reach the Library of Congress, but you also can search libraries in other countries. You can gather information from sources not available in any library anywhere. While you do need to be especially critical of the source of your facts, using the Internet effectively to gather information can give you a tremendous competitive advantage.

- Database software provides a convenient way to collect information.

Once you have gathered the facts, you will want to store them in some organized fashion so you can retrieve them readily when needed. *Database software* will help you immensely here. If your company is interested in developing a new product for a newly defined market niche, you may want to collect articles about the targeted market, potential suppliers of components of your new product, sites for producing the product, projected labor costs, etc. You could do this simply by entering the facts of

FIGURE 16-4   Illustration of a Tool for Collecting Data

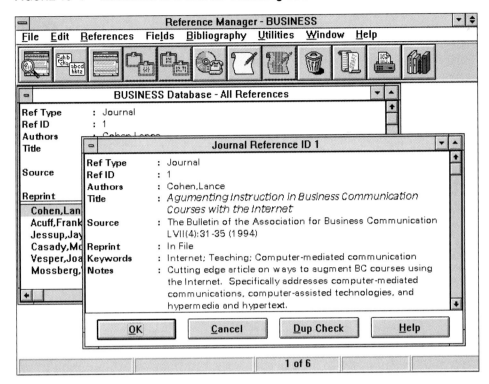

publication and abstracted information in your individually designed form created with database software. The source information you have collected will be available whenever you need it. You can search and sort it on any of the categories (called fields) you set up on your data entry screen.

Variations of the generic database are the specialty tools such as ProCite, Reference Manager, Endnote, and others. These specialty programs allow you to collect information and enter it manually as you do with database software; and they allow you to enter it automatically as you download from a wide variety of on-line catalogs and services as well as CD-ROM and diskette-based services. Figure 16–4 gives you an example of this type of data manager.

• Specialty tools help you collect facts, too.

In Chapter 19, which discusses business research methods, you will learn about other on-line information providers for business information. The major point to remember is that in business it is not necessarily what you know that really counts, but what you can find out. No one can know all there is to know about a subject, but those who can use a computer to gather and collect facts when they need them will find it a real asset.

Computer Tools for Analyzing and Organizing

Three tools that writers find useful in analyzing data are statistics, graphics, and spreadsheet software. Since sometimes you cannot say very much about raw numbers, combining them or viewing them in different ways gives you a clearer picture of their meaning. Today, some very sophisticated *statistical software* has been made user-friendly, allowing those with little computer expertise to use them easily. Some programs will even query you about the nature of your data and recommend which statistical tests to use. Also, most *spreadsheet software* will compute a broad range of statistics that allows writers to give meaningful interpretations to data.

• Computer software helps analyze and interpret data with statistics and graphics.

Graphics software helps writers in several ways. First, graphics reveal trends and relationships in data that are often hard to picture from raw data. This helps writers interpret clearly the meaning of their data. Second, graphics software helps writers explain more clearly to readers what the data mean. For example, you can direct the reader to look at the red and blue lines for the last five years on a line chart, noting the trend of increasing rate of profits. You can create graphics easily with all three tools. Also, most of these tools have features that allow you to annotate the graphic, directing the reader's attention to some particular aspect of the graph. You no longer have to be a graphic artist to create clear, good-looking graphics.

Outlining or *brainstorming software* is an organizing tool for the writer as well as a planning tool. Once you have captured your ideas and grouped related ideas, you can rearrange items into a meaningful order, organizing with the reader in mind. You can also collapse or expand the outline to view as few or as many levels as you want. This lets you see a macro view or big picture of your document as well as a micro or detailed view, so you can check for consistency at all levels.

Computer Tools for Writing

Word processing software is clearly the dominant writing tool of most writers. Today's word processors are becoming more and more document-centric, allowing you to use other writing tools from within the word processor. Other computer writing tools that help writers include *spelling checkers, electronic thesauruses, grammar and style checkers, electronic references,* and *graphics and drawing packages.* The following discussion of these computer writing tools will point out how they can be used as well as caution you about any limitations.

Word Processing Software.   By liberating them from tiresome chores, word processing gives writers time to spend their energy on revising, editing, and other document-polishing efforts. Some of the most common features of word processing software for revising and editing include insert/delete, move and copy, and search and replace.

Insert allows the writer to add characters at any point while delete lets the writer delete characters. One of the nicest features of recent releases of major word processing programs is being able to change your mind and undo the most recent insert and delete changes. Some writers rarely delete text, moving the text to the end of the file or to another file for possible future use. The search and replace feature can be used several ways. One way might be to search for the name in a file of someone who got married, who retired, or who was promoted and replace that name with the new name. Most software lets the writer decide whether to replace automatically every occurrence of the item or to decide on each occurrence. The search feature is usually used to find a particular word, name, or place. However, sometimes writers add asterisks or other symbols to mark copy or to add remarks or reminders—similar to the way one would use the bookmark feature. Later they search for those symbols to find the points in the document that need attention. You will find that these common features will be useful over and over.

Two other useful features of word processing are basic math and simple sorting. The basic math feature lets the writer enter columns or rows of numbers, leaving the calculation job for the software. The sorting feature lets the writer enter columns or rows of words, leaving the alphabetic sorting for the software. While these are useful features of word processing software, the writer has to be careful to enter or mark the copy exactly the way the software needs it to do the proper calculating or sorting.

The tables feature is another feature that enables you to do simple math and sort. It works similarly to a spreadsheet by allowing you to enter formulas in table cells, freeing you from the math. You can also link a spreadsheet to a table. When numbers change in the linked spreadsheet, they are automatically changed in the table with which they are linked. The tables feature allows formatting of individual cells, rows, and columns. It is useful for presenting data as well as textual material in rows and columns.

- Outlining software helps organize your information.

- Word processing helps you capture, manipulate, edit, and revise your messages.

- Insert, delete, move and copy, and search and replace enable you to do what the terms suggest.

- Basic math calculates columns and sorting arranges information in an order.

- The tables feature also allows you to do simple math with data and to sort them.

Another nice feature of many word processing programs is the hidden comment or remark feature. If you insert the proper symbol, the comments that follow will be recorded in the file but not printed unless you tell the software to print them. Teachers can use this feature to put test answers in files but not on the test; later they can print a second copy and direct the software to print the comments. This feature can be used for reminders, detailed information, and such. For example, one might note that the vice president directed that an exception to ordinary practice be granted under some special circumstances. Or one might leave a reminder to verify the statistics presented at a particular point in a document. In Figure 16–5 you can see both the display of a comment and the printed document without the comment.

- The hidden comment feature permits inserting information that is not printed until you choose to print it.

Two additional editing features involve the physical presentation of documents. These features are hyphenation and format change. Both help you change how the physical output looks. Hyphenation, for example, is a feature that helps the right margin appear less ragged than when it is not used. A ragged margin does not usually bother most people on a full page with full length lines; however, when one is using a short line without hyphenating, the right margin can be distracting if it appears ragged. The example of column text in Figure 16–6 with and without hyphenation illustrates how hyphenation can smooth out a ragged right margin. Format change also helps you change margins, tabs, spacing, etc. Formatting is particularly useful when you are changing letterheads, type styles, or binding. It allows you to experiment easily to find the most appropriate form to present the document to the reader.

- Hyphenation and format change enable you to control evenness of right margin.

Since revising and editing are extremely important to turning out well-written business documents, these are tools you will find you use often.

A couple of other word processing features that make the writing job easier are footnoting and index building. Most high-end word processors include the footnoting feature. It allows the writer to mark the place where the footnote occurs, entering the footnote at that point. The software then keeps track of the line count, placing the footnote at the bottom of the page on which it occurs, as well as numbering the footnotes consecutively. Also, the software will move the footnote if the text associated with it is moved. Another chore word processing software assists with is index building. The writer simply tags the words to be indexed, including cross-references, or creates a list of words and the software builds an alphabetic index with associated page numbers. This procedure is particularly helpful with long, frequently referenced documents.

- The footnote feature helps you to fit footnotes within the page layout. Index building enables you to compile an index easily.

Word processing also has three other features that save the writer from having to re-enter the same information. These features are merge, macros, and headers and footers. The merge feature permits you to combine one form document with a document containing variable data. Merge is particularly useful in early and late-stage collection letters, where names and amounts are variable but the message is the same. Another feature, called *macros,* allows you to enter any characters you want to call up at the command of a few keystrokes. This feature is useful for calling up form paragraphs for answering commonly occurring questions as well as bringing up repeatedly used memo headings or letter closings. Macros can be attached to buttons so they can be played with a single click. Headers and footers also let the software enter repeated information at the top and bottom of pages as well as count and print the page numbers.

- Using advanced word processing features saves time.

There are also special features of word processing software for using columns, fonts, importing graphics and spreadsheet files, etc. Knowing how to exploit the features of the word processing software you use will definitely make writing and revising easier for you.

Spelling Checkers. Along with AutoCorrect and QuickCorrect, spelling checkers are relied on daily by business writers. However, they are only effective if the writer uses them. One study found that 75 percent of the spelling errors in student letters could have been caught by spelling checkers.[1] While this finding points out the value of

- Spelling checkers supplement proofreading but do not replace it.

FIGURE 16–5   Illustration of a Writing Tool

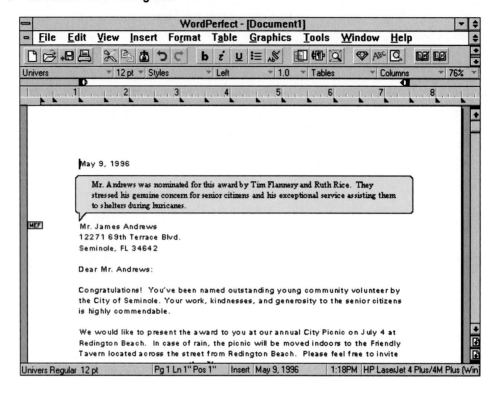

FIGURE 16–6   Illustration of a Writing Tool

Computers, Human Intellect, and Organizational Nervous Systems

An executive provides vision and direction, makes decisions, diagnoses and solves problems, negotiates, convinces, and selects and coaches people. All these actions depend on the excutive's ability to think creatively and communicate clearly; clear communication and creative thinking can be enhanced by the use of computers.

Unfortunately, most people don't realize this. The computer's role as a valuable thinking tool seems to be a secret. Instead, many intellegent people, even today, believe that computers are best suited to clerical and administrative tasks. They see the computer as only a convenience or an operational necessity. I see the computer as an extension of the human brain.

An understanding of the connection between the evolution of the human mind and computers takes us back in time.

Note the ragged margin in this example of text without the hyphenation feature turned on.

Computers, Human Intellect, and Organizational Nervous Systems

An executive provides vision and direction, makes decisions, di-agnoses and solves problems, nego-tiates, convinces, and selects and coaches people. All these actions depend on the excutive's ability to think creatively and communicate clearly; clear communication and creative thinking can be enhanced by the use of computers.

Unfortunately, most people don't realize this. The computer's role as a valuable thinking tool seems to be a secret. Instead, many intellegent people, even to-day, believe that computers are best suited to clerical and adminis-trative tasks. They see the comput-er as only a convenience or an op-erational necessity. I see the com-puter as an extension of the hu-man brain.

An understanding of the con-nection between the evolution of the human mind and computers takes us back in time.

Note that when the hyphenation feature is used, the right margin is smoothed out.

using a spelling checker, it also shows that 25 percent of the spelling errors would not have been found by spelling checkers. Mistakes you will want to watch out for include wrong word errors such as "compliment" for "complement" or "imply" for "infer." A spell checker will also miss errors such as "desert" for "dessert" or misused words such as "good" for "well." Therefore, careful proofreading is still in order after a document has been checked with a spelling program.

Thesaurus Software.   Serious writers usually have a bound thesaurus on hand. But they can use an electronic thesaurus with great ease and efficiency. The ease of popping up a window with suggested synonyms is hard to beat. Most word processors

• The electronic thesaurus gives easy access to synonyms.

---

[1] Berle Haggblade. "Has Technology Solved the Spelling Problem?" *The Bulletin of the Association for Business Communication,* March 1988, p. 23.

A Word of Advice: BACK UP FREQUENTLY!

Some programs will create an automatic backup file, but most leave the responsibility with the writer. Some writers back up every 15 minutes or so while others back up every page. Most writers know how difficult it is to create a document, much less recreate it; so they are willing to spend a few seconds regularly to protect their investment. To further protect your documents, alternate the backup floppies you use. If one disk should be damaged or become infected with a virus, you'll still have another copy. Using different colored floppies for different days or using an odd numbered floppy on an odd-dated day and an even numbered one on an even-dated day are techniques some writers use to make their backup procedures safer. Other writers also grandfather their files by giving each revision a new name in order to help recreate the document from earlier drafts should the current file become unusable for any reason.

include a thesaurus; however, several good independent programs are available. One thesaurus included with a popular word processor gives the part of speech and meaning along with the synonyms. You can page through different uses of the word, selecting the synonym from a new list for each different use. The thesaurus is a powerful tool, and the computer has made it faster to use and easier to access.

- Grammar and style checkers are only suggestion systems.

Grammar and Style Checkers.   The value of grammar and style checkers is often debated. Unlike spelling programs, which are easily able to identify "wrong" words (words that are not in their dictionaries), grammar and style checkers identify "possible problems" with "suggestions" for revision. It is then your responsibility to decide whether the "possible problem" is a problem and whether the "suggestion" is the best solution. However, these programs are improving rapidly, adding expert system techniques to identify "possible problems" in context more accurately.

- They also evaluate a variety of other elements of writing quality.

In addition to checking grammar, style, word usage, and punctuation, these programs now report readability, strength, descriptive, and jargon indexes. They also perform sentence structure analysis, suggesting that you use simpler sentences, vary the sentence beginnings, use more or fewer prepositional phrases, and make various other changes. Grammar and style checkers also identify "possible problems" with specific words that might be slang, jargon, misspelled, misused, or difficult for readers to understand. These programs also give word counts such as average length of sentences, longest sentence, shortest sentence, number of words in a document, and number of times each word is used. An example of the interactive use of one grammar checker is shown in Figure 16–7.

- Although often critized, this software is improving.

While the debate goes on, the tool is getting better. Recent versions address some of the issues concerning writers. For example, recent versions of grammar and style checkers are much more flexible than older versions. If you are writing in an informal environment where your boss finds beginning sentences with "And" and "But" acceptable, you can turn off the rule that would identify those beginnings as problems. Also, you can choose the level of writing your intended audience wants. These are just a few examples of the flexibility in the newest versions of grammar and style checkers.

Grammar and style checkers are definitely an important tool for the business writer. But, like any tool, the more appropriately you use it the better job it does for you.

- A wide variety of reference books are available for easy access.

Reference Software.   Reference software is just what its name suggests—software that presents reference books such as dictionaries, style manuals, zip code directories,

FIGURE 16–7   Illustration of a Writing Tool

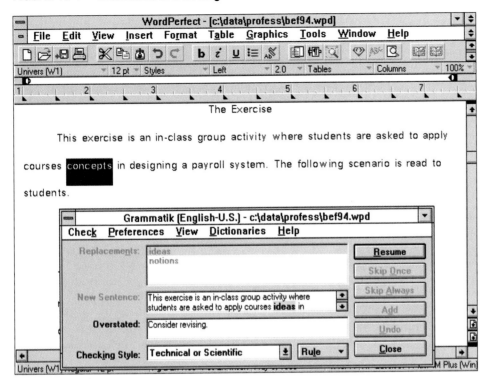

etc. A few of these reference programs are on floppy disks, but the larger ones containing dictionaries, thesauruses, books of quotations, Zip code directories, the world almanac, and several other references are on compact disks. These CD-ROM references include such things as pronunciation of words in audio form and pictures, including video and animation.

Graphics and Draw Tools.   Graphics and draw tools are becoming more important tools for the writer every day. Not only are these programs becoming easier to use, but you also can now launch them from within your word processor. In some cases, your drawing is pasted in your document at the point you left it. The introduction of ready-made graphs and pictures (called clip art) and low-cost scanners, which will copy from any printed source, have made it easier to supplement text with professional-looking graphics. Also, the cost of color output is dropping, making it more desirable to use colored graphics and drawings. In Chapter 13, you learned how to use graphics effectively. The important point to remember here is that the computer enables you to enhance textual communication with graphics.

* Graphics and draw programs assist in supplementing textual materials with visuals.

As you have learned, technology is certainly an important tool for the writer in constructing messages. While word processing is the writer's primary tool in constructing a message, a wide variety of other tools will help in the planning, gathering and collecting, analyzing and organizing, and writing stages.

TOOLS FOR PRESENTING MESSAGES

After you have completed the document, you need to consider how to present it. This decision involves both software and hardware choices.

Software

- Using its layout and design features, desktop publishing software helps present your messages in their best form.

Publishing software for print and electronic documents, enables you to prepare professional-looking documents. You'll find this software particularly useful for long reports, newsletters, policy and procedure manuals, and proposals. This software, called desktop publishing software for print documents and portable document publisher for electronic documents, combines three basic elements—text, graphics, and design. Electronic documents have an additional element—hypertext links. Initially, the first software to combine these elements was desktop publishing software. However, most word processors are now capable of doing nearly 80 percent of what full-featured desktop publishing software can do if you take advantage of their features. To do so effectively, you need some knowledge of the basic elements of design.

Ironically, professionals engaged in designing documents for publication have the same major objective as writers—to communicate effectively. Professionals aim for designs that attract the reader but do not distract. Also, they understand that the most successful publications are those in which the design enhances or complements the meaning of the writer.

With publishing software, you can break out of the traditional-looking page with its roots in the typewriter era to give the reader the best looking, most readable document possible. However, to do this, you need to know about some basic design principles. These principles cover three areas: layout, typography, and art.

- Writers can control the look of their messages through effective layout.

Basic Layout Principles.   Roger Parker, a nationally recognized expert on design, defines layout as simply "the arrangement of text and graphics on a page." Suzanne West, another expert, goes further with, "A layout is a composition of interrelated elements on a page." While similar, the latter implies that the writer has some control over the results through careful composition of the elements. These elements include *white space, text, visuals,* and *graphic design elements* such as circles, lines, and bullets.

- White space adds emphasis and affects readability.

You might find surprising that today a commonly accepted ratio of white space to text is 1:1. That means half of your page is devoted to text and half to white space. This ratio provides optimum readability. Readability is also improved by using lines 35 to 40 characters long. Therefore, with these two factors in mind, you can clearly see in Figure 16–8 that instead of using a full page of long, double-spaced lines it is better to use short lines with less spacing between them. This deliberate shifting of the white space to the margins keeps the 1:1 ratio but improves the readability.

- Use white space consistently.

In planning the placement of white space in documents with facing pages, you will want to be sure your elements line up at the top and at the left. The example in Figure 16–9 shows a facing page layout with consistent use of white space in margins and between the lines.

- Use it to give emphasis.

White space can also be used for emphasis. As you've already learned, space denotes importance. When you are writing about a topic, the more space you give it the more emphasis it gets. The same principle applies to white space. If you leave more white space around certain text or graphics, you will be giving that text or graphic more emphasis.

- Type size and style also affect readability.

Another way to get emphasis in the text is through type size and style. Of course, you want headings to stand out, but they should be balanced with the rest of the text. The size of your main heading will also be governed by the number of levels of subheadings you plan to use. And you will want to use a type size smaller than your text type size for captions and footnotes so they do not distract the reader from the text. Type style elements such as bold, italic, or bold italic can also be added to headings, subheadings, text, captions, and footnotes for more emphasis.

One means of emphasis that should be used sparingly is all uppercase. Using both uppercase and lowercase in headings makes the headings easier to read. However, all uppercase in short phrases will work effectively.

FIGURE 16–8   Illustration of a Presentation Tool

Before
Double-spaced with long lines

After
Short lines with white space moved to margins

FIGURE 16–9   Illustration of a Presentation Tool

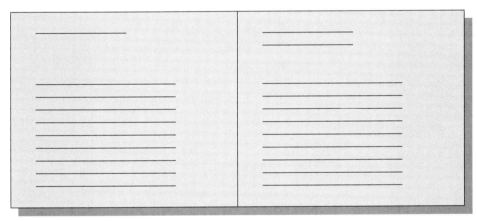

This facing, double-page spread illustrates copy aligned at top and left, the way our eye has been trained to read pages.

Good layout always includes careful planning of visuals—graphics and drawings. In planning them, give attention to placement and size as well as content. Also, be sure you plan space for the captions in your layout.

A final element of layout is the graphic device. Lines or rules around text or separating text from visuals or white space can be a very effective tool for directing the eye to where you want it to go. The thickness of a line can be varied to give differing degrees of emphasis to the material it is highlighting. Tints or shading are other graphic devices that attract attention. Usually these are used to separate related copy in the same text. *Business Week* often uses this device. For example, it may run a story on General Motors Corporation, including a brief profile of a GM executive in a shaded box accompanying the article. Or it may be reporting on a specific industry in general, detailing explicit facts on specific companies in a table in a shaded box.

- Graphic devices can direct the eye, giving attention to particular parts of the message.

- Plan them to enhance the text.

Graphic devices should enhance the text, not distract from it. If your reader just reads the shaded boxes and overlooks the primary content of the report, your layout is not successful. Careful planning for effective use of graphic devices is a prerequisite to effective layout as discussed in Chapter 13.

When the layout is good, it works well with the typography and art. While we have touched on the importance of type size and style in planning the textual component of layout, let us look at some basic principles of typography.

- Understanding type and its terminology helps you communicate with publishing professionals.

Typography Basics.   Although you may not be doing much yourself with the technical aspect of type in the majority of documents you produce, knowing the concepts and basic vocabulary is important. Not only will you be able to communicate more effectively with those who work on your documents, but you also will help them to produce better layouts for you.

- A *point* is $1/72$ inch; a *pica* is 12 points.

Many word processing terms for measuring, such as pitch and space, are carryovers from the typewriter era. However, the publishing and typesetting world measures in *points and picas.* A point is about $1/72$ of an inch, and a pica is 12 points, or about $1/6$ of an inch. When you are specifying type size, generally 14-point type and smaller is considered appropriate for text while type larger than 14 points is usually used for headings. Some software gives you the choice of specifying in inches, centimeters, or picas. If you are working closely with people in the publishing world, you would be wise to work with the terminology they understand.

- *Kerning* is the spacing between characters.

Another term from this area is *kerning.* Kerning refers to the spacing between characters. While standard typewriters and dot matrix printers generally use equal spacing for each character, in publishing this space is variable. For example, in the word "The" a publishing system would allow the T to overhang, moving the h in for an even-appearing spacing. A fixed pitch printer, on the other hand, would place the h after the overhang, appearing to leave more space between the T and h than between the h and e. Also, if copy doesn't quite fit the page, you can squeeze it or stretch it by tightening or loosening the kerning or spacing between characters.

- *Leading* is the spacing between lines.

Leading is similar to kerning except that it refers to vertical spacing rather than horizontal. When your lines are too close together, you can increase the leading to add more white space between lines. As with kerning, you can adjust the leading to fit copy to the space available.

One other term commonly used in the publishing industry is *typeface.* Typeface refers to the design of the entire uppercase and lowercase set of letters. While there are hundreds of typefaces available today, two common typefaces in use are Times Roman and Arial (see Figure 16–10). Times Roman is a serif type, having feet (cross-lines) at the end of the main strokes. Arial is a sans serif type, having no feet at the ends of its main strokes.

- Computer people use the term *font* for typeface.

When you are talking to computer-oriented people about publishing, you may hear the term *font* used for typeface. However, a font means one typeface in one size and style. Therefore, if you wanted to use a Arial type with standard, bold, and italics in

---

FIGURE 16–10   Illustration of a Presentation Tool

R

Times Roman (Serif)

R

Arial(SansSerif)

four sizes, you would need 12 fonts—one for each size and one for each style. Today we often use scalable fonts, fonts that can be changed in size within a range. The most commonly used fonts today for the Mac and Windows-based systems are Postscript and TrueType. Numerous font libraries are available for purchase, allowing you to prepare a custom-looking document.

Since type is a key element in most business documents, you'll want to pay special attention to it. Usually, it will account for more than 90 percent of your document. Your care in selecting and using type will have a big impact on the effectiveness of your design.

Art Fundamentals.   Art as used here in its broadest sense refers to drawings, graphs, photos, and other illustrations. As a writer you primarily need to remember that art should always serve a message's purpose; it must never serve its own. Whenever you are about to place an art element on a page, ask yourself what purpose does it serve. As noted in Chapter 13, need is the sole criterion for including a graphic in a document.

* Art should serve the message's purpose.

One purpose of art is to break up large blocks of text. While we often try to conjure up an idea for drawings, graphs, or photos, we can also use the space to emphasize a key idea. By quoting from within the document and setting it off in larger type with ruling lines, we use a technique called a *pull quote.*

* Use it to break up blocks of text.

Whatever the reason we have for our art, we should also strive to use the best art possible. Look for interesting photos, not merely mug shots. Crop photos, cutting out any extraneous material that does not work to enhance the text. Choose your art with the reader in mind. In some cases these suggestions might mean using cartoons or illustrations you scan in an import from various clip art software, and in other cases it might mean using high-quality color photos or significant pull quotes. Of course, you need to be sure you do not violate copyrights.

* Choose art for the best communication effect.

Good design expertly integrates layout, typography, and art elements. You will probably want to begin with either some very basic applications or the prepared templates or style sheets bundled with the publishing software. You will get better with practice. Also, you will get better if you read books and magazines on design, pay attention to the designs of others noting what seems to work, and keep a file of ideas. By always keeping the reader in mind as you design your documents, you will be effective in communicating your message.

* Effective design integrates layout, type, and art.

Hardware

Software is just one component of presenting a message; hardware is another. If the software has features your printer or other output device cannot print, the features are useless. On the other hand, if your hardware has features your software cannot produce, they, too, are useless. Both must work together to produce your message.

* Your choice of output hardware is critical to the appearance of your message.

The most common output device is still the printer. Depending on the formality of your communication, you may find yourself using dot printers for one type of message, inkjets for another, and laser printers for yet another. In circumstances where you must have the best-looking documents, you may even use typeset output. Appearance does convey a message, and the hardware you choose to complete the presentation of your document is an important consideration.

* Print and some electronic documents give the writer control of appearance.

Electronic documents have different hardware considerations. Portable document publishers such as Envoy and Acrobat prepare documents to be used across platforms. Readers will read them on screens, not paper. And because they have the ability to create hypertext links within the document, the paths readers take through a document may vary substantially from someone reading the same document in print form. Keeping readers appraised of where they are at all times within a document is important. Also, it is important to always give a reader ways to move around the document; including both buttons and keystroke alternatives is essential.

Another type of electronic document is one that is posted to a computer system and read by readers using browsers. Microsoft's recent introduction of this technology both with its inclusion of HTML (hypertext markup language) formatting in Word and its inclusion of a browser in Windows indicates this method of information presentation will be a growing one. However, unlike the other forms, the reader rather than the writer controls such things as font, size, and color of the text. The writer's job is focused on identifying headings, content, and links to other information. But it is still up to the writer to test documents on the most commonly used browsers to assure that the visual look of their document (at least in the default mode) does not distract from or interfere with the message content.

- Documents created for browser use turn over some control of visual aspects to the reader.

······························

TOOLS FOR TRANSMITTING MESSAGES

- The medium you choose to send your message communicates.

Transmitting means to send the message. The medium you choose to transmit a message communicates to the receiver the importance you attach to the message. Usually a written message gets more attention than an oral message, and a special delivery message gets more attention than an ordinary mailed message. Even the method of special delivery chosen conveys a message. The client who sends you electronically the document you requested is perceived differently from the client who sends it on paper through Federal Express. Knowing what technologies are available to transmit the message assists you in deciding which is the best medium to use.

- Cellular technology expands the physical environment of the message sender.

Technologies for sending a variety of oral and visual messages are widely used in business. One booming technology for oral communication is the cellular phone. While predominantly used in cars, it can be used in any area of the country equipped for it. With a phone that fits in the palm of the hand, businesspeople can now be reached for important calls as well as conduct business from otherwise inaccessible places. While you are delayed in a traffic jam on your way to the airport, you can call your office, your important client, or your company's central word processing center. Cellular phones enable businesspeople to make more productive use of their time.

- Voice messaging systems are gaining business use.

As was mentioned in Chapter 14, another oral communication technology gaining wide acceptance by businesspeople is the voice messaging system. Not only do these systems answer phones, direct calls, and take messages, but they also act as voice stor-

WAISGLASS/COULTHART
Still haven't figured out the electronic-mail system, huh, Bob?
(FARCUS Reprinted by Permission: Universal Press Syndicate)

Transmitting messages by cellular allows you and your receiver the freedom to move around.

age systems. For example, you can ask the system to retrieve messages for a particular date or from a particular person. You can also take a message you receive, annotate it with your voice message, and pass it along to another person's voice mailbox. You can even record a message for the system to deliver to several people's voice mailboxes at a specified time. By eliminating telephone tag and interruptions, this technology, too, improves the productivity of those using it.

One technology that combines oral and video communication effectively is videoconferencing. While it has been around for a while, new developments in optical fibers, satellite transmission, and software and chip technology may push them into even more favor. New developments are making the systems better and lowering the costs. Videoconferencing systems save travel time and expense, and they help eliminate many scheduling problems. Even small companies or medium-sized companies with not enough use to justify setting them up are using them through providers such as Kinkos.

- Videoconferencing combines oral and video media.

Technology also gives us the option of adding sound to our written documents. The sounds can be words dictated and attached to a document, or they can be sounds from other sources such as sound clip libraries. Sounds can be used to add interest, emphasis, and clarity to a document. As more offices get computer systems equipped with sound capabilities, we will see a growth in the use of the compound document.

- Technology enables us to add sound to our written documents.

Written communication, on the other hand, can be transmitted effectively with two proven technologies—electronic mail and facsimile. Electronic mail transmission works with computer systems, sending documents to an electronic mailbox. These electronic mailboxes can be set up on a company's mini or mainframe computer, on a local area network (LAN), on a bulletin board system, or on a private subscriber information service. In any case, you need to know the electronic address of the receiver and how to access the system in order to send the document. Also, the receiver needs to check the electronic mailbox to receive the document. Facsimile transmission (fax) uses telephone lines to send a copy of the document. Faxing is much like photocopying or printing, but the copy is delivered elsewhere. Similarly, you need to know the telephone number of the receiving fax in order to send the message, and someone on the receiving end needs to check the fax and deliver the message.

- Electronic mail and facsimile transmission are gaining use for transmitting written messages.

Both of these technologies are being effectively used for transmitting written messages. However, while both have the advantage of immediacy, they are both less formal than sending a formal document. You need to evaluate carefully the need for formality in choosing your transmission medium.

- Although they communicate in writing, they are viewed as informal.

- So use them appropriately.

Knowing that you have a choice of media for transmitting the message and knowing how to use it are both important in order to choose the most appropriate medium. Because this technology is developing rapidly, you need to make it a priority to keep up-to-date on the latest developments.

TOOLS FOR COLLABORATIVE WRITING

- Computer tools assist groups on a wide variety of tasks.

As discussed in Chapter 10, collaborative writing or group writing tasks occur regularly in business, and they vary widely in the form and nature of the work. However, there is a wide range of computer tools to support various aspects of the process. A recent study reviewing computer-supported collaborative work group writing tools divided them into two classifications: asynchronous and synchronous.[2] Asynchronous tools automate the traditional groups; synchronous tools, on the other hand, create a new kind of group environment.

Asynchronous Computer Tools

- Several computer tools assist the traditional group.

Asynchronous tools include word processing, conferencing systems, electronic mail systems, portable document publishers, and group authoring systems. Word processing features useful in group writing include commenting, strikeouts, and redlining. Commenting allows you to insert comments in a document written by someone else. Strikeout and redlining allow you to identify text you would like to delete or insert. A lead writer in a group might distribute a document draft to members of the group; they would use these features of their word processor and return the disk to the leader. The leader would then review the documents and edit the original. Electronic document publishers work similarly. However, the leader tells the software to compile all the comments.

- Computer conferencing is useful when distance or time make getting together difficult.

Another group writing tool is computer conferencing. As noted in Chapter 14, this tool is useful when groups have a difficult time meeting due to distance and time. To begin, the lead writer would enter some text. Others would access the system, review the comments, and enter their own. All comments can be reviewed by all members of the group. In some systems, group members have anonymity, but others maintain audit trails so comments can be attributed to specific group members.

- Electronic mail permits communicating to intended receivers only.

Electronic mail systems provide a means for one writer to send a message to others. Unlike conferencing, in these systems access to others' mailboxes is restricted. While you can distribute messages to a whole group, you do not have access to messages one member sends to someone else.

- Collaborative writing is helped by group authoring software.

Group authoring systems are software programs designed specifically for group work. While different products have varied features, most are designed to allow document versions to be compared, to allow comments and suggestions to be entered at appropriate places, and to allow the use of common editing tools such as insert, delete, paragraph, stet, etc.

All these tools are designed to work the way groups have traditionally worked. The planning, writing, and revising occur much the way they occur in traditional groups.

---

[2] Annette Easton, George Easton, Marie Flatley, and John Penrose, "Supporting Group Writing with Computer Software," *The Bulletin of the Association for Business Communication,* June 1990, p. 34.

However, the tools contribute to improvements in both speed and the quality of the final documents.

Synchronous Computer Tools

Synchronous computer tools are used by all group members at the same time. However they can be used either at the same place or at different places. Same-place tools are generally referred to as electronic meeting systems (EMS). Different-place tools are sometimes called whiteboard or cooperative tools.

- Collaborative tools change the group process and improve its output quality.

With the same-place EMS tools, a facilitator conducts the meeting and operates the software that runs on a network. The facilitator may start the group with a question or statement. The group members will comment on the statement through their computers simultaneously and anonymously. For example, one member may propose a new policy statement. The other members then would comment about it. The the group under the direction of the facilitator might use other EMS tools to group related comments, rank order of them, and write the final policy statement. This kind of EMS group writing tool has been shown to produce significantly higher quality documents than manual group writing.[3]

With the different-place cooperative tools, one member of the group initiates the process either on a network or through modem connections. This tool often provides both a chat box, where users can talk to each other, and a whiteboard or place where the shared document can be viewed and edited. The software can be set for different levels and types of editing. The technology is advancing to include a window where the group can view others they are working with. As the hardware comes into greater use in business, we are likely to see much more use of distributed teams working on writing projects together.

A LOOK TO THE FUTURE

In addition to the technological developments discussed thus far, you can anticipate further rapid development. Bill Gates, CEO of Microsoft, in his *"Information at Your Fingertips 2005"* speech at Comdex, presented a futuristic vision of pervasive technology in the next decade. These systems will be friendlier and seamlessly blended. He predicted that exponential improvements will continue, empowering people with rich sets of communication tools. Digital convergence, where all information is in digital form, will provide the vehicle for on-demand transactions of all types. We can also expect to see improvements in display technology, higher speed wired and wireless networks, and simpler authoring tools. You are likely to see more voice and handwriting input, too. Some of the early signposts that we are moving this way are wider use of CDs and on-line services. You must make it a priority to keep abreast of these developments in order to identify tools that will make your job easier.

- Computer tools will continue to enhance the communication process, . . .

However, whatever form these developments take, human minds will continue to control message formulation. In fact, there is no evidence whatsoever that the need for messages communicated in writing and speaking will decrease. Even more important, there is absolutely no evidence that these messages can be handled in a way that does not require basic writing and speaking skills. Business communication is here to stay. In fact, the increasing advancement of the technology of the future is likely to require more—not less—of it.

- . . . but the human mind still controls it.

---

[3] Annette Easton, Nancy Eickelmann, and Marie Flatley, "The Effects of an Electronic Meeting System Group Writing Tool on the Quality of Written Documents," *Journal of Business Communication,* Spring 1994.

SUMMARY ▶ by Chapter Objectives

① Explain how technology helps in constructing messages.

1. Technology helps a writer construct messages through every step of the writing process including:
   - Planning,
   - Gathering and collecting information,
   - Analyzing and organizing information, and
   - Writing and rewriting.

② Identify appropriate software tools for different stages in the writing process.

2. Each stage of the writing process has a set of software tools most appropriate for the tasks in that stage. These include the following:
   - Outlining or brainstorming, project management, and personal information management programs for planning,
   - Communications and database programs for gathering and collecting information,
   - Statistical, spreadsheet, graphics, and outlining or brainstorming software for analyzing and organizing information, and word processing, spelling, thesaurus, grammar and style checking, reference, and graphics and draw programs for writing.

③ Discuss how technology helps in the presentation of messages.

3. Technology helps in the presentation of documents with both sophisticated hardware and software.
   - Hardware contributes in the printing of documents.
   - Software contributes with publishing features that combine text and graphics and promote good layout and design.

④ Explain basic concepts of document layout and design.

4. Layout and design refers to the arrangement of text and graphics on a page. Layout involves the careful composition of these basic elements:
   - White space for manipulating emphasis and readability,
   - Text for emphasis and balance as well as for visual clues of organization,
   - Visuals such as graphics and drawings, and
   - Graphic design elements to direct the eye.

   Layout and design are also affected by typography. Aspects writers need to know about include:
   - Points and picas, which represent height,
   - Kerning, which determines the spacing between letters,
   - Leading, which determines the spacing between lines, and
   - Typeface, which refers to the design of an entire set of letters.

   Art is a final aspect of layout and design. Its main purpose is always to serve a message's purpose.

⑤ Discuss various ways to transmit messages and the hardware curently used.

5. Communicators have a variety of choices of media for transmitting their messages.
   - Oral messages can be sent by cellular phone, voice messaging systems, and sound clips.
   - Videoconferencing technology combines oral and visual messages.
   - Written messages can be transmitted by electronic mail or fax.

⑥ Describe how technology assists in collaboration.

6. A range of software tools assists groups of writers in asynchronous and synchronous writing environments.
   - Asynchronous tools automate traditional groups with such tools as word processing, conferencing systems, electronic mail, portable document publishers, and group authoring systems.
   - Synchronous tools automate a group environment where writers work on a document at the same time. Electronic meeting system tools are used for same-time/same-place writing, and cooperative tools are used for same-time/different-place writing.

⑦ Discuss what impact the future developments might have on business communication.

7. Future developments expect to integrate present technologies more smoothly, making them easier to use. Digital convergence will provide the vehicle for bringing us on-demand transactions. Future developments will likely mean more need for good basic communication skills.

CRITICAL THOUGHT QUESTIONS

1. Explain how technology can help the writer with both creative and tedious writing tasks.
2. Identify specific software tools that assist with constructing written messages. Explain what each does.
3. Word processing software is the writer's primary tool. Identify five basic features and two advanced features useful to business writers.
4. Discuss the advantages and disadvantages of spelling checkers and grammar and style checkers.
5. Describe ways graphics software helps writers.
6. Explain what a writer should know about layout and design and why it is important.
7. Identify various ways business writers can transmit oral and written messages.
8. How can technology assist in group writing?
9. What can we expect to see in future technological developments that will impact business communication?

CRITICAL THINKING EXERCISES

1. Investigate the school and/or local libraries to determine what current (or future) computer systems will help one find information for business. Report your findings to the class.
2. Compile an annotated list of at least five local or regional BBSs. Include name, number, type, and access information, along with a descriptive statement on the nature of the board.
3. Locate six examples of electronic clip art and sound clips you might use in a business document. Print the examples along with a brief explanation of a good use in a business document.
4. Identify where computers, printing equipment, and faxes are available at or around your college. Prepare a table with this information, listing times available as well as any costs. Also, be sure to include computer configurations and software available.
5. Choose a feature from your word processor (such as index, table of contents, templates, macros, etc.) that you have not used much. Learn how to use it and create an example of its use in a business document. Write a brief description of its application.
6. Select a dozen idioms from a reference book (found in your library or bookstore) that seem common to you. Type these into your word processor and run the file through a grammar and style checker. Print a copy of the results and bring it to class for discussion.
7. From a current computer magazine, find an article that relates to communication in business. Write a one-paragraph reaction to it and send your paragraph electronically (e-mail) to someone selected by your instructor.

17

Techniques of Cross-Cultural Communication

Upon completing this chapter, you will be able to describe the major barriers to cross-cultural communication and how to overcome them. To reach this goal, you should be able to

1. Explain why communicating clearly across cultures is important to business.

2. Define culture and explain its effects on cross-cultural communication.

3. Describe cultural differences in body positions and movements and use this knowledge effectively in communicating.

4. Describe cultural differences in attitudes toward time, space, odors, and such and use this knowledge effectively in communicating.

5. Explain the language equivalency problem as a cause of miscommunication.

6. Describe what one can do to overcome the language equivalency problem.

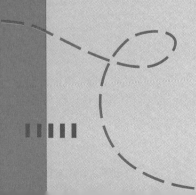

▷ to Cross-Cultural Communication

To introduce yourself to this chapter, assume the position of assistant to the president of Thatcher-Stone and Company, a small manufacturer of computer components. Your boss, gregarious old Vernon Thatcher, invited you to join him at a luncheon meeting with a group of Asian business executives in which negotiations for the sale of Thatcher-Stone products would be opened. Because Thatcher-Stone's domestic sales have been lagging, the company badly needs these customers.

As the Asian guests entered the room, bowing as introductions were made, Mr. Thatcher attempted to put them at ease. "No need to do that," he said. "I'm just plain Vernon Thatcher. Just relax and make yourself at home." You noticed that the Asians appeared bewildered. They appeared even more bewildered when early in the meeting Mr. Thatcher made this statement: "We've only got the lunch hour, gents. I know you'll appreciate getting right down to business."

Throughout the meeting Mr. Thatcher was in his best conversational mood—laughing, back-slapping, telling jokes. But none of this seemed to make an impression on the guests. They seemed confused to you. They smiled and were extremely polite, but they seemed to understand little of what Mr. Thatcher was saying. Although he tried again and again to move to business talk, they did not respond. The meeting ended pleasantly, but without a sale.

"They're a strange people," Mr. Thatcher commented when he got back to his office. "They have a lot to learn about doing business. It doesn't look like they're going to deal with us, does it?" Mr. Thatcher was right in his last comment. They did not.

As you review the meeting, you cannot help but feel that Mr. Thatcher spoiled the deal, for he failed miserably in communicating with the Asians. The fact is that there is much to know about communicating in international settings. The goal of this chapter is to introduce this issue to you. ■

Technological advances in communication, travel, and transportation have made business increasingly global. This trend is expected to continue in the foreseeable future. Thus, the chances are good that you will have to communicate with people from other cultures.

• Business has become more global.

Both large and small businesses want you to be able to communicate clearly with those from other cultures for several reasons. Many businesses sell their products and services both domestically and internationally. Being able to communicate with others helps you be more successful in understanding customers' needs, communicating how your company can meet these needs, and winning their business. In addition to being a more productive worker, you will be more efficient both within and outside your company. You will be able to work harmoniously with those from other cultures, creating a comfortable workplace. With cultural barriers broken down, you will be able to hire good people despite their differences. Also, you will avoid problems stemming solely from misinterpretations. Your attention to communicating clearly with those from other cultures will enrich both your business and your personal lives.[1]

• Communicating across cultures effectively improves your productivity and efficiency and promotes harmonious work environments.

In preparing to communicate with people from other cultures, you might well begin by reviewing the instructions given in this book. Most of them fit all people. But many do not, especially those involving letter writing. To determine which do not, you must study the differences among cultures, for cultural differences are at the root of the exceptions. In addition, you must look at the special problems that our language presents to those who use it as a second language. It is around these two problem areas that this review of cross-cultural communication is organized.

• Cross-cultural communication involves understanding cultural differences and overcoming language problems.

---

[1] Sondra Thiederman, *Bridging Cultural Barriers for Corporate Success: How to Manage the Multicultural Work Force* (Lexington, MA: Lexington Books, 1991), p. xviii.

PROBLEMS OF CULTURAL DIFFERENCES

A study of the role of culture in international communication properly begins with two qualifying statements. First, culture is often improperly assumed to be the cause of miscommunication. Often it is confused with the other human elements involved. We must remember that communication between people of different cultures involves the same problems of human behavior that are involved when people of the same culture communicate. In either case, people can be belligerent, arrogant, prejudiced, insensitive, or biased. The miscommunication these types of behavior cause is not a product of culture.

Second, one must take care not to overgeneralize the practices within a culture. We say this even though some of the statements we make in the following paragraphs are overgeneralized. But we have little choice. In covering the subject, it is necessary to make generalizations such as "Latin Americans do this" or "Arabs do that" in order to emphasize a point. But the truth of the matter is that in all cultures, subcultures are present; and what may be the practice in one segment of a culture may be unheard of by other segments. Within a culture townspeople differ from country dwellers, the rich differ from the poor, and the educated differ from the uneducated. Clearly, the subject of culture is highly complex and should not be reduced to simple generalizations. Keep this point in mind as you read the following material.

Culture has been defined in many ways. The classic definition most useful in this discussion is one derived from anthropology: *Culture* is "a way of life of a group of people . . . the stereotyped patterns of learning behavior, which are handed down from one generation to the next through the means of language and imitation."[2] A more contemporary definition is that "Culture is an agreed-upon set of rules that consists of components ranging from seemingly inconsequential edicts about how to shake hands or dress on a date to more cosmic ideas about the existence of God or the nature of man."[3] In other words, people living in different geographic areas have developed different ways of life. They have developed different habits, different values, and different ways of relating to one another.

These differences are a major source of problems when people of different cultures try to communicate. Unfortunately, people tend to view the ways of their culture as normal and the ways of other cultures as bad, wrong, peculiar, or such. Specifically, communication between people of different cultures is affected by two major kinds of differences: (1) differences in body positions and movements and (2) differences in attitudes toward various factors of human relationships (time, space, intimacy, and so on).

Body Positions and Movements

At first thought, one might think that the positions and movements of the body are much the same for all people. But such is not the case. These positions and movements differ by culture, and the differences can affect communication. For example, in our culture most people sit when they wish to remain in one place for some time, but in much of the world people hunker (squat). Because we do not hunker, we tend to view hunkering as primitive. This view obviously affects our communication with people who hunker, for what we see when we communicate is a part of the message. But how correct is this view? Actually, hunkering is a very normal body position. Our children hunker quite naturally—until their elders teach them to sit. Who is to say that sitting is more advanced or better?

---

[2] V. Barnouw, *Culture and Personality* (Chicago: Dorsey Press, 1963), p. 4.

[3] Sondra Thiederman, *Profiting in America's Multicultural Marketplace: How to Do Business Across Cultural Lines* (New York: Lexington Books, 1991) p. 2.

- Two qualifying statements begin this study of culture: (1) It is improperly blamed for some miscommunication.

- (2) It is easy to overgeneralize cultural practices.

- Culture is the way people in an area view human relationships.

- Two major kinds of cultural differences affect communication.

- Body positions and movements differ among cultures. For example, in some cultures, people sit; in other cultures, they hunker.

Carefully Present and Receive the Business Card in Japan

In Japan, it is considered bad manners to go to a business meeting without the business card or *Meishi*. While there are a number of ways to present it, receiving it is an art, too. If you want to make a good impression on the presenter, receive it in both hands, especially when the other party is senior in age or status or a potential customer. Be careful not to fiddle with the card or put it in your rear pocket—that is considered crude. Put it in some distinctive case. Those who do business in both countries often have their business card translated on the back, as the examples here show.

For another example, people from our culture who visit certain Asian countries are likely to view the fast, short steps taken by the inhabitants as peculiar or funny and to view our longer strides as normal. And when people from our culture see the inhabitants of these countries bow on meeting and leaving each other, they are likely to interpret the bowing as a sign of subservience or weakness. Similarly, people from our culture see standing up as the appropriate thing to do on certain occasions (as when someone enters the room) whereas people from some other cultures do not.

As you know, movements of certain body parts (especially the hands) are a vital form of human communication. Some of these movements have no definite meaning even within a culture. But some have clear meanings, and these meanings may differ by culture. To us an up-and-down movement of the head means yes and a side-to-side movement of the head means no. These movements may mean nothing at all or something quite different to people from cultures in which thrusting the head forward, raising the eyebrows, jerking the head to one side, or lifting the chin are used to convey similar meanings. For another example, the two-fingered "victory" sign is as clear to us as any of our hand signs. To an Australian, whose culture is not vastly different from ours, the sign has a most vulgar meaning. The "OK" sign is terribly rude and insulting in such diverse places as Russia, Germany, and Brazil.[4] In Japan, a similar

• Manners of walking differ among cultures.

• Communication with body parts (hands, arms, head, etc.) varies by culture.

[4] Roger E. Axtell, *Gestures: The Do's and Taboos of Body Language Around the World* (New York: John Wiley & Sons, Inc., 1993), p. 41.

sign represents money. If a businessperson completing a contract gave this sign, the Japanese might think they needed to give more money, perhaps even a bribe. Even the widely used "thumbs up" sign for "things are going well" could get you into trouble in countries from Nigeria to Australia.[5] And so it is with many of our other body movements. They differ widely, even within cultures.

• Eye movements differ by culture.

The movements of our eyes also vary by culture. We in North America are taught to look our audience in the eye in formal speechmaking. In informal talking, however, we are encouraged to look but not stare. Although not everyone in our culture conforms to these standards, we regard them as desirable. In cultures such as Indonesia, looking at people, especially those older or in higher positions, is considered to be disrespectful. On the other hand, our practices of eye contact are not so rigorous as with the British and Germans. Unless one understands these cultural differences, how one looks or does not look can be interpreted as being impolite on the one hand and being shy on the other.

• So do touching and handshaking.

Touching and particularly handshaking differences are important to understand. This is made difficult by others adopting Western greetings. However, some cultures, like the Chinese, do not like touching much and will give a handshake you might perceive as weak while other cultures like touching and will give you greetings ranging from full embraces and kisses to nose rubbing. If you can avoid judging others from different cultures on their greeting based on your standards for others like you, you can seize the opportunity to access the cultural style of the worker. Here are some types of handshakes.[6]

Culture	Handshakes
Americans	Firm
Germans	Brusk, firm, repeated upon arrival and departure
French	Light, quick, not offered to superiors, repeated upon arrival and departure
British	Soft
Hispanics	Moderate grasp, repeated frequently
Middle Easterners	Gentle, repeated frequently
Asians	Gentle; for some, shaking hands is unfamiliar and uncomfortable (an exception to this is the Korean, who generally has a firm handshake)

• A smile can be a sign of weakness, and the left hand may be taboo.

In our culture, smiles are viewed positively in most situations. But in some other cultures (notably African cultures), a smile is regarded as a sign of weakness in certain situations (such as bargaining). Receiving a gift or touching with the left hand is a serious breach of etiquette among Muslims, for they view the left hand as unclean. We attach no such meaning to the left hand. And so it is with other body movements—arching the eyebrows, positioning the fingers, raising the arms, and many more. All cultures use body movements in communicating, but in different ways.

Attitudes toward Factors of Human Relationships

• Differing attitudes toward various factors of human relationships cause communication problems.

Probably causing even more miscommunication than differences in body positions and movements are the different attitudes of different cultures toward various factors of human relationships. For illustrative purposes, we will review seven major factors: time, space, odors, frankness, relationships, values, and social behavior.

---

[5] *Ibid.*, pp. 47–50.

[6] Thiederman, *Bridging Cultural Barriers,* p. 138.

The classic "ugly American" was traveling in a faraway land. He had been critical of much of what he experienced—the food, the hotels, the customs in general. One day he came upon a funeral. He observed that the mourners placed food on the grave—and left it there.

"What a stupid practice!" he exclaimed to his native host. "Do your people actually think that the dead person will eat the food?"

At this point, the host had taken all the insults he could handle for one day. So he replied, "Our dead will eat the food as soon as your dead smell the flowers you place on their graves."

Time. In our culture, people tend to regard time as something that must be planned for the most efficient use. They strive to meet deadlines, to be punctual, to conduct business quickly, and to work on a schedule.

In some other cultures (especially those of the Middle East and some parts of Asia), people view time in a more relaxed way. They see planning as unwise and unnecessary. Being late to a meeting, a social function, or such is of little consequence to them. In fact, some of them hold the view that important people should be late to show that they are busy. In business negotiations, the people in these cultures move at a deliberately slow pace, engaging in casual talk before getting to the main issue. It is easy to see how such different views of time could cause people from different cultures to have serious miscommunication problems.

• Views about time differ widely. Some cultures stress punctuality; some do not.

Space. People from different cultures often vary in their attitudes toward space. North Americans tend to prefer about two feet or so of distance between themselves and those with whom they speak. But in some cultures (some Arabian and South American cultures), people stand closer to each other; not following this practice is considered impolite. For another example, North Americans view personal space as a right and tend to respect this right of others; thus, they stand in line and wait their turn. People from some other cultures view space as belonging to all. Thus, they jostle for space when boarding trains, standing at ticket counters, shopping in stores, and such. In encounters between people whose cultures have such different attitudes toward space, actions are likely to be misinterpreted.

• Space is viewed differently by different cultures. In some cultures, people want to be far apart; in other cultures, they want to be close.

Odors. People from different cultures may have different attitudes toward body odors. To illustrate, Americans work hard to neutralize body odors or cover them up and view those with body odors as dirty and unsanitary. On the other hand, in some Asian cultures people view body odors not as something to be hidden but as something that friends should experience. Some of the people from these cultures feel that it is an act of friendship to "breathe the breath" of the person with whom they converse and to feel their presence by smelling. Clearly, encounters between people with such widely differing attitudes could lead to serious miscommunication.

• Some cultures view body odors as bad; others view them as normal.

Frankness. North Americans tend to be relatively frank in their relationships with others, quickly getting to the point and perhaps being blunt and sharp in doing so. Asians tend to be far more reticent and sometimes go to great lengths not to offend. Thus, Asians may appear evasive, roundabout, and indecisive to North Americans; and North Americans may appear harsh, impolite, and aggressive to Asians. Telephone customs may be an exception, especially among the Chinese, who tend to end telephone calls abruptly after their purpose has been accomplished. North Americans, on

• Some cultures are more direct, more blunt than others.

Knowing how those from other cultures regard touching or hand-shakes helps you avoid misinterpreting them.

the other hand, tend to move on to friendly talk and clearly prepare the listener for the end of the call.

Relationships.   In many cultures, strict social classes exist, and class status determines how intimately people are addressed and treated in communication. For this reason, a person from such a culture might quiz a person from another culture to determine that person's class status. Questions concerning occupation, income, title, and such might be asked. People from cultures that stress human equality are apt to take offense at such questioning and in fact at the notion of class status. This difference in attitude toward class status is also illustrated by differences in the familiarity of address. Some Americans are quick to get on a first-name basis. This practice is offensive to people from some other cultures, notably the English and the Germans, who expect such intimate address only from long-standing acquaintances.

- Intimacy among people varies in different cultures.

Similarly, how people view superior–subordinate relations can vary by culture. The dominant view in Latin America, for example, is of the necessity for a strong boss with weak subordinates doing as the boss directs. In sharp contrast is the somewhat democratic work arrangement of the Japanese in which much of the decision making is by consensus. Most in our culture view as appropriate an order between these extremes. These widely differing practices have led to major communication problems in joint business ventures involving people from these cultures.

- How people view superior–subordinate relations also differs.

The role of women varies widely by culture. In North America, we continue to move toward a generally recognized goal of equality. In many Islamic cultures, the role of women is quite different. In our view, the practices of the people of these other cultures suggest severe restriction of rights. In the view of the people of these cultures,

- So does the role of women.

their practices are in accord with their religious convictions. They see us as being the ones out of step.

Values.   Also differing by culture are our values—how we evaluate the critical matters in life. Americans, for example, have been indoctrinated with the Puritan work ethic. It is the belief that if one puts hard work ahead of pleasure, success will follow. The product of this thinking is an emphasis on planning, working efficiently, and maximizing production. Of course, not all of us subscribe to this ethic, but it is a strong force in the thinking of those in our culture. The prevailing view in some other cultures is quite different. In some, the major concern is for spiritual and human well-being. The view of work is relaxed, and productivity is, at best, a secondary concern.

> • Each culture has different values—concerning such matters as attitude toward work,

Views about the relationships of employers and employees also may differ by culture. North American workers expect to change companies in their career a number of times; and they expect companies to fire them from time to time. Employees expect to move freely from job to job, and they expect employers to hire and fire as their needs change. Expectations are quite different in some other cultures. In Japan, for example, employment tends to be for a lifetime. The workplace is viewed much like a family with loyalty expected from employees and employer. Differences such as this have caused misunderstandings in American–Japanese joint ventures.

> • employee–employer relations,

How employees view authority is yet another question that cultures view differently. We North Americans generally accept authority, yet we fiercely maintain the rights of the individual. In many Third World cultures, workers accept a subservient role passively. Autocratic rule is expected—even wanted.

> • and authority.

Social Behavior.   From culture to culture, differences in social behavior develop. To illustrate, in some Asian cultures public displays of affection are strongly frowned upon—in fact, considered crude and offensive. Westerners, on the other hand, accept at least a moderate display of affection. To Westerners, laughter is a spontaneous display of pleasure, but in some cultures (Japanese, for one), laughter can also be a controlled behavior—to be used in certain social situations. Even such emotional displays as sorrow are influenced by culture. In some Middle Eastern cultures, sorrow is expressed with loud, seemingly uncontrolled wailing. In similar situations, Westerners typically respond with subdued and controlled emotions.

> • Social behavior varies by culture such as practices concerning affection, laughter, and emotion.

We all have observed the emotion and animation people of the Mediterranean cultures display as they communicate. And we have seen the more subdued communication of others—notably northern Europeans. The first group tends to see the second as disinterested and lacking in friendliness. The second sees the first as excitable, emotional, perhaps even unstable.

> • Included is the degree of animation displayed.

Many more such practices exist. Some cultures combine business and social pleasure; others do not. Some expect to engage in aggressive bargaining in business transactions; others prefer straightforward dealings. Some talk loudly and with emotion; others communicate orally in a subdued manner. Some communicate with emphasis on economy of expression; others communicate with an abundance of verbiage.

> • Many more such practices exist.

The comparisons could go on and on, for there are countless differences in cultures. But it is not necessary to review them all. What is important is that we recognize their existence, that we look for them, and that we understand them. Always we should guard against ethnocentrism, using our cultural practices as standards for determining meaning in cross-cultural communication.

> • We must recognize them, look for them, and understand them.

Effects on Business Communication Techniques

The foregoing examples illustrate only a few of the numerous differences that exist among cultures. Books have been written on the subject. Our objective here is only to establish the point that the differences among cultures affect communication between people of different cultures.

> • Cultural differences affect communication.

Multilingual Word Processors: Tools for Communicating Effectively in Other Languages

Accent is a multilingual word processor that lets you create documents in over 30 languages. You simply click on the appropriate flag and begin writing with the characters that language needs. A drop-down key map shows you which characters are mapped to which keys. In fact, you can even write right to left if needed. Most of the languages have spell checkers as well as hyphenation and thesaurus support. And the major languages have on-line help in their language. While not intended as a translator, Accent has a built-in translation tool that you see illustrated here. You simply enter the word in your strongest language and the Berlitz translator presents it in the other languages. The translation tool has over 60,000 words in its vocabulary. With the necessary second-language skills, this tool can help you do business with customers who speak other languages.

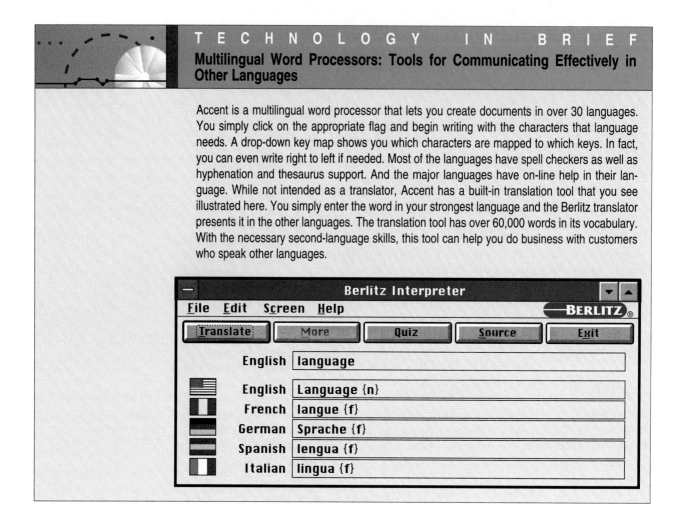

- Our letter-writing techniques are not universally acceptable.

The communication techniques presented in this book should be modified in light of cultural differences, but it is difficult to say how this should be done. You simply have to apply your knowledge of the culture involved to each of these techniques. For example, the Japanese have difficulty saying no emphatically. They often see it as a personal attack, so they give a *tatemae* response. This response is what they think should be said, not necessarily the whole truth. They believe this will help save face for all involved.[7] A major cultural phenomenon that is important to understand when doing business with Mexicans is the *mañana* syndrome. While it is often used derogatorily to imply that Mexicans are lazy, understanding how and when it is used will help you communicate deadlines clearly.[8] As you can see, much that is acceptable in our business communication must be modified for readers from other cultures.

- These techniques do not work with all English-speaking people.

Cultural differences even cause communication problems among people using the same language. For example, even though the United States and other countries have a common language, communication problems occur between them. Such small differences as calling an elevator a *lift* or the hood of a car a *bonnet* can be very confusing. Just telling time with a 24-hour clock can be very confusing. The Canadian who told you he fell asleep at *22:00* on the *chesterfield* can be easily misunderstood.

---

[7] Diana Rowland, *Japanese Business Etiquette,* 2nd ed. (New York: Warner Books, 1993), pp. 49–51.

[8] Jay and Maggie Jessup, *Doing Business in Mexico: Your Guide to Exporting, Importing, Investing and Manufacturing in the World's Fastest-Growing Economy* (Rocklin, CA: Prima Publishing, 1993), p. 34.

Without question, cultural differences can cause communication problems. But there is a way to overcome those problems. You can become a student of cultures— that is, you can learn about the cultures of the people with whom you communicate. In doing so, you must take care not to overgeneralize or oversimplify, for cultural differences are highly complex. You must also take care not to exaggerate the effects of cultural differences. Not all miscommunication between people of different cultures results from cultural differences. While there are many variations and exceptions within and between cultures, there are similarities, too. As a student of cultures, you understand that finding those similarities will help you communicate clearly. This effort is not easy, and it will never be completely successful, but it is the only solution available.

- Overcome communication problems stemming from cultural differences by learning about cultures.

PROBLEMS OF LANGUAGE

The people on earth use more than 3,000 languages. Because few of us can learn more than one or two other languages well, problems of miscommunication are bound to occur in international communication.

- Communication problems are caused by the existence of many languages.

Lack of Language Equivalency

Unfortunately, wide differences among languages make precisely equivalent translations difficult. One reason for such differences is that languages are based on the concepts, experiences, views, and such of the cultures that developed them. And different cultures have different concepts, experiences, views, and such. For example, we think of a *florist* as someone who sells flowers and related items in a store. In some cultures, however, flowers are sold by street vendors, mainly women and children. Obviously, our *florist* does not have a precise equivalent in the language of such cultures. Similarly, our *supermarket* has no equivalent in some languages. The French have no word to distinguish between *house* and *home, mind* and *brain,* and *man* and *gentleman.* The Spanish have no word to distinguish between a *chairman* and a *president* while the Italians have no word for *wishful thinking.* And Russians have no words for *efficiency, challenge,* and *having fun.* However, the Italians have nearly 500 words for types of macaroni, and the Eskimos have over 100 words for types of snow. And so it is with words for many other objects, actions, concepts, and such (for example, *roundup, interview, strike, tough, monopoly, domestic, feminine, responsible, aloof*).

- Differences among languages make equivalent translations difficult.

Another explanation for the lack of language equivalency is the grammatical and syntactic differences among languages. Some languages (Urdu, for example) have no gerunds, and some have no adverbs and/or adjectives. Not all languages deal with verb mood, voice, and tense in the same way. The obvious result is that even the best translators often cannot find literal equivalents between languages.

- Grammar and syntax differences add to the difficulty.

Adding to these equivalency problems is the problem of multiple word meanings. Like English, other languages have more than one meaning for many words. Think, for example, of our numerous meanings for the simple word *run* (to move fast, to compete for office, a score in baseball, a break in a stocking, a fading of colors, and many more). Or consider the multiple meanings of such words as *fast, cat, trip, gross, ring,* and *make.* The Oxford English Dictionary uses over 15,000 words to define *what.* Unless one knows a language well, it is difficult to know which of the meanings is intended.

- So do the multiple meanings of words.

Overcoming such language problems is difficult. The best way, of course, is to know more than one language well; but the competence required is beyond the reach of most of us. Thus, your best course is first to be aware that translation problems exist and then to ask questions—to probe—to determine what the other person understands.

- Overcome such language problems by knowing languages well and by questioning.

- Use back translating for important communications.

- English is the primary language of international business.

- But many foreigners have problems using English.

- Two-word verbs are hard for foreigners to understand,

- as in these combinations.

For very important oral messages, documents, or such, you might consider using a procedure called *back translating*. This procedure involves using two translators, one with first-language skills in one of the languages involved and one with first-language skills in the other language. The first translator translates the message into his or her language, and the second translator then translates the message back into the original. If the translations are good, the second translation matches the original.

Difficulties in Using English

Fortunately for us, English is the primary language of international business. This is not to say that other languages are not used in international business, for they are. When business executives from different countries have a common language, whatever it may be, they are likely to use it. For example, an executive from Iraq and an executive from Saudi Arabia would communicate with each other in Arabic, for Arabic is their common language. For the same reason, an executive from Venezuela would use Spanish in dealing with an executive from Mexico. However, when executives have no common language, they are likely to use English. The members of the European Free Trade Association conduct all their business in English even though not one of them is a native English speaker. And when a Swiss company and a Swedish company merged, they decided to make English the official company language.[9]

Although we can take comfort from knowing that ours is the primary language of international business, we must keep in mind that it is not the primary language of many of those who use it. Since many of these users have had to learn English as a second language, they are likely to use it less fluently than we and to experience problems in understanding us. Some of their more troublesome problems are reviewed in the following pages.

Two-Word Verbs. One of the most difficult problems to nonnative speakers of English involves the use of two-word verbs. By *two-word verbs* we mean a wording consisting of (1) a verb and (2) a second element that, combined with the verb, produces a meaning that the verb alone does not have. For example, take the verb *break* and the word *up*. When combined, they have a meaning quite different from the meanings the words have alone. And look how the meaning changes when the same verb is combined with other words: *break away, break out, break in, break down*. Dictionaries are of little help to nonnatives who are seeking the meanings of these word combinations.

There are many two-word verbs—so many, in fact, that a special dictionary of them has been compiled.[10] Following are a few of them arranged by the more common words that combine with the verbs:

VERB PLUS "AWAY"	VERB PLUS "BACK"
give away	cut back
keep away	feed back
lay away	keep back
pass away	play back
put away	read back
throw away	take back
	turn back
	win back

---

[9] Bill Bryson, *The Mother Tongue: English & How it Got That Way* (New York: William Morrow and Company, Inc., 1990), p. 12.

[10] George A. Meyer, *The Two-Word Verb* (The Hague, Netherlands: Mouton, 1975).

VERB PLUS "DOWN"

calm down

die down

hand down

keep down

let down

lie down

mark down

pin down

play down

put down

run down

shut down

sit down

wear down

VERB PLUS "IN"

cash in

cave in

close in

dig in

give in

run in

take in

throw in

VERB PLUS "OFF"

break off

brush off

buy off

check off

clear off

cool off

cut off

finish off

let off

mark off

pay off

run off

send off

show off

shut off

sound off

start off

take off

write off

VERB PLUS "OUT"

blow out

clean out

clear out

crowd out

cut out

die out

dry out

even out

figure out

fill out

find out

give out

hold out

lose out

pull out

rule out

tire out

wear out

work out

VERB PLUS "OVER"

check over

do over

hold over

pass over

put over

run over

stop over

take over

talk over

think over

win over

VERB PLUS "UP"

blow up

build up

call up

catch up

cover up

dig up

end up

fill up

get up

hang up

hold up

VERB PLUS "UP"

keep up

look up

mix up

pick up

save up

shake up

shut up

slow up

split up

wrap up

VERB PLUS MISCELLANEOUS WORDS

bring about

catch on

get across

pass on

put across

put forth

roll over

set forth

stop over

• Use two-word verbs sparingly. Find substitutes, as shown here.

Of course, foreigners studying English learn some of these word combinations, for they are part of the English language. But many of them are not covered in language textbooks or listed in dictionaries. It is apparent that we should use these word combinations sparingly when communicating with nonnative speakers of English. Whenever possible, we should substitute for them words that appear in standard dictionaries. Following are some two-word verbs and suggested substitutes:

TWO-WORD VERBS	SUGGESTED SUBSTITUTES
give up	surrender
speed up, hurry up	accelerate
go on, keep on	continue
put off	defer
take off	depart, remove
come down	descend
go in, come in, get in	enter
go out, come out, get out	exit, leave
blow up	explode
think up	imagine
figure out	solve
take out, take away	remove
go back, get back, be back	return

• Some two-word verbs have noun and adjective forms. Use these sparingly.

Additional problems result from the fact that some two-word verbs have noun and adjective forms. These also tend to confuse nonnatives using English. Examples of such nouns are *breakthrough, cover-up, drive-in, hookup, show-off,* and *sit-in.* Examples of such adjectives are *going away* (a going-away gift), *cover-up* (cover-up tactics), *cleanup* (cleanup work), and *turning-off* (turning-off place). Fortunately, some nouns and adjectives of this kind are commonly used and appear in standard dictionaries (words such as *hookup, feedback, breakthrough, lookout,* and *takeover*). In writing to nonnative readers, you will need to use sparingly those that do not appear in standard dictionaries.

• Culturally derived words, especially slang, cause problems.

Culturally Derived Words. Words derived from our culture also present problems. The most apparent are the slang expressions that continually come into and go out of use. Some slang expressions catch on and find a place in our dictionaries (*brunch, hobo, blurb, bogus*). But most are with us for a little while and then are gone.

OBEDIENCE SCHOOL

Today, class, we're going to discuss cultural diversity. . . .
From *The Wall Street Journal,* with permission of Cartoon
Features Syndicate

Examples of such short-lived slang expressions are the "twenty-three skiddoo" and "oh you kid" of the 1920s and the *ritzy, scram, natch, lousy, soused, all wet, hep, in the groove,* and *tops* of following decades. More recent ones that are probably destined for the same fate include *nerd, wimp, earth pig, pig out, waldo, squid, grimbo,* and *dexter.*

Most slang words are not in dictionaries or on the word lists that non-English speaking people study to learn English. The obvious conclusion is that you should not use slang in cross-cultural communication.

- So avoid slang.

Similar to and in fact overlapping slang are the words and expressions that we derive from our various activities—sports, social affairs, work, and the like. Sports especially have contributed such words, many of which are so widely used that they are part of our everyday vocabulary. From football we have *kickoff, goal-line stand,* and *over the top.* Baseball has given us *out in left field, strike out, touch base, off base, right off the bat, a steal, squeeze play, balk,* and *go to bat for.* From boxing we have *knockout, down for the count, below the belt, answer the bell,* and *on the ropes.* From other sports and from sports in general we have *jock, ace, par, stymie, from scratch, ballpark figure,* and *get the ball rolling.*

- Words derived from sports, social activities, and so on cause problems.

Similar to these words and expressions are words and expressions developed within our culture (colloquialisms). Some of these have similar meanings in other cultures, but most are difficult for foreigners to understand. Following are some examples:

- Colloquialisms also cause problems.

head for home	in the groove
have an itching palm	nuts (crazy)
grasp at straws	grand (thousand)
flat-footed	circle the wagons
on the beam	shoot from the hip
out to pasture	tuckered out
sitting duck	gumption
crying in his beer	tote (carry)
in orbit	in a rut
a honey	pump priming
a flop	make head or tail of it
dope (crazy)	tearjerker
hood (gangster)	countdown
up the creek without a paddle	shortcut
a fish out of water	educated guess
a chicken with its head cut off	

• We use such words in everyday communication. But avoid them in cross-cultural correspondence.

If you are like most of us, many of these words and expressions are a part of your vocabulary. You use them in your everyday communicating, which is all right. They are colorful, and they can communicate clearly to those who understand them. Nonnative English speakers are not likely to understand them, however, so you will need to eliminate such words and expressions in communicating with them. You will need to use words that are clearly defined in the dictionaries that these people are likely to use in translating your message. Following are some examples:

NOT THIS	BUT THIS
We were caught flat-footed.	We were surprised.
He frequently shoots from the hip.	He frequently acts before he thinks.
We would be up the creek without a paddle.	We would be in a helpless situation.
They couldn't make heads or tails of the report.	They couldn't understand the report.
The sales campaign was a flop.	The sales campaign was a failure.
I'll touch base with you on this problem in August.	I'll talk with you about this problem in August.
Take an educated guess on this question.	Answer this question to the best of your knowledge.
Your sales report put us in orbit.	Your sales report pleased us very much.
We will wind down manufacturing operations in November.	We will end manufacturing operations in November.
Your prediction was right on the beam.	Your prediction was correct.

A General Suggestion for Communicating across Cultures

• Use simple, basic English.

In addition to the specific suggestions for improving your communication in English with nonnative English speakers, you should follow one general suggestion: talk (or write) simply and clearly. Talk slowly and enunciate each word. Remember that as most of these people learned English in school, they are acquainted mainly with primary dictionary meanings and are not likely to understand slang words or shades of difference in the meanings we give words. Thus, they will understand you better if you use simple, basic English.

• Word questions carefully to elicit the response intended.

You will also communicate better if you carefully word your questions. Be sure your questions are not double questions. Avoid "Do you want to go to dinner now or wait until after the rush hour is over?" Also, avoid the yes/no question that some cultures may have difficulty answering directly. Use more open-ended questions such as, "When would you like to go to dinner?" Also, avoid the negative question such as, "Aren't you going to dinner?" In some cultures a yes response confirms whether the questioner is correct; in other cultures the response is directed toward the question being asked.

• Continually check the accuracy of the communication.

Finally, try to check and clarify your communication through continuous confirmation. Additionally, written summaries are also a good idea, and today's technology enables parties to do this on the spot. It allows you to be certain you've conveyed your message and received theirs accurately. Even in Britain, a culture similar to ours, similar words can have vastly different meanings. For example, we use a billion to mean 1,000,000,000 where the British use it to mean 1,000,000,000,000. Continually checking for meaning and using written summaries can help ensure the accuracy of the communication process.

SUMMARY ▶ by Chapter Objectives

1. Businesses are becoming increasingly global in their operations.
   - Being able to communicate across cultures is necessary in these operations.
   - Specifically, it helps in gaining additional business, in hiring good people, and generally in understanding and satisfying the needs of customers.
2. *Culture* may be defined as "the way of life of a group of people."
   - Cultures differ.
   - People tend to view the practices of their culture as right and those of other cultures as peculiar or wrong.
   - These views cause miscommunication.
3. Variations in how people of different cultures use body positions and body movements is a cause of miscommunication.
   - How people walk, gesture, smile, and such varies from culture to culture.
   - When people from different cultures attempt to communicate, each may not understand the other's body movements.
4. People in different cultures differ in their ways of relating to people.
   - Specifically, they differ in their practices and thinking concerning time, space, odors, frankness, relationships, values, and social behavior.
   - We should not use our culture's practices as standards for determining meaning.
   - Instead, we should try to understand the other culture.
5. Language problems are another major cause of miscommunication in international communication.
   - About 3,000 languages are used on Earth.
   - They differ greatly in grammar and syntax.
   - Like English, most have words with multiple meanings.
   - As a result, equivalency in translation is difficult.
6. Overcoming the language equivalency problem involves hard and tedious work.
   - The best advice is to master the language of the nonnative English speakers with whom you communicate.
   - Also, you should be aware of the problems caused by language differences.
   - Ask questions carefully to make sure you are understood.
   - For important communications, consider back translation—the technique of using two translators, the first to translate from one language to the other and the second to translate back to the original.
   - Check the accuracy of the communication with written summaries.

1 Explain why communicating clearly across cultures is important to business.

2 Define culture and explain its effects on cross-cultural communication.

3 Describe cultural differences in body positions and movements and use this knowledge effectively in communicating.

4 Describe cultural differences in attitudes toward time, space, odors, and such and use this knowledge effectively in communicating.

5 Explain the language equivalency problem as a cause of miscommunication.

6 Describe what one can do to overcome the language equivalency problem.

CRITICAL THOUGHT QUESTIONS

1. "Just as our culture has advanced in its technological sophistication, it has advanced in the sophistication of its body signals, gestures, and attitudes toward time, space, and such. Thus, the ways of our culture are superior to those of most other cultures." Discuss this view.

2. What are the prevailing attitudes in our culture toward the following, and how can those attitudes affect our communication with foreigners? Discuss.
   a. Negotiation methods
   b. Truth in advertising
   c. Company–worker loyalty
   d. Women's place in society

3. Some of our letter-writing techniques are said to be unacceptable to people from such cultures as those of Japan and England.
   a. Which techniques in particular do you think would be most inappropriate in these cultures?
   b. Why?

4. Think of English words (other than text examples) that probably do not have a precise equivalent in some other culture. Tell how you would attempt to explain each of these words to a person from that culture.

5. Select a word with at least five meanings. List those meanings and tell how you would communicate each of them to a foreigner.

6. From newspapers or magazines, find and bring to class 10 sentences containing words and expressions that a nonnative English speaker would not be likely to understand. Rewrite the sentences for this reader.

7. Is conversational style appropriate in writing to foreign readers? Discuss.

CRITICAL THINKING EXERCISES

Instructions: Rewrite the following sentences for a nonnative English speaker.

1. Last year our laboratory made a breakthrough in design that really put sales in orbit.

2. You will need to pin down Mr. Wang to put across the need to tighten up expenses.

3. Recent losses have us on the ropes now, but we expect to get out of the hole by the end of the year.

4. We will kick off the advertising campaign in February, and in April we will bring out the new products.

5. Jamison gave us a ballpark figure on the project, but I think he is ready to back down from his estimate.

6. We will back up any of our products that are not up to par.

7. Mr. Maghrabi managed to straighten out and become our star salesperson.

8. Now that we have cut back on our advertising, we will have to build up our personal selling.

9. If you want to improve sales, you should stay with your prospects until they see the light.

10. We should be able to bring about a saving of about 8 or 10 grand.

18

Correctness of Communication

Upon completing this chapter, you will be able to use the accepted standards of English grammar and punctuation in written business communications. To reach this goal, you should be able to

1 Use punctuation marks correctly.

2 Write complete, grammatically correct sentences, avoiding such problems as awkward construction, dangling modifiers, and misuse of words.

3 Determine when to spell out numbers and when to express them in numeral form according to standards of correctness.

4 Spell words correctly by applying spelling rules and using the dictionary or spell checker.

5 Use capital letters for all proper names, first words of sentences, and first words of complimentary closes.

▷ to the Effects of Correctness on Communication

Play the role of a purchasing agent for Stockwell Machine Works and read through today's mail. The first letter comes from Joe Spivey, sales manager, B and B Manufacturing Company. You have not met the writer, though you talked to him on the telephone a few days ago. At that time, you were favorably impressed with Spivey's enthusiasm and ability, and with B and B. In fact, you assumed that after he gave you the information you needed about B and B's products and services, you would begin buying from it.

As you read Spivey's letter, however, you are startled. "Could this be the same person I talked with?" you ask yourself. There in the first paragraph is an *it don't,* a clear error of subject-verb agreement. Farther down, an *it's* is used to show possession rather than *it is.* Spivey apparently uses the sprinkle system for placing commas—that is, he sprinkles them wherever his whims direct. His commas often fall in strange places. For example, he writes, "Our salespeople, say the Rabb Company engineers, will verify the durability of Ironskin protective coating," but you think he means "Our salespeople say the Rabb Company engineers will verify the durability of Ironskin protective coating." The two sentences, which differ only in their punctuation, have distinctly different meanings. Spivey's letter is filled with such errors.

In general, you now have a lower opinion of Spivey and his company. Perhaps you'll have to take a long look at B and B's products and services. After all, the products and services that a company provides are closely related to the quality of its people.

The problem just described is a very real one in business. Image does influence the success of both companies and people. And correctness in writing influences image. Thus, you will want to make certain that your writing is correct, so that it helps form a favorable image both of you and of your company. The material presented in the pages that follow should help you in that effort. ■

The correctness of your communication will be important to you and your company. It will be important to you because people will judge you by it, and how they judge you will help determine your success in life. It will be important to your company because it will help convey the image of competence that companies like. People judge a company by how its employees act, think, talk, and write. Company executives want such judgments to be favorable.

- People judge you and your company by the correctness of your communication.

THE NATURE OF CORRECTNESS

Not all people agree that there are standards for correct communication. In fact, some people think there should be no general standards of this kind, that whatever communicates in a given case is all right. Businesspeople, however, generally accept the standards for correct usage that educated people have developed over the years. These are the standards that you have studied in your English composition classes and that appear in textbooks. Businesspeople expect you to follow them.

- Businesspeople expect you to follow the generally accepted standards of English.

These standards of correctness have one basic purpose: to assist in communicating. To some people the standards of correctness appear arbitrary or unnecessary. But such is not the case. They are designed to reduce misunderstanding—to make communication more precise. It is only in this light that we can justify studying them.

- These standards of correctness assist in communicating.

The practical value of these standards is easily illustrated. Take, for example, the following two sentences. Their words are the same; only their punctuation differs. But what a difference the punctuation makes!

"The teacher," said the student, "is stupid."
The teacher said, "The student is stupid."

What's the latest dope?
What's the latest, dope?

The butler was asked to stand by the door and call the guests names as they arrived.
The butler was asked to stand by the door and call the guests' names as they arrived.

A clever dog knows it's master.
A clever dog knows its master.

Everyone, I know, has a problem.
Everyone I know has a problem.

Do not break your bread or roll in your soup.
Do not break your bread, or roll in your soup.

She ate a half-fried chicken.
She ate a half fried chicken.

I left him convinced he was a fool.
I left him, convinced he was a fool.

In the parade will be several hundred children, carrying flags and many important officials.
In the parade will be several hundred children, carrying flags, and many important officials.

The play ended, happily.
The play ended happily.

Thirteen people knew the secret, all told.
Thirteen people knew the secret; all told.

Or what about the following pair of sentences? Who is speaking, the Democrats or the Republicans? The commas make a difference.

The Democrats, say the Republicans, will win.
The Democrats say the Republicans will win.

Here are two more sentences. The difference here needs no explanation.

He looked at her stern.
He looked at her sternly.

• The following review covers the major standards. They are coded for your convenience.

Because the standards of correctness are important to your communication in business, this chapter will review them. The review is not complete, for much more space would be needed for complete coverage. But the major standards are covered, those that most often present problems in your writing. For your convenience, the standards are coded with symbols (letters and numbers). You should find these symbols useful in identifying the standards. Your instructor should find them useful as grading marks to identify errors in your writing.

• Take the self-analysis test to determine your present knowledge of the standards.

You probably already know many of the standards of correctness, so the following information will not all be new to you. To help you determine how much you know and do not know, you should take the self-analysis test at the end of the chapter. It should indicate what you know and do not know. This will enable you to study the standards selectively. Because the self-analysis test covers only the more frequently used standards, however, you would be wise to review the entire chapter.

STANDARDS FOR PUNCTUATION

The following explanations cover the most important standards for correctness in punctuation. For reasons of accuracy, the explanations use some technical words. Even so, the illustrations should make the standards clear.

Apostrophe: Apos 1

Use the apostrophe to show the possessive case of nouns and indefinite pronouns. If the word does not end in *s*, add an apostrophe and an *s*. If the word ends in *s*, add only an apostrophe.

- Use the apostrophe to show possession.

NOMINATIVE FORM	POSSESSIVE FORM
company	company's
employee	employee's
companies	companies'
employees	employees'

Proper names and singular nouns ending in *s* sounds are exceptions. To such words you may add either an apostrophe and an *s* or just an apostrophe. Add only an apostrophe to the nominative plural.

NOMINATIVE FORM	POSSESSIVE FORM
Texas (singular)	Texas', Texas's
Jones (singular)	Jones', Jones's
Joneses (plural)	Joneses'
countess (singular)	countess', countess's

Apos 2

Use an apostrophe to mark the place in a contraction where letters are omitted.

- Mark omissions in contractions with the apostrophe.

it is = it's
has not = hasn't
cannot = can't

Brackets: Bkts

Set off in brackets words that you wish to insert in a quotation.

- Use brackets to set off words that you insert in a quotation.

"The use of this type of supervisor [the trained correspondence expert] may still be increasing."
"Direct supervision has diminished in importance during the past decade [the report was written in 1994], when 43 percent of the reporting business firms that started programs used teams."

Colon: Cln 1

Use the colon to introduce a statement of explanation, an enumeration, or a formal quotation.

- Use the colon to introduce formal statements.

Enumeration: Working in this department are three classes of support: clerical support, computer support, and customer support.
Formal quotation: President Hartung had this to say about the proposal: "Any such movement that fails to get the support of the rank-and-file worker in this plant fails to get my support."

CHAPTER 18 Correctness of Communication

571

Explanation: At this time the company was pioneering a new marketing idea: It was attempting to sell its products directly to consumers by means of vending machines.

Cln 2

- Do not use the colon when it breaks the thought flow.

Do not use the colon when the thought of the sentence should continue without interruption. If introducing a list by a colon, the colon should be preceded by a word that explains or identifies the list.

Below standard: Cities in which new sales offices are in operation are: Fort Smith, Texarkana, Lake Charles, Jackson, and Biloxi.
Acceptable: Cities in which new sales offices are in operation are Fort Smith, Texarkana, Lake Charles, Jackson, and Biloxi.
Acceptable: Cities with new sales offices are as follows: Fort Smith, Texarkana, Lake Charles, Jackson, and Biloxi.

Comma: Cma 1

- Use the comma to separate clauses connected by *and, but, or, nor, for.*

Use the comma to separate principal clauses connected by a coordinating conjunction. The coordinating conjunctions are *and, but, or, nor,* and *for.* (A principal clause has a subject and a verb and stands by itself. A coordinating conjunction connects clauses, words, or phrases of equal rank.)

Only two components of the index declined, and these two account for only 12 percent of the total weight of the index.
New automobiles are moving at record volumes, but used-car sales are lagging behind the record pace set two years ago.

Make exceptions to this rule, however, in the case of compound sentences consisting of short and closely connected clauses.

We sold and the price dropped.
Sometimes we win and sometimes we lose.

Cma 2.1

- Use the comma to separate (1) items in a series and

Separate the items listed in a series by commas. In order to avoid misinterpretation of the rare instances in which some of the items listed have compound constructions, it is always good to place the comma between the last two items (before the final conjunction).

Good copy must cover fact with accuracy, sincerity, honesty, and conviction.
Direct advertising can be used to introduce salespeople, fill in between salespeople's calls, cover territory where salespeople cannot be maintained, and keep pertinent reference material in the hands of prospects.
A survey conducted at the 1996 automobile show indicated that green, white, blue, and black cars were favored by the public.

Cma 2.2

- (2) adjectives in a series.

Separate coordinate adjectives in a series by commas if they modify the same noun and if no *and* connects them. A good test to determine whether adjectives are coordinate is to insert an *and* between them. If the *and* does not change the meaning, the adjectives are coordinate.

Miss Pratt has been a reliable, faithful, efficient employee for 20 years.
We guarantee that this is a good, clean car.
Blue office furniture is Mr. Orr's recommendation for the clerical pool. (Office furniture is practically a compound noun; blue modifies both words.)
A big Dawson wrench proved to be best for the task. (The *and* won't fit between *big* and *Dawson.*

(PEANUTS reprinted by permission of UFS, Inc.)

Cma 3

Set off nonrestrictive modifiers by commas. By a *nonrestrictive modifier* we mean a modifier that could be omitted from the sentence without changing its meaning. Restrictive modifiers (those that restrict the words they modify to one particular object) are not set off by commas. A restrictive modifier cannot be left out of the sentence without changing its meaning.

• Use commas to set off nonrestrictive modifiers (those that could be left out without changing the meaning of the sentence).

Restrictive: The salesperson who sells the most will get a bonus. [*Who sells the most* restricts the meaning to a particular salesperson.]
Nonrestrictive: James Smithers, who was the company's top salesperson for the year, was awarded a bonus. [If the clause *who was the company's top salesperson for the year* is omitted, the meaning of the sentence is not changed.]
Restrictive: J. Ward & Company is the firm that employs most of the physically disabled in this area.
Nonrestrictive: J. Ward & Company, the firm that employs most of the physically disabled in this area, has gained the admiration of the community.

Notice that some modifiers can be either restrictive or nonrestrictive, depending on the writer's intended meaning.

Restrictive: All the suits that were damaged in the fire were sold at a discount. (Implies that some of the suits were not damaged.)
Nonrestrictive: All the suits, which were damaged by the fire, were sold at a discount. (Implies that the entire stock of suits was damaged.)

Cma 4.1

Use commas to set off parenthetic expressions. A parenthetic expression consists of words that interrupt the normal flow of the sentence. In a sense, they appear to be "stuck in." In many instances, they are simply words out of normal order. For example, the sentence "A full-page, black-and-white advertisement was run in the *Daily Bulletin*" contains a parenthetic expression when the word order is altered: "An advertisement, full-page and in black and white, was run in the *Daily Bulletin.*"

• Use commas to set off (1) parenthetic expressions (comments "stuck in"),

This practice, it is believed, will lead to ruin.
The Johnston Oil Company, so the rumor goes, has sharply reduced its exploration activity.

Although you may use the dash and the parenthesis for similar reasons, the three marks differ in the degree to which they separate the enclosed words from the rest of the sentence. The comma is the weakest of the three, and it is best used when the material set off is closely related to the surrounding words. Dashes are stronger marks than commas and are used when the material set off tends to be long or contains internal punctuation marks. Parentheses, the strongest of the three, are primarily used to enclose material that helps explain or supplement the main words of the sentence.

Cma 4.2

• (2) apposition words (words explaining another word),

Use commas to set off an appositive (a noun or a noun and its modifiers inserted to explain another noun) from the rest of the sentence. In a sense, appositives are parenthetic expressions, for they interrupt the normal flow of the sentence.

The Baron Corporation, our machine-parts supplier, is negotiating a new contract.
St. Louis, home office of our Midwest district, will be the permanent site of our annual sales meeting.
President Cartwright, a self-educated woman, is the leading advocate of our night school for employees.

But appositives that identify very closely are not set off by commas.

The word *liabilities* is not understood by most laboring men.
Our next shipment will come on the ship *Alberta*.

Cma 4.3

• (3) certain parenthetic words (*therefore, however*), and

Set off parenthetic words such as *therefore, however, in fact, of course, for example,* and *consequently* with commas.

It is apparent, therefore, that the buyers' resistance has been brought about by an overvigorous sales campaign.
After the first experiment, for example, the traffic flow increased 10 percent.
The company will, however, be forced to abandon the old pricing system.

Included in this group of parenthetic words may be introductory interjections (*oh, alas*) and responsive expressions (*yes, no, surely, indeed, well,* and so on). But if the words are strongly exclamatory or are not closely connected with the rest of the sentence, they may be punctuated as a sentence. (*No. Yes. Indeed.*)

Yes, the decision to increase production has been made.
Oh, contribute whatever you think is adequate.

Cma 4.4

• (4) units in a date or address.

When more than one unit appears in a date or an address, set off the units by commas.

One unit: December 30 is the date of our annual inventory.
One unit: The company has one outlet in Ohio.
More than one unit: December 30, 1906, is the date the Johnston Company first opened its doors.
More than one unit: Richmond, Virginia, is the headquarters of the new sales district.

Cma 5.1

• Use the comma after (1) introductory subordinate clauses and

Use the comma after a subordinate clause that precedes the main clause.

Although it is durable, this package does not have eye appeal.
Since there was little store traffic on Aisle 13, the area was converted into office space.

Cma 5.2

• (2) introductory verbal phrases.

Place a comma after an introductory verbal phrase. A verbal phrase is one that contains some verb derivative, a gerund, a participle, or an infinitive.

Participle phrase: Realizing his mistake, the foreman instructed his workers to keep a record of all salvaged equipment.
Gerund phrase: After gaining the advantage, we failed to press on to victory.
Infinitive phrase: To increase our turnover of automobile accessories, we must first improve our display area.

Cma 6.1

Use the comma only for good reason. It is not a mark to be inserted indiscriminately at the writer's whim. As a rule, the use of commas should be justified by one of the standard practices previously noted.

- Do not use the comma without good reason,

Cma 6.1.1

Do not be tripped into putting a comma between the subject and the verb.

The thought that he could not afford to fail spurred him on. [No comma after *fail*]

- such as between the subject and the verb.

Cma 6.2

Take exception to the preceding standards wherever the insertion of a comma will help clarity of expression.

- Use the comma wherever it helps clarity.

Not clear: From the beginning inventory methods of Hill Company have been haphazard.
Clear: From the beginning, inventory methods of Hill Company have been haphazard.
Not clear: Ever since she has been a model worker.
Clear: Ever since, she has been a model worker.

Dash: Dsh

Use the dash to set off an element for emphasis or to show interrupted thought. In particular, use it with long parenthetic expressions or parenthetic expressions containing internal punctuation (see Cma 4.1). Most word processing software will usually allow you to insert a dash with a special character code. Depending on the software, you either insert the code through a combination of keystrokes or by selecting the character from a character map. With some word processing software, make the dash by striking the hyphen twice, without spacing before or after.

- Use the dash to show interruption or emphasis.

Budgets for some past years—1994, for example—were prepared without consulting the department heads.
The test proved that the new process is simple, effective, accurate—and more expensive.
Only one person—the supervisor in charge—has authority to issue such an order.
If you want a voice in the government—vote.

Exclamation Mark: Ex

Use the exclamation mark at the end of a sentence or an exclamatory fragment to show strong emotion. But use it sparingly; never use it with trivial ideas.

- Use exclamation marks to show strong feeling.

We've done it again!
No! It can't be!

Hyphen: Hpn 1

Use the hyphen to indicate the division of a word at the end of the line. You must divide between syllables. It is generally impractical to leave a one-letter syllable at the end of a line (*a-bove*) or to carry over a two-letter syllable to the next line (*expens-es*).

- Mark word divisions with hyphens.

If you turn on the hyphenation feature of your word processing software, you can let it automatically take care of hyphenating words. Several programs permit you to set a hyphenation range. The wider the range the fewer words that will be hyphenated and the more ragged your margin; the narrower the range the more words that will be hyphenated and the smoother your right margin. Some have the option of allowing you to control the hyphenation you desire. You can accept what the program recommends, suggest a different place to hyphenate, or tell it not to hyphenate. Most programs will use their internal dictionaries for determining where to hyphenate words; some programs allow you to use an external dictionary for hyphenating words. These external dictionaries usually can be modified to suit your needs and preferences.

Hpn 2

• Place hyphens between the parts of compound words.

Place hyphens between the parts of some compound words. Generally, the hyphen is used whenever its absence would confuse the meaning of the words.

Compound nouns: brother-in-law, cure-all, city-state

Compound numbers twenty-one through ninety-nine: fifty-five, seventy-seven
Compound adjectives (two or more words used before a noun as a single adjective): *long-term* contract, *50-gallon* drum, *door-to-door* selling, *end-of-month* clearance.
Prefixes (most have been absorbed into the word): co-organizer, ex-chairperson, anti-inflation

Hpn 2.1

• Do not place hyphens between (1) proper names and

A proper name used as a compound adjective needs no hyphen or hyphens to hold it together as a visual unit for the reader. The capitals perform that function.

Correct: A Lamar High School student
Correct: A United Airlines pilot

Hpn 2.2

• (2) words that only follow each other.

Two or more modifiers in normal grammatical form and order need no hyphens. Particularly, a phrase consisting of an unmistakable adverb (one ending in *ly*) modifying an adjective or participle that in turn modifies a noun shows normal grammatical order and is readily grasped by the reader without the benefit of the hyphen. But an adverb not ending in *ly* had better be joined to its adjective or participle by the hyphen.

No hyphen needed: A poorly drawn chart.
Use the hyphen: A well-prepared chart

Italics: Ital 1

• Use italics for (1) publication titles,

For the use of italics for book titles, see QM 4. Note that italics are also used for titles of periodicals, works of art, long musical compositions, and names of naval vessels and aircraft.

Ital 2

• (2) foreign words and abbreviations, and

Italicize rarely used foreign words—if you must use them (*déjà vu, bon vivant, pro bono publico, ich dien*). After a foreign word is widely accepted, however, it does not need to be italicized (bon voyage, pizza, rancho). A current dictionary is a good source for information on which foreign words are italicized.

Ital 3

• (3) a word used as its own name.

Italicize a word, letter, or figure used as its own name. Without this device, we could not write this set of rules. Note the use of italics throughout to label name words.

The little word *sell* is still in the dictionary.
The pronoun *which* should always have a noun as a clear antecedent. [Without the italics, this one becomes a fragment ending in midair.]

Reference Software Tools Made Easier with Multitasking

Reference software, like reference books, are tools for looking up facts when you need them. All kinds of reference materials are available electronically from dictionaries, grammar and style guides, encyclopedias, ZIP code directories, quotations databases, maps, and much, much more. These programs vary widely in their similarities to and differences from traditional reference books.

Often they enhance the printed form, giving the user more ways to use them. Electronic dictionaries let you search for words the traditional way, search for them with wildcards or sound alikes when you don't know the spelling, and search for them by words in their definition. You could ask for the word with yellow and flower in its definition. The electronic dictionary will provide you with a list of all words with yellow and flower in its definition. The electronic dictionaries even have sound clips that tell you how to pronounce words simply by clicking on a sound icon.

While these programs have been around for years, their use is growing for two reasons. First, they are getting better, serving the user more fully and much more easily. Second, the power of the hardware lets users multitask—keep more than one application open at a time. This feature allows you to use your word processor while opening your reference material whether on your system, a server, or another computer.

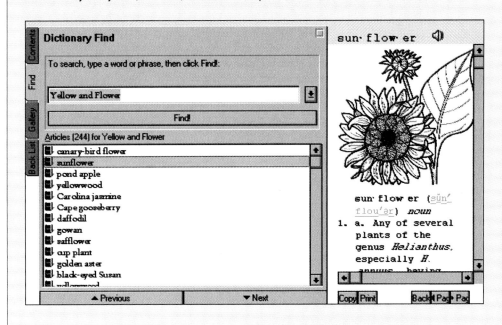

Parentheses: Parens

Use the parenthesis to set off words that are parenthetic or are inserted to explain or supplement the principal message (see Cma 4.1).

• Set off parenthetic words with parentheses.

Dr. Samuel Goppard's phenomenal prediction (*Business Week,* June 22, 1994) has made some business forecasters revise their techniques.
As soon as Smith was elected chairperson (the vote was almost 2 to 1), he introduced his plan for reorganization.

Period: Pd 1

Use the period to indicate the end of a declarative sentence, an imperative statement, and a courteous request.

Declarative sentence: The survey will be completed and returned by October 26.
Imperative statement: Complete and return the survey by October 26.
Courteous request: Will you please complete and return the survey by October 26.

Pd 2

Use periods after abbreviations or initials.

Ph.D., Co., Inc., a.m., A.D., etc.

But omit the periods and use all capitals in names of agencies, networks, associations, and such: IRS, NBC, OPEC.

Pd 3

Use ellipses (a series of periods) to indicate the omission of words from a quoted passage. If the omitted part consists of something less than a sentence, three periods are customarily placed at the point of omission (a fourth period is added if the omission is a sentence or more). If the omitted part is a paragraph or more, however, a full line of periods is used. In all cases, the periods are separated by spaces.

Logical explanations, however, have been given by authorities in the field. Some attribute the decline . . . to recent changes in the state's economy. . . .
Added to the labor factor is the high cost of raw material, which has tended to eliminate many marginal producers. Moreover, the rising cost of electric power in recent years may have shifted the attention of many industry leaders to other forms of production.

Question Mark: Q

Place a question mark at the end of sentences that are direct questions.

What are the latest quotations on Disney common stock?
Will this campaign help sell Microsoft products?

But do not use the question mark with indirect questions.

The president was asked whether this campaign would help sell Microsoft products.
He asked me what the latest quotations on Disney common stock were.

Quotation Marks: QM 1

Use quotation marks to enclose the exact words of a speaker or, if the quotation is short, the exact words of a writer.

Short written quotations are quotations of four lines or less, though authorities do not agree on this point. Some suggest three lines—others up to eight. Longer written quotations are best displayed without quotation marks and with additional indented right and left margins (double indent).

Short written quotation: H. G. McVoy sums up his presentation with this statement: "All signs indicate that automation will be evolutionary, not revolutionary."
Verbal quotation: "This really should bring on a production slowdown," said Ms. Kuntz.

If a quotation is broken by explanation or reference words, each part of the quotation is enclosed in quotation marks.

"Will you be specific," he asked, "in recommending a course of action?"

QM 2

Enclose a quotation within a quotation with single quotation marks.

President Carver said, "It has been a long time since I have heard an employee say, 'Boss, I'm going to beat my quota today.'"

• Use single quotation marks for a quotation within a quotation.

QM 3

Always place periods and commas inside quotation marks. Place semicolons and colons outside the quotation marks. Place question marks and exclamation points inside if they apply to the quoted passage only and outside if they apply to the whole sentence.

"If we are patient," he said, "prosperity will arrive someday." (The comma and the period are within the quotation marks.)
"Is there a quorum?" he asked. (The question mark belongs to the quoted passage.)
Which of you said, "I know where the error lies"? (The question mark applies to the entire sentence.
I conclude only this from the union's promise to "force the hand of management": Violence will be its trump card.

• Periods and commas go inside quotation marks; semicolons and colons go outside; question marks and exclamation points go inside when they apply to the quoted part and outside when they apply to the entire sentence.

QM 4

Enclose in quotation marks the titles of parts of publications (articles in a magazine, chapters in a book). But italicize the titles of whole publications. If your software or printer will not italicize, use underscoring.

The third chapter of the book *Elementary Statistical Procedure* is titled "Concepts of Sampling."
Joan Glasgow's most recent article, "A Union Boss Views Automation," appears in the current issue of *Fortune*.

• Use quotation marks to enclose titles of parts of a publication.

Semicolon: SC 1

Use the semicolon to separate independent clauses that are not connected by a conjunction.

Cork or asbestos sheeting must be hand-cut; polyurethane may be poured into a mold.
The new contract provides substantial wage increases; the original contract emphasized shorter hours.

Covered by this standard are independent clauses connected by conjunctive adverbs such as *however, nevertheless, therefore, then, moreover,* and *besides*.

The survey findings indicated a need to revise the policy; nevertheless, the president vetoed the amendment.
Small-town buyers favor the old model; therefore, the board concluded that both models should be manufactured.

• Use the semicolon to separate independent clauses not connected by a conjunction.

SC 2

You may use the semicolon to separate independent clauses joined by *and, but, or, for,* or *nor* (coordinating conjunctions) if the clauses are long or if they have other punctuation in them. In such situations, you may also use the semicolon for special emphasis.

The FTU and the IFL, rivals from the beginning of the new industry, have shared almost equally in the growth of membership; but the FTU predominates among workers in the petroleum-products crafts, including pipeline construction and operation, and the IFL leads in memberships of chemical workers.
The market price was $4; but we paid $7.

• You may choose to separate with a semicolon independent clauses joined by a conjunction.

Get It Right!

Don't use no double negative.
Make each pronoun agree with their antecedent.
Join clauses good, like a conjunction should.
About them sentence fragments.
When dangling, watch your participles.
Verbs has to agree with their subjects.
Just between you and I, the case is important too.
Don't write run-on sentences they are hard to read.
Don't use commas, which aren't necessary.
Its important to use your apostrophe's correctly.
Proofread your writing to see if you any words out.
Correct spelling is esential.

SC 3

• Use the semicolon to separate items in a list when the items contain commas.

Separate by semicolons the items in a list when the items have commas in them.

The following gains were made in the February year-to-year comparison: Fort Worth, 7,300; Dallas, 4,705; Lubbock, 2,610; San Antonio, 2,350; Waco, 2,240; Port Arthur, 2,170; and Corpus Christi, 1,420.
Elected for the new term were Anna T. Zelnak, attorney from Cincinnati; Wilbur T. Hoffmeister, stockbroker and president of Hoffmeister Associates of Baltimore; and William P. Peabody, a member of the faculty of the University of Georgia.

SC 4

• Use the semicolon only between equal units.

Use the semicolon between equal (coordinate) units only. Do not use it to attach a dependent clause or phrase to an independent clause.

Below standard: The flood damaged much of the equipment in Building 113; making it necessary for management to stop production and lay off all production workers.
Acceptable: The flood damaged much of the equipment in Building 113, making it necessary for management to stop production and lay off all production workers.
Acceptable: The flood damaged much of the equipment in Building 113; thus, it was necessary for management to stop production and lay off all production workers.

Standards for Grammar

Like the review of punctuation standards, the following summary of grammatical standards is not intended as a complete handbook on the subject. Rather, it is a summary of the major trouble spots encountered by business writers. If you learn these grammatical principles, you should be able to write with the correctness expected in business.

Adjective-Adverb Confusion: AA

• Do not use adjectives for adverbs.

Do not use adjectives for adverbs or adverbs for adjectives. Adjectives modify only nouns and pronouns; and adverbs modify verbs, adjectives, or other adverbs.

Possibly the chief source of this confusion is statements in which the modifier follows the verb. If the modifier refers to the subject, an adjective should be used. If it refers to the verb, an adverb is needed.

Below standard: She filed the records *quick.*
Acceptable: She filed the records *quickly.* [Refers to the verb.]
Below standard: John doesn't feel *badly.*
Acceptable: John doesn't feel *bad.* [Refers to the noun.]
Below standard: The new cars look *beautifully.*
Acceptable: The new cars look *beautiful.* [Refers to the noun.]

It should be noted that many words are both adjective and adverb (*little, well, fast, much*). And some adverbs have two forms, of which one is the same as the adjective and the other adds *ly* (*slow* and *slowly, cheap* and *cheaply, quick* and *quickly*).

Acceptable: All our drivers are instructed to drive *slow.*
Acceptable: All our drivers are instructed to drive *slowly.*

Subject–Verb Agreement: Agmt SV

Nouns and their verbs must agree in number. A plural noun must have a plural verb form; a singular noun must have a singular verb form.

- Verbs must agree in number with their subjects.

Below standard: Expenditures for miscellaneous equipment *was* expected to decline. [*Expenditures* is plural, so its verb must be plural.]
Acceptable: Expenditures for miscellaneous equipment *were* expected to decline.
Below standard: The *president,* as well as his staff, *were* not able to attend. [*President* is the subject, and the number is not changed by the modifying phrase.]
Acceptable: The *president,* as well as his staff, *was* not able to attend.

Compound subjects (two or more nouns joined by *and*) require plural verbs.

- Compound subjects require plural verbs.

Below standard: The *salespeople* and their *manager is* in favor of the proposal. [*Salespeople* and *manager* are compound subjects of the verb, but *is* is singular.]
Acceptable: The *salespeople* and their *manager are* in favor of the proposal.
Below standard: Received in the morning delivery *was* a *word processing program* and two *reams* of letterhead paper. [*Word processing program* and *reams* are the subjects; the verb must be plural.]
Acceptable: Received in the morning delivery *were* a *word processor* and *two reams* of letterhead paper.

Collective nouns may be either singular or plural, depending on the meaning intended.

- Collective nouns may be singular or plural.

Acceptable: The *committee have* carefully *studied* the proposal. [*Committee* is thought of as separate individuals.]
Acceptable: The *committee has* carefully *studied* the proposal. [The *committee* is thought of as a unit.]

As a rule, the pronouns *anybody, anyone, each, either, everyone, everybody, neither, nobody, somebody,* and *someone* take a singular verb. The word *none* may be either singular or plural, depending on whether it is used to refer to one unit or to more than one unit.

- The pronouns listed here are singular.

Acceptable: Either of the advertising campaigns *is* costly.
Acceptable: Nobody who watches the clock *is* successful.
Acceptable: None of the boys *understands* his assignment.
Acceptable: None of the boys *understand* their assignments.

Adverbial Noun Clause: AN

Do not use an adverbial clause as a noun clause. Clauses beginning with *because, when, where, if,* and similar adverbial connections are not properly used as subjects, objects, or complements of verbs.

- Do not use an adverbial clause as a noun clause.

Not this: The reason was *because* he did not submit a report.
But this: The reason was *that* he did not submit a report.
Not this: A time-series graph is *where* (or *when*) changes in an index such as wholesale prices are indicated.
But this: A time-series graph is the picturing of . . .

Awkward: Awk

• Avoid awkward writing.

Avoid awkward writing. By *awkward writing* we mean word arrangements that are unconventional, uneconomical, or simply not the best for quick understanding.

Dangling Modifiers: Dng

• Avoid dangling modifiers (those that do not clearly modify a specific word).

Avoid the use of modifiers that do not logically modify a word in the sentence. Such modifiers are said to dangle. They are both illogical and confusing. You can usually correct sentences containing dangling constructions by inserting the noun or pronoun that the modifier describes, or by changing the dangling part to a complete clause.

Below standard: Believing that credit customers should have advance notice of the sale, special letters were mailed to them.
Acceptable: Believing that credit customers should have advance notice of the sale, we mailed special letters to them. (Improvement is made by inserting the pronoun modified.)
Acceptable: Because we believed that credit customers should have advance notice of the sale, we mailed special letters to them. (Improvement is made by changing the dangling element to a complete clause.)

Dangling modifiers are of four principal types: participial phrases, elliptical clauses, gerund phrases, and infinitive phrases.

Below standard: Believing that District 7 was not being thoroughly covered, an additional salesperson was assigned to the area. [Dangling participial phrase.]
Acceptable: Believing that District 7 was not being thoroughly covered, the sales manager assigned an additional salesperson to the area.
Below standard: By working hard, your goal can be reached. [Dangling gerund phrase.]
Acceptable: By working hard, you can reach your goal.
Below standard: To succeed at this job, long hours and hard work must not be shunned. (Dangling infinitive phrase.)
Acceptable: To succeed at this job, one must not shun long hours and hard work.
Below standard: While waiting on a customer, the radio was stolen. (Dangling elliptical clause—a clause without a noun or verb.)
Acceptable: While the salesperson was waiting on a customer, the radio was stolen.

• Some introductory phrases are permitted to dangle.

There are, however, a few generally accepted introductory phrases that are permitted to dangle. Included in this group are *generally speaking, confidentially speaking, taking all things into consideration,* and such expressions as *in boxing, in welding,* and *in farming.*

Acceptable: Generally speaking, business activity is at an all-time high.
Acceptable: In farming, the land must be prepared long before planting time.
Acceptable: Taking all things into consideration, this applicant is the best for the job.

Sentence Fragment: Frag

• Avoid sentence fragments (words used as a sentence that are not a sentence).

Avoid the sentence fragment. Although the sentence fragment may sometimes be used to good effect, as in sales writing, it is best avoided by all but the most skilled writers. The sentence fragment consists of any group of words that are used as if they were a sentence but are not a sentence. Probably the most frequent cause of sentence fragments is the use of a subordinate clause as a sentence.

Below standard: Believing that you will want an analysis of sales for November. We have sent you the figures.
Acceptable: Believing that you will want an analysis of sales for November, we have sent you the figures.
Below standard: He declared that such a procedure would not be practical. And that it would be too expensive in the long run.
Acceptable: He declared that such a procedure would not be practical and that it would be too expensive in the long run.

Pronouns: Pn 1

Make certain that the word each pronoun refers to (its antecedent) is clear. Failure to conform to this standard causes confusion, particularly in sentences in which two or more nouns are possible antecedents or the antecedent is far away from the pronoun.

Below standard: When the president objected to Mr. Carter, he told him to mind his own business. [Who told whom?]
Acceptable: When the president objected to Mr. Carter, Mr. Carter told him to mind his own business.
Below standard: The mixture should not be allowed to boil, so when you do it, watch the temperature gauge. [*It* doesn't have an antecedent.]
Acceptable: The mixture should not be allowed to boil, so when conducting the experiment, watch the temperature gauge.
Below standard: The Model V is being introduced this year. Ads in *Time, The Saturday Evening Post,* and big-city newspapers over the country are designed to get sales off to a good start. It is especially designed for the novice boater who is not willing to pay a big price.
Acceptable: The Model V is being introduced this year. Ads in *Time, The Saturday Evening Post,* and big-city newspapers over the country are designed to get sales off to a good start. The new model is especially designed for the novice boater who is not willing to pay a big price.

> • A pronoun should refer clearly to a preceding word.

Confusion may sometimes result from using a pronoun with an implied antecedent.

Below standard: Because of the disastrous freeze in the citrus belt, it is necessary that most of them be replanted.
Acceptable: Because of the disastrous freeze in the citrus belt, most of the citrus orchards must be replanted.

Except when the reference of *which, that,* and *this* is perfectly clear, it is wise to avoid using these pronouns to refer to the whole idea of a preceding clause. Many times you can make the sentence clear by using a clarifying noun following the pronoun.

> • Usually avoid using *which, that,* and *this* to refer to broad ideas.

Below standard [following a detailed presentation of the writer's suggestion for improving the company suggestion-box plan]: This should be put into effect without delay.
Acceptable: This suggestion-box plan should be put into effect right away.

Pn 2

The number of the pronoun should agree with the number of its antecedent (the word it stands for). If the antecedent is singular, its pronoun must be singular. If the antecedent is plural, its pronoun must be plural.

> • The number of a pronoun should be the same as that of the word to which the pronoun refers.

Below standard: Taxes and insurance are necessary evils in any business, and it must be considered carefully in anticipating profits.
Acceptable: Taxes and insurance are necessary evils in any business, and they must be considered carefully in anticipating profits.
Below standard: Everybody should plan for their retirement. [Such words as *everyone, everybody,* and *anybody* are singular.]
Acceptable: Everybody should plan for his or her retirement.

Pn 3

Take care to use the correct case of the pronoun. If the pronoun serves as the subject of the verb, or if it follows a form of the infinitive *to be,* use a pronoun in the nominative case. (The nominative personal pronouns are *I, you, he, she, it, we,* and *they*).

> • Use the correct case of pronoun.

Acceptable: He will record the minutes of the meeting.
Acceptable: I think it will be he.

If the pronoun is the object of a preposition or a verb, or if it is the subject of an infinitive, use the objective case. (The objective personal pronouns are *me, you, him, her, it, us, them.*)

Below standard: This transaction is between you and *he.* [*He* is nominative and cannot be the object of the preposition *between.*]
Acceptable: This transaction is between you and *him.*
Below standard: Because the investigator praised Ms. Smith and *I,* we were promoted.
Acceptable: Because the investigator praised Ms. Smith and *me,* we were promoted.

The case of a relative pronoun (*who, whom*) is determined by the pronoun's use in the clause it introduces. One good way of determining which case to use is to substitute the personal pronoun for the relative pronoun. If the case of the personal pronoun that fits is nominative, use *who.* If it is objective, use *whom.*

Acceptable: George Cutler is the salesperson *who* won the award. [*He* (nominative) could be substituted for the relative pronoun; therefore, nominative *who* should be used.]
Acceptable: George Cutler is the salesperson *whom* you recommended. [Objective *him* could be substituted; thus, objective *whom* is used.]

The possessive case is used for pronouns that immediately precede a gerund (a verbal noun ending in *ing*).

Acceptable: *Our* selling of the stock frightened some of the conservative members of the board.
Acceptable: *Her* accepting the money ended her legal claim to the property.

Parallelism: Prl

- Express equal thoughts in parallel (equal) grammatical form.

Parts of a sentence that express equal thoughts should be parallel (the same) in grammatical form. Parallel constructions are logically connected by the coordinating conjunctions *and, but,* and *or.* Care should be taken to see that the sentence elements connected by these conjunctions are of the same grammatical type. That is, if one of the parts is a noun, the other parts should also be nouns. If one of the parts is an infinitive phrase, the other parts should also be infinitive phrases.

Below standard: The company objectives for the coming year are to match last year's production, higher sales, and improving consumer relations.
Acceptable: The company objectives for the coming year are to match last year's production, to increase sales, and to improve consumer relations.
Below standard: Writing copy may be more valuable experience than to make layouts.
Acceptable: Writing copy may be more valuable experience than making layouts.
Below standard: The questionnaire asks for this information: number of employees, what is our union status, and how much do we pay.
Acceptable: The questionnaire asks for this information: number of employees, union affiliation, and pay scale.

Tense: Tns

- The tense of each verb should show the logical time of happening.

The tense of each verb, infinitive, and participle should reflect the logical time of happening of the statement: Every statement has its place in time. To communicate that place exactly, you must select your tenses carefully.

Tns 1

- Use present tense for current happenings.

Use present tense for statements of fact that are true at the time of writing.

Below standard: Boston was not selected as a site for the aircraft plant because it *was* too near the coast. [Boston is still near the coast, isn't it?]
Acceptable: Boston was not selected as a site for the aircraft plant because it *is* too near the coast.

Tns 2

Use past tense in statements covering a definite past event or action.

Below standard: Mr. Burns *says* to me, "Bill, you'll never make an auditor."
Acceptable: Mr. Burns *said* to me, "Bill, you'll never make an auditor."

* Use past tense for past happenings.

Tns 3

The time period reflected by the past participle (*having been . . .*) is earlier than that of its governing verb. The present participle (*being . . .*) reflects the same time period as that of its governing verb.

Below standard: These debentures are among the oldest on record, *being* issued in early 1937.
Acceptable: These debentures are among the oldest on record, *having been* issued in early 1937.
Below standard: Ms. Sloan, *having been* the top salesperson on the force, was made sales manager. [possible but illogical]
Acceptable: Ms. Sloan, *being* the top salesperson on the force, was made sales manager.

* The past participle (*having been . . .*) indicates a time earlier than that of the governing verb, and the present participle (*being . . .*) indicates the same period as that of the governing verb.

Tns 4

Verbs in subordinate clauses are governed by the verb in the principal clause. When the main verb is in the past tense, you should usually also place the subordinate verb in a past tense (past, past perfect, or present perfect).

Acceptable: I *noticed* [past tense] the discrepancy, and then I *remembered* [same time as main verb] the incidents that had caused it.

If the time of the subordinate clause is earlier than that of the main verb in past tense, use past perfect tense for the subordinate verb.

Below standard: In early July, we *noticed* [past] that he *exceeded* [logically should be previous to main verb] his quota three times.
Acceptable: In early July, we *noticed* that he *had exceeded* his quota three times.

The present perfect tense is used for the subordinate clause when the time of this clause is subsequent to the time of the main verb.

Below standard: Before the war we *contributed* [past] generously, but lately we *forget* [should be a time subsequent to the time of the main verb] our duties.
Acceptable: Before the war we *contributed* generously, but lately we *have forgotten* our duties.

* Verbs in the principal clause govern those in subordinate clauses.

* Present perfect tense (*have . . .*) refers to the indefinite past.

*

Tns 5

The present perfect tense does not logically refer to a definite time in the past. Instead, it indicates time somewhere in the indefinite past.

Below standard: We *have audited* your records on July 31 of 1994 and 1995.
Acceptable: We *audited* your records on July 31 of 1994 and 1995.
Acceptable: We *have audited* your records twice in the past.

* Use of present perfect tense indicates time somewhere in the indefinite past.

Word Use: WU

Misused words call attention to themselves and detract from the writing. The possibilities of error in word use are infinite; the following list contains only a few of the common errors of this kind.

* Use words correctly.

DON'T USE	USE
a long ways	a long way
and etc.	etc.
anywheres	anywhere
continue on	continue
different than	different from
have got to	must
in back of	behind
in hopes of	in hope of
in regards to	in regard to
inside of	within
kind of satisfied	somewhat satisfied
nowhere near	not nearly
nowheres	nowhere
off of	off
over with	over
seldom ever	seldom
try and come	try to come

Wrong Word: WW

• Check the spelling and meanings of words carefully.

Wrong words refer to meaning one word and using another. Sometimes these words are confused by their spelling and sometimes by their meanings. Here are a few examples:

affect	effect
among	between
capital	capitol
cite	sight
collision	collusion
complement	compliment
cooperation	corporation
deferential	differential
desert	dessert
except	accept
implicit	explicit
imply	infer
principal	principle
stationary	stationery

Standards for the Use of Numbers: No

Quantities may be spelled out or expressed as numerals. Whether to use one form or the other is often a perplexing question. It is especially perplexing to business writers, for much of their work deals with quantitative subjects. Because the proper expression of quantities is vital to business writers, the following notes on the use of numbers are presented.

No 1

Although authorities do not agree on number usage, business writers would do well to follow the rule of nine. By this rule, you spell out numbers nine and below. You use figures for numbers above nine.

Correct: The auditor found 13 discrepancies in the stock records.
Correct: The auditor found nine discrepancies in the stock records.

Apply the rule to both ordinal and cardinal numbers:

Correct: She was the seventh applicant.
Correct: She was the 31st applicant.

• Spell out numbers nine and under, and use figures for higher numbers, except as follows:

No 2

Make an exception to the rule of nine when a number begins a sentence. Spell out all numbers in this position.

Correct: Seventy-three bonds and six debentures were destroyed.
Correct: Eighty-nine men picketed the north entrance.

• Spell out numbers that begin a sentence.

No 3

In comparisons, keep all numbers in the same form. If any number requires numeral form, use numerals for all the numbers.

Correct: We managed to salvage 3 lathes, 1 drill, and 13 welding machines.

• Keep in the same form all numbers in comparisons.

No 4

Use numerals for all percentages.

Correct: Sales increases over last year were 9 percent on automotive parts, 14 percent on hardware, and 23 percent on appliances.

Concerning whether to use the percent sign (%) or the word, authorities differ. One good rule to follow is to use the sign in papers that are scientific or technical and the word in all others. Also, it is conventional to use the sign following numbers in graphics. The trend in business appears to be toward using the sign. Consistent use of either is correct.

• Use numerals for percentages.

No 5

Present days of the month in figure form when the month precedes the day.

Correct: July 3, 1995

When days of the month appear alone or precede the month, they may be either spelled out or expressed in numeral form according to the rule of nine.

Correct: I will be there on the 13th.
Correct: The union scheduled the strike vote for the eighth.
Correct: Ms. Millican signed the contract on the seventh of July.
Correct: Sales have declined since the 14th of August.

• Use figures for days of the month when the month precedes the day.

No 6

Present money amounts as you would other numbers. If you spell out the number, also spell out the unit of currency.

Twenty-seven dollars

• Present amounts like other numbers, spelling units when numbers are spelled and using appropriate symbols or abbreviations when in figures.

If you present the number as a figure, use the $ symbol with Canadian and U.S. currency and the appropriate abbreviation or symbol with other currencies.

U.S. and Canada	$27.33
France	Fr 743.21
Germany	DM 45.72
Great Britain	£231.91

No 7

• For dates, use either day, month, year or month, day, year sequence, the latter with year set off by commas.

Use either of the two orders for date information. One, preferred by the *Chicago Manual of Style,* is day, month, and year:

29 June 1995

The other is the conventional sequence of month, day, and year. This order requires that the year be set off by commas:

On June 29, 1995, we began production.

No 8

• Usually spell rounded numbers.

Usually spell out rounded numbers.

Correct: Over a million people live there.
Correct: The current population is about four hundred thousand.

No 9

• Use the word form for a number that begins a sentence.

Use the word form for a number that begins a sentence.

Correct: Thirty-nine men and 77 women reported for work.
Correct: Nineteen ninety-five was our best year.

No 10

• Do not use both word and figure except for legal reasons.

Except in legal documents, do not express amounts in both figures and words.

Appropriate for legal purposes: 25 (twenty-five)
Appropriate for business use: either the figure or the word, depending on circumstance

Spelling: SP

• Spell words correctly. Use the dictionary.

Misspelling is probably the most frequently made error in writing. And it is the least excusable. It is inexcusable because all one needs to do to eliminate the error is to use a dictionary or a spell checker.

• See Figure 18–1 for the 80 most commonly misspelled words.

Unfortunately, we must memorize to spell. Thus, becoming a good speller involves long and hard work. Even so, you can improve your spelling significantly with relatively little effort. Studies show that fewer than 100 words account for most spelling errors. So if you will learn to spell these most troublesome words, you will go a long way toward solving your spelling problems. Eighty of these words appear in Figure 18–1. Although English spelling follows little rhyme or reason, a few helpful rules exist. You would do well to learn and use them.

Rules for Word Plurals

• These three rules cover plurals for most words.

1. To form the plurals of most words, add *s.*

   cat, cats
   dog, dogs

FIGURE 18–1 Eighty of the Most Frequently Misspelled Words

absence	desirable	irritable	pursue
accessible	despair	leisure	questionnaire
accommodate	development	license	receive
achieve	disappear	misspelling	recommend
analyze	disappoint	necessary	repetition
argument	discriminate	newsstand	ridiculous
assistant	drunkenness	noticeable	seize
balloon	embarrassment	occasionally	separate
benefited	equivalent	occurrence	sergeant
category	exceed	panicky	sheriff
cede	existence	parallel	succeed
changeable	forty	paralyze	suddenness
committee	grammar	pastime	superintendent
comparative	grievous	persistent	supersede
conscience	holiday	possesses	surprise
conscious	incidentally	predictable	truly
coolly	indispensable	privilege	until
definitely	insistent	proceed	vacuum
dependent	irrelevant	professor	vicious
description	irresistible	pronunciation	weird

2. To form the plurals of words ending in *s*, *sh*, *ch*, and *x*, usually add *es* to the singular.

   glass, glasses
   dish, dishes
   bunch, bunches
   ax, axes

3. To form the plural of words ending in *y*, if a consonant precedes the *y*, drop the *y* and add *ies*. But if the *y* is preceded by a vowel, add *s*.

   pony, ponies
   chimney, chimneys

Other Spelling Rules

1. Words ending in *ce* or *ge* do not drop the *e* when adding *ous* or *able*.

   charge, chargeable
   change, changeable
   notice, noticeable
   service, serviceable

   • These rules cover four other trouble areas of spelling.

2. Words ending in *l* do not drop the *l* when adding *ly*.

   final, finally
   principal, principally

3. Words ending in silent *e* usually drop the *e* when adding a suffix beginning with a vowel.

   have, having
   believe, believable
   dive, diving
   time, timing

4. Place *i* before *e* except after *c*.

relieve	conceive
believe	receive

Exception: when the word is sounded as long *a*.

neighbor	weigh

Exceptions:

either	Fahrenheit	height
seize	surfeit	efficient
sufficient	neither	foreign
leisure	ancient	seizure
weird	financier	codeine
forfeit	seismograph	sovereign
deficient	science	counterfeit

Capitalization: Cap

• Capitalize all proper names and the beginning words of sentences.

Use capitals for the first letters of all proper names. Common examples are these:

Streets: 317 East Boyd Avenue
Geographic places: Chicago, Indiana, Finland
Companies: Berkowitz Manufacturing Company, Inc.
Title preceding names: President Watkins
Titles of books, articles, poems: *Lesikar's Basic Business Communication*
First words of sentences and complimentary closes
The word *number* (or its abbreviation) when used with a figure to identify something: Number 1, Oak Circle

As noted earlier, other standards are useful in clear communication. But those covered in the preceding pages will help you through most of your writing problems. By using them, you can give your writing the precision that good communication requires.

Correct any punctuation or grammar errors you can find in the following sentences. Explain your corrections.

1. Charles E. Baskin the new member of the advisory committee has been an employee for seven years.

2. The auditor asked us, "If all members of the work group had access to the petty cash fund?"

3. Our January order consisted of the following items; two dozen Norwood desk calendars, note size, one dozen desk blotters, 20 by 32 inches, and one dozen bottles of ink, permanent black.

4. The truth of the matter is, that the union representative had not informed the workers of the decision.

5. Sales for the first quarter were the highest in history, profits declined for the period.

6. We suggest that you use a mild soap for best results but detergents will not harm the product.

7. Employment for October totaled 12,741 an increase of 3.1 percent over September.

8. It would not be fair however to consider only this point.

9. It is the only water-repellent snagproof and inexpensive material available.

10. Todd Thatcher a supervisor in our company is accused of the crime.

11. Mr. Goodman made this statement, "Contrary to our expectations, Smith and Company will lose money this year."

12. I bought and he sold.

13. Soon we saw George Sweeney who is the auditor for the company.

14. Sold in light medium and heavy weight this paper has been widely accepted.

15. Because of a common belief that profits are too high we will have to cut our prices on most items.

16. Such has been the growth of the cities most prestigious firm, H.E. Klauss and Company.

17. In 1994 we were advised in fact we were instructed to accept this five year contract.

18. Henrys goofing off has got him into trouble.

19. Cyrus B. Henshaw who was our leading salesperson last month is the leading candidate for the position.

20. The sales representative who secures the most new accounts will receive a bonus.

21. The word phone which is short for telephone should be avoided in formal writing.

22. In last months issue of Modern Business appeared Johnson's latest article What Systems Theory Means to You.

23. Yes he replied this is exactly what we mean.

24. Why did he say John it's too late?

25. Place your order today, it is not too late.

26. We make our plans on a day to day basis.

27. There is little accuracy in the 60 day forecast.

28. The pre Christmas sale will extend over twenty six days.

29. We cannot tolerate any worker's failure to do their duty.

30. An assortment of guns, bombs, burglar tools, and ammunition were found in the cellar.

31. If we can be certain that we have the facts we can make our decision soon.

32. This one is easy to make. If one reads the instructions carefully.

33. This is the gift he received from you and I.

34. A collection of short articles on the subject were printed.

35. If we can detect only a tenth of the errors it will make us realize the truth.

36. She takes criticism good.

37. There was plenty of surprises at the meeting.

38. It don't appear that we have made much progress.

39. The surface of these products are smooth.

40. Everybody is expected to do their best.

41. The brochures were delivered to John and I early Sunday morning.

42. Who did he recommend for the job.

43. We were given considerable money for the study.

44. He seen what could happen when administration breaks down.

45. One of his conclusions is that the climate of the region was not desirable for our purposes.

46. Smith and Rogers plans to buy the Moline plant.

47. The committee feels that no action should be taken.

48. Neither of the workers found their money.

49. While observing the employees, the work flow was operating at peak perfection.

50. The new building is three stories high, fifteen years old, solid brick construction, and occupies a corner lot.

51. They had promised to have completed the job by noon.

52. Jones has been employed by the Sampson Company for twenty years.

53. Wilson and myself will handle the job.

54. Each man and woman are expected to abide by this rule.

55. The boiler has been inspected on April 1 and May 3.

56. To find problems and correcting them takes up most of my work time.

57. The carton of canned goods were distributed to the employees.

58. The motor ran uneven.

59. All are expected except John and she.

60. Everyone here has more ability than him.

The following test is designed to give you a quick measure of your ability to handle some of the most troublesome punctuation and grammar situations. First, correct all the errors in each sentence. Then turn to Appendix A for the recommended corrections and the symbols for the punctuation and grammar standards involved. Next, study the standards that you violate.

1. An important fact about this keyboard is, that it has the patented "ergonomic design".

2. Goods received on Invoice 2741 are as follows; three dozen white shirts, size 15-33, four mens felt hats, brown, size 7, and five dozen assorted ties.

3. James Silver president of the new union started the campaign for the retirement fund.

4. We do not expect to act on this matter however until we hear from you.

5. Shipments through September 20, 1995 totaled 69,485 pounds an increase of 17 percent over the year ago total.

6. Brick is recommended as the building material but the board is giving serious consideration to a substitute.

7. Markdowns for the sale total $34,000, never before has the company done anything like this.

8. After long experimentation a wear resistant high grade and beautiful stocking has been perfected.

9. Available in white green and blue this paint is sold by dealers all over the country.

10. Julie Jahn who won the trip is our most energetic salesperson.

11. Good he replied, sales are sure to increase.

12. Hogan's article Retirement? Never!, printed in the current issue of Management Review, is really a part of his book A Report on Worker Security.

13. Formal announcement of our pre Labor Day sale will be made in thirty-two days.

14. Each day we encounter new problems. Although they are solved easily.

15. A list of models, sizes, and prices of both competing lines are being sent to you.

16. The manager could not tolerate any employee's failing to do their best.

17. A series of tests were completed only yesterday.

18. There should be no misunderstanding between you and I.

19. He run the accounting department for five years.

20. This report is considerable long.

21. Who did you interview for the position?

22. The report concluded that the natural resources of the Southwest was ideal for the chemical industry.

23. This applicant is six feet in height, 28 years old, weight 165 pounds, and has had eight years' experience.

24. While reading the report, a gust of wind came through the window, blowing papers all over the room.

25. The sprinkler system has been checked on July 1 and September 3.

19

Business Research Methods

C H A P T E R   O B J E C T I V E S

Upon completing this chapter, you will be able to design and implement a plan for conducting the research needed for a business-report problem. To reach this goal, you should be able to

1 Explain the difference between primary and secondary research.

2 Describe appropriate procedures for direct and indirect library research.

3 Describe the procedures for searching through company records and conducting experiments.

4 Design an experiment for a business problem.

5 Design an observational study for a business problem.

6 Explain sampling as it relates to conducting a survey.

7 Discuss the techniques for constructing a questionnaire, developing a working plan, and conducting a pilot test for a survey.

8 Analyze and interpret information clearly and completely for your reader.

▷ **to Business Research Methods**

Introduce yourself to this chapter by assuming the position of administrative assistant to Carmen Bergeron, the vice president for human resources for Mammoth Industries. Today at a meeting of plant administrators, someone commented about the low morale in the production departments. The production vice president immediately came to the defense of his area, claiming that there is no proof of the statement—that in fact the opposite is true. Others joined in with their views, and in time a heated discussion developed. In an effort to ease tensions, Ms. Bergeron suggested that her office conduct a survey of plant personnel "to learn the truth of the matter." The administrators liked the idea.

After the meeting, Ms. Bergeron called you in to tell you that you would be the one to do the research. And she wants the findings in report form in time for next month's meeting. She didn't say much more. No doubt she thinks your college training equipped you to handle the assignment.

Now you must do the research. This means you will have to work out a plan for a survey. Specifically you will have to design a sample, construct a questionnaire, devise an interview procedure, conduct interviews, record findings—and more. All these activities require much more than a casual understanding of research. There are right ways and wrong ways of going about them. How to do them right is the subject of this chapter. ■

You can collect the information needed for your report by using the two basic forms of research—secondary research and primary research. Secondary research is research utilizing material that someone else has published—through periodicals, brochures, books, electronic publication, and such. Commonly called *library research,* secondary research may be the first form of research that you use in some problems (see "Preliminary Investigation," Chapter 10). Primary research is research that uncovers information firsthand. It is research that produces new findings.

- The two basic forms of research are secondary research (getting information from printed sources) and primary research (getting information firsthand).

To be effective as a report writer, you should be familiar with the techniques of both secondary and primary research. A brief summary of each appears in the following pages.

SECONDARY RESEARCH

Secondary research materials are potentially the least costly, the most accessible, and the most complete source of information. However, to take full advantage of the available materials, you must know what you are looking for and where and how to find it.

- Secondary research can be a rich source of information if you know what to look for and where to look.

The task can be complex and challenging. You can meet the challenge if you become familiar with the general arrangement of a library or other repositories of secondary materials and if you learn the techniques of finding those materials. Also, research must be orderly if it is to be reliable and complete.

In the past, researchers used a card system to help them keep track of the sources they identified. This card system can be combined with and adapted to a computer system quite easily. The manual system of organization required that the researcher complete two sets of cards. One set was simply a bibliography card set, containing complete information about sources. A researcher numbered these cards consecutively as the sources were identified. A second set of cards contained the notes from each source. Each of these cards was linked to its source through the number of the source in the bibliography card set.

- Keep track of the sources you gather in an orderly way.

Since the computer systems in today's libraries often allow users to print the citations they find from the indexes and databases, it makes the most sense to number the source on the printout rather than recopy it to a card. Not only is it usually more legible than one's handwriting, but it is also complete. Some writers will cut their printouts apart and tape them to a master sheet. Others will enter these items in databases they build. And still others will download items directly into specialty databases, letting the software organize and number them. With the widespread use of notebook and laptop computers, many researchers are taking notes on computers rather than cards. These notes can be linked to the original source by number as in the manual system.

No matter whether you use a manual, combined, or computer system, using one is essential.

Finding Publication Collections

The first step in an orderly search for printed information is to determine where to begin. The natural place, of course, is a library. However, as different types of libraries offer different kinds of collections, it is helpful to know what types of libraries are available and to be familiar with their contents.

General libraries are the best known and the most accessible. General libraries, which include college, university, and most public libraries, are called *general* to the extent that they contain all kinds of materials. Many general libraries, however, have substantial collections in certain specialized areas.

Libraries that limit their collections to one type or just a few types of material are considered *special libraries.* Many such libraries are private and do not invite routine public use of their materials. Still, they will frequently cooperate on research projects that they consider relevant and worthwhile.

Among the special libraries are the libraries of private businesses. As a rule, such libraries are designed to serve the sponsoring company and provide excellent information in the specialized areas of its operations. Company libraries are less accessible than other specialized libraries, but a letter of inquiry explaining the nature and purpose of a project or a letter of introduction from someone known to the company can help you gain access to them.

Special libraries are also maintained by various types of associations—for example, trade organizations, professional and technical groups, chambers of commerce, and labor unions. Like company libraries, association libraries may provide excellent coverage of highly specialized areas. Although such libraries develop collections principally for members or a research staff, they frequently make resources available to others engaged in reputable research.

A number of public and private research organizations also maintain specialized libraries. The research divisions of big-city chambers of commerce and the bureaus of research of major universities, for example, keep extensive collections of material containing statistical and general information on a local area. State agencies collect similar data. Again, though these materials are developed for a limited audience, they are often made available upon request.

Now, how do you determine what these research centers and special libraries offer and whom to contact for permission to use their collections? Several guides are available in the reference department of most general libraries. The *American Library Directory* is a geographic listing of libraries in the United States and Canada. It gives detailed information on libraries, including special interests and collections. It covers all public libraries as well as many corporate and association libraries. The Special Libraries Association has chapters in many large cities that publish directories for their chapter areas. Particularly helpful in identifying the information available in research centers is *The Research Centers Directory.* Published by Gale Research Company, it lists the research activities, publications, and services of 7,500 university-related and other nonprofit organizations. It is supplemented between editions by a related publication, *New Research Centers.*

Gale Research also publishes three comprehensive guides to special library collections. *The Directory of Special Libraries and Information Centers* describes the contents and services of 16,500 information centers, archives, and special and research libraries. Each entry includes the address and telephone number of the facility and the name and title of the individual in charge. A companion guide, *Subject Directory of*

- A library is the natural place to begin secondary research.

- General libraries offer the public a wide variety of information sources.

- Special libraries have limited collections and limited circulation.

- Consult a directory to determine what special libraries offer.

Special Libraries and Information Centers, organizes the same information by subject. The third guide, *New Special Libraries,* is a periodic supplement of the first.

Taking the Direct Approach

When you have found the appropriate library for your research, you are ready for the next challenge. With the volume of material available, how will you find what you need? Many cost-conscious businesses are hiring professionals to find information for them. These professionals' charges range from $40 to $80 per hour in addition to any on-line charges incurred. Other companies like to keep their information gathering more confidential; some employ company librarians and others expect their employees to gather the information. If you know nothing about how material is arranged in a library, you will waste valuable time on a probably fruitless search. However, if you are familiar with certain basic reference materials, you may be able to proceed directly to the information you seek. And if the direct approach does not work, there are several effective indirect methods of finding the material you need.

- Begin your research using the direct approach. Look up the information you need. But some companies hire specialists to do this work.

Taking the direct approach is advisable when you seek quantitative or factual information. The reference section of your library is where you should start. There, either on your own or with the assistance of a research librarian, you can discover any number of timely and comprehensive sources of facts and figures. Although you cannot know all these sources, as a business researcher you should be familiar with certain basic ones. These sources are available in either print or electronic forms. You should be able to use both.

Encyclopedias. Encyclopedias are the best-known sources of direct information and are particularly valuable when you are just beginning a search. They offer background material and other general information that give you a helpful introduction to the area under study. Individual articles or sections of articles are written by experts in the field and frequently include a short bibliography.

- Encyclopedias offer both general and detailed information.

Of the general encyclopedias, two worthy of special mention are *The Encyclopedia Americana* and the *Encyclopaedia Britannica.* Others gaining wide use and acceptance are Grolier's *Academic American Encyclopedia* and Microsoft *Encapta.* These are available either on several information services and updated every three months, for sale in software outlets, or even bundled with multimedia computer systems. Also helpful are such specialized encyclopedias as the *Encyclopaedia of the Social Sciences, The Encyclopedia of Accounting Systems, Encyclopedia of Banking and Finance,* and *The Encyclopedia of Management.*

Biographical Directories. A direct source of biographical information about leading figures of today or of the past is a biographical directory. The best-known biographical directories are *Who's Who in America* and *Who's Who in the World,* annual publications that summarize the lives of living people who have achieved prominence. Similar publications provide coverage by geographic area: *Who's Who in the East* and *Who's Who in the Midwest,* for example. For biographical information about prominent Americans of the past, the *Dictionary of American Biography* is useful. Specialized publications will help you find information on people in particular professions. Among the most important of these are *Who's Who in Finance and Industry; Standard & Poor's Register of Corporations, Directors, and Executives; Dun & Bradstreet's Reference Book of Corporate Management; Who's Who in Labor; Who's Who in Economics; The Rand McNally International Bankers Directory; Who's Who in Insurance;* and *Who's Who in Computer Education and Research.* Nearly all business and professional areas are covered by some form of directory.

- Biographical directories offer information about influential people.

Almanacs. Almanacs are handy guides to factual and statistical information. Simple, concise, and selective in their presentation of data, they should not be underestimated as references. *The World Almanac and Book of Facts,* published by Funk &

- Almanacs provide factual and statistical information.

Much secondary research can be done through the use of computers.

Wagnalls Corp. is an excellent general source of facts and statistics. The *Information Please Almanac* is another excellent source for a broad range of statistical data. One of its strongest areas is information on the labor force. The *Universal Almanac* presents much of its data in charts and graphs. It has excellent coverage of business and the economy. If you need business and investment data, *Irwin Business & Investment Almanac* provides comprehensive coverage of timely information. Some of the information you will find in it is a chronological presentation of business events during the past year, industry surveys, financial general business and economic indicators, stock market data, a glossary, and much more.

- Trade directories publish information about individual businesses and products.

Trade Directories.　For information about individual businesses or the products they make, buy, or sell, directories are the references to consult. Directories are compilations of details in specific areas of interest and are variously referred to as *catalogs, listings, registers,* or *source books.* Some of the more comprehensive directories are indispensable in general business research. The more useful ones include *The Million Dollar Directory* (a listing of U.S. companies compiled by Dun & Bradstreet), *Thomas Register of American Manufacturers,* and *The Datapro Directory.* Some directories that will help you determine linkages between parent and subsidiaries include *America's Corporate Families* and *Who Owns Whom* (both compiled by Dun & Bradstreet) as well as the *Directory of Corporate Affiliations.* Literally thousands of directories exist—so many, in fact, that there are two directories of directories (*Trade Directories of the World* and *Directory of Directories*).

- Governments (national, state, provincial, etc) publish extensive research materials.

Government Publications.　Governments (national, state, provincial, etc.) publish hundreds of thousands of titles each year. In fact, the U.S. government is the world's largest publisher. Surveys, catalogs, pamphlets, periodicals—there seems to be no limit to the information that various bureaus, departments, and agencies collect and make available to the public. The challenge of working with government publications, therefore, is finding your way through this wealth of material to the specifics you need. That task can sometimes be so complex as to require indirect research methods. However, if you are familiar with a few key sources, the direct approach will often be productive.

In the United States, it may be helpful to consult the *Monthly Catalog of U.S. Government Publications.* Issued by the Superintendent of Documents, it includes a comprehensive listing of annual and monthly publications and an alphabetical index of the issuing agencies. It can be searched on-line. The Superintendent of Documents also issues *Selected United States Government Publications,* a monthly list of general-interest publications that are sold to the public.

• The U.S. government publishes guides to its publications.

Routinely available are a number of specialized publications that are invaluable in business research. These include *Census of Population, Census of Housing, Annual Housing Survey, Consumer Income and Population Characteristics, Census of Governments, Census of Retail Trade, Census of Manufacturers, Census of Agriculture, Census of Construction Industries, Census of Transportation, Census of Service Industries, Census of Wholesale Trade,* and *Census of Mineral Industries.* The *Statistical Abstract of the United States* is another invaluable publication, as are the *Survey of Current Business,* the *Monthly Labor Review,* the *Occupational Outlook Quarterly,* and the *Federal Reserve Bulletin.* To say the least, government sources are extensive.

• These government publications are invaluable in business research.

Dictionaries. Dictionaries are helpful for looking up meanings, spellings, and pronunciations of words or phrases. Electronic dictionaries add another option; they let you find words when you know the meaning. Dictionaries are available in both general and specialized versions. While it might be nice to own an unabridged dictionary, an abridged collegiate or desk dictionary will answer most of your questions. You should be aware that the name *Webster* can be legally used by any dictionary publisher. Also, dictionaries often include added features such as style manuals, signs, symbols, and weights and measures. Because dictionaries reflect current usage, you want to be sure the one you use is up to date. Not only are new words being added but spellings and meanings change, too. Several good dictionaries are the *American Heritage Dictionary, Funk & Wagnalls Standard Dictionary,* the *Random House Webster's Collegiate Dictionary,* and *Webster's New Collegiate Dictionary.*

• Dictionairies provide meanings, spellings, and pronunciations for both general and specialized words and phrases.

Specialized dictionaries concentrate on one functional area. Some business dictionaries are the *Dictionary of Management,* the *MBA's Dictionary, The Dictionary of Business and Management,* the *McGraw-Hill Dictionary of Modern Economics,* and the *Computer Glossary.* There are also dictionaries of acronyms and abbreviations. Two of these are *Acronyms, Initialisms, and Abbreviations Dictionary* and *Abbreviations Dictionary.*

Statistical Sources. Today's businesses rely heavily on statistical information. Not only is this information helpful in the day-to-day operations of their businesses, but it also is helpful in planning future products, expansions, and strategies. Today a good deal of statistical information is available on-line; some is only available on-line. Sometimes it is available on-line long before the data can be printed and distributed. In any case, there are several sources of statistical information you should be aware of. These sources are both public and private.

• Statistical information is available both on-line and in printed form.

In order to facilitate the collection and retrieval of statistical data for industry, the US government developed a classification system, called the SIC (Standard Industrial Classification) code. This system uses a four-digit code for all manufacturing and nonmanufacturing industries.

Some of the basic comprehensive publications include the *Handbook of Basic Economic Statistics,* the *Statistical Abstract of the United States,* the *Predicasts Basebook,* and *Standard & Poor's Statistical Service.* These sources are a starting point when you are not familiar with a more specialized source. These publications

• Basic publications provide broad coverage and source listings for more detailed statistics.

include historical data on American industry, commerce, labor and agriculture; industry data by SIC codes; numerous indexes such as producer/price indexes, housing indexes, and stock price indexes. Additionally, the *Statistical Abstract of the United States* contains an extremely useful "Guide to Sources of Statistics."

If you are not certain where to find statistics, you may find various guides useful. The *American Statistics Index* is an index to statistics published by all government agencies. It identifies the agency, describes the statistics, and provides access by category. The *Encyclopedia of Business Information Sources* provides a listing of information sources along with names of basic statistical sources. The *Statistical Reference Index* is a good source of statistics published by sources other than the government, such as trade and professional associations. *Predicasts Forecasts* is useful for current forecasting statistical sources. It documents the source of the data as well. And it has a source directory arranged by title, geographic index, and SIC codes. These directories will help direct you to specialized statistics when you need them.

- Private business services collect and publish data. Many such reports are available in public and university libraries.

Business Information Services. Business services are private organizations that supply a variety of information to business practitioners, especially investors. Libraries also subscribe to their publications, giving business researchers ready access to yet another source of valuable, timely data.

Moody's Investors' Service, one of the best known of such organizations, publishes a weekly *Manual* in each of six business areas: transportation, industrials, OTC (over-the-counter) industrials, public utilities, banks and finance, and municipals and governments. These reports summarize financial data and operating facts on all the major American companies, providing information that an investor needs to evaluate the investment potential of individual securities or of fields as a whole. *Corporation Records,* published by Standard & Poor's Corporation, presents similar information in loose-leaf form. Both Moody's and Standard & Poor's provide a variety of related services, including *Moody's Investors' Advisory Service* and Standard & Poor's *Value Line Investment Service.*

Two other organizations whose publications are especially helpful to business researchers are Predicasts, Inc., and Gale Research Company. Predicasts, Inc., provides seven separate business services, although it is best known for publications featuring forecasts and market data by country, product, and company (*Predicasts, World-Regional-Casts, World-Product-Casts,* and *Expansion and Capacity Digest*). Similarly, Gale Research Company provides numerous services to business researchers.

- Some provide loose-leaf and audiotape services.

Another type of business service provides loose-leaf services and audiotapes. For keeping up to date on particular topics, services offer excellent loose-leaf publications with weekly and biweekly supplements that report on topics such as personnel and labor, legal rules, and other areas.

- Document delivery services provide the information for a fee.

Technology has brought us another kind of business service—document delivery services. These services will fax, e-mail, or mail copies of articles to you. They are particularly helpful both for getting information quickly and getting information your local library does not have on hand. They charge both for their services, and for any copyright fees the publisher charges.

- Statistical information for the international business environment is available in a wide range of documents.

International Sources. In today's global business environment, we often need information outside our borders. Many of the sources we have discussed have counterparts with international information. *Principal International Businesses* lists basic information on major companies located around the world. *Major Companies of Europe* and *Japan Company Handbook* are two sources providing facts on companies in their respective areas. The *International Encyclopedia of the Social Sciences* covers all important areas of social science, including biographies of acclaimed persons in these areas. General and specialized dictionaries are available, too. *The Multilingual*

Commercial Dictionary and the *International Business Dictionary in Nine Languages* include commonly used business terms in several languages. You will even be able to find trade names in the *International Trade Names Dictionary* published by Gale Research. For bibliographies and abstracts, available sources include *International Business Reference Sources, Business International Index,* the *Foreign Commerce Handbook,* and several more. Even statistical information is available in sources such as the *Index to International Statistics, Statistical Yearbook,* and *Worldcasts.* In addition, libraries usually contain many references for information on international marketing, exporting, tax, and trade.

Using Indirect Methods

If you cannot move directly to the information you need, you must use indirect methods to find it. The first step in this approach is preparing a bibliography, or a list of prospective sources. The next two steps are gathering the publications in your bibliography and systematically checking them for the information you need.

> • When you cannot find secondary materials directly, try the indirect approach. Start by preparing a bibliography of sources that may include the information you need.

These two steps are elementary, but nonetheless important. Your acquisition of secondary materials must be thorough. You should not depend solely on the material you find on the shelves of your library. Use interlibrary loan services, database and Internet searches, and send away for company or government documents. Your check of the sources you gather must also be thorough. For each source, review the pages cited in your bibliographic reference. Then take some time to learn about the publication. Review its table of contents, its index, and the endnotes or footnotes related to the pages you are researching. You should be familiar with both the source and the context of all the information you plan to report; they are often as significant as the information itself.

> • Gather all available publications. Check each systematically for the information you need.

However, the first step, preparing the bibliography, is still the most demanding and challenging task in indirect research. It is therefore helpful to review what this task involves.

Prepared Bibliographies.   You should begin the preparation of your own bibliography by looking for one that has already been prepared. Lists of published materials are available through a number of sources, and finding such a list may save you the time and trouble of developing a bibliography from scratch.

> • Try to find a prepared bibliography. It will save you time and trouble.

Start your search in the reference section of your library. Prepared bibliographies are sometimes published as reference books, and individual entries in these books often include a description. In the reference section you may also find bibliographies that have been compiled by associations or government agencies. Encyclopedias are also a helpful source of published materials; most encyclopedia articles conclude with a brief bibliography.

Another way to discover prepared bibliographies is to consult texts, articles, and master's and doctor's theses that deal with your subject. If books include bibliographies, it is so noted in the on-line catalog. Academic studies routinely include complete bibliographies. Articles present the most challenging task, for not all of them list their sources. However, since those that do are likely to include very timely and selective listings, it is worth the trouble to check articles individually.

The On-line Catalog.   If you are not able to locate a prepared bibliography, or if the bibliographies you have identified are inadequate, you must set about developing your own list of prospective sources. Here the on-line catalog is very helpful.

> • The on-line catalog is another resource for developing a bibliography.

If the catalog you are using is composed of cards, it offers three distinct ways of identifying and locating desired references: by author, by title, and by subject. However, today many libraries are using electronic catalogs, giving you numerous ways to locate sources. As you can see from the main menu screen of one system in

> • On-line catalogs list the holdings of each library.

Figure 19–1, in some ways electronic catalogs are similar to card catalogs. You can still locate sources by author, title, and subject. In addition, the electronic catalogs give you more main options and more options within each choice. The options you have will depend on the system installed and the way your librarians decided to set it up.

Two options you need to understand clearly are *keywords in titles* and *subject.* When the *keywords in titles* option is selected, the system will ask you for the keywords and then search only the titles for those keywords. This means the items it finds will likely be on the subject you need. However, it misses all those whose titles do not contain the words you keyed in. For example, if you wanted to know more about cross-cultural communication, using keywords in title would find only those items with those exact words in the title. It would miss titles with the words *intercultural communication, international communication,* and *global communication.* If you did multiple searches using all the similar terms you could think of, it would still miss those titles without the keywords, such as Robert Axtell's *Dos and Taboos Around the World.*

The subject search, on the other hand, is broader. Using the subject *intercultural communication,* you will find items on the subject, whether or not the exact words are indicated in the title. For example, you might find a management book with a chapter on *intercultural* communication; however, the book's emphasis might be on something else, such as crisis management or conflict resolution.

The electronic catalog never gets tired. If you key in the words accurately, it will always produce a complete and accurate list of sources. Let us look at a few results from a subject search on *intercultural* communication. Notice in Figure 19–2 that the system found 174 sources. That is more than you really want, so you decide to select the other options shown at the bottom of the screen to limit your search. This system then gives you some options for limiting your search (see Figure 19–3). You decide to limit the search by year, telling it you want it to find all sources after 1993 (see Figure 19–4). As you can see in Figure 19–5, 20 entries were found. When you ask the system to display the title and author, it brings up the screen shown in Figure 19–6. Not only will you find the title and author, but you will also find complete bibliographic information, the call number, and the status along with subjects this book fits. Furthermore, the system gives you the option of browsing through other books nearby on the shelf.

The on-line catalog is a useful source of information for your library's holdings. Learning how to use it effectively will save you time and will help your searches be fast and accurate.

Periodical Indexes.   The on-line catalog helps you identify books for your bibliography. To identify articles published in newspapers, magazines, or journals, you will need to consult an index, either a general one or one that specializes in the field you are researching. Regularly updated indexes are available in the reference section of most libraries.

If you are like most business researchers, you will start your search for periodical literature with the *Business Periodicals Index.* Issued monthly and cumulated yearly, this index covers articles in 300 major business periodicals and indexes, by subject headings and company references. Another index that you may find useful is the *United States Predicasts F & S Index,* which covers over 700 business-oriented periodicals, newspapers, and special reports. A third index that may be helpful is the *Public Affairs Information Service Bulletin.* It lists by subject information relating to economics and public affairs. In addition, you may find useful such specialized indexes as *Findex: the Directory of Market Research; Reports, Studies, and Surveys; Marketing Information Guides;* and the *Accountant's Index.*

Infotrak, Wilsonline, and University Microfilms are providers of CD-ROM products on business information. The CD-ROMs give the researcher a simple citation, an abstract, or even full text. For business information, the *Academic Index* and the

- Understanding how the catalog systems work will help you gather information efficiently.

- To identify articles for your list of prospective sources, consult a periodical index.

- Excellent business indexes are available on CD-ROMs.

FIGURE 19–1   A Menu for an On-line Catalog

```
                        Welcome to the SDSU Library            SDSU PAC
                      Public Access Catalog (the PAC)

        You may search for library materials by any of the following:

                    A > AUTHOR
                    T > TITLE
                    W > WORDS in the TITLE
                    S > SUBJECT
                    J > JUVENILE BOOK SUBJECTS

                    C > CALL #/DOC #

                    R > RESERVE Lists
                    I > Library INFORMATION
                    V > VIEW your Library Circulation Record
                    D > DISCONNECT
                        Choose one (A,T,W,S,J,C,R,I,V,D)
```

FIGURE 19–2   Illustration of On-line Search Results

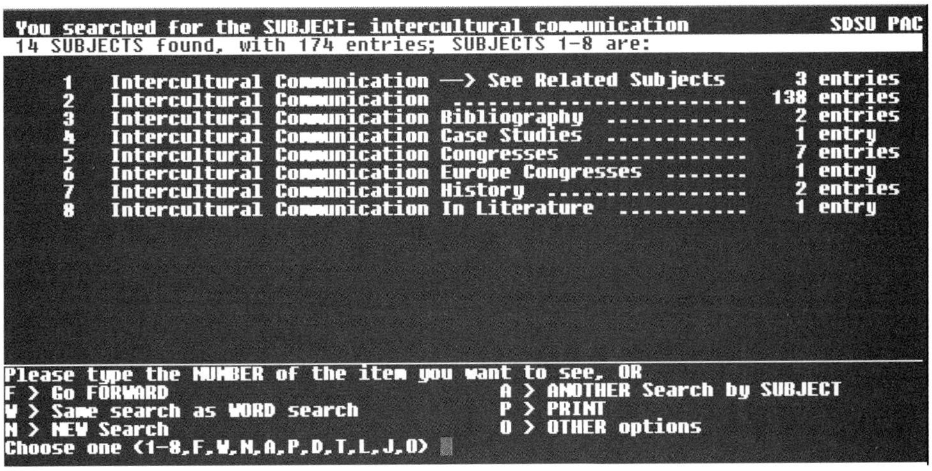

```
You searched for the SUBJECT: intercultural communication       SDSU PAC
14 SUBJECTS found, with 174 entries; SUBJECTS 1-8 are:

    1    Intercultural Communication —> See Related Subjects      3 entries
    2    Intercultural Communication  ----------------------    138 entries
    3    Intercultural Communication Bibliography  -----------     2 entries
    4    Intercultural Communication Case Studies  -----------     1 entry
    5    Intercultural Communication Congresses  -------------     7 entries
    6    Intercultural Communication Europe Congresses  ------     1 entry
    7    Intercultural Communication History  ----------------     2 entries
    8    Intercultural Communication In Literature  ----------     1 entry



Please type the NUMBER of the item you want to see, OR
F > Go FORWARD                             A > ANOTHER Search by SUBJECT
W > Same search as WORD search             P > PRINT
N > NEW Search                             O > OTHER options
Choose one (1-8,F,W,N,A,P,D,T,L,J,O)
```

FIGURE 19–3   Some Options for Limiting a Search

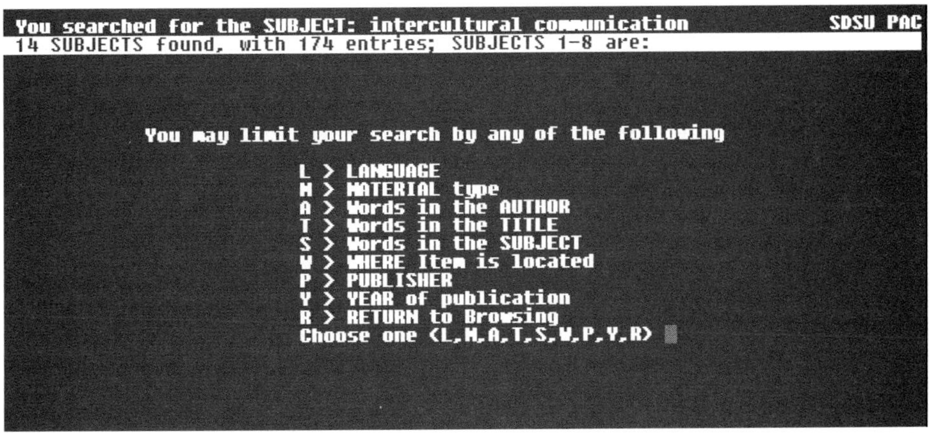

```
You searched for the SUBJECT: intercultural communication       SDSU PAC
14 SUBJECTS found, with 174 entries; SUBJECTS 1-8 are:


        You may limit your search by any of the following

                    L > LANGUAGE
                    M > MATERIAL type
                    A > Words in the AUTHOR
                    T > Words in the TITLE
                    S > Words in the SUBJECT
                    W > WHERE Item is located
                    P > PUBLISHER
                    Y > YEAR of publication
                    R > RETURN to Browsing
                    Choose one (L,M,A,T,S,W,P,Y,R)
```

FIGURE 19-4   Additional Options for Use in Searching

```
You searched for the SUBJECT: intercultural communication      SDSU PAC
14 SUBJECTS found, with 174 entries; SUBJECTS 1-8 are:
   YEAR of publication AFTER 1993



                    F > Find items with above limits

                    A > AND   (Limit further)
                    O > OR    (Expand retrieval)
                    R > RETURN to Previous Screen
                    Choose one (F,A,O,R) █
```

FIGURE 19-5   Results with Time Limit

```
You searched for the SUBJECT: intercultural communicationLIMITED TO AFTER 199
20 entries found, entries 1-8 are:                              CALL #
Intercultural Communication
   1   Between worlds : interpreters, guides,  P306.9 .K37 1994
   2   Crosstalk and culture in Sino-American  PL1074 .Y68 1994
   3   Disney discourse : producing the magic  PN1999.W27 D57 1994
   4   Doing business in Asia's booming "China HF3836.5 .E53 1994
   5   Doing business internationally : the gu HD31 .B7235 1995
   6   Effective communication in multicultura R118 .K729 1994
   7   Globalwork : bridging distance, culture HD62.4 .O36 1994
   8   Improving intercultural interactions :  GN345.6 .I46 1994


Please type the NUMBER of the item you want to see, OR
F > Go FORWARD              A > ANOTHER Search by SUBJECT      J > JUMP
R > RETURN to Browsing      P > PRINT
N > NEW Search              D > DISPLAY Title and Author
Choose one (1-8,F,R,N,A,P,D,J)
```

FIGURE 19-6   Illustration of a Retrieved Record

```
You searched for the SUBJECT: intercultural communicationLIMITED TO AFTER 199
AUTHOR      Brake, Terence.
TITLE       Doing business internationally : the guide to cross-cultural
                success / Terrence Brake, Danielle Medina Walker, Thomas (Tim)
                Walker.
PUBLISHER   Burr Ridge, Ill. : Irwin Professional Pub., c1995.
DESCRIPTION xiv, 282 p. : ill. ; 24 cm.
NOTE(S)     Includes bibliographical references and index.
SUBJECT(S)  Industrial management —Cross-cultural studies.
            Intercultural communication.
            Negotiation in business —Cross cultural studies.
            Success in business.
CALL #      HD31 .B7235 1995.

    LOCATION          CALL #                        STATUS
1 > Book Stacks       HD31 .B7235 1995              NOT CHECKD OUT

R > RETURN to Browsing          A > ANOTHER Search by SUBJECT
F > FORWARD browse              Z > Show Items Nearby on Shelf
B > BACKWARD browse             S > SHOW items with the same SUBJECT
N > NEW Search                  P > PRINT
Choose one (R,F,B,N,A,Z,S,P)
```

Business Index from Infotrak are particularly useful. *Wilson Business Abstracts* from Wilsonline is an excellent source for general business information. *ABI/INFORM* and *Business Dateline* are good business CD-ROM indexes from University Microfilms.

On-line Databases. Computers offer the most advanced method of conducting secondary research. As you know, the capacity of computers to collect and retrieve information has been expanding phenomenally. Business research has been a primary beneficiary of that expansion. Much of the information routinely recorded in printed form and accessed through directories, encyclopedias, bibliographies, indexes, and the like is now collected and stored in computer files as well. When these files of related information, known collectively as *databases,* are accessed by computer, the result is research that can be more extensive, complete, and accurate than any conducted manually.

* Computers organize and store vast amounts of data.

Databases, many of which are produced by private information services, offer a variety of materials essential to business research. For example, Knight-Ridder Information Services, Inc., includes in its selection of 450 databases the *American Statistics Index,* the *Encyclopedia of Associations,* a number of Predicasts services (*PTS F&S Indexes, International Forecasts,* and *Promt*), and *Standard & Poor's News.* Two other private information services, Bibliographic Retrieval System (BRS) and LEXIS/NEXIS, offer many of the same information files. In addition, prominent business resources, including Dow Jones & Company, the *Harvard Business Review,* the *New York Times,* and Standard & Poor's, now offer computer access to their data and files.

Most public, college, and university libraries offer database searching services, usually for a fee that reflects the computer time employed and the number of items identified. They also usually require you to work closely with trained staff to design a strategy that will use computer time effectively and retrieve mostly relevant information. However, considering the potential advantages of computer-assisted research, the cost of the service and the initial inconvenience of designing a computer search strategy are a small price to pay. Many of these information providers, such as Knight-Ridder and Dow Jones News Retrieval Services, offer special price packages. You can search their databases during off-peak times at reduced rates or you can subscribe to some services for a flat fee. Developing your own searching skills will also help to keep costs down.

* Many libraries offer facilities for computer-searching of databases.

You can keep costs down several ways. One way is by planning carefully before you go on-line to shorten the amount of time you need to be connected to the database. Another way is to choose the correct database the first time. Some database providers have a selection utility you can use. First you tell it the subject you need, then it recommends appropriate databases to use. Using these kinds of "assistants" will pay off by eliminating trial-and-error charges. A third way to cut costs is to know what to do when your search contains too many or two few citations.

* Developing good search strategies will help you keep costs down when using on-line systems.

If your search gives you more citations than you can handle, be prepared to limit the search. Know ahead of time how you might do this. Most systems let you limit your search by language and year. Sometimes you can add a NOT term, which eliminates citations with a particular term from your search. If your search comes up short, you need to check for spelling errors and narrow terms. If you have a hard time adding terms to broaden your search, look at the keywords or descriptors of the items that have already been identified. Often these will give you ideas of terms to broaden the search. Be sure to keep track of the strategies that work so you can use them in future searches. Learning how to extract information efficiently from databases will pay off immensely, putting information at your fingertips.

The Internet. The Internet is a network of networks. It runs off a backbone provided by the National Science Foundation. However, no one organization owns or runs this globally connected network. Its users work together to develop standards. On the network are a wide variety of resources, including many useful to business. Since no one

* A wide variety of business sources are available through the Internet.

is officially in charge, finding information on the Internet can be difficult. But this network of loosely organized computer systems does provide some search tools.

- Using on-line search tools such as WebCrawler will help find files and text.

These tools can search for files as well as text on various topics. They can search titles as well as the documents themselves. The World Wide Web is a growing medium for publishing documents. Web browsers are tools that help you view these web documents as well as use other Internet tools such as ftp, gopher, and telnet. Microsoft's Windows 95 includes a web browser. Using a web browser, you can reach various search engines. The WebCrawler, one such search tool, is shown in Figure 19–7. To use it, simply type your search terms in the space provided. As you can see in Figure 19–8, the search for the terms *cross-cultural* and *communication* found 68 hits and displayed 35. The displayed hits are linked to their locations. To find the information, the user simply clicks on the hit and the system will take you there.

· ·
PRIMARY RESEARCH

- Primary research employs four basic methods.

When you cannot find the information you need in secondary sources, you must get it firsthand. That is, you must use primary research, which employs four basic methods:

1. Search through company records.
2. Experimentation.
3. Observation.
4. Survey.

Searching through Company Records

- Company records are an excellent source of firsthand information.

Since many of today's business problems involve various phases of company operations, a company's internal records—production data, sales records, merchandising information, accounting records, and the like—are frequently an excellent source of firsthand information.

- Make sure you (1) have a clear idea of the information you need, (2) understand the terms of access and confidentially, and (3) cooperate with company personnel.

There are no set rules on how to find and gather information through company records. Record-keeping systems vary widely from company to company. However, you are well advised to keep the following standards in mind as you conduct your investigation. First, as in any other type of research, you must have a clear idea of the information you need. Undefined, open-ended investigations are not appreciated—nor are they particularly productive. Second, you must clearly understand the ground rules under which you are allowed to review materials. Matters of confidentiality and access should be resolved before you start. And third, if you are not intimately familiar with a company's records or how to access them, you must cooperate with someone who is. The complexity and sensitivity of such materials require that they be reviewed in their proper context.

Conducting the Experiment

- Experimentation develops information by testing variable factors.

The experiment is a very useful technique in business research. Originally perfected in the sciences, the experiment is an orderly form of testing. In general, it is a form of research in which you systematically manipulate one variable factor of a problem while holding all the others constant. You measure quantitatively or qualitatively any changes resulting from your manipulations. Then you apply your findings to the problem.

For example, suppose you are conducting research to determine whether a new package design will lead to more sales. You might start by selecting two test cities, taking care that they are as alike as possible on all the characteristics that might affect the problem. Then you would secure information on sales in the two cities for a specified time period before the experiment. Next, for a second specified time period, you

FIGURE 19–7   Ilustration of a Popular Internet Search Tool

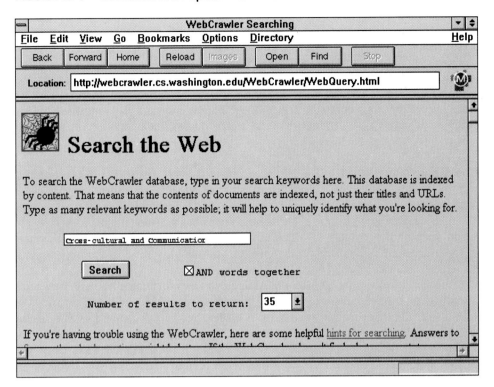

FIGURE 19–8   Illustration of Internet Search Results

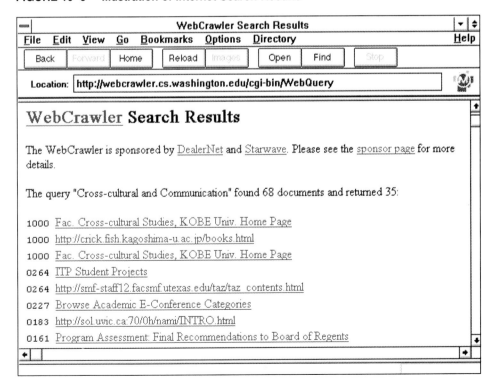

would use the new package design in one of the cities, and continue to use the old package in the other. During that period, you would keep careful sales records and check to make sure that advertising, economic conditions, competition, and other factors that might have some effect on the experiment remain unchanged. Thus, when the experimentation period is over, you can attribute any differences you found between the sales of the two cities to the change in package design.

Each experiment should be designed to fit the individual requirements of the problem. Nonetheless, a few basic designs underlie most experiments. Becoming familiar with two of the most common designs—the before-after and the controlled before-after—will give you a framework for understanding and applying this primary research technique.

- Design each experiment to fit the problem.

The Before-After Design. The simplest experimental design is the before-after design. In this design you select a test group of subjects, measure the variable in which you are interested, and then introduce the experimental factor. After a specified time period, during which the experimental factor has presumably had its effect, you again measure the variable in which you are interested. If there are any differences between the first and second measurements, you may assume that the experimental factor is the cause. Figure 19–9 illustrates this design.

- The before-after design is the simplest. You use just one test group.

Consider the following application. Assume you are conducting research for a retail store to determine the effect of point-of-sale advertising. Your first step is to select a product for the experiment, Brand Y razor blades. Second, you record sales of Brand Y blades for one week, using no point-of-sale advertising. Then you introduce the experimental variable—the Brand Y point-of-sale display. For the next week you again record sales of Brand Y blades; and at the end of that week, you compare the results for the two weeks. Any increase in sales would presumably be explained by the introduction of the display. Thus, if 500 packages of Brand Y blades were sold in the first week and 600 were sold in the second week, you would conclude that the 100 additional sales can be attributed to point-of-sale advertising.

You can probably recognize the major shortcoming of the design. It is simply not logical to assume that the experimental factor explains the entire difference in sales between the first week and the second. The sales of Brand Y razor blades could have changed for a number of other reasons—changes in the weather, holiday or other seasonal influences on business activity, other advertising, and so on. At best, you have determined only that point-of-sale advertising *could* influence sales.

- The changes recorded in a before-after experiment may not be attributable to the experimental factor alone.

FIGURE 19–9   The Before-After Design

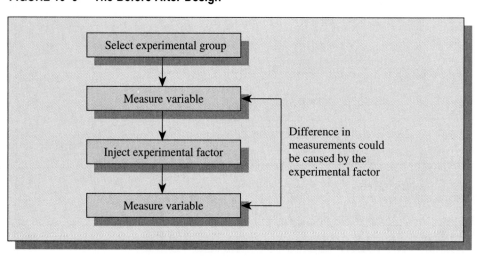

PART 7   Special Topics in Business Communication

The Controlled Before-After Design. To account for influences other than the experimental factors, you may use designs more complex than the before-after design. These designs attempt to measure the other influences by including some means of control. The simplest of these designs is the controlled before-after design.

In the controlled before-after design, you select not one group, but two—the experimental group and the control group. Before introducing the experimental factor, you measure in each group the variable to be tested. Then you introduce the experimental factor into the experimental group only.

When the period allotted for the experiment is over, you again measure in each group the variable being tested. Any difference between the first and second measurements in the experimental group can be explained by two causes—the experimental factor and other influences. But the difference between the first and second measurements in the control group can be explained only by other influences, for this group was not subjected to the experimental factor. Thus, comparing the "afters" of the two groups will give you a measure of the influence of the experimental factor. The controlled before-after design is diagrammed in Figure 19–10.

In a controlled before-after experiment designed to test the point-of-sale application, you might select Brand Y razor blades and Brand X razor blades and record the sales of both brands for one week. Next you introduce point-of-sale displays for Brand Y only and you record sales for both Brand Y and Brand X for a second week. At the end of the second week, you compare the results for the two brands. Whatever difference you find in Brand Y sales and Brand X sales will be a fair measure of the experimental factor, independent of the changes that other influences may have brought about.

For example, if 400 packages of Brand X blades are sold the first week, and 450 packages are sold the second week, the increase of 50 packages (12.5 percent) can be attributed to influences other than the experimental factor, the point-of-sale display. If 500 packages of Brand Y blades are sold the first week, and 600 are sold the second week, the increase of 100 can be attributed to both the point-of-sale display and other influences. To distinguish between the two, you note that other influences accounted for the 12.5 percent increase in the sales of Brand X blades. Because of the experimental control, you attribute 12.5 percent of the increase in Brand Y sales to other influences as well. An increase of 12.5 percent on a base of 500 sales is 63 sales, indicating that 63 of the 100 additional Brand Y sales are the result of other influences. However, the sale of 37 additional packages of Brand Y blades can be attributed to point-of-sale advertising.

- In the controlled before-after experiment, you use two identical test groups. You introduce the experimental factor into one group, then compare the two groups. You can attribute any difference between the two to the experimental factor.

FIGURE 19–10   The Controlled Before-After Design

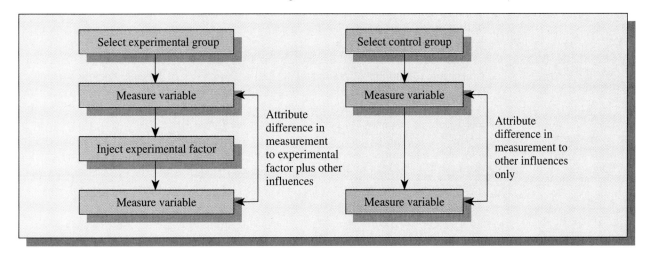

Using the Observation Technique

• Research by observation involves watching phenomena and recording what is seen.

Like the experiment, observation is a technique perfected in the sciences that is also useful in business research. Simply stated, observation is seeing with a purpose. It consists of watching the events involved in a problem and systematically recording what is seen. In observation, you do not manipulate the details of what you observe; you take note of situations exactly as you find them.

• This form of observation does not involve experimentation.

Note that observation as an independent research technique is different from the observation you use in recording the effects of variables introduced into a test situation. In the latter case, observation is a step in the experiment, not an end in itself. The two methods, therefore, should not be confused.

To see how observation works as a business technique, consider this situation. You are a grocery supplier who wants to determine how shoppers are responding to a new line of foods. A review of sales records would certainly give some information, as would a survey of store patrons. However, observing customers as they shop may reveal important information that you might overlook if you used alternative techniques.

• Observation requires a systematic procedure for observing and recording.

Like all primary research techniques, observation must be designed to fit the requirements of the problem being considered. However, the planning stage generally requires two steps. First, you construct a recording form; second, you design a systematic procedure for observing and recording the information of interest.

• The recording form should enable you to record details quickly and accurately.

The recording form may be any tabular arrangement that permits quick and easy recording of that information. Though observation forms are hardly standardized, one commonly used arrangement (see Figure 19–11) provides a separate line for each observation. Headings at the top of the page mark the columns in which the observer will place the appropriate mark. The recording form identifies the characteristics that are to be observed and requires the recording of such potentially important details as the date, time, and place of the observation and the name of the observer.

• An effective observation procedure ensures the collection of complete and representative information.

The observation procedure may be any system that ensures the collection of complete and representative information. But every effective observation procedure includes a clear focus, well-defined steps, and provisions for ensuring the quality of the information collected. For example, an observation procedure for determining what style of clothing men wear in a certain city would include a detailed observation schedule for all appropriate sections of the city, detailed observing instructions, and provisions for dealing with all the complications that the observer might encounter. In short, the procedure would leave no major question unanswered.

Collecting Information by Survey

• You can best determine certain information by asking questions.

The premise of the survey as a method of primary research is simple: You can best determine certain types of information by asking questions. Such information includes personal data, opinions, evaluations, and other important material. It also includes information necessary to plan for an experiment or an observation or to supplement or interpret the data that result.

• Decide which survey format and delivery will be most effective in developing the information you need.

Once you have decided to use the survey for your research, you have to make decisions about a number of matters. The first is the matter of format. The questions can range from spontaneous inquiries to carefully structured interrogations. The next is the matter of delivery. The questions can be posed in a personal interview, asked over the telephone, or presented in printed or electronic form.

• Also decide whom to interview. If the subject group is large, select a sample.

But the most important is the matter of whom to survey. Except for situations in which a small number of people are involved in the problem under study, you cannot reach all the people involved. Thus, you have to select a sample of respondents who represent the group as a whole as accurately as possible. There are several ways to select that sample, as you will see.

FIGURE 19–11   Excerpt of a Common Type of Observation Recording Form

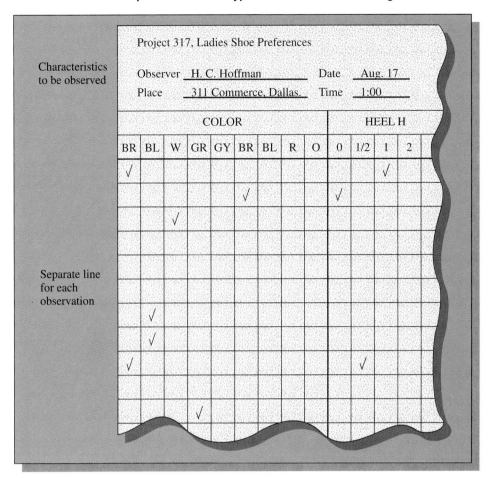

Sampling as a Basis.   Sampling theory forms the basis for most research by survey, though it has any number of other applications as well. Buyers of grain, for example, judge the quality of a multi-ton shipment by examining a few pounds. Quality-control supervisors spot-check a small percentage of products ready for distribution to determine whether production standards are being met. Judges at county fairs take a little taste of each entry of homemade jam to decide which entry will win a blue ribbon.

• Survey research is based on sampling.

Sampling is generally used for economy and practicality. However, for a sample to be representative of the whole group, it must be designed properly. Two important aspects to consider in the design of a survey are *reliability* and *validity*. You want the results to be reliable, free from random error. A test of a survey's reliability is its repeatability with similar results. You also want your survey to be valid, measuring what it is supposed to measure.

• Good samples are reliable, valid, and controlled for sampling error.

Another aspect of sample design is controlling for sampling error and bias. Sampling error results when the sample is not representative of the whole group. While all samples have some degree of sampling error, you can reduce the error through techniques used to construct representative samples. These techniques fall into two groups—probability and nonprobability sampling.

Probability Sampling Techniques.   Probability samples are based on chance selection procedures. Every element in the population has a known nonzero probability of

T E C H N O L O G Y   I N   B R I E F

Survey Project Software: Specialty Tools for Business Research

Since client and customer surveys are effective tools for eliciting meaningful information, tools for helping business researchers execute them well are extremely useful. These programs are designed for those who want to conduct productive surveys and report results quickly and accurately.

Survey project software supports the questionnaire design, data entry, and analysis steps in the research process. Survey Pro, illustrated here, helps you create a questionnaire through special entry screens. The software does all the arranging on the screen; the user simply fills in a template. The software even keeps track of the appropriate statistics to use when analyzing the results. And this product lets users create a library of questions, questions that can be reused or modified for future projects. It can generate professional-looking, easy-to-comprehend reports. It even allows you to report results from open-ended questions.

Businesses might use survey project software for some of these types of applications:

- Before and after evaluations of training programs.
- Employee feedback.
- Longitudinal studies of groups.
- Marketplace needs determination.
- Opinion surveys.
- Recurring surveys on customer satisfaction.

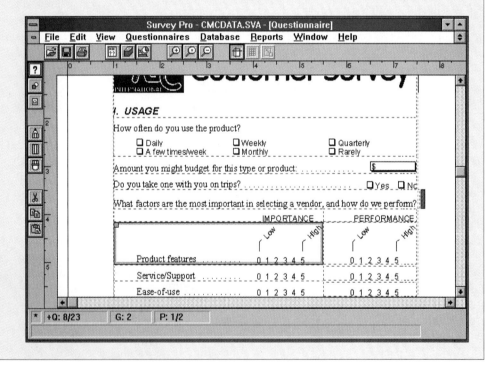

The survey is a widely used form of primary research in business. It is especially useful for gathering marketing information.

selection.[1] These techniques include simple random sampling, stratified random sampling, systematic sampling, and cluster or area sampling.

Random sampling. Random sampling is the technique assumed in the general law of sampling. By definition, it is the sampling technique that gives every member of the group under study an equal chance of being included. To assure equal chances, you must first identify every member of the group and then, using a list or some other convenient format, record all the identifications. Next, through some chance method, you select the members of your sample.

- In random sampling, every item in the subject group has an equal chance of being selected.

For example, if you are studying the job attitudes of 200 production workers and determine that 25 interviews will give you the information you need, you might put the names of each worker in a container, mix them up, and draw out 25. Since each of the 200 workers has an equal chance of being selected, your sample will be random and can be presumed to be representative.

Stratified random sampling. Stratified random sampling subdivides the group under study and makes random selections within each subgroup. The size of each subgroup is usually proportionate to that subgroup's percentage of the whole. If a subgroup is too small to yield meaningful findings, however, you may have to select a disproportionately large sample. (Of course, when the study calls for statistics on the group as a whole, the actual proportion of such a subgroup must be restored.)

- In stratified random sampling, the group is divided into subgroups and the sample is randomly selected from each subgroup.

---

[1] William G. Zikmund, *Business Research Methods,* 2nd ed. (Chicago: The Dryden Press, 1988), p. 346.

Assume, for example, that you are attempting to determine the curriculum needs of 5,000 undergraduates at a certain college and that you have decided to survey 20 percent of the enrollment, or 1,000 students. To construct a sample for this problem, first divide the enrollment list by academic concentration: business, liberal arts, nursing, engineering, and so forth. Then draw a random sample from each of these groups, making sure that the number you select is proportionate to that group's percentage of the total undergraduate enrollment. Thus, if 30 percent of the students are majoring in business, you will randomly select 300 business majors for your sample; if 40 percent of the students are liberal arts majors, you will randomly select 400 liberal arts majors for your sample; and so on.

Systematic sampling. Systematic sampling, though not random in the strictest sense, is random for all practical purposes. It is the technique of taking selections at constant intervals (every *n*th unit) from a list of the items under study. The interval used is based, as you might expect, on the size of the list and the size of the desired sample. For example, if you want a 10 percent sample of a list of 10,000, you might select every 10th item on the list.

However, your sample would not really be random. By virtue of their designated place on the original list, items do not have an equal chance of being selected. To correct that problem, you might use an equal-chance method to determine what *n* to use. Thus, if you selected the number 7 randomly, you would draw the numbers 7, 17, 27, and so on to 9,997 to make up your sample. Or, if you wanted to draw every 10th item, you might first scramble the list and then select from the revised list numbers 10, 20, 30, and so on up to 10,000 and make up your sample that way.

Area or cluster sampling. In area sampling, the items for a sample are drawn in stages. This sampling technique is appropriate when the area to be studied is large and can be broken down into progressively smaller components. For example, if you want to draw an area sample for a certain city, you may use census data to divide the city into homogeneous districts. Using an equal-chance method, you then select a given number of districts to include in the next stage of your sample. Next you divide each of the selected districts into subdistricts—city blocks, for example. Continuing the process, you randomly select a given number of these blocks and subdivide each of them into households. Finally, using random sampling once more, you select the households that will constitute the sample you will use in your research.

Area or cluster sampling is not limited to geographic division, however. It is adaptable to any number of applications. For example, it is an appropriate technique to use in a survey of the workers in a given industry. An approach that you may take in this situation is to randomly select a given number of companies from a list of all the companies in the industry. Then, using organization units and selecting randomly at each level, you break down each of these companies into divisions, departments, sections, and so on until you finally identify the workers you will survey.

Nonprobability Sampling Techniques. Nonprobability samples are based on an unknown probability of any one of a population being chosen. These techniques include convenience sampling, quota sampling, and referral sampling.[2]

Convenience sampling. A convenience sample is one whose members are convenient and economical to reach. When professors use their students as subjects for their research, they are using a convenience sample. Researchers generally use this sample to reach a large number quickly and economically. This kind of sampling is best used for exploratory research.

A form of convenience sampling is *judgment* or *expert* sampling. This technique relies on the judgment of the writer to identify appropriate members of the sample. Illustrating this technique is the common practice of predicting the outcome of an election, based on the results in a bellwether district.

- In systematic sampling, the items are selected from the subject group at constant intervals.

- Select the interval randomly or scramble the order of the subject group if you want your systematic sample to be random.

- For an area or cluster sample, draw items from the subject group in stages. Select randomly at each stage.

- Convenience samples are chosen for their convenience, their ease and economy of reaching, and their appropriateness.

---

[2] Ibid., p. 346.

Quota sampling. Quota sampling is a nonrandom technique. Also known as *controlled sampling,* it is used whenever the proportionate makeup of the universe under study is available. The technique requires that you refer to the composition of the universe in designing your sample, selecting items so that your sample has the same characteristics in the same proportion as that universe. Specifically, it requires that you set quotas for each characteristic that you want to consider in your research problem. Within those quotas, however, you will select individual items randomly.

• Setting quotas assures that the sample reflects the whole. Choose items randomly within each quota.

Let us say that you want to survey a college student body of 4,000 using a 10 percent sample. As Figure 19–12 illustrates, you have a number of alternatives for determining the makeup of your sample, depending on the focus of your research. Keep in mind, though, that no matter what characteristic you select, the quotas the individual segments represent must total 100 percent and the number of items in the sample must total 400. Keep in mind also that within these quotas you will use an equal-chance method to select the individual members of your sample.

Referral sampling. Referral samples are those whose members are identified by others from a random sample. This technique is used to locate members when the population is small or hard to reach. For example, you might want to survey rolle bolle players. To get a sample large enough to make the study worthwhile, you could ask those from your town to give you the names of other players. Perhaps you were trying to survey the users of project management software. You could survey a user's group and ask those members for names of other users. You might even post your announcement on a bulletin board system; users of the system would send you the names for your sample.

• Referral samples are used for small or hard-to-reach groups.

Constructing the Questionnaire. Most orderly interrogation follows a definite plan of inquiry. This plan is usually worked out in a printed form, called the *questionnaire.* The questionnaire is simply an orderly arrangement of the questions, with appropriate spaces provided for the answers. But simple as the finished questionnaire may appear to be, it is the subject of careful planning. It is, in a sense, the outline of the analysis of the problem. In addition, it must observe certain rules. These rules sometimes vary with the problem. The more general and by far the more important ones follow.

FIGURE 19–12 Alternative Quota Sample

	Number in Universe	Percent of Total	Number to Be Interviewed
Total student enrollment	4,000	100	400
Sex			
Men students	2,400	60	240
Women students	1,600	40	160
Fraternity, sorority membership			
Members	1,000	25	100
Nonmembers	3,000	75	300
Marital status			
Married students	400	10	40
Single students	3,600	90	360
Class rank			
Freshman	1,600	40	160
Sophomores	1,000	25	100
Juniors	800	20	80
Seniors	400	10	40
Graduates	200	5	20

• Avoid leading questions (questions that influence the answer).

• Word the questions so that all the respondents understand them.

• Vagueness of expression, difficult words, and two questions in one cause misunderstanding.

• Avoid questions of a personal nature.

• But if personal questions are necessary, use less direct methods.

• Seek factual information whenever possible.

• Ask only for information that can be remembered.

Avoid leading questions. A leading question is one that in some way influences the answer. For example, the question "Is Dove your favorite bath soap?" leads the respondent to favor Dove. Some people who would say yes would name another brand if they were asked, "What is your favorite brand of bath soap?"

Make the questions easy to understand. Questions not clearly understood by all respondents lead to error. Unfortunately, it is difficult to determine in advance just what respondents will not understand. As will be mentioned later, the best means of detecting such questions in advance is to test the questions before using them. But you can be on the alert for a few general sources of confusion.

One source of confusion is vagueness of expression, which is illustrated by the ridiculous question "How do you bank?" Who other than its author knows what the question means? Another source is using words not understood by the respondents, as in the question "Do you read your house organ regularly?" The words *house organ* have a specialized, not widely known meaning, and *regularly* means different things to different people. Combining two questions in one is yet another source of confusion. For example, "Why did you buy a Ford?" actually asks two questions: "What do you like about Fords?" and "What don't you like about the other automobiles?"

Avoid questions that touch on personal prejudices or pride. For reasons of pride or prejudices, people cannot be expected to answer accurately questions about certain areas of information. These areas include age, income status, morals, and personal habits. How many people, for example, would answer no to the question "Do you brush your teeth daily?" How many people would give their ages correctly? How many solid citizens would admit to fudging a bit on their tax returns? The answers are obvious.

But one may ask, "What if such information is essential to the solution of the problem?" The answer is to use less direct means of inquiry. To ascertain age, for example, investigators could ask for dates of high school graduation, marriage, or the like. From this information, they could approximate age. Or they could approximate age through observation, although this procedure is acceptable only if broad age approximations would be satisfactory. They could ask for such harmless information as occupation, residential area, and standard of living and then use that information as a basis for approximating income. Another possibility is to ask range questions such as "Are you between 18 and 24, 25 and 40, or over 40?" This technique works well with income questions, too. People are generally more willing to answer questions worded by ranges rather than specifics. Admittedly, such techniques are sometimes awkward and difficult. But they can improve on the biased results that direct questioning would obtain.

Seek facts as much as possible. Although some studies require opinions, it is far safer to seek facts whenever possible. Human beings simply are not accurate reporters of their opinions. They are often limited in their ability to express themselves. Frequently, they report their opinions erroneously simply because they have never before been conscious of having them.

When opinions are needed, it is usually safer to record facts and then to judge the thoughts behind them. This technique, however, is only as good as the investigators' judgment. But a logical analysis of fact made by trained investigators is preferable to a spur-of-the-moment opinion.

A frequent violation of this rule results from the use of generalizations. Respondents are sometimes asked to generalize an answer from a large number of experiences over time. The question "Which magazines do you read regularly?" is a good illustration. Aside from the confusion caused by the word *regularly* and the fact that the question may tap the respondent's memory, the question forces the respondent to generalize. Would it not be better to phrase it in this way: "What magazines have you read this month?" The question could then be followed by an article-by-article check of the magazines to determine the extent of readership.

Ask only for information that can be remembered. Since the memory of all human beings is limited, the questionnaire should ask only for information that the respondents can be expected to remember. To make sure that this is done, a knowledge of certain fundamentals of memory is necessary.

Recency is the foremost fundamental. People remember insignificant events that occurred within the past few hours. By the next day, they will forget some. A month later they may not remember any. One might well remember, for example, what one ate for lunch on the day of the inquiry, and perhaps one might remember what one ate for lunch a day, or two days, or three days earlier. But one would be unlikely to remember what one ate for lunch a year earlier.

The second fundamental of memory is that significant events may be remembered over long periods. One may long remember the first day of school, the day of one's wedding, an automobile accident, a Christmas Day, and the like. In each of these examples there was an intense stimulus—a requisite for retention in memory.

A third fundamental of memory is that fairly insignificant facts may be remembered over long time periods through association with something significant. Although one would not normally remember what one ate for lunch a year earlier, for example, one might remember if the date happened to be one's wedding day, Christmas Day, or one's first day at college. Obviously, the memory is stimulated, not by the meal itself, but by the association of the meal with something more significant.

Plan the physical layout with foresight.   The overall design of the questionnaire should be planned to facilitate recording, analyzing, and tabulating the answers. Three major considerations are involved in such planning.

First, answers should be allowed sufficient space for recording. When practical, a system for checking answers may be set up. Such a system must always provide for all possible answers, including conditional answers. For example, a direct question may provide for three possible answers: Yes _____, No _____, and Don't know _____.

Second, adequate space for identifying and describing the respondent should be provided. In some instances, such information as the age, sex, and income bracket of the respondent is vital to the analysis of the problem and should be recorded. In other instances, little or no identification is necessary.

Third, the best possible sequence of questions should be used. In some instances, starting with a question of high interest value may have psychological advantages. In other instances, it may be best to follow some definite order of progression. Frequently, some questions must precede others because they help explain the others. Whatever the requirements of the individual case may be, however, careful and logical analysis should be used in determining the sequence of questions.

Use scaling when appropriate.   It is sometimes desirable to measure the intensity of the respondents' feelings about something (an idea, a product, a company, and so on). In such cases, some form of scaling is generally useful.

Of the various techniques of scaling, ranking and rating deserve special mention. These are the simpler techniques and, some believe, the more practical. They are less sophisticated than some others,[3] but the more sophisticated techniques are beyond the scope of this book.

The ranking technique consists simply of asking the respondent to rank a number of alternative answers to a question in order of preference (1, 2, 3, and so on). For example, in a survey to determine consumer preferences for toothpaste, the respondent might be asked to rank toothpastes A, B, C, D, and E in order of preference. In this example, the alternatives could be compared on the number of preferences stated for each. This method of ranking and summarizing results is reliable despite its simplicity. There are various more complicated ranking methods (such as the use of paired comparison) and methods of recording results.

- Memory is determined by three fundamentals: (1) recency.

- (2) intensity of stimulus, and

- (3) association.

- Design the form for each recording.

- Provide sufficient space.

- Provide adequate identification space.

- Arrange the questions in logical order.

- Provide for scaling when appropriate.

- Ranking of responses is one form.

---

[3] Equivalent interval techniques (developed by L. L. Thurstone), scalogram analysis (developed by Louis Guttman), and the semantic differential (developed by C. E. Osgood, G. J. Suchi, and P. H. Tannenbaum) are more complex techniques.

FIGURE 19–13 Illustration of a Rating Question

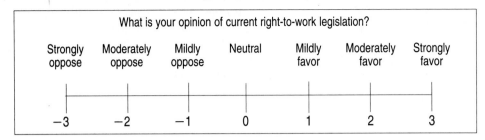

What is your opinion of current right-to-work legislation?

Strongly oppose	Moderately oppose	Mildly oppose	Neutral	Mildly favor	Moderately favor	Strongly favor
−3	−2	−1	0	1	2	3

FIGURE 19–14 Comparison of Data Collection Methods

	Personal	Telephone	Mail
Data collection costs	High	Medium	Low
Data collection time required	Medium	Low	High
Sample size for a given budget	Small	Medium	Large
Data quantity per respondent	High	Medium	Low
Reaches widely dispersed sample	No	Maybe	Yes
Reaches special locations	Yes	Maybe	No
Interaction with respondents	Yes	Yes	No
Degree of interviewer bias	High	Medium	None
Severity of non-response bias	Low	Low	High
Presentation of visual stimuli	Yes	No	Maybe
Field worker training required	Yes	Yes	No

Source: Pamela L. Alreck and Robert B. Settle, *The Survey Research Handbook* (Burr Ridge, Il: Richard D. Irwin, 1995, p. 32).

• Rating is another.

The rating technique graphically sets up a scale showing the complete range of possible attitudes on a matter and assigns number values to the positions on the scale. The respondent must then indicate the position on the scale that indicates his or her attitude on that matter. Typically, the numeral positions are described by words, as the example in Figure 19–13 illustrates.

Because the rating technique deals with the subjective rather than the factual, it is sometimes desirable to use more than one question to cover the attitude being measured. Logically, the average of a person's answers to such questions gives a more reliable answer than does any single answer.

• Select the way of asking the questions (by personal contact, telephone, or mail) that gives the best sample, the lowest cost, and the best results.

Selecting the Manner of Questioning.   You can get answers to the questions you need answered in three primary ways: by personal (face-to-face) contact, by telephone, or by mail (print or electronic). You should select the way that in your unique case gives the best sample, the lowest cost, and the best results. By *best sample* we mean respondents who best represent the group concerned. And *results* are the information you need. As you can see in Figure 19–14, other factors will influence your choice.

• Develop a working plan that covers all the steps and all the problems.

Developing a Working Plan.   After selecting the manner of questioning, you should carefully develop a working plan for the survey. As well as you can, you should

...ing. Why are you *really*

...n Features Syndicate.)

antic_____ problem. If you are conduct-
ing a _____ __ __ __ ___ develop an explanatory message that
move. ___ subjects to respond, tells them what to do, and answers all the questions
they are likely to ask. If you are conducting a personal or telephone survey, you need
to cover this information in instructions to the interviewers. You should develop your
working plan before conducting the pilot study discussed in the following section.
You should test that plan in the pilot study and revise it based on the knowledge you
gain from the pilot study.

Conducting a Pilot Study.   Before doing the survey, it is advisable to conduct a pilot
study on your questionnaire and working plan. A pilot study is a small-scale version
of the actual survey. Its purpose is to test what you have planned. Based on your experience in the pilot study, you modify your questionnaire and working plan for use in
the full-scale survey that follows.

- Test the questionnaire and the working plan. Make any changes needed.

Analyzing and Interpreting Data

Gathering information is one step in processing facts for your report. The secondary
information you gather needs to be analyzed carefully. Ask yourself questions about
the writer's credibility, including methods of collecting facts and ability to draw inferences from the facts presented. Does the author draw conclusions that can be supported by the data presented? Are the sources reliable? Is the data or interpretation
biased in any way? Are there any gaps or holes in the data or interpretation? Be a good
judge of the material and feel free to let it go if it does not meet your standard for quality. Hold this secondary information to the same high standards you would your own
primary data.

- Carefully evaluate the secondary information you find.

   In this chapter, you have learned how to plan and carry out primary data collection
properly. Now that you have good data to work with, you must interpret it accurately
and clearly for your reader (see Chapter 10 for interpreting procedure). If you are

- Report statistics from primary research clearly and completely.

FIGURE 19–15   SPSS Sample Screen

									jobcat	minority	sexrace
								5	Colleg	White	White m
								0	Exempt	White	White m
3	632	10200	Mal	83	31			8	Exempt	White	White m
4	633	8700	Mal	93	31			3	Colleg	White	White m
5	635	17400	Mal	83	41			0	Exempt	White	White m
6	637	12996	Mal	80	29			2	Colleg	White	White m
7	641	6900	Mal	79	28.00	16080	15	3.17	Clerical	White	White m
8	649	5400	Mal	67	28.75	14100	15	.50	Clerical	White	White m
9	650	5040	Mal	96	27.42	12420	15	1.17	Clerical	White	White m
10	652	6300	Mal	77	52.92	12300	12	26.42	Securit	White	White m
11	653	6300	Mal	84	33.50	15720	15	6.00	Clerical	White	White m
12	656	6000	Mal	88	54.33	8880	12	27.00	Clerical	White	White m
13	657	10500	Mal	93	32.33	22000	17	2.67	Colleg	White	White m

SPSS for Windows - [c:\spsswin\bank.sav]

File   Edit   Data   Transform   Statistics   Graphs   Utilities   Window   Help

Frequencies...
Descriptives...
Explore...
Crosstabs...

List Cases...
Report Summaries in Rows...
Report Summaries in Columns...

Summarize
Custom Tables
Compare Means
ANOVA Models
Correlate
Regression
Loglinear
Classify
Data Reduction
Scale
Nonparametric Tests
Time Series
Survival
Multiple Response

unsure of your reader's level of expertise in understanding descriptive statistics such as measures of central tendency and cross-tabulations, give the statistic and tell the reader what it means. In general, you can expect to interpret the statistics from univariate, bivariate, and multivariate analyses. In many cases, graphics help tremendously. Not only do they show trends and relationships, but they also do it ably. Statistical programs such as SPSS, which is illustrated in Figure 19–15, help you analyze and graph your data. Finally, you have an ethical responsibility to present your data honestly and completely. Omitting an error or limitation of the data collection is often viewed as seriously as hiding errors or variations from accepted practices. Of course, the deliberate distortion of the data is unethical. It is your responsibility to communicate the findings of the report as accurately and as clearly as possible.

SUMMARY ▶ by Chapter Objectives

1 Explain the difference between primary and secondary research.

1. Primary research is firsthand research. You can conduct primary research in four major ways:
   - Looking through company records
   - Conducting an experiment
   - Recording observations
   - Conducting a survey
   Secondary research is secondhand research or library research. You conduct secondary research in either a general library (usually public) or a special library (usually private).

2. If you need quantitative or factual information, you may be able to go directly to it, using such sources as the following:
   - Encyclopedias
   - Biographical directories
   - Almanacs
   - Trade directories
   - Government publications
   - Dictionaries
   - Statistical sources
   - Business information services

   When you cannot go directly to the source, you use indirect methods. You may begin by searching the following sources:
   - Prepared bibliographies in books, theses, research periodicals, or such
   - The on-line catalog
   - Periodical indexes
   - Databases
   - The Internet

3. Company records are usually confidential. You must either ask the person responsible for the information for it or gather it yourself from company databases.

4. An experiment is an orderly form of testing. It can be designed using the before-after design or the controlled before-after design.
   - The simplest is the before-after design. It involves selecting a group of subjects, measuring the variable, introducing the experimental factor, and measuring the variable again. The difference between the two measurements is assumed to be the result of the experimental factor.
   - The controlled before-after design involves selecting two groups, measuring the variable in both groups, introducing the experimental factor in one group, and then measuring the variable again in both groups. The second measurement enables you to determine the effect of the experimental factor and of other factors that might have influenced the variable between the two measurements.

5. The observation method may be defined as seeing with a purpose. It consists of watching the events involved in a problem and systematically recording what is seen. The events observed are not manipulated.

6. A sample is a group representative of the whole group. The procedure for selecting the sample is called sampling. A good sample is reliable, valid, and controlled for sampling error. You may use any of a variety of sample designs. Those discussed in this chapter include probability and nonprobability sampling.
   - Probability sampling is based on chance selection procedures. Every element in the population has a known nonzero probability of selection. Some of the techniques discussed are described below.
     —Simple random sampling involves chance selection, giving every member of the group under study an equal chance of being selected.
     —Stratified random sampling involves proportionate and random selection from each major subgroup of the group under study.
     —Systematic sampling involves taking selections at constant intervals (every fifth one, for example) from a complete list of the group under study.
     —Cluster or area sampling involves dividing into parts the area that contains the sample, selecting from these parts randomly, and continuing to subdivide and select until you have your desired sample size.
   - Nonprobability sampling is based on an unknown probability of any one of a group being studied. Some of the techniques discussed are described below.

2 Describe appropriate procedures for direct and indirect library research.

3 Describe the procedures for searching through company records and conducting experiments.

4 Design an experiment for a business problem.

5 Design an observational study for a business problem.

6 Explain sampling as it relates to conducting a survey.

—Convenience sampling involves selecting members that are convenient, easy to reach, and appropriate as judged by the researcher.

—Quota sampling requires that you know the proportions of certain characteristics (sex, age, education, etc.) in the group under study. You then select respondents in the same proportions.

—Referral sampling involves building your sample from other participants' referrals.

⑦ Discuss the techniques for constructing a questionnaire, developing a working plan, and conducting a pilot test for a survey.

7. The questions you ask should follow a definite plan, usually in the form of a questionnaire. You should construct the questionnaire carefully, following these general rules.
   - Avoid leading questions.
   - Make the questions easy to understand (avoid vagueness, difficult words, technical words).
   - Avoid questions that touch on personal prejudices or pride.
   - Seek facts as much as possible.
   - Ask only for what can be remembered (consider the laws of memory, recency, intensity, and association).
   - Plan the layout with foresight (enough space for answers and identifying information, proper sequence of questions).
   - Use scaling when appropriate.

   You develop a working plan for conducting the questioning—one that covers all the possible problems and clearly explains what to do. It is usually advisable to test the questionnaire and working plan through a pilot study. This enables you to make changes in the questionnaire and improve the working plan before conducting the survey.

⑧ Analyze and interpret information clearly and completely for your reader.

8. You need to evaluate the facts you gather from secondary research carefully before you include them in your report. Check to make sure they meet the following tests.
   - Can the author draw the conclusions from the data presented?
   - Are the sources reliable?
   - Has the author avoided biased interpretation?
   - Are there any gaps in the facts?

   You must present the primary information you collect clearly and completely. It is your responsibility to interpret statistics the reader may not understand.

CRITICAL THOUGHT QUESTIONS

1. Suggest a hypothetical research problem that would make good use of a specialized library. Justify your selection.
2. What specialized libraries are there in your community? What general libraries?
3. Under what general condition are investigators likely to be able to proceed directly to the printed source of the information sought?
4. Which index is most likely to contain information on each of the following subjects?
   a. Labor-management relations.
   b. Innovation in sales promotion.
   c. Accident proneness among employees.
   d. Recent advances in computer technology.
   e. Trends in responsibility accounting.
   f. Labor unrest in the 1800s.
   g. Events leading to enactment of a certain tax measure in 1936.
   h. Textbook treatment of business writing in the 1930s.
   i. Viewpoints on the effect of deficit financing by governments.
   j. New techniques in office management.
5. What advice would you give an investigator who has been assigned a task involving analysis of internal records of several company departments?
6. Define *experimentation*. What does the technique of experimentation involve?
7. Explain the significance of keeping constant all factors other than the experimental variable of an experiment.

8. Give an example of (*a*) a problem that can best be solved through a before-after design, and (*b*) a problem that can best be solved through a controlled before-after design. Explain your choices.
9. Define *observation* as a research technique.
10. Select an example of a business problem that can be solved best by observation. Explain your choice.
11. Point out violations of the rules of good questionnaire construction in the following questions. The questions do not come from the same questionnaire.
    a. How many days on the average do you wear a pair of socks before changing?
    b. (The first question in a survey conducted by Coca-Cola.) Have you ever drunk a Diet Coke?
    c. Do you consider the ideal pay plan to be one based on straight commission or straight salary?
    d. What kind of gasoline did you purchase last time?
    e. How much did you pay for clothing in the past 12 months?
    f. Check the word below that best describes how often you eat dessert with your noon meal.
       Always
       Usually
       Sometimes
       Never
12. Explain the difference between random sampling and convenience sampling.
13. Discuss the writer's responsibility in analyzing and interpreting data.

CRITICAL THINKING EXERCISES

1. Using your imagination to supply any missing facts you may need, develop a plan for the experiment you would use in the following situations.
   a. The Golden Glow Baking Company has for many years manufactured and sold cookies packaged in attractive boxes. It is considering packaging the cookies in recyclable bags and wants to conduct an experiment to determine consumer response to this change.
   b. The Miller Brush Company, manufacturers of a line of household goods, has for years sold its products through conventional retail outlets. It now wants to conduct an experiment to test the possibility of selling through catalogs (or home shopping networks or the Internet).
   c. A national chain of drugstores wants to know whether it would profit by doubling the face value of coupons. It is willing to pay the cost of an experiment in its research for an answer.
   d. The True Time Watch Company is considering the use of automated sales displays ($29.50 each) instead of stationary displays ($14.50 each) in the 2,500 retail outlets that sell True Time watches. The

   company will conduct an experiment to determine the relative effects on sales of the two displays.
   e. The Marvel Soap Company has developed a new cleaning agent that is unlike current soaps and detergents. The product is well protected by patent. The company wants to determine the optimum price for the new product through experimentation.
   f. National Cereals, Inc., wants to determine the effectiveness of advertising to children. Until now, it has been aiming its appeal at parents. The company will support an experiment to learn the answer.
2. Using your imagination to supply any missing facts you may need, develop a plan for research by observation for these problems.
   a. A chain of department stores wants to know what causes differences in sales by departments within stores and by stores. Some of this information it hopes to get through research by observation.
   b. Your university wants to know the nature and extent of its parking problem.
   c. The management of an insurance company wants to determine the efficiency and productivity of its data entry department.

d. Owners of a shopping center want a study to determine shopping patterns of their customers. Specifically they want to know such things as what parts of town the customers come from, how they travel, how many stores they visit, and so on.

e. The director of your library wants a detailed study of library use (what facilities are used, when, by whom, and so on).

f. The management of a restaurant wants a study of its workers' efficiency in the kitchen.

3. Using your imagination to supply any missing facts you may need, develop a plan for research by survey for these problems.

a. The American Restaurant Association wants information that will give its members a picture of its customers. The information will serve as a guide for a promotion campaign designed to increase restaurant eating. Specifically it will seek such information as who eats out, how often, where they go, how much they spend. Likewise, it will seek to determine who does not eat out and why.

b. The editor of your local daily paper wants a readership study to learn just who reads what.

c. The National Beef Producers Association wants to determine the current trends in meat consumption. The association wants such information as the amount of meat people consume, whether people have reduced their meat consumption, and so on.

d. The International Association of Publishers wants a survey of the reading habits of adults in the United States and Canada. It wants such information as who reads what, how much, when, where, and so on.

Corrections for the Self-Administered Diagnostic Test of Punctuation and Grammar

Following are the corrected sentences for the diagnostic test at the end of Chapter 18. The corrections are underscored, and the symbols for the standards explaining the correction follow the sentences.

1. An important fact about this keyboard is‚ that it has the patented "ergonomic design"‚
   An important fact about this keyboard is that it has the patented "ergonomic design." *Cma 6.1, QM 3*

2. Goods received on invoice 2741 are as follows‚ three dozen white shirts, size 15–33‚ four mens felt hats, brown, size 7‚ and five dozen assorted ties.
   Goods received on Invoice 2741 are as follows: three dozen white shirts, size 15–33; four men's felt hats, brown, size 7; and five dozen assorted ties. *Cln 1, Apos 1, SC 3*

3. James Silver__president of the new union__started the campaign for the retirement fund.
   James Silver, president of the new union, started the campaign for the retirement fund. *Cma 4.2*

4. We do not expect to act on this matter__however__until we hear from you.
   We do not expect to act on this matter, however, until we hear from you. *Cma 4.3*

5. Shipments through September 20, 1995__totaled 69,485 pounds__an increase of 17 percent over the year__ago total.
   Shipments through September 20, 1995, totaled 69,485 pounds, an increase of 17 percent over the year-ago total. *Cma 4.4, Cma 4.1, Hpn 2*

6. Brick is recommended as the building material__but the board is giving serious consideration to a substitute.
   Brick is recommended as the building material, but the board is giving serious consideration to a substitute. *Cma 1*

7. Markdowns for the sale total $34,000‚ never before has the company done anything like this.
   Markdowns for the sale total $34,000; never before has the company done anything like this. *SC 1*

8. After long experimentation a wear__resistant __high__grade__and beautiful stocking has been perfected.
   After long experimentation a wear-resistant, high-grade, and beautiful stocking has been perfected. *Hpn 2, Cma 2.2*

9. Available in white__green__and blue__this paint is sold by dealers all over the country.
   Available in white, green, and blue, this paint is sold by dealers all over the country. *Cma 2.1, Cma 3*

10. Julie Jahn__who won the trip__is our most energetic salesperson.
    Julie Jahn, who won the trip, is our most energetic salesperson. *Cma 3*

11. __Good__he replied__sales are sure to increase.
    "Good," he replied. "Sales are sure to increase." *QM 1, Pd 1*

12. Hogan's article__Retirement? Never!,__printed in the current issue of <u>Management Review</u>, is really a part of his book__<u>A Report on Worker Security</u>.
Hogan's article, "Retirement? Never!," printed in the current issue of *Management Review,* is really a part of his book, *A Report on Worker Security. Cma 4.2, QM 4, Ital 1*

13. Formal announcement of our Labor Day sale will be made in <u>thirty-two</u> days.
Formal announcement of our Labor Day sale will be made in 32 days. *No 1*

14. Each day we encounter new problems.__Although they are solved easily.
Each day we encounter new problems, although they are solved easily. *Cma 5.1, Frag*

15. A list of models, sizes, and prices of both competing lines <u>are</u> being sent you.
A list of models, sizes, and prices of both competing lines is being sent you. *Agmt SV*

16. The manager could not tolerate any employee's failing to do <u>their</u> best.
The manager could not tolerate any employee's failing to do his or her best. *Pn 2*

17. A series of tests <u>were</u> completed only yesterday.
A series of tests was completed only yesterday. *Agmt SV*

18. There should be no misunderstanding between you and <u>I</u>.
There should be no misunderstanding between you and me. *Pn 3*

19. He <u>run</u> the accounting department for five years.
He ran the accounting department for five years. *Tns 2*

20. This report is <u>considerable</u> long.
This report is considerably long. *AA*

21. <u>Who</u> did you interview for the position?
Whom did you interview for the position? *Pn 3*

22. The report concluded that the natural resources of the Southwest <u>was</u> ideal for the chemical industry.
The report concluded that the natural resources of the Southwest are ideal for the chemical industry. *Agmt SV, Tns 1*

23. This applicant is six feet in height, __ 28 years old, weighs 165 pounds, and has had eight years' experience.
This applicant is six feet in height, is 28 years old, weighs 165 pounds, and has had eight years' experience. *Prl*

24. While__reading the report, a gust of wind came through the window, blowing papers all over the room.
While she was reading the report, a gust of wind came through the window, blowing papers all over the room. *Dng*

25. The sprinkler system <u>has been</u> checked on July 1 and September 3.
The sprinkler system was checked on July 1 and September 3. *Tns 5*

B

Physical Presentation of Letters, Memos, and Reports

The appearance of a letter, memo, or report plays a significant role in communicating the message. Attractively presented messages reflect favorably on the writer and the writer's company. They give an impression of competence and care; and they build credibility for the writer. Their attractiveness tells the readers that the writer thinks they are important and deserving of a good-looking document. On the other hand, sloppy work reflects unfavorably on the writer, the company, and the message itself. Thus, you should want your messages to be attractively displayed.

Recent advances in word processing have finally relieved us of much of the tedious, repetitive tasks involved in presenting documents. Yesterday's hot feature in word processing software was a feature called styles. Styles allowed writers to define and apply a set of commands or keystrokes to a single style just once and then reuse the style. Writers could format a level-one heading once and reuse its style each time they needed to format a level-one heading. Also, if a writer decided to change the level-one formatting, only the style needed to be changed for the software automatically changed all occurrences linked to the styles. While styles let writers create formatting for use anywhere within a document, today's templates let you create the formatting for the entire document.

Templates have several advantages. Since they let you create documents from a previously defined shell, your documents will be consistent over time. Also, templates enable a company to be consistent across the company. They help assure that a professional image is being presented through the look of all types of documents the company uses. This continuity helps show the reader that a company is stable and probably reliable, too.

In addition to creating a professional image consistently, companies that use templates usually are more productive. Not only will the company save time formatting documents, but the templates also can act as prompts to the writer. This can help ensure that all components are included. Most major word processors include a full range of templates, but templates can be customized to serve the precise needs of a business. The templates can include text, graphics, macros, styles, keyboard assignments, and custom toolbars.

An add-on product, HotDocs, works with several word processors to help users create custom templates from models of documents. The user simply identifies the variables and the boilerplate text. HotDocs will build the template, a process similar to reverse engineering that's long been part of manufacturing.

Furthermore, templates are easy to use. Both Word and WordPerfect use *wizards* or *experts* to lead one through the use of most of the basic templates. This is helpful for the first time one creates a document with a template and for those documents that one creates infrequently. Figures B–1 and B–2 illustrate the process of creating a letter using the *expert* and the *wizard* tools. Notice that the writer simply fills in text, clicks buttons, or checks boxes or radio buttons.

BASICS FOR ALL DOCUMENT PREPARATION

To understand the templates most effectively, you should know the basic components and how they are used for the documents you create. These basic components are presented here after a discussion of elements that are common to all documents—layout, type, and media.

FIGURE B–1   These Steps are Involved in Creating a Basic Business Letter Using Novell WordPerfect's *Expert.*

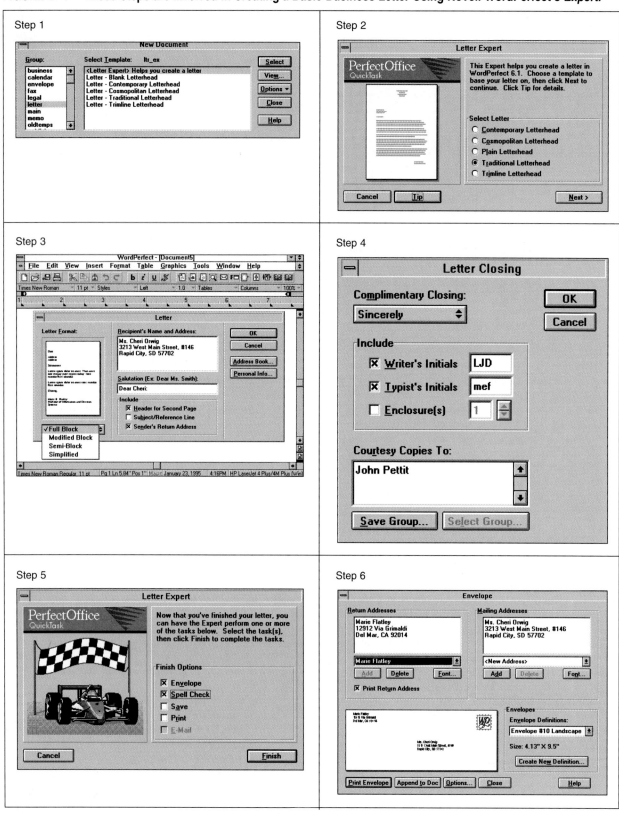

FIGURE B–2   These Steps are Followed in Creating a Basic Business Letter Using Microsoft Word's *Wizard*.

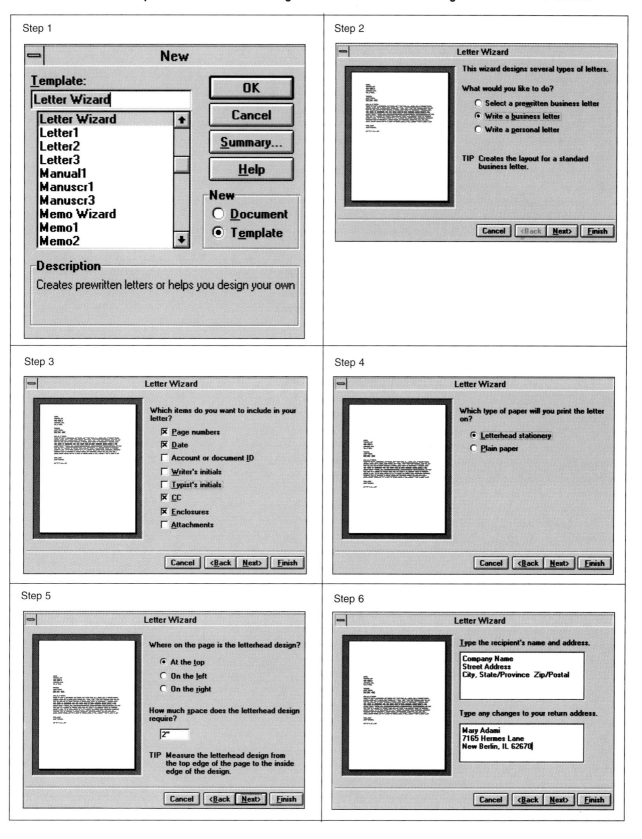

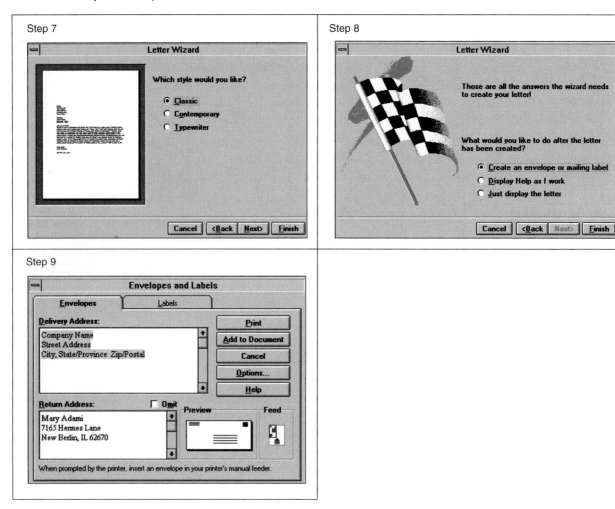

Layout

Common layout decisions involve grids, spacing, and margins. Grids are the nonprinted horizontal and vertical lines that determine placement of your document on the page. They allow you to plan the placement of your text and graphics on the page for consistency. The examples shown in Figure B–3 illustrate the placement of text on two-, three-, and six-column grids. You can readily see how important it is to plan for this element. Templates will illustrate the layouts you can choose from when creating documents.

To make your document look its best, you must consider both external and internal spacing. External spacing is the white space—the space some never think about carefully. Just as space denotes importance in writing, white space denotes importance. Surrounding text or a graphic with white spaces sets it apart, emphasizing it to the reader. Used effectively, white space has also been shown to increase the readability of your documents, giving your readers' eyes a rest. Ideally, white space should be a careful part of the design of your document.

As discussed in Chapter 16, internal spacing refers to both the vertical and horizontal spacing. The spacing between letters on a line is called kerning. With word processing software, you can adjust how close the letters are to each other. This software also allows you to adjust how close the lines are to each other vertically, called leading. Currently, many are still referring to spacing in business documents as single or double spaced. However, this is a carryover from the typewriter era when a vertical line space was always ⅙ inch or when six lines equaled an inch. Today's software and hardware allow you to control this aspect of your document as well.

FIGURE B–3 Layout illustrations on Different Grids

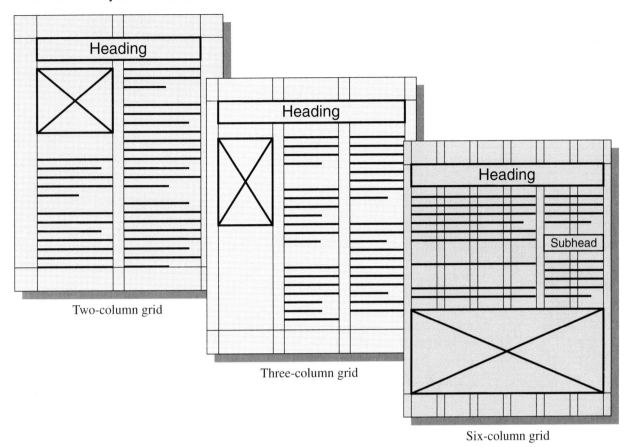

Two-column grid

Three-column grid

Six-column grid

Deciding on the best spacing to use depends on the typeface you decide to use. In any case, you need to make a conscious decision about the spacing aspect of the layout of your documents.

Another aspect of layout is your margin settings. Ideally, you should like your document to look like a framed picture. This arrangement calls for all margins to be equal. However, some businesses use a fixed margin on all documents regardless of their length. Some do this to line up with design features on their letterhead; others believe it increases productivity. In either case, the side margins will be equal. And with today's software you easily make your top and bottom margins equal by telling the software to center the document vertically on the page. Although all margins will not be equal, the page will still have horizontal and vertical balance. And some word processors are adding "make it fit" experts. With this feature, the writer tells the software the number of pages, letting the software select such aspects as margins, font size, and spacing to fit the message to the desired space.

Today's software also has the capability to align your type at the margins or in the center. This is called *justification*. Left justification aligns every line at the left, right justification aligns every line at the right, full justification aligns every line at both the left and the right (see Figure B–4). Unless you are using a proportional font, full justification takes the extra spaces between the last word and the right margin and distributes them across the line. This adds extra white spaces across the line, stopping most readers' eyes a bit. Therefore, it is usually best to set a left-justified margin and ignore the resulting ragged right margin. However, if your document's right margin is distracting, you may want to turn on the hyphenation feature. Your software will then hyphenate words at the end of lines, smoothing the raggedness of the right margin.

Type

Type is purported to influence the appearance of your document more than any other aspect. You need to make decisions on the typeface, the type style, and the type size. Typeface refers

FIGURE B–4   Different Forms of Justification

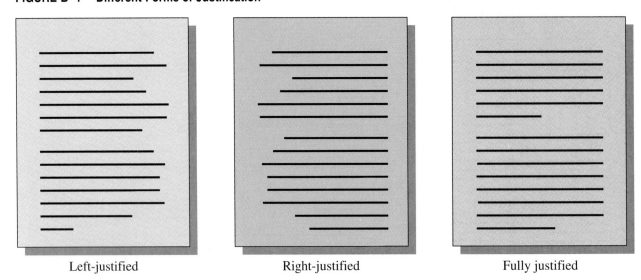

Left-justified   Right-justified   Fully justified

to the font or shape of the characters. Although thousands of fonts are available, they are generally classified as *serif* or *sans serif.* Serif typefaces have feet; sans serif do not. You can see this clearly in the examples below.

New Century Schoolbook and Times Roman are serif typefaces.

Helvetica and ITC Avant Garde Gothic Book are sans serif typefaces.

Since readers use the visual cues they get from the feet to form the words in their minds, they find the text of documents easier to read if a serif typeface is used. Sans serif typefaces are particularly good for headings where clear, distinct letters are important.

Type style refers to the way the typeface can be modified. The most basic styles include normal, **bold,** *italic,* and ***bold italic.*** Depending on your software and printer, you may have other options such as outline or shadow. You will usually decide to use modifications for specific reasons. For example, you may want all actions you want the reader to take to appear in boldface type. Or you may decide to apply different styles to different levels of headings. In any case, use of type styles should be planned, not random or haphazard.

Finally, you will need to decide on size of type. Type is measured in points. Characters one inch high are 72 points. While this is a standard measure, different typefaces in the same size often appear to be a different size. You need to consider your typeface in choosing size for your documents. Generally, body text is between 9 and 14 points, and headings are 15 points and larger.

Media

The media you choose to transmit your documents also communicates. Most electronic mailboxes today are perceived as an informal medium. But using this medium tells the reader that you are a user of computer technology and may imply that you are also up to date in your business. Choosing to send your message by fax may also imply your currency with the technology. However, because you cannot be assured of the quality of the output of the fax at the other end, your document may suffer in appearance due to either print quality or paper quality. By choosing paper as your medium, you will have control over the appearance while relinquishing control over delivery to company and mail delivery systems.

Today, paper is still the top choice of media. In the United States, standard business paper size is 8½ by 11 inches; in international business its measurements are metric, resulting in paper sized slightly narrower than 8½ inches and slightly longer than 11 inches. Occasionally, half-size (5½ × 8½) or executive size (7¼ × 10½) is used for short messages. Other than these standards, you have a variety of choices to make for color, weight, texture, and such.

The most conservative color choice is white. Of course, you will find that there are numerous variations of white. In addition, there are all the colors of the palette and many tints of these colors. You want your paper to represent you and your business but not distract your reader from the message. The color you choose for the first page of your document should also be the color you use for the second and continuing pages. This is the color you would usually use for envelopes, too.

Some businesses even match the color of the paper with the color of their typewriter or printer ink and the color of their postage meter ink. This, of course, communicates to the reader that the writer or company is detail conscious. Such an image would be desirable for accountants or architects where attention to detail is perceived as a positive trait.

The weight and texture of your paper also communicate. While "cheap" paper may denote control of expenses to one reader, it may denote cost cutting to another. Usually businesses use paper with a weight of 16 to 20 pounds and a rag or cotton content of 25 to 100 percent. The higher the numbers the higher the quality. And, of course, many readers often associate a high-quality paper with a high-quality product or service.

The choice of medium to use for your documents is important because it, too, sends a message. By being aware of these subtle messages, you will be able to choose the most appropriate medium for your situation.

With the basics taken care of, now we can move on to the specifics for the letter, memo, or report.

FORM OF BUSINESS LETTERS

The layout of a letter (its shape on the page) accounts for a major part of the impression made by the appearance of the letter. A layout that is too wide, too narrow, too high, too low, or off-center may impress the reader unfavorably. The ideal letter layout is one that has the same shape as the space in which it is formed. It fits that space much as a picture fits a frame. That is, a rectangle drawn around the processed letter has the same shape as the space under the letterhead. The top border of the rectangle is the dateline, the left border is the line beginnings, the right border is the average line length, and the bottom border is the last line of the notations.

As to the format of the layout, any generally recognized one is acceptable. Some people prefer one format or another, and some people even think the format they prefer is the best. Templates allow you to choose your own format preferences. Generally, the most popular formats are block, modified block, and AMS simplified. These are illustrated in Figure B–5. In all formats, single-spacing is the general rule. The standard templates bundled with word processors give users a choice of layout. Figure B–6 shows the standard choices available in WordPerfect.

Agreement has not been reached on all the practices for setting up the parts of the letter. The suggestions below, however, follow the bulk of authoritative opinion.

Dateline. You should use the conventional date form, with month, day, and year (December 19, 1995). When you are using a word processor's date feature, be sure to select the appropriate one. If you insert a date code, the date will be updated each time you retrieve the letter. If you use the date text feature, you insert the date the letter was created, and it does not change when you retrieve the letter in the future. Thus, when it is important that you have a record of the date you created the letter, this is the date feature you should use. Abbreviated date forms such as 12-19-95 or Dec. 9, '95 are informal and leave unfavorable impressions on some people. Most word processors allow you to set up your preference and will use that preference when you use the date feature.

Return Address. In most cases, your return address is printed on the letterhead or filled in on or by the template.

Inside Address. The mailing address, complete with the title of the person being addressed, makes up the inside address. Preferably, form it without abbreviations, except for commonly abbreviated words (*Dr., Mr., Mrs., Ms.*).

Attention Line. Some executives prefer to emphasize the company address rather than the individual offices. Thus, they address the letter to the company in the inside address and then use an attention line to direct the letter to a specific officer or department. The attention line is placed a double space after the inside address and a double space before the salutation. When used, the typical form of attention lines is

Attention: Mr. William O'Brien, Vice President

FIGURE B–5 Standard Letter Formats

Full Block
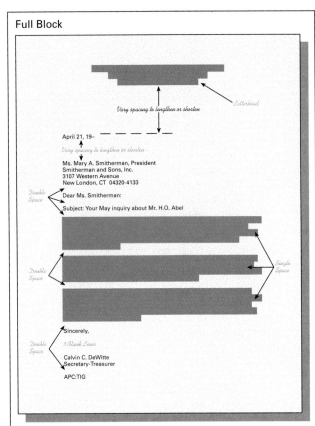

Modified Block, Blocked Paragraphs
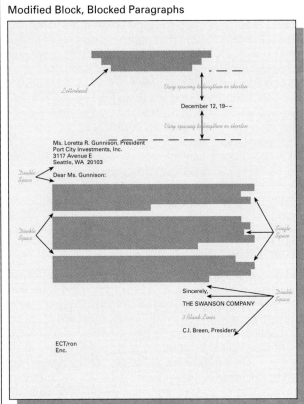

Modified Block, Indented Paragraphs
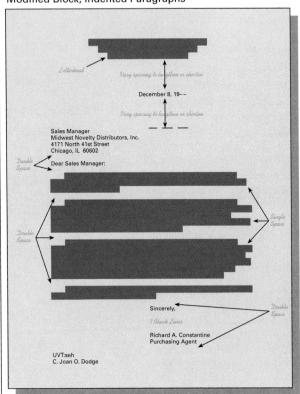

AMS Simplified
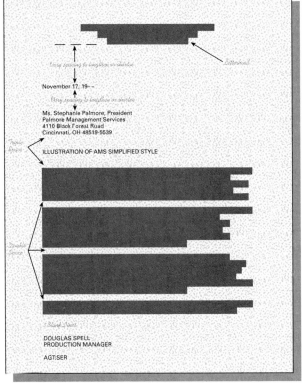

FIGURE B–6   Dialogue Box Illustrating the Standard Choices Writers Have for Letter Layout Formats

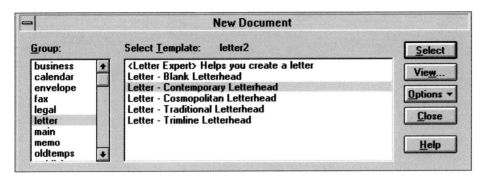

Salutation.   The salutation you choose should be based on your familiarity with the reader and on the formality of the situation. As a general rule, remember that if the writer and the reader know each other well, the salutation may be by first name (*Dear Joan*). A salutation by last name (*Dear Mr. Baskin*) is appropriate in most cases.

If you do not know and cannot find out the name of the person to whom you are sending the letter, use a position title. By directing your letter to Director of Personnel or Public Relations Manager, you are helping your letter reach the appropriate person.

The women's movement has sharply reduced the use of *Mrs.* and *Miss.* Why distinguish between married and single women, the group argues, when we make no such distinction between married and single men? The logical solution advanced by this movement is to use *Ms.* for all women, just as *Mr.* is used for all men. If you know that the woman you are writing has another preference, however, you should adhere to that preference.

Mixed or Open Punctuation.   The punctuation following the salutation and the closing is either mixed or open. Mixed punctuation employs a colon after the salutation and a comma after the complimentary close. Open punctuation, on the other hand, uses no punctuation after the salutation and none after the complimentary close. These two forms are used in domestic communication. In international communication, you may see letters with closed punctuation— punctuation distinguished by commas after the lines in the return and inside addresses and a period at the end of the complimentary close.

Subject Line.   So that both the sender and the receiver may quickly identify the subject of the correspondence, many offices use the subject line in their letters. The subject line tells what the letter is about. In addition, it contains any specific identifying material that may be helpful— date of previous correspondence, invoice number, order number, and the like. It is usually placed a double space below the salutation, though some companies prefer to place it higher— often in the upper right corner of the letter layout. The block may be headed in a number of ways, of which the following are representative:

Subject: Your July 2nd inquiry about . . .
RE: Please refer to File H-320.

Second Page Heading.   When the length of a letter must exceed one page, you should set up the following page or pages for quick identification. Always print such pages on plain paper (no letterhead). These two forms are the most common:

Ms. Helen E. Mann   2   May 7, 1996

Ms. Helen E. Mann
May 7, 1996
Page 2

Most standard templates automatically insert this information—name of addressee, date, and page number—on the second and following pages of your letter.

Closing.   By far the most commonly used complimentary close is *Sincerely. Sincerely yours* is also used, but in recent years the *yours* has been fading away. *Truly* (with and without the *yours*) is also used, but it has also lost popularity. Such closes as *Cordially* and *Respectfully* are

FIGURE B–7   A Letter Template that Allows the Writer to Select a Closing

appropriate when their meanings fit the writer–reader relationship. A long-standing friendship, for example, would justify *Cordially;* the writer's respect for the position, prestige, or accomplishments of the reader would justify *Respectfully.* WordPerfect's letter template has an insert feature that allows the writer to select the letter's closing (see Figure B–7).

Signature Block.   The printed signature conventionally appears on the fourth line below the closing, beginning directly under the first letter for the block form. Most templates will insert the closing. A short name and title may appear on the same line, separated by a comma. If either the name or title is long, the title appears on the following line, blocked under the name. The writer's signature appears in the space between the closing and the printed signature.

Some people prefer to have the firm name appear in the signature block. The conventional form for this arrangement places the firm name in solid capitals and blocked on the second line below the closing phrase. The typed name of the person signing the letter is on the fourth line below the firm name.

Information Notations.   In the lower left corner of the letter may appear abbreviated notations for enclosures (*Enc., Enc.*—3, and so on) and for the initials of the writer and the typist (*WEH:ga*). Indications of copies prepared for other readers may also be included (*cc. William E. Sutton, Copy to William E. Sutton*). Originally, the initials of the person who wrote the letter were useful in helping readers decipher illegible signatures. Now with printed signatures, these initials are less useful, but many firms still use them. The initials of the typist are useful for office records although document summaries can maintain this information (see Figure B–8).

Postscripts.   Postscripts, commonly referred to as the *PS,* are placed after any notations. While rarely used in most business letters because they look like afterthoughts, they can be very effective for added punches in sales letters.

Folding.   The carelessly folded letter is off to a bad start with the reader. Neat folding will complete the planned effect by (1) making the letter fit snugly in its cover, (2) making the letter easy and handy for the reader to remove, and (3) making the letter appear neat when opened.

FIGURE B–8   A Template that Can Help Writers Complete and Format Closings and Notations

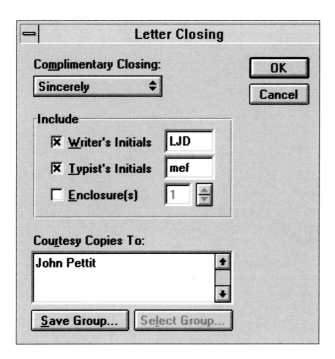

The two-fold pattern is the easiest. It fits the standard sheet for the long (Number 10) envelope as well as some other envelope sizes.

As shown in Figure B–9, the first fold of the two-fold pattern is from the bottom up, taking a little less than a third of the sheet. The second fold goes from the top down, taking exactly the same panel as the bottom segment. (This measurement will leave the recipient a quarter-inch thumbhold for easy unfolding of the letter.) Thus folded, the letter should be slipped into its envelope with the second crease toward the bottom and the center panel at the front of the envelope.

The three-fold pattern is necessary to fit the standard sheet into the commonly used small (Number 6¾) envelope. Its first fold is from the bottom up, with the bottom edge of the sheet riding about a quarter inch under the top edge to allow the thumbhold. (If the edges are exactly even, they are harder to separate.) The second fold is from the right side of the sheet toward the left, taking a little less than a third of the width. The third fold matches the second: from the left side toward the right, with a panel of exactly the same width. (This fold will leave a quarter inch thumbhold at the right, for the user's convenience.) So that the letter will appear neat when unfolded, the creases should be neatly parallel with the top and sides, not at angles that produce "dog-ears" and irregular shapes. In the three-fold form, it is especially important for the side panels produced by the second and third folds to be exactly the same width; otherwise, the vertical creases are off-center and tend to throw the whole carefully planned layout off-center.

The three-fold letter is inserted into its cover with the third crease toward the bottom of the envelope and the loose edges toward the stamp end of the envelope. From habit, most recipients of business letters slit envelopes at the top and turn them facedown to extract the letter. The three-fold letter inserted as described thus gives its reader an easy thumbhold at the top of the envelope to pull it out by and a second one at the top of the sheet for easy unfolding of the whole.

Envelope Address.   So that optical character recognition equipment may be used in sorting mail, the U.S. Postal Service requests that all envelopes be typed as follows (see Figure B–10):

1. Place the address in the scannable area as shown in the white box in Figure B–10.

2. Use a block address format.

FIGURE B–9 Two Ways of Folding and Inserting Letters (See Text Descriptions for Dimensions)

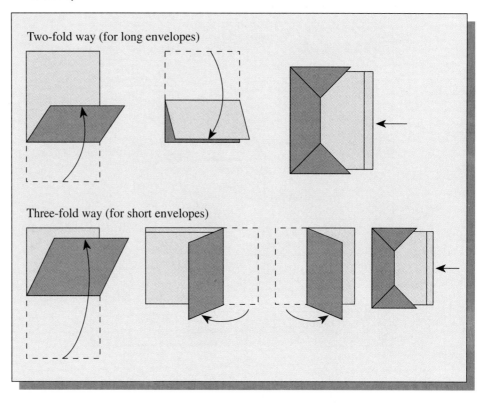

FIGURE B–10 Form for Addressing Envelopes Recommended by the U.S. Postal Service

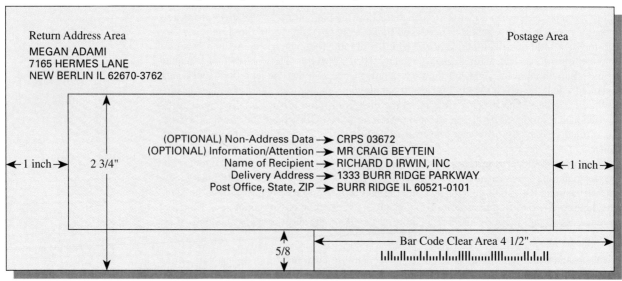

3. Single-space.

4. Use all uppercase letters (capitals).

5. Do not use punctuation, except for the hyphen in the nine-digit ZIP code.

6. Use these two-letter abbreviations for the U.S. states and territories and the Canadian provinces:

STATES AND TERRITORIES OF THE UNITED STATES

Alabama	AL	Missouri	MO
Alaska	AK	Montana	MT
American Samoa	AS	Nebraska	NE
Arizona	AZ	Nevada	NV
Arkansas	AR	New Hampshire	NH
California	CA	New Jersey	NJ
Colorado	CO	New Mexico	NM
Connecticut	CT	New York	NY
Delaware	DE	North Carolina	NC
District of Columbia	DC	North Dakota	ND
Federated States of		Northern Mariana	
Micronesia	FM	Islands	MP
Florida	FL	Ohio	OH
Georgia	GA	Oklahoma	OK
Guam	GU	Oregon	OR
Hawaii	HI	Palau	PW
Idaho	ID	Pennsylvania	PA
Illinois	IL	Puerto Rico	PR
Indiana	IN	Rhode Island	RI
Iowa	IA	South Carolina	SC
Kansas	KS	South Dakota	SD
Kentucky	KY	Tennessee	TN
Louisiana	LA	Texas	TX
Maine	ME	Utah	UT
Marshall Islands	MII	Vermont	VT
Maryland	MD	Virginia	VA
Massachusetts	MA	Virgin Islands	VI
Michigan	MI	Washington	WA
Minnesota	MN	West Virginia	WV
Mississippi	MS	Wyoming	WY

CANADIAN PROVINCES & TERRITORIES

Alberta	AB	Nova Scotia	NS
British Columbia	BC	Ontario	ON
Manitoba	MB	Prince Edward Island	PE
New Brunswick	NB	Quebec	PQ
Newfoundland	NF	Saskatchewan	SK
Northwest Territories	NT	Yukon Territory	YT

Use other address abbreviations as shown in the most recent edition of the *Post Office Directory.*

7. The last line of the mailing address should contain no more than 28 characters. The city should be 13 or fewer characters. Also, there should be one space between city and state; two spaces for the state or province abbreviation; two spaces between the state and ZIP code; and 10 characters for the ZIP + 4 code.

8. When the return address must be typed (it is usually printed), block it in the left corner, beginning on the second line from the top of the envelope and three spaces from the left edge of the envelope.

9. Type any on-arrival instructions ("Confidential," "Personal") four lines below the return address.

10. Place all notations for the post office ("Special Delivery") below the stamp and at least three lines above the mailing address.

FORM OF MEMORANDUMS

Memorandums (memos) have basic components in common, but their form varies widely from organization to organization. The basic components are the heading and body. The heading has four elements: *To, From, Date,* and *Subject.* These elements are arranged in various placements, but all are present.

The body of the memo is usually single-spaced with double-spacing between paragraphs. First-level headings are frequently used in memos. And notations for writer, typist, and enclosures are included just as they are in letters. An example of typical template format choices is shown in Figure B–11.

FORM OF LETTER AND MEMORANDUM REPORTS

As letter reports are actually letters, the review of letter form presented earlier in this chapter applies to them. Memorandum reports, however, are somewhat different. The conventional memorandum form uses the introductory information: *To, From, Date, Subject.* Many large companies have stationery on which this information is printed or standard macros, templates, or styles. The report text follows the introductory information.

Both letter and memorandum reports may use headings (captions) to display the topics covered. The headings are usually displayed in the margins, on separate lines, and in a different style. Memorandum and letter reports may also differ from ordinary letters by having illustrations (charts, tables), an appendix, and/or a bibliography.

FORM OF FORMAL REPORTS

Like letters, formal reports should be pleasing to the eye. Well-arranged reports give an impression of competence—of work professionally done. Because such an impression can affect the success of a report, you should make good use of the following review of report form.

FIGURE B–11   A Standard Template Available for Memos

FIGURE B–12 Report Format Options by Templates

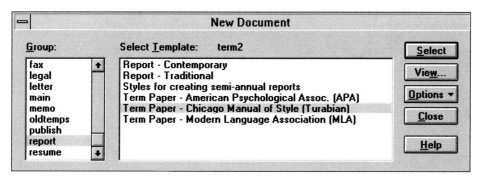

FIGURE B–13 Recommended Page Layouts

Double-spaced Page

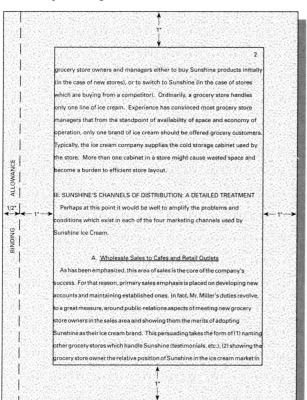

Single-spaced Page

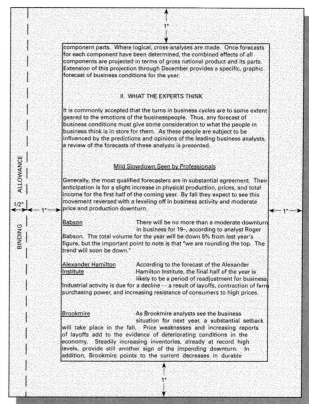

FIGURE B–14 Example of a Template that Requests Information Needed to Create a Title Page

Template Information		
Name of Institution:	University of South Florida	OK
Title of Report:	Diversity Training Proposal	Cancel
Report Submitted To:	James A. Flatley	Next Field
Course Name:	Business Communication	
Date of Report:	September 17, 1996	Personal Info...
		Help

General Information on Report Presentation

Your formal reports are likely to be prepared with word processing software. You will not need to know the general mechanics of manuscript preparation if you use report templates such as those shown in Figure B–12. However, even if you do not have to format your own reports, you should know enough about report presentation to be sure your work is done right. You cannot be certain that your report is in good form unless you know good form.

Conventional Page Layout.   For the typical text page in a report, a conventional layout appears to fit the page as a picture fits a frame (see Figure B–13). This eye-pleasing layout, however, is arranged to fit the page space not covered by the binding of the report. Thus, you must allow an extra half inch or so on the left margins of the pages of a left-bound report and at the top of the pages of a top-bound report.

Special Page Layouts.   Certain text pages may have individual layouts. Pages displaying major titles (first pages of chapters, tables of contents, executive summaries, and the like) conventionally have an extra half inch or so of space at the top. Figure B–14 illustrates that some special pages can be created with templates.

Letters of transmittal and authorization may also have individual layouts. They are arranged in any conventional letter form. In the more formal reports, they may be carefully arranged to have the same general shape as the space in which they appear using the "make-it-fit" feature.

Choice of Form.   It is conventional to double-space reports. This procedure stems from the old practice of double-spacing to make typed manuscripts more readable to the proofreader and printer. The practice has been carried over into work that is not to be reproduced. Advocates of double-spacing claim that it is easier to read than single-spacing, as the reader is less likely to lose line place.

In recent years, single-spacing has gained in popularity. The general practice is to single-space within paragraphs, double-space between paragraphs, and triple-space above all centered heads. Supporters of single-spacing contend that it saves space and facilitates reading, as it is like the printing that most people are accustomed to reading.

Patterns of Indentation.   You should indent the paragraph beginnings of double-spaced typing. On the other hand, you should block single-spaced typing, because its paragraph headings are clearly marked by extra line spacing.

No generally accepted distance of indentation exists. Some sources suggest 4 spaces, some prefer 5, some like 8, and others like 10 and more. Any decision as to the best distance to use is up to you, though you would do well to follow the practice established in the office, group, or school for which you write the report. Whatever your selection, you should be consistent.

Numbering of Pages.   Two systems of numbers are used in numbering the pages of the written report. Arabic numerals are conventional for the text portion, normally beginning with the first page of the introduction and continuing through the appendix. Small Roman numerals are standard for the pages preceding the text. Although these prefatory pages are all counted in

FIGURE B–15   A Report Template Formats for the *Chicago Manual of Style*

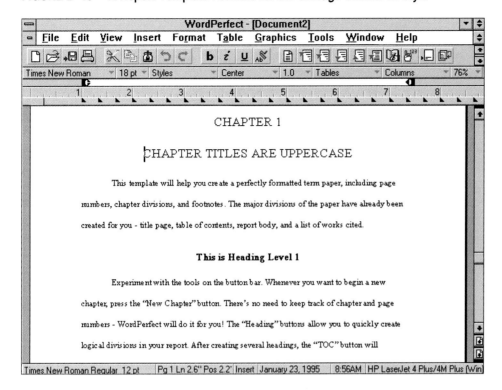

the numbering sequence, the numbers generally do not appear on the pages before the table of contents.

Placement of the numbers on the page varies with the binding used for the report. In reports bound at the top of the page, you should center all page numbers at the bottom of the page, a double or triple space below the layout used in the body.

For left-sided binding, you should place the numbers in the upper right corner, a double or triple space above the top line and in line with the right margin. Exception to this placement is customarily made for special-layout pages that have major titles and an additional amount of space displayed at the top. Such pages may include the first page of the report text; the executive summary; the table of contents; and, in very long and formal works, the first page of each major division or chapter. Numbers for these pages are centered a double or triple space below the imaginary line marking the bottom of the layout.

In documents printed back-to-back, page numbers are usually placed at the top of the page even with the outside margin. Today's word processing programs are capable of automatically placing page numbers this way if directed.

Display of Headings.   Headings (captions) are the titles of the parts of the report. Designed to lead the readers through the report, they must show at a glance the importance of the information they cover.

In showing heading importance by position, you have many choices. If your software and printer make available a variety of typefaces, you can select various progressions of font sizes and styles to fit your needs. Your goal, of course, should be to select forms that show differences in importance at first glance—much as is done in the printing of this book.

You can use any combination of form and position that clearly shows the relative importance of the headings. The one governing rule to follow in considering form and positions of headings is that no heading may have a higher-ranking form or position than any of the headings of a higher level. But you can use the same form for two successive levels of headings as long as the positions vary. And you can use the same position for two successive levels as long as the forms vary. You can also skip over any of the steps in the progression of form or position. If you had selected the report template for the *Chicago Manual of Style* format, the headings would be set up for you (See Figure B–15).

page, the first area of identification covers the report title. Preferably, use the highest-ranking form used in the report.

The second area of identification names the individual (or group) for whom the report has been prepared. Precede it with an identifying phrase indicating that individual's role in the report, such as "Prepared for" or "Submitted to." In addition to the recipient's name, include the identification of the recipient by title or role, company, and address, particularly if you and the recipient are from different companies.

The third area of identification names you, the writer of the report. It is also preceded by an identifying phrase—"Prepared by," "Written by," or similar wording describing your role in the report—and it may also identify title or role, company, and address. As a final part of this area of information, you may include the date of publication. Placement of the three areas of identification on the page should make for an eye-pleasing arrangement. Most word processing software will help you place this page vertically.

Letters of Transmittal and Authorization. As their names imply, the letters of transmittal and authorization are actual letters. You should print them in any acceptable letter form. If the report is important, you should give the letter an ideal layout. An ideal layout is one that fits the letter into a rectangle of the same shape as the space within which it is printed.

Acknowledgments. When you are indebted to the assistance of others, it is fitting that you acknowledge the indebtedness somewhere in the report. If this number is small, you may acknowledge them in the introduction of the report or in the letter of transmittal. In the rare event that you need to make numerous acknowledgments, you may construct a special section for this purpose. This section, bearing the simple title "Acknowledgments," has the same layout as any other text page in which a title is displayed.

Table of Contents. The table of contents is the report outline in its polished, finished form. It lists the major report headings with the page numbers on which those headings appear. Although not all reports require a table of contents, one should be a part of any report long enough to make such a guide helpful to the readers. Most word processors are capable of generating a table of contents—complete with page numbers.

The table of contents is appropriately titled "Contents" or "Table of Contents." The layout of the table of contents is the same as that used for any other report page with a title display. Below the title, set up two columns. One contains the outline headings, generally beginning with the first report part following the table of contents. You have the option of including or leaving out the outline letters and numbers.

In the table of contents, as in the body of the report, you may vary the form to distinguish different heading levels. But the form variations of the table of contents need not be the same as those used in the text of the report. The highest level of headings is usually distinguished from the other levels, and sometimes typeface differences are used to distinguish second-level headings from lower-level headings. It is acceptable to show no distinction by using plain capitals and lowercase for all levels of headings.

Table of Illustrations. The table (list) of illustrations may be either a continuation of the table of contents or a separate table. Such a table lists the graphics presented in the report in much the same way as the table of contents lists the report parts.

In constructing this table, head it with an appropriately descriptive title, such as "Table of Charts and Illustrations," or "List of Tables and Charts," or "Table of Figures." If you place the table of illustrations on a separate page, layout for this page is the same as that for any other text page with a displayed title. And if you place it as a continued part of the table of contents, you should begin it after the last contents entry.

The table consists of two columns—the first for the graphics titles and the second for the pages on which the graphics appear. Head the second column "Page." And connect the two columns by leader lines of spaced periods. The periods should be aligned vertically. Line spacing in the table of illustrations is optional, again depending on the line lengths of the entries. Preceding the title of each entry, place that entry's number; and should these numbers be Roman or otherwise require more than one digit, align the digits at the right. If your report contains two or more illustration types (tables, charts, maps, and the like) and you have given each type its own numbering sequence, you should list each type separately.

References (or Bibliography). Anytime you use another's idea, you need to give credit to the source. Sometimes business writers interweave this credit into the narrative of their text. But often these sources are listed in a reference or bibliography section at the end of the report.

Typically, these sections are organized alphabetically, but they can also be organized by date, subject, or type of source.

The format and content of citations vary by style used as described in Appendix E. Among the widely used formats are *The Chicago Manual of Style, The MLA Style Sheet,* and the *Publication Manual of the American Psychological Association.* The content for most items on the list of references is similar to the footnote. This format can be set up by the report format.

Need to Improvise.   The foregoing review covers most of the problems of form you will encounter in preparing reports. But there will be others. When you encounter other problems, you simply improvise an arrangement that appears right to the eye. After all, what appears right to the eye is the basis of conventional report form.

C

A Grading Checklist
for Letters

THE OPENING

O Ind *Indirectness needed.* This opening gets to the goal too fast.

O Dir *Directness needed.* This opening is too slow in getting to the goal.

O Qual *Quality.* This opening could be improved by making it more (1) on subject, (2) logical, or (3) interesting.

COVERAGE

C Inc *Incomplete.* You have not covered all the important information.

C Ex *Excess information.* You have included more information than is needed.

C Exp *Explanation.* More or better explanation is needed here.

C Id *Identification.* Completely identify the situation, either in the letter or in a subject line.

ENDING

E AC *Action close.* A drive for action is appropriate in this situation.

E AC S *Action strong.* This action drive is too strong.

E AC W *Action weak.* This action drive is too weak.

E IT *Individually tailored.* Make your close fit the one case.

E OS *Off subject.* An off-subject close is best for this case. These words recall unpleasant things in the reader's mind.

TECHNIQUE

Adp *Adaptation.* Your words should be adapted to the one reader. Here yours are (1) above or (2) below your reader.

Awk *Awkward word arrangement.*

Bky *Bulky arrangement.* Make your paragraphs more inviting by breaking them into shorter units of thought.

Chop *Choppy writing.* A succession of short sentences produces an irritating effect.

DL *Dull writing.* Bring your writing back to life with vivid, concrete words.

Emp + *Emphasis, too much.*

Emp − *Emphasis, too little.* Here you have given too much or too little (as marked) emphasis by (1) placement, (2) volume, or (3) words or mechanical means.

Intp *Interpretation.* Do more than just present facts. In this situation, something more is needed. Make the data meaningful in terms of the reader's situation.

Los *Loose writing.*   Use words more economically. Write concisely.

Ord *Order of presentation.*   This information does not fall into a logical order. The information is mixed up and confusing.

RS *Rubber-stamp expression.*   Timeworn words from the past have no place in modern business writing.

Trans *Transition.*   Abrupt shift of thought here.

EFFECT

Conv *Conviction.*   This is less convincing than it should be. More fact or a more skillful use of words is needed.

GW *Goodwill.*   The letter needs more goodwill. Try to make your words convey friendliness. Here you tend to be too dull and matter-of-fact.

Hur *Hurried treatment.*   Your coverage of the problem appears to be hurried. Thus, it tends to leave an effect of routine or brusque treatment. Conciseness is wanted, of course, but you must not sacrifice your letter's objectives for it.

Log *Logic.*   Is this really logical? Would you do it this way in business?

Neg *Negative effect.*   By word or implication, this part is more negative than it should be.

Pers + *Too persuasive.*   Your words are too high-pressure for this situation.

Pers − *Not persuasive enough.*   More persuasion, by either words or facts, would help your letter.

Ton *Tone of the words.*   Your words create a bad impression on the reader. Words work against the success of your letter if they talk down, lecture, argue, accuse, and the like.

YVP *You-viewpoint.*   More you-viewpoint wording and adaptation would help the overall effect of your letter.

D

A Grading Checklist
for Reports

The following checklist should serve both as a guide for preparing reports and as a tool for grading reports. (Your instructor can use the symbols to mark errors.) The checklist covers all types of reports—from simple memorandums to long analytical reports. For each report type, you need only use the items that apply.

TITLE (T)

T 1   Complete? The title should tell what the report contains. Use the five Ws as a check for completeness *(who, what, where, when, why—sometimes how).*

T 2   Too long. This title is longer than it needs to be. Check it for uneconomical wording or unnecessary information.

LETTER OF TRANSMITTAL (LT)

LT 1   More directness needed in the opening. The letter should present the report right away.

LT 2   Content of the letter needs improvement. Comments that help the readers understand or appreciate the report are appropriate.

LT 3   Do not include findings unless the report has no executive summary.

LT 4   A warm statement of your attitude toward the assignment is appropriate—often expected. You either do not make one, or the one you make is weak.

LT 5   A friendlier, more conversational style would improve the letter.

EXECUTIVE SUMMARY (ES)

ES 1   *(If the direct order is assigned)*   Begin directly—with a statement of finding, conclusion, or recommendation.

ES 2   *(If the indirect order is assigned)*   Begin with a brief review of introductory information.

ES 3   The summary of highlights should be in proportion and should include major findings, analyses, and conclusions. Your coverage here is *(a)* scant or *(b)* too detailed.

ES 4   Work for a more interesting and concise summary.

ORGANIZATION—OUTLINE (O)

O 1   This organization plan is not the best for this problem. The main sections should form a logical solution to the problem.

O 2   The order of the parts of this outline is not logical. The parts should form a step-by-step route to the goal.

O 3   Do not let one major section account for the entire body of the report.

O 4   One-item subdivisions are illogical. You cannot divide an area without coming up with at least two parts.

O 5   These parts overlap. Each part should be independent of the other parts. Although some repetition and relating of parts may be desirable, outright overlap is a sign of bad organization.

O 6   More subparts are needed here. The subparts should cover all the information in the major part.

O 7   This subpart does not fit logically under this major part.

O 8   These parts are not equal in importance. Do not give them equal status in the outline.

O 9   *(If talking headings are assigned)*   These headings do not talk well.

O 10   Coordinate headings should be parallel in grammatical structure.

O 11   This (these) heading(s) is (are) too long.

O 12   Vary the wording of the headings to avoid monotonous repetition.

INTRODUCTION (I)

I 1   This introduction does not cover exactly what the readers need to know. Although the readers' needs vary by problem, these topics are usually important: *(a)* origin of the problem, *(b)* statement of the problem, *(c)* methods used in researching the problem, and *(d)* preview of the presentation.

I 2   Coverage of this part is *(a)* scant or *(b)* too detailed.

I 3   Important information has been left out.

I 4   Findings, conclusions, and other items of information are not a part of the introduction.

COVERAGE (C)

C 1   The coverage here is *(a)* scant or *(b)* too detailed.

C 2   More analysis is needed here.

C 3   Here you rely too heavily on a graphic. The text should cover the important information.

C 4   Do not lose sight of the goal of the report. Relate the information to the problem.

C 5   Clearly distinguish between fact and opinion. Label opinion as opinion.

C 6   Your analyses and conclusions need the support of more fact and authoritative opinion.

WRITING (W)

W 1   This writing should be better adapted to your readers. It appears to be *(a)* too heavy or *(b)* too light for your readers.

W 2   Avoid the overuse of passive voice.

W 3   Work for more conciseness. Try to cut down on words without sacrificing meaning.

W 4   For this report, more formal writing is appropriate. You should write consistently in impersonal (third-person) style.

W 5   A more personal style is appropriate for this report. That is, you should use more personal pronouns *(I's, we's, you's)*.

W 6   The change in thought is abrupt here.

(a)   Between major parts, use introductions, summaries, and conclusions to guide the readers' thinking.

(b)   Use transitional words, phrases, or sentences to relate minor parts.

W 7   Your paragraphing is questionable. Check the paragraphs for unity. Look for topic sentences.

GRAPHICS (GA)

GA 1   You have *(a)* not used enough graphics or *(b)* used too many graphics.

GA 2   For the information presented, this graphic is *(a)* too large or *(b)* too small.

GA 3   This type of graphic is not the best for presenting the information.

GA 4   Place the graphic near the place where its contents are discussed.

GA 5   The text must tell the story; so don't just refer the reader to a figure or table and let it go at that.

GA 6   The appearance of this graphic needs improvement. This may be your best work, but it does not make a good impression on the readers.

GA 7   Refer the readers to the graphics at the times that the readers should look at them.

GA 8   Interpret the patterns in the graphic. Note central tendencies, exceptions, ranges, trends, and such.

GA 9   Refer to the graphics incidentally, in subordinate parts of sentences that comment on their content (for example, ". . . as shown in Chart 5" or "see Chart 5").

LAYOUT AND MECHANICS (LM)

LM 1   The layout of this page is *(a)* too fat, *(b)* too skinny, or *(c)* too low, high, or off-center (as marked).

LM 2   Neat? Smudges and light type detract from the message.

LM 3   Make the margins straighter. The raggedness here offends the eye.

LM 4   The spacing here needs improvement. *(a)* Too much space here. *(b)* Not enough space here.

LM 5   Your page numbering is not the best. See the text for specific instructions.

LM 6   This page appears *(a)* choppy or *(b)* heavy.

LM 7   Your selection of type placement and style for the headings is not the best.

LM 8   This item or form is not generally acceptable.

E

Documentation and the Bibliography

In writing reports, you will frequently use information from other sources. As this material is not your own, you may need to acknowledge it. Whether and how you should acknowledge it are the subject of this brief review.

WHEN TO ACKNOWLEDGE

Your decision to acknowledge or not acknowledge a source should be determined mainly on the basis of giving credit where credit is due. If you are quoting the words of another, you must give credit. If you are paraphrasing (using someone else's ideas in your own words), you should give credit unless the material covered is general knowledge.

HOW TO ACKNOWLEDGE

Acknowledge sources by citing them in the text, using one of a number of reference systems. Three of the most commonly used systems are the Chicago (*The Chicago Manual of Style*), MLA (Modern Language Association), and APA (American Psychological Association). Although all are similar, they differ somewhat in format, as you will see in the following pages. Because the Chicago system is the most widely used in business books and journals, we will review it first. Then we will illustrate the MLA and APA systems to note primary differences.

After you have selected a system, you must choose a method of acknowledgment. Two methods are commonly used in business: (1) parenthetic author-date references within the text, and (2) footnote references. A third method, endnote references, is sometimes used, although it appears to be losing favor. Only the first two are discussed here.

The Parenthetic Author-Date Method

In recent years, the author-date method has become the most popular reference method in business. It involves placing the author's last name and year of publication in parentheses immediately following the material cited:

(Calahan 1994)

The reference is keyed to a list of all the publications cited (a bibliography), which appears at the end of the report (see discussion of the bibliography in a following section). If specific page numbers are needed, they follow the date:

(Calahan 1994, 117–18)

The last names are listed of works with two or three authors:

(Smith, Corley, and Doran 1993, 31)

For works with more than three authors, "et al." is used:

(Clovis et. al. 1991)

When no author is listed, as in unsigned publications issued by a company, government agency, labor union, or such, the author's name is the organization name:

(U.S. Department of Labor 1992)
(American Federation of Labor 1991, 31)

As noted earlier, these references are keyed to a bibliography that appears at the end of the report. To find the details of a reference, the reader turns to the bibliography and traces the reference through the alphabetical listing. For the reference "(Sanders 1992)," for example, the reader would find Sanders in its alphabetical place. If more than one publication by Sanders is listed, the reader would refer to the one written in 1992.

The Footnote Method

The traditional method of acknowledging sources (preferred in the humanities) is by footnotes; that is, the references are placed at the bottom of the page and are keyed to the text material by superscripts (raised Arabic numbers). The numbering sequence of the superscripts is consecutive—by page, by chapter, or by the whole work. The footnotes are placed inside the page layout, single-spaced, and indented or blocked just as the text is typed.

Although footnote form varies from one source to another, one generally accepted procedure is presented here. It permits two structures: an abbreviated structure that is used with a bibliography in the report and a structure that is used when the report has no bibliography.

In the abbreviated structure (not accepted by everyone), the footnote reference needs to contain only these parts: (1) author's surname; (2) title of the article, bulletin, or book; and (3) page number.

[3] Wilson, *The Report Writer's Guide*, 44 (book reference).
[4] Allison, "Making Routine Reports Talk," 71 (periodical reference).

For the complete reference (usually preferred), the descriptive points are listed in the order mentioned below. Capitals are used only with proper nouns, and abbreviations are acceptable if used consistently.

In the following lists, all the items that could be placed in each type of entry are named in the order of arrangement. Items that are unavailable or unimportant should be passed over. In other words, the following lists give, in order, all the possible items in an entry. The items listed should be used as needed.

Book Entry:

1. *Superscript.* Arabic numeral keyed to the text reference and placed before the first part of the entry without spacing.

2. *Name of the author, in normal order.* If a source has two or three authors, all are named. If a source has more than three authors, the name of the first author followed by the Latin "et al." or its English equivalent "and others" may be used.

3. *Capacity of the author.* Needed only when the person named is actually not the author of the book but an editor, compiler, or the like.

4. *Chapter name.* Necessary only in the rare instances in which the chapter title helps the reader find the source.

5. *Book title.* Book titles are placed in italics. In typewritten work, italics are indicated by underscoring.

6. *Edition.*

7. *Location of publisher.* If more than one city is listed on the title page, the one listed first should be used. If the population exceeds half a million, the name of the city is sufficient; otherwise, the city and state (or province) are best given.

8. *Publishing company.*

9. *Date.* Year of publication. If revised, year of latest revision.

10. *Page or pages.* Specific page or inclusive pages on which the cited material is found.

The following are examples of book entries:

A TYPICAL BOOK:

[1] Cindy Burford, Aline Culberson, and Peter Dykus, *Writing for Results*, 4th ed., New York: Charles Storm Publishing Company, 1992, 17–18.

A BOOK WRITTEN BY A STAFF OF WRITERS UNDER THE DIRECTION
OF AN EDITOR
(chapter title is considered helpful):
[2] W. C. Butte and Ann Buchanan, ed., "Direct Mail Advertising," *An Encyclopedia of Advertising*,
New York: Binton Publishing Company, 1994, 99.
A BOOK WRITTEN BY A NUMBER OF COAUTHORS:
[3] E. Butler Cannais et al., *Anthology of Public Relations*, New York: Warner-Bragg, Inc., 1994, 137.

Periodical Entry:

1. *Superscript.*

2. *Author's name.* Frequently, no author is given. In such cases, the entry may be skipped, or if it is definitely known to be anonymous, the word *anonymous* may be placed in the entry.

3. *Article title.* Typed within quotation marks.

4. *Periodical title.* Set in italics, which are indicated by underscoring.

5. *Publication identification.* Volume number in Arabic numerals followed by date of publication (month and year or season and year). Volume number is not needed if complete (day, month, year) date is given. See examples below for punctuation differences with and without complete date.

6. *Page or pages.*

Examples of periodical entries are shown below:

[1] Mildred C. Kinnig, "A New Look at Retirement," *Modern Business*, July 31, 1993, 31–32.
[2] William O. Schultz, "How One Company Improved Morale," *Business Leader*, August 31, 1994, 17.
[3] Mary Mitchell, "Report Writing Aids," *ABCA Bulletin*, 46 (October 1984): 13.

Newspaper Article:

1. *Superscript.*

2. *Source description.* If article is signed, give author's name. Otherwise, give description of article, such as "Associated Press dispatch" or "Editorial."

3. *Main head of article.* Subheads not needed.

4. *Newspaper title.* City and state (or province) names inserted in brackets if place names do not appear in newspaper title. State (or province) names not needed in case of very large cities, such as New York, Toronto, and Los Angeles.

5. *Date of publication.*

6. *Page (p.) and column (col.).* May be used—optional.

The following are typical newspaper article entries:

[1] Associated Press dispatch, "Rival Unions Sign Pact," *Morning Advocate* [Baton Route, Louisiana], September 3, 1996.
[2] Editorial, "The North Moves South," *Austin* [Texas] *American*, February 3, 1995, p. 2-A, col. 3.

Letters or Documents:

1. *Nature of communication.*

2. *Name of writer.*

3. *Name of recipient.*

$\left[\begin{array}{l}\text{With identification by title and}\\\text{organization where helpful.}\end{array}\right]$

4. *Date of writing.*

5. *Where filed.*

An example of an entry citing a letter is given below:

[1] Letter from J. W. Wells, president, Wells Equipment Co., to James Mattoch, secretary-treasurer, Southern Industrialists, Inc., June 10, 1990, filed among Mr. Mattoch's personal records.

Electronic Documentation:

As research using electronic media is recent, standards for referencing it are in the development stage. Li and Crane's 1993 *Electronic Style: A Guide to Citing Electronic Information* presents techniques that appear to be useful and logical. Using Li and Crane's work as a base, APA suggests the following forms for referencing electronic sources.

Abstract on CD-ROM:

Easton, Annette C., Eickelmann, Nancy S., and Marie E. Flatley (1994). Effects of an electronic meeting system group writing tool on the quality of written documents. [CD-ROM]. *Journal of Business Communication.* 31. 27–40. Abstract from: ProQuest File: ABI/Inform Item: 00861581

On-line abstract:

Easton, Annette C., Eickelmann, Nancy S., and Marie E. Flatley (1994). Effects of an electronic meeting system group writing tool on the quality of written documents. [CD-ROM]. *Journal of Business Communication.* 31. 27–40. Abstract from: DIALOG File: ABI/Inform Item: 00861581 On-line Journal, General Access

Gopher:

Murrmann, Suzanne K. (1992 September). The Americans with Disabilities Act: Perspectives on Reasonable Accommodation. *Journal of the International Academy of Hospitality Research* [On-line serial], Issue 5. Available Gopher: Hostname: borg.lib.vt.edu Select: Journal of International Academy of Hospitality Research. Select: JIAHR5

World Wide Web:

Soderland, S. and Lehnert, W. (1994). Wrap Up: A Trainable Discourse Module for Information Extraction. *Journal of Artificial Intelligence Research* [On-line serial], Volume 2, pages 131–158. Available World Wide Web: URL:http://www.cs.washington.edu/research/jair/home.html

The types of entries discussed in the preceding paragraphs are those most likely to be used. Yet many unusual types of publications (not books or periodicals) are likely to come up. When they do, you should classify the source by the form it most closely resembles—a book or a periodical. Then you should construct the entry that describes the source most correctly. Frequently, you will need to improvise—to use your best judgment in determining the source description.

Standard Reference Forms

Certain forms are conventionally used in handling repeated references in footnotes. The more common of these are the following:

Ibid. Literally, *ibid.* means "in the same place." It is used to refer the reader to the preceding footnote. The entry consists of the superscript, *ibid.*, and the page number if the page number is different as shown in these entries:

[1] Janice Smith, *How to Write the Annual Report,* Chicago: Small-Boch, Inc., 1993, 173.
[2]*Ibid.,* 143 (refers to Smith's book).

Op. cit. ("in the work cited") and **loc. cit.** ("in the place cited") also can refer to references cited earlier in the paper. But they are rarely used today. It is better to use in their place a short reference form (author's last name, date).

Other abbreviations used in footnote entries are as follows:

ABBREVIATION	MEANING
cf.	Compare (directs reader's attention to another passage)
cf. ante	Compare above
cf. post	Compare below
ed.	Edition
e.g.	For example
et al.	And others
et passim	And at intervals throughout the work
et seq.	And the following
f, ff.	Following page, following pages
i.e.	That is
infra	Below
l., ll.	Line, lines

ABBREVIATION	MEANING
MS, MSS	Manuscript, manuscripts
n.d.	No date
n.n.	No name
n.p.	No place
p., pp.	Page, pages
supra	Above
vol., vols.	Volume, volumes

DISCUSSION FOOTNOTES

In sharp contrast with source footnotes are discussion footnotes. Through discussion footnotes the writer strives to explain a part of the text, to amplify discussion on a phase of the presentation, to make cross-references to other parts of the report, and the like. The following examples illustrate some possibilities of this footnote type.

CROSS-REFERENCE:
[1] See the principle of focal points on page 72.

AMPLIFICATION OF DISCUSSION AND CROSS-REFERENCE:
[2] Lyman Bryson says the same thing: "Every communication is different for every receiver even in the same context. No one can estimate the variation of understanding that there may be among receivers of the same message conveyed in the same vehicle when the receivers are separated in either space or time." See *Communication of Ideas*, 5.

COMPARISON:
[3] Compare with the principle of the objective: Before starting any activity, one should make a clear, complete statement of the objective in view.

PLACEMENT OF QUOTED AND PARAPHRASED INFORMATION

You may use data obtained from secondary sources in two ways. You may paraphrase the information (cast it in your own words), or you may use it verbatim (exactly as the original author worded it). In typing paraphrased material, you need not distinguish it from the remainder of the report text. Material you use verbatim, however, must be clearly distinguished.

The procedure for marking this difference is simple. If the quoted passage is short (about eight lines or less), place it within the text and with quotation marks before and after it. Set off longer quotations from the margins, without quotation marks, as shown in the example below. If the text is double-spaced, further distinguish the quoted passage by single-spacing it.

Several other authorities have voiced their objections. Supporting Warren's view, Perlick presents this argument:

> In theory, this reasoning seems perfectly legitimate. The managers control the business, and the stockholders control the managers. In practice, however, it does not always hold true. There are wide differences among stockholders. They often live far apart, they often have quite different educational backgrounds, and their knowledge of the business is not always the same. Thus, it becomes very difficult for any small group of stockholders to hold the management of the firm truly accountable for its actions. (358)

As noted previously, stockholders want either dividends or price appreciation on their investments.

To the extent that the management of the firm wants to keep the stockholders happy . . . .

Frequently, you will find it best to break up or use only fragments of the quoted author's work. Because omissions may distort the meaning of a passage, you must clearly indicate them, using ellipsis points (a series of three periods typed with intervening spaces) where material is left out. If an omission begins after the end of a sentence, you must use four periods—one for final punctuation plus the ellipsis points. A passage with such omissions is the following:

> Many companies have undertaken to centralize in the hands of specially trained correspondents the handling of the outgoing mail. Usually, centralization has been accomplished by the firm's employment of a correspondence supervisor. . . . The supervisor may guide the work of correspondents . . . , or the company may employ a second technique.

In long quotations it is conventional to show omission of a paragraph or more by a full line of periods, typed with intervening spaces (see example in Pd 3, Chapter 18).

THE BIBLIOGRAPHY

A bibliography is an orderly list of material on a particular subject. In a formal report the list covers references on the subject of the report. The entries in this list closely resemble footnotes, but the two must not be confused. The bibliography normally appears as an appended part of a formal report and is placed after the appendix. It may be preceded by a fly page containing the one word *bibliography*. The page that begins the list bears the main heading *"Bibliography,"* usually typed in capital letters. Below this title the references are listed by broad categories and in alphabetical order within the categories. Such listed categories as *books, periodicals,* and *bulletins* may be used. But the determination of categories should be based solely on the types of publications collected in each bibliography. If, for example, a bibliography includes a large number of periodicals and government publications plus a wide assortment of diverse publication types, the bibliography could be divided into these categories: *periodicals, government publications,* and *miscellaneous publications.* As with footnotes, variations in bibliographic style are numerous. A simplified form recommended for business use follows the same procedure as described above for footnotes, with four major exceptions:

1. The author's name is listed in reverse order—surname first—for the purpose of alphabetizing. If an entry has more than one author, however, only the name of the first author is reversed.

2. The entry is generally typed in hanging-indention form. That is, the second and subsequent lines of an entry begin some uniform distance (usually about five spaces) to the right of the beginning point of the first line. The purpose of this indented pattern is to make the alphabetized first line stand out.

3. The entry gives the inclusive pages of articles, but not for books, and does not refer to any one page or passage.

4. Second and subsequent references to publications of the same author are indicated by a uniform line (see bibliography illustration). In typed manuscripts, this line might be formed by striking the underscore 10 consecutive times. But this line may be used only if the entire authorship is the same in the consecutive publications. For example, the line could not be used if consecutive entries have one common author but different coauthors.

Following is an example of a bibliography:

Bibliography

Books

Burton, Helen. *The City Fights Back.* New York: Citadel Press, 1991.
Caperton, Hudson D. *The Business of Government.* Boston: Sherman-Kaufman Company, 1959.
Chapman, Kenneth W., Harvey H. Heinz, and Robert V. Martinez. *The Basics of Marketing.* 4th ed. New York: Barrow-Dore, Inc., 1939.
Kiernan, Gladys M. *Retailers Manual of Taxes and Regulation.* 12th ed. New York: Institute of Distribution, Inc., 1994.
Surrey, N.M.M. *The Commerce of Louisiana during the French Regime, 1699–1763.* New York: Columbia University Press, 1916.

Government Publications

U.S. Bureau of the Census. "Characteristics of the Population." *Twentieth Census of the United States: Census of Population,* Vol. 2, part 18. Washington, D.C.: U.S. Government Printing Office, 1991. 248 pp.
_____. *Statistical Abstract of the United States.* Washington D.C.: Government Printing Office, 1990. 1056 pp.
U.S. Department of Commerce. *Business Statistics: 1990.* Washington, D.C.: U.S. Government Printing Office, 1991. 309 pp.
_____. *Survey of Current Business: 1991 Supplement,* Washington, D.C.: U.S. Government Printing Office, 1991. 271 pp.

Periodicals

Montgomery, Donald E. "Consumer Standards and Marketing." *Journal of Distribution* (May 1994). 141–49.
Phillips, Emily F. "Some Studies Needed in Marketing." *Journal of Marketing 9* (July 1980). 16–25.
_____. "Major Areas of Marketing Research." *Journal of Marketing 18* (July 1992), 21–26.

Miscellaneous Publications

Bradford, Ernest S. *Survey and Directory, Marketing Research Agencies in the United States.* New York: Bureau of Business Research, College of the City of New York, 1992. 137 pp.
Reference Sources on Chain Stores. New York: Institute of Distribution, Inc., 1994. 116 pp.
Smith, Lynn T. *Farm Trade Center in Louisiana, 1901 to 1990.* Louisiana Bulletin no. 234. Baton Rouge: Louisiana State University, 1993. 56 pp.

THE ANNOTATED BIBLIOGRAPHY

Frequently, in scholarly writing each bibliography entry is followed by a brief comment on its value and content. That is, the bibliography is annotated. The form and content of annotated bibliographies are illustrated in these entries:

Donald, W.T., ed. *Handbook of Business Administration.* New York: Shannon-Dale Book Co., Inc., 1994.
　　Contains a summary of the activities in each major area of business. Written by foremost authorities in each field. Particularly useful to the business specialist who wants a quick review of the whole of business.
Braden, Shelby M., and Lillian Como, eds. *Business Leader's Handbook.* 4th ed. New York: Mercer and Sons, Inc., 1993.
　　Provides answers to most routine problems of executives in explicit manner and with good examples. Contains good material on correspondence and sales letters.

DIFFERENCES IN APA AND MLA FORMATS

As noted previously, the APA and MLA systems differ somewhat from that presented in preceding pages. The primary differences are evident from the following illustrations.

Parenthetic References:

Chicago and MLA:

(Burton 1991)

APA:

(Burton, 1991)

Footnotes:

Books
Chicago:

[2] Helen Burton, *The City Fights Back,* New York: Citadel Press, 1991, 17.

MLA:

[2] Helen Burton, *The City Fights Back* (New York: Citadel Press, 1991), 17.

APA: Does not use footnotes.

Periodicals
Chicago:

[3] Donald E. Montgomery, "Consumer Standards and Marketing," *Journal of Distribution,* May 1994, 144.

MLA

[3] Donald E. Montgomery, "Consumer Standards and Marketing," *Journal of Distribution*, May 1994: 144.

APA: Does not use footnotes.

Bibliography:

Books
Chicago:

Burton, Helen. *The City Fights Back*. New York: Citadel Press. 1991.

MLA:

Burton, Helen. *The City Fights Back*. New York: Citadel Press, 1991.

APA:

Burton, H. (1991). *The city fights back*. New York: Citadel Press.

Periodicals
Chicago:

Montgomery, Donald E. "Consumer Standards and Marketing." *Journal of Distribution*, (May 1994). 141–49.

MLA:

Montgomery, Donald E. "Consumer Standards and Marketing." *Journal of Distribution*, May 1994: 141–49.

APA

Montgomery, D. E. (1994). Consumer standards and marketing. *Journal of Distribution*, 15(5), 141–149.

In place of the specific date of publication, APA style uses volume and number—in this example 15(5).

Any of these systems are appropriate in business. Of course, you should use only one in a paper.

Index

Photo Credits

Chapter 1

1-A Tim Brown/Tony Stone Images
1-B Chuck Savage/The Stock Market
1-C Superstock

Chapter 2

2-A Lawrence Migdale/Photo Researchers, Inc.
2-B Bob Daemmrich/The Image Works

Chapter 3

3-A Larry Dale Gordon/The Image Bank
3-B David Woo/Stock Boston

Chapter 4

4-A Alan Carey/The Image Works
4-B Bob Daemmrich/The Image Works

Chapter 5

5-A P. Rivera/Superstock
5-B Donovan Reese/Tony Stone Images
5-C Frank Herholdt/Tony Stone Images

Chapter 6

6-A Comstock, Inc.
6-B Jon Feingersh/The Stock Market
6-C Miro Vintoniv/Stock Boston

Chapter 8

8-A William Taufic/The Stock Market
8-B Frank Herholdt/Tony Stone Images
8-C Larry Dale Gordon/The Image Bank

8-D Courtesy Credit Union National Association, Inc.

Chapter 9

9-A Loren Santow/Tony Stone Images
9-B Superstock

Chapter 10

10-A Roger Tully/Tony Stone Images
10-B David R. Frazier/Tony Stone Images
10-C Superstock

Chapter 11

11-A David Young Wolff/Tony Stone Images
11-B Dan Bosler/Tony Stone Images

Chapter 12

12-A David de Lossy/The Image Bank
12-B Bryan F. Peterson/The Stock Market

Chapter 13

13-A HMS Images/The Image Bank

Chapter 14

14-A Jeff Smith/The Image Bank
14-B Bob Daemmrich/Stock Boston
14-D Donovan Reese/Tony Stone Images

Chapter 15

15-A Courtesy Morris Massey Associates, Inc.

15-B Catherine Ursillo/Photo Researchers, Inc.
15-C Jose L. Palaez/The Image Bank

Chapter 16

16-B Courtesy Fujitsu Ltd. All rights reserved.

Chapter 17

17-A Jon Feingersh/The Stock Market

Chapter 19

19-A Courtesy Laurie Stevensen/ Knowledge Systems & Research, Inc.
19-B Bob Daemmrich

Part One	Greg Pease/Tony Stone Images
Part Two	Jon Riley/Tony Stone Images
Part Three	Jose L. Pelaez/The Stock Market
Part Four	Real Life/The Image Bank
Part Five	Superstock
Part Six	Frank Herholdt/Tony Stone Images
Part Seven	Jon Riley/Tony Stone Images

PUNCTUATION

Apostrophe

Use the apostrophe:

Apos 1	to show possession
Apos 2	to mark omissions in contractions

Brackets

Use brackets:

Bkts	to set off author's words in quotations

Colon

Use the colon:

Cln 1	to introduce formal statements
Cln 2	not when it breaks thought flow

Comma

Use the comma:

Cma 1	to separate clauses connected by *and, but, or, nor, for*
Cma 2.1	to separate items in series
Cma 2.2	to separate adjectives in series
Cma 3	to set off nonrestrictive modifiers
Cma 4.1	to set off parenthetic expressions
Cma 4.2	to set off appositional words
Cma 4.3	to set off parenthetic words
Cma 4.4	to set off units in a date
Cma 5.1	to set off a subordinate clause preceding a main clause
Cma 5.2	after introductory verbal phrases
Cma 6.1	only for good reason
Cma 6.1,1	not between subject and verb
Cma 6.2	to aid clarity

Dash

Use the dash:

Dsh	to show interruption or emphasis

Exclamation Mark

Use the exclamation mark:

Ex	to show strong feeling

Hyphen

Use the hyphen:

Hpn 1	to show word division
Hpn 2	between compound words
Hpn 2.1	not between proper names used as compound adjective
Hpn 2.2	not between words that just follow each other

Italics

Use italics:

Ital 1	for book titles
Ital 2	for foreign words and phrases
Ital 3	for a word, letter, or figure used as its own name

Parentheses

Use parentheses:

Paren	to set off parenthetic words

Period

Use the period:

Pd 1	at ends of declarative sentences
Pd 2	after abbreviations or initials
Pd 3	in a series (ellipses) to show omissions

Question Mark

Use the question mark:

Q	at the end of a question